Communications
in Computer and Information Science   70

Vinu V Das   R. Vijayakumar   Narayan C. Debnath
Janahanlal Stephen   Natarajan Meghanathan
Suresh Sankaranarayanan   P.M. Thankachan
Ford Lumban Gaol   Nessy Thankachan (Eds.)

Information Processing and Management

International Conference
on Recent Trends in Business Administration
and Information Processing, BAIP 2010
Trivandrum, Kerala, India, March 26-27, 2010
Proceedings

Springer

Volume Editors

Vinu V Das
Engineers Network, Trivandrum, India
E-mail: vinuvdas@gmail.com

R. Vijayakumar
NSS College of Engineering, Palakkadu, India
E-mail: kiran2k6@bsnl.in

Narayan C. Debnath
Winona State University, Winona, MN, USA
E-mail: ndebnath@winona.edu

Janahanlal Stephen
Viswajiyithi College Engineering, Muvattupuzha, India
E-mail: drlalps@gmail.com

Natarajan Meghanathan
Jackson State University, Jackson, MS, USA
E-mail: natarajan.meghanathan@jsums.edu

Suresh Sankaranarayanan
University of West Indies, Kingston, Jamaica
E-mail: pessuresh@hotmail.com

P.M. Thankachan
CGM, ACEEE, Pattom, India
E-mail: thankachan@engineersnetwork.org

Ford Lumban Gaol
University of Indonesia, Depok, Indonesia
E-mail: fordlg@gmail.com

Nessy Thankachan
College of Engineering, Trivandrum, India
E-mail: nessythankachan@gmail.com

Library of Congress Control Number: 2010923029

CR Subject Classification (1998): D.2, H.4, J.1, H.3, K.4.4, C.2

ISSN   1865-0929
ISBN-10   3-642-12213-2 Springer Berlin Heidelberg New York
ISBN-13   978-3-642-12213-2 Springer Berlin Heidelberg New York

springer.com

© Springer-Verlag Berlin Heidelberg 2010
Printed in Germany

Typesetting: Camera-ready by author, data conversion by Scientific Publishing Services, Chennai, India
Printed on acid-free paper   06/3180

Preface

It is my pleasure to write the preface for Information Processing and Management. This book aims to bring together innovative results and new research trends in information processing, computer science and management engineering.

If an information processing system is able to perform useful actions for an objective in a given domain, it is because the system knows something about that domain. The more knowledge it has, the more useful it can be to its users. Without that knowledge, the system itself is useless.

In the information systems field, there is conceptual modeling for the activity that elicits and describes the general knowledge a particular information system needs to know. The main objective of conceptual modeling is to obtain that description, which is called a conceptual schema. Conceptual schemas are written in languages called conceptual modeling languages. Conceptual modeling is an important part of requirements engineering, the first and most important phase in the development of an information system.

Furthermore, many researchers have put forward, many times, a vision in which the conceptual schema is the only important description that needs to be created in the development of an information system. According to this vision, the building of information systems is completely automated. The only things to be done are to determine the functions that the information system has to perform and to define its conceptual schema. The huge potential economic benefit of this vision justifies the research and development efforts currently devoted to it, which are being made mainly in the framework of OMG's Model-Driven Architecture. The progress made in other branches of computer science (especially in the field of databases) makes this vision feasible in the mid-term.

Following this approach, the book is organized in two parts. The first part covers the new results and systems in the field of Computer Science and Information Processing, E-Marketing, E-Commerce, Information Technology, Software and Web Engineering, Computational Management, and System Administration, E-financial Analysis. The second part deals with BPO, Business Administration, Management, E-Marketing, Computational Management, and System Administration, E-financial Analysis.

I would like to express my gratitude to Springer LNCS-CCIS for publishing the proceedings of the International Conference on Recent Trends in Business Administration and Information Processing (BAIP 2010) which was held during March 26–27, 2010 in Trivandrum, Kerala, India.

Vinu V Das

Organized by

Table of Contents

SVD and Neural Network Based Watermarking Scheme

Swanirbhar Majumder[1], Tirtha Shankar Das[2], Vijay H. Mankar[2], and Subir K. Sarkar[2]

[1] Department of ECE, NERIST (Deeed University), Arunachal Pradesh 791109, India
swanirbhar@gmail.com
[2] Department of ETCE, Jadavpur University, Kolkata, West Bengal, India
tirthasankardas@yahoo.com, sksarkar@etce.jdvu.ac.in

Abstract. Presently the WWW phenomenon has brought the world in to the personal computer. Digital media is thereby given high priority. But this has increased the frequency of security breach of intellectual properties. Therefore copyright protections and content integrity verification are highly recommended. What we need is newer data hiding techniques that must be imperceptible, robust, highly secured, etc. Digital image watermarking is one of the ways that is resilient to various attacks on the image based digital media where data authentication is done by embedding of a watermark in image characteristics. This work incorporates singular value decomposition (SVD) based image watermarking. Here unlike previous work done by researchers, error control coding (ECC) and artificial neural networks (ANN) for the authentication purposes have been used. ECC and ANN increase the robustness of the method against malicious attacks.

Keywords: SVD, Error control coding, Artificial Neural Network, Watermark.

1 Introduction

Till date a lot of digital watermarking techniques, for copyright protection of multimedia data, have been proposed to avoid their misuse [1] [2]. Implementation of these watermarking schemes requires main focus on robustness, trustworthiness and imperceptibility [3] [4]. In a broader sense, the embedding of watermark for any multimedia data (audio, video or image) is either in spatial or in the transform domain [5].

In the spatial domain, embedding of watermark is implemented by directly adding it to the data in terms of any particular algorithm. It is faster than the latter, due to its simpler operations and implementation, but is less robust. Therefore for noise, filtering or compression mechanisms, it is better to go for the transform domain, despite of higher computing cost to attain higher robustness of the watermark [6]. Various transforms, as well as their hybrids have been used for getting better robustness than each other comparatively. Here SVD has been used along with error control coding and back propagation neural networks to enhance the performance at the cost of algorithmic complexity.

The singular value decomposition (SVD) technique is a generalization of the eigen-value decomposition, used to analyze rectangular matrices. This mathematical

V.V Das et al. (Eds.): BAIP 2010, CCIS 70, pp. 1–5, 2010.

technique has been used in various fields of image processing. The main idea of the SVD is to decompose a rectangular matrix into three simple matrices (two orthogonal matrices and one diagonal matrix) [5] [6]. It has been widely studied and used for watermarking by researchers for long.

When SVD is undergone on an image (I_{MxN}) matrix it produces 3 matrices (U_{MxM}, S_{MxN} and V_{NxN}). The main image characteristics are in the S. U and V contain the finer details respective to the Eigen values at S. By using any rank R, the U_{MxM} becomes U_{MxR} and S_{MxN} becomes S_{RxR} and V_{NxN} becomes V_{NxR}. Their resultant operation is image I'_{MxN} , where I' is the image generated from U_{MxR}, S_{RxR} and V_{NxR}. This I' does have approximately similar features as I for optimum value of R.

Here SVD is used to hide the logo for watermarking, in its Eigen values. To improve the robustness error control coding is applied, for which the convolution encoder is used with Vitrebi decoder as per a particular polynomial and code trellis has been implemented [7].

Along with the SVD and the error control coding scheme the next important technique employed is the back propagation algorithm based neural network. This is because among different learning algorithms, back-propagation algorithm is a widely used learning algorithm in Artificial Neural Networks. The Feed-Forward Neural Network architecture is capable of approximating most problems with high accuracy and generalization ability [8] [9]. This algorithm is based on the error correction learning rule. Error propagation consists of two passes through the different layers of the network, a forward pass and a backward pass. In the forward pass the input vector is applied to the sensory nodes of the network and its effect propagates through the network layer by layer. Finally a set of outputs is produced as the actual response of the network. During the forward pass the synaptic weight of the networks are all fixed. During the back pass the synaptic weights are all adjusted in accordance with an error-correction rule. The actual response of the network is subtracted from the desired response to produce an error signal. This error signal is then propagated backward through the network against the direction of synaptic conditions. The synaptic weights are adjusted to make the actual response of the network move closer to the desired response.

2   Watermark Embedding

The prerequisites for image watermarking are the subjective watermark (logo image) and the host image for data concealment. After generation of the code trellis, the watermark is passed through an error control convolution encoder to obtain an encoded logo data stream. The singular value decomposition (SVD) of host image is performed to obtain the matrices U, S, and V. The S matrix consisting of the diagonal values is converted to one dimension via zig zag scan, done in order to add the logo near the most significant Eigen values. This leads to a matrix S'

$$S'_{1D} = S_{zigzag1D} + key \times Logo_{1D} \tag{1}$$

Since the number of bits in **S** is greater than that of the logo, number of bits in **S'** is same as that of **S**. Moreover, to reduce the intensity of the logo, it is multiplied with a number '*key*', which is less than 1. This reduces the intensity of logo in the **S** matrix and does not degrade the host image significantly.

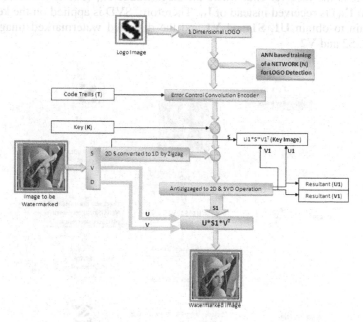

Fig. 1. Watermark embedding steps

This one dimensional **S'** is then converted back to two dimensional (2D) form using the anti-zigzag algorithm. On having the 2D **S'** the SVD operation is applied on it for the second time to have **S1**, **U1** and **V1** as output of the SVD operation on **S'**. The **S1** of second SVD operation along with the earlier extracted **U** and **V** from the first operation are incorporated to obtain the watermarked image **I_W** from equation 2.

$$I_W = U \times S1 \times V^T \qquad (2)$$

Now using the leftover matrices **U1**, **S** and **V1** we get the key image **I_K** given by:

$$I_K = U1 \times S \times V1^T \qquad (3)$$

Further the 16x16 logo (watermark) is divided into blocks of 4x4 pixels, with eight bits in each pixel. Then a back propagation based neural network is used to train the neurons to identify the logo by weight adjustment of the synapse. This is applied on the normalized pixel bits (in range 0 to 1). Thereby with some amount of pixel alteration the network can still identify the logo (that it has been trained to recognize).

3 Watermark Extraction

The detection of the watermarked logo from the stego image is just the opposite of the embedding method. This is of non-oblivious type, as the *key* and Key image I_K are to be available at the receiver end, where the stego image I'_W (due to malicious attacks I_W turns to I'_W) is received instead of I_W. Therefore, SVD is applied on the key image I_K to obtain to obtain **U1**, **S1** and **V1** and the distorted watermarked image I'_W to obtain **U2**, **S2** and **V2**.

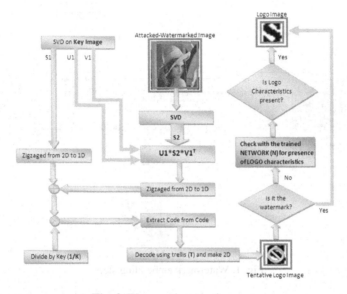

Fig. 2. Watermark extraction steps

Here **S1** is replaced by **S2** and the inverse SVD is performed to obtain **D** where:

$$D = U1 \times S2 \times V1^T \tag{4}$$

Now, this **D** and the previously obtained **S1** from key image are reshaped to one dimension by zigzag operation. Then at the receiver end, encoded logo code **C** is estimated.

$$C = 1/key \times (D - S1) \tag{5}$$

The difference of the two arrays is multiplied by the reciprocal of *key* to reinstate the lost intensity of code in the decoder. This extracted code is further decoded using a hard Viterbi decoder with the same trellis structure used during encoding.

But the problem is that sometimes due to heavy duty attacks; even the presence of error control coding cannot help the recognition of the logo. In these conditions the tentative logo is checked via the back propagation based neural network (BPNN) trained during the embedding process. In case nominal logo characteristics are present in the tentative logo it is recognized, as in the figure below. Else it is considered to be a malicious logo with no characteristics of the logo that was embedded.

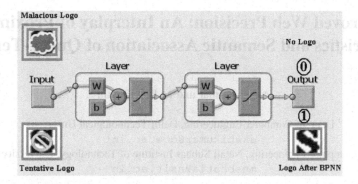

Fig. 3. BPNN pre-trained with the logo during the embedding process that detects tentative logo and rejects malicious ones

4 Conclusion

In this paper a method of watermarking logo using the SVD technique has been proposed. This scheme has been enhanced with the use of error control coding as well as back propagation neural network. This method can be checked for results by Checkmark 1.2. So for these standard attacks the robustness of the watermarking method may thereby be judged.

References

1. Acken, J.M.: How watermarking adds value to digital content. Commun. ACM 41(7), 74–77 (1998)
2. Low, S.H., et al.: Document identification for copyright protection using centroid detection. IEEE Trans. Commun. 46, 372–383 (1998)
3. Liu, R., Tan, T.: A SVD-based watermarking scheme for protecting rightful ownership. IEEE transactions on multimedia 4, 121–128 (2002)
4. Swanson, M.D., Kobayashi, M., Tewfik, A.H.: Multimedia data embedding and watermarking technologies. Proc. IEEE 86, 1064–1087 (1998)
5. Macq, B.R., Pitas, I.: Special issue on water making. Signal Process. 66(3), 281–282 (1998)
6. Zhu, X., et al.: A digital watermarking algorithm and implementation based on improved SVD. In: Proceedings of the ICPR 2006 (2006)
7. Majumder, S., et al.: SVD and Error Control Coding based Digital Image Watermarking. In: Proceedings of ACT 2009, pp. 60–63. IEEE CS, Los Alamitos (2009)
8. Haykin, S.: Neural Networks, A Comprehensive Foundation, 2nd edn.
9. Anna Durai, S., Anna Saro, E.: Image Compression with Back-Propagation Neural Network using Cumulative Distribution Function. International Journal for Applied Science and Engg. Technology, 185–189

Improved Web Precision: An Interplay of Proximity Heuristics and Semantic Association of Query-Terms

Akshi Kumar and M.P.S. Bhatia

[1] Dept. of Computer Engineering, Delhi Technological University
akshikumar@dce.ac.in
[2] Dept. of Computer Engineering, Netaji Subhas Institute of Technology, University of Delhi
mpsbhatia@nsit.ac.in

Abstract. This paper expounds a method to improve the precision of Web retrieval based on proximity and semantic association of terms for a multi-term query. We implement the three proximity measures: first appearance term distance (FTD), minimum term distance (MTD), and local occurrence density (LOD); and study the effectiveness of these measures from the perspective of semantic association of query terms. The experimental evaluation show that for the topic modifying type query terms, the MTD method has a remarkable effect on improving Web retrieval precision and for the topic collocating type query terms the LOD method has a remarkable effect on improving Web retrieval precision.

Keywords: Term Proximity, Term Distance, Semantic Associations, Web Precision, Query Terms.

1 Introduction

One of the fundamental questions in Web information retrieval is how to operationally define the notion of relevance so that we can score a document with respect to a query appropriately. In the past a few decades, many different retrieval models have been proposed and tested, including vector space models, classic probabilistic models and statistical language models [1, 2]. In most existing retrieval models, documents are scored primarily based on various kinds of term statistics such as within-document frequencies, inverse document frequencies, and document lengths. Search results often contain a large number of pages that are only weakly relevant to either of the keywords. One solution is to focus on the proximity of keywords in the search results. That is, in addition to purely occurrence-based relevance models, term proximity has been frequently used to enhance retrieval quality of keyword-oriented retrieval systems [3, 4, 5]. For example, when we use a two-term query "Indian Music" and "Classical Singer" for the search, we acquire not only Web pages about Indian Classical Music singers, but also those about Indian music forms other than classical and also International classical singers who are not involved with Indian Music in the highly ranked results. This is caused by the keywords appearing in remote places on Web pages and weak semantic relationship between them. One method of removing

V.V Das et al. (Eds.): BAIP 2010, CCIS 70, pp. 6–11, 2010.
© Springer-Verlag Berlin Heidelberg 2010

such noise is to focus attention on the proximity & semantic association of the query terms. Intuitively, the proximity of matched query terms in a document can also be exploited to promote scores of documents in which the matched query terms are close to each other [6]. Such a proximity heuristic, however, has been largely under-explored in the literature; it is unclear how we can model proximity and incorporate a proximity measure into an existing retrieval model. In this paper, we propose and study the effectiveness of three different proximity measures, each modeling prox-imity from a different perspective.

2 Query Term Proximity Heuristic and Semantic Associations

2.1 Multi-term Query

Query, which entails a group of keywords, plays a quintessential role in the Web search paradigm. Recent studies claim that queries involving one or two keywords are most common in Web searches. While most Web Search engines perform very well for a single-keyword query, their precision is not good for query involving two or more keywords because the search results usually contain a large number of pages with weak relevance.

Mathematically, we define a Multi-term query as:

A query $Q = t_1\ t_2\ ...\ t_n$ of n terms, where t_i $(1<= i<=n)$ is the ith term of Q.

2.2 Semantic Association between Query Terms

Words which are related semantically and belong to the same semantic domain tend to be used together to describe the same topics. The relationship between query terms of a multi-term query can be mainly categorized into the following two types [5]:

Topic Modifying
One query term represents a particular topic and the other modifies it. For example, "India Currency", belong to the subject modifying type. This type of keywords is used when a user wants to do a search about a particular aspect of a subject. The query terms are subordinating. Thus, if X & Y are two query terms, then Topic Modifying queries take the general form of "Y of X", i.e., "Currency of India".

Topic Collocating
Here the query terms represent individual topic. For example, the query keywords "Data Mining, Knowledge Discovery", where a user wants to search about the corre-spondence between two different topics. Thus, if X & Y are two query terms, then Topic Collocating queries take the general form of "X and Y", i.e., "Data Mining and Knowledge Discovery".

2.3 Term Proximity Measures

The query keywords are submitted to the Web search engine to acquire the search results. The morphological analysis on the results is then done to further analyze the measures for term- proximity. Three measures of term proximity, namely, the First

Appearance Term Distance (FTD), Minimum Term Distance (MTD) and the Local Occurrence Density (LOD), can be taken into account depending on the type of multi-term query.

First-Appearance Term Distance (FTD)
FTD means the term distance (TD) between the first appearances of X and Y in a document. The reason for using FTD is based on the hypothesis that important terms always appear in the forefront of a document, i.e, query terms emerge at the top of a document when they are contained in the subject of the document.

$$\text{FTD (X, Y)} = \text{TD (first (X), first (Y))}$$

where, first(A) : The first appearance of A in a Web page. In this method, the original results of a Web search engine are re-ranked based on the FTD of query keywords. The search results are sorted and ranked in ascending order of FTD. Thus, smaller the FTD higher is the result ranking.

Minimum Term Distance (MTD)
MTD means the smallest of all the term distances between X and Y in a document. The reason for using MTD as a proximity measure is based on the hypothesis that related terms appear in close proximity.

$$\text{MTD (X, Y)} = \min (\{\text{TD (X, Y)}\})$$

where, TD(X, Y): The term distance between X and Y. The MTD measure is superior for topic modifying type query keywords and shows remarkable effect on improving Web retrieval precision. In this method, the original results of a Web search engine are re-ranked based on the MTD of query keywords. The search results are sorted and ranked in ascending order of MTD. Thus, smaller the MTD higher is the result ranking.

Local Occurrence Density (LOD)
LOD is defined as a ratio of *the sum of two keywords (A and B)* to *the sum of all terms* appearing between the first and last appearance keywords. The reason for using LOD is based on a hypothesis that important terms appear repeatedly in a Web page. In this method, the search results are sorted and ranked in descending order of LOD. Higher the LOD higher is the result ranking.

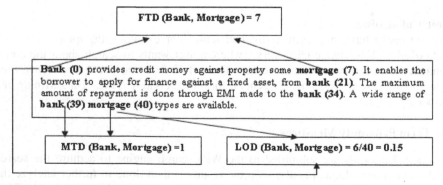

Fig. 1. An Example of Proximity Heuristics (FTD; MTD; LOD)

3   Experimental Evaluation

We performed the experiment with 20 pairs of topic modifying type and 10 pairs of topic collocating type query keywords. We set the number of search results acquired from Google as 20. In the experiments, we applied each measure to the top 20 search results acquired from Google.

Table 1. Improvement in Precision for Topic Modifying Query Type

Topic Modifying	Top 5	Top 10	Top 15	Average
FTD	3.0	4.0	1.5	4.0
MTD	**20**	**9.0**	**3.0**	**10.7**
LOD	9.0	7.5	0.2	4.6

The resultant Table 1 depicts that the MTD measure is superior for topic modifying type query keywords and shows remarkable effect on improving Web retrieval precision. The improvement with the MTD method is more significant than that with either the FTD or LOD methods. The average improvement was 4.0 points with the FTD method and 4.6 points with the LOD method. Though the improvement is trivial, it appears to have a certain level of effect. Figure 2 illustrates the respective Web Precision Improvement.

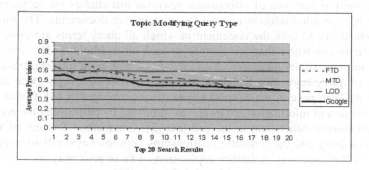

Fig. 2. Results for Topic Modifying Query Type

As depicted by the following Table 2, for the topic collocating type query keywords, LOD measure has the most remarkable effect on improving Web retrieval precision. In the MTD method, the average improvement was 7.2, and this is the next significant improvement with the LOD method. On the other hand, in the FTD method, the average improvement was -3.7, i.e., the average precision with FTD is inferior to Google's. Figure 3 illustrates the respective Web Precision Improvement.

Table 2. Improvement in Precision for Topic Collocating Query Type

Topic Collocating	Top 5	Top 10	Top 15	Average
FTD	-10	-1	-3.3	-3.7
MTD	6.0	8.0	4.0	7.2
LOD	**20**	**15**	**5. 3**	**13.0**

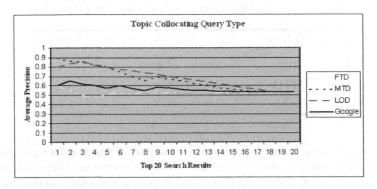

Fig. 3. Results for Topic Collocating Query Type

4 Related Works

Term proximity is one area of information retrieval that studies the relationship between the term position information and the relevance of documents. The intuition is that we would like to rank the document in which all query terms are close to each other above the one where they are apart from each other. MinDist [3] is one of state-of-the-art term proximity measures. As a method of Web page retrieval based on the proximity of query keywords, Sadakane and Imai developed a high-speed algorithm to extract the Web page in which most keywords appear together [4]. Callan showed that the precision of information retrieval was improved by performing the retrieval in a restricted domain rather than in the full text [5]. Our method focuses attention on both the proximity and the semantic relationships between keywords to improve the precision of Web retrieval. A further application of these proximity measures is presented in the Contextual Proximity Model defined in [7].

5 Conclusion

We demonstrate the effectiveness of proximity heuristics and semantic association of query terms in a multi-term query. In order to provide empirical evidence we implement the three proximity measures and conclude that the MTD measure is superior for topic modifying type query keywords and shows remarkable effect on improving Web retrieval precision whereas the LOD measure has the most remarkable effect on improving Web retrieval precision for the topic collocating type query keywords.

References

1. Kobayashi, M., Takeda, K.: Information Retrieval on the Web. ACM Computing Surveys 32(2), 144–173 (2000)
2. Bhatia, M.P.S., Kumar, A.: A Primer on the Web Information Retrieval Paradigm. Journal of Theoretical and Applied Information Technology (JATIT) 4(7), 657–662 (2008)
3. Tao, T., Zhai, C.X.: An Exploration of Proximity Measures in Information Retrieval. In: SIGIR 2007: Proceedings of the 30th Annual International ACM SIGIR Conference on Research and Development in Information Retrieval (2007)
4. Sadakane, K., Imai, H.: On k-word Proximity Search. IPSJ SIG Notes 99-AL-68 (1999)
5. Callan, J.: Passage-level Evidence in Document Retrieval. In: Proceedings of the 17th Annual International ACM SIGIR Conference, pp. 302–309 (1994)
6. Bhatia, M.P.S., Kumar, A.: Contextual Proximity Based Term-Weighting for Improved Web Information Retrieval. In: Zhang, Z., Siekmann, J.H. (eds.) KSEM 2007. LNCS (LNAI), vol. 4798, pp. 267–278. Springer, Heidelberg (2007)
7. Bhatia, M.P.S., Kumar, A.: Contextual Paradigm for Ad-hoc Retrieval of User-Centric Web-Data. IET Software 3(4), 264–275 (2009)

Network Management Initialization for Wired and Wireless Communication: A Real Time Study

Navneet Tiwari[1], Siddarth Jain[1], Saifuddin A. Tariwala[1], and Ankit Salgia[2]

[1] Department of Electronics & Communication
Medi-Caps Institute of Technology & Management, Indore, India
{navneet1231,siddarth.m.jain,saiftari}@gmail.com
[2] Department of Biomedical Engineering
G. S. Institute of Technology and Science, Indore, India
ankit.salgia06@gmail.com

Abstract. We are presenting a detailed study for the administering and monitoring of the existing IT Infrastructure for SAP. The SAP Infrastructure requirements like the users involved in the transaction, the real time monitoring and bandwidth management, are the crucial issues for the designing of the existing IT Infrastructure. Redesigning is done in such a way that, network becomes simple and secure. During the implementation phase, we have explored different methodology for the PIX firewall implementation involved in the different security profiles of the wired and wireless network. In the design and implementation phase, some of the prime solutions are proposed for the effective utilization of the available resources.

Keywords: Firewall, IT Infrastructure, Network Management, SAP, Security.

1 Introduction

The emergence of SAP R/3 technology has created an opportunity to ensure information and business process equality both at organizational and global levels. SAP R/3 a catalyst for information integration within and beyond the organizational scope through its standardized software modules, while at the same time working as a vehicle for transferring best practice business processes. The scope of this project is the methods used to implement a network for SAP needs and different configurations made right from implementing internet backbone to the SAP network using CISCO 2500 router to securing SAP network using CISCO PIX 515E Keeping all the servers in the DMZ. Other work in administering this network is by monitoring the bandwidth, implementing failover solution for monitoring using SAP GUI component and VPN authentication in Cisco PIX 515E. The project involves implementing and securing wireless infrastructure, understanding the existing network and incorporating Wireless access to their existing infrastructure. Understanding of the RF Technology, Site Survey and Implementing Wireless network with different security profiles is required. It also involved in implementing Wireless network with Radius Authentication and implementing High Availability for redundancy. This gave clearer understanding of the networking devices and the way to configure and test.

V.V Das et al. (Eds.): BAIP 2010, CCIS 70, pp. 12–16, 2010.
© Springer-Verlag Berlin Heidelberg 2010

2 Overview of the Infrastructure Modules

The project focuses on implementing effective IT infrastructure for SAP network from implementing and configuring effective for the SAP servers to configuring router for internet gateway and giving a solution for securing SAP network by integrating Cisco PIX to that network. This includes providing VIP authentication for the branch office to login to the server, designing a failover module for effective transaction thereby providing effective connectivity. The whole process involves understanding the existing network and provides a solution considering future expansions.

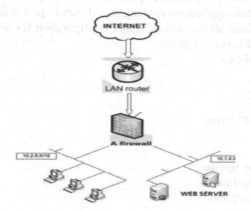

Fig. 1. Demonstration of the layout of the back bone

3 Adaptive Security Algorithm

In Adaptive security algorithm levels, the security level designates whether an interface is inside (trusted) or outside un-trusted) relative to another interface. An interface is considered inside in relation to another interface if its security level is higher than the other interface's security level, and is considered outside in relation to another interface if its security level is lower than the other interface's security level.

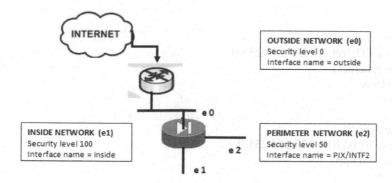

Fig. 2. Network diagram explaining ASA Levels

4 Back Bone Implementation

While implementing backbone, there are lot many factors that we have considered like understanding the current infrastructure for integration with the new one, current requirement, scope for expansion etc.. Since this network requires SAP servers run in the DMZ zone and considering the application used for the external users for effective bandwidth, we started on implementing 256 kbps internal bandwidth. This leased line implementation involves last mile cabling, router configuration for internet bandwidth.

A typical data center for small business is where security risk is not an issue. These servers will be running user programmed application listening to a specific port for data pulling. A visual basic application running in a dynamic port will keep listening to the port for the data from all the outlets, router configuration for allocated internet bandwidth done during this project phase.

Configuration is as follows:

```
Café# sh run
Building configuration...
Current configuration: 842 bytes
!
Version 12.2
service timestamps debug uptime
service timestamps log uptime
no service password-encryption
!
hostname café
!
logging console errors
enable secret 5 $1$w003$71Ou5TY7Tg3ohoNCMsMsMvr0
enable password cafe05sap
!
ip subnet-zero
ip name-server 202.138.96.2
ip name-server 202.138.96.3
!
!
!
Interface Ethernet0
ip address 192.168.1.1 255.255.255.0
interface Ethernet1
no ip address
shutdown
!
interface Serial0
ip address 10.10.10.1 255.255.255.0
encapsulation ppp
no keepalive
!
```

```
interface Serial1
no ip address
encapsulation ppp
no keepalive
!
ip default-gateway 10.10.10.2
ip classless
ip route 0.0.0.0.0.0.0.0 10.10.10.2
ip route 0.0.0.0.0.0.0.0 192.168.1.0
ip http server
ip pim bidir-enable
!
!
line con 0
line aux 0
line vty 0 4
exec-timeout 300 0
password cafe005sap
login
!
end
```

Host name of this router is Café. Password is enabled and enable secret will give access to the privileged mode. However the only difference is the secret command is used if the password has to be encrypted. DNS of the service provider is mentioned by sing the command ip name-server followed by the ip address. Ip address 10.10.10.1 should be in the same subnet of the gateway provided by the service provider. Here, encapsulation is ppp. PPP is used to provide data encapsulation, link integrity and authentication. Default gateway for the connection is specified by the command ip default-gateway and followed by the ip address of the gateway.

Command ip route 0.0.0.0.0.0.0.0 10.10.10.2
        ip route 0.0.0.0.0.0.0.0 192.168.1.0

here 0.0.0.0 (any) to the gateway 10.10.10.2. This will route all packet from the loacal LAN to service provider gateway and is otherwise called as default route.

5 Performance Management

SAP performance management is not a tool, but rather a proactive approach to monitor and manage the performance of the individual and collective subsystems that make up an SAP solution the hardware, OS, database, and SAP applications, along with third-party bolt-on systems that, combined, solve business problems.

Benefits of performance management include:

1. Extends the life of the current technology stack
2. Assists in identifying pending performance bottlenecks, helping to justify when and to what extent an investment is required to stave off performance – robbing problems.

3. Enables predictive capacity planning, helping an IT organization plan for potentially large capital outlays.
4. Helps minimize IT headcount requirements.

6 Conclusion and Future Work

The successful initialization and management is carried out for the minimal infrastructure bottleneck. The different aspects of the wired and wireless networks are analyzed for better understanding of the enterprise wireless devices. We have proposed the placing and successful modulation of the low cost Linux box for the concurrent Login with the Virtual Privacy Network. In the future work, we will try to extend our work over the automatic load balancing needs to be addressed between two different service providers.

References

1. Tiwari, N., Saraf, J., Jain, S.: WsVsSenNet: An Era of Enhanced Vision Based Sensing Capability. In: International Conference on Computer Technology and Development, 2009. ICCTD, vol. 1, pp. 383–387 (2009)
2. Leimbach, T.: The SAP Story: Evolution of SAP within the German Software Industry. IEEE Annals of the History of Computing 30(4), 60–76 (2008)
3. Jianguo Ding Balasingham, I., Bouvry, P.: Management challenges for emerging networks and services. In: International Conference on Ultra Modern Telecommunications & Workshops, ICUMT 2009, pp. 1–8 (2009)
4. Qiu, L., Varghese, G., Suri, S.: Fast Firewall Implementations for Software and Hardware-based Routers. In: Proceedings of 9th International Conference on Network Protocols (ICNP 2001) (November 2001)

IMM-I46: Inter Mobility Management for an Integrated IPv4 and IPv6 Network

J. Gnana Jayanthi[1] and S. Albert Rabara[2]

[1] Dept. of Computer Science, Holy Cross College (Autonomous),
Tiruchirappalli, Tamilnadu, India-620 002
jgnanamtcy@yahoo.com
[2] Dept. of Computer Science, St.Joseph's College (Autonomous),
Tiruchirappalli, Tamilnadu, India-620 002
a_rabara@yahoo.com

Abstract. Mobility is becoming ubiquitous now-a-days. Mobility management has been a growing concern in IPv6 with numerous problems originating from roaming between IPv6 and IPv4 access networks owing to ever-growing research. The various architectures concerning transition / mobility among IPv6 and IPv4 are studied. The study reveals that only IPv6 initiated communications (from IPv6 based network) with IPv4 nodes (in IPv4 based network) are considered. The existing architectures in the study do not consider the scenarios such as the IPv6 nodes visiting IPv4 network; IPv4 nodes visiting IPv6 network; IPv4 initiated communications with other nodes irrespective of IP version of network. The newly proposed mobility management system for the integrated IPv4 and IPv6 networks is referred to as IMM-I46 and provides a detailed solution that can be implemented immediately. The proposed IMM-I46 system helps IPv6 mobile users to roam freely also into IPv4 based networks besides roaming in IPv6 networks, get serviced, connected with internet and vice versa.

Keywords: Mobility Architecture, IPv4-IPv6 Interoperability, Address Mapping, Mixed Network, IPv4 to IPv6 Address Mapping.

1 Introduction

IPv4 and IPv6 are two independent networks, each having their own service providers and customers. The Telecom Regulatory Authority of India (TRAI) report of the year 2006, briefs that Europe, China, Japan, Korea and USA deployed IPv6 networks in their countries [1]. Therefore in the real world scenario, the whole transition from IPv4 Internet to IPv6 will not be in over-night [2, 3].

Due to the co-existence of IPv4 and IPv6 networks, there arises some issues like IPv6 addressing in IPv4 network, IPv4 addressing in IPv6 network, communication

V.V Das et al. (Eds.): BAIP 2010, CCIS 70, pp. 17–21, 2010.
© Springer-Verlag Berlin Heidelberg 2010

establishment when IPv6 node roaming in IPv4 network and vice-versa. Also, a mobile user should not be restricted to roam only in the native network i.e. an IPv6 MN can roam into IPv4 network and vice-versa; get serviced even in the different IP version of the network and connected with the Internet. This serves as the motivation for this paper to endeavor a new mechanism.

2 Literature Review

Internet Protocols (IPv4 and IPv6) need to coexist with each other during the complete migration from IPv4 to IPv6. Three main transition mechanisms proposed by NGTRANS [4] for managing the transition from IPv4 to IPv6 are the *Dual Stack, Tunneling and Translation.* A number of architectures have been proposed by other researchers implementing the above three mechanisms which are categorized in the study as Dual Stack Implemented Architectures *such as* DSTM[5], DSMIPv4[6], DSMIPv6 [7] etc., Tunneling Implemented Architectures such as RoamIP[8], Virtual Overlay[9], 64 Translation as Residential Gateway[10] etc., Network Level Translation Implemented Architectures such as NAT-PT [11], NAPT-PT [12], SIIT [13], BIS[14], BDMS[15], [16] etc., Transport Level Translation Implemented Architectures such as TRT [17] and SOCKS64 [18] etc, and Application Level Translation Implemented Architectures such as BIA[19] architecture and MIP–ALG [20].

Having analyzed the translation architectures, the study reveals that none of them consider a scenario like IPv6 nodes roaming in IPv4 network; IPv4 nodes roaming in IPv6 network and initiate communications with other nodes irrespective of IP version of network. The proposed system IMM-I46 meets these issues by providing inter-mobility as well as inter-operability while integrating IPv4 and IPv6 networks. The IMM-I46 system permits both IPv4 and IPv6 mobile users to roam freely either into IPv4 based networks or IPv6 based networks, get serviced and connected with internet.

3 Proposed System

The proposed IMM-I46 architecture consists of Domain Name System (DNS4 and DNS6) server, v6 and v4 Enabled Gateway Translator such as (v6EGT) installed in v4 border router, (v4EGT) installed in v6 border router, native IPv4 nodes located in the IPv4 Domain, and IPv6 nodes located in the IPv6 Domain. An IPv6 mobile user A from IPv6 network is assumed to move into IPv4 network and while roaming in IPv4 network, referred to as A' as depicted in fig. 1. Similarly IPv4 mobile user B from IPv4 network is assumed to move into IPv6 network referred to as B'. While roaming so, IPv6 node is assumed to obtain its Care-of-Address (CoAv6) from IPv4 network using the addressing mechanism P46CGA [21] and IPv4 node is assumed to obtain its Care-of-Address (CoA) from IPv6 network using the addressing mechanism P46A [22].

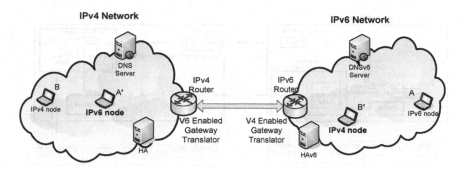

Fig. 1. Proposed IMM-I46 System

3.1 Processing IPv6 Initiated Communications in V6EGT

IPv6 node A' in the IPv4 network initiates communication with IPv4 node that may be either in IPv4 network or in IPv6 network. The destined IPv4 node cannot recognize this IPv6 source address. IPv4 Router when finds that the source address is not an IPv4 address, it enables the V6EGT. V6EGT identifying the source address as the IPv6 address, searches into its table for the presence of MNv6 entry. If present, immediately it checks for the entry of the destined IPv4 address for the corresponding MNv6 entry. If the destined IPv4 address and the table entry are different then V6EGT updates the current destined IPv4 address and forwards the packet to the correct destined network environment. In the absence of MNv6 entry in the 6Gateway Table, the V6EGT temporarily assigns an IPv4 address to the P46CGA of MNv6; assumes this temporarily assigned IPv4 address as the source address and forwards the packet to the correct destined network environment. Soon after assigning a temporary IPv4 address to MNv6 address, the information is recorded into v6 Enabled Gateway Table.

3.2 Processing IPv4 Initiated Communications in V4EGT

IPv4 node B' in the IPv6 network initiates communication establishment with IPv6 node that may be either in IPv6 network or in IPv4 network. The IPv4 source address must be converted into IPv6 address in order to transmit packets to IPv6 destined nodes. IPv6 Router when finds that the source address is not an IPv6 address, it enables the V4EGT. V4EGT identifying the source address as the IPv4 address, searches into its table for the presence of MNv4 entry. If present, immediately it checks for the entry of the destined IPv6 address corresponding to MNv4. If the destined IPv6 address and the table entry are different then V4EGT updates the current destined IPv6 address and forwards the packet to the correct destined network environment. In the absence of destined IPv6 address corresponding to MNv4 entry in the 4Gateway Table, the V4EGT converts the IPv4 source into IPv4 compatible IPv6 address; assumes this IPv4 compatible IPv6 address as the source address, the information is recorded into 6Gateway Table and forwards the packet to the correct destined network environment.

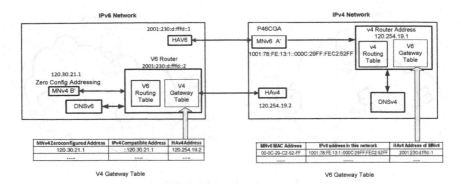

Fig. 2. Proposed IMM-I46 Architecture

3.3 Processing IPv6 Destined Communications in V6EGT

If the source address is IPv4 and the destination is IPv6 node then IPv4 router enables the V6EGT. Then the V6EGT checks for the presence of an incoming IPv4 source address entry. If the entry is not present, then the IPv4 source address is converted into IPv4 compatible IPv6 address which is recorded into the v6-Gateway Table.

4 Implementation

Mobile Network can implement the simulation for its dissemination technique. By using NS2 simulator [23], a performance analysis will be carried out for the proposed model. The proposed architecture is clearly depicted in fig. 2.

5 Conclusion

The paper dealt with the issue of inter-mobility and inter-operability IPv6 and IPv4 nodes irrespective of being in IPv4 or IPv6 networks. The proposed IMM-I46 mobility architecture facilitates either IPv6 or IPv4 nodes to roam freely without restricting to roam only in their IP version based networks. The proposed architecture guarantees for both IPv6 and IPv4 initiated communication establishment. Further, there is no need of additional equipment to be included in the existing IPv4 and IPv6 network. Hence the proposed approach is scalable. For future work, the performance of the proposed implementation procedure will be evaluated using NS2 simulator. Furthermore, the issue of security for IPv6 and IPv4 nodes during connection establishment may be considered as further research.

References

1. Recommendations on Issues Relating to Transition from IPv4 to IPv6 in India, Telecom Regulatory Authority of India, 09-01-2006 (2006)
2. Dunn, T.: The IPv6 Transition, Market place. IEEE Internet Computing 6(3), 11–13 (2002)

3. Sanjaya: IPv4 is Running out, How to craft the Internet beyond, January 22 (2009), http://www.sanog.org/resources/sanog13/sanog-13-ipv4-ipv6-sanjaya.pdf
4. http://go6.net/ipv6-6bone/ngtrans/
5. Bound, J., Toutain, L., Richier, J.L.: Dual Stack IPv6 Dominant Transition Mechanism (DSTM), draft-bound-dstm-exp-04.txt, October 17 (2005)
6. Tsirtsis, G., Park, V., Soliman, H.: Dual Stack Mobile IPv4, Internet Draft draft-ietf-mip4-dsmipv4-06, IETF (February 2008)
7. Solima, H.: Mobile IPv6 support for dual stack Hosts and Routers, Internet Draft draft-ietf-mext-nemo-v4traversal-03, IETF (May 2008)
8. Turanyi, Z.R., Szabo, C.: Global Internet Roaming with RoamIP. ACM journal on Mobile Computing and Communications Review 4(3), 58–68 (2001)
9. Liu, C.: Support Mobile IPv6 in IPv4 Domains. In: IEEE Proceedings of the International conference on Vehicular Technology (VTC), May 2004, pp. 2700–2704 (2004) ISBN 7803-8255-2/04
10. Seo, S.-H., Kong, I.-Y.: A Performance Analysis Model of PC-based Software Router Supporting IPv6-IPv4 Translation for Residential Gateway. In: Proceedings of the Fourth Annual ACIS International Conference on Computer and Information Science (ICIS 2005), 0-7695-2296-3/05 (2005)
11. Srisuresh, P., Egevang, K.: Traditional IP Network Address Translator (Traditional NAT), RFC 3022 (January 2001)
12. Bangnulo, M., Matthews, P., van Beijnum, I.: NAT64/DNS64: Network Address and Protocol Translation from IPv6 Clients to IPv4 Servers, draft-bagnulo-behave-nat64-00 (June 2008)
13. E. Nordmark: Stateless IP/ICMP Translation Algorithm (SIIT), RFC 2765 (February 2000)
14. Mackay, M., Edwards, C., Dunmore, M., Chown, T., Carvalho, G.: A Scenario-Based Review of IPv6 Transition Tools: IEEE Internet Computing, 1089-7801/03, May - June 2003, pp. 27–35 (2003)
15. Mellor, J., AlJa'afreh, R., Kamala, M., Kasasbeh, B.: Bi-Directional Mapping System as a New IPv4/IPv6 Translation Mechanism. In: IEEE Proceedings of the Tenth International Conference on Computer Modeling and Simulation, pp. 40–45 (2008) ISBN 0-7695-3114-8
16. Ra'ed AlJa'afreh, John Mellor, and Irfan Awan.:Implementation of IPv4/IPv6 BDMS Translation Mechanism: IEEE Second UKSIM European Symposium on Computer Modeling and Simulation, PP 512-517 (2008) ISBN 978-0-7695-3325-4/08
17. Hagino, J., Yamamoto, K.: An IPv6-to-IPv4 Transport Relay Translator, RFC 3142 (June 2001)
18. Kitamura, H.: A SOCKS-based IPv6/IPv4 Gateway Mechanism, RFC 3089 (April 2001)
19. Lee, S., Shin, M.-K., Kim, Y.-J., Nordmark, E., Durand, A.: Dual Stack Hosts Using "Bump-in-the-API" (BIA), RFC3338 (October 2002)
20. Choi, H.H., Cho, D.H.: Mobility management based on mobile IP in mixed IPv4/IPv6 networks. In: IEEE 58th Proceedings of VTC 2003-Fall, October 2003, pp. 2048–2052 (2003)
21. Gnana Jayanthi, J., Albert Rabara, S.: IPv6 Addressing in IPv4 Network. In: Paper accepted for the publication of the IEEE Proceedings of the International Conference on Communication Software and Networks. ICCSN 2010, Singapore, February 26-28 (in press, 2010)
22. Gnana Jayanthi, J., Albert Rabara, S.: IPv4 Addressing Architecture in IPv6 Network. In: Paper accepted for the publication of the Proceedings of the 2nd IEEE International Conference on Advanced Computer Control (ICACC 2010), Shenyang, China, March 27-29 (in press, 2010)

An Efficient Multicast Hybrid Routing Protocol for MANETs

Srinivas Sethi[1] and Siba K. Udgata[2]

[1] Dept. of Computer Science & Engineering, Indira Gandhi Institute of Technology,
Sarang, India
srinivas_sethi@igitsarang.ac.in
[2] Dept. of Computer & Information Sciences, University of Hyderabad, Hyderabad, India
udgatacs@uohyd.ernet.in

Abstract. Multicasting reduces communication cost for applications which need to send same data packets to multiple destinations instead of sending via multiple unicasts. It also reduces the required channel bandwidth, sender and router processing and delivery delay. This paper compares the performance of an efficient multicast hybrid routing protocol with the existing one. i.e. MAODV. We explore the reliability as well as proactive approaches of Multicast Hybrid Distance Vector (MHDV) for MANETs, which are used to improve the Packet Delivery Ratio (PDR) in all possible mobility rates as compared with MAODV. It is also observed that, the PDR and end-to-end delay of proposed routing protocol are better for less number of senders.

Keywords: Multicasting, Hybrid, MANET, Reliable, Proactive.

1 Introduction

Hybrid routing protocols is the combination of advantages of proactive and reactive routing protocols. In Proactive routing protocol, at all times, routes to all destinations are ready to use and as a consequence initial delays before sending data are small. Keeping routes to all destinations up-to-date is a disadvantage with regard to the usage of bandwidth and other network resources. Reactive routing protocol is designed to overcome the undesired effort in maintaining unused routes. It creates and maintains routes only to meet the current demand. This strategy is suitable for high mobility networks. In hybrid routing protocols, routing is initially established with some discovered proposed routes in proactive manner and then uses on-demand method from additional activated nodes through reactive flooding. It provides a better compromise between communication overhead and delay.

Multicasting reduces the required channel bandwidth, delivery delay and the communication cost for applications which need sending same data packets to multiple destinations instead of sending via multiple unicasts. Multicast Ad hoc On demand Distance Vector (MAODV) [1][2], On Demand Multicast Routing Protocol (ODMRP) [3] etc., are examples of multicast routing protocols in MANET.

V.V Das et al. (Eds.): BAIP 2010, CCIS 70, pp. 22–27, 2010.
© Springer-Verlag Berlin Heidelberg 2010

Destination Sequenced Distance Vector (DSDV) [4] is a proactive routing protocol which has no sleeping nodes. So it has high overhead as, most of the routing information are never used. In terms of route learning capability, Dynamic Source Routing (DSR) [5] [6] can learn more routing information from the traffic, because DSR packets contain complete route information. In DSR, source routes carried in data packets are likely to cause significant overhead in larger networks where routes are longer. Control overhead can be reduced by creating a route maintenance mechanism between only those nodes which need the services to transmit. AODV [7] [8] [9] is reactive, uniform and destination routing protocol. It minimizes the number of required broadcasts, by creating routes on demand basis. AODV does not maintain any routing information. It takes more time to discover the route.

MAODV [1] [2] is multicast version of AODV, which discovers Multicast routes on demand. The multicast is similar to unicast route request and route reply propagates back from the nodes that are members of multicast group. RMAODV [10] describes the reliable use of Packet Delivery Ratio (PDR) for multicast routing protocol. But it is ignored the important performance evaluation parameters like Normalized Routing Load (NRL) and end-to-end delay while increasing the PDR.

In this paper we investigate a novel multicast hybrid routing protocol named as MHDV, which aims to acquire a better PDR, end-to-end delay as well as overhead. We also analyze the multicast performance MHDV with varying number of senders for different receivers groups.

The rest of the paper is organized as follows: a proposed protocol discussed in section-2. Detailed discussion on the performance evaluations are done in section-3. Section-4 describes the simulation environment and parameters. Observations and discussions are described in section-5. Section-6 describes the conclusions.

2 Proposed Protocol

Multicast Hybrid Distance Vector (MHDV) routing protocol has enhanced the reliability and proactive approach of MAODV. As nodes join the group, a multicast tree consisting of group members is created. Each multicast group has a group leader whose responsibility is to maintain the group sequence number, which is used to ensure freshness of routing information [1]. It enables dynamic, self-starting, multi-hop routing between participating mobile nodes wishing to join or participate in a multicast group within an ad hoc network. The members of these multicast groups are free to change during the lifetime of the network. It responds quickly to link breaks in multicast trees by repairing in time. Multicast trees are established independently in each partition, and trees for the same multicast group are quickly connected if required. The Route Request (RREQ) and Route Reply (RREP) packet types are similar to that of MAODV [1] [2]. It discovers the root only when it is required. When a mobile node wants to join a multicast group a Route Request (RREQ) is originated. It also asks for termination in its group membership. Every multicast group is identified by its own unique address and group sequence number. If it has the information, the data packets are forwarded towards the next hop; otherwise, it will send an unsolicited RREP back to the source node. If the node itself is a tree member, it will follow its Multicast Route Table to forward the packets. When using the Unicast Route Table to forward multicast data packets, we use the MAC layer detection to detect link breakage on the route and use the unsolicited RREP to inform the source node to revoke it and discover another route if necessary. Group-Hello message (GRPH) broadcasted throughout the whole network, to indicate the existence of group. Then each node must update its Group Leader Table to indicate group leader when the non-member node received GRPH first time. A group leader must be selected for partitioned tree or when the group leader revokes its group membership.

In MHDV, RREQ is used for unicast route discovery, maintenance of route for reaching a specific node and also maintenance of route for reaching a multicast group when a node is not part of multicast tree but has multicast data packet to send to multicast group. By RREQ-J, the non multicast member joined to multicast group and link breakage.

Apart from these, it will test for reliability of packet delivery. The use of reliability is expected to increase the packet delivery ratio. The basic function of reliability is to check whether the data packet is received correctly or not. If not then the data packet will be retransmitted again only once. It ensures guaranteed data packet transmission to the receiver node. It will improve the data packet delivery ratio at the cost of slightly increase in average End-to-End delay as compared with MAODV. We added the proactive features for the tree maintenance in MHDV protocol. The basic idea is to predict the link breakage time of an active link in tree before the breakage. Then a new connection is constructed in a proactive manner before the old one becomes unavailable, in order to avoid the loss of data packets on the link.

Since multicast hybrid routing protocol deal with number of receivers and senders with retransmitting of failure packets to destinations, the end-to-end delay is expected to be more in comparison to simple multicast routing protocol. But it can be avoided by using proactive approach, which is used to minimize the initial delay for searching the route. The MHDV performance is better than MAODV in terms of Packet Delivery Ratio (PDR) and End-to-End delay.

3 Performance Evaluation

Packet delivery ratio (PDR) in this simulation is defined as the percentage of the ratio between the number of packets sent by constant bit rate (CBR) sources and the number of received packets by the CBR sinks at destination. This parameter measures effectiveness, reliability and efficiency of a routing protocol.

$$PDR = \frac{\sum \text{No. of received packet by CBR sink}_i}{\sum \text{No. packets sent by CBR source}_i} * 100$$

End-to-End delay is the average overall delay for a packet to traverse from a source node to all destination nodes. It is used to measure as the time elapsed from the time when a multicast data packet is originated from a source and it is successfully received by all multicast receivers.

Normalized Routing Load is the sum of all transmissions of routing packets per total delivery packets.

In this paper, exhaustive simulation experiments are carried out with different mobility rates for comparison between MHDV and MAODV. Again it is examined the performance of MHDV with different senders for varying the number of receivers in the MANET.

4 Simulation Environment and Parameters

To evaluate the performance of MHDV in comparison with MAODV, we have implemented in the simulator NS-2 [11] and carried out the simulation using the parameters as per Table-1 for different mobility rate and traffic load of MHDV and MAODV routing protocol. Only multicast traffic exists in this simulation.

Table 1. Simulation Parameters for different mobility and traffic load of MHDV and MAODV

S.No.	Parameters	Values
1	Area size	600x600 m
2	Transmission range	250 meters.
3	Nodes	50 Nos.
4	Simulation time	500 secs.
5	Nodes speed	1,5,10,15,20 m/s
6	Pause times	10 s
7	Data rate	5 Kbps
8	Traffic load in terms of No. of multicast senders	1,2,3,5,10 senders
9	No. of experiments	5 times.

5 Observations and Discussions

It is observed from figure-1 that, the PDR of MHDV is better than MAODV for all possible combination of mobility rate and much better for 20 m/s. This shows that the MHDV perform better as compared to MAODV. Figure-2 shows that, less end-to-end delay is observed for MHDV in all cases except for the mobility rate 15 m/s. So it can be concluded that the end-to-end delay of MHDV is comparatively better than MAODV. From figure-3, it is observed that, NRL of MAODV is little better than MHDV in different mobility rates in all case except 5 m/s mobility rates. Since the proposed protocol is proactive and based on retransmission approaches, the NRL is expected to be high in comparison to MAODV. But it is minimized due to on-demand approach of proposed protocol. From figure-4 and figure-5, it is observed that fewer senders yields better performance in terms of PDR and end-to-end delay. So it can be concluded that the proposed MHDV is better than MAODV.

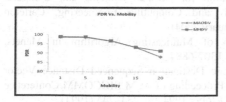

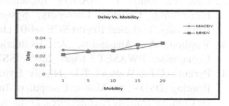

Fig. 1. PDR Vs. Mobility rate for 1 sender and 10 receivers

Fig. 2. Delay Vs. Mobility rate for 1 sender and 10 receivers

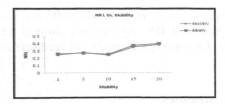

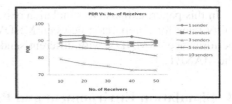

Fig. 3. NRL Vs. Mobility rate for 1 sender and 10 receivers

Fig. 4. PDR Vs. No. of receivers for Mobility rate 15 m/s

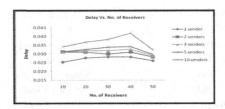

Fig. 5. Delay Vs. No. of receivers for Mobility rate 15 m/s

6 Conclusions

The data delivery services and end-to-end delay are important for a MANET. These are more challenging in case of multicast routing protocols. In this paper, we proposed a multicast hybrid routing protocol and experimental results show better performance of multicast hybrid routing protocol over the multicast ad hoc on demand routing protocol. The performance of proposed Multicast Hybrid Distance Vector (MHDV) in term of PDR and End-to-End delay are better as comparison to the MAODV. While the performance for low mobility and few multicast senders are always better, the proposed protocol performance degrades for more number of multicast senders in presence of high mobility rate or higher traffic.

References

1. Royer, E.M., Perkins, C.E.: Multicast Ad hoc On- Demand Distance Vector (MAODV) Routing, IETF, Internet Draft: draft- ietf-manet-maodv- 00.txt (2000)
2. Zhu, Y., Kunz, T.: MAODV Implementation for NS-2.26 Systems and Computer Engineering Carleton University, Systems and Computing Engineering, Carleton University, Technical Report SCE-04-01 (January 2004)
3. Vasiliou, A., Anastasios, A.: Evaluation of Multicasting Algorithm in Manets. Economides, PWASET 5 (April 2005), ISSN 1307-6884
4. Perkins, C.E., Watson, T.J.: Highly Dynamic Destination Sequenced Distance Vector Routing (DSDV) for Mobile Computers. In: Proceeding of ACM SIGCOMM Conference on Communications Architectures, London, October 1994, pp. 234–244 (1994)
5. Johnson, D.B., Maltz, D.A., Hu, Y.-C.: The Dynamic Source Routing Protocol for Mobile Ad Hoc Networks (DSR), Internet draft, draft-ietf-manet-dsr-09.txt (April 2003)

6. Johnson, D.B., Maltz, D.A.: Dynamic Source Routing in Ad Hoc Wireless Networks. Mobile Computing 353 (1996)
7. Perkins, C.E., Royer, E.M.: Ad-Hoc On-Demand Distance Vector Routing. In: Proc. Workshop Mobile Computing Systems and Applications (WMCSA 1999), pp. 197–211 (1999)
8. Perkins, C.E., Belding-Royer, E.M., Chakeres, I.D.: Ad Hoc On Demand Distance Vector (AODV) Routing, IETF Internet draft (October 2003)
9. Perkin, C.E., Royer, E.M.: Ad hoc on Demand Distance Vector Routing. In: Proceeding 2nd IEEE Workshop, Mobile Computing, Sys. Apps., pp. 90–100 (1999)
10. Baolin, S., Layuan, L.: Reliability of MAODV in Ad Hoc Networks. In: IEEE International Symposium on Microwave, Antenna, Propagation and EMC Technologies for Wireless Communications proceeding (2005)
11. Ns-2 Manual, internet draft (2009), http://www.isi.edu/nsnam/ns/ns-documentation.html
12. Xie, A.D., Nandi, S., Gupta, A.K.: Improving the reliability of IEEE 802.11 broadcast scheme for multicasting in mobile ad hoc networks. JIEE, Proc. Commun. 153(2) (April 2006)
13. Özkasap, Ö., Birman, K.P.: Throughput Stability of Reliable Multicast Protocols. In: Yakhno, T. (ed.) ADVIS 2000. LNCS, vol. 1909, pp. 159–169. Springer, Heidelberg (2000)
14. Jayakumar, G., Gopinath, G.: Performance Comparision of MANET Protocols Based on Manhattan Grid Mobility Model. Journal of Mobile Communication 2(1), 18–26 (2008); ISSN, 1990- 794X, Medwell Journals

Applications of Graph Theory in Face Biometrics

Dakshina Ranjan Kisku[1,*], Phalguni Gupta[2], and Jamuna Kanta Sing[3]

[1] Department of Computer Science and Engineering,
Dr. B. C. Roy Engineering College,
Durgapur, India – 713206
drkisku@ieee.org, drkisku@gmail.com
[2] Department of Computer Science and Engineering,
Indian Institute of Technology Kanpur,
Kanpur, India – 208016
pg@cse.iitk.ac.in
[3] Department of Computer Science and Engineering,
Jadavpur University,
Kolkata, India – 700032
jksing@ieee.org

Abstract. Biometric systems are considered as human pattern recognition systems that can be used for individual identification and verification. The decision on the authenticity is done with the help of some specific measurable physiological or behavioral characteristics possessed by the individuals. Robust architecture of any biometric system provides very good performance of the system against rotation, translation, scaling effect and deformation of the image on the image plane. Further, there is a need of development of real-time biometric system. There exist many graph matching techniques used to design robust and real-time biometrics systems. This paper discusses two graph matching techniques that have been successfully used in face biometric traits.

Keywords: Biometrics, Graphs, SIFT features, Face recognitions.

1 Introduction

There exist several graph matching techniques [1], [2], [3] for identity verification of biometric samples which can solve problems like orientation, noise, non-invariant, etc that often occurred in face. Different graph topologies are successfully used for feature representations of these biometric cues [1], [2], [4]. Graph algorithms [5] can be considered as a tool for matching two graphs obtained from feature sets extracted from two biometric cues. To describe the topological structure of biometric pattern, the locations at which the features are originated or extracted are used to define a graph. The small degree of distortions of features can easily be computed during matching of two graphs based on the position and distances between two nodes of the graph and also with the adjacency information of neighbor's features.

---

* Corresponding author.

V.V Das et al. (Eds.): BAIP 2010, CCIS 70, pp. 28–33, 2010.

This paper makes an attempt and explains the way a graph can be used in the designing efficient biometric systems. Section 2 discusses a robust face recognition using complete graph topology. Next section proposed a probabilistic graph based face recognition. Experimental results are presented in Section 4 and concluding remarks are made in the last section.

2 Face Recognition Using Graph Matching Constraint

This section presents a face recognition system [6] which uses graph topology drawn on SIFT (Scale Invariant Feature Transform) [7] extracted from face images. SIFT features are invariant to scale, rotation, partial illumination and 3D projective transform. Four major filtering stages, namely, scale-space extrema detection, keypoints localization, orientation assignment and keypoint descriptor generation can be used to detect and extract the set of image feature based on SIFT.

2.1 Reduced Point Based Match Constraint for Face Recognition

Usually, false matches are obtained due to multiple assignments [6] while more than one point are assigned to a single point on another face, or due to existence of one way assignments. The false matches due to multiple assignments are eliminated by pairing the points with the minimum distance. The false matches due to one way assignments are eliminated by removing the correspondence links that do not have any corresponding assignment from the other face. With this consideration, the false matches due to multiple assignments are eliminated by choosing the match pair with the minimum distance. The false matches due to one way assignments are eliminated by removing the links which do not have any corresponding assignment from the other side. False matches, due to multiple assignments, are removed by choosing the match with the minimum distance between two face images.

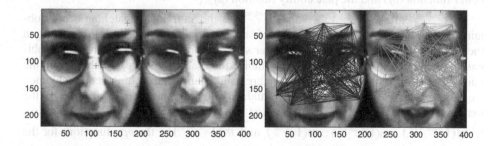

Fig. 1. Reduced Point based Match Constraint

The dissimilarity scores on reduced points between two face images for nodes and edges, are computed in the same way as for the gallery image based match constraint. Finally, the weighted average score is computed by using Gaussian Empirical Rule [6]. All matches computed from left face to right face are shown in Figure 1(a) while resulted graphs with few false matches are shown in Figure 1(b).

3   Face Recognition Using Probabilistic Graph

This section proposes a novel local feature based face recognition technique which makes use of dynamic (mouth) and static (eyes, nose) salient features of face obtained through SIFT operator [7]. Differences in facial expression, head pose, illumination, and partly occlusion may result to variations of facial characteristics and attributes. To capture the face variations, face characteristics of dynamic and static parts are further represented by incorporating repetitive probabilistic graph relaxations drawn on SIFT features extracted from localized mouth, eyes and nose facial parts.

To localize the major facial features such as eyes, mouth and nose, positions are automatically located by applying the technique in [8], [9]. A circular region of interest (ROI) centered at each extracted facial landmark location is considered to determine the SIFT features of the landmark. The face recognition system can use SIFT descriptor for extraction of invariant features from each facial landmark (Kisku, et. al., in press), namely, eyes, mouth and nose.

In order to interpret the facial landmarks with invariant SIFT points and graph relaxation topology [10], each extracted feature can be thought as a node and the relationship between invariant points can be considered as an edge between two nodes. At the level of feature extraction, invariant SIFT feature points are extracted. Relaxation graphs [10] are then drawn on the features extracted from these landmarks. These relaxations are used for matching and verification. Detail discussion about probabilistic graph matching is given in.

3.1   Fusion of Matching Scores

The Dempster-Shafer decision theory [11] which is applied to combine the matching scores obtained from individual landmark is based on combining the evidences obtained from different sources to compute the probability of an event. This is obtained by combining three elements: the basic probability assignment function (bpa), the belief function (bf) and the plausibility function (pf).

Let $\Gamma^{left-eye}$, $\Gamma^{right-eye}$, Γ^{nose} and Γ^{mouth} be the individual matching scores obtained from the four different matching of salient facial landmarks. In order to obtain the combine matching score from the four salient landmarks pairs, Dempster combination rule has been applied. First, we combine the matching scores obtained from the pairs of left-eye and nose landmark features and then the matching scores obtained from the pairs of right-eye and mouth landmark features are combined. Finally, the matching scores determined from the first and second processes are fused. Also, let $m(\Gamma^{left-eye})$, $m(\Gamma^{right-eye})$, $m(\Gamma^{nose})$ and $m(\Gamma^{mouth})$ be the bpa functions for the Belief measures $Bel(\Gamma^{left-eye})$, $Bel(\Gamma^{right-eye})$, $Bel(\Gamma^{nose})$ and $Bel(\Gamma^{mouth})$ for the four classifiers, respectively. Then the Belief probability assignments (bpa) $m(\Gamma^{left-eye})$, $m(\Gamma^{right-eye})$, $m(\Gamma^{nose})$ and $m(\Gamma^{mouth})$ can be combined together to obtained a Belief committed to a matching score set $C \in \Theta$ using orthogonal sum rule [11].

The final decision of user acceptance and rejection can be established by applying threshold to the final match score.

4   Experimental Results

To verify the efficacy and robustness of graph matching techniques in biometric discussed in the paper, several biometric databases such as BANCA [12], ORL [13] and IIT Kanpur [14] face databases are used. This paper is described two identity verification and recognition techniques and they are invariant face recognition through complete graph topology and face recognition by fusion of invariant features of salient landmarks using probabilistic graphs. The experimental results are given as follows.

4.1   Face Recognition Using RPbMC

The graph matching technique has used the BANCA database [12] with the proposed matching constraint. BANCA face database is a challenging, realistic and large face database that has variations of face instances. Face images have recorded in controlled, degraded and adverse conditions with over 12 different sessions spanning three months. In total, face images of 52 subjects are taken from 26 male participants and 26 female participants. For this experiment, the Matched Controlled (MC) protocol [12] is followed where the images from the first session are used for training and second, third, and fourth sessions are used for testing and generating client and impostor scores. The testing images are divided into two groups, *G1* and *G2*, of 26 subjects each. The Prior Equal Error Rate (PEER) [6], Weighted Error Rate (WER) and client-specific threshold are computed using the procedure presented in.

Prior Equal Error Rates for *G1* and *G2* are presented in Table 1 showing the weighted equal error rates for three different values of R (R is defined as the cost ratio for three different operating points, namely, R=0.1, R=1 and R=10).

Table 1. Weighted Equal Error rates for the proposed face recognition system

WER ↓ Method →	RPbMC
WER (R=0.1) on G1	7.09
WER (R=0.1) on G2	2.24
WER (R=1.0) on G1	6.66
WER (R=1.0) on G2	1.92
WER (R=10) on G1	6.24
WER (R=10) on G2	1.61

4.2   Face Recognition by Fusion of Salient Invariant Features

The IITK face database [14] consists of 1200 face images with four images per person (300X4). These images are captured under control environment with ±20 degree changes of head pose and with at most uniform lighting and illumination conditions and with almost consistent facial expressions. For the face matching, all probe images are matched against all target images. From the ROC curve in Figure 2 it has been observed that the recognition accuracy is 93.63%, with the false accept rate (FAR) of 5.82%.

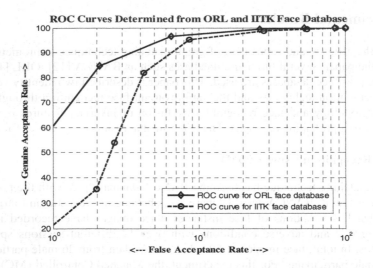

Fig. 2. ROC Curves

The ORL face database [13] consists of 400 images taken from 40 subjects. Out of these 400 images, 200 face images are considered for experiment. It has been observed that there exist changes in orientation in images which lying between -20^0 and 30^0. The face images are found to have the variations in pose and facial expression (smile/not smile, open/closed eyes). The original resolution of the images is 92 x 112 pixels. However, for the experiment, the resolution is set to 120×160 pixels. From the ROC curve in Figure 2 it has been observed that the recognition accuracy for the ORL database is 97.33%, yielding 2.14% FAR. The relative accuracy of the matching strategy for ORL database increases of about 3% over the IITK database.

5 Conclusion

In this paper, two face recognition systems have been presented using complete graph topology and probabilistic graph respectively. The proposed systems exhibit robustness towards recognize the users. The results of the Reduced Point based Match Constraint show the capability of the system to cope for illumination changes and occlusions occurring in the database or the query face image. From the second face recognition it has been determined that when the face matching accomplishes with the whole face region, the global features (whole face) are easy to capture and they are generally less discriminative than localized features. In the face recognition method, local facial landmarks are considered for further processing. The optimal face representation using graph relaxation drawn on local landmarks allows matching the localized facial features efficiently by searching the correspondence of keypoints using iterative relaxation.

References

1. Wiskott, L., Fellous, J.M., Kruger, N., Von der Malsburg, C.: Face Recognition by Elastic Bunch Graph Matching. IEEE Transactions on Pattern Analysis and Machine Intelligence 19(7), 775–779 (1997)
2. Fazi-Ersi, E., Zelek, J.S., Tsotsos, J.K.: Robust Face Recognition through Local Graph Matching. Journal of Computers 2(5), 31–37 (2007)
3. Liu, J., Liu, Z.-Q.: EBGM with Fuzzy Fusion on Face. In: Zhang, S., Jarvis, R.A. (eds.) AI 2005. LNCS (LNAI), vol. 3809, pp. 498–509. Springer, Heidelberg (2005)
4. Li, S.Z., Jain, A.K. (eds.): Handbook of Face Recognition. Springer, Heidelberg (2005)
5. Conte, D., Foggia, P., Sansone, C., Vente, M.: Graph Matching Applications in Pattern Recognition and Image Processing. In: International Conference on Image Processing (2003)
6. Kisku, D.R., Rattani, A., Grosso, E., Tistarelli, M.: Face Identification by SIFT-based Complete Graph Topology. In: 5th IEEE International Workshop on Automatic Identification Advanced Technologies, pp. 63–68 (2007)
7. Lowe, D.G.: Object Recognition from Local Scale Invariant Features. In: International Conference on Computer Vision, pp. 1150–1157 (1999)
8. Gourier, N., James, D.H., Crowley, L.: Estimating Face Orientation from Robust Detection of Salient Facial Structures. In: FG Net Workshop on Visual Observation of Deictic Gestures (2004)
9. Smeraldi, F., Capdevielle, N., Bigün, J.: Facial Features Detection by Saccadic Exploration of the Gabor Decomposition and Support Vector Machines. In: 11th Scandinavian Conference on Image Analysis, pp. 39–44 (1999)
10. Kisku, D.R., Mehrotra, H., Gupta, P., Sing, J.K.: Probabilistic Graph-based Feature Fusion and Score Fusion using SIFT Features for Face and Ear Biometrics. In: SPIE International Symposium on Optics and Photonics, vol. 7443, p. 744306 (2009)
11. Bauer, M.: Approximation Algorithms and Decision-making in the Dempster-Shafer Theory of Evidence—An Empirical Study. International Journal of Approximate Reasoning 17, 217–237 (1997)
12. Bailly-Baillire, E., Bengio, S., Bimbot, F., Hamouz, M., Kitler, J., Marithoz, J., Matas, J., Messer, K., Popovici, V., Pore, F., Ruiz, B., Thiran, J.P.: The BANCA database and evaluation protocol. In: International Conference on Audio – and Video-Based Biometric Person Authentication, pp. 625–638 (2003)
13. Samaria, F., Harter, A.: Parameterization of a Stochastic Model for Human Face Identification. In: IEEE Workshop on Applications of Computer Vision (1994)
14. Kisku, D.R., Rattani, A., Tistarelli, M., Gupta, P.: Graph Application on Face for Personal Authentication and Recognition. In: 10th IEEE International Conference on Control, Automation, Robotics and Vision, pp. 1150–1155 (2008)

Substitution-Diffusion Based Image Cipher Using Chaotic Standard Map and 3D Cat Map

Anil Kumar and M.K. Ghose

Computer Science and Engineering Dept.
Sikkim Manipal Institute of Technology, Sikkim, India
dahiyaanil@yahoo.com

Abstract. This paper proposes a substitution-diffusion based image cipher using chaotic standard maps and 3D cat map. The first stage consists of stretches of plain image using arnold cat map, XOR-ing with synthetic image which is generated using chaotic standards map and total number of rounds are controlled by secret key and plain image. Then in second stage further diffusion and confusion is obtained in the horizontal and vertical pixels by mixing the properties of the horizontally and vertically adjacent pixels, respectively, with XORing by generating an intermediate chaotic key stream (CKS)image in a novel manner with the help of chaotic standard map and total numbers of rounds are controlled by secret key and plain image. The performance is done such as entropy analysis, difference analysis, statistical analysis, key sensitivity analysis,, key space analysis, speed analysis. This proposed technique is trade of between security and time. The experimental results illustrate that performance of this is highly secured.

1 Introduction

The traditional encryption schemes [2] fails to protect multimedia data due to some special properties and some specific requirements of multimedia processing systems, such as mammoth size and strong redundancy of uncompressed data.

Many chaos-based encryption systems also proposed [1],[3],[4]. Many chaos-based cryptography schemes have been successfully cryptanalyzed [5],[6].

In this paper, we have proposed a new symmetric image encryption by using the chaotic 2D standard map and 3D cat map in such a way that it incorporating nonlinearity which is the main limitation of the patidar et al [1].

2 Proposed Method

First, the generation of synthetic images explained in section 2.1, in second stage image stretching and XORing explained in section 2.2, in third stage of diffusion and XORing explained in section 2.3, and decryption discussed in Section 2.4.

2.1 Generation of Synthetic Images

Here, the generation of the synthetic images is discussed and also calculating the number of rounds which will be used in rotation and mixing stage.

V.V Das et al. (Eds.): BAIP 2010, CCIS 70, pp. 34–38, 2010.

1. The secret key consists of three floating point numbers and one integer (X_0, Y_0, K, N) where $X_0, Y_0 \in (0, 2\pi)$, K can have any real value greater than 18.0 and N is any integer value, ideally should be greater than 100.

$$X_{n+1} = X_n + K * \sin Y_n$$
$$Y_{n+1} = Y_n + X_{n+1}$$

(1)

2. Read the image, let the size of image is $* H$. XOR all the bytes of the image let it be IXOR.
3. Generate the pseudorandom sequence by iterating the equation (1) by $W * H + N$ times and the pseudorandom sequence generated as *XKey1* and *XKey2* take last $W * H$ values. Scale the key using Algorithm as stated

```
program Synthetic images generation ()
begin
      repeat
         XKey1(i) = (XKey1(i)/2pi)* 256;
         XKey2(i) = (XKey2(i)/2pi)* 256;
      until i = W*H
      SImage1=reshape(XKey1,W,H);
      SImage2=reshape(XKey2,W,H);
end.
```

4. Take XOR of the all values of key *XKey1* as *KXOR1* and for *XKey2* as *KXOR2*.

2.2 Image Stretching and XORing

Here, in the proposed chaos based encryption technique, the concept image stretching, XOR (SImage1) is used.

The 2D Arnold cat map including two control parameters [7] is as follows:

$$\begin{pmatrix} x' \\ y' \end{pmatrix} = \begin{pmatrix} 1 & a \\ b & ab+1 \end{pmatrix} \begin{pmatrix} x \\ y \end{pmatrix} mod(N)$$

Where *a and b* are two positive integers and $x, y \in \{0, 1, 2, \dots, N-1\}$. 3D cat map is extended by introducing another two control parameters *c and d* [8].

$$\begin{pmatrix} x' \\ y' \\ z' \end{pmatrix} = \begin{pmatrix} 1 & a & 0 \\ b & ab+1 & 0 \\ c & d & 1 \end{pmatrix} \begin{pmatrix} x \\ y \\ z \end{pmatrix} mod(N)$$

In Liu scheme [9], *x, y and x', y'* in map are considered as positions of image before and after mapping, *z and z'* as grey values of image before and after mapping.

In this way, Liu change *z into p* and transform the form of map as follows:

$$\begin{pmatrix} x' \\ y' \end{pmatrix} = \begin{pmatrix} 1 & a \\ b & ab+1 \end{pmatrix} \begin{pmatrix} x \\ y \end{pmatrix} mod(N)$$

$$p' = (cx + dy + p)mod(M)$$

Where, N is the width and height of image, M is the color level. Hence, shuffling and substitution achieved using 3D cat map.

Steps for the first stage: The image $[N * N]$ elements are regarded as a set and are fed into an $N * N$ matrix.

1. i=1;
2. Apply the cat map, $c = XKey1(i)$ and $d = XKey2(i)$.
3. XOR transformed data with synthetic image $SImage1$.
4. Repeat above steps $N1$ times, $i = i + 1$ in order to get completely disordered data.

2.3 Diffusion and XORing

In cryptography, diffusion plays most important part especially in images, where the redundancy is large, the process of diffusion is a necessary requirement to develop a secure encryption technique. This removes the possibility of differential attacks by comparing the pair of plain and cipher images.

1. Modify second row by XORing of the first row and second row, modify third row by XORing of the modified second row and third row and the process continues till last row, which in turn gives the vertical diffusion.
2. Modify second column by XORing of the first column and second column, modify third column by XORing of the modified second column and third column and the process continues till last column, which in turn gives the horizontal diffusion.
3. XOR transformed data with synthetic image $SImage2$.
4. The number of rounds $N2=XOR(IXOR,KXOR2)$ times, in order to get completely diffusion.

2.4 Decryption

Decryption can be obtained as exact reverse of the encryption as discussed in above sections.

3 Security and Performance Analysis

An robust encryption scheme should resist against all kinds of attacks such as cryptanalytic attacks: ciphertext only attack, known plaintext attack, statistical attacks, brute-force attacks, etc. Results of the security and performance analysis performed on the proposed image encryption technique.3.1 Statistical analysis.

Histograms of encrypted image:
In example of such histogram analysis is shown in (Fig. 1). In the left column, we have shown the plain image *Lena (256 * 256 pixels)* and its histogram right column, cipher image of the image *Lena* obtained using the secret key, ($X_0 = 4.94785238984676$, $Y_0 = 0.31256128342389$, $K = 131.7183545564243$, and $N = 110$) and its histogram has been shown.

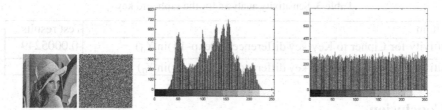

Fig. 1. Histogram Analysis: (a) Lena Image (b) Encrypted Image (c) Histogram of Lena Image (d) Histogram of Encrypted Image

Table 1. Correlation coefficients for the two adjacent pixels in the original and encrypted shown in (Fig. 1)

	Original Image	Encrypted Image
Horizontal	0.9187	-0.00048501
Vertical	0.9511	0.0024
Diagonal	0.8934	-0.0052

Table 2. Correlation between the plain image 'Lena' and its cipher image

Plain vs Encrypted image	Correlation
	-0.0013

3.1 Sensitivity Analysis of the Encryption

A good encryption algorithm must possess the property that a slight change in the key changes the encrypted file almost completely different.

1. Encrypted image is very sensitive to the secret key.Results are shown in (Table 3).
2. The encrypted image is not be decrypted correctly even if there is slight difference between the encryption and decryption keys.
   - First by changing least significant bit of X_0 key 4.94785238984676 to 4.94785238984675. The resulting image (Fig. 2(b)).
   - After that changing the least significant bit of Y_0 key 0.31256128342389 to 0.31256128342388. The resulting image (Fig 2(c))

Fig. 2. Sensitivity analysis for the cipher to keys when decrypt with slightly different key (a) Original key (b) Change in x (c) Change in y

Table 3. Sensitivity analysis for the cipher to key

Test item	Test results
Sensitivity for Cipher to Key(key difference(10exp-14)in X_0)	-0.0005249
Sensitivity for Cipher to Key(key difference(10exp-14)in Y_0)	-0.0059

4 Conclusion

The improved encryption concept is proposed using the stretching, diffusion, and numbers of rounds for both stages depends upon plain image and key combination. This method is immune to various types of cryptographic attacks like known-plain text, chosen plain text attacks. It is lossless also. The proposed scheme paper has high level security, and fast speed.

Acknowledgments

This work is part of the Research Project funded by All India Council of Technical Education (Government of India) vide their office order: F.No:8023/BOR/RID/RPS-236/2008-09.

References

1. Schneier, B.: Applied cryptography: protocols algorithms and source code in C. Wiley, New York (1996)
2. Patidar, V., Pareek, N.K., Sud, K.K.: A new substitution diffusion based image cipher using chaotic standard and logistic maps. Commun. Nonlinear Sci. Numer Simulat. 14, 3056–3075 (2009)
3. Tong, X., Cui, M.: Image encryption with compound chaotic sequence cipher shifting dynamically. Image and Vision Computing 26, 843–850 (2008)
4. Wang, Y., Wong, K.-W., Liao, X., Xiang, T., Chen, G.: A chaos based image encryption algorithm with variable control parameters. Chaos, Solitons and Fractals 41, 1773–1783 (2009)
5. Li, C., Li, S., Chen, G., Halang, W.A.: Cryptanalysis of an image encryption scheme based on a compound chaotic sequence. Image and Vision Computing 27, 1035–1039 (2009)
6. Rhouma, R., Solak, E., Belghith, S.: Cryptanalysis of a new substitution-diffusion based image cipher. Commun. Nonlinear Sci. Numer. Simulat. (2009) (in press) doi:10.1016/j.cnsns.2009.07.007
7. Chen, G., Mao, Y., Chui, C.: A symmetric image encryption scheme based on 3D chaotic cat maps. Chaos, Solitons and Fractals, 741–749 (2004)
8. Zhong, X., Liu, J., Huang, X.: An Image Encryption Algorithm Based on chaotic Cat Map. Chinese Microelectronics and Computer 282, 131–134 (2007)
9. Liu, H., Zhu, Z., Jiang, H.: A Novel Image Encryption Algorithm Based on Improved 3D Chaotic Cat Map. In: 9th International Conference for Young Computer Scientists, pp. 3016–3021 (2009)

Hybrid Activities of AODV for Wireless Ad hoc Sensor Network

Srinivas Sethi[1], Ashima Rout[2], Dipti Mohanta[3], Aayush Behera[4],
and Manmath N. Sahoo[5]

[1] Department of Computer Science and Engineering,
srinivas_sethi@igitsarang.ac.in
[2,3,4,5] Department of Electrical and Electronics Engineering,
IGIT, Sarang, Orissa, India
ashimarout@yahoo.com,
dipti.igit@gmail.com, aayushbehera05@gmail.com,
manmath.igit@gmail.com

Abstract. With upcoming availability of low cost short ranges along with advances in wireless networking it is expected that Wireless Ad hoc Sensor Network will become commonly deployed. Many applications for wireless communication networks such as wireless sensors, industrial control and monitoring, intelligent agriculture, inventory tracking, and security would benefit from a communication protocol. Routing has important role in these types of scenarios. In this paper a hybrid routing protocol named as Hybrid-AODV has been proposed. The goal of this paper is to characterize the performance of proposed protocol based on ad hoc sensor network. An exhaustive simulation experiment reveals that, the proposed Hybrid-AODV protocol performs better than AODV in terms of PDR and end-to-end delay for all mobility rates and various area grid sizes.

Keywords: Wireless Ad hoc Sensor Network, AODV, Proactive, Hybrid.

1 Introduction

Wireless Ad hoc Sensor Network (WASN) has become popular in recent years because of their easy deploybility, less infrastructure requirement, short range radios and suitability for applications such as catastrophic management, war frontier, office networks, and taxicab networks along others. All sensor nodes behave as routers and take part in discovery and maintenance of the route to other sensor node(s) in the network. Without the fixed base station the mobile sensor nodes dynamically exchange the data among themselves.

Routing protocols have vital role in these types of scenarios. Mainly three different types of routing protocols are available and they are proactive, reactive and hybrid routing protocols. Proactive routing protocols periodically exchange messages. At all times the routes to all destinations are ready to use and as a consequence initial delays before sending data are small. However it requires regular

V. V Das et al. (Eds.): BAIP 2010, CCIS 70, pp. 39–44, 2010.

routing updates which may consume a large portion of limited resources. Keeping routes to all destinations up-to-date, even if they are not used, is a disadvantage with regard to the usage of bandwidth and of network resources. WRP, OLSR are examples of this type of protocol. Whereas, the on-demand(reactive) routing protocol finds a route when required. The main disadvantage of such algorithms is high latency time in route discovery. Examples of reactive algorithms are AODV, DSR etc. The combination of advantages of table driven and on-demand protocols are seen in hybrid routing protocol. It has better scalability as compared to others. CBRP, ZRP are examples of hybrid routing protocols.

In terms of route learning capability, Dynamic Source Routing (DSR) [3][4] can learn more routing information from the traffic because DSR packets contain complete route information. Control overhead can be reduced by creating a route maintenance mechanism between only those nodes which needs the services to transmit. Route cache can also help to cut the overhead burden.

Destination Sequenced Distance Vector (DSDV)[2] is a proactive routing protocol. It is a hop-by-hop distance vector routing protocol requiring each node to periodically broadcast routing updates. It has no sleeping nodes. So it has high overhead because most of the routing information are never used.

AODV [1][6][10] combines the use of destination sequence numbers in DSDV [2] with the on-demand route discovery technique in DSR [3][4] to formulate a loop-free, on-demand, single path, distance vector protocol. Unlike DSR, which uses source routing, AODV is based on hop-by-hop routing approach. AODV is an uniform and destination based reactive routing protocol.

The evaluation of performance of AODV routing protocol is observed with random based entity mobility model and pursue group mobility model in respect to PDR, Delay and Throughput [11]. The pursue group mobility model performs better than random based entity mobility models.

TORA[12] seems to be the worst performer in terms of routing packet overhead. So in this paper, AODV is considered for comparison with proposed Hybrid-AODV for wireless ad hoc sensor network. The packet delivery ratio is significantly improved along with end-to-end delay.

The remaining part of the paper is organized as follows: section-2 has a detailed discussion on the proposed work. In Section-3, we describe the performance evaluations parameters followed by simulation parameter in section-4. Observations and discussions are described in section-5 followed by conclusions in Section-6.

2 Proposed Protocol

Hybrid-AODV (Hybrid Ad-hoc On Demand Distance Vector) is extension of AODV [1][6][10] with proactive capability in wireless ad hoc sensor network. When a traffic source needs a route to a destination, it initiates a route discovery process. Route discovery typically involves a network-wide flood of route request (RREQ) packets targeting the destination and waiting for a route reply (RREP). An intermediate node receiving a RREQ packet first sets up a reverse path to the source using the previous hop of the RREQ as the next hop on the reverse path. If a valid route to the destination is available, then the intermediate node generates a RREP else the RREQ is rebroadcasted. When the destination receives a RREQ, it also generates a RREP. As the RREP proceeds towards the source, a forward path to the destination is established. Route maintenance is done using route error (RERR) packets. When a link failure is detected, a RERR is sent back via separately maintained predecessor links to all sources using that failed link. When a traffic source receives a RERR, it initiates a new route discovery if the route is still needed.

It maintains the highest known sequence numbers for each destination in the routing table called "destination sequence numbers". Destination sequence numbers are tagged on all routing messages, thus providing a mechanism to determine the relative freshness of two pieces of routing information.

The Hybrid-AODV protocol maintains an invariant destination sequence number that monotonically increases along a valid route, thus preventing routing loops. A node can receive a routing update via a RREQ or RREP packet either forming or updating a reverse or forward path. We refer to such routing updates received via a RREQ or RREP as "route advertisements."

It is the extended proactive capability of AODV, so that route discovery delays to be reduced which are main disadvantages of on-demand routing protocols. All the nodes are not in sleep mode. They are always active and send the "hello" message to indicate their aliveness, so that no delay to discover the route for destination.

3 Performance Evaluation Parameters

We used PDR and delay the performance matrices to the effect of each scheduling algorithm. **Packet Delivery Ratio (PDR)** is used to measure the reliability, effectiveness and efficiency of routing protocols. It is defined as the percentage of data packets delivered at receiver end to that of no. of data packets sent for that node.

$$PDR = \frac{\sum_i No. of \ packets \ delivered \ at \ receiver}{\sum_i No. packets \ sent \ to \ receiver} * 100$$

End-to-End delay: This includes all possible delays caused by buffering during route discovery delay, queuing at the interface, queuing transmission delays at MAC, propagation and transfer times of data packets from source to destination. In this paper, through simulation we measured all these parameters for performance comparison purpose. Exhaustive simulation experiments are carried out with different mobility rates and number of nodes in the wireless ad hoc sensor network.

4 Simulation Parameters

The performance evaluation and comparisons are carried out using NS-2[13] [14] under Linux operating system as the simulation parameters described Table-1.

Table 1. Simulation Parameters

S. No.	Parameters	Values
1	Area size	500x500m,1000x1000m, 1500x1500m, 2000x2000m
2	Transmission range	250 meters.
3	Simulation time	600 sec.
4	Mobility Rates	1,5,10,15,20 m/s
5	Pause time	10 s
6	Data rate	1 Kbps
7	No. of experiments	5 times.

5 Observation and Discussion

It is observed that as regards to PDR, Hybrid-AODV proves to be better than AODV for all combinations of mobility rate and grid sizes. Hence the proposed protocol of Hybrid-AODV outperforms AODV.

Figure-1 shows that PDR of Hybrid-AODV achieves a better result as compared to AODV in respect to various mobility rates. Similarly Figure-2 reveals that the result in terms of PDR obtained by simulation for Hybrid-AODV found to be better with respect to various grid sizes. It is observed that Hybrid-AODV performs better than AODV in terms of end-to-end delay. As per Figure-3, the end-to-end delay of Hybrid-AODV is better in respect to all mobility rates. Figure-4 shows that performance of Hybrid-AODV in terms of end-to-end delay better than AODV. In case of various mobility rate and different area in grid sizes, Hybrid-AODV performs better than AODV in respect to end-to-end delay.

From the above discussion, we observed that our proposed work Hybrid-AODV routing protocol is better than AODV for wireless ad hoc sensor networks.

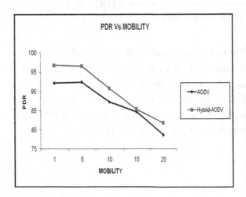 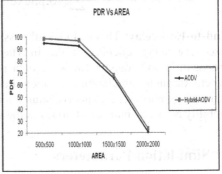

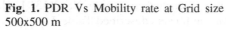

Fig. 1. PDR Vs Mobility rate at Grid size 500x500 m

Fig. 2. PDR Vs Area in grid size at mobility rate 5 m/s

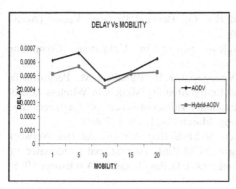

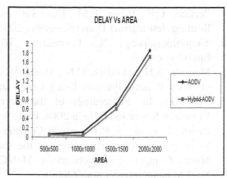

Fig. 3. Delay Vs Mobility rate at Grid size 500x500 m

Fig. 4. Delay Vs Area in grid size at mobility rate 5 m/s

6 Conclusion

In this paper, the performance of Hybrid Ad hoc On Demand Distance Vector (Hybrid-AODV) in terms of Packet Delivery Ratio has been discussed. Comparison of the Hybrid-AODV with AODV routing protocols under different mobility rates and area in grid size reveal that PDR is much better in case of proposed Hybrid-AODV with improvement of end-to-end delay as compared to AODV. Thus, it can be concluded that Hybrid-AODV protocol is suitable for Wireless Ad hoc Sensor Network where reliability and time sensitive is an important issue.

References

1. Perkin, C.E., Royer, E.M.: Ad Hoc On Demand Distance Vector Routing. In: Proceeding 2nd IEEE Workshop, Mobile Computing, Sys. Apps., pp. 90–100 (1999)
2. Perkins, C.E., Watson, T.J.: Highly Dynamic Destination Sequenced Distance Vector Routing (Dsdv) For Mobile Computers. In: Proceeding of ACM Sigcomm Conference on Communications Architectures, London, October 1994, pp. 234–244 (1994)
3. Johnson, D.B., Maltz, D.A.: Dynamic Source Routing in Ad Hoc Wireless Networks. Mobile Computing 353 (1996)
4. Johnson, D.B., Maltz, D.A., Hu, Y.-C.: The Dynamic Source Routing Protocol For Mobile Ad Hoc Networks (Dsr). Internet Draft, Draft-Ietf-Manet-Dsr-09.Txt (April 2003)
5. Jayakumar, G., Gopinath, G.: Performance Comparision of Manet Protocols Based on Manhattan Grid Mobility Model. Journal of Mobile communication 2(1), 18–26 (2008)
6. Perkins, C.E., Belding-Royer, E.M., Chakeres, I.D.: Ad Hoc On Demand Distance Vector (Aodv) Routing. Ietf Internet Draft (November 2003)
7. Meng, L., et al.: A Novel Ad Hoc Routing Protocol Based On Mobility Prediction. Information Technology Journal 7(3); In: 12th International Conference on Information Technology. Asian Network For Scientific Information 2008, pp. 537–540 (2008) ISSN 1812-5638
8. Wan, C.-Y., Campbell, A.T., Krishnamurthy, L.: Psfq: A Reliable Transport Protocol For Wireless Sensor Networks. In: WSNA 2002, Atlanta, Georgia, September 28. ACM, New York (2002), 1-58113-589-0/02/0009

9. Perkins, C.E., Royer, E.M., Das, S.R.: Ad Hoc On Demand Distance Vector (Aodv) Routing, Ietf Internet Draft (November 2000)
10. Thepvilojanapong, N.: Connecting Wireless Sensor in Ubiquitous Computing Environments
11. Manjula, S.H., Abhilash, C.N., Shaila, K., Venugopal, K.R., Patnaik, L.M.: Performance of Aodv Routing Protocol Using Group and Entity Mobility Models in Wireless Sensor Networks. In: Proceedings of the International Multiconference of Engineers and Computer Scientists, IMECS 2008, Hong Kong, March 19-21, vol. I (2008)
12. Broch, J., et al.: A Performance Comparison of Multi-Hop Wireless Ad Hoc Network Routing Protocols: Proceedings of the fourth ACM/IEEE International Conference on Mobile Computing and Networking (MobiCom 1998), Dallas, Texas, USA (October 1998)
13. Ns-2 Manual, internet draft (2009),
    http://www.isi.edu/nsnam/ns/ns-documentation.html
14. Downard, I.: Simulating Sensor Networks in Ns-2, Naval Research Laboratory, internet draft,
    http://www.cs.itd.nrl.navy.mil/pubs/docs/nrlsensorsim04.pdf

Design and Evaluation of a Fuzzy-Based CPU Scheduling Algorithm

Shatha J. Kadhim[1] and Kasim M. Al-Aubidy[2]

[1] Computer Eng. Dept, Al-Blaqa' Applied University, Al-Salt, Jordan
[2] Computer Eng. Dept, Philadelphia University, Amman, Jordan
kma@philadelphia.edu.jo

Abstract. Scheduling in computer science means determining which tasks run when there are multiple runnable tasks. Several CPU scheduling algorithms have different features, and no single one is ideal absolutely for every application. This paper presents an attempt to apply fuzzy logic in the design and implementation of a rule-based scheduling algorithm to solve the shortcoming of well-known scheduling algorithms. Results given in this paper demonstrate that the average waiting time and the average turnaround time in the proposed algorithm are better than that obtained using priority scheduling, and closed to that obtained from shortest-job-first (SJF) scheduling. The new proposed algorithm is a dynamic scheduling algorithm which deals with both task priority and its execution time, while the SJF algorithm doesn't.

Keywords: Task Scheduling; Fuzzy Decision Making; Operating Systems; Real-Time Systems.

1 Introduction

A real time system is the one whose applications are mission-critical, where real-time tasks should be scheduled to be completed before their deadlines [1,2]. Most real-time systems control unpredictable environments and may need operating systems that can handle unknown and changing task populations. In this case, not only a dynamic task scheduling is required, but both system hardware and software must adapt to unforeseen configurations [3].

In computer science, a scheduling algorithm is the method by which tasks, processes, threads or data flow are given access to system resources [2]. The need for a scheduling algorithm arises from the requirement for most modern systems to perform more than one process at a certain time. Operating systems, such as Windows NT, have sophisticated CPU scheduling algorithms. Windows NT-based operating systems use a multilevel feedback queue with 32 priority levels and users can select 5 of these priorities and assign them to a running application. The kernel may change the priority level of a thread depending on its I/O and CPU usage and whether it is interactive. It usually raises the priority of interactive of I/O bounded processes and lowering that of CPU bound processes, to increase the responsiveness of interactive applications. The scheduler was modified in Windows Vista to use the cycle counter register of modern processors to keep track of exactly how many CPU cycles a thread

V. V Das et al. (Eds.): BAIP 2010, CCIS 70, pp. 45–52, 2010.

has executed, rather than just using an interval-timer interrupt routine. Vista also uses a priority scheduler for the I/O queue so that disk defragmenters and other such programs don't interfere with foreground operations [2,4].

Operating systems may feature up to three distinct types of schedulers: a long-term scheduler, a mid-term or medium-term scheduler and a short-term scheduler. The short-term scheduler (also called dispatcher) decides which of the ready, in-memory processes are to be executed. Thus the short-term scheduler makes scheduling decisions much more frequently than the long-term or mid-term schedulers. This scheduler can be preemptive, implying that it is capable of forcibly removing processes from a CPU when it decides to allocate that CPU to another process, or non-preemptive, in which case the scheduler is unable to "force" processes off the CPU [2]. So far, a number of research works have been performed on CPU scheduling problems for different applications. Swin and his group [3] addressed the difficult problem of dynamic task scheduling in real-time distributed systems. An enhanced SJF scheduling algorithm was suggested by Shahzad and Afzal [5] to ensure that higher tasks are not going to starve, and each task is executed in a certain definite time.

Limited amounts of literature have addressed the application of fuzzy logic to CPU scheduling problems. There are four main approaches reported in the literature for the fuzzy scheduling problems; fuzzifying directly the classical dispatching rules [6], using fuzzy ranking [7], fuzzy dominance relation methods[8], and solving mathematical models to determine the optimal schedules by heuristic approximation methods[9] including genetic algorithms[10]. In this paper, an attempt will be made to apply fuzzy logic in the design and implementation of a modified scheduling algorithm to overcome the shortcoming of well-known scheduling algorithms.

2 Scheduling Algorithms

Scheduling means determining which tasks run when there are multiple runnable tasks. There are several competing goals that scheduling algorithms aim to fulfill. These includes; throughput, turnaround, response time, and others. Before discussing these goals and features of the proposed scheduling algorithm, three types of the well-known scheduling algorithms need to be identified.

2.1 First-Come, First-Served (FCFS)

The first-come first-service (FCFS) is non-preemptive, and its implementation can be considered as a simple first-in first-out (FIFO) queue. This scheduler runs each task until it either terminates or leaves the task due to an input/output or other resource blockage. Now consider six tasks (T_1-T_6) with run times as given in Table 1. By running these tasks in that order, the turnaround times for these tasks are 34, 56, 74, 86, 92, 96, for an average of 73. It is clear that the FCFS scheduler is usually unsatisfactory for interactive systems as it favors long tasks.

2.2 Shortest-Job-First (SJF)

The shortest-job-first (SJF) scheduler is non-preemptive, and tries to improve response for short tasks over FCFS. However, it requires explicit information about the service time requirements for each task. The task with the shortest time

Table 1. An example

Task No.	T_1	T_2	T_3	T_4	T_5	T_6
Run Time	34	22	18	12	6	4
Priority	5	3	2	6	1	4

Table 2. Fuzzy rules

		Pre-Priority (P_o)				
		VHP_o	HP_o	MP_o	LP_o	VLP_o
Execution Time (Tx)	VBT	MP_n	LP_n	VLP_n	VLP_n	VLP_n
	BT_x	MP_n	MP_n	LP_n	LP_n	VLP_n
	MT_x	HP_n	MP_n	LP_n	LP_n	LP_n
	ST_x	VHP_n	HP_n	HP_n	MP_n	MP_n
	VST_x	VHP_n	VHP_n	HP_n	HP_n	MP_n

requirement is chosen. Operating system will change tasks if the next CPU burst is less than what is left of the current one. Now, consider running the six tasks given in Table 1 using SJF algorithm. The turnaround times are 4, 10, 22, 40, 62, 96, for an average of 39.

It is clear that the SJF algorithm performance is better than that for FCFS algorithm for the given tasks[11]. One problem with SJF is that long processes wait a long time or suffer starvation. Short tasks are treated very favorably. Another problem with SJF is that there has to be some way of estimating the time requirement; which will be based on the previous performance.

2.3 Priority Scheduling (PrS)

Priority scheduling requires that each task is assigned a priority. At each scheduling event, the task queue is sorted according to priority, and the task of highest priority chosen first. Tasks of equal priority are scheduled as FCFS. Again, consider running of the same tasks given in Table 1 using priority scheduling algorithm, lower numbers represent higher priorities. The turnaround times are 6, 24, 46, 50, 84, 96, for an average of 50.333. It is clear that the main problem with priority scheduling algorithm is the blocking of low-priority tasks. To prevent this, it is required to modify the scheduling algorithm. Forms of priority scheduling are used in interactive systems, real-time systems, and in batch systems. In many real-time systems, it is necessary to have some priority mechanism.

As mentioned above, different scheduling algorithms have different features, and no single one is ideal absolutely for every situation. It is required to specify techniques for quantifying the characteristics of each algorithm in order to investigate a new scheduler to overcome the mentioned drawbacks of the available scheduling algorithms. To make a scheduler very efficient, we need to specify the quantitative metrics that may include;

- CPU Utilization: keep CPU utilization as high as possible.
- Throughput: number of tasks completed per unit time.
- Turnaround Time: mean time from submission to completion of task.
- Waiting Time: amount of time spent ready to run but not running.
- Response Time: time between submission of requests and first response to the request.

3 Fuzzy-Based Scheduling (FuzS)

A modified rule-based fuzzy scheduler that deals with both task priority and its execution time is presented in this section. A fuzzy-based decision maker (FDM) has

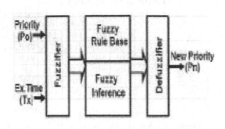

Fig. 1. Fuzzy decision maker layout

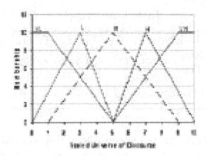

Fig. 2. Universe of discourse of the variables

been proposed to compute the new priority (Pn) of all CPU tasks according to the task pre-priority (Po) and its execution time (Tx), as shown in Fig.(1). The measured variables are inverted into suitable linguistic variables. In this application, the following linguistic variables are used for pre-priority (Po), and new calculated priority (Pn); Very Low (VL), Low (L), Medium (M), High (H), and Very High(VH). The fuzzy sets definition for execution time (Tx) are; Very Short (VS), Short (S), Medium (M), Big (B), and Very Big (VB). Figure (2) shows the universe of discourse and fuzzy sets of these variables. Fuzzy sets can have a variety of shapes. However, a triangular or a trapezoid can often provide an adequate representation of the knowledge [11].

The proposed fuzzy decision maker is a collection of linguistic rules which describe the relationships between measured variables (Po & Tx), and calculated output (Pn). Table 2 contains 25 rules, since we have five fuzzy sets for each variable. Each rule is represented by IF and THEN statement such as;

IF MPo and STx THEN HPn

This means that if the pre-priority is medium (MPo) and the execution time is short (STx), then the new calculated priority is high (HPn). The Mamdani-style inference process is used[11], and the center of gravity defuzzification method is applied to convert the fuzzy output into a crisp value that represents the new priority of a task.

It is clear that the average waiting time and average turnaround time obtained from the FuzS algorithm are better than that obtained from the PrS algorithm and close to that obtained from the SFJ algorithm.

4   Results and Performance Evaluation

To demonstrate the applicability and performance of the fuzzy-based scheduling algorithm, it is compared with two well-known scheduling algorithms; SFJ and PrS algorithms. Four case studies were considered in this comparison in terms of average waiting time (WT) and average turnaround time (TA).

Table 3. Case study 1

Task No.	T_1	T_2	T_3	T_4	T_5	T_6
Priority	10	9	1	10	5	8
Execute Time	30	1	20	3	5	10
New priority	4.151	6.413	3.562	6.541	5.500	5.090

Table 4. Tasks time specifications, case study1

Task No.	T_1	T_2	T_3	T_4	T_5	T_6	Average
W Time	0	33	49	30	44	34	31.66
TA Time	30	34	69	33	49	44	43.166

(a) using priority scheduling algorithm

Task No.	T_1	T_2	T_3	T_4	T_5	T_6	Average
W Time	39	0	19	1	4	9	12.0
TA Time	69	1	39	4	9	19	23.5

(b) using SFJ scheduling algorithm

Task No.	T_1	T_2	T_3	T_4	T_5	T_6	Average
W Time	39	3	19	0	4	9	12.333
TA Time	69	4	39	3	9	19	23.833

(c) using fuzzy-based scheduling algorithm

T_1	T_2	T_3	T_4	T_5	T_6
0	30 33 34		44 49		69

(a) using priority scheduling algorithm

T_2	T_4	T_5	T_6	T_3	T_1
0 1	4	9	19	39	69

(b) using SFJ scheduling algorithm

T_4	T_2	T_5	T_6	T_3	T_1
0 3	4	9	19	39	69

(c) using fuzzy-based scheduling algorithm

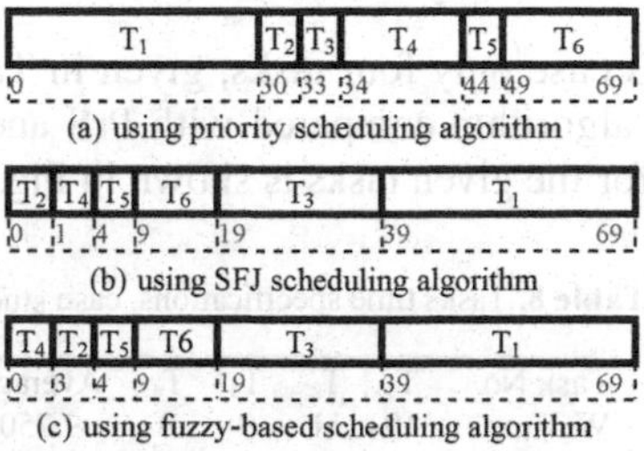

Fig. 3. The Gant chart of CPU time for case-study 1

4.1   Case-Study 1

Consider the running of the six tasks given in Table 3 using three scheduling algorithms; PrS, SFJ and FuzS. Figure 4 shows the Gant chart of CPU time for the given tasks.

Table 5. Case study 2

Task No.	T_1	T_2	T_3	T_4	T_5
Priority	6	5	1	4	2
Execute Time	3	24	6	9	8
New priority	5.961	4.407	4.891	5.081	4.967

Table 6. Tasks time specifications, case study 2

Task No.	T_1	T_2	T_3	T_4	T_5	Average
W Time	0	3	44	27	36	22
TA Time	3	27	50	36	44	32

(a). using priority scheduling algorithm.

Task No.	T_1	T_2	T_3	T_4	T_5	Average
W Time	0	26	3	17	9	11.000
TA Time	3	50	9	26	17	21.000

(b). using SFJ scheduling algorithm.

Task No.	T_1	T_2	T_3	T_4	T_5	Average
W Time	0	26	20	3	12	12.200
TA Time	3	50	26	12	20	22.200

(c). using fuzzy-based scheduling algorithm.

T_1	T_2	T_4	T_5	T_3
0 3	27	36	44	50

(a). using priority scheduling algorithm.

T_1	T_3	T_5	T_4	T_2
0 3	27	36	44	50

(b). using SFJ scheduling algorithm.

T_1	T_4	T_5	T_3	T_2
0 3	12	20	26	50

(c). using fuzzy-based scheduling algorithm.

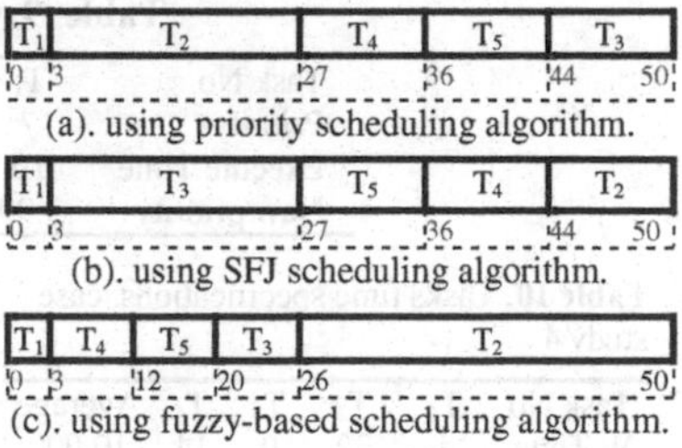

Fig. 4. The Gant chart of CPU time, case study 2

Table 7. Case study 3

Task No.	T_1	T_2	T_3	T_4
Priority	0	5	8	10
Execute Time	20	8	2	9
New priority	2.70	4.96	6.50	5.72

4.2 Case-Study 2

Now consider the running of tasks given in Table 5 using the same scheduling algorithms; PrS, SFJ and FuzS. The Gant chart of the CPU time for the given tasks is shown in Fig. 4.

4.3 Case-Study 3

In this case only four tasks, given in Table 7, are considered to test the ability of the FuzS algorithm compared with PrS and SFJ algorithms. The Gant chart of the CPU time for the given tasks is shown in Fig. 5.

Table 8. Tasks time specifications, case study 3

Task No.	T_1	T_2	T_3	T_4	Average
W Time	19	11	9	0	9.750
TA Time	39	19	11	9	19.500

(a) using priority scheduling algorithm

Task No.	T_1	T_2	T_3	T_4	Average
W Time	19	2	0	10	7.750
TA Time	39	10	2	19	17.500

(b) using SFJ scheduling algorithm

Task No.	T_1	T_2	T_3	T_4	Average
W Time	19	11	0	2	8.000
TA Time	39	19	2	11	17.750

(c) using fuzzy-based scheduling algorithm

(a) using priority scheduling algorithm

(b) using SFJ scheduling algorithm

c) using fuzzy-based scheduling algorithm

Fig. 5. The Gant chart of CPU time, case study 3

4.4 Case-Study 4

Again four tasks are considered in this case but with different priorities and execution times, as in Table 9. The Gant chart of the CPU time for the given tasks is shown in Fig. 6.

Table 9. Case study 4

Task No.	T_1	T_2	T_3	T_4
Priority	7	1	15	4
Execute Time	10	5	4	8
New priority	3.90	4.27	5.80	2.95

Table 10. Tasks time specifications, case study 4

Task No.	T_1	T_2	T_3	T_4	Average
W Time	4	22	0	14	10.000
TA Time	14	27	4	22	16.750

(a) using priority scheduling algorithm

Task No.	T_1	T_2	T_3	T_4	Average
W Time	17	4	0	9	7.500
TA Time	27	9	4	17	14.250

(b) using SFJ scheduling algorithm

Task No.	T_1	T_2	T_3	T_4	Average
W Time	19	4	0	9	8.000
TA Time	27	9	4	19	14.750

(c) using fuzzy-based scheduling algorithm

(a) using priority scheduling algorithm

(b) using SFJ scheduling algorithm

(c) using fuzzy-based scheduling algorithm

Fig. 6. The Gant chart of CPU time, case study 4

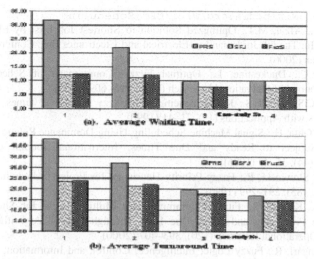

Fig. 7. Comparisons between SJF, PrS and FuzS

5 Conclusion

This paper addresses different problems of task scheduling in computer-based systems. In some applications, SJF scheduling algorithm is more suitable than PrS algorithm since it provides less waiting time and less turnaround time. In real-time applications, PrS algorithm must be used to deal with different priorities, since each task has a priority order.

In order to obtain an efficient scheduling algorithm, a rule-based fuszzy decision maker deals with both task priority and its execution time is designed and evaluated to overcome the shortcoming of well-known scheduling algorithms. As illustrated in Fig. 7, a simple comparison between fuzzy-based scheduling algorithms with other mentioned scheduling algorithms (PrS and SFJ), the following points can be pointed out:

- Several CPU scheduling algorithms have different characteristics, and no single one is ideal for absolutely every application.
- The average waiting time and the average turnaround time in the FuzS algorithm are better than that obtained using priority scheduling, and closed to that obtained from shortest-job-first scheduling.
- The FuzS algorithm is a dynamic scheduling algorithm deals with task priority, while the SJF doesn't.

References

1. Blazewicz, J., Ecker, K.H., Pesch, E., Schmidt, G., Weglarz, J.: Scheduling Computer and Manufacturing Processes. Springer, Berlin (2001)
2. Stallings, W.: Operating Systems Internals and Design Principles, 5th edn. Prentice-Hall, Englewood Cliffs (2004)
3. Swin, B.R., Tayli, M., Benmaiza, M.: Prospects for Predictable Dynamic Scheduling in RTDOS. Journal King Saud University, Computer & Information Science 9, 57–93 (1997)

4. http://en.wikipedia.org/wiki/CPU_Scheduling
5. Shahzad, B., Afzal, M.T.: Optimized Solution to Shortest Job First by Eliminating the Starvation. In: The 6th Jordanian Inr. Electrical and Electronics Eng. Conference (JIEEEC 2006), Jordan (2006)
6. Ozelkan, E.C., Duckestine, L.: Optimal Fuzzy Counterparts of Scheduling Rules. European Journal of Operational Research (113), 593–609 (1999)
7. McCahon, C.S., Lee, E.S.: Job Sequencing with Fuzzy Processing Times. Computers & Mathematics with Applications (19), 31–41 (1990)
8. Asano, M., Ohta, H.: Signal Machine Scheduling Using Dominance Relation to Minimize Earliness Subject to Ready and Due Times. International Journal of Production Economics (44), 35–43 (1996)
9. Hapke, M., Slowinski, R.: Fuzzy Priority Heuristics for Project Scheduling. Fuzzy Sets and Systems (83), 291–299 (1996)
10. Sakawa, M., Kubota, R.: Fuzzy Programming for Multi-objective Job Shop Scheduling with Fuzzy Processing and Fuzzy Due Date Through Genetic Algorithms. European Journal of Operational Research (120), 393–407 (2000)
11. Yen, J., Langari, R.: Fuzzy Logic; Intelligence, Control, and Information. Prentice Hall, Englewood Cliffs (1999)

Object Location in Cluster Based Mobile Ad Hoc Networks

Prasad Naik Hamsavath[1], G.V. Singh[1], and Sanjay K. Dhurandher[2]

[1] School of Computer and System Sciences, Jawaharlal Nehru University,
New Delhi, India
naikphd@gmail.com, gvs10@hotmail.com
[2] Division of Information Technology, Netaji Subhas Institute of Technology,
University of Delhi, New Delhi, India
dhurandher@rediffmail.com

Abstract. Object[1] location Services (OLS) in MANET is a challenging issue due to limitation of the applications of MANET such as bandwidth, mobility, battery power, memory etc.., For more significance and efficient results we have worked out on the clustering architecture for location services in MANET. We brief in this paper about location services in MANET. Due to frequent mobility of the mobile hosts the physical topology of the network continuously changes as result frequent link breaks of existing paths. The absence of any centralized, dedicated servers to maintain the location information of the mobile hosts in Mobile ad-hoc networks is a challenging issue. Therefore location management becomes an important issue. Location management refers to updating and searching the "whereabouts" of mobile nodes in a network. The proposed algorithm for object location in MANET using clustering has shown effective and better results when comparing with the very well known location protocol that is GLS (Grid Location Services). The algorithm also registers and updates the location information of mobile nodes as well as searches their current location in ClusterHead tables. The simulation results show that lesser overhead cost of object location and better throughput are achieved when using the clustering methodologies by implementing a mechanism to track the location of other Mobile nodes (MN) in the network topology.

Keywords: Mobile Ad hoc Networks, Mobile Node, Cluster, Object location.

1 Introduction

Location service [3-4], [8], [11], [17], [19] consists of location registration, location updates, searches and search-updates. Registration occurs when a mobile host initially joins in the network. Updates occur when a mobile host changes location; searches occur when a mobile host wants to communicate with a mobile host whose location is unknown to the requesting host and search-updates occur after a successful search, when the requesting host updates the location information corresponding to the

---

[1] In our research work we define object as a Mobile node in MANET.

V. V Das et al. (Eds.): BAIP 2010, CCIS 70, pp. 53–59, 2010.
© Springer-Verlag Berlin Heidelberg 2010

mobile host. The goal of a good location management scheme should be to provide efficient searches and updates.

As per the survey, few proposed location information services which are existing [5] in the literature to date is listed below. We briefly derive all the existing location services in three classified categories. Those as referred in [8]. Proactive location services (*Table-based*), Reactive location services (*On demand*) and the Hybrid location services (*Proactive and Reactive*). Proactive location services are those protocols that have nodes exchange location information periodically. Reactive location services query location information on an as needed basis. Hybrid location services are combination of proactive and reactive features.

A location service should have the following characteristics:

  a. It should efficiently and accurately provide a node with the location(s) when it needs to make routing decisions.
  b. It should be distributed, and should not rely on any special hardware or setup.
  c. It should be self-configuring.
  d. It should not introduce too much overhead.

Location services [6] can be classified by the number of nodes that host the service (*Some* or *all* nodes act as location servers) and by the amount of information hosted on each location server (each location server contains information about *some* or *all* nodes of the network). As an example, in a traditional cellular network several dedicated location servers maintain location information of all nodes in the network. Thus, a cellular network can be classified as *some-for-all* approach. So, location database system would be classified as an *all-for-some* approach and location dissemination system would be classified as an *all-for-all* approach. In location services we may classify this as *Mauve classification [18]*.

2 Previous Work

Location information[2] has recently been applied to MANET [14] routing protocols [2], [9]. Using routing protocols the location information exchange takes place between source and destination when they transmit/receive packets. However, there are few protocols which are only location based protocols [8], [15-20] exist in MANET which are designed for location information services such as the Grid Location Service [7] (GLS), the Simple Location Service (SLS), the DREAM Location Service (DLS), and the Reactive Location Service (RLS). Home Region Location Services (HRLS), Quorum based Location Services (QLS). These protocols are combination of proactive, reactive and hybrid. However, we compared our simulation work with Grid Location Services (GLS) due to this algorithm works similar to cluster-based location services in MANET [20]. This is the main motivation behind to select this protocol for simulation results comparison with our algorithm.

---

[2] Location Information, Location Services, Object Location are used in an interchangeable way in our research paper.

3 Assumptions Made

1. The Network to be covered is heavily populated with mobile nodes.
2. Heavy traffic (Dense) is expected within the network (i.e., multiple simultaneous communications among nodes are possible). If network is not dense it may cause Dead-end[3] situation.
3. Every node is equipped with GPS (Global Positioning System) capability that provides its current location.
4. There exists a universal Hash-function that maps every node to a specific cluster-zone based on the node's identifier.
5. We assume bidirectional (two-way) links and same transmission range for the entire network. The transmission range is determined by the transmission power and the radio propagation properties.
6. IEEE 802.11 MAC (Media Access Control) layer (RTS (Request To Send) /CTS (Clear To Send) (CSMA/CA- Carrier Sense Multiple Access with Collision Avoidance)) is used to avoid collisions due to hidden/exposed terminal nodes.

4 Algorithm

In order to exchange location information on the network, four special types of packets have been used. These packets are exchanged in the same way as data packets. These are LOCK, LREQ, LREP and LACK packets which have 8 bits in each field and contain three fields in each packet.

1. A LOCN (Location) packet is used to inform its location address and ID to its neighbors, and in return all nodes who receive the LOCN packet must acknowledge by using LACK (LOCN ACKnowledgement) packet.
2. When a source node wants to find a destination node location, it first records the field of LREQ packet and broadcasts a Location Request (LREQ) to its cluster head.
3. If a ClusterHead itself wants to find a destination address, it keeps the LREQ field in its location table and broadcast LREQ packet to its nearest Gateway [1].
4. If a Gateway itself wants to find a destination address, it keeps the LREQ field in its routing table and broadcast LREQ packet to its nearest Cluster heads.
5. If a cluster head receives a LREQ packet, it checks the identification field of the packet with its location table list to find whether it has previously seen the LREQ packet. If it has, it discards the packet. Otherwise, if the destination node is a member of its cluster, it unicasts the Location Reply (LREP) packet to the source node. Else, it first records the address of the LREQ packet in its location table list and rebroadcasts the LREQ packet to its nearest Gateway node.
6. If more than two gateways exist, the CH decides which gateway to be its chief for broadcasting the packet to destination is based on the shortest path algorithm nearest to its location.
7. If a Gateway receives a LREQ packet, it stores the information and broadcast the LREQ packet to its nearest cluster heads.

---

[3] If no neighbor node is closer to the packet's destination than the node currently holding the packet, then the packet has reached a "dead-end" situation.

8. When the cluster head receives the LREQ packet, if the destination address is its member, it stores the destination address and location in its table and broadcast a LREP message back to the source via its closest neighbors.
9. If the source node does not receive any LREP after sending out a LREQ for a set period of time, it goes into an exponential back off[4] before re-transmitting the LREQ.
10. It is important to note that the path traversed by the LREP may be different from that traveled by the LREQ.
11. If the source node receives the LREP packet from the destination node before the timer expires, it will record the address of the node and terminates the algorithm, else repeat step 1~11.

5 Maintenance of Location Information

1. The algorithm is suitable for heterogeneous networks because it maintains and updates [10] the location information of the source and the destination every time the pairs send or receive data and acknowledge packets.
2. The source updates its location information before sending each data packet. When the destination receives the data packet, its location information is updated and an acknowledgment packet is sent to the source.

6 Metrics Used

Location registration cost: Every LOCN packet broadcasts a node before registering its location with its ClusterHead; minimum nodes in clusters will reduce the location registration overhead.

Location updation cost: Every LOCN packet broadcasted by a node will have to register its location by each neighbor in its transmission range and CH; hence location updation cost will increase in its cluster.

Location finding cost: Every source node which uses the LREQ packet for finding a destination node using intermediate nodes, this implies the location finding cost in its shortest route for all nodes which involved for finding the route to destination. A shortest path will decrease the routing delay as well as location finding overhead on intermediate nodes.

Location maintenance cost: Every ordinary node and ClusterHead has to maintain LOCN packets upto date in its table this cause the high memory for its tables.

These above four metrics we considered as one metric under overhead cost (Location registration cost, Location query cost, Location updation cost, Location maintenance cost).

Throughput: The overall system throughput in location discovery needs to be maximized for better performance of the network.

---

[4] Exponential backoff is an algorithm that uses feedback to multiplicatively decrease the rate of some process, in order to gradually find an acceptable rate. It is often used in network congestion avoidance to help determine the correct sending rate. It means that there is an exponentially increasing time interval between successive automatic retries.

7 Simulation Results

For our simulations, we used GloMoSim (Global Mobile Information System Simulator-Zeng et al., 1998). GloMoSim [12] is a discrete event parallel environment based on PARSEC (PARallel Simulation Environment for Complex systems) [13] (Bagrodia, 1998). In this simulation work we have compared the metrics with Grid Location Services (GLS). Out result shows that the average location overhead cost at 550 nodes when mobility rate at 10 m/s comparing with GLS such as:

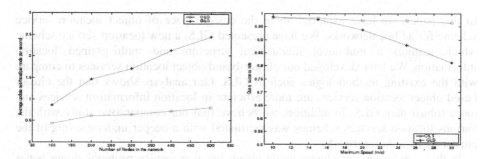

Fig. 1. Average Location Update cost at 550 nodes

Fig. 2. Average location overhead success ratio at mobility of 10m/s

Figure 1 shows the average overall cost for both OLS and GLS. However, it is clear that OLS exhibits higher location overhead costs; Its overall cost scales much better than GLS.

Figure 2 shows the average location update cost over all the nodes in the network. In OLS, we see, the location update cost grows much more slowly than GLS so we can define as $O \, (v \, log \, N)$ vs. $O \, (v\sqrt{N})$. When number of nodes (N) of the network density (order O) grows, the number of location update cost (v log N) also grows along with the varied network density.

Figure 3 show that both OLS and GLS can distribute location overhead cost uniformly across the network. It is calculated as the total number of successful queries

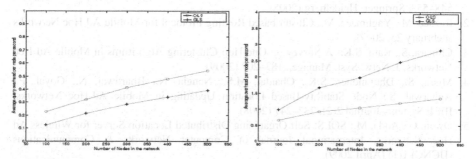

Fig. 3. Average Overhead cost at 550 nodes at mobility 10m/s

Fig. 4. Average Throughput of 550 nodes

divided by the total number of queries requested in a simulation run. It is observed that OLS shows the better result than GLS.

Figure 4 shows that average throughput of the network are much maximum in GLS when compare to OLS, for getting better throughput in GLS we may increase the clusters range to get better throughput in our proposed algorithm. Presently we are focusing on this issue in our future work.

8 Conclusion and Future Work

In this paper, we have explored about the design space of object location service scheme for ad hoc networks. We have presented GLS, a new location service scheme which features a multilevel hierarchical structure and multi-grained location information. We have developed our cluster-based object location services to compare with the existing methodologies such as GLS. Our analysis shows that the cluster based object location services are more efficient in location information services and more robust than GLS. In addition, we believe that our comparative study with the various location services schemes was facilitated with a deeper understanding of the clustering in ad hoc networks.

In this simulation, our cluster-based object location service protocol shows better results when compared to Grid Location Services (GLS) in MANETs, with respect to overhead-cost (Location registration cost, Location query cost, Location updation cost, Location maintenance cost), and throughput.

After brief examination of the location services in ad hoc networks, we have kept the issues open for further study on when a node is associated with a position, location privacy is difficult to achieve. Since none of the surveyed location services consider anonymity, future research in this area is essential. Finally we will be taking advantage of this work and are in the process of applying on a real ad hoc infrastructure.

References

1. Shivapraksh, T., Aravinda, C., Deepak, A.P., Kamal, S., Mahantesh, H.L., Venugopal, K.R., Patnaik, L.M.: Efficient Passive Clustering and Gateway Selection in MANETs, pp. 548–553. Springer, Heidelberg (2005)
2. Rezaee, M., Yaghmaee, M.: Cluster based Routing Protocol for Mobile Ad Hoc Networks (February 23, 2009)
3. Chinara, S., Rath, S.K.: A Survey on One-Hop Clustering Algorithms in Mobile Ad Hoc Networks. J. Netw. Syst. Manage., 183–207 (2009)
4. Misra, S., Dhurandher, S.K., Obaidat, M.S., Nangia, N., Bhardwaj, N., Goyal, P., Aggarwal, S.: Node Stability-Based Location Updating in Mobile Ad-Hoc Networks. IEEE Systems Journal 2(2), 237–247 (2008)
5. Owen, G., Adda, M.: SOLS: Self Organizing Distributed Location Server for Wireless Ad Hoc Networks. International Journal of Computer Networks & Communications (IJCNC) 1(1) (April 2009)
6. Sivavakeesar, S., Pavlou, G.: Scalable Location Services for Hierarchically Organized Mobile Ad hoc Networks. In: MobiHoc 2005, Urbana-Champaign, Illinois, USA, May 25–27. Copyright ACM, New York (2005)

7. Guba, N.K., Camp, T.: GLS: a Location Service for an Ad Hoc Network. IEEE ACM Journal (2002)
8. Camp, T.: Location Information Services in Mobile Ad Hoc Networks. MCS-03-15, the Colorado School of Mines (October 2003)
9. Abolhasan, M., Winsock, T., Dutkiewicz, E.: A review of routing protocols for mobile ad hoc networks. Elsevier, Amsterdam (2003)
10. Abraham, I., Dolev, D., Malkhi, D.: LLS: a Locality Aware Location Service for Mobile Ad Hoc Networks, pp. 75–84. ACM, New York (2004)
11. Ko, Y.-B., Vaidya, N.H.: Location-Aided Routing (LAR) in mobile ad hoc networks. Wireless Networks 6, 307–321 (2000)
12. Nuevo, J.: INRS - Universite du Quebec nuevo@inrs-telecom.uquebec.ca.: Comprehensible GloMoSim Tutorial (March 2004)
13. Meyer, R.A., Bagrodia, R.: PARSEC User Manual for PARSEC. Release 1.1 (revised, September 1999), http://pcl.cs.ucla.edu/
14. C. Kopp.: Ad Hoc Networking (1999, 2002), Carlo Kopp. arlo.Kopp@aus.net
15. Cheng, H., Cao, J. (Senior Member, IEEE), Chen, H.-H. (Senior Member, IEEE), Zhang, H.: GrLS: Group-Based Location Service in Mobile Ad Hoc Networks. IEEE Transactions on Vehicular Technology 57(6), 3693–3707 (2008)
16. Kieß, W., Füßler, H., Widmer, J., Mauve, M.: Hierarchical Location Service for Mobile Ad-Hoc Networks. Mobile Computing and Communications Review 1(2)
17. Camp, T., Boleng, J., Wilcox, L.: Location Information Services in Mobile Ad Hoc Networks. NSF Grants ANI-9996156 and ANI-0073699
18. Liao, W.-H., Sheu, J.-P., Tseng, Y.-C.: GRID: A Fully Location-Aware Routing Protocol for Mobile Ad Hoc Networks. Telecommunication Systems 18(1-3), 37–60 (2001)
19. Li, S., Zhao, G., Liao, L.: User Location Service over an 802.11 Ad-Hoc Network. songli, galaxy, liaolin@cs.washington.edu
20. Sivavakeesar, S., Pavlou, G.: Cluster-Based Location-Services For Scalable Ad Hoc Network Routing. Center for communication systems research, University of Surrey, Guildford, and Surrey GU2 7XH, United Kingdom

Performance Analysis of Coded OFDM for Various Modulation Schemes in 802.11a Based Digital Broadcast Applications

Alok Joshi and Davinder S. Saini

Jaypee University of Information Technology, Waknaghat, Solan, India
{20.alok,dsaini76}@gmail.com

Abstract. In wireless communication, concept of parallel transmission of symbols is applied to achieve high throughput and better transmission quality. Orthogonal Frequency Division Multiplexing (OFDM) is one of the techniques for parallel transmission. The performance of uncoded orthogonal frequency division multiplexing (OFDM) over fading channels is generally improved by introducing some kind of channel coding. Coded OFDM (COFDM) has therefore been chosen for two recent new standards for broadcasting namely DAB and DVB-T. Different coding schemes for OFDM have been reported in the literature. In this paper our aim is to evaluate COFDM performance using block interleaver/Reed Solomon (RS) codes with convolution code and result is compared with uncoded OFDM. The performance parameter used for evaluation is BER with AWGN channel assumption. All other parameters used are as per IEEE 802.11a specification.

Keywords: OFDM, COFDM, BER, RS codes, SNR, DAB.

1 Introduction

Orthogonal frequency division multiplexing (OFDM) is a special case of multicarrier transmission, where a single datastream is transmitted over a number of lower rate subcarriers. OFDM is most preferred for high speed communication in multipath environment due to its immunity to ISI. OFDM avoids ISI problem by sending many low speed transmissions simultaneously. OFDM is presently used in a number of commercial wired and wireless applications. One of the wired applications is digital subscriber line (DSL). For wireless, OFDM is used for several digital video and digital audio broadcast applications [1-2] such as eureka 147DAB and European digital television. Coded OFDM is a modified version of conventional OFDM where OFDM is combined with channel coding techniques, resulting in to higher data transmission rates or lower BER in wireless fading medium [3-4]. COFDM is currently most preferred choice for both DAB and DVB applications. In this paper the performance of COFDM is analyzed for combinations (*a*) RS and 1/2 convolution codes (*b*) RS and 2/3 convolution codes and (*c*) block interleaving with 1/2 convolution codes. The result is compared with uncoded OFDM system. The paper is organized as follows.

V. V Das et al. (Eds.): BAIP 2010, CCIS 70, pp. 60–64, 2010.
© Springer-Verlag Berlin Heidelberg 2010

Section 2 describes IEEE 802.11a specifications. Section 3 deals with implementation of coded OFDM system. Section 4 verifies the superiority of the coded OFDM system and paper is concluded in section 5.

2 IEEE 802.11a Specifications

IEEE 802.11[5] is a set of standards carrying out wireless local area network (WLAN) computer communication in the 2.4, 3.6 and 5 GHz frequency bands.The IEEE 802.11a standard specifies an OFDM physical layer (PHY) that splits an information signal across 52 separate subcarriers. Four of the subcarriers are pilot subcarriers. The remaining 48 subcarriers provide separate wireless pathways for sending the information in a parallel fashion. The resulting subcarrier frequency spacing is 0.3125 *MHz* (for a 20 *MHz* with 64 possible subcarrier frequency slots).The basic parameters for OFDM systems as per IEEE 802.11*a* standard are given in Table 1.

Table 1. OFDM Time base parameters in IEEE 802.11a

Parameter	Value
FFT size (*nFFT*)	64
Number of digital subcarriers (*nDSC*)	52
FFT Sampling frequency	20*MHz*
Subcarrier spacing	312.5 *KHz*
Used subcarrier index	{-26 to -1, +1 to +26}
Cyclic prefix duration, T_{cp}	0.8μs
Data symbol duration, T_d	3.2μs
Total Symbol duration, T_s	4μs
Modulation schemes	BPSK,QPSK,16-QAM, 64-QAM

3 Implementing Coded Orthogonal Frequency Division Multiplexing Based System

COFDM is most preferred choice in proposed European telecommunication Standard Institute (ETSI) standards DVB and DAB. The coded OFDM system used in this paper is given Fig.1.

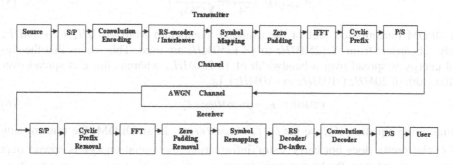

Fig. 1. Coded-OFDM system with RS /Interleaver and convolution code

The cyclic prefix symbols are 25% of the IFFT/FFT size. The (n,k) [6] RS encoder/decoder is designed as per Table 2.

Table 2. RS-encoder/decoder parameters

Parameter	value	Range
m	Number of bits/ symbol	3-16
n	Symbols/ code word	$3-2^{m-1}$
k	Symbols/ data word	$k<n$ ($n-k$ should be even)
t	Number of errors	$(n-k)/2$

The most widely used mapping schemes used in OFDM as per IEEE 802.11a standard are BPSK, QPSK, 16-QAM and 64-QAM. The theoretical expressions of SER [6] for various uncoded OFDM schemes are given in following equations.

For BPSK system,

$$P_{s(or\ b),bpsk} = \frac{1}{2} erfc\left(\sqrt{\frac{E_S}{N_0}}\right) \quad (1)$$

For QAM system,

$$P_{s,M-QAM} \cong 2\left(1 - \frac{1}{\sqrt{M}}\right) erfc\left(\sqrt{\frac{3E_S}{2(M-1)N_0}}\right) \quad (2)$$

Since each symbol carries k bits, the symbol to noise ratio (E_s/N_0) is k times the bit to noise ratio (E_b/N_0), i.e. $E_s/N_0 = k(E_b/N_0)$. The above discussion leads to bit error rate for the various QAM schemes.

$$For\ QPSK\ system,\ P_{b,QPSK} = \frac{1}{2} erfc\left(\sqrt{\frac{E_b}{N_0}}\right) \quad (3)$$

This shows that BER for QPSK and BPSK is same. For 16-QAM and 64-QAM the BER is

$$P_{b,16-QAM} = \frac{3}{8} erfc\left(\sqrt{\frac{4E_b}{10N_0}}\right) \quad (4)$$

$$P_{b,64-QAM} = \frac{7}{24} erfc\left(\sqrt{\frac{18Eb}{126N_0}}\right) \quad (5)$$

In OFDM transmission, out of the available bandwidth from $-10MHz$ to $+10MHz$, only subcarriers from $-8.1250MHz$ to $+8.1250MHz$ are used. This means that the signal energy is spread over a bandwidth of $16.250MHz$, whereas noise is spread over bandwidth of $20MHz$ ($-10MHz$ to $+10MHz$), i.e.

$$(20MHz) \times E_s = (16.25MHz) \times E_b \quad (6)$$

Simplifying equation (6), we get $E_s/E_b = nDSC/nFFT$. In an OFDM, the transmission of cyclic prefix does not carry 'extra' information, the signal energy is spread over time $T_d + T_{cp}$ whereas the bit energy is spread over the time T_d i.e. $E_s/E_b = T_d/(T_d + T_{cp})$. Combining the above two aspects and converting in to decibels

$$\frac{E_s}{N_0}dB = \frac{E_b}{N_0}dB + 10\log_{10}\left(\frac{nDSC}{nFFT}\right) + 10\log_{10}\left(\frac{T_d}{T_d + T_{CP}}\right) + 10\log_{10}(k) \tag{7}$$

4 Simulation Results

We compare BER performance of the uncoded OFDM and coded OFDM for BPSK, QPSK, 16-QAM and 64-QAM modulation schemes. Fig. 2(*a*) compares BER for COFDM and OFDM, where block interleaving and 1/2 convolution codes are used. Fig. 2(*b*) compares the BER for RS codes and 1/2 convolution codes. Fig. 3 compares the BER with RS codes and 2/3 convolution codes. The schemes BPSK, QPSK, 16-QAM uses (15,13) RS codes and 64-QAM use (60,58) which are the nearest values of (*n*, *k*) as per Table 2, rest of the parameters are as per Table 1.

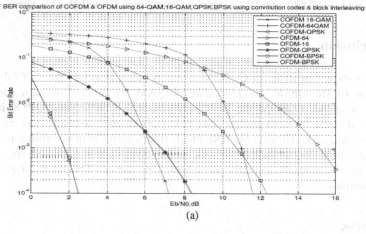

(a)

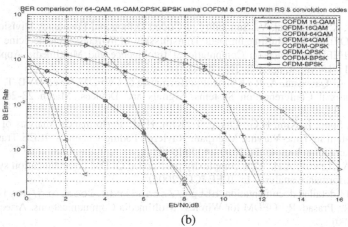

(b)

Fig. 2. Coded-OFDM Vs OFDM system (a) Convolution 1/2 with interleaving (b) Convolution 1/2 with Reed Solomon codes

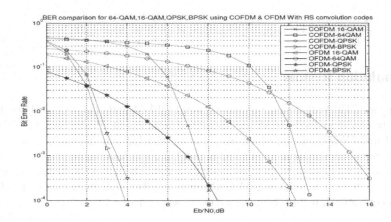

Fig. 3. Coded-OFDM Vs OFDM system for Convolution 2/3 with Reed Solomon codes

5 Conclusion

The results show that BER for COFDM is much better than OFDM. In COFDM and OFDM the BPSK, QPSK, 16-QAM and 64-QAM are ordered as increasing BER. However in uncoded OFDM the BER performance of BPSK and QPSK is almost same. The RS and 1/2 convolution code pair performance is better than the RS and 2/3 convolution code. However simple block interleaving with convolution code can give slightly better performance provided suitable interleaving, is used, the choice is arbitrary. So above results strongly recommend the use of COFDM for digital broadcast applications.

References

1. Thenmozhi, K., Prithiviraj, V.: Suitability of Coded Orthogonal Frequency Division Multiplexing (COFDM) for Multimedia Data Transmission in Wireless Telemedicine Applications. In: IEEE Conference on Computational Intelligence and Multimedia Applications, December 13-15, vol. 4, pp. 288–292 (2007)
2. Daoud, O., Al-Qawasmi, A.-R.: Efficient performance of COFDM-based DVB-T. In: IEEE 6th International Conference on Systems, Signals and Devices, March 23-26, pp. 1–4 (2009)
3. Kim, Y.H., Song, I., Kim, H.G., Chang, T., Kim, H.M.: Performance Analysis of a Coded OFDM System in Time-Varying Multipath Rayleigh Fading Channels. IEEE Transactions on Vehicular Technology 48(5), 1610–1615 (1999)
4. Shah, S.F.A., Tewfik, A.H.: Low complexity post-coded OFDM communication system design and performance analysis. In: IEEE ICC (2006)
5. IEEE 802.11 detailed documentation, http://standards.ieee.org/getieee802
6. Van Nee, R., Prasad, R.: OFDM for Wireless Multimedia Communications. Artech House, Boston (2000)

Fast OVSF Code Assignment Scheme for WCDMA Wireless Networks

Davinder S. Saini, Vipin Balyan, Kanika Mittal, Mansi Saini, and Manika Kishore

Jaypee University of Information Technology, Waknaghat, Solan, India
{davinder.saini,vipin.balyan}@juit.ac.in,
{kanu.angel,zenith.soleil}@gmail.com,saini.mansi@ymail.com

Abstract. In 3G and beyond wireless networks orthogonal variable spreading factor (OVSF) codes are used to handle multimedia rates. These codes suffer from code blocking limitation which reduces the throughput and spectral efficiency of the system. Also, real time calls suffer from call processing delay. We propose a single OVSF code assignment design which utilizes offline optimum code selection algorithm so that the optimum code is available at the arrival of new call. The design finds the optimum code using a variable *code index* for all the parents of the available vacant codes. If a tie occurs for two or more parents for *code index*, the parent with the higher *code index* is chosen. The procedure repeats till a unique solution is reached. If still tie is not resolved the average elapse time of busy children of these parents can be used to choose single optimum code option.

Keywords: *WCDMA, OVSF* codes, spreading factor (*SF*), code blocking, code (channel) placement and replacement.

1 Introduction

All 3G and beyond networks use OVSF codes for data spreading in both uplink and downlink transmission. Due to the use of shared channel in the downlink, efficient use of OVSF codes is essential. One of the important features of OVSF code is that if a code is used, none of its parents and children can be used. This is because a code is not orthogonal to its parents and children. This leads to code blocking and new call blocking. The data rates for WCDMA [1] downlink varies from 7.5 kbps (*R* kbps) to 960 kbps. The channel chip rate in WCDMA is always 3.84 *Mcps*. To facilitate this OVSF spreading factor is varied from 4 (for 960 kbps) to 128 (for 7.5 kbps).

As discussed earlier, in the forward link transmission, wideband CDMA standard defines an 8-layer OVSF code tree [2]. The spreading factors from layers 1, 2, 4,...., 8 are 512, 256, 128,...., 4 respectively. The corresponding data rates handled are *R*, 2*R*, 4*R*,...., 128*R*, where *R* is the basic data rate (typically 7.5 kbps). The code with smaller *SF* can be used for user with relatively higher data rate so that the overall bandwidth (chip rate equal to 3.84 *Mcps*) of the system is same. As explained earlier, code blocking is the major drawback of OVSF-CDMA system. According to

V. V Das et al. (Eds.): BAIP 2010, CCIS 70, pp. 65–70, 2010.

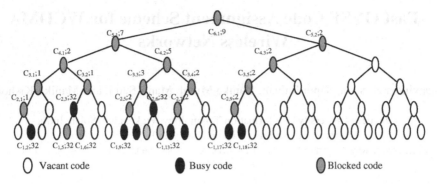

Fig. 1. Illustration of code blocking using 6 layer OVSF code tree

definition, a new call can not be supported even if the system has enough capacity to handle it. To demonstrate code blocking limitation, consider Figure 1 with 6 layer OVSF code tree. The maximum, used and remaining capacity of the code tree is $32R$, $11R$ and $21R$. Every code is represented by vector $[C_{l,n} \; I_{l,n}]$, where $C_{l,n}$ is the code in layer l with branch number n $(1 \leq l \leq 5, 1 \leq n \leq 2^{5-l})$ and $I_{l,n}$ is the code index signifying number of busy children with root $C_{l,n}$. When a new call of $16R$ arrives, there is no vacant code with rate $16R$ available even though the system has $21R$ remaining capacity. This leads to code blocking and new call blocking.

A large number of code assignment schemes are proposed in literature. Leftmost code assignment (LCA) [3], crowded first assignment (CFA) [3], fixed set partitioning (FSP) [4] and dynamic code assignment (DCA) [5] are single code assignment schemes. In the leftmost code assignment scheme, the code assignment is done from the left side of the code tree. In crowded first assignment, the code is assigned to new user such that the availability of vacant higher rate codes in future is more. In the fixed set partitioning, the code tree is divided into a number of sub trees according to the input traffic distribution. In dynamic code assignment scheme, the blocking probability is reduced using reassignments based on the cost function. The DCA scheme requires extra information to be transmitted to inform the receiver about code reassignments. The DCA scheme with different QoS requirements is given in [6]. The performance of fixed and dynamic code assignment schemes with blocking probability constraint is given in [7].

2 Proposed Design

Consider an OVSF system with L (In WCDMA L is 8) layer code tree. The proposed design aims to nullify the requirement of code searches at the arrival of new call. The identifier *code index* $I_{l,n}$ for code $C_{l,n}$ facilitates this and has following properties.

- If a code, $C_{l,n}$ is chosen to be assigned to a new call $2^{l-1}R$ then its *code index* becomes $I_{l,n}=2^{L-1}$ (equal to the number of leaves in the code tree).
- All the children of the code $C_{l,n}$ are assigned code index value 2^{L-1}. The parents of the node $C_{l,n}$ incremented its *Code Indices* by 1. The parents and children of the code $C_{l,n}$ are given in Table 1.

Table 1. Parents and children blocked for a code $C_{l,n}$

Parents Blocked	Children Blocked
$C_{l+1,\lceil n/2 \rceil}$ in layer $l+1$	$C_{l-1,2n-1}, C_{l-1,2n}$ in layer l-1
$C_{l+2,\lceil n/2^2 \rceil}$ in layer $l+2$	$C_{l-2,2^2 n-3}, C_{l-2,2^2 n}$ in layer l-2
$C_{l+3,\lceil n/2^3 \rceil}$ in layer $l+3$	$C_{l-3,2^3 n-7}, C_{l-3,2^3 n}$ in layer l-3
....	....
$C_{L-1,\lceil n/2^{L-l-2} \rceil}$ in layer L-	$C_{2,2^{l-2} n-2^{l-2}+1}, C_{2,2^{l-2} n}$ in layer
$C_{L,\lceil n/2^{L-l-1} \rceil}$ in layer L	$C_{1,2^{l-1} n-2^{l-1}+1}, C_{1,2^{l-1} n}$ in layer 1

- When a code $C_{l,n}$ gets free at call completion, then its *code index* and its children *code indices* becomes 0 and the *code index* of all its parents is decremented by 1.

The algorithm of the proposed scheme is given in Figure 2 and is described as follows.

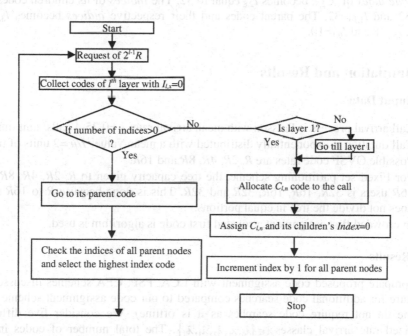

Fig. 2. Flowchart representation of the proposed design

1. Suppose a new request of call $2^{l-1}R$ requiring a code from layer l arrives. We go to layer l and search for all the codes with *code indices* $I_{l,n}$ value of 0.
2. a) If there is no code in layer l with $I_{l,n}$ value 0 then the new call cannot be assigned to any code.

b) If there is only one code with $I_{l,n}$ value 0, then assign this code to the call and then go to step 7.

c) If there are more than one code with $I_{l,n}$ value 0 go to step 3.

3. Go one layer up to $l+1$. We now compare the *code indices* of all these immediate parent nodes and pick the one with highest *code index*.

4. If there are more than one codes having same highest *code index* then repeat step 3 maximum $L-l$ steps (till root node) to get unique result. The child code of selected code in layer l (say $C_{l,n}$) shall be assigned to the new call of $2^{l-1}R$.

5. All the children of $C_{l,n}$ will be assigned *code indices* value 2^{L-1} and the *code indices* of the parents of $C_{l,n}$ will be incremented by 1.

For Illustration, consider the 6 layer shown in Figure 1. If a new request of $2R$ arrives, go to layer 2. The codes in this layer with *code indices* 0 are $C_{2,2}$, $C_{2,4}$, $C_{2,8}$ and $C_{2,10}$---- $C_{2,16}$. Since there are many codes with *code indices* 0, go to their parents in layer 3. In layer 3 the best parent codes (with highest *code indices*) the mentioned codes are $C_{3,4}$ and $C_{3,5}$ with *code indices* 2. To resolve tie go to their respective parents in layer 4. There code id and *indices* are $C_{4,2}$, $C_{4,3}$ and 5 and 2. Since $C_{4,2}$ has the highest *index* $I_{4,2}$ equal to 5 we assign its child code $C_{2,8}$ to this new call of $2R$. The *code index* of $C_{2,8}$, becomes $I_{2,8}$ equal to 32. The *Indices* of its children codes are $I_{1,15}=32$ and $I_{1,16}=32$. The parent codes and their respective *indices* becomes $I_{3,4}=3$, $I_{4,2}=6$, $I_{5,1}=8$ and $I_{6,1}=10$.

3 Simulation and Results

3.1 Input Data

- Call arrival process is Poisson with mean arrival rate, λ =0.25-4 calls/ unit time.
- Call duration is exponentially distributed with a mean value, $1/\mu$ =2 units of time.
- Possible OVSF code rates are R, $2R$, $4R$, $8R$ and $16R$.
- For Fixed set partitioning scheme, the tree capacity given to R, $2R$, $4R$, $8R$ and $16R$ users is $32R$, $16R$, $16R$, $32R$ and $32R$. This is done because R to $16R$ rates does not divide the tree in equal portions.
- In crowded first assignment, crowded first code is algorithm is used.

3.2 Results

We compare proposed code assignment with LCA, FSP, CFA schemes discussed in literature for additional code searches compared to our code assignment scheme (our scheme do not require code searches as it is offline). We consider five different quantized rate arrival classes $\lambda \in \{\lambda_0, \lambda_1, \lambda_2, \lambda_3, \lambda_4\}$. The total number of codes in the system is, $G_0 + G_1 + G_2 + ...G_4$, where G_x is the total number of codes corresponding to class x in the system. The service time is $1/\mu$ for all traffic classes. As discussed earlier, the calculation of number of code searched is measure of speed of the code assignment scheme. The searches comparison is done for different call rate distributions. Let the rate distribution is given by $[p_1, p_2, p_3, p_4, p_5]$, where p_i is the probability of user with rate $2^{i-1}R$. The distributions considered are

- [12.5, 12.5, 25, 25, 25], i.e. the percentage probability for rate R, $2R$, $4R$, $8R$, $16R$ is 12.5, 12.5, 25, 25, 25. High rates dominate in this distribution.
- [25, 25, 25, 12.5, 12.5], i.e. low rates dominate traffic.
- [25, 12.5, 12.5, 25, 25] and
- [12.5, 37.5, 25, 12.5, 12.5]

The additional code searches results are given in Fig. 3(a), 3(b), 3(c) and 3(d) for fixed set portioning scheme (FSP), leftmost first code assignment scheme (LCA and crowded first assignment (CFA), dynamic code assignment (DCA) and multi code with CFA (MCCFA) schemes. As discussed our design do not require any code searches. The blocking probability of our design is same as the blocking probability of crowded first assignment scheme.

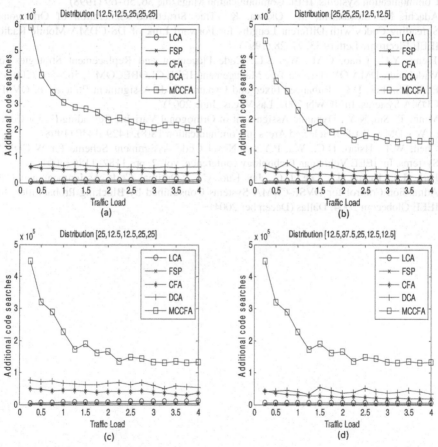

Fig. 3. Additional code searches required in existing single code and multi code schemes compared to proposed scheme

4 Conclusion

The WCDMA wireless networks require different treatment of real time and non real time calls. The important QoS parameters of real time calls are call processing delay and jitter. The proposed code assignment scheme can be utilized for networks dominated by real time calls as the time required for selection of appropriate code is zero. Although this requires the availability of buffers at BS and UE end. Work can be done to optimize the code assignment scheme for traffic environment consisting of real time as well as non real time calls.

References

1. Adachi, F., Sawahashi, M., Suda, H.: Wideband CDMA for Next Generation Mobile Communication Systems. IEEE Communication Magazine 36, 56–69 (1998)
2. Adachi, M., Sawahashi, M., Okawa, K.: Tree Structured Generation of Orthogonal Spreading Codes with Different Lengths for Forward Link of DS-CDMA Mobile Radio. IEEE Electronic Letters 33, 27–28 (1997)
3. Tseng, Y.C., Chao, C.M., Wu, S.L.: Code Placement and Replacement Strategies for Wideband CDMA OVSF Code Tree Management. IEEE GLOBECOM 1, 562–566 (2001)
4. Park, J.S., Lee, D.C.: Enhanced Fixed and Dynamic Code Assignment Policies for OVSF-CDMA Systems. In: ICWN 2003, Las Vegas (June 2003)
5. Minn, T., Siu, K.Y.: Dynamic Assignment of Orthogonal Variable Spreading Factor Codes in W-CDMA. IEEE J. Selected Areas in Communication 18(8), 1429–1440 (1998)
6. Chen, W.T., Hsiao, H.C., Wu, P.Y.: A Novel Code Assignment Scheme for W-CDMA Systems. In: IEEE Vehicular Technology conference, vol. 2, pp. 1182–1186 (2001)
7. Park, J.S., Huang, L., Lee, D.C., Jay Kuo, C.C.: Optimal Code Assignment and Call Admission Control for OVSF-CDMA Systems Constrained by Blocking Probabilities. In: IEEE Globecom 2004, Dallas (December 2004)

A Closed Form Slew Evaluation Approach Using Burr's Distribution Function for High Speed On-Chip RC Interconnects

Rajib Kar, Vikas Maheshwari, Md. Maqbool, A.K.Mal, and A.K.Bhattacharjee

Department of Electronics & Communication Engg.,
National Institute of Technology, Durgapur, West Bengal, India
rajibkarece@gmail.com

Abstract. This work presents an accurate and efficient closed form model to compute the slew metric of on-chip RC interconnects of high speed CMOS VLSI circuits. Our slew metric computation is based on the Burr's distribution function. The Burr's distribution is used to characterize the normalized homogeneous portion of the step response. The simulation results performed on the practical industrial nets justifies the accuracy of our approach.

Keywords: Slew Calculation, Distribution Function, Interconnect, Moment Matching, VLSI, Burr's Distribution.

1 Introduction

As integrated circuit feature sizes continue to scale well below 0.18 μm [2], active device counts are reaching hundreds of millions. Slew rate determines the ability of a device to handle the varying signals. Determination of the slew rate to a good proximity is thus essential for efficient design of high speed CMOS integrated circuits. As the design parameters like gate oxide thickness, channel length reach their threshold, computation of slew metric and interconnect delay become crucial for both performance and physical design optimization for high speed CMOS integrated circuits.

We present a closed form slew metric based on the Burr's distribution using moment matching technique. Our approach is different with respect to the proposals made in [1], [7] in the way that our slew calculation does not require any look-up table. We have proposed the Slew metric, BSM (Burr's Slew Metric) using the first two moments of the impulse response. The effectiveness and accuracy of the Burr's metric is justified on nets from an industrial design.

2 Basic Theory

Let h (t) is the circuit impulse response in the time domain and let H (s) be the corresponding transfer function.

$$H\ (s\ ) = \int_0^\infty h\ (t\ )e^{-st}\ dt \tag{1}$$

V. V Das et al. (Eds.): BAIP 2010, CCIS 70, pp. 71–75, 2010.

Applying a Taylor series expansion of e^{-st} about s = 0 yields:

$$H(s) = \int_0^\infty h(t)\left\{1 - st + \frac{1}{2!}s^2t^2 - \frac{1}{3!}s^3t^3 + \dots\right\} dt = \sum_{i=0}^\infty \frac{(-1)^i}{(i)!}s^i \int_0^\infty t^i h(t)dt \quad (2)$$

The ith circuit-response moment [4], m_i is defined as:

$$\hat{m}_i = \frac{(-1)^i}{(i)!}\int_0^\infty t^i h(t)dt \quad (3)$$

The mean of the impulse response is given by:

$$\mu = \frac{\int_0^\infty th(t)dt}{\int_0^\infty h(t)dt} = \frac{-m_1}{m_0} \quad (4)$$

It is straightforward to show that the first few central moments can be expressed in terms of circuit moments as follows [3]:

$$\mu_0 = m_0, \mu_1 = 0, \mu_2 = 2m_2 - \frac{m_1^2}{m_0}, \mu_3 = -6m_3 + \frac{6m_1m_2}{m_0} - 2\frac{m_1^3}{m_0^2} \quad (5)$$

The second and third central moments [3] are always positive for RC tree impulse responses. The positiveness of the second order central moment is obvious from its definition:

$$\mu_2 = \int_0^\infty (t - \mu)^2 h(t)dt \quad (6)$$

The impulse response, h (t), at any node in an RC tree is always positive. Hence the second central moment, μ_2 is always positive.

3 Properties of Burr's Distribution

In theory, Elmore's distribution interpretation can be extended beyond simply estimating the median by the mean if higher order moments can be used to characterize a representative distribution function. Once characterized, the slew can be approximated via table-lookup of the median value for the representative distribution family. In our work we have proposed the slew estimation technique using Burr's distribution function. The probability density function of the burr's distribution $f_{c,k}(x)$, is a function of one variable x and two parameters c and k (positive real numbers.)[6] and is given as,

$$f(x) = \frac{kcx^{c-1}}{(1 + x^c)^{k+1}} \quad (7)$$

Mean and Median for the burr distribution is given by,

$$Mean \quad (E(x)) = kB\left(k - \frac{1}{c}, 1 + \frac{1}{c}\right) \quad \text{and} \quad Median = \left[2^{\frac{1}{k}} - 1\right]^{\frac{1}{c}} \quad (8)$$

Where B (x, y) is Beta function and $E(x^2)$ is given in terms of Beta function as,

$$E(x^2) = kB\left[k - \frac{2}{c}, 1 + \frac{2}{c}\right] \quad (9)$$

By using the Gamma function approximation [5], we get,

$$\Gamma(az+b)=\sqrt{2\pi}\,e^{-az}(az)^{az+b-\frac{1}{2}}$$ (10)

By using the definition of Beta function, we get the Mean as,

$$E(x)=k\left[\frac{\Gamma\left(k-\frac{1}{c}\right)\Gamma\left(1+\frac{1}{c}\right)}{\Gamma(k+1)}\right]$$ (11)

By using equation (10) we get

$$\Gamma\left(k-\frac{1}{c}\right)=\sqrt{2\pi}\,e^{-k}(k)^{k-\frac{1}{c}-\frac{1}{2}} \quad\text{and}\quad \Gamma\left(1+\frac{1}{c}\right)=\sqrt{2\pi}\,e^{-1}$$ (12)

And

$$\Gamma(k+1)=\sqrt{2\pi}\,e^{-k}(k)^{k+\frac{1}{2}}$$ (13)

By substituting equations (12), (13) in (11) we get,

$$Mean\quad=E(x)=0.9196\quad(k)^{\frac{1}{c}}$$ (14)

Similarly, we get $E(x^2)$ as,

$$E(x^2)=k\frac{\Gamma\left(k-\frac{2}{c}\right)\Gamma\left(1+\frac{2}{c}\right)}{\Gamma(k+1)}$$ (15)

By using equation (10) we get,

$$\Gamma\left(k-\frac{2}{c}\right)=\sqrt{2\pi}\,e^{-k}(k)^{k-\frac{2}{c}-\frac{1}{2}}\quad\text{and}\quad \Gamma\left(1+\frac{2}{c}\right)=\sqrt{2\pi}\,e^{-\frac{2}{c}}\left(\frac{2}{c}\right)^{\frac{2}{c}+\frac{1}{2}}$$ (16)

Substituting (13), (16) in (15) we get,

$$E(x^2)=(k)^{-\frac{2}{c}}\sqrt{2\pi}\left(\frac{2}{c}\right)^{\frac{2}{c}+\frac{1}{2}}e^{\frac{-2}{c}}$$ (17)

Now using the definition of the Variance and using (14) and (17) we get,

$$Variance\quad(\sigma^2)=\sqrt{2\pi}\,k^{\frac{-2}{c}}\left(\frac{2}{c}\right)^{\frac{2}{c}+\frac{1}{2}}e^{\frac{-2}{c}}-\left(0.9196\;k^{\frac{1}{c}}\right)^2$$ (18)

Now equating the mean and variance of the distribution function to that of the circuit moments we get,

$$E(x)=-m_1\quad and\quad Variance\quad=2m_2-m_1^2$$ (19)

By solving for the values of c and k, we get,

$$c=\frac{2}{3}\ln\left(\frac{2.4709}{m_2\,m_1^2}\right)\quad\text{and}\quad k=\left[\frac{-m_1}{0.9196}\right]^{\frac{2}{3}\ln\left(\frac{2.4709}{m_2 m_1^2}\right)}$$ (20)

4 Proposed Slew Metric Model

Burr's cumulative distribution function [6] as a function of t is given by

$$F(t)=1-\frac{1}{(1+t^c)^k}\quad t\geq 0$$ (21)

If F (t) satisfies the following conditions, they are

$$0 \le F(t) \le 1 \quad and \quad \lim_{t \to \infty} F(t) = 1 \quad , \lim_{t \to 0} F(t) = 0$$

We can write the above equation (21) as, after applying Binomial approximations [5]

$$t \approx \left[\frac{1}{k} F(t)\right]^{\frac{1}{c}} \tag{22}$$

Now, let T_{LO} and T_{HI} be 10% and 90% delay points, respectively. Matching to these points to the CDF yields from equation (22):

$$T_{LO} = \left[\frac{0.1}{k}\right]^{\frac{1}{c}} \quad and \quad T_{HI} = \left[\frac{0.9}{k}\right]^{\frac{1}{c}} \tag{23}$$

The Burr's slew metric is calculated by using equations (23) and given as,

$$BSM = T_{HI} - T_{LO} = \left[\frac{0.9}{k}\right]^{\frac{1}{c}} - \left[\frac{0.1}{k}\right]^{\frac{1}{c}} \tag{24}$$

By substituting the values of the c and k from the equations (30) and (31) in the equation (24) we get:

$$BSM = \frac{0.9196}{-m_1}\left[(0.9)^{\frac{3}{2\ln\left(\frac{2.4709}{m_2 m_1^2}\right)}} - (0.1)^{\frac{3}{2\ln\left(\frac{2.4709}{m_2 m_1^2}\right)}}\right] \tag{25}$$

This is our proposed closed form model for the slew metric for the on-chip VLSI interconnects based on the Burr's Distribution. From the above equation it can be seen that Slew Metric [BSM] is the mere function of the first two circuit moments.

5   Experimental Result

In order to verify the efficiency of our model, we have extracted 208 routed nets containing 1026 sinks from an industrial ASIC design in 0.18 μm technology. We choose the nets so that the maximum sink delay is at least 10 ps and the delay ratio between closest and furthest sinks in the net is less than 0.2. It ensures that each net has at least one near end sink. We classify the 1026 sinks into the following three categories: 503 far-end sinks have delay greater or equal to 75% of the maximum delay to the furthest sink in the net. 347 mid-end sinks which have delay between 25% and 75% of the maximum delay , 176 near-end sinks which have delay less than or equal to 25% of the maximum delay. For each sink we compute the slew using SPICE simulator. We compare our slew metric with [1], [7] and [8]. We call these metrics as EDS, BakS and WbS, respectively. The comparison of our slew metric (BSM) with BakS, WbS and EDS is shown in Table 1. From Table 1, we find that our proposed model provides the best slew estimation compared to other approaches and results an average error of less than 2% for lower value of driver resistance and less than 5% for higher value of driver resistance.

Table 1. Comparison for Burr's Slew Metric

Driver Resistance=0Ω							
Average % Relative error				% Standard Deviation			
sinks	BaKs	EDS	WbS	BSM	BaKs	EDS	WbS	BSM
Near	65.45	786.13	43.72	36.89	44.25	615.1	27.38	17.97
Mid	11.76	24.27	4.65	3.651	7.832	23.62	4.59	3.36
Far	9.23	11.23	2.831	1.437	6.96	10.30	3.1	2.28
Total	9.23	11.23	2.831	1.597	6.96	10.30	3.1	2.28

Driver Resistance=100Ω							
Average % Relative error				% Standard Deviation			
sinks	BaKs	EDS	WbS	BSM	BaKs	EDS	WbS	BSM
Near	17.25	143.23	15.34	10.87	18.3	98.9	15.66	11.52
Mid	12.3	31.2	7.87	6.19	10.23	26.56	7.67	6.54
Far	9.45	16.6	6.78	5.32	7.12	78.65	6.98	5.69
Total	10.35	29.4	7.23	5.67	10.54	78.65	6.98	5.71

6 Conclusion

We have proposed Burr's Distribution function based closed form Slew Metric model for the generalized RC trees that is a simple function of two moments of impulse response. Our model has Elmore delay as upper bound but with significantly less error. We find that our proposed model provides the best slew estimation compared to other approaches. The novelty of our approach is justified by the calculated from the experiments performed on the industrial nets.

References

1. Elmore, W.C.: The Transient Response of Damped Linear Networks with Particular Regard to Wideband Amplifiers. J. Applied Physics 19(1), 55–63 (1948)
2. Wu, S.-Y., Liew, B.K., Young, K.L., Yu, C.H.: Analysis of Interconnect Delay for 0.18um Technology and Beyond. In: IEEE International Conference on Interconnect Technology, pp. 68–70 (1999)
3. Gupta, R., Tutuianu, B., Pileggi, L.: The Elmore Delay as Bound for RC Trees Generalized input Signals. IEEE Trans. Computer-Aided Design 16(1), 95–104 (1997)
4. Celik, M., Pileggi, L., Odabasioglu, A.: IC Interconnect Analysis. Kluwer Academic Publishers, Dordrecht (2002)
5. Kendall, M.G., Stuart, A.: The Advanced Theory of Statistics. Distribution Theory, vol. 1. Hafner, New York (1969)
6. Tadikamalla, P.R.: A Look at the Burr and Related Distributions. International Statistical Review 48(3), 337–344 (1980)
7. Bakoglu, H.B.: Circuits, Interconnects, and Packaging for VLSI. Addison-Wesley Publishing Company, Reading (1990)
8. Kar, R., Mal, A.K., Bhattacharjee, A.K.: An Accurate Slew Metric for on-chip VLSI Interconnect using Weibull Distribution Function. In: ACM ICAC3, January 2009, pp. 601–604 (2009)

Wavelet-Domain L^∞-Constrained Two-Stage Near-Lossless EEG Coder

K. Srinivasan and M. Ramasubba Reddy

Bio-Medical Engineering Group, Department of Applied Mechanics,
IIT Madras, Chennai, India
srinivasan.sivam@gmail.com, rsreddy@iitm.ac.in

Abstract. In this paper, a two-stage coder based near-lossless compression of Electroencephalogram (EEG) is discussed. It consists of wavelet based lossy coding layer (until bitplane n_d) followed by entropy coding of the wavelet domain residuals. L^∞-error bound is fixed in wavelet domain and the corresponding time-domain absolute error variation is studied. Studies show that intermediate demarcating bit-planes (n_d) register a higher compression and gives a nearly constant time-domain error. Both the normal and epileptic EEG registered a comparable compression performance.

1 Introduction

Electroencephalogram (EEG) signal is a record of electrical activity of the brain, is widely used in sleep studies, diagnose brain disorders and brain research. International standard for EEG measurement employs 10-20 electrode system (21 electrodes) for EEG signal acquisition. Brain Computer Interface(BCI) and sleep study generates a huge amount of data, thereby imposing a need for application driven flexible compression systems.

EEG, being a random signal, quantitative distortion measures fails to exactly quantify the loss of information when lossy compression algorithm is used. But, from legal and diagnostic point of view clinicians require lossless reconstruction as a prominent requirement [1]. Unfortunately, lossless compression algorithms suffers from low compression ratio and high encoding/decoding time and hence it will be difficult to use it under real-time environments.

The near-lossless compression algorithms provides a trade-off between compression and distortion, and places a tight local bound in the allowable distortion. Near-lossless compression of EEG signals is being reported in [4, 5], which employs different kind of predictors in their first stage, followed by residual quantization to achieve a better compression. The efficiency of the above mentioned techniques depend mainly on context-modeling and estimation, which is usually obtained with significant computational efforts.

Here, we discuss a two-stage wavelet encoder similar to [8], with SPIHT as lossy layer and arithmetic coding for residuals. The idea is to study the variation of time-domain error and compression performance with varying bitplane and

V.V Das et al. (Eds.): BAIP 2010, CCIS 70, pp. 76–80, 2010.
© Springer-Verlag Berlin Heidelberg 2010

quantization step size. This study will give an idea on the selection of separating bitplane for the two-stage coder.

2 Techniques Used

2.1 Lifting Scheme

Lifting scheme is a method to build and realize wavelets exploiting spatial domain correlation. Every wavelet or subband transform can be obtained as the Lazy wavelet followed by a finite number of primal and dual lifting steps and a scaling [2], a general version of which is shown in Fig. 1. The inverse transform, is obtained by flipping the signs and reversing the steps of forward transform. Integer transform can be realized by quantization/truncation of intermediate results.

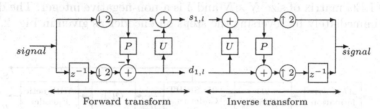

Forward transform   Inverse transform

Fig. 1. Forward and inverse wavelet transform using lifting (P-Prediction & U-Update)

2.2 SPIHT Encoding Algorithm

Set Partitioning in Hierarchical Trees (SPIHT) [3] achieved a notable success in the field of lossy image coding. It takes wavelet coefficients as input and produces an embedded bit-stream, where i.e., a message of R_0 bits always forms the first R_0 bits of message encoded at rate $R_1 \geq R_0$. The same set-partitioning rule is being shared by the encoder and decoder and they have nearly same computational complexity. The set formation and division is based on the temporal or spatial orientation trees, which is governed by the number of decomposition level and Rate-Distortion performance depends on the energy compaction property of wavelet base and signal characteristics [2].

3 Compression Algorithm

The compression algorithm consists of a wavelet based lossy layer followed by an entropy encoder (Arithmetic coder) for wavelet-domain residuals is shown in Fig. 2. In pre-processing EEG (S) is arranged in 2D matrix ($N \times N$) form, to improve the rate-distortion (R-D) performance of the integer transforms especially at low bit-rates and reduce the coding time [6].

  2D matrix is subjected to Integer lifting Wavelet transform (ILWT), followed by 2D SPIHT until bitplane n_d, referred as demarcating bitplane. SPIHT algorithm will become inefficient while coding the lower bit-planes as subbands is devoid of structural similarity [8]. Hence, the wavelet domain residuals (R_w) are entropy coded by Arithmetic coder after quantization (R_{enc}). The quantizer and de-quantizer is denoted by $Q(.)$ & $Q_d(.)$ is given by,

$$Q(x) = \lfloor \frac{x + \delta}{2\delta + 1} \rfloor \tag{1}$$

$$Q_d(x) = x \times (2\delta + 1) \tag{2}$$

where $\lfloor . \rfloor$ denotes the integer part of the argument. With x being integer, $\delta = 0$ corresponds to *lossless* case. When residual (R_w) is subjected to above quantization it satisfies L^∞- error bound in wavelet domain given by,

$$\|W - \widehat{W}\|_\infty = \max_{0 \le x, y < N} |W(x, y) - \widehat{W}(x, y)| \le \delta \tag{3}$$

where $W \& \widehat{W}$ are original and reconstructed wavelet coefficients corresponding to a 2D EEG matrix of size $N \times N$ and δ is a non-negative integer. The decoder follows immediately by reversing the steps on encoder as given in Fig. 2.

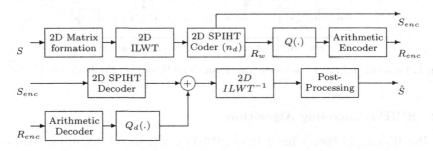

Fig. 2. Block diagram of Encoder (top) and Decoder (bottom)

4   Experiments

The experiments utilize EEG Datasets from university of Bonn, Germany with $f_s = 173\,Hz$ and amplitude resolution of 12 bits. Here *bior*2.6 is chosen as wavelet base, because of its good performance in our previous work [7]. It is difficult to derive the relationship between the absolute error in wavelet and time domain [8]. Experiments were performed to study CR, time-domain absolute error and percent root mean square distortion (PRD) variation with demarcating bit-plane(n_d) and quantization step size (δ) for a fixed L^∞-error in wavelet domain. PRD and absolute error can be expressed as:

$$PRD(\%) = \sqrt{\frac{\sum_{i=1}^{N} [S(i) - \hat{S}(i)]^2}{\sum_{i=1}^{N} S^2(i)}} \tag{4}$$

$$Absolute\ Error = \max\{|S - \hat{S}|\} \tag{5}$$

where S and $\hat{S}$ is the original and reconstructed signals respectively.

5 Results and Discussion

The two-stage coder shown in Fig. 2 is tested with the university of Bonn datasets and the results were summarized in Fig. 3. As expected CR increased with increasing wavelet-domain allowable error (δ). A low CR is registered at lower and higher bit-planes. At lower bitplanes, the wavelet residuals lacks structural similarity, making SPIHT inefficient. Large symbol size and inability to utilize the structural similarity by entropy coder leads to a fall in CR at higher bitplanes. Good compression ratio is obtained in intermediate bit-planes, where structural similarity and i.i.d nature of residual are utilized fully.

Absolute error in time-domain is higher than fixed wavelet-domain error bound. A nearly constant error is noticed for most of the lower bitplanes and reduces only at higher bitplane, as the range increases. Considering these facts, intermediate bit-planes can be considered as a good choice as a demarcating bitplane between SPIHT and entropy coder.

The L^∞-error bound in wavelet-domain gives a tight control over the error, which is reflected as a near fixed error in time-domain as given in Tab. 1. The inconsistency of PRD is reflected here, as it gives different values for the same absolute error of different datasets.

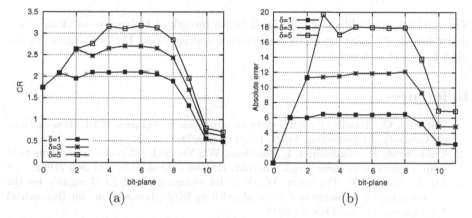

(a)   (b)

Fig. 3. Variation of (a) Compression Ratio (CR) (b) absolute time-domain error with demarcating bitplane and δ

Table 1. Compression performance improvement with increasing δ for various datasets

Dataset	CR		PRD(%)		Abs. Error	
	$\delta = 1$	$\delta = 5$	$\delta = 1$	$\delta = 5$	$\delta = 1$	$\delta = 5$
F	2.31	3.64	0.21	1.59	6	18
N	2.33	3.68	0.21	1.64	6	18
O	2.05	3.02	0.12	0.98	6	18
S	1.55	2.05	0.01	0.06	6	18
Z	2.25	3.48	0.26	1.98	6	18

Compression performance of the two-stage coder for various datasets with increasing δ is given in Table 1. A higher CR is obtained for Dataset F&N, which is a mix of epileptic and normal data, compared to normal datasets (O&Z) and purely epileptic (S). CR and PRD change commensurate for all the datasets with the increase in time domain absolute-error except the epileptic one. The value of PRD is well below 5%, which is often a good bound for bio-medical signals.

6   Conclusion

In this paper we studied a 2D based, two-stage coder for near-lossless and lossless EEG signal compression with a fixed wavelet domain L^∞-error bound. The time-domain error and CR variation is studied with different bitplane. Intermediate bit-planes gave a higher CR and a stabilised time domain-error compared to lower and higher bitplanes. This study will give an idea about the bitplane selection for the two-stage coder. A good compression performance is noticed for normal and mixed epileptic EEG, whereas pure epileptic EEG need specific techniques for improvement.

Acknowledgement

The authors would like to thank Dr.R.G.Andrzejak of University of Bonn, Germany for kindly allowing us to make use of datasets and Dr. N.Sriraam for his kind help and suggestions.

References

1. Antoniol, G., Tonella, P.: EEG data compression techniques. IEEE Transactions on Biomedical Engineering 44(2), 105–114 (1997)
2. Calderbank, R., Daubechies, I., Sweldens, W., Yeo, B.L.: Wavelet transforms that map integers to integers. Appl. Comput. Harmon. Anal. 5(3), 332–369 (1998)
3. Lu, Z., Kim, D.Y., Pearlman, W.: Wavelet compression of ECG signals by the set partitioning in hierarchial trees algorithm. IEEE Transactions on Biomedical Engineering 47(7), 849–855 (2000)
4. Memon, N., Kong, X., Cinkler, J.: Context-based lossless and near-lossless compression of EEG signals. IEEE Transactions on information technology in Biomedicine 3(3), 231–238 (1999)
5. Sriraam, N., Eswaran, C.: Performance evaluation of neural network and linear predictors for near-lossless compression of EEG signals. IEEE Transactions on Information Technology in Biomedicine 12(1), 87–93 (2008)
6. Srinivasan, K., Reddy, M.R.: Efficient pre-processing technnique for real-time lossless EEG compression. IET Electrionics Letters (in press)
7. Srinivasan, K., Reddy, M.R.: Selection of optimal wavelet for lossless EEG compression for real-time applications. In: 2nd National conference on Bio-mechanics, IIT Roorke, India (March 2009)
8. Yea, S., Pearlman, W.: A wavelet-based two stage near lossless coder. IEEE transactions in Image processing 15(11), 3488–3500 (2006)

Fuzzy Based Bandwidth Management for Wireless Multimedia Networks

J.D. Mallapur[1], Syed Abidhusain[2], Soumya S. Vastrad[1], and Ajaykumar C. Katageri[1]

[1] Department of Electronics and Communications Engineering,
Basaveshwar Engineering College, Bagalkot-587102, India
abidsyed4u@gmail.com
[2] Department of Electronics and Communications Engineering,
BLDEA's college of Engineering and Technology, Bijapur-586101, India
bdmallapur@yahoo.co.in, soumyav4@gmail.com,
ajaykatageri@yahoo.co.in

Abstract. After finding wide range of applications in the field of communications over decades, the wired networks are replaced by mobile and wireless networks and have become ubiquitous in the recent past. This is mainly due to the dynamic nature of these wireless networks. The interesting feature of the wireless communications is the need for connectivity at any place and at any time, which leads to frequent handoff. Due to larger bandwidth of wireless communications, the cell phones are not only used to communicate voice, but also to send and receive text, video and pictures. This requires some QoS criteria such as bandwidth utilization and time delay to be managed. In this paper, we present a novel approach for designing a high performance QoS management scheme that exploits attractive features of fuzzy logic and provide adaptation to dynamic cellular environment.

Keywords: Fuzzy Logic, Wireless Multimedia Networks, Bandwidth.

1 Introduction

Wireless/Mobile networking is one of the rapidly growing area in todays communication technology. Advancement in interactive multimedia applications, such as audio phone, movie/video on demand, video conference, video games, and so on has resulted in spectacular strides in the progress of wireless communication systems. In multimedia applications, data needs to be transmitted continuously thus demanding for larger bandwidth. Since bandwidth is the critical resource in wireless multimedia networks, it is necessary to employ mechanisms for efficient utilization of the available bandwidth. Due to the presence of inherent load variations in mobile multimedia network, there is a greater demand for efficient distribution of available bandwidth depending upon priority of calls, specially that for handoff call. Thus, there should be a mechanism to deal with these problems, which should not only deal with efficient distribution of bandwidth but should also take care of minimizing delay encountered

V.V Das et al. (Eds.): BAIP 2010, CCIS 70, pp. 81–90, 2010.

by accepted calls. In this paper we present one such mechanism for bandwidth allocation using fuzzy based techniques.

In Fuzzy-based bandwidth allocation scheme, we assume that the multimedia applications can tolerate transient fluctuations in the QoS and allows for the temporary borrowing of bandwidth from existing connections in order to accommodate new and handoff call connections. Some of the users may move out of the cell thus releasing the allocated bandwidth for those specific users. The same can be redistributed with minimal disturbance to all of the existing users.

This paper is structured into 6 major sections, where section 2 explains the previous works related to bandwidth management for wireless multimedia networks. Section 3 describes proposed scheme that highlights the Fuzzy based bandwidth management for wireless multimedia networks. Section 4 and 5 describes the simulations and results. Section 6 concludes the paper.

2 Related Work

Previously published works relating to bandwidth management for wireless multimedia networks are briefly explained in this section. Developing a mobility and traffic model for multimedia mobile radio network according to measures from two considered services areas and analyzing by simulation is done in [1]. In [2], the problem of finding the reservation scheme that would minimize the amount of time for which bandwidth has to be allocated in a cell while meeting the QoS constraint is explored, hence an optimal time based bandwidth reservation and call admission scheme is proposed. The work in [3] examines QoS guarantees for bandwidth in mobile wireless networks, with a focus on reducing dropped connections on handoff. It develops a framework for analyzing issues relevant to handoff, and the main principal for this is the use of an arbitrary planar graph to model the adjacency relationships of cells in the network.

The scheme in [4] investigates the issue of Optimal-Complete-Partitioning (OCP) policy, by introducing a conservative level of sharing into OCP, such that those sharing would have least adverse impact on the overall partitioning policy. The scheme in [5] proposes an on-line bandwidth reservation algorithm that adjusts bandwidth reservations adaptively based on existing network conditions. The major contribution of this work is an adaptive algorithm that is able to resolve conflicting performance criteria-bandwidth utilization, call dropping and call blocking probabilities. In [6], the different aspects of handoff and handoff related features of cellular systems are discussed. Several system deployment scenarios that dictate specific handoff requirements are illustrated. The policy proposed in [7] is a threshold-based bandwidth reservation policy, which gives priority to handoff calls over new calls and prioritizes between different classes of handoff calls according to their QoS constraints by reserving a maximum occupancy, i.e., a threshold, to each call class. The work in [8] proposes and evaluates a simple distributed adaptive bandwidth reservation scheme and a connection admission test for multimedia cellular networks that limit handover dropping probability to a prespecified target value.

3 Proposed Work

Mobile multimedia services have got enormous potential in the recent communication scenario. Since bandwidth and other resources like buffer, power consumption, etc are extremely valuable and scarce resources in these wireless multimedia networks, effective management of these resources is necessary to provide high quality service to users with different requirements. If the bandwidth required by each application is not available then the call dropping increases. Hence for efficient utilization of the bandwidth in order to avoid dropping of calls, we propose a fuzzy based bandwidth management scheme. In this section, we present the network environment, fuzzy based bandwidth allocation, dropping scheme and the algorithm for bandwidth management.

3.1 Network Environment

A cell is considered to have several users operating in it. There is a chance of additional users joining the existing ones from adjacent cells due to handoff. New calls can also be generated within the cell by the existing users. Bandwidth allocation scheme exists at the base station. Which allocates bandwidth to new/handoff call according to certain criteria.

We consider a borrowing-based bandwidth allocation scheme. Here we assume that the multimedia applications can tolerate transient fluctuations in the QoS and allows for the bandwidth to be borrowed temporarily from the existing connections in order to accommodate new/handoff connections. In other situation where the user moves out of the cell, the bandwidth is released. This bandwidth can be redistributed to all the existing users with minimal disturbance.

3.2 Bandwidth Allocation

The difference between the required and expected amount of bandwidth of a connection is the actual borrowable bandwidth (shown in figure 1) and the cell may borrow some of these bandwidth from an existing connection in order to accommodate other incoming connections.

The proposed fuzzy based bandwidth management scheme shown in figure 2 is located at the base station. This scheme comprises of QOS manager, fuzzy based dropper, bandwidth allocator, application database and fuzzy based allocator. The functions of each block are given below.

- **QoS manager:** It receives the request for the application connection from handoff/new calls with required specifications such as bandwidth, delay, etc. The fuzzy scheme computes the Dropping Factor (DF) and sends back to the QoS manager. QoS manager checks if DF=99, then it drops the call, otherwise it gives the output to Bandwidth Allocator. It allocates the bandwidth for requested applications, considering the input from QoS manager and also access allocation factor from the fuzzy allocator. If the bandwidth of requested application is less than the amount of bandwidth available or less than the total bandwidth borrowable from the pool of all the requests already being served, then the application will be accepted, otherwise rejected. It updates the application database with call information (bandwidth allocated, time delay).

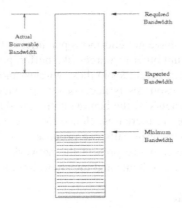

Fig. 1. Bandwidth borrowing

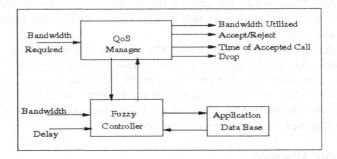

Fig. 2. Fuzzy based bandwidth management

- **Fuzzy dropper:** It accesses the parameters from database and calculates the dropping factor. The calculated dropping factor is used as an input to the QoS manager. Since handoff calls are given the highest priority, dropping factor for these calls is zero.
- **Fuzzy allocation:** It calculates the allocation factor for requesting application and decides whether to accept or reject calls by the help of time of entry of call request from the database.
- **Application database:** It is a database of all existing calls, containing information like bandwidth required, bandwidth allocated, delay associated with each call, type of call, bandwidth borrowable from each call, and so on. This information is given to bandwidth allocator, fuzzy dropper and fuzzy allocator.

3.3 Fuzzy Based Bandwidth Allocation

Fuzzy controlled bandwidth allocation scheme consists of Fuzzification, Inference and Defuzzification steps, as shown in figure 3.

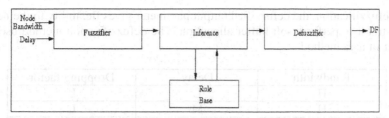

Fig. 3. Fuzzy based dropping factor estimator

Fuzzy inputs like priority, packet size and rate of flow are considered in our proposed work for computing allocation factor. A single crisp value can take more than one linguistic values if the membership values overlap. In the Inference step, a set of rules called rule-base, which emulates the decision-making process of a human expert is applied to the linguistic values of the inputs to infer the output sets which represents the actual control signal for the process. Here we give the membership functions [G (BW), G (D) and G (AF)] for each of the considered fuzzy parameter and their range of linguistic values as depicted in figure 4.

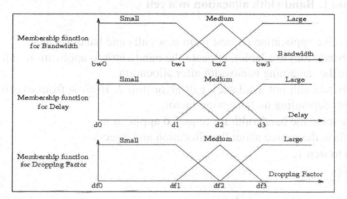

Fig. 4. Membership function for input and output linguistic parameters (dropping)

- **Bandwidth:** For bandwidth BW, its linguistic values are low (bw0 to bw2), medium (bw1 to bw3) and high (bw2 to bw4).
- **Delay:** For delay D, its linguistic values are low (d0 to d2), medium (d1 to d3) and high (d2 to d4).
- **Dropping factor:** For dropping factor DF, its linguistic values are low (df0 to df2), medium (df1 to df3) and high (df2 to df4).

The fuzzy bandwidth allocation scheme forms a fuzzy set of dimension G(BW) * G(D) * G(AF). The membership values of the assigned fuzzy variables depends on the network administrator, i.e., he/she can assign the different values at different instants of time depending upon the network conditions. To decide an appropriate output membership function, the strength of each rule must be considered. For this reason, the output membership function is a complicated function and hence center of area method is used for defuzzification. This method finds the center point of the fuzzy output membership function which is used for allocating buffer for requesting application. The fuzzy rule base table shown in figure 5 considers 9 different rules.

In Defuzzification, the defuzzified output parameter gives flexibility to the network administrator to perform soft buffer allocation. The defuzzification method used here is center of area method.

Bandwidth	Delay	Dropping factor
H	L	L
H	M	L
H	H	L
M	L	L
M	M	L
M	H	H
L	L	H
L	M	H
L	H	H

Fig. 5. Fuzzy rule base table for dropping factor computation

Algorithm 1: Bandwidth allocation in a cell

Begin
- Receive application request from new calls and handoff calls.
- if(bandwidth available), allocate the bandwidth to application request, calculate the remaining bandwidth after allocation.
- if(bandwidth not available), call algorithm 2. Borrow from existing applications depending on borrowing factor.
- Compute the bandwidth for requeted application.
- Inform the source about the allocation and rejection.
- go to step 1.
- Stop.

End.

Algorithm 2: Computation of dropping factor

Begin
- Intialize fuzzy controller with delay of application, bandwidth allotted to the connection.
- Find the membership function of each delay and bandwidth allocatted.
- Find the dropping factor membership from above information.
- Inform to bandwidth allocator.
- Go to Algorithm 1.
- Stop.

End.

4 Simulation

4.1 Simulation Model

A single cell environment with an area of (x,y) meters is considered. N number of users are generated in a cell comprising of both handoff and new calls. Maximum bandwidth of a cell is assumed to be BW_{max} Mbps, Maximum delay bound T msec. Bandwidth requests for each call generated randomly in the range BW_{req1} to BW_{req2} Mbps. The application requests may be from either new or handoff calls. Each application is having a priority p having linguistic values low (p0 to p2), medium (p1 to p3) and high (p2 to p4) that are randomly selected at the time of connection. Allocation factor is considered in the range (af0 to af2) for low, (af1 to af3) for medium and (af2 to af4) for high.

4.2 Simulation Procedure

The simulation procedure consists of following steps,

- Generate a cellular network.
- Generate the application/call requests.
- Apply the proposed scheme.
- Compute the performance of the end system.

4.3 Simulation Inputs

Single cell environment with an area of (x,y) sq.Kms. Each cell is divided into grids of size z sq.Km., z = 1 sq.Kms. f % grids are in the blocking range, f = 10 %. The mobile nodes are randomly placed in any of the grids within the cell. Mobile nodes can move in any of eight directions: N, S, E, W, NE, NW, SE, SW. Speed of the mobile is randomly selected among the following: low(1 mt/sec.,pedestrian), medium(50 mts/sec., medium vehicle speed), and high(100 mts/sec., speedy vehicle). Bandwidth of the cell M = 50Mbps. Application request types from mobile nodes: Handoff and new calls. Minimum, maximum bandwidth requests for each call are generated randomly between [0.6 max, max], where max is randomly generated between 0.5 to 1 Mbps, 1 to 2 Mbps, 1.5 to 3 Mbps for low, medium and high delay of applications respectively. Maximum of n = 150 users are considered in a cell. Among the active users a % move within the cell and b % users are handoff from neighboring cells. Among the generated call requests 75 % are new calls and the rest are handoff calls. An accepted call lives upto its duration or gets dropped if moves into the blocking range or if bandwidth borrowed causes its share of bandwidth to be less than its minimum requirement.

4.4 Performance Parameters

The performance parameters measured are as follows:

- **Dropping probability:** it is defined as the total Number of call request dropped at the base station.
- **Bandwidth utilization:** it is defined as the ratio of bandwidth utilized to the maximum size of bandwidth available at base station.
- **Calls accepted:** it is defined as the ratio of calls accepted to the total Number of calls arrived.
- **Time of new calls accepted:** It is defined as the ratio of time of new calls accepted to the total time of all calls generated.

5 Results

The results that we obtained as a consequence of using the above stated approach one can clearly demonstrate the worthfulness of adopting fuzzy approach for bandwidth allocation. Further we show that by adopting the fuzzy approach, various QOS parameter viz., Bandwidth Utilization, number of call acceptance, etc increases as compared to non fuzzy approach. By observing the figure 6 we can notice that better bandwidth utilization is achieved through fuzzy approach. Figure 7 shows how number of calls accepted increases if we use fuzzy approach, as compared to non fuzzy. Figure 8 shows how the number of calls dropped decreases if we use fuzzy approach. In fuzzy approach the time required to accept the call is less as compared to non fuzzy approach and is as depicted in Figure 9.

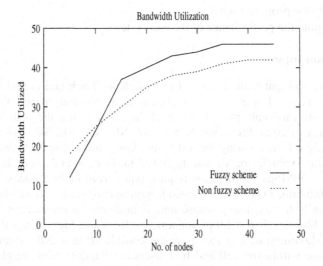

Fig. 6. Bandwidth Utilization

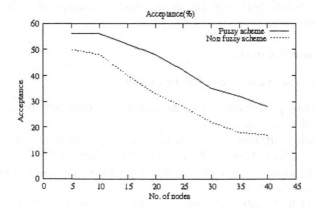

Fig. 7. Acceptance of Calls

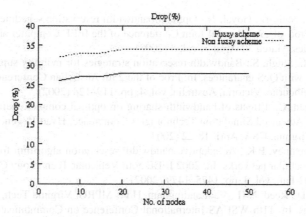

Fig. 8. Dropping of Calls

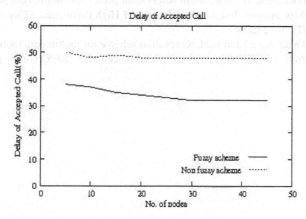

Fig. 9. Call Acceptance Time

6 Conclusions

In this paper we proposed a scheme for Bandwidth allocation for multimedia applications by using fuzzy logic. The main objective is to use the available Bandwidth efficiently and decrease the rejection and drop of calls. One important characteristic of this bandwidth allocation scheme is that dropping & allocation is done looking at some fuzzy parameters of each application. Parameters considered are amount of bandwidth required and time delay. Extensive simulation results reveal that the scheme proposed features very low call dropping probability, low call rejecting probability, and good bandwidth utilization as compared to a traditional bandwidth allocation scheme.

References

[1] Rejeb, S.B., Tabbane1, S., Choukairieure, Z.: Mobility model used for QoS management for wireless multimedia network. International Journal of Wireless and Mobile Computing 2(4), 350–361 (2007)

[2] Ganguly, S., Nath, B., Goyal, N.: Optimal bandwidth reservation schedule in cellular networks. In: Proc. of 22nd Annual Joint Conference of the IEEE Computer and Communications Societies, March 30-April 3, vol. 3 (2003)

[3] Hutchens, R., Singh, S.: Bandwidth reservation strategies for mobility support of wireless connections with QoS guarantees. In: Proc of the 25th Australian Conference on Computer Science, Melbourne, Victoria, Australia, vol. 4, pp. 119–128 (2002)

[4] Li, L., Chigan, C.: Effects of bandwidth sharing on optimal complete partitioning policy. In: Proc. of Advanced Simulation Technologies Conference, Hyatt Regency, Crystal City, Arlington Virginia, USA, April 18-22 (2004)

[5] Kim, S., Varshney, P.K.: An adaptive bandwidth reservation algorithm for QoS sensitive multimedia cellular networks. In: 2002 IEEE 56th Vehicular Technology Conference, Proc of VTC 2002-Fall, vol. 3, pp. 1475–1479 (2002)

[6] Tripathi, N.D., Reed, N.H., VanLandingham, H.F.: MPRG, Virginia Tech, Handoff in cellular systems. In: 11th WSEAS International Conference on Communications, Agios Nikolaos, Crete Island, Greece, vol. 11, pp. 366–370 (2007)

[7] Nasser, N., Hassanein, H.: Bandwidth reservation policy for multimedia wireless cellular networks and its analysis. International Journal of High Performance Computing and Networking 4(1/2), 3–12 (2006)

[8] Kim, H.B.: An adaptive bandwidth reservation scheme for multimedia mobile cellular networks. In: Proc. of IEEE International Conference, May 2005, vol. 5, pp. 3088–3094 (2005)

A Novel Digital Algorithm for Sobel Edge Detection

Jagadish H. Pujar[1] and D.S. Shambhavi[2]

[1] Faculty, Department of EEE, B V B College of Engg. & Tech., Hubli, India
jhpujar@bvb.edu
[2] Student, Department of EEE, B V B College of Engg. & Tech., Hubli, India
shambhavids@gmail.com

Abstract. To go with today's technology there is need of improving network communication performance. Its number of bits required to store an image that decides the speed of transmission of that image, in network communication. Here comes the need to reduce the number of bits required to represent an image. Many scholars have discovered that the most of the vital information lies in the edge of the image. Edges being the local property of a pixel and its immediate neighborhood, characterizes boundary. When image is represented as edge, the number of bits or pixels required to store an image reduces and also has a property of reducing the redundancy when restored. Hence one of the techniques for edge detection is proposed called as "Sobel edge detection".

Keywords: x-direction convolution mask G_x, y-direction convolution mask G_y, Convolution, absolute magnitude gradient, Sobel operator.

1 Introduction

Edge detection is a process of indentifying an edge. The sharp change in image pixel intensity is identified as the edge of the image. Edges correspond to points in the image where the gray value changes significantly from one pixel to the next pixel. Edge detection extracts useful information from the image, which is significant in understanding the image features. It reduces significantly the size of the image and filters out the information that may be regarded as less relevant, preserving the important structural features of the image. Most images contain some amount of redundancies that can sometimes be removed when edges are detected and replaced, when it is reconstructed. Eliminating the redundancy could be done through edge detection. When image edges are detected, every kind of redundancy present in the image is removed. Hence the size of the image is reduced, while retaining the image's vital information with high frequency [2].

Many scholars have discovered that the most of the vital information lies in the edge of the image. Edges being the local property of a pixel and its immediate neighborhood, characterizes boundary. They correspond to object boundaries, changes in surface orientation and describe defeat by a small margin. Representing an image as its edge has the fundamental advantages such as the size of the image is as reduced significantly. Thus, detecting Edges help in extracting useful information characteristics of the image where there are abrupt changes. Edge detection is advantageous in fields

V.V Das et al. (Eds.): BAIP 2010, CCIS 70, pp. 91–95, 2010.
© Springer-Verlag Berlin Heidelberg 2010

such as image segmentation, internet communication, feature detection, Machine vision applications, inspection of missing parts, Bio-medical image processing applications and Seismic image analysis. Edge detection is done using various methods such as gradient method and laplacion method. This paper deals with the gradient method using sobel operator hence the name Sobel edge detection.

2 Functional Description

The input taken is gray image, which is operated with sobel operator. Sobel is gradient based edge detection algorithm. It uses convolution mask to find the gradient in x-direction and y-direction. The convolution mask used in this paper is of order 3x3, hence for every iteration the considered pixel 8-neighbours are extracted which from a 3x3 matrix and convolved with the convolution mask and gradients are obtained. Then resultant magnitude is computed from the above two gradient.

Some of criterions for detection are to be considered such as the optimal detector must decrease the false positivity and false negativity, minimize the local maxima around the true edge, threshold value is taken into consideration such that information about the object of interest in not lost ,here the maximum and minimum pixel value of the absolute magnitude gradient matrix is found and difference of this is added to the minimum value and resultant is taken as threshold value [2].

-1	0	1
-2	0	2
-1	0	1

Horizontal mask

-1	-2	-1
0	0	0
1	2	1

Vertical mask

Fig. 1. Horizontal and vertical convolution mask used for convolving

3 Sobel Edge Detection

Sobel edge detection method uses gradient method to find the edge. Most edge detection methods work on the assumption that the edge occurs where there is a discontinuity in the intensity function or a very steep intensity gradient in the image. Commonly used method for detecting edges is to apply derivative operators on images. Derivative based approaches can be categorized into two groups, namely first and second order derivative methods. First order derivative based techniques depend on computing the gradient several directions and combining the result of each gradient. The value of the gradient magnitude and orientation is estimated using two convolution masks [1].

Sobel uses the derivative approximation to find edges, if one take the derivative of the intensity value across the image and find points where the derivative is maximum and then the edge could be located. The gradient is a vector, whose components measure how rapid pixel value are changing with distance in the x and y direction. Thus, the components of the gradient may be found using the following approximation [1]:

$$\frac{\partial f(x,y)}{\partial x} = \Delta x = \frac{f(x+dx,y)-f(x,y)}{dx} \tag{1}$$

$$\frac{\partial f(x,y)}{\partial y} = \Delta y = \frac{f(x,y+dy)-f(x,y)}{dy} \tag{2}$$

Where dx and dy *measure* distance along the x and y directions respectively. In discrete images, one can consider dx and dy in terms of numbers of pixel between two points. $dx = dy = 1$ (pixel spacing) is the point at which pixel coordinates are (i, j) thus,

$$\Delta x = f(i+1,j)-f(i,j) \tag{3}$$

$$\Delta y = f(i,j+1)-f(i,j) \tag{4}$$

In order to detect the presence of a gradient discontinuity, one could calculate the change in the gradient at (i, j) .This can be done by finding the following magnitude measure.

$$M = \sqrt{\Delta x^2 + \Delta y^2} \tag{5}$$

and the gradient direction θ is given by

$$\theta = \tan^{-1}\left[\frac{\Delta y}{\Delta x}\right] \tag{6}$$

The Sobel operator is a discrete differentiation operator, computing an approximation of the gradient of the image intensity function. The different operators in eq. (3) and (4) correspond to convolving the image with the following mask:

$$\Delta x = \begin{bmatrix} -1 & 1 \\ 0 & 0 \end{bmatrix} \qquad \Delta y = \begin{bmatrix} -1 & 0 \\ 1 & 0 \end{bmatrix}$$

When this is done, then:

- The top left-hand corner of the appropriate mask is super-imposed over each pixel of the image in turn, A value is calculated for Δx or Δy by using the mask coefficients in a weighted sum of the value of pixels $(i, j$) and its neighbors'.
- These masks are referred to as convolution masks or sometimes convolution kernels. Instead of finding approximate gradient components along the x and y directions, approximation of the gradient components could be done along directions at 45 degree and 135 degree to the axes respectively as show in (3) & (4).The corresponding convolution masks are given by:

$$\Delta x = \begin{bmatrix} -1 & 1 \\ 0 & 0 \end{bmatrix} \qquad \Delta y = \begin{bmatrix} -1 & 0 \\ 1 & 0 \end{bmatrix}$$

An advantage of using a larger mask size is that the errors due to the effects of noise are reduced by local averaging within the neighborhoods of the mask. An advantage of using a mask of odd size is that the operators are centered and can therefore provide an estimate that is based on a center pixel *(i,j)*. One important edge operator of this type is the Sobel edge operator. The Sobel edge operator masks are given as:

$$\Delta x = \begin{bmatrix} -1 & 0 & 1 \\ -2 & 0 & 2 \\ -1 & 0 & 1 \end{bmatrix} \qquad \Delta y = \begin{bmatrix} -1 & -2 & -1 \\ 0 & 0 & 0 \\ 1 & 2 & 1 \end{bmatrix}$$

The operator calculates the gradient of the image intensity at each point, giving the direction of the largest possible increase from light to dark and the rate of change in that direction. The result therefore shows how "abruptly" or "smoothly" the image changes at that point and therefore how likely it is that part of the image represents an edge, as well as how that the edge is likely to be oriented. In practice, the magnitude calculation is more reliable and easier to interpret than the direction calculation. Mathematically, the gradient of a two-variable function at each image point is a 2D vector with the components given by the derivatives in the horizontal and vertical directions. At each image point, the gradient vector points to the direction of largest possible intensity increase, and the length of the gradient vector corresponds to the rate of change in that direction. This implies that the result of the Sobel operator at any image point which is in a region of constant image intensity is a zero vector and at a point on an edge is a vector which points across the edge, from darker to brighter values.

3.1 Block Diagram

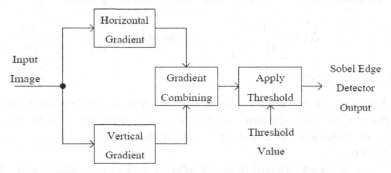

Fig. 2. Block diagram representation for Sobel edge detection technique

3.2 Algorithm for Sobel Edge Detection Method

Step 1: Accept the input image
Step 3: Start row and column for loop
Step 4: Consider each pixel, excluding the boundaries'.
Step 5: Apply a vertical odd 3 X 3 convolution mask and calculate G_x

Step 6: Apply a horizontal odd 3X3 convolution mask and calculate G_y
Step 7: Find the absolute magnitude gradient and store it in the resultant matrix
Step 8: Calculate an threshold and apply to the resultant matrix

3.3 Results

Fig. 3. Input image   **Fig. 4.** Output image before threshold   **Fig. 5.** Output image after threshold

4 Conclusion

The Sobel operator performs a *2-D* spatial gradient measurement on an image. Typically it is used to find the approximate absolute gradient magnitude at each point I of an input grayscale image. Transferring a 2-D pixel into statistically uncorrelated data set reduces the no of bits required to store an image and also reduces the redundant data when reconstructed, hence network communication speed is increased to large extent and optimizes the network bandwidth. Even though it is slower ,it smoothens the input to larger extent when used with higher order convolution mask.

References

1. Vincent, O.R.: A Descriptive Algorithm for Sobel Image Edge Detection. In: Proceedings of Informing Science & IT Education Conference (InSITE), Clausthal University of Technology, Germany and University of Agriculture, Abeokuta, Nigeria. Folorunso Department of Computer Science, University of Agriculture, Abeokuta, Nigeria (2009)
2. Czajkowski, K., Fitzgerald, S., Foster, I., Kesselman, C.: Grid Information Services for Distributed Resource Sharing. In: 10th IEEE International Symposium on High Performance Distributed Computing, pp. 181–184. IEEE Press, New York (2001)
3. Sobel, I.: Camera Models and Perception, Ph.D. thesis. Stanford University, Stanford, CA (1970)
4. Davis, L.S.: Edge detection techniques. Computer Graphics Image Process. (4), 248–270 (1995)
5. Gonzalez, R., Woods, R.: Digital image processing, 2nd edn., pp. 567–612. Prentice-Hall Inc., Englewood Cliffs (2002)

Efficient Intrusion Detection with Reduced Dimension Using Data Mining Classification Methods and Their Performance Comparison

B. Kavitha[1], S. Karthikeyan[2], and B. Chitra[3]

[1] Research Scholar, Bharathiar University
[2] College of Applied Sciences, Sohar, Sultanatae of Oman
(ACEEE Senior Member No: 7000490)
[3] Department of Computer Applications, SNMV College of Arts and Science

Abstract. Intrusion Detection System (IDS) is the science of detection of malicious activity on a computer network. Due to the enormous volume existing and newly appearing network data, Data Mining classification methods are used for Intrusion Detection System. In this paper the classifying methods used are ID3, J48, Naive Bayes and OneR. The data set used for this experiment is kddcup1999. The dimensionality reduction is being performed from 41 attributes to 7 and 14 attributes based on Best First Search method and the 4 classifying methods are being applied. The result shows that ID3 and J48 method carry the highest accuracy and sensitivity with 7 and 14 attributes. Naive Bayes holds the highest degree of specification for all three dimensionalities. OneR has the worst Sensitivity with 7 and 14 attributes but the time taken by OneR for classification is very less. It is found that the optimal algorithm may vary based on the dimensionality.

Keywords: Intrusion Detection System, Best first Search, ID3, J48, Naive Bayes, OneR, Classifier Performance Evaluator, Cross Validation.

1 Introduction

In this paper, 4 different classification algorithms namely ID3, J48, Naïve Bayes and OneR have been used. From the result it is observed as to how these algorithms are used in the classification of Intrusion Detection Attacks. In the dataset dimension, reduction is applied using Best First search because of which the feature selection has been reduced from 41 attributes to 7 and 14 potential attributes for classification. With the selected attributes the performance is compared based on Accuracy, Specificity, Sensitivity and the correctly classified instance percentage.

2 Related Work

In [2] is being presented, a data mining-based network intrusion detection framework in real time (NIDS). In [3], a new hybrid model RSC- is being presented, for, the

V.V Das et al. (Eds.): BAIP 2010, CCIS 70, pp. 96–101, 2010.
© Springer-Verlag Berlin Heidelberg 2010

problem of identifying important features in building an intrusion detection system. The model [4,5] is implemented and tested on sample data with 40 variables and the results are documented in the paper.

3 Dataset Description

In this paper, Kddcup'99 data set is used which is based on the 1998 DARPA[6]. Normal connections are created to profile that those expected in a military network and attacks fall into one of the following four categories namely Denial of Service (DoS), Remote to Local (R2L), User to Root (U2R) and Probe.

The various types of attack in our experimental dataset which are classified into four categories are shown in the following table.

Table 1. Various Attack Types

Categories	Attack Types
DOS	Apache2, Back, Land, Mail bomb, Neptune, Pod, process Table, Smurf, Tear drop, Udpstrom
PROBE	IPsweep, Mscan, nMap, Portsweep, Saint, Satan
U2R	Buffer Overflow, http tunnel, load module, perl, root kit, ps, sqlattack, xterm
R2L	Ftpwrite, guesspasswd, imap, multihop, named, phf, send mail, snmp getattack, snmpguess, warezmaster, worm, xlock, xsnoop

The KDDCup'99 Intrusion Detection benchmark is comprised of 3 components which are detailed in Table 2. Only "10% KDD" dataset is employed for the purpose of training. This dataset is comprised of 22 attack types and is a more concise version of the "Whole KDD" dataset. Because of their nature, denial of service attacks account for the majority of the dataset.

Table 2. Intrusion Detection benchmark

Data set	DoS	Probe	U2r	R2l	Normal
10% KDD	391458	4107	52	1126	97277
KDD Corrected	229853	4166	70	16347	60593
Whole KDD	3883370	41102	52	1126	972780

On the other hand, a dataset with different statistical distributions than either "10% KDD" or "Whole KDD" is provided by the "Corrected KDD" and is comprised of 14 additional attacks. Hence, the "Corrected KDD" dataset is being used for our experiment. The value of each connection is being predicted by this task.

3.1 Exclusion of Dataset

65000 records have been selected as sample dataset out of 3, 11,029 Corrected KDD dataset connections for the work done by us. However, because the sample number of Probe, U2R, and R2L is being less, the number of records of above attack types will be constant in any sample rate. The remaining records out of 65,000 are 44,417 which are the outcome of excluding the Probe, U2R and R2L types of records. Out of 44417, 20% of Normal connection is selected, and remaining 80% of the dataset is accounted by the Dos. The data sampling number and ratio are shown in Table 3.

Table 3. Amount and ratio of data sampling

Category	Corrected Dataset		Randomly Selected Sampled Records	
Normal	60593	19.48%	8883	13.67%
Probe	4166	1.34%	4166	6.4%
DOS	229853	73.9%	35534	54.67%
U2R	158	.02%	70	.11%
R2L	16347	5.26%	16347	25.15%
Total	3,11,029	100%	65000	100%

4 Estimation of Model Performance

The classification models can be evaluated using 10 fold cross validation method, criteria for evaluation [10], confusion matrix and ROC curve [11].

5 Performance Evaluation

The software used for this performance is Weka Tool kit [7]. The work is begun with the dimensionality reduction of original dataset which is comprised of 41 attributes and one class label. Two sets of potential dimensionalities, 7 and 14 attributes are obtained by Best First Search.

5.1 Dimensionality Reduction

The original dataset is comprised of 41 attributes and one class label.Using Best First Search method we obtained two set of reduced dimensionalities. 7 potential attributes and 14 potential attributes which are listed as follows

7 Attributes: Protocol Type, Service,Srcbytes, Dstbytes,count, diff_srv_rate, dest_host_srv_count.

14 Attributes: duration, service, flag, src_bytes, dst_bytes, count, srv _ count, serror_rate, rerror_rate, dst _ host _ same _ srv _ count, dst_host_srv_rate, dst _ host _ rerror _ rate, dst _ host _ diff _ srv_byte, dst_host_ same _ src _port_rate.

6   Result

The analysis and interpretation of classification is a time consuming process for which a deep understanding of statistics is required.

6.1   ROC Statistical Result

The result of above table 4 shows that ID3 and J48 method had highest accuracy and sensitivity with 7 and 14 attributes. Naive Bayes had highest specificity for all three dimensionalities. OneR had worst Sensitivity with 7 and 14 attributes.

Table 4. Sensitivity, specificity and accuracy based on 7, 14 and 41 feature selections

	Sensitivity			Specificity			Accuracy		
	7	14	41	7	14	41	7	14	41
ID3	97%	100%	98%	97%	98%	100%	97%	99%	99%
J48	97%	99.5%	97.8%	97%	97.5%	99.9%	97%	99%	99.9%
Naïve Bayes	92%	94%	98%	99%	100%	100%	96%	97%	99%
OneR	74%	72%	98%	99%	92%	99.7%	86%	97%	99.5%

6.2   Performance Comparison of Weka Explorer and Knowledge Flow

The Tables 5 is obtained through the Weka Explorer and Table 6 was an outcome of the Weka Knowledge Flow. The resultant tables show that the improvement in the performances of all the four classifiers of Weka Knowledge Flow compared to Weka Explorer is shown in the resultant tables.

Table 5. Comparison of 7 and 14 attributes based on class label using weka explorer

	ID3		J48		NaïveBayes		OneR	
	7	14	7	14	7	14	7	14
Time Taken in Seconds	1.49	4.01	1.20	1.86	0.05	0.09	0.05	0.16
Correctly Classified	89.15%	91.99 %	89.15%	91.96%	88.08%	90.16%	72.48 %	72.48%
Incorrectly Classified	10.75%	7.74%	10.85%	8.04%	11.92%	9.84%	27.52%	27.52%
Kappa Statistics	0.88	0.91	0.87	0.91	0.86	0.89	0.65	0.67
Mean Abs Error	0.01	0.01	0.01	0.01	0.01	0.01	0.01	0.01
Unclassified	0.09%	0.27%	-	-	-	-	-	-

Table 6. Comparison of 7 and 14 attributes based on class label using Weka Knowledge Flow

	ID3		J48		NaïveBayes		OneR	
	7	14	7	14	7	14	7	14
Correctly Classified	89.16%	4.01	98.1%	98.7%	88.05%	90.16%	89.95 %	89.97%
Incorrectly Classified	10.75%	92 %	1.94%	1.31%	11.95%	9.84%	10.54%	10.03%
Kappa Statistics	0.88	7.74%	0.98	0.98	0.86	0.89	0.88	0.88
Mean Abs Error	0.01	0.91	0.00	0.00	0.01	0.01	0.01	0.01
Unclassified	0.09%	0.01	-	-	-	-	-	-

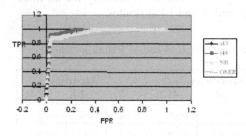

Fig. 1. ROC Curve for 7 Attributes   **Fig. 2.** ROC Curve for 14 Attributes

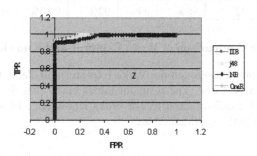

Fig. 3. ROC Curve for 41 Attributes

From the above three ROC Curves it is observed that the performance of all the four classification models namely ID3, j48, Naïve Bayes, OneR is said to be better in Roc Curve based on 14 attributes.

7 Conclusion

From the result, it is observed that better performance in classification and accuracy in all three dimensions are being given by ID3 and j48. The highest specificity for all three dimensionalities is possessed by the Naive Bayes. The worst Sensitivity with 7 and 14 attributes is possessed by OneR but the time taken by OneR for classification is very less when compared to all other models.

References

1. KDDCup99datasets, The UCI KDD Archive,
   http://kdd.ics.ucs.edu/databases/kddcup99/kddcup99.html
2. Peng, T., Zuo, W.: Data Mining for Network Intrusion Detection System in Real Time. Journal of Computer Science and Network Security 6(2), 173–177
3. Hybrid Model. International Journal of Computer Science and Network Security 9(10), 23–33 (October 2009)
4. Prasad, G.V.S.N.R.V., Dhanalakshmi, Y., Vijaya Kumar, V., Ramesh Babu, I.: Modeling. Modeling An Intrusion Detection System Using Data Mining and Genetic Algorithms Based on Fuzzy Logic 8(7), 319–325 (2008)
5. Panda, M., Patra, M.R.: A Comparative Study of Clustering Algorithms for Building a Network Intrusion Detection Model. Journal of Computer Science
6. MIT Lincoln Lab., Information Systems Technology Group, The 1998 Intrusion detection off-line evaluation plan (March 25, 1998)
7. WEKA: Data Mining Software in Java (2008),
   http://www.cs.waikata.ac.nz/ml/weka
8. J48 classifier, http://www.d.umn.edu/~padhy005/Chapter5.html
9. Zhang, H.: The Optimality of Naive Bayes. In: FLAIRS 2004 conference (2004),
   http://www.resample.com/xlminer/help/NaiveBC/
   class1NB_intro.htm
10. Ross, P.: OneR: the simplest method
11. ROC Signal detection theory and ROC analysis in psychology and diagnostics : collected papers; Swets (1996)

Recognition of Isolated Indian Sign Language Gesture in Real Time

Anup Nandy, Jay Shankar Prasad, Soumik Mondal, Pavan Chakraborty,
and G.C. Nandi

Robotics & AI Lab, Indian Institute of Information Technology, Allahabad
{iro2008005,jsp,iro2009012,pavan,gcnandi}iiita.ac.in

Abstract. Indian Sign Language (ISL) consists of static as well as dynamic hand gestures for communication among deaf and dumb persons. Most of the ISL gestures are produced using both hands. A video database is created and utilized which contains several videos, for a large number of signs. Direction histogram is the feature used for classification due to its appeal for illumination and orientation invariance. Two different approaches utilized for recognition are Euclidean distance and K-nearest neighbor metrics.

Keywords: Indian Sign Language, Direction Histogram, Gestures, K-nearest neighbor and Euclidean distance metric.

1 Introduction

Sign Language enhances the understanding ability for the challenging persons in speech and hearing all over the world. It employs complete sign which is made with hand, facial expression and other parts of our body. Every country uses their own native language as per sign language is concerned about their own syntactical and grammatical meaning. Like British Sign Language (BSL) and American Sign Language (ASL), the language which is being used in India is called Indian Sign Language henceforth ISL [1,2]. Still ISL is not the official sign language of India in spite of 6 millions deaf and dumb populations.

Several techniques have been followed for gesture recognition and classification including vision based using one or more camera [2-9]. Extraction of visual information in the form of feature vector is an important part in gesture recognition problem [6]. There are some difficult problems like tracking of hand, segmentation of hand from the background and environment, illumination variation, occlusion, movements, and position etc [5, 8]. Several techniques have been developed for pattern classification towards dynamic gestures in real time [3, 4, and 7]. Dynamic gesture implies moving gesture, represented by sequence of images. Classification in Indian sign language is most complicated task for preserving the necessary information about hand motions [3]. The prior work is based on recognition of Indian sign language reported in [2] was with a limited set of ISL samples. The classification approach is based on the hand gestures trajectory, hand shape and hand motion [6]. HMM would be used as a robust classifier for gesture recognition [7, 8]. This paper

V.V Das et al. (Eds.): BAIP 2010, CCIS 70, pp. 102–107, 2010.
© Springer-Verlag Berlin Heidelberg 2010

demonstrates the statistical techniques for recognition of ISL gestures in real time which comprises of both the hands. Next section discusses the experimental setup for static and dynamic ISL gesture capture method.

2   Generation of ISL Video Training Samples

We used constant background while recording the video with different frame rate per seconds (30 fps) and different sizes because we found background removal is computationally complex task and it affects the recognition result in real time [2]. As the feature extraction technique is concerned about the gray scale images so the background was chosen dark. Every ISL gesture implies some class or word which could be captured by waving both hands in a very appropriate manner [7]. We created repository of training and testing samples with huge number of images (sequence of images) of 22 specific kind of ISL class/word under various light illumination condition as shown in Fig. 1. Methodology is discussed in next section.

ISL	Training	Testing	Start Frame	End Frame	ISL	Training	Testing	Static Frame
Above	13	11			Ascend	12	12	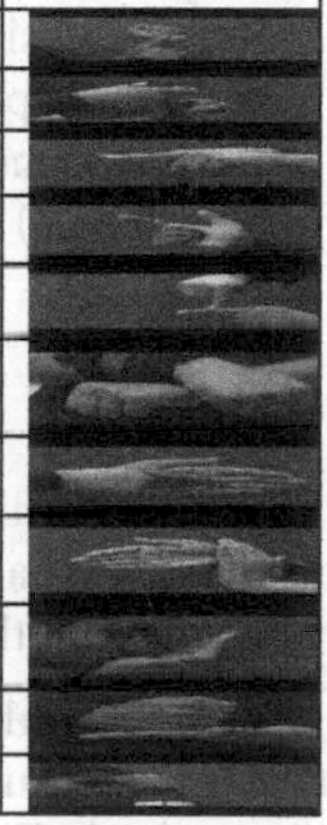
Across	17	15			Hang	12	10	
Advance	11	9			Marry	22	12	
Afraid	16	16			Moon	12	10	
All	19	15			Middle	12	12	
Alone	16	14			Prisoner	12	12	
Arise	17	12			Beside	12	12	
Bag	17	13			Flag	12	12	
Below	16	15			Drink	14	12	
Bring	18	17			Aboard	14	12	
Yes	22	12			Anger	12	12	

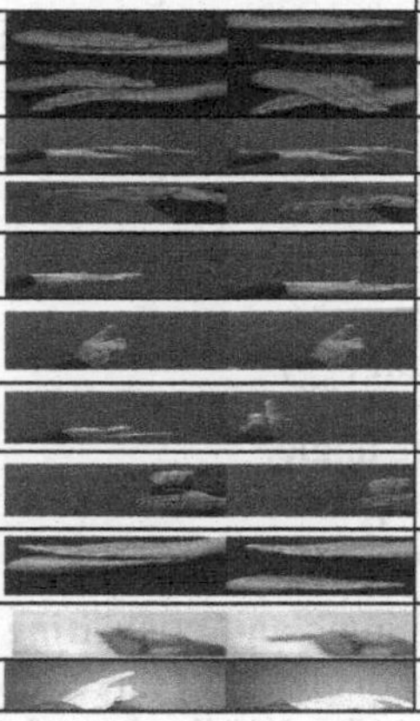

Fig. 1. ISL dynamic and static gestures under different light illumination conditions

3   Methodology

The real time classification of ISL is shown in Fig. 2. The ISL videos were split into image frames. All the image frames were converted into gray scale images. Blurring the gray scale images with Gaussian filter and normalization is applied. As per

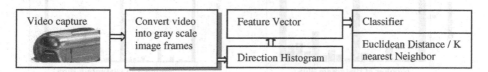

Fig. 2. Methodology for real time ISL classification

dynamic gesture is concerned and the gesture is performed in different light conditions so features would be selected in a very intelligent way so that position of the hand, changing the light condition along with the scene illumination effect would be invariance definitely[8].It is totally rotation dependent.

4 Feature Extraction

Several types of features have been suggested by the researchers for real time gesture recognition. The hand trajectory is utilized as a feature vector for DTW [2], hand contour [3], combination of color, motion and hand position is utilized for hand gesture recognition [4, 7]. The hand skin color information is used for extracting the histogram [5] .The histogram of the local direction of edges in an image contributes an important feature [9, 10]. Direction histogram needs computation of gradient with the help of filter and generation of histogram in desired number of directions [10]. We found that the same frames at different position of gestures would produce the same feature vectors. The overall algorithm is as follows [9]:

Step 1: Find the frames from video.
Step 2: Convert all the frames into gray-scale images.
Step 3: Resize all the images into 160 x120 pixels. Normalise the image sequences.
Step 4: Apply 3 tap derivative filter kernels: U direction = {0 -1 1}, V direction = {0 1 -1} and Gradient of image X is computed at each point (u, v), given $dv = X(u, v + 1) - X(u, v - 1)$ and $du = X(u + 1, v) - X(u - 1, v)$.

$$g(u, v) = \sqrt{du^2 + dv^2} \tag{1}$$

$$\Phi(u, v) = \operatorname{atan}\left(\frac{dv}{du}\right) \tag{2}$$

Where g is the magnitude and Φ is the angle.
Step 5: Quantize angle obtained in step 4 into T numbers of bins and normalize the values. Store the values as feature vector.

Rearrange the image blocks into columns and converting the column matrix with the radian values to degrees in order to display the direction histogram of the image like a plot in Fig. 3 and Fig. 4 is showing the distribution of values grouped according to their numeric range. Each group is called as one bin. The training patterns have been constructed with feature vector having 18 and 36 elements which is being consisted of direction histogram of the ISL motion gestures.

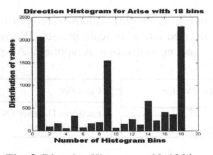

Fig. 3. Direction Histogram with 18 bins

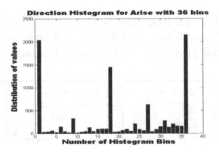

Fig. 4. Direction Histogram with 36 bins

Direction histograms are used to characterize images. In this 2 D histogram given an angular displacement Φ the (x, y) value of matrix indicates how many pixel couples at Φ angle distance consists of gray level x and y respectively. Gray level histogram is 1 D in nature where as images is 2D. In the case of 1-D, pattern matching is found using vector distance method. When feature space is a subset of real number and the distance among two feature vectors is their absolute difference ,we define it alternatively as:

Theorem 1: Assume $s(f)$ and $t(f)$ be two direction histograms from the subset of real numbers, where an alpha function specifies the location of a point. Alpha function α is such that $\int_{-\epsilon}^{\epsilon} \alpha(f)df = 1$ for all $\epsilon > 0$. The requirement of same number of points is described by $\int_{-\infty}^{\infty} s(f)df = \int_{-\infty}^{\infty} t(f)df$. Distance between feature vector is given by the absolute difference, the pattern match distance between s and t is $\int_{-\infty}^{\infty} \left| \int_{-\infty}^{f} s(u)du - \int_{-\infty}^{f} t(u)du \right| df$.

Define $S(f) = \int_{-\infty}^{f} s(u)du$; $T(f) = \int_{-\infty}^{f} t(u)du$. $S(f)$ is number of points in direction histograms S having values $\leq f$, similarly for $T(f)$ also. In linear case, points are coupled for matching. Thus for every u the number of points with values less than u paired with points with values greater than u is $|S(u) - T(u)|$. Hence $\int_{-\infty}^{\infty} |S(u) - T(u)|$ is equal to the sum of all pair wise distance in pattern matching.

Theorem 2: If D is a set of descriptors having the metric u. Suppose $s; D \rightarrow R$ be a function from D to real numbers, denoting the direction histogram values i.e. frequency of each descriptor $d \in D$ and $\sum_{d \in D} s(d) = C$, where C is constant. For direction histogram this restriction implies that only images of equal C can be compared. Metric can be Euclidean distance or city block or some other else.

5 Classification and Result Analysis

As explained in Fig.1. All the above step has to be followed for every training and testing gestures. For testing pattern based on the feature vector obtained we used two different classifiers Euclidean Distance and K-nearest neighbor. K nearest neighbor gives very good classification result. We achieved up to 100 % recognition. The classification result of 36 bins are more accurate. In real time, the training time using 36 bins direction histogram is more. Some of the ISL we considered are complex and many frames are similar hence the recognition result is poor in few cases as shown in Table 1. We used limited number of gestures for training, the classification and recognition result can be improved by incorporating more number of training samples. To handle the situation where two gestures are similar for example "Advance" and "Arise" use of other features will improve the recognition rate.

Table 1. Recognition result using Euclidean and K nearest neighbor classifier

Class	Recognition (%) using Euclidean Distance		Recognition (%) using K- nearest neighbor		Class	Recognition (%) using Euclidean Distance		Recognition (%) using K-nearest neighbor	
	18 bins	36 bins	18 bins	36 bins		18 bins	36 bins	18 bins	36 bins
Above	99.42	99.81	100	100	Ascend	100	100	100	100
Across	100	100	94.71	99.82	Hang	94	92	92	91
Advance	93.83	94.25	97.03	98.63	Marry	93	92	91.6	90.8
Afraid	100	100	100	100	Moon	92.8	92	92.6	92.8
All	71.85	79.51	71.58	66.12	Middle	97.14	86	100	97.14
Alone	96.39	85.9	77.05	74.1	Prisoner	100	100	79.25	100
Arise	68.08	64.42	63.1	61.93	Beside	96	100	100	100
Bag	51.35	65.99	60.02	48.42	Flag	99.02	100	100	100
Below	86.11	84.47	73.05	70.42	Drink	90.58	94	54.11	91.76
Bring	100	100	100	100	Aboard	100	100	100	100
Yes	100	100	100	100	Anger	92.4	92	93	92.6

6   Conclusion and Future Work

The underlying statistical techniques give efficient recognition accuracy for a limited set of dynamic ISL gestures. It comprises the comprehensive results for Euclidean distance and K-Nearest neighbor metrics. Recognition has been entertained by choosing the closest pattern among all the training set of patterns.   Future work implies addition of more features and recognition with Hidden Markov Model technique in order to keep temporal information for each dynamic gesture in real time for continuous gestures. The system can be used with humanoid robot in future for training the robot in real time in a reactive manner. Another important aspect includes integration with Natural Language, so that robot could easily understand the ISL gestures and accordingly respond to them.

References

1. Dasgupta, T., Shukla, S., Kumar, S., Diwakar, S., Basu, A.: A Multilingual Multimedia Indian Sign Language Dictionary Tool. In: The 6th Workshop on Asian Language Resources, pp. 57–64 (2008)
2. Bhuyan, M.K., Ghoash, D., Bora, P.K.: A Framework for Hand Gesture Recognition with Applications to Sign Language. In: 2006 Annual IEEE, pp. 1–6 (2006)
3. Incertis, I.G., Bermejo, J.G.G., Casanova, E.Z.: Hand Gesture Recognition for Deaf People Interfacing. In: 18th Int. Conf. on Pattern Recognition (ICPR 2006), vol. 2, pp. 100–103 (2006)
4. Coogan, T., Awad, G., Han, J., Sutherland, A.: Real time hand gesture recognition including hand segmentation and tracking. In: 2nd Int. Symposium on Visual Computing, Lake Tahoe, NV, USA (2006)
5. Stefan, A., Wang, H., Athitsos, V.: Towards automated large vocabulary gesture search. In: Proc. of the 2nd int. Conf. on Pervasive Technologies Related to Assistive Environments, Corfu, Greece (2009)
6. Kelly, D., Delannoy, R., Mc Donald, J.: A framework for continuous multimodal sign language recognition. In: Proc. of the int. Conf. on Multimodal interfaces, Cambridge, Massachusetts, USA, pp. 351–358 (2009)

7. Prasad, J.S., Nandi, G.C.: Clustering Method Evaluation for Hidden Markov Model Based Real-Time Gesture Recognition. In: IEEE ARTCom. Advances in Recent Technologies in Communication and Computing, October 27-28, pp. 419–423 (2009)
8. Ionescu, B., Coquin, D., Lambert, P., Buzuloiu, V.: Dynamic hand gesture recognition using the skeleton of the hand. EURASIP J. Appl. Signal Process. 2005(1), 2101–2109 (2005)
9. Hninn, T., Maung, H.: Real-Time Hand Tracking and Gesture Recognition System Using Neural Networks. WASET 50, 466–470 (2009)
10. Freeman, W.T., Roth, M.: Orientation histograms for hand gesture recognition. In: Intl. Workshop on Automatic Face- and Gesture- Recognition, pp. 296–301. IEEE Computer Society, Zurich (1995)

Power-Efficient Cache Design Using Dual-Edge Clocking Scheme in Sun OpenSPARC T1 and Alpha AXP Processors

Megalingam Rajesh Kannan, M. Arunkumar, V. Arjun Ashok, Krishnan Nived,
and C.J. Daniel

Department of ECE, Amrita School of Engineering, Amrita Vishwa Vidyapeetham,
Amritapuri Campus, Kollam, Kerala, India 690525
{megakannan,arunkumar.m,arjunashok619,nivedkrish}@ieee.org,
daniel.cj228@gmail.com

Abstract. Power efficiency in VLSI design is in prime focus in today's state of the art. A simple method of reducing power consumption in cache memories and other logic is presented here. We make use of both edges of clock signals to perform cache accesses in order to enable the reduction of operating frequency - and thus, dynamic power - without affecting performance to a large extent. Experimental results are presented, making use of the OpenSPARC T1 and Alpha AXP 21064 processor caches.

Keywords: CMOS, dynamic power dissipation, dual-edge clocking, OpenSPARC T1, Alpha AXP 21064.

1 Introduction

One of the highest demands on VLSI design in today's world is the need for power efficiency. With the rise of ubiquitous computing, power efficiency directly translates into extended battery life for portable devices. It also makes better environmental sense. Cache memories can consume a major portion of the power drawn by a processor [1].

Here, we explore a method of dividing cache access between the rising and falling edges of the clock signal, so that we are in a position to reduce the overall operating frequency of the module [2]. This contributes to a reduction in dynamic power dissipation, since the switching frequency of a logic circuit is closely related to the amount of dynamic power dissipated.

We then present results obtained when this method was applied to the caches specified for the OpenSPARC T1 and Alpha AXP 21064 processors.

2 Power Consumption in CMOS

During switching in a CMOS circuit, current is typically drawn directly from the supply [3], [4]. The more transitions a CMOS circuit or memory experiences, more

V.V Das et al. (Eds.): BAIP 2010, CCIS 70, pp. 108–113, 2010.

the dynamic power it dissipates. It is known that clock signals in CMOS circuits have the highest toggling rates of all signals. The expression for dynamic power, P_D, has load capacitance, C_L, supply voltage, V_{DD} and clock frequency, f_C, as factors.

$$P_D = C_L V_{DD}^2 f_C \tag{1}$$

Each of the terms in the above expression needs to be carefully minimized, particularly clock frequency, f_C, ensuring the circuit's performance does not suffer.

3 Dual-Edge Clocking Methodology

Caches and other memories are essentially banks of registers which trigger on the same edge, either rising or falling. Here, we propose a simple method where we make use of both edges of the clock.

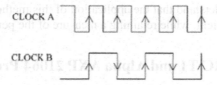

Fig. 1. A comparison of traditional clocking and dual-edge clocking. The most interesting result is that both of these have the same number of triggering edges, even though the frequencies differ by a factor of two.

It can be seen from Fig. 1 that the two clocks, one of frequency f and the other of frequency f/2, have edges at the same instants of time, albeit with a change in the sense. If one D flip-flop consumes power P watts at operating frequency f, it will consume power P/2 watts at frequency f/2, as in equation (1).

Applying a design scheme where accesses are staggered over sequential clock edges to large scale memories and other circuits would mean large gains in power efficiency. One of the possible applications is in cache memory.

4 Application of Dual-Edge Clocking in Caches

To apply the proposed method to memories in general, and caches in particular, we consider a direct-mapped cache [5]. We then divide the architecture into two banks, each containing only either odd or even locations [2]. Even-numbered locations are always accessed on a particular edge of the clock, and odd-numbered locations are always accessed on the opposite edge. The clock frequency can then be made half. The arrangement is illustrated in Fig. 2.

A caveat of this method is that trying to address a location on the wrong edge will cause a delay, equal in duration to a single cycle of the original clock [1]. This, however, is not as serious as a cache miss. The required data becomes available at the next edge without going to the level below in the memory hierarchy. The situation can be rectified to an extent by intelligently queuing requests, so that accesses always alternate between odd and even locations.

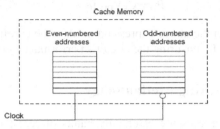

Fig. 2. The proposed organization of cache memory is shown. Odd and even addresses are accessed on different clock edges.

It is important to understand that the application of this method results in logic that are twice as power efficient, while retaining a measure of the performance.

5   The OpenSPARC T1 and Alpha AXP 21064 Processor Caches

The OpenSPARC T1 processor was designed by Sun Microsystems [6]. Each SPARC core has a 16 KB 4-way set-associative primary instruction cache and an 8 KB 4-way set-associative primary data cache. Our dual-edge technique was applied as a modification to the 8 KB primary data cache, Fig. 3. Our aim was to compare the power consumption of the two and establish the veracity of our technique.

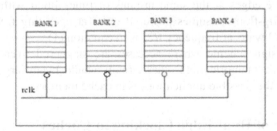

Fig. 3. Simplified representation of the OpenSPARC T1 data cache. *rclk* is the original clock signal.

The Alpha AXP 21064 processor was developed by Digital Equipment Corporation, [9]. We used the instruction cache memory defined for this processor to illustrate our dual-edge scheme. The instruction cache is specified to be direct-mapped for single-cycle access, 8 KB in size, with data being stored in blocks of 32 B each.

5.1 Modification Using Dual-Edge Clocking

Read and write processes take place on the positive edge of the clock when one set of banks are involved. The other set of banks are accessed on the falling edge.

In these modified caches, the clock frequency to carry out cache transactions is now reduced to half of that of the original clock, called *rclk,* used in the original design. The new clock is named *dclk.* A simplified schematic of the modification for the OpenSPARC T1 data cache is shown in Fig 4.

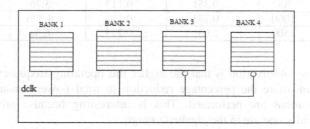

Fig. 4. Simplified representation of the modified OpenSPARC T1 data cache. *dclk* is the new clock signal.

5.2 Experimental Results and Analysis

Both designs were synthesised using Xilinx 10.1 ISE [8] for Virtex 5 FPGA devices. Using Xilinx XPower Analyzer, the power consumption for various clock frequencies was analyzed in each case. The results indicate that a significant amount of power consumed is reduced by the use of the proposed cache design. Tables 1 and 2 show the power consumption statistics for OpenSPARC T1 and Alpha AXP 21064 caches respectively.

Table 1. Power consumption by the OpenSPARC T1 processor data cache

Freq. (MHz)		Dynamic Power (W)		Total Power (W)	
rclk	dclk	Original	Modified	Original	Modified
1200	600	1.284	1.014	1.636	1.353
1300	650	1.389	1.096	1.746	1.438
1400	700	1.494	1.178	1.857	1.524
1500	750	1.600	1.261	1.969	1.612
1600	800	1.707	1.345	2.081	1.700
1700	850	1.815	1.430	2.196	1.790
1800	900	1.925	1.517	2.311	1.881
1900	950	2.305	1.605	2.429	1.974
2000	1000	2.148	1.696	2.548	2.069

Table 2. Power consumption by the Alpha AXP 21064 processor instruction cache

Freq.(MHz)		Dynamic Power (W)		Total Power (W)	
rclk	*dclk*	Original	Modified	Original	Modified
50	25	0.038	0.007	3.313	3.27
100	50	0.062	0.013	3.347	3.279
200	100	0.106	0.026	3.409	3.296
300	150	0.145	0.037	3.465	3.312
400	200	0.181	0.049	3.516	3.329
500	250	0.213	0.06	3.562	3.344
1000	500	0.351	0.113	3.76	3.419
2000	1000	0.783	0.184	4.396	3.52
3000	1500	2.001	0.273	6.34	3.647

An interesting observation is that the higher the operating frequency the original design works in, more the percentage reduction in total power consumption when dual-edge operations are performed. This is interesting because processor cache memories typically operate in the gigahertz range.

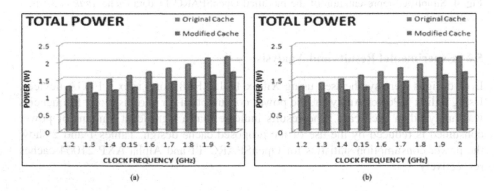

Fig. 5. Comparison of total power dissipated in the *(a)* original and modified OpenSPARC T1 processor data cache, *(b)*Alpha AXP 21064 instruction cache

The power consumption statistics given in Tables 1 and 2 are represented graphically in Fig. 5.

6 Conclusion

It is obvious that the dual-edge clocking scheme is quite efficient in reducing power consumption, and that it can be applied to cache systems to reduce the dynamic power dissipation without largely compromising performance.

However, this technique is not without its caveats. The experimental results seem to indicate that the method is economical only at high frequencies. Also, it is more useful where long sequences of data are expected to be accessed, for example, in data caches used in multimedia devices, where sequential access of data can be exploited to its fullest extent. It is obvious that a request on the wrong edge can increase the delay before the processor receives its data. This can be rectified to some extent using intelligent addressing techniques, where accesses are fully alternated between dual-edge triggered banks to maximize throughput.

Acknowledgments

We gratefully acknowledge the Almighty God who gave us strength and health to successfully complete this venture. The authors wish to thank Amrita Vishwa Vidyapeetham, for access to their research facilities.

References

1. Zhang, C.: An Efficient Direct Mapped Instruction Cache for Application-Specific Embedded Systems, Jersey City, New Jersey, USA (2005)
2. Megalingam, R.K., Krishnan, N., Arjun Ashok, V., Arunkumar, M.: Highly Power Efficient, Uncompromised Performance Cache Design Using Dual-Edged Clock. In: 2nd IEEE ICCSIT 2009, Beijing, China (2009)
3. Weste, H., Eshraghian, K.: Principles of CMOS VLSI Design
4. Kang, S.-M., Leblebici, Y.: CMOS Digital Integrated Circuits, 3rd edn. Tata McGraw-Hill, New York (2003)
5. Mano, M.: Computer System Architecture, 3rd edn.
6. Sun Microsystems: OpenSPARC T1 Microarchitecture Specification (2006)
7. OpenSPARC, http://www.opensparc.net/
8. Xilinx, http://www.xilinx.com/
9. Hennessy, J.L., Patterson, D.A.: Computer Organization and Design – The Hardware-Software Interface. Morgan Kaufman, San Francisco (1997)
10. Mathur, A., Wang, Q., Dimri, V.: Power Reduction Techniques at the RTL and System Level. In: 22nd International Conference on VLSI Design, January 5-9 (2009)
11. Tirumalashetty, V., Mahmoodi, H.: Clock Gating and Negative Edge Triggering for Energy Recovery Clock (2007)
12. Abella, J., González, A.: Power Efficient Data Cache Designs. In: Proceedings of the 21st International Conference on Computer Design, ICCD 2003 (2003)

Power Consumption Analysis of Direct, Set Associative and Phased Set Associative Cache Organizations in Alpha AXP 21064 Processor

Megalingam Rajesh Kannan, K.B. Deepu, Joseph P. Iype, Ravishankar Parthasarathy, and Popuri Gautham

Department of Electronics and Communication Engineering
Amrita School Of Engineering, Amritapuri
rajeshm@am.amrita.edu, deepu13589@gmail.com,
iype_06ec24@students.amrita.ac.in, partha_parthu@yahoo.co.in,
gautham.dondbz@gmail.com

Abstract. The power consumption of the integrated circuits have become increasingly a central topic of today's research. The need for low power has caused a major paradigm shift where power dissipation has become as important as performance and area. In this paper the original direct mapped cache of Alpha AXP 21064 processor is modified into set associative and phased set associative caches. The experimental results show that phased set associative cache is more power efficient than set associative cache. These three designs namely direct mapped, set associative and phased set associative caches are modeled using Verilog HDL, simulated in Modelsim and synthesized in Xilinx ISE 10.1. The power estimation and analysis is done using Xilinx XPower Analyser.

Keywords: Direct mapped, set associative, phased set associative, Alpha AXP 21064, miss rate.

1 Introduction

Cache memory is an extremely fast memory that is built into the central processing unit (CPU), or located next to it on a separate chip. The CPU uses cache memory to store instructions that are repeatedly required to run programs, improving overall system speed, and reducing power consumption. But as the size of on-chip cache started increasing, the energy dissipation per unit area also started increasing proportionately. The various ways for reducing cache energy dissipation includes the use of alternative cache organizations, way predictions, selective turning-off of various parts of cache, feeding the cache with different voltages and low power design based on value frequencies[1][2][3][4][6]. The direct mapped instruction cache of Alpha AXP 21064 processor is modified to set associative and phased set associative cache designs. First part of the paper gives brief idea about the three cache mapping techniques. The next section explains Alpha AXP 21064 processor's instruction cache, and the modified cache. Finally experimental results are provided for both original and modified cache designs.

V.V Das et al. (Eds.): BAIP 2010, CCIS 70, pp. 114–119, 2010.

2 Direct Mapped Cache Architecture

In a direct mapped cache, every block in the main memory is mapped to a particular line in the cache. Every line of the cache corresponds to more than one block of main memory [7]. There is no replacement algorithm and if a particular line is preoccupied, it has to be replaced by a new incoming block. This leads to resource wastage when it comes to continuous replacement of a particular line in the cache even if other lines are empty and this is called cache thrashing [7]. This cache mapping technique consumes less power compared to other techniques.

3 Set Associative Cache Architecture

In conventional set associative cache, the chance for cache thrashing is very less. The tag is checked sequentially or in parallel and simultaneously the data is read into the bus but the valid bit is set only when a hit occurs. When the CPU generates an address, it first searches the cache for data or instruction. If it is found in the cache, then it is a hit and if not found it is a miss. The address generated by the CPU is split into tag, set and word [7]. The corresponding set is selected with the generated set address and the tag of each line in the set is compared with the generated tag and at the same time the data will be available in the bus but the valid bit will not be set. If there is a tag match then it is a hit and if none of the tag matches then it is a cache miss and the data or instruction should be fetched form the memory. If there is a hit the valid bit will be set and the required data can be accessed from the bus.

4 Phased Set Associative Cache Architecture

In phased cache, the tag array and data array are separate. Tags of all the ways are compared sequentially or in parallel in the first stage. If there is a hit then the corresponding data is accessed and fed to the input of the buffer in second stage. The corresponding buffer will be enabled in the same clock cycle and data will be available in

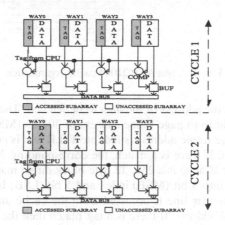

Fig. 1. Phased Cache [5]

the data bus. Phased cache will reduce the power consumption by avoiding unnecessary access of data sub array. Disadvantage of phased cache is that it takes two clock cycles to access the data.

Fig.1 shows a phased cache. The tag sub arrays of all the ways are accessed simultaneously and compared with the tag from CPU. If there is a match then the data sub array of the matched way is accessed and is fed to the input of the buffer. The corresponding buffer is enabled and the requested data will be available in the data bus in two clock cycles. In Fig.1 it is clear that the number of comparators needed is equal to the number of ways in a set. Here we need four comparators as our cache is four way set associative. In the first clock cycle all the tags in a set are compared with the tag from the CPU. If there is a tag match then in the next clock cycle the data is accessed and will be available in the data bus.

5 The Alpha AXP 21064 Processor

Alpha is a 64 bit processor developed by Digital Equipment Corporation (DEC). The Instruction Translation Look aside Buffer (ITLB) and Instruction Cache (ICache) of Alpha processor is shown in Fig 2. ITLB outputs the physical address corresponding to a page-frame address. This physical address is the input to ICache and the data is retrieved from the cache.

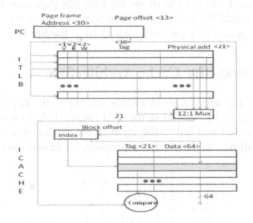

Fig. 2. Alpha AXP 21064 cache organization

The CPU generates the address of the data to be fetched. The 43 bit address generated by the CPU is split in to page frame address of 30 bits (MSB) and page offset of 13 bits (LSB). The page frame address is fed into ITLB and is compared with the tags whose valid bit is high. If there is a match, the corresponding 21 bit physical address is fed into ICache. The ICache is a 256, 32 byte block direct mapped memory. The 13 bit page offset is split into 8 bit (MSB) index and 5 bit (LSB) block offset in ICache. With this index a particular line is accessed from the cache and its tag is compared with the input physical address. If there is a tag match then the corresponding data is read using block offset.

6 Implementation and Experimental Results

The direct mapped ICache of Alpha AXP 21064 and its variations namely set associative and phased set associative cache are modeled using Verilog HDL and synthesized in Xilinx ISE 10.1 The power analysis is done using Xilinx Xpower analyzer. The results show that the set associative cache consumes a maximum of 91% more power than the direct mapped cache whereas the phased four way set associative cache consumes a maximum of 76.6% power than the direct mapped cache. We can also note that the four way phased set associative cache results in a maximum of 63.1% less power than the four way set associative cache design.

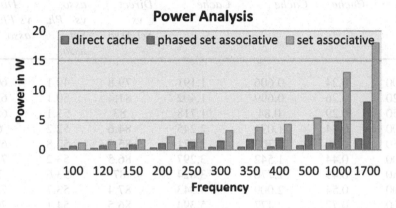

Fig. 3. Comparison of direct, phased set associative and set associative caches

Fig.3 shows the comparison of direct cache, the set associative cache and phased set associative cache. The power consumption by all the cache designs for various frequencies are found out and plotted. The figure shows that the power consumption of the set associative cache is very high when compared to other two designs. The phased cache consumes much less power than the conventional set associative cache. If we use phased set associative cache instead of the conventional set associative cache we get a maximum reduction in power consumption of 63.1% without compromising the miss rate.

Table 1 shows the power analysis of the direct cache, set associative cache and phased set associative caches. The set associative cache shows an average increase of 85.6% power compared to the direct mapped cache. The maximum increase in power consumption of 91% occurs at a frequency of 1GHz and the minimum increase in power consumption of 79.8% occurs at a frequency of 100MHz. The phased set associative cache shows an average increase of 68.5% power compared to the direct mapped cache. The maximum increase in power consumption of 76.6% occurs at a frequency of 1.7GHz and the minimum increase in power consumption occurs at a frequency of 100MHz. The phased set associative cache shows an average reduction in power consumption of 53.4% compared to conventional four way set associative cache. The maximum reduction in power consumption is found to be 63.1% at a frequency of 1GHz. The minimum reduction in power consumption is found to be 49.1% at a frequency of 100MHz.

The total miss rate of the 8KB direct mapped cache is 0.046 and the miss rate of the 8KB four way set associative cache is 0.035 [7]. If we use the phased four way set associative cache instead of the conventional set associative cache, the power consumption is reduced without compromising the miss rate.

Table 1. Details of power analysis done using Xilinx Xpower analyzer

Clock (in MHz)	Power Consumed (in Watts)			% Increase in Power Consumption		
	Direct Cache	Ph.SetAsso. Cache	Set.Asso. Cache	Direct vs Set Asso.	Set asso. vs Ph. Set asso.	Direct vs Ph. Set asso.
100	0.24	0.606	1.191	79.8	49.1	60.2
120	0.26	0.699	1.402	81.4	50.1	62.7
150	0.29	0.84	1.718	83	51.1	65.2
200	0.34	1.074	2.245	84.6	52.2	68
250	0.39	1.308	2.771	85.7	52.8	69.8
300	0.44	1.542	3.297	86.5	53.2	71.1
350	0.49	1.776	3.824	87	53.6	72
400	0.54	2.009	4.343	87.4	53.7	72.7
500	0.72	2.477	5.394	86.5	54.1	70.6
1000	1.16	4.817	13.05	91	63.1	75.8
1700	1.88	8.092	18.041	89.5	55.2	76.6

7 Conclusion

Of all the three cache categories, the direct mapped cache consumes less power. The power consumption of the phased set associative cache is found to be very less, compared to the conventional set associative cache. If power is the major concern we can opt for direct mapped cache. But direct mapped cache has high miss rate. If we can compromise performance for power, phased set associative cache is a good option rather than conventional set associative cache.

References

[1] Calder, B., Grunwald, D., Emer, J.: Predictive Sequential Associative Cache. In: Proceedings of Second International Symposium on High-Performance Computer Architecture, February 1996, pp. 244–253 (1996)
[2] Chang, J.H., Chao, H., So, K.: Cache design of a sub-micron cmos system/370. In: 14th Annual International Symposium on Computer Architecture, SIGARCH Newsletter, June 1987, pp. 208–213 (1987)

[3] Koji, I., Tohru, I., Kazuaki, M.: Way Predicting Set Associative Cache for High Performance and Low Energy Consumption. In: ISLPED 1999, San Diego, CA, USA (1999)

[4] Hasegawa, A., et al.: SH3: High Code Density, Low Power. IEEE Micro 15(6), 11–19 (1995)

[5] Megalingam, R.K., Deepu, K.B., Joseph, I.P., Vikram, V.: Phased Set Associative Cache Design For Reduced Power Consumption. In: 2nd IEEE ICCSIT 2009, Beijing, China (2009)

[6] Kin, J., Gupta, M., Mangione-Smith, W.H.: The Filter Cache: An Energy Efficient Memory Structure. In: IEEE/ACM International Symposium on Microarchitecture (MICRO-30), pp. 184–193 (1997)

[7] Patterson, D.A., Hennesy, J.L.: Computer Organization and Design, 2nd edn.

Role of Resolution in Noisy Pattern Matching

Alex Pappachen James[*] and Sima Dimitrijev

Queensland microtechnology Facility, QMNC, Griffith University, Australia
{a.james,s.dimitrijev}@griffith.edu.au

Abstract. Natural variability and limited number of library instances influence the matching performance and robustness of automatic pattern analysis methods. A data representation method that utilizes the local structures from the original data with a focus to effectively use the full resolution of data vector is presented. Using plant and face database, the issue of resolution, limitations in the number of library instances, and variability were addressed. Interestingly, the method shows an automatic matching improvement of over 22% under noisy and difficult matching condition.

Keywords: Gaussian Noise, Filtering.

1 Introduction

Data and pattern analysis is widely used in studies involving medicine, subject classification, sequence detection, volumetric image analysis and biometric time signal analysis [7,10,14,11]. Numerical mapping of data from real-world measurements is the first process involved in any pattern analysis systems [6]. The selection of a proper representation is not considered as a trivial task, and has been very often debated over the subject of practice and theoretical meaning [5]. Often linked with the idea of curse of dimensionality, most statistical methods find the use of full-resolution, of large dimensional data, unnecessary and redundant [15,1].

In this paper, we present a method that uses full resolution of the available data in a typical data classification process. The method presents local feature normalization and selection scheme providing a way to use the resolution of data without removing the useful information from its inherent structure.

2 The Approach

The main approach in this paper involves using the local structures in the data without the knowledge of inherent distribution of the data. To extract the feature intensities locally, relative variations between the features are calculated by using change detection filters such as gradients, standard deviation, and range filter [2,17,18,19,9,8].

---

[*] Dr A.P. James is the corresponding author of this paper. He is a research fellow with QMNC, Griffith University.

V.V Das et al. (Eds.): BAIP 2010, CCIS 70, pp. 120–124, 2010.
© Springer-Verlag Berlin Heidelberg 2010

Local standard deviation filtering is used as a proposed approach to transform the N-dimensional vector I using a N-dimensional kernel operation:

$$\sigma(i_1 \ldots i_N) = \sqrt{\frac{1}{m_1 \ldots m_N} \sum_{z_1=-a_1}^{a_1} \cdots \sum_{z_N=-a_N}^{a_N} \cdots \left[I(i_1 + z_1 \ldots i_N + z_N) - \overline{I(i_1 \ldots i_N)} \right]} \qquad (1)$$

where $a_N = (m_N - 1)/2$, over a N-dimensional window of size $m_1 \times .. m_{N-1} \times m_N$. The local mean $\overline{I(i_1 .. i_N)}$ used in (1) is calculated by the following equation:

$$\overline{I(i_1 .. i_N)} = \frac{1}{m_1 .. m_N} \sum_{z_1=-a_1}^{a_1} .. \sum_{z_N=-a_N}^{a_N} I(i_1 + z_1 .. i_N + z_N) \qquad (2)$$

The resulting feature vector σ maintains the same resolution as the original feature vector I. Further, these local features can be boosted by readjusting the local mean of the data. The normalized features x are calculated using the following equation:

$$x(i, j) = \frac{\sigma(i, j)}{\overline{\sigma}} \qquad (3)$$

where the spatial change features σ are normalized using the local mean is calculated using Eq. (2) with different values for $m_1 .. m_N$ and σ instead of I.

An example of obtaining such a data representation is shown in Fig 1. It can be seen from this example that the original instance has 4 features (represented by 4 numbers), which when using the new data representation is transformed to 16 features via the process of filtering. Also, note that more number of window descriptors can be defined and used to further increase the number of features in the modified data.

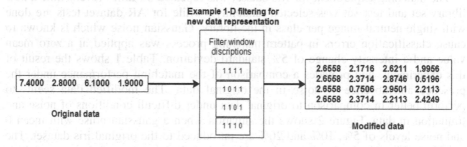

Fig. 1. The illustration shows the process of creating a local data representation from an original data using the Eq. (1), (2) and (3). The window descriptors select the moving window of elements used for the filtering calculations. The original data instance having 4 feature values is shown in this example is a random selection of an instance from the iris plant dataset [4].

In a typical classification problem, a known set of features representing different classes are stored in the library. An unknown instance called a test instance is compared with the instances in the library to determine the class of the test instance through a process of best match. The process of matching becomes a difficult problem if: (1) the number of instances in the library per class is limited to one and/or (2) the inter-class similarities and intra-class differences are high.

The matching process involves the use of a similarity or a distance calculation between the comparing instances from a N-dimensional test vector x_t to that from a N-dimensional library x_l. The simplest measure of distance calculation having a good theoretical and practical foundation is the Euclidean distance measure [16, 3]. The feature level description of such a distance is merely the inter-feature differences:

$$L_1(i_1..i_N) = |x_t(i_1..i_N) - x_l(i_1..i_N)| \qquad (4)$$

These local distances can be used to calculated the global distance by aggregating the local distances. For example the global distance can be represented as:

$$L_g = \sum_{i_1} .. \sum_{i_N} L_1(i_1...i_N) \qquad (5)$$

Equation (5) can be used for finding the best match by ranking the distances obtained as a result of comparison of a test instance with many library instances. The lowest value of the distance implies the highest similarity and provides the best match for the test instance in the library.

3 Experimental Results

We used iris plant dataset [4] is a classical classification database and a high-dimensional dataset of face images (AR database [12, 13]) for our experiments[1]. From the original-iris and AR dataset, one instance per class was randomly selected to form the library set. The remaining instances form the test set[2].

The matching experiment for Iris dataset was repeated 30 times (every time a new library set and test set was selected randomly), while for AR dataset tests are done with single neutral image per class in the library. Gaussian noise which is known to cause classification errors in pattern matching process was applied at a zero mean value and a intensity change of 5% standard deviation. Table 1 shows the result of this experiment, and provides a comparison of the matching performance under the presence and absence of noise in the original data. The modified data seems to perform better in comparison to original data under difficult conditions of noise and limitation in data. Figure 2 shows the situation when a gaussian noise with mean 0 and noise levels of 5%, 10% and 20% are introduced to the original iris dataset. The modified data obtained when using this noisy dataset showed better matching performance at every situation depicted in Fig 2. The mean matching accuracy is higher for modified data than for original data. As an example the average accuracy at 20% noise level for modified data is $68 \pm 4\%$, while for original data this is $36 \pm 4\%$.

---

[1] Images of 100 persons from the AR dataset form the database for our experiments.

[2] The main parameter in the classification experiment using the proposed method was the selection of the local filter window, in the experiments a size of 1×4 was selected for Iris dataset and 3×3 was selected for AR dataset, as any window size larger than 1×1 would increase the total feature numbers with respect to the original data.

This showed that increased resolution of features has the ability to provide better immunity towards natural variability and can be a viable option irrespective of limitations in library data.

Table 1. A comparison of matching accuracy for single instance per library problem. The gaussian noise has a mean 0 and 5% standard deviation on intensities of the original data.

Noise addition	Data type	Matching accuracy (%)
No	Original Iris	88 ± 4
	Modified Iris	88 ± 4
	Original AR	61 ± 0
	Modified AR	82 ± 0
Yes	Original Iris	38 ± 10
	Modified Iris	64 ± 4
	Original AR	41 ± 0
	Modified AR	70 ± 0

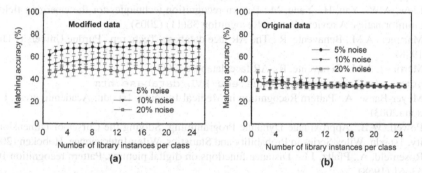

Fig. 2. A comparison with respect to matching accuracy between original data and modified data under the presence of gaussian noise at various levels: (a) shows the accuracies for modified data obtained as a result of processing noise added original data using proposed method, (b) shows the accuracies for noise added original data.

4 Conclusion

This paper presented a method that has the ability to utilize the full-resolution of the original features using a method of analyzing local features. The general assumption on the use of feature resolution is that it does not provide robustness in matching problems, on contrary we find that local features can utilize resolution and provided better robustness. Local information revealed the structure and uniqueness of the pattern which became useful for the feature matching. The approach followed in this method was modular and was easy to scale in both software and hardware.

Acknowledgments. The support of Qs Semiconductors is gratefully acknowledged.

References

1. Bellman, R.: Adaptive Control Processes: A Guided Tour. Princeton University Press, Princeton (1961)
2. Castleman, K.R.: Digital Image Processing. Prentice Hall, Englewood Cliffs (1996)
3. Danielsson, P.E.: Euclidean distance mapping. CGIP 14(3), 227–248 (1980)
4. Fisher, R.A.: The use of multiple measurements in taxonomic problems. Annual Eugenics, 179–188 (1936)
5. Hand, D.J.: Statistics and the theory of measurement (with discussion). Journal of the Royal Statistical Society, Series A 159, 445–492 (1996)
6. Hand, D.J.: Measurement Theory and Practice: The World Through Quantification. Wiley, Chichester (2004)
7. Jagota, A.: Data Analysis and Classification for Bioinformatics. Bioinformatics By the Bay, 1st edn. (2000)
8. James, A.P.: Face Recognition, ch. 1, pp. 1–22. INTech Pub. (2010)
9. James, A.P., Dimitrijev, S.: Face recognition using local binary decisions. IEEE Signal Processing Letters 15, 821–824 (2008)
10. Jones, N.C.: An Introduction to Bioinformatics Algorithms (Computational Molecular Biology), 1st edn. The MIT Press, Cambridge (2004)
11. Liew, A.W., Yan, H., Yang, M.: Pattern recognition techniques for the emerging field of bioinformatics: A review. Pattern Recognition 38(11) (2005)
12. Martinez, A.M., Benavente, R.: The AR face database. Tech. rep., Purdue University (June 1998)
13. Martinez, A.M., Benavente, R.: AR face database (2000),
    http://rvl.www.ecn.purdue.edu/RVL/database.htm
14. Meyer-Baese, A.: Pattern Recognition in Medical Imaging, 1st edn. Academic press, London (2003)
15. Powell, W.B.: Approximate Dynamic Programming: Solving the Curses of Dimensionality, 1st edn. Wiley Series in Probability and Statistics. Wiley-Interscience, Hoboken (2007)
16. Rosenfeld, A., Pfaltz, J.L.: Distance functions on digital pictures. Pattern recognition 1(1), 33–61 (1968)
17. Russ, J.C.: The Image Processing Handbook. CRC Press, Boca Raton (1995)
18. Serra, J.: Image Analysis and Mathematical Morphology. Academic Press, London (1982)
19. Verbeek, P., Vrooman, H., Vliet, L.V.: Low-level image processing by max-min filters. Signal Processing 15, 249–258 (1988)

Integrating an Efficient Authorization Protocol with Trigon-Based Authentication Mechanism for Improving Grid Security

V. Ruckmani[1] and G. Sudha Sadasivam[2]

[1] Senior Lecturer, Department of MCA, Sri Ramakrishna Engineering College,
Coimbatore, Tamilnadu, India
ruckmaniv@yahoo.com
[2] Professor, Department of Computer Science and Engineering, PSG College of Technology,
Coimbatore, Tamilnadu, India
sudhasadhasivam@yahoo.co.in

Abstract. Security is a vital part of an integrated grid application in which heterogeneous services and resources belonging to multiple domains are distributed dynamically. Authentication and authorization are the major security concerns in grid environment. Most of the grid security mechanisms stress on authentication, and not on authorization. This paper proposes to integrate an authorization protocol with the effective trigon-based authentication technique based on the user's role. This integrated trigon-based authentication – authorization protocol provides effective grid security in an efficient manner.

Keywords: Security, Trigon-based Authentication, Authorization, Authorization Protocol, Grid.

1 Introduction

The major concern of grid computing is to provide collaborative resource sharing between virtual organizations. Grid Security Infrastructure (GSI) [1] ensures secure communication between the entities on the grid. Existing grid security mechanisms are based on authentication and do not lay emphasis on authorization. As an example, the effective trigon-based grid security mechanism is composed only for authentication and not for authorizing the grid users. Though, the trigon-based mechanism is effective in authenticating the grid users, the grid security violates as it is not providing any authorization mechanism.

Grid authentication frameworks use the standard SSL authentication protocol (SAP) or a certificate free authentication protocol [2]. A flexible and meaningful policy-driven, two-level, credential-based authorization system [3] controls access to the Globus Computational GRAM service. Authorization can be provided by Role-Based Grid Delegation Model (RB-GDM) [4] framework that delegates admittance in grids.

V.V Das et al. (Eds.): BAIP 2010, CCIS 70, pp. 125–129, 2010.

This paper proposes the integration of a simple authorization technique with the novel trigon-based authentication scheme. The integrated authorization technique authorizes the users based on access rights. Hence, by integrating, the trigon-based authentication with authorization the grid security is enhanced by providing effective authentication and authorization. The rest of the paper is organized as follows. Section 2 details the authorization protocol with required illustration and also construes about integration of the protocol with the trigon-based authentication. Section 3 discusses the simulation results and Section 4 concludes the paper.

2   The Authorization Protocol and Its Integration with the Trigon-Based Authentication Protocol

The trigon-based authentication protocol [5] authenticated the user based on authentication server and back-end server. $T_{vo}^{(i)}$ token is issued on the basis of the role of the registered users with the authentication/main server. $T_{vo}^{(i)}$ is provided by the database maintained in the main server which is comprised of the available roles, resources identities and their weights. Let, $[r_0 \quad r_1 \quad r_2 \quad \cdots \quad r_{n-1}]$ be the vector of roles that are available in the grid, where, n is the total number of roles, $[w_{r_0} \quad w_{r_1} \quad w_{r_2} \quad \cdots \quad w_{r_{n-1}}]$ be the vector of weight of each role, where, $w_{r_a} \neq w_{r_b}$ and $w_{r_a}, w_{r_b} \in [w_r]$.

The valid users authenticated by the authentication protocol can play only the registered roles. Let, $[R_0 \quad R_1 \quad R_2 \quad \cdots \quad R_{m-1}]$ be the vector of resources available in the grid and $[w_{R_0} \quad w_{R_1} \quad w_{R_2} \quad \cdots \quad w_{R_{m-1}}]$ be the vector of the weight of each resource, where, $w_{R_a} \neq w_{R_b}$ and $w_{R_a}, w_{R_b} \in [w_R]$. The information vectors $[r], [w_r], [R]$ and $[w_R]$ are maintained in the database of the main server. Authorization information is requested by the authorization server (VO manager). The integrated trigon-based authentication-authorization protocol performs authorization as shown in Fig 1.

Once the authentication had been performed, the main server issues the $T_{vo}^{(i)}$ to the valid user. The $T_{vo}^{(i)}$ for a particular user can be calculated using

$$T_{vo}^{(i)} = \frac{w_r(u_i)}{\sum_{l=0}^{n-1} w_{r_l}} \tag{4}$$

$T_{vo}^{(i)}$ is sent by the valid user to the authorization server along with the job J to be performed. The necessary resources needed to perform the job is then identified by the authorization server.

Authorization server sends the vector of recognized resources $[R_{req}]_i$ to the Main server, where, $R_{req}(j) \in [R]$ and $0 \leq j \leq n_R^{(J_i)}$. The code for the resource access $[C_R]_i$ is then determined by the Main server for each resource in the $[R_{req}]_i$ as follows which is sent to the authorization server.

$$C_R(j) = \frac{w_{R_{req}}(j)}{\sum_{l=0}^{m-1} w_{R_l}} \tag{5}$$

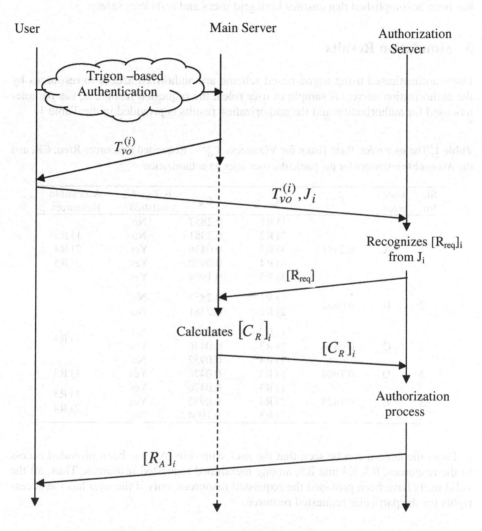

Fig. 1. Proposed Role-based Authorization Protocol

Then the user is authorized by the authorization server by providing access to the jth resource using the criteria $T_{vo}^{(i)} \geq C_R(j)$. Thus the authorization server provided the user to access the eligible resources using the key $[R_A]_i$. This authorization is thus based on the registered role of the user with the main server. For this purpose u_i, pw_i and role of access has been provided by the user at the time of registration. In the trigon-based authentication protocol, the main server authenticated the user to access the resources. The proposed trigon-based authorization protocol, the authorization server authorized the valid users to access the right resources. Thus by integrating both the authentication and authorization protocol, an efficient security mechanism has been accomplished that ensures both grid users and resources safety.

3 Simulation Results

Users authenticated using trigon-based scheme are authorized access to resources by the authorization server. A sample of user roles, the requested resources, the parameters used for authorization and the authorization results is provided in the Table 1.

Table 1. The user roles, their Token for VO access $T_{vo}^{(i)}$, Requested Resources Rreq, CR, and the Accessible resources for the particular user after its authorization

Sl. No	User roles	T_{vo}	R_{req}	C_R	Is $T_{vo} > C_R$ satisfied?	Accessible Resources
1	A	0.2381	1) R1	0.2857	No	
			2) R2	0.2381	No	1) R3
			3) R3	0.0476	Yes	2) R4
			4) R4	0.0952	Yes	3) R5
			5) R5	0.1904	Yes	
2	B	0.0952	1) R1	0.2857	No	
			2) R2	0.2381	No	
3	C	0.0476	1) R2	0.2381	No	1) R3
			2) R3	0.0476	Yes	
			3) R4	0.0952	No	
4	D	0.1904	1) R3	0.0476	Yes	1) R3
5	E	0.1429	1) R3	0.0476	Yes	1) R3
			2) R4	0.0952	Yes	2) R4
			3) R5	0.1904	No	

From the table it can be seen that the user with role 'A', has been provided access to the resources, R3, R4 and R5, among mentioned requested resources. Thus, all the valid users have been provided the requested resources, only if the user has the access rights for the particular requested resource.

4 Conclusion

The integration of the authorization protocol with the trigon-based authentication technique enhances grid security. The implementation results have shown that the resources are denied to any adversaries and the right resources are provided to the right users on the basis of their roles. Hence, by incorporating the aforesaid authorization protocol with the trigon-based authentication technique has made the grid more secure.

Acknowledgments. We authors would like to thank Mr. K. V. Chidambaram, Director, Data Infrastructure & Cloud Computing Group, Yahoo Software Development India Pvt Ltd., and Dr. R. Rudramoorthy, Principal, PSG College of Technology, Coimbatore for their support in carrying out the research work. We also thank the management of Sri Ramakrishna Engineering College for their support.

References

1. Foster, I., Kesselman, C., Tsudik, G., Tuecke, S.: A Security Architecture for Computational Grids. In: Proceedings of the ACM Conference on Computers and Security, pp. 83–91 (1998)
2. Koshutanski, H., Lazouski, A., Martinelli, F., Mori, P.: Enhancing grid security by fine-grained behavioral control and negotiation-based authorization. International Journal of Information Security 8(4), 291–314 (2009)
3. Hongweia, L., Shixina, S., Haomiaoa, Y.: Identity-based authentication protocol for grid. Journal of Systems Engineering and Electronics 19(4), 860–865 (2008)
4. Geethakumari, G., Negi, A., Sastry, V.N.: A Cross - Domain Role Mapping and Authorization Framework for RBAC in Grid Systems. International Journal of Computer Science and Applications 6(1), 1–12 (2009)
5. Ruckmani, V., Sudha Sadasivam, G.: A novel trigon-based authentication protocol for enhancing security in grid environment. International Journal of Computer Science and Information Security 6(3), 64–72 (2009)

Bandwidth Estimation Scheme for Mobile Adhoc Network

Deepak Vidhate, Anita Patil, and Supriya Sarkar

Department of Information Technology,
Padmashri Dr. Vithalrao Vikhe Patil College of Engineering, Ahmednagar, India

Abstract. Routing protocols for mobile ad hoc networks (MANETs) have been explored extensively in recent years. Much of this work is targeted at finding a feasible route from a source to a destination without considering current network traffic or application requirements. Therefore, the network may easily become overloaded with too much traffic and the application has no way to improve its performance under a given network traffic condition. While this may be acceptable for data transfer, many real-time applications require quality-of-service (QoS) support from the network. We believe that such QoS support can be achieved by either finding a route to satisfy the application requirements or offering network feedback to the application when the requirements cannot be met. The novel part of this QoS-aware routing is the use of the approximate bandwidth estimation to react to network traffic.

Keywords: We Mobile Ad hoc Network (MANET), Quality of Service (QoS), Bandwidth Estimation.

1 Introduction

Mobile ad-hoc network consists of wireless mobile hosts that communicate with each other over wireless link, in the absence of a fixed infrastructure, or centralized administration. When a host tries to send packets to destination that is out of range it can't send packets to destination directly. In such an environment, it may be necessary for one mobile host to enlist the aid of other hosts in forwarding a packet to its destination. Thus each node has to perform the function of host and router, to relay packets to nodes out of direct communication range. Under these circumstances, routing is much more complex than in conventional networks. It is unknown which of the routing techniques is likely to perform better for different types of traffic or mobility patterns as network size grows. It is also unclear that any existing ad-hoc routing protocol can be used to successfully route data over the many hops that will be necessary in large scale wireless networks. In this paper the performance evaluation of certain protocols are carried out and their performances are analyzed. Numerous protocols have been developed for Ad Hoc mobile networks, which include high power consumption, low bandwidth and high error rates.

V.V Das et al. (Eds.): BAIP 2010, CCIS 70, pp. 130–135, 2010.
© Springer-Verlag Berlin Heidelberg 2010

With the constraints, Hard QoS (e.g., guaranteed constant bit rate and delay) is difficult to achieve. The reasons are as follows.

- To support QoS, in principle, the end host should have precise knowledge of the global status of the network. The dynamic nature of MANETs makes it difficult for hosts to determine information about their local neighborhood.
- It is hard to establish cooperation between neighboring hosts to determine a transmit schedule for guaranteed packet delivery without centralized control. In MANETs, all hosts share the same physical channel, and each host's transmissions will interfere with neighboring hosts' transmissions.
- The wireless channel's main deficiency is its unreliability caused by various reasons such as fading and interference.

Thus, aim is to develop a routing protocol that provides Soft QoS [1] or better than best-effort service, rather than guaranteed hard QoS. However, if the topology changes too frequently, the source host cannot detect the network status changes and cannot make the corresponding adjustment to meet the specific QoS requirements, rendering the QoS meaningless. Some applications require minimum bandwidth support. If the minimum bandwidth cannot be met, all data will be useless. Thus, it is better not to transmit data in this case, because it will just waste network bandwidth and energy. Therefore, an admission control scheme is also embedded into our QoS-aware routing protocol to address this issue. Another challenge of QoS is medium access control (MAC)-layer design. We argue that the IEEE 802.11MAC is not the best MAC for supporting QoS. However, it is widely adopted in the wireless local area network (WLAN) community, and many devices have been commercialized with IEEE 802.11.

2 QOS-Aware Routing

QoS is an agreement to provide guaranteed services, such as bandwidth, delay, delay jitter, and packet delivery rate to users. Supporting more than one QoS constraint makes the QoS routing problem NP-complete [11]. Therefore, only consider the bandwidth constraint when studying QoS-aware routing for supporting real-time video or audio transmission. It is proposed a QoS-aware routing protocol that either provides feedback about the available bandwidth to the application (feedback scheme), or admits a flow with the requested bandwidth (admission scheme). Both the feedback scheme and the admission scheme require knowledge of the end-to- end bandwidth available along the route from the source to the destination. Thus, bandwidth estimation is the key to supporting QoS. This work focuses on exploring different ways to estimate the available bandwidth, incorporating a QoS-aware scheme into the route discovery procedure and providing feedback to the application through a cross-layer design.

A. Bandwidth Estimation
To offer bandwidth-guaranteed QoS, the available end-to-end bandwidth along a route from the source to the destination must be known. The end-to-end throughput is a concave parameter [12], which is determined by the bottleneck bandwidth of the intermediate hosts in the route. Therefore, estimating the end-to-end throughput can be

simplified into finding the minimal residual bandwidth available among the hosts in that route. However, how to calculate the residual bandwidth using the IEEE 802.11 MAC is still a challenging problem, because the bandwidth is shared among neighboring hosts, and an individual host has no knowledge about other neighboring hosts' traffic status. One method is for hosts to listen to the channel and estimate the available bandwidth based on the ratio of free and busy times ("Listen" bandwidth estimation).

1) "Listen" Bandwidth Estimation: To estimate the available bandwidth, intuitively, each host can listen to the channel to track the traffic state and determine how much free bandwidth it has available every second. The IEEE 802.11 MAC utilizes both a physical carrier sense and a virtual carrier sense [via the network allocation vector (NAV)], which can be used to determine the free and busy times. The MAC detects that the channel is free when following three requirements are met:

1. NAV's value is less than the current time;
2. Receive state is idle; & 3. Send state is idle.

A host estimates its available bandwidth for new data transmissions as the channel bandwidth times the ratio of free time to overall time, divided by a weight factor. The weight factor is introduced due to the nature of IEEE 802.11. This overhead makes it impossible in a distributed MAC competition scheme to fully use the available bandwidth for data transmission. Using the "Listen" method to estimate residual bandwidth is straightforward. However, using this approach, the host cannot release the bandwidth immediately when a route breaks, because it does not know how much bandwidth each node in the broken route consumes. "Listen" only counts the used bandwidth, but does not distinguish the corresponding bandwidth cost for each flow. This greatly affects the accuracy of bandwidth estimation when a route is broken.

2) "Hello" Bandwidth Estimation: In the "Hello" bandwidth estimation method, the sender's current bandwidth usage as well as the sender's one-hop neighbors' current bandwidth usage is piggybacked onto the standard "Hello" message. Each host estimates its available bandwidth based on the information provided in the "Hello" messages and knowledge of the frequency reuse pattern. This approach avoids creating extra control messages by using the "Hello" messages to disseminate the bandwidth information. The actual upper bound of bandwidth in the two-hop circle varies with the topology and the traffic status, but the raw channel bandwidth is the soft upper bound of total bandwidth. With the above frequency reuse pattern, we can simplify the bandwidth calculation problem to determining the residual bandwidth within the two-hop neighborhood range. Therefore, each host can approximate its residual bandwidth information based on information from hosts within two-hops (the interference range).

ID	Consumed Bandwidth	Timestamp
Neighbor ID 1	Consumed Bandwidth	Timestamp
:	:	:
:	:	:
Neighbor ID n	Consumed Bandwidth	Timestamp

Fig. 1. Hello structure. The bold item in the first row is the host's own information. The following rows are the host's neighbors' information.

Using this approach to gather the first and second neighboring hosts' information is imprecise. Fig. 2 shows an example topology that will result in imprecise information. The outside big circle indicates host A's interference range, and the other small-size dotted circles indicate host A and its neighbors' transmission ranges. Host E is not in A's transmission range, but it is in A's interference range. In addition, E does not fall into any of A's neighbors' transmission range. In this situation, A will never know E's status. If E transmits data, A's knowledge of available bandwidth is imprecise. However, this "hidden node" problem does not happen frequently since it has to meet strict requirements to "hide" the host. Even if this situation occurs, it can be overcome by using a conservative bandwidth estimate that leaves some extra bandwidth to conceal this "hidden node" effect. Once a host receives a "Hello" message from its neighbors, it determines whether this "Hello" is an updated one by examining the message's timestamp. Cache structure shown in Fig. 3 is used, which includes a first neighbor table and a second neighbor table. The second neighbors are linked with their corresponding first neighbors in the cache. It needs to divide the residual bandwidth by a weight factor due to the IEEE 802.11 MAC's nature and some overhead required by the routing protocol. In the MAC layer, ready-to-send (RTS), clear-to-send (CTS), and acknowledgment (ACK) packets consume bandwidth, the backoff scheme cannot fully use the entire bandwidth, and packets can collide, resulting in packet retransmissions.

Fig. 2. Hidden node scenario. The big circle indicates host A's interference range. The small circles indicate host A and its first neighboring hosts' transmission range. Hosts B, C, and D are A's first neighbors, and hosts F, G, H, and I are host A's second neighbors. Host E is in host A's interference range, but it is hidden to A.

B. Incorporating QoS with Bandwidth Estimation
Differentiate SENSE BUSY state from BUSY state: Let us first review a wireless node's four basic states: Transmitting, if it is currently emitting through its antenna; Receiving, if there is any node transmitting within its transmission range; Sensing, when the medium is sensed busy but no frame is being received because the energy level is below the receive power threshold. The other time the node is Idle. According to its influence on the surrounding media, it define that a node is BUSY when it is in the state of Transmitting or Receiving, and SENSE BUSY when it is in the state of Sensing. The other time the node is IDLE. The 'AB' estimated by a single node can be written as

$$AB = \frac{T_I}{T} \times C = \frac{T - T_B - T_S}{T} \times C \qquad (1)$$

where TI ; TB; TS are the time duration of IDLE, BUSY and SENSE BUSY states, respectively, in the measurement period T. C is the maximum capacity of the link. We consider the typical scenario in Fig. 3a where N1 is transmitting to N2, where the radius of the carrier sense range is supposed to be more than twice that of the transmission range. Fig. 3b depicts the basic IEEE 802.11 frame exchange sequence & the channel states sensed by all the nodes. Note that nodes within the transmission range of N1 can successfully decode a packet from it & thus know the exact time it takes to finish transmitting this packet. During this time they are in the state of Receiving and thus BUSY. Although we arbitrarily define N1 is IDLE in 'Interval a', this period cannot be used by nodes within its carrier sense range for the coming packet to be sent successfully.

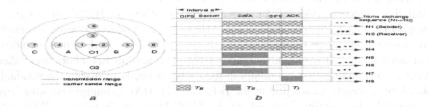

Fig. 3. From frame exchange sequence to channel occupation

3   Simulation Results

In a 1300X1100 m area we evenly deploy 100 nodes, among which 10 sender-receiver pairs are randomly picked out. Each sender-receiver pair has a flow with a constant bandwidth x. We set T in (1) equal to 1s as [3] does, and the maximum capacity 1.6 Mbit/s. The transmission range and carrier sense range is 250 m and 550 m, respectively. We then add two more nodes, s and r with co-ordinate of (525 m, 550 m) and (775 m, 550 m), respectively, into the network. Co-ordinates ensure that they are in the centre of the network and can just communicate directly to represent a one-hop link. Let s and r evaluate the 'AB' on Link (s, r) as a function of x. Keep the network load below 90% so that collision rates do not have a high influence on the problem that we are evaluating. The average values of estimated 'AB' by AAC, ABE and the proposed approach, with the legend of 'IAB Estimation' are plotted in Fig. 4. The results clearly show that IAB outperforms the estimations achieved by AAC and ABE

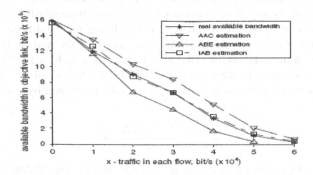

Fig. 4. Simulation validation

just by considering the dependence of the two adjacent nodes' channel occupations and giving a more accurate estimation on the overlap probability of their idle periods.

4 Conclusion

This paper proposes incorporating QoS into routing, and introduces bandwidth estimation by disseminating bandwidth information through "Hello" messages. A cross-layer approach, including an adaptive feedback scheme and an admission scheme to provide information to the application about the network status, are implemented. This paper rethinks the problems of available bandwidth estimation in IEEE 802.11-based ad hoc networks. The estimation accuracy is increased by improving the calculation accuracy of the probability for two adjacent nodes' idle periods to overlap.

References

1. Chen, S., Nahrstedt, K.: Distributed quality-of-service in ad hoc networks. IEEE J. Sel. Areas Commun. 17(8) (August 1999)
2. Chakrabarti, S.: QoS issues in ad hoc wireless networks. IEEE Commun. Mag. 39(2), 142–148 (2007)
3. Zhang, Y.: Very low bit rate video coding standards. Proc. Vis. Commun. Image Process. 2501, 1016–1023 (1995)
4. Coete, G., Erol, B., Gallant, M., Kossentini, F.: H.263+: Video coding at low bit rates. IEEE Trans. Circuits Syst. Video Technol. 8(7), 849–866 (2008)
5. Servetto, S., Ramchandran, K., Vaishampayan, V., Nahrstedt, K.: Multiple-description wavelet based image coding. In: Proc. IEEE Int. Conf. Image Process., pp. 659–663 (1998)
6. Ad hoc on demand distance vector (AODV) routing, IETF Internet Draft, Work in Progress. adov.03.txt (June 1999)
7. Perkins, C., Royer, E.: Ad hoc on-demand distance vector routing. In: Proc. 2nd IEEE Workshop Mobile Comput. Syst. Appl., pp. 90–100 (1999)
8. Johnson, D., Maltz, D.: Dynamic source routing in ad hoc wireless networks. Mobile Comput., 153–181 (1996)
9. Perkins, C., Bhagwat, P.: Highly dynamic destination sequenced distance vector routing (DSDV) for mobile computers. In: Proc. ACMSIGCOM M 1994, October 1994, pp. 234–244 (1994)
10. Park, V.D., Corson, M.S.: A highly adaptive distributed routing algorithm for mobile wireless networks. In: Proc. INFOCOM, April 1997, pp. 1405–1413 (1997)
11. Chen, S.: Routing support for providing guaranteed end-to-end quality-of-service. Ph.D. dissertation, Univ. Illinois at Urbana–Champaign, Urbana–Champaign, IL (1999)
12. Mohapatra, P., Li, J., Gui, C.: QoS in mobile ad hoc networks. IEEE Wireless Commun. Mag., 44–52 (2003)

Multimodal Biometric Invariant Moment Fusion Authentication System

P. Viswanathan, P. Venkata Krishna, and S. Hariharan

VIT University, Vellore 632014
{pviswanathan,pvenkatakrishna,s.hariharan}@vit.ac.in

Abstract. The authentication based on biometric is more reliable and secure because of using the unique physical feature of human. Initially, mono biometric system was used for authentication but it has some error rate and hence multimodal biometric system was introduced to reduce the error. The constraint of using these systems is to maintain more information. Without reducing the error rate and maintain the above constraint a new algorithm has been developed which is based on the invariant moment information of fingerprint and face which is fused using variation. In this algorithm the fingerprint and face is segmented and the invariant moment information is extracted. The invariants are fused into a single identification value by using coefficient variance. This single value is authenticated by calculating the difference, evaluated using the threshold value which is set as 90% for fingerprint and 70% for face, provides low error rate of FAR and FRR. The algorithm is tested under cooperative and non cooperative condition and obtained less complexity, storage, execution time, high reliability and secure authentication system.

Keywords: Fusion, FAR, FRR, variation, invariant, coefficient, STFT, face, fingerprint.

1 Introduction

The recent advancement in technology resulted more threats to personal data and national security due to large amount of electronic data processing. The information transmitted through online can be easily hacked and overridden the authorised user by the hackers. There are many traditional methods such as password, watermarking, cryptography based systems to protect the data's from the hackers. But they were not up to the safe mark because they could be easily cracked by the brute force method [3].

The biometric based authentication was introduced to avoid the brute force attack. It means the authentication was performed by the unique physical features of human like fingerprint [4] or Iris. It gives high secured systems than the traditional methods. Initially, the mono biometric[1] authentication system was used. In this, the authentication was performed by single biometric system [5] and resulted in large no of error rates when there were many features which were similar.

In order to overcome the large error rates, the multimodal biometric system has been developed. It means more than one biometric [6] is used simultaneously to

V.V Das et al. (Eds.): BAIP 2010, CCIS 70, pp. 136–143, 2010.
© Springer-Verlag Berlin Heidelberg 2010

validate the user and need to maintain more information for security purpose. It resulted in high complexity, storage and execution time. The new fused biometrics system has been introduced to solve the above constraints. This system means the features of the multiple biometrics are combined into a single feature and the authentication is performed by having some threshold value.

In this paper, a new simple and robust fusion technique called the multimodal biometric invariant moment fusion authentication system has been introduced and it provides better adaptation of genuine and imposter among various test data sets. The fused algorithm gives a single identification decision (data sets) using coefficients which may solve the problem of timely constraints and storage space [2]. This approach provides better results than by score, feature and decision-level fusion technique.

2 Related Work

There are many fusion methods based upon decision, score and feature level were used in biometric authentication system. These techniques differ upon what biometric information is going to be fused and how the fusing has been done. In decision level fusion techniques [7] the biometric image was divided into equal small squares from which the local binary pattern is fused to single global features pattern. The performance of this techniques leads to 95% of accuracy. The score level fusion technique [8] is fusing the PCA analysis of the face and fingerprint into single identification system and in this the error rate reaches more than 11%. The feature level fusion techniques [9] fuse the feature points of the fingerprint and the face provides 97% efficiency but none of the previous fusion techniques provides zero error rates.

3 Multimodal Biometric System

In the multimodal biometric system, more than one biometric system is used for the authentication. Usually, both mono and multimodal systems commonly perform the two major operations namely, Enrolment and authentication. During enrolment the distinct information of the biometric is stored in the database which is used for verification. After enrolment, the authentication is performed by comparing the information with the stored information. Depending upon the ratio of similar or non similar data the genuine or imposter must be identified. This process is called the biometric based authentication system.

Problem Definition
The multimodal biometric system leads to maintain more information for authentication so it takes more time for authentication and storage capability.

The fused multi biometric system leads to increase the error rate for authentication due to more similar features.

4 Invariant Moment Fusion System

The invariant moment fusion system is the multimodal biometric system in which the invariant moment from face and fingerprint are extracted and fused into a single identification system.

Goals and Objectives
The introduced technology will secure the system more effectively from unlawful intervention with minimum storage and less timely constraints.

This method reduces the error rate, means the reduction of FAR (False Accept Rate) and FRR (False Reject Rate) [10]. This paper is organized as 4.1. Fingerprint 4.2. Face and 4.3. Fusion.

4.1 Fingerprint

The architecture of the fingerprint system is shown in fig (1). In the initial stages, an approach called STFT analysis [11] is used for enhancing the fingerprint image to have reliable extraction of features from poor quality fingerprints shown in fig (2). The enhancement algorithm simultaneously estimates several intrinsic properties of the fingerprint such as the foreground region mask, local ridge orientation and local frequency substituted in equation (1) to have an enhanced image shown in fig (3).

$$X(\tau_1,\tau_2,\omega_1,\omega_2) = \int\limits_{-\infty}^{\infty}\int\limits_{-\infty}^{\infty} I(x,y)w^*(x-\tau_1,y-\tau_2)e^{-j(\omega_1 x+\omega_2 y)}dxdy \qquad (1)$$

The central fingerprint is located by means of the core point using Gaussian function [12]. The noise was filtered by Gaussian low pass filter using equation (2). The horizontal gradient equation (4) and vertical gradient equation (5) are computed using simple gradient operator to obtain the orientation of the fingerprint using equation (6). After positioning the core part the fingerprint is cropped of size 64*64 is shown in fig (4).

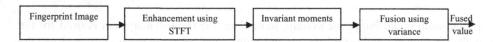

Fig. 1. Fingerprint System

Fig. 2. Original Imag   **Fig. 3.** Enhanced Image   **Fig. 4.** Cropped Image

$$f(x,y) = e^{-(\frac{(x-x_0)^2}{2\sigma^2 x}+\frac{(y-y_0)^2}{2\sigma^2 y})} \qquad (2)$$

$$G(x,y) = \frac{1}{2\pi\sigma^2}e^{-\frac{x^2+y^2}{2\sigma^2}} \qquad (3)$$

$$G_{xy} = \sum_{u\in W}\sum_{v\in W} 2G_x(u,v)G_y(u,v) \qquad (4)$$

$$G_{xx} = \sum_{u\in W}\sum_{v\in W} G_x^2(u,v)-G_y^2(u,v) \qquad (5)$$

$$\theta = \frac{1}{2}\tan^{-1}\left(\frac{G_{xy}}{G_{xx}}\right) \qquad (6)$$

The segmented approach is used for extracting the information of the fingerprint [13]. The fingerprint is segmented with reference to the core point. The seven invariant moments are extracted by using the following equations and sample test data are shown in table (1).

The mean is calculated using the following equations

$$m_{0,0}=\sum_{i,j=1}^{n} f \quad \bar{x}=\frac{m_{1,0}}{m_{0,0}} \quad \bar{y}=\frac{m_{0,1}}{m_{0,0}} \quad m_{1,0}=\sum_{i=1}^{n} x\cdot f \quad m_{0,1}=\sum_{j=1}^{n} y\cdot f \quad m_{1,1}=\sum_{i,j=1}^{n} x\cdot y\cdot f$$

$$m_{2,0}=\sum_{i=1}^{n} x^2\cdot f \quad m_{0,2}=\sum_{j=1}^{n} y^2\cdot f \quad m_{1,2}=\sum_{i,j=1}^{n} x\cdot y^2\cdot f \quad m_{3,0}=\sum_{i=1}^{n} x^3\cdot f \quad m_{0,3}=\sum_{j=1}^{n} y^3\cdot f \quad m_{2,1}=\sum_{i,j=1}^{n} x^2\cdot y\cdot f$$

The orientation is computed by the following equations

$$\xi_{1,1}=\frac{(m_{1,1}-\bar{y}\cdot m_{1,0})}{m_{0,0}^2} \qquad \xi_{2,0}=\frac{(m_{2,0}-\bar{x}\cdot m_{1,0})}{m_{0,0}^2} \qquad \xi_{0,2}=\frac{(m_{0,2}-\bar{y}\cdot m_{0,1})}{m_{0,0}^2}$$

$$\xi_{3,0}=\frac{(m_{3,0}-3\bar{x}\cdot m_{2,0}+2\cdot \bar{x}^2\cdot m_{1,0})}{m_{0,0}^{2.5}} \qquad \xi_{0,3}=\frac{(m_{3,0}-3\bar{y}\cdot m_{0,2}+2\cdot \bar{y}^2\cdot m_{0,1})}{m_{0,0}^{2.5}}$$

$$\xi_{2,1}=\frac{(m_{2,1}-2\bar{x}\cdot m_{1,1}+\bar{y}\cdot m_{2,0}+2\bar{x}^2\cdot m_{0,1})}{m_{0,0}^{2.5}} \qquad \xi_{2,1}=\frac{(m_{1,2}-2\bar{y}\cdot m_{1,1}-\bar{x}\cdot m_{0,2}+2\bar{y}^2\cdot m_{1,0})}{m_{0,0}^{2.5}}$$

Invariant moments are evaluated by the following equations: $\varphi(1)=\xi_{2,0}+\xi_{0,2}$

$$\varphi(2)=(\xi_{2,0}+\xi_{0,2})^2+(4\xi_{1,1}^2) \quad \varphi(3)=(\xi_{3,0}-3\xi_{1,2})^2+(3\xi_{2,1}-\xi_{0,3})^2 \quad \varphi(4)=(\xi_{3,0}-\xi_{1,2})^2+(\xi_{2,1}+\xi_{0,3})^2$$

$$\varphi(5)=(\xi_{3,0}-3\xi_{1,2})(\xi_{3,0}+\xi_{1,2})((\xi_{3,0}+\xi_{1,2})^2-3(\xi_{2,1}+\xi_{0,3})^2+(3\xi_{2,1}-\xi_{0,3})(\xi_{2,1}+\xi_{0,3})(3(\xi_{3,0}+\xi_{1,2})^2-(\xi_{2,1}+\xi_{0,3})^2))$$

$$\varphi(6)=(\xi_{2,0}-\xi_{0,2})((\xi_{3,0}+\xi_{1,2})^2-(\xi_{2,1}+\xi_{0,3})^2)+4\xi_{1,1}(\xi_{3,0}+\xi_{1,2})(\xi_{2,1}+\xi_{0,3})$$

$$\varphi(7)=(3\xi_{2,1}-3\xi_{0,3})(\xi_{3,0}+\xi_{1,2})((\xi_{3,0}+\xi_{1,2})^2-3(\xi_{2,1}+\xi_{0,3})^2+(3\xi_{1,2}-\xi_{3,0})(\xi_{2,1}+\xi_{0,3})(3(\xi_{3,0}+\xi_{1,2})^2-(\xi_{2,1}+\xi_{0,3})^2))$$

Table 1. Data sets of trained Image Database (**Fingerprint**) Example

Data sets	Train Image Database						
Fing1	6.6739	24.1707	30.6781	30.3368	66.175	42.5687	60.8585
Fing2	6.6439	21.8419	26.9747	30.2023	60.5443	41.5152	58.8209
Fing3	6.6444	14.9212	28.2185	28.0322	57.1951	35.5803	58.8439
Fing4	6.5548	14.7008	29.5278	28.9722	59.2708	37.7285	58.6214
Fing5	6.6496	23.3503	30.7699	31.9627	64.0907	48.2492	63.8234
Fing6	6.6524	23.6642	30.9556	30.0366	62.4862	43.1547	60.855

4.2 Face

The architecture of the face fusion system is shown in fig (5). The eigen faces were extracted from the face and has been used for authentication [14]. Initially, the mean and difference of each image in the training set has been computed by using equations (7) and (8). Then the entire centralized image T has been merged using mean gives the result $A,$ the merged value for computing the surrogate covariance matrix L using equation (9). The diagonal elements of covariance matrix were taken as eigen faces using equation (10). Sorting and elimination of eigen vectors takes place by checking the eigen element > 1. Finally the six invariant features are extracted from the faces using equation (11)

The high dimensionality makes a good face recognition algorithm. The sample tested face features fusion is shown in table (2)

$$mean = \frac{1}{n}\sum_{i=1}^{n} X_i \quad (7) \qquad A_i = T_i\text{-mean} \quad (8) \qquad L = A'\times A(X_i\text{-mean}) \quad (9)$$

$$[V\ D] = Eig(L) \quad (10) \qquad \text{Variant} = L \times A \quad (11)$$

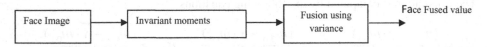

Fig. 5. Face Fusion

4.3 Fusion

The data sets are independently computed by the described variants of face and fingerprint [15]. The variants are fused together using the coefficient variance using equations (12) and (13). The calculated data set of every test image was enrolled in the database for authorizing the user.

Table 2. Data sets of trained Image Database (**Face**) Example

Data sets	Train Image Database					
Face 1	-0.0861	0.0292	0.2199	0.0595	-0.1391	-0.0263
Face 2	0.1025	-0.0871	0.0046	0.0363	-0.1580	0.0161
Face 3	-0.0021	-0.2707	0.0512	-0.0392	0.0847	0.2199
Face 4	0.3195	-0.0552	0.1880	-0.3034	-0.1184	-0.1025
Face 5	-0.3618	-0.0130	0.3020	-0.2350	0.4339	-0.2700
Face 6	-0.4902	0.8825	-0.2266	-1.0756	-0.1895	1.0297

This type of fusion increases the robustness and efficiency of authentication of user by providing single validation entry which is shown in table (3). It manages less storage, time and complexity than the other ones.

$$SD = \sqrt{\frac{\sum_{I=1}^{N}(x_i - \mu)^2}{N}} \quad (12) \qquad \qquad Variation = \frac{Mean}{SD} \quad (13)$$

Table 3. Fused value of Face and Fingerprint

Fusion	FP-value	Face-value	Fused Value
ID-1	1.78773441	-0.424068667	0.436
ID-2	1.78854862	0.199364642	0.8845
ID-3	1.66374867	0.472983786	1.2688
ID-4	1.67129004	-0.609705682	0.3291
ID-5	1.79835985	-0.059927557	0.6615
ID-6	1.82625854	0.333900078	1.0235

5 Authentication

The multimodal biometric authentication is one of the new breed of authentication system performed by means of more than one biometric to validate the user. The architecture of our authentication system is shown in Fig (6). The trained set of input in which invariant moment is extracted then fused and enrolled in the database. Now during authentication the test data input image of fingerprint and face scanned by the user is fused and compared with the fused value in the database by considering the differences of the fused value computed using equation (14).

The resultant difference value is evaluated by using the threshold value to validate the user using equation (15). The threshold value is based upon the sensitive of the system. If the difference is low then the similarity will be higher and it crosses the threshold limit to validate the user, otherwise the user is not validated. This multimodal biometric authentication system performed more than 99% of the accurate system and the resultant evaluation is shown in Fig (7) for valid user and Fig (8) for invalid user.

$$D = \text{Fused}_{\text{scanned}} - \text{Fused}_{\text{Enrolled}} \tag{14}$$

$$A = \begin{cases} \dfrac{100-D}{100} \times 100 > Th = Authenticated \\[2mm] \dfrac{100-D}{100} \times 100 < Th = Notauthehticated \end{cases} \tag{15}$$

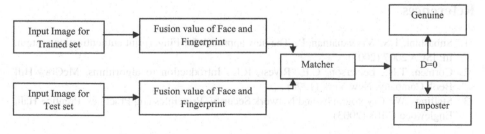

Fig. 6. Face and Fingerprint Fusion Authentication

Fig. 7. Authentication   **Fig. 8.** Not Authenticated

6 Conclusion

The variance based multimodal biometric authentication was performed by using various data sets and got accurate results. The fusion technique used in this work was very simple and it provides less complexity and time to perform authentication. Also the information maintained for authentication was compressed into single identification data which means large amount of biometric data could be maintained easily. The maximum FAR and FRR was maintained less than 1%. From the above results we conclude that the multimodal biometric invariant moment fusion authentication system provides good storage, less execution time and accurate authentication result. This system was the improved version having the system reliability, robustness and good performance in personnel authentication system.

Acknowledgement

The achievement of the real life project of watermarking would not have been feasible without the timely help given by the research candidates to whom we wisdom to oblige. I express my thankfulness to Dr.Venkata Krishna.P, Associate Professor, VIT University, for the priceless idea's and timely advice during the proposed work. I also thankful to Dr S Hariharan, Assistant professor in school of Advances sciences. We also express gratitude for the staff and friends for their very useful guidance and for constant hold up and encouragement.

References

1. Subashini, T.S., Viswanathan, P.: The new approach for Fingerprint authentication system. In: ISCA 2007 (2007)
2. Cormen, T.H., Leiserson, C.E., Rivest, R.L.: Introduction to algorithms. McGraw-Hill Book Company, New York (1998)
3. Stallings, W.: Cryptography and Network Security- Principles and Practices. Prentice-Hall, Englewood Cliffs (2003)

4. Jea, T., Govindaraju, V.: A Minutia-Based Partial Fingerprint Recognition System. In: To appear in Pattern Recognition 2005 (2005)
5. Jea, T., Chavan, V.K., Govindaraju, V., Schneider, J.K.: Security and matching of partial fingerprint recognition systems. In: Proceeding of SPIE, vol. 5404, pp. 39–50 (2004)
6. Besbes, F., Trichile, H., Solaiman, B.: Multimodal biometric system based on fingerprint identification and Iris recognition 978-1-4244-1751-3©2008. IEEE, Los Alamitos (2008)
7. Chen, C.: Decision level fusion of hybrid local features for face Recognition Neural network and signal processing 2008. IEEE, Los Alamitos (2008)
8. Marcialis, G.L., Roli, F.: Score-level fusion of fingerprint and face matchers for personal verification under "stress" conditions. In: 14th International Conference on Image Analysis and Processing (ICIAP 2007) 0-7695-2877-5/07 $25.00 © 2007. IEEE, Los Alamitos (2007)
9. Rattani, A., Kisku, D.R., Bicego, M., Tistarelli, M.: Feature level fusion of face and fingerprint biometrics 978-1-4244-1597-7/07/$25.00 ©2007. IEEE, Los Alamitos (2007)
10. Jea, T.-Y., Govindaraju, V.: A minutia-based partial fingerprint recognition system. Submitted to Pattern Recognition (2004)
11. Subashini, T.S., Viswanathan, P.: Fingerprint Image Enhancement using SOFT Analysis. In: SCT 2006 (2006)
12. Maio, D., Maltoni, D.: Direct gray scale minutia detection in fingerprints. Transactions on PAMI 19(1) (1997)
13. Watson, C.I., Candela, G.T., Grother, P.J.: Comparison of fft fingerprint filtering methods for neural network classification. NISTIR, 5493 (1994)
14. Belhumeur, P.N., Hespanha, J., Kriegman, D.J.: Eigenfaces vs. Fisherfaces: Recognition using class specific linear projection. In: Buxton, B.F., Cipolla, R. (eds.) ECCV 1996. LNCS, vol. 1065, pp. 45–58. Springer, Heidelberg (1996)
15. Maio, D., Maltoni, D.: Direct gray scale minutia detection in fingerprints. Transactions on PAMI 19(1) (1997)

Histogram Equalization for Class-Identification of Dental Disease Using Digital Radiography

Anjali Naik[1], Shubhangi Vinayak Tikhe[1], and S.D. Bhide[2]

[1] Department of Computer Engineering, Cummins College of Engineering for Women,
Karve Nagar, Pune, India
anjalm@gmail.com, svtikhe@rediffmail.com
[2] Department of Electronics and Telecommunication Engineering,
Cummins College of Engineering for Women, Karve Nagar, Pune, India
sd_bhide@hotmail.com

Abstract. Digital radiography is the latest advancement in dental imaging. It is more comfortable in terms of technique and interpretation. Dynamic appearance of digital radiograph is supportive for image analysis and enhancements like image sharpening, coloring, contrast and density adjustments, depending on the diagnostic task. Histogram equalization is useful in images with backgrounds and foregrounds that are both bright or both dark. Equalization can lead to better views of bone structure in radiographic images, and to show details in over or under-exposed photographs. The objective of the paper is to study use of histogram equalization to enhance the digital radiographs for classifying various problems in dental care.

Keywords: Digital radiology, dental care, image processing techniques, histogram equalization, image filtering.

1 Introduction

Traditionally, dental surgeons and clinicians have been using x-ray imaging for identifications of varied dental deformities for diagnosis and its line of treatment. A digital radiography has become available where dental image is obtained directly on computer screen. Dynamic appearance of digital radiograph is supportive to accurate and faster diagnosis using image analysis and enhancements like image sharpening, coloring, contrast and density adjustments, depending on the diagnostic task. Digital image enhancement techniques when applied to digital radiograph in dentistry provide improvement in the visual quality of diagnostic images in various branches of dentistry, like conservative dentistry (endodontic), pediatric dentistry, periodontics, maxillofacial surgery, etc. Several studies have shown that various digital image enhancements increase diagnostic accuracy in the detection and monitoring of lesions [1, 2, 3, 4, 5] and estimation of lesion depth and improve detection of thin file tips in root canal treatment [6]. Improvement can also be found in analysis of gum diseases, finding deformity of head-neck-face, enhancing features of trauma to facial bone, finding progress in cancer of oral region and deciding treatment involving dental diseases of

V.V Das et al. (Eds.): BAIP 2010, CCIS 70, pp. 144–151, 2010.
© Springer-Verlag Berlin Heidelberg 2010

children. Image enhancements like digital contrast enhancement and filtering, modify attributes of an image to make it more suitable for a given task and to a specific observer. However, this does not imply that for any given task there is some image processing operation for improving diagnostic efficiency.

It is interesting to find why digital radiography is more accepted advancement in dental field over conventional radiography. Understanding of anatomy of the teeth and commonly found dental diseases according to dental clinicians and surgeons help to find diagnostic applicability. The paper gives information about effect of low pass filter, high pass filter and histogram equalization for image enhancements of dental radiographs. The focus is on use of histogram equalization of digital radiograph to help identifying class of routine dental diseases.

1.1 Advantages of Direct Digital Radiography Compared with Conventional Film

Digital images are dynamic. According to dental surgeon, coloring facilities for image enhancement help in accurate diagnosis. Digital images do not require wet processing using chemical solutions as needed by conventional film helping to reduce retakes and also the environmental problems. It reduces human and processing error as compared to film radiographs, as, majority times conventional films are processed manually. The cost of film and chemicals is eliminated. Working time needed right from image exposure to display is reduced considerably. As compared to conventional radiography, the direct digital systems require 50% of the dose needed to create an acceptable image quality. Further, the x-ray tube will last longer [1]. Actually, the harm to patients is much less as they get exposed to doses only once than a dental surgeon as dental surgeon get exposed to indirect radiation for multiple times. Digital image data storing and communication is easier with digital networking. Digital radiograph is useful as a proof in medico-legal matter. One of the main advantages of digital intraoral radiography is that image characteristics may be improved by digital processing algorithms [6].

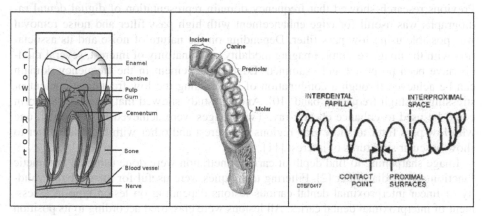

Fig. 1. Tooth anatomy   **Fig. 2.** Right half of   **Fig. 3.** Proximal tooth surfaces and
lower dental arch,   spaces
seen from above

1.2 Routine Dental Diseases

Fig. 1 shows the cross section of a tooth and figs. 2 and 3 give naming convention of tooth. Majority of the times patient goes to a dental surgeon when there is tooth decay (caries), pain in teeth, gum diseases, traumatic injuries to the teeth and/or the surrounding regions, or need of routine checkup.

Of all these diseases which affect the teeth and surrounding areas, caries remains one of the most common class of diseases throughout the world. It is the primary pathological cause of tooth loss in children. Around 29% to 59% of adults over the age of fifty experience caries. Dental surgeons classify caries in to five classes according to the surfaces where they are seen [7].

In dental terminology an "impacted" tooth refers to a tooth that has failed to emerge fully into its expected position. Most commonly impacted tooth is the wisdom tooth (third molar). The failure to erupt properly might occur because there may not be enough room in the person's jaw to accommodate the tooth, or because the angulations of the tooth are improper. These impacted teeth may cause damage to the adjacent teeth. Hence their removal becomes necessary.

Any trauma to jaws can cause fracture of bones and/or teeth. Normal film radiography allows visualization of the fracture line. However, the disadvantage of this conventional film is that, it also shows artifacts, ghost images, and superimposition of surrounding structure. In contrast to this, digital radiograph allows visualizing only the area of interest with much better clarity and the added advantage of zooming.

Pathological conditions like cyst or tumor, routine checkup or overall evaluation are all special cases.

When patient is examined, some clinical findings indicate that there is a need for radiographic examination. Radiographs are prescribed by dental surgeon to gather useful information which will influence the plan of treatment. Clinical information is used to select the type of radiograph and later to aid in their interpretation [8].

1.3 Digital Image Processing Radiographs

Previous research showed that frequency domain representation of digital dental radiographs was useful for edge enhancement with high pass filter and noise removal was possible using low pass filter. Depending on the nature of noise and its association with the image receptor, imaging modality, and anatomy of interest, several models have been proposed and examined. Edge enhancement in the frequency domain can be achieved through a combination of suppressing the low frequency content or stressing the high frequency band [10]. Another study showed that wavelet transform could be used to enhance chest x-ray. Two images were achieved in this study, one with low pass filter to show gray regions of interest and other with high pass filter to show vascular structures of interest [11].

Image sharpening to find depth of caries penetration were done using an arithmetic function and median filter [2]. Filtering techniques were useful for the studying validity of linear interproximal dental carious lesions depending on lesion type in assessment of interproximal dental caries. All lesions were classified according to its position on dentine or enamel. Use of the filter resulted in a reduced underestimation of CD (central depth) measurements in enamel lesions. [3]. A study demonstrated use of two image enhancement procedures watershed and modification of SVM (supporting vector machine) kernel function for improving the diagnosis accuracy in initial approximal caries. Watershed algorithm for Image segmentation was applied to the histogram of tooth image to make initial caries visible and easier. The method enhanced the grey-level image into a pseudo-color image to find decayed [4].

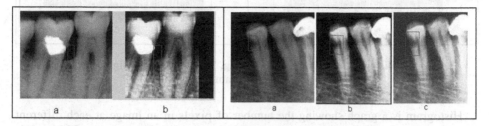

Fig. 4. a: Original image showing bone loss, b: Image after histogram equalization

Fig. 5. a: Original image showing caries, b: Image after histogram equalization in frequency domain, c: Image after histogram equalization in spatial domain

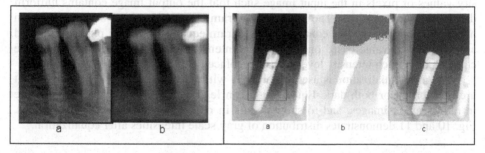

Fig. 6. a: Gaussian high pass filter applied on figure 5, b: Gaussian low pass filter applied on figure 5.

Fig. 7. a: Original: bone healing after implant, b: Image after histogram equalization in frequency domain, c: Image after histogram equalization in spatial domain

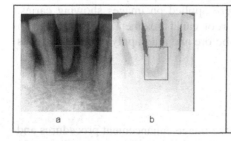

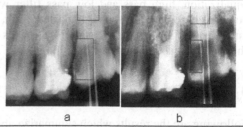

Fig. 8. a: Original image showing periapical lesions, b: Image after histogram equalization in frequency domain

Fig. 9. a: Original image showing root canal procedure, b: Image after histogram equalization in frequency domain

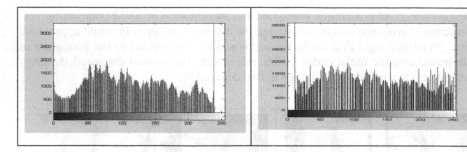

Fig. 10. Histogram of figure 8a   **Fig. 11.** Histogram of figure 8b after histogram equalization

Histogram is a graph showing the number of pixels in an image at each different intensity value found in that image. For an 8-bit grayscale image there are 256 intensities. The histogram of a gray scale image graphically displays 256 levels showing the distribution of pixels amongst those grayscale values. Histogram equalization is the technique by which the dynamic range of the histogram of an image is increased. The histogram equalization is operated on a histogram of an image and assigns the intensity values of pixels in the input image such that the output image contains uniform distribution of intensities. The goal of histogram equalization is to obtain a uniform histogram and improve the contrast. In histogram equalization, each pixel is assigned a new intensity value based on its previous intensity level. New intensity values are calculated for each intensity levels and are replaced [9].

Histogram equalization is useful in images with backgrounds and foregrounds that are both bright or both dark. Equalization can lead to better views of bone structure in radiographic images, and to show details in over or under-exposed photographs. Fig. 10 and 11 demonstrates distribution of gray scale intensities after equalization.

2   Method

MatLab 6.5 software was used to process digital radiographic images showing common diseases. Various filters like Gaussian low pass, Gaussian high pass, and histogram equalization methods were used to study images in frequency domain. Histogram equalization, high pass and low pass filter were applied on images showing caries, bone loss, periapical lesions, impacted teeth, root canal treatment and images with implants [11]. Visual representation of images before and after applying functions was shown to dental clinicians for their judgment.

3   Results

Following are the results which summarize above image enhancement procedures and their sensitivity to improve area of interest in visual aspects of superior diagnosis. Problem areas in the figures are marked by red rectangle.

The digital radiographic images give good quality pictures. Thus, the noise in image is almost negligible. Low pass filter blurs the image and is powerful for known noise removal [10]. When low pass filter was applied on images showing routine dental diseases mentioned above, blurring of the image was observed. Fig. 6b shows Gaussian low pass filter applied on fig. 5. This effected in loss of image features. Thus low pass filter was not much useful to improve visual effects.

Fig. 4a is an image showing bone loss. After sharpening the image with histogram equalization clear view of bone loss is seen in fig. 4b. Fig. 5a shows caries. The decay touching the pulp area is seen clear in the enhanced image 5b. fig. 5c shows histogram equalization in special domain. Fig. 5b and 5c results are similar. Fig 6a shows Gaussian high pass filter applied on figure 5. Though the image is sharpened, its clarity is less as compared to histogram equalization method. Fig 6b shows Gaussian low pass filter applied on figure 5. The image is blurred and surrounding features are lost. Fig. 7 shows image showing bone healing after implant, 7b shows image after histogram equalization in frequency domain, 7c shows image after histogram equalization in spatial domain. Implant is a metallic material whose intensity is different as compared to intensity of oral region. Thus histogram equalization shows loss in image data. Fig. 8 and fig. 9 show cases regarding periapical lesions and root canal treatment. In both the cases details regarding infection at root and thin tip at root of tooth are not enhanced up to mark using histogram equalization.

4   Discussion

Low pass filtering, high pass filtering and histogram equalization was carried on few images showing caries, implants, and bone loss. Histogram equalization was useful in enhancement of caries. Further enhancement techniques can be explored to clearly identify the need of root canal treatment.

The discussion below will focus on diseases mentioned in Introduction-1.2 and a need of image enhancement techniques for accurate diagnosis. The diseases selected for this paper are more common problems found with the patient. Out of many researches, selection of above mentioned enhancements may be useful in routine work. In majority of these cases of caries, radiography is necessary and its enhancement adds to more accuracy in diagnosis and treatment planning.

Radiography plays a part in monitoring lesion development over time, since early treatment procedures can arrest or reverse progression of the lesion. The evidence for dental caries is not restricted to the levels of surface cavitation, and radiography can add information about many of the clinical stages of the caries process at proximal surfaces and the more advanced stages on occlusal surfaces.

In impacted teeth problem, digital radiograph will definitely show the position and angulations of the impacted teeth. When surgery for such problem is planned, it is important to visualize properly the relation of the tooth with surrounding structures like arteries and nerves. In radiographic image its clear visualization is not possible. This can be done using image enhancement techniques. These enhanced images will be a guideline for a dental surgeon to plan a surgery.

In case of accidents involving the facial bones, image enhancements are useful to visualize and enhance minute details and smallest cracks in the bone which may be missed on a plain film radiograph.

Gum diseases, also called as gingivitis, are an infection to gum. In this disease, there is a severe loss of bone surrounding the teeth. The level of bone loss can be visualized in a better manner in digital radiograph. When the treatment is complete in gum diseases or cyst trouble, patient is recalled at periodic intervals for assessment of bone healing. Digital radiographs taken at such periodic intervals helps the surgeons to monitor the effectiveness of the treatment rendered to the patient. Digital radiograph definitely gives good view of bone healing. Various image comparison algorithms could be considered as an area of interest for researchers.

Pathological condition like cyst or tumor, routine checkup or overall evaluation are all special cases and can be considered as separate areas of research. These diseases require radiographic helps to visualize the exact extent of these pathologies. Radiographic images of these diseases give precise view of bone destruction caused by tumor or cyst. These cases are not considered here.

Surgeon's diagnosis becomes more accurate because of his/her intelligence, knowledge, tremendous hard work and abundant experience. Findings were that though using enhancements were beneficial, selecting the proper one could be time consuming. Using enhancements requires the surgeons to browse through enhancement techniques and subjectively select those that have the best possibilities for perfect diagnoses [10]. To give this similar intelligence of a dental surgeon and expertise, to a soft tool for selecting proper enhancement technique automatically, various parameters need be considered by a program. Thus, this will require various techniques like data mining algorithms, use of artificial neural network, use of fussy logic techniques and content based image data retrieval.

5   Conclusion

Digital imaging has become the standard in dental radiology. Histogram equalization, low pass filtering and high pass filtering are not just enough procedures for better visualization of digital radiograph. Various image enhancement algorithms are required to process radiographs for classification of dental diseases. Histogram equalization was useful in enhancement of caries. In case of images with implants, loss of image data was observed. Further enhancement techniques need to be explored to classify dental diseases.

Further work is needed to investigate the effects of single and multiple enhancements to assist the diagnosis of each of the above class of disease. It may be that dental surgeons are awaiting some computer automated intelligence which will work on multiple radiographs at a time as per daily needs to manage and assist image data.

Acknowledgment

The authors wish to express their sincere gratitude to Dr. Mrs. Madhavi Vaze (B. D. S.) and Dr. Suhas Vaze (M. D. S, oral and maxillofacial surgery) for sharing their experiences of past twenty five years in the field of dentistry. Dr. Kapil Kshirsagar (P. G. Oral and maxillofacial surgery) for sharing his views and domain expertise, and Dr. Rohit Behare (Postgraduate Student, Oral Medicine and Radiology) for sharing valuable information on dental caries.

References

[1] Wenzel, A.: Digital radiography and caries diagnosis. Dentomaxillofacial Radiology 27, 3±11 (1998)

[2] Shrout, M.K., Russell, C.M., Potter, B.J., Powell, B.J., Hildebolt, C.F.: Digital enhancement of radiographs: can itimprove caries diagnosis? J. Am. Dent. Assoc. 127, 469–473 (1996)

[3] Seneadza, V., Koob, A., Kaltschmitt, J., Staehle, H.J., Duwenhoegger, J., Eickholz, P.: Digital enhancement of radiographs for assessment of interproximal dental caries. Dentomaxillofacial Radiology 37, 142–148 (2008)

[4] Kuang1, W., Ye, W.: A Kernel-Modified SVM Based Computer-aided Diagnosis System in Initial Caries. IEEE, 206–209 (2008), doi:10.1109/IITA.2008.206

[5] Gakenheimer, D.C.: The efficacy of a computerized caries detector in intraoral digital radiography. J. Am. Dent. Assoc. 133, 883–890 (2002)

[6] Li, G., Sanderink, G.C.H., Welander, U., McDavid, W.D., Nasstrom, K.: Evaluation of endodontic files in digital radiographs before and after employing three image processing algorithms. Dentomaxillofacial Radiology 33, 6–11 (2004)

[7] http://en.wikipedia.org/wiki/Dental_caries

[8] White, P.: Oral Radiology Principles and interpretation, 5th edn. Elsevier, Amsterdam

[9] Gonzalez, R.C., Woods, R.E.: Digital Image Processing, ch.1, 4, 2nd edn., Person Education Asia

[10] Analoui, M.: REVIEW Radiographic digital image enhancement. Part II: transform domain techniques. Dentomaxillofacial Radiology 30, 65–77 (2001)

[11] Gonzalez, R.C., Woods, R.E.: Digital Image Processing using MATLAB. Person Education Asia

Comparison of Histogram and Spatiograms for Content Based Retrieval of Remote Sensing Images

Bikesh Kr. Singh[1], G.R. Sinha[2], and Imroze Khan[1]

[1] National Institute of Technology, Raipur (C.G)
bikesh_020581@yahoo.co.in
[2] SSCET, Bhilai (C.G)

Abstract. The problem of content-based retrieval of remotely sensed images presents a major challenge not only because of the surprisingly increasing volume of images acquired from a wide range of sensors but also because of the complexity of images themselves. In this paper, a software system for content-based retrieval of remote sensing images, using spatiograms is introduced. In addition, we also compare our results with histogram based content retrieval. Finally we illustrate the effect and relation of quantization bins on the retrieval efficiency of histogram & spatiogram based content retrieval system. Bhattacharyya coefficient is obtained in order to make comparisons between histogram & spatiogram of two images. Experimental results show that the integration of spatial information in histogram improves the image analysis of remote sensing data and the proposed method is simple, accurate and costs much less time than the traditional ones.

Keywords: Content based image retrieval, histogram, spatiogram, color.

1 Introduction

Image databases and collections can be enormous in size, containing hundreds, thousands or even millions of images. The conventional method of image retrieval is searching for a keyword that would match the descriptive keyword assigned to the image by a human categorizer [1]. Currently under development, even though several systems exist, is the retrieval of images based on their content, called *Content Based Image Retrieval, CBIR*. While computationally expensive, the results are far more accurate than conventional image indexing. Hence, there exists a tradeoff between accuracy and computational cost.

There is rapid increase in image databases of remote sensing images due to image satellites with high resolution, commercial applications of remote sensing & high available bandwidth. Satellite remote sensing is an evolving technology with the potential for contributing to studies of the human dimensions of global environmental change by making globally comprehensive evaluations of many human actions possible. Remotely sensed image data enable direct observation of the land surface at repetitive intervals and therefore allow mapping of the extent and monitoring of the changes in land cover. This information, combined with results of case studies or surveys, can provide helpful input to informed evaluations of interactions among the

V.V Das et al. (Eds.): BAIP 2010, CCIS 70, pp. 152–156, 2010.
© Springer-Verlag Berlin Heidelberg 2010

various driving forces. Thus remote sensing image (RSI) is one kind of important images in present image resources. RSI contents abundant details and its data size is very large.

The paper is organized as follows: In section two we give a brief overview of histogram and spatiogram along with their relationship, in section 3 & 4 we explain the methodology & results followed by conclusions in section 5.

2 Overview of Histogram and Spatiogram

2.1 Histogram

A digital image, in general, is a two dimensional mapping I: $x \rightarrow v$ from M × N *pixels* $x = [i, j]^T$ to values v. The histogram of an image can be found as

$$r_b = \sum_{i=1}^{M} \sum_{j=1}^{N} S_b(i, j), \qquad \forall b = 1, 2, .. \qquad (1)$$

where $S_b(i, j) = 1$ if the value v at pixel location $[i, j]$ falls in bin b, and $S_b(i, j) = 0$ otherwise and B is number of bins in the histogram [2]. Histograms have proved themselves to be a powerful representation for image data in a region. Discarding all spatial information, they are the foundation of classic techniques such as histogram equalization and image indexing [3]. Color histograms are flexible constructs that can be built from images in various color spaces, whether RGB, rg chromaticity or any other color space of any dimension. The color histogram of an image is relatively invariant with translation and rotation about the viewing axis, and varies only slowly with the angle of view [4]. By comparing histograms signatures of two images and matching the color content of one image with the other, the color histogram is particularly well suited for the problem of recognizing an object of unknown position and rotation within a scene. Color Histograms are a commonly used as appearance-based signature to classify images for content-based image retrieval systems (CBIR) [5]. In remote sensing, color histograms are typical features used for classifying different ground regions from aerial or satellite photographs.

The main drawback of histograms for classification is that the representation is dependent of the color of the object being studied, ignoring its shape and texture.

2.2 Spatiogram

Birchfield and Rangarajan have extended the popular concept of histograms with spatial layout information, yielding spatiograms. Unlike histograms, in spatiograms the spatial layout for each attribute bin is part of the model as well. A limited amount of information regarding the domain may be retained by obtaining higher order moments of binary function. A histogram is a zeroth-order spatiogram, while second-order spatiograms contain spatial means and covariance's for each histogram bin. This spatial information still allows quite general transformations, as in histogram, but captures richer description increase robustness in tracking. Promising results have been obtained with the tracking of local features in video [6]. We define the k_{th} order spatiogram to be tupe of all the moments up to order k. The second-order spatiogram of an image may be then represented by

$$h_I^{(2)}(b) = [n_b, \mu_b, \Sigma_b] \qquad b=1, 2, \ldots, B \qquad (2)$$

Where n_b is the number of pixels whose value is that of the b_{th} bin, μ_b and Σ_b are the mean vector and covariance matrix respectively of the co-ordinates of those pixels and B is the number of bins in the spatiogram. It can be noted that

$$h_I^{(0)}(b) = [n_b] \qquad b=1, 2, \ldots, B \qquad (3)$$

is just histogram of I. From probabilistic point of view a spatiogram captures the probability density function (PDF) of the image values

$$P(I(x) = v) = p(x, v) = p(x/v)\, p(v) \qquad (4)$$

where p(x, v) and p (v) joint PDF and marginal PDF respectively. For zeroth – order spatiogram i.e. histogram, there is no spatial dependency hence p(x, v) = p (v).

3 Methodology

Experiments were conducted on database of 600 remote sense images. A system is developed for image retrieval using histogram and spatiogram using MATLAB 7.0.1 version. Then the query image is taken and images similar to the query images are found on the basis of histogram and spatiogram similarity. The main tasks of the system are histogram and spatiogram determination and similarity distance computation between the query image and database images. A histogram of an image is produced first by discretization of the colors in the image into a number of bins, and counting the number of image pixels in each bin.

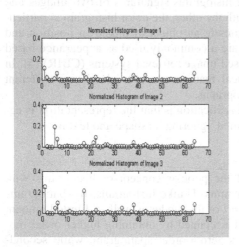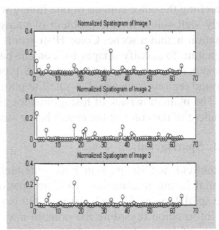

Fig. 1. 4×4×4 Color histogram and Spatiogram of three different remote sense images. No. of bins = 4

Figure 1 shows histogram and spatiogram of three different images shown in figure 2 from database. It can be observed that the histogram and spatiogram are different for these images.

For image retrieval a query image is input to the system. Bhattacharyya coefficient [7] is then used for similarity distance calculation between query image & each image in the database. Bhattacharyya coefficient is a measure of the amount of overlap between two statistical samples or populations. The coefficient can be used to determine the relative closeness of the two samples being considered. It is used to measure the separability of classes in classification. Calculating the Bhattacharyya coefficient involves a rudimentary form of integration of the overlap of the two samples. The interval of the values of the two samples is split into a chosen number of partitions, and the number of members of each sample in each partition is used in the following formula,

$$\text{Bhattacharyya Coefficient} = \sum_{i=1}^{n} (\textstyle\sum a_i \sum b_i)^{\frac{1}{2}} \qquad (5)$$

where considering the samples a and b, n is the number of partitions, and a_i, b_i are the number of members of samples a and b in the i'th partition. The output from the system is the stored database image with maximum similarity with query image.

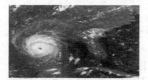

Fig. 2. Three different remote sensing images from database used in Fig.1 & Fig.2

4 Results

Table 1 and Table 2 show the Histogram & Spatiogram similarity using Bhattacharyya coefficient of image 1 with nine other images of database for different number of bins.

Table 1. Histogram similarity using Bhattacharyya coefficient of one image with nine other images of database for different number of bins

Bins → Image Id↓	4	8	16	32
I1	1	1	1	1
I2	0.619	0.439	0.327	0.261
I3	0.777	0.424	0.292	0.228
I4	0.645	0.504	0.436	0.382
I5	0.761	0.571	0.452	0.373
I6	0.657	0.508	0.409	0.326
I7	0.656	0.489	0.341	0.255
I8	0.659	0.390	0.258	0.173
I9	0.637	0.457	0.322	0.224
I10	0.582	0.295	0.159	0.102

Table 2. Spatiogram similarity using Bhattacharyya coefficient of one image with nine other images of database for different number of bins

Bins → Image Id↓	4	8	16	32
I1	1	1	1	1
I2	0.392	0.237	0.146	0.087
I3	0.632	0.290	0.171	0.097
I4	0.489	0.361	0.294	0.228
I5	0.558	0.395	0.292	0.223
I6	0.472	0.329	0.240	0.169
I7	0.490	0.321	0.179	0.103
I8	0.514	0.302	0.177	0.090
I9	0.528	0.351	0.220	0.132
I10	0.509	0.251	0.111	0.049

It can be observed from the table that both histogram as well as spatiogram is efficient for retrieval of remote sensing images of our database. However spatiogram is more effective than histogram as in former similarity value for two different images is obtained to be much less. Further the retrieval efficiency of the proposed system can be increased by increasing number of quantization bins but at small cost of time.

5 Conclusions

We have implemented the concept that extends the familiar histogram in a natural way by capturing a limited amount of spatial information between the pixels contributing to the histogram bins for content retrieval of remote sensing images. This spatiogram, as we call it, is a generalization of a histogram to higher-order moments and is more efficient for content based retrieval of remote sensing images. The main drawback of histograms for classification is that the representation is dependent of the color of the object being studied, ignoring its spatial information. The efficiency of the proposed system can thus be increased by including spatial information such as spatiograms, texture based CBIR, and shape based CBIR etc.

References

1. Linda, G.S., George, C.S.: Computer Vision. Prentice-Hall, Englewood Cliffs (2001)
2. Nilsson, M., Bartunek, J.S., Nordberg, J., Claesson, I.: On Histograms and Spatiograms - Introduction of the Mapogram. In: ICIP, pp. 973–976 (2008)
3. Birchfield, S.T., Rangarajan, S.: Spatiograms versus Histograms for Region-Based Tracking. In: CVPR 2005 (2005)
4. Linda, G.S., George, C.S.: Computer Vision. Prentice-Hall, Englewood Cliffs (2003)
5. Stricker, M., Swain, M.: The Capacity of Color Histogram Indexing, Computer Vision and Pattern Recognition. In: Proceedings of IEEE Computer Society Conference on CVPR, pp. 704–708 (1994)
6. Adrian, U., Christoph, L., Daniel, K.: Spatiogram-Based Shot Distances for Video Retrieval
7. Djouadi, A., Snorrason, O., Garber, F.: The quality of Training-Sample estimates of the Bhattacharyya coefficient. IEEE Transactions on Pattern Analysis and Machine Intelligence, 92–97 (1990)
8. Venteres, C.C., Cooper, M.: A Review of Content-Based Image Retrieval Systems
9. Shengjiu, W.: A Robust CBIR Approach Using Local Color Histograms. Department of Computer Science, University of Alberta, Edmonton, Alberta, Canada, Tech. Rep. TR 01-13 (October 2001)
10. Bjorn, J.: QBIC (Query By Image Content), http://www.isy.liu.se/cvl/Projects/VISIT-bjojo/survey/surveyonCBIR/node26.html
11. Manjunath, B.S.: Color and texture descriptors. IEEE Trans. CSVT 11(6), 703–715 (2001)
12. Stanchev, P.L., Green Jr., D., Dimitrov, B.: High level color similarity retrieval. Int. J. Inf. Theories Appl., 363–369 (2003)

Vector Quantization for Tumor Demarcation of Mammograms

H.B. Kekre[1], Tanuja K. Sarode[2], and Saylee M. Gharge[3]

[1] Senior Professor, MPSTME, NMIMS University, Vile-Parle (w), Mumbai-56, India
[2] Ph.D. Scholar, MPSTME, NMIMS University, Assistant Prof., TSEC, Mumbai-50, India
[3] Ph.D. Scholar, MPSTME, NMIMS University, Lecturer, V.E.S.I.T, Mumbai-400071, India

Abstract. Segmenting mammographic images into homogeneous texture regions representing disparate tissue types is often a useful preprocessing step in the computer-assisted detection of breast cancer. Hence new algorithm to detect cancer in mammogram breast cancer images is proposed. In this paper we proposed segmentation using vector quantization technique. Here Linde Buzo Gray (LBG) for segmentation of mammographic images is used. Initially a codebook (CB) of size 128 was generated for mammographic images. These code vectors were further clustered in 8 clusters using same algorithm. These 8 images were displayed as a result. The codebook of size 128 clustered to 16 code vectors, codebook of size 128 clustered to 8 code-vectors using LBG algorithm is compared with watershed algorithm. The proposed approach does not lead to over segmentation or under segmentation with less complexity with more accuracy.

Keywords: mammographic images, LBG, Segmentation, Vector Quantization.

1 Introduction

Breast cancer is among the most common and deadly of all cancers. Mammography is a uniquely important type of medical imaging used to screen for breast cancer. All women at risk go through mammography screening procedures for early detection and diagnosis of tumor. A typical mammogram is an intensity X-ray image with gray levels showing levels of contrast inside the breast that which characterize normal tissue and different calcifications and masses. The contrast level of a typical mammogram image is proportional to the difference in X-ray attenuation between different tissues. Important visual clues of breast cancer include preliminary signs of masses and calcification clusters. A mass is a localized collection of tissue seen in two different projections, and calcifications are small calcium deposits. Unusually smaller and clustered calcifications are associated with malignancy while there are other calcifications (diffuse, regional, segmental and linear) that are typically benign. Such calcifications are termed as microcalcifications (MC). In the early stages of breast cancer, these signs are subtle and hence make diagnosis by visual inspection difficult. With millions undergoing mammography procedures, the need for quick and reliable computer based tools is strongly desired.

V.V Das et al. (Eds.): BAIP 2010, CCIS 70, pp. 157–163, 2010.
© Springer-Verlag Berlin Heidelberg 2010

Computer-aided diagnostic (CAD) methods have been proposed as one low cost tool to aid radiologists in film interpretation [1]. CAD can be used to alert radiologists to locations of suspicious lesions and provides a second reading which has been found to reduce misdiagnosis. However, a well-trained computer program (which can screen a large volume of mammograms accurately and reproducibly) is needed in order for CAD to become practical in clinical settings. Such a program has yet to be developed. The fundamental step in many CAD methods is the segmentation of possible target signals in the input image. For mammograms manifesting masses this corresponds to the detection of suspicious mass regions.

Different approaches have been proposed for enhancing and segmenting microcalcifications, including various filtering and local thresholding methods [2], mathematical morphology [3], neural networks [4], the stochastic models [5], the stochastic fractal model [6], pyramidal multiresolution image representation [7], and the contour-based approach [8]. It is observed that most of the enhancement techniques used in the past research works not only enhanced microcalcifications, but also enhanced background structure and noise. Clustering algorithms, such as k-means and Iterative Self-Organizing Data Analysis Techniques (ISODATA), operate in an unsupervised mode and have been applied to a wide range of classification problems [9]. In previous research work a set of existing texture features [10-13] which can provide good discriminating power and are easy to compute as compare to GLCM [14] are used. The choice of a particular technique depends on the application, on the nature of the images available and on the primitives to be extracted. The choice between manual, semiautomatic or fully automatic methods depends on the quality of the images, the numbers of objects need to be segmented, the amount of available user time, and the required accuracy of the segmentation.

The a segmentation process which identifies on a mammogram the opaque areas, suspect or not, present in the image using vector quantization which consumes moderate time but provide good accuracy with less complexity is proposed. Watershed algorithm has a drawback of over-segmenting the image making it obscure for identification of tumor.

2   Algorithms for Segmentation

In this section segmentation by basic watershed algorithm [15,16] and proposed method using Linde Buzo Gray (LBG) algorithm [17,18] which are used for comparative performance of tumor detection is explained.

2.1   Watershed Algorithm

Watershed segmentation [15] classifies pixels into regions using gradient descent on image features and analysis of weak points along region boundaries. The image feature space is treated, using a suitable mapping, as a topological surface where higher values indicate the presence of boundaries in the original image data. It uses analogy with water gradually filling low lying landscape basins. The size of the basins grows with increasing amount of water until they spill into one another. Small basins (regions) gradually merge together into larger basins. Regions are formed by using local geometric structure to associate the image domain features with local extremes measurement. Watershed techniques produce a hierarchy of segmentations, thus the resulting segmentation has to be selected using either some a priory knowledge or manually. These methods are well suited for different measurements fusion and they are less sensitive to user defined thresholds. watershed algorithm for mammographic images as mentioned in [16] is implemented. Results for mammographic images are displayed in Fig 4(a).

2.2 Vector Quantization

Vector Quantization (VQ) [19-25],[33-35] is an efficient technique for data compression and has been successfully used in a variety of research fields such as image segmentation [26-29], speech data compression [30], content based image retrieval CBIR [31,32] etc.

Vector Quantization is a technique in which a codebook is generated for each image. A codebook is a representation of the entire image containing a definite pixel pattern which is computed according to a specific VQ algorithm. The method most commonly used to generate codebook is the Linde-Buzo-Gray (LBG) algorithm which is also called as Generalized Lloyd Algorithm (GLA)[17,18].

Using this algorithm initially a codebook of size 128 was generated for the given images. These code-vectors were further clustered in 8 clusters using same LBG algorithm. The 8 images were constructed using one code-vector at a time. These 8 images display different segments depending on the textural property of the image (Fig.1(b)-(i)). It is observed that the image constructed using first code vector displays tumor clearly.

3 Results

Mammography images from mini-mias database [36] were used in this paper for implementation of Watershed and proposed method using LBG algorithm for tumor demarcation. Fig.1(a) shows original image with tumor. It has fatty tissues as background. Class of abnormality present is CIRC which means well-defined/ circumscribed masses. This image has malignant abnormality. Location of the center of abnormality is (338, 314) for x, y image co-ordinates. Approximate radius is 56 (in pixels) of a circle enclosing the tumor. For this image codebook of size 128 using LBG algorithm is generated. Further these code-vectors were clustered in 8 clusters using same algorithm. Then 8 images were constructed using one code-vector at a time as shown in Fig.1(b)-(i) for LBG algorithm. Then for the same image the codebook of size 8 is generated and the results are displayed in Fig.3(a)-(h). For more details in the image and to find out the effect of codebook size variation codebook size of 128 is generated and then these codevectors are further clustered in 16 clusters using LBG algorithm. Then 16 images were constructed using one code vector at a time. For comparison first 8 codevector images are shown in Fig.2(a)-(h). Fig. 4(a) shows superimposed edge map on original image using watershed algorithm, Fig.4(b) indicates result for superimposed image for first code-vector amongst 8 code-vectors using LBG algorithms. To locate the tumor it is necessary to find the boundaries and the center point co-ordinates in pixels using standard x,y co-ordinate system for images. For this we have found the max and min values for the boundaries as obtained by using these algorithms. The results obtained are given in Table 1.

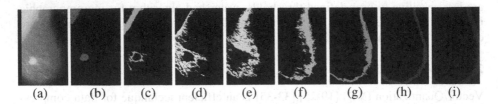

(a)   (b)   (c)   (d)   (e)   (f)   (g)   (h)   (i)

Fig. 1. Original mammogram image with tumor and results of 128 codebook size obtained from LBG clustered to 8 code-vectors using LBG. (a) Breast tumor image, (b) Image for first codevector, (c) Image for second codevector, (d) Image for third codevector, (e) Image for fourth codevector, (f) Image for fifth codevector, (g) Image for sixth codevector, (h) Image for seventh codevector, (i) Image for eighth codevector.

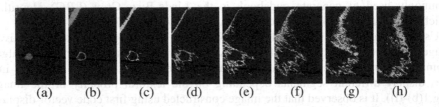

(a)   (b)   (c)   (d)   (e)   (f)   (g)   (h)

Fig. 2. Results of 128 codebook obtained from LBG clustered to 16 code-vectors using LBG. (a)-(h) Images for first eight code-vectors separately for image Fig.1(a)

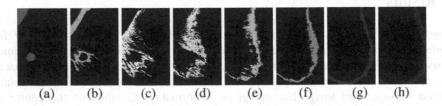

(a)   (b)   (c)   (d)   (e)   (f)   (g)   (h)

Fig. 3. Results using LBG for codebook size 8. (a)-(h) Images for eight code-vectors separately for image Fig.1(a)

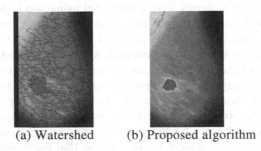

(a) Watershed   (b) Proposed algorithm

Fig. 4. Results of Segmentation using watershed and proposed algorithm

Table 1. Co-ordinates of boundary and center point

Co-ordinates	Name of the algorithm			
	Watershed	LBG		
		128 to 8 codebook	Codebook of size 8	128 to 16 codebook
Xmax	468	388	388	383
Xmin	255	286	280	287
Ymax	300	363	368	359
Ymin	220	275	272	282
Xc	362	337	334	335
Yc	260	319	320	321

4 Conclusion

In this paper vector quantization which is commonly used for data compression is used for segmentation. Basically vector quantization is a clustering algorithm and can be used for texture analysis. Here the results of LBG algorithms for tumor detection in mammographic images for different sizes of codebook are given. The results are compared with well known watershed algorithm. LBG shows far better results for the same(Fig.4). The original values of center point co-ordinates are Xc=338, Yc=314. It is seen that proposed method using LBG with 128 codebook size clustered to 8 codevectors gives the best prediction where as watershed prediction is off the mark (Table 1). It is observed that watershed gives over segmentation while LBG shows far better results for the same. This approach does not lead to over segmentation or under segmentation with less complexity.

Acknowledgments

Authors sincerely would like to thank Dr. Manisha Mundhe for identifying tumor and approving the results.

References

1. Kegelmeyer, W.P.: Computer detection of stellate lesions in mammograms. In: Proc. SPIE Biomed. Image Processing, vol. 1660, pp. 446–454 (1992)
2. Qian, W., Clarke, L.P., Kallergi, M., Li, H., Velthuizen, R., Clark, R.A., Silbiger, M.L.: Tree-structured nonlinear filter and wavelet transform for microcalcification segmentation in mammography. In: SPIE Biomed. Image Processing and Biomed. Visual., vol. 1905, pp. 509–520 (1993)
3. Zhao, D.: Rule-based morphological feature extraction of microcalcifications in mammograms. In: SPIE Med. Imag., vol. 1095, pp. 702–715 (1993)
4. Lo, S.C., Chan, H.P., Lin, J.S., Li, H., Freedman, M.T., Mun, S.K.: Artificial convolution neural network for medical image pattern recognition. Neural Networks 8(7/8), 1201–1214 (1995)
5. Karssemeijer, N.: Recognition of clustered microcalcifications using a random field model. In: SPIE Med. Imag., vol. 1905, pp. 776–786 (1993)

6. Lefebvre, F., Benali, H., Gilles, R., Kahn, E., Paola, R.D.: A fractal approach to the segmentation of microcalcification in digital mammograms. Med. Phys. 22(4), 381–390 (1995)
7. Yoshida, H., Doi, K., Nishikawa, R.M.: Automated detection of clustered microcalcifications in digital mammograms using wavelet transform techniques. In: SPIE Image Processing, vol. 2167, pp. 868–886 (1994)
8. Laine, F., Schuler, S., Fan, J., Huda, W.: Mammographic feature enhancement by multiscale analysis. IEEE Trans. Med. Imag. 13(4), 725–740 (1994)
9. Tou, J., Gonzalez: Pattern Recognition Principles. Addison-Wesley Publishing Company, Reading (1974)
10. Kekre, H.B., Gharge, S.: Selection of Window Size for Image Segmentation using Texture Features. In: Proceedings of International Conference on Advanced Computing & Communication Technologies (ICACCT 2008) Asia Pacific Institute of Information Technology SD India, Panipat, November 08-09 (2008)
11. Kekre, H.B., Gharge, S.: Image Segmentation of MRI using Texture Features. In: Proceedings of International Conference on Managing Next Generation Software Applications, School of Science and Humanities, Karunya University, Coimbatore, Tamilnadu, December 05-06 (2008)
12. Kekre, H.B., Gharge, S.: Statistical Parameters like Probability and Entropy applied to SAR image segmentation. International Journal of Engineering Research & Industry Applications (IJERIA) 2(IV), 341–353
13. Kekre, H.B., Gharge, S.: SAR Image Segmentation using co-occurrence matrix and slope magnitude. In: ACM International Conference on Advances in Computing, Communication and Control (ICAC3 2009), Fr. Conceicao Rodrigous College of Engg., Mumbai, January 23-24, pp. 357–362 (2009) (Available on ACM portal)
14. Haralick, R.M.: IEEE Proceedings of Statistical and Structural Approaches to Texture 67(5) (May 1979)
15. Shafarenko, L., Petrou, M.: Automatic Watershed Segmentation of Randomly Textured Color Images. IEEE Transactions on Image Processing 6(11), 1530–1544 (1997)
16. Alhadidi, B., Mohammad, H., et al.: Mammogram Breast Cancer Edge Detection Using Image Processing Function. Information Technology Journal 6(2), 217–221 (2007)
17. Linde, Y., Buzo, A., Gray, R.M.: An algorithm for vector quantizer design. IEEE Transactions on Communication COM-28, 85–94 (1980)
18. Gray, R.M.: Vector quantization. IEEE ASSP Magazine 1, 4–29 (1984)
19. Kekre, H.B., Sarode, T.K.: New Fast Improved Clustering Algorithm for Codebook Generation for Vector Quantization. In: International Conference on Engineering Technologies and Applications in Engineering, Technology and Sciences, Computer Science Department, Saurashtra University, Rajkot, Gujarat, India, Amoghsiddhi Education Society, Sangli, Maharashtra, India, January 13-14 (2008)
20. Kekre, H.B., Sarode, T.K.: New Fast Improved Codebook Generation Algorithm for Color Images using Vector Quantization. International Journal of Engineering and Technology 1(1), 67–77 (2008)
21. Kekre, H.B., Sarode, T.K.: Fast Codebook Generation Algorithm for Color Images using Vector Quantization. International Journal of Computer Science and Information Technology 1(1), 7–12 (2009)
22. Kekre, H.B., Sarode, T.K.: An Efficient Fast Algorithm to Generate Codebook for Vector Quantization. In: First International Conference on Emerging Trends in Engineering and Technology, ICETET 2008, Raisoni College of Engineering, Nagpur, India, July 16-18, pp. 62–67 (2008), IEEE Xplore

23. Kekre, H.B., Sarode, T.K.: Fast Codebook Generation Algorithm for Color Images using Vector Quantization. International Journal of Computer Science and Information Technology 1(1), 7–12 (2009)
24. Kekre, H.B., Sarode, T.K.: Fast Codevector Search Algorithm for 3-D Vector Quantized Codebook. WASET International Journal of cal Computer Information Science and Engineering (IJCISE) 2(4), 235–239 (Fall 2008), http://www.waset.org/ijcise
25. Kekre, H.B., Sarode, T.K.: Fast Codebook Search Algorithm for Vector Quantization using Sorting Technique. In: ACM International Conference on Advances in Computing, Communication and Control (ICAC3 2009), Fr. Conceicao Rodrigous College of Engg., Mumbai, January 23-24, pp. 317–325 (2009) (Available on ACM portal)
26. Kekre, H.B., Sarode, T.K., Raul, B.: Color Image Segmentation using Kekre's Fast Codebook Generation Algorithm Based on Energy Ordering Concept. In: ACM International Conference on Advances in Computing, Communication and Control (ICAC3 2009), Fr. Conceicao Rodrigous College of Engg., Mumbai, January 23-24, pp. 357–362 (2009) (Available on ACM portal)
27. Kekre, H.B., Sarode, T.K., Raul, B.: Color Image Segmentation using Kekre's Algorithm for Vector Quantization. International Journal of Computer Science (IJCS) 3(4), 287–292 (Fall 2008), http://www.waset.org/ijcs
28. Kekre, H.B., Sarode, T.K., Raul, B.: Color Image Segmentation using Vector Quantization Techniques Based on Energy Ordering Concept. International Journal of Computing Science and Communication Technologies (IJCSCT) 1(2), 164–171 (2009)
29. Kekre, H.B., Sarode, T.K., Raul, B.: Color Image Segmentation Using Vector Quantization Techniques. Advances in Engineering Science Sect. C (3), 35–42 (2008)
30. Kekre, H.B., Sarode, T.K.: Speech Data Compression using Vector Quantization. WASET International Journal of Computer and Information Science and Engineering (IJCISE) 2(4), 251–254 (Fall 2008), http://www.waset.org/ijcise
31. Kekre, H.B., Sarode, T.K., Thepade, S.D.: Image Retrieval using Color-Texture Features from DCT on VQ Codevectors obtained by Kekre's Fast Codebook Generation. ICGST-International Journal on Graphics, Vision and Image Processing (GVIP) 9(5), 1–8 (2009), http://www.icgst.com/gvip/Volume9/Issue5/P1150921752.html
32. Kekre, H.B., Sarode, T.K., Thepade, S.D.: Color-Texture Feature based Image Retrieval using DCT applied on Kekre's Median Codebook. International Journal on Imaging (IJI), http://www.ceser.res.in/iji.html
33. Kekre, H.B., Sarode, T.K.: Vector Quantized Codebook Optimization using K-Means. International Journal on Computer Science and Engineering (IJCSE) 1(3), 283–290 (2009), http://journals.indexcopernicus.com/abstracted.php?level=4&id_issue=839392
34. Kekre, H.B., Sarode, T.K.: 2-level Vector Quantization Method for Codebook Design using Kekre's Median Codebook Generation Algorithm. Advances in Computational Sciences and Technology (ACST) 2(2), 167–178 (2009), http://www.ripublication.com/Volume/acstv2n2.htm
35. Kekre, H.B., Sarode, T.K.: Bi-level Vector Quantization Method for Codebook Generation. In: Second International Conference on Emerging Trends in Engineering and Technlogy, G. H. Raisoni College of Engineering, Nagpur, December 16-18 (2009) (this paper will be uploaded online at IEEE Xplore)
36. Clark, A.F.: The mini-MIAS database of mammograms, http://peipa.essex.ac.uk/info/mias.html (Last updated on July 31, 2003) (referred on 16-09-2009)

Selective Encryption of Video Using Multiple Chaotic Maps

L.M. Varalakshmi[1] and G. Florence Sudha[2]

[1] Dept.of ECE, Sri Manakula Vinayagar Engineering College, Puducherry, India
varalakshmi_1@yahoo.co.in
[2] Dept.of ECE, Pondicherry Engineering College, Puducherry, India
gfsudha@pec.edu

Abstract. Selective encryption exploits the relationship between encryption and compression to reduce the encryption requirements, saving in complexity and facilitating new system functionality. Selective encryption of MPEG video stream have been proposed in a number of variations, yet has seen little application to date. Similarly chaos is another area which has not been focused much for video. In this paper, a video encryption scheme based on the widely used substitution–diffusion architecture which utilizes the chaotic 2D standard map and 1D logistic map is proposed. Hence, the advantages of both, selective encryption and chaos has been combined in this work with no impact on compression efficiency, and a cryptanalytic approach is performed for validating the security.

Keywords: selective encryption, compression, chaos, video security.

1 Introduction

With the development of multimedia and network technology, digital TV, video mail, visual telephone etc. have become more and more popular and now have a widespread and profound influence on our lives. Because video streams are often subject to malicious attacks such as information divulgence, information theft, and data distortion, the security of video stream has become a hot research topic. Many methods for encrypting and decrypting video data have been proposed [1]. However, there are many drawbacks in the current schemes in respect of security and real-time performance [2].

Encrypting the entire multimedia content imposes a heavy computational burden due to the large data size [3]. Several selective encryption schemes have been proposed as a possible solution, where only a specific portion of the multimedia data is selected for encryption [4]. Most existing selective encryption schemes are based on the encryption of DCT coefficients and motion vectors, since it carries more important semantic information.

Very recently, an increasing attention has been devoted to the usage of chaotic functions to implement the encryption process. The chaotic systems have attracted the attention of cryptographers due to their fundamental features such as ergodicity, mixing property and sensitivity to initial conditions/system parameters. Most of the chaotic

V.V Das et al. (Eds.): BAIP 2010, CCIS 70, pp. 164–168, 2010.
© Springer-Verlag Berlin Heidelberg 2010

encryption schemes focus only on images [5][6]. Less attention is being paid to chaotic video encryption, in-spite of its superior performance. In this paper, a video encryption scheme based on the widely used substitution–diffusion architecture which utilizes the chaotic 2D standard map and 1D logistic map is proposed. The scheme discussed earlier for images[7] has been implemented for video and its performance is analyzed. The rest of the paper is organized as follows: The detailed algorithm of the proposed encryption procedure is discussed in Section 2. In Section 3, the security of the proposed cipher is analyzed and its performance is evaluated through various statistical analysis. Finally, Section 4 concludes the paper.

2   Encryption Scheme

A compressed video sequence consists of three kinds of frames namely I-frame, B-frame and P-frame. The encryption of an I frame can greatly influence the relevant B-frames, P-frames and entire video. Hence the I-frames alone are scrambled and encrypted in the proposed encryption scheme. The initial condition, system parameter of the chaotic standard map and number of iterations together constitute the secret key of the algorithm. The proposed algorithm comprises of four rounds: two for the substitution and two for the diffusion. The first round of substitution/confusion is achieved with the help of intermediate XORing keys calculated from the secret key. Then two rounds of diffusion namely the horizontal and vertical diffusions are completed by mixing the properties of horizontally and vertically adjacent pixels, respectively. In the fourth round, a robust substitution/confusion is accomplished by generating an intermediate chaotic key stream (CKS). The secret key in the proposed encryption technique is a set of three floating point numbers and one integer (x_0, y_0, K, N), where $x_0, y_0 \in (0, 2\pi)$, K can have any real value greater than 18.0 and N is any integer value, ideally should be greater than 100. The original video is taken and the above operations are performed as shown in fig.1.

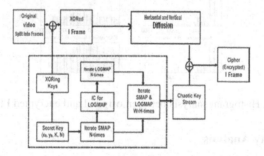

Fig. 1. Encryption scheme

3   Experimental and Performance Analysis

The experiments are simulated using MATLAB software (ver7.5) in HP computer with Pentium processors. News.avi is the test video sequence used. The key in the proposed encryption technique is composed of four parts: three floating point numbers and one integer (x_0, y_0, K, N), where $x_0, y_0 \in (0, 2\pi)$, K can have any real value greater than 18.0 and N is any integer value, ideally should be greater than 100. The output at various stages of encryption are shown in Fig.2. Only I frames are encrypted selectively and simulation results are analyzed.

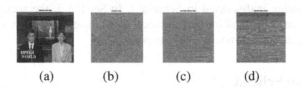

(a)   (b)   (c)   (d)

Fig. 2. Steps of encryption process. (a)original video. (b)confused I frame (c) Diffused I frame (d) Encrypted I frame.

3.1 Histogram Analysis

The histogram illustrates how pixels are distributed by plotting the number of pixels at each color intensity level. The histogram of the original I frame and the encrypted I frame obtained using the secret key ($x_0 = 2.65318934456704$, $y_0 = 1.90890233561695$, $K = 126.348932136745$ and $N = 101$) is shown in Fig.3. It is clear that the histograms of the encrypted frame are fairly uniform and significantly different from the respective histograms of the plain video and hence does not provide any clue to employ statistical attack on the encryption scheme.

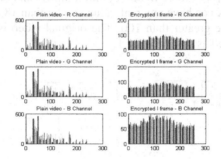

Fig. 3. Histogram analysis between original and encrypted I frame

3.2 Key Sensitivity Analysis

Extreme key sensitivity is an essential feature for any good cryptosystem which guarantees the security of the cryptosystem against the brute-force attack. The key sensitivity of a cryptosystem can be observed by decrypting the cipher video by using slightly different keys and observing the output. As there are four different parts (three floating point numbers and one integer) in the secret key of the proposed encryption technique, the sensitivity is tested with respect to each part of the secret key. In the first step, a test video sequence (news.avi) is encrypted using the secret

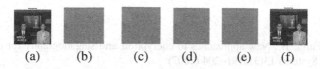

(a)   (b)   (c)   (d)   (e)   (f)

Fig. 4. Key sensitivity analysis. (a) Original video.(b),(c),(d),(e).Decrypted using slightly different x_0, y_0, K and N. (f) Decrypted using correct key.

key (x_0 =2.65318934456704, y_0 =1.90890233561695, K = 126.348932136745 and N = 101) Now, in the second step, the same plain video sequence is decrypted with four slightly different keys: (i) (x_0=2.65318934456705, y_0 =1.90890233561695, K = 126.348932136745andN= 101), (ii) (x_0 =2.65318934456704, y_0 =1.90890233561696, K=126.348932136745andN=101(iii)(x_0=2.65318934456704, y_0 =1.90890233561695, K=126.348932136743andN=101)and(iv)(x_0=2.65318934456704,y_0=1.90890233561695, K = 126.348932136745 and N = 100). In each of the secret keys used in second step, at least three parts are exactly same as used in the first step, however the remaining fourth one differs by 10^{-14} (if it is a floating point number) or by 1 (if it is an integer). The encrypted I frames produced in the second step are shown in frames (b), (c), (d) and (e) of Fig. 4. This shows that even with a slight change in key the original video cannot be decrypted. Only when all four parameters are the same, the original picture is obtained as shown in Fig.4(f).

3.3 Key Space Analysis

The key space is the total number of different keys that can be used in the encryption/decryption procedure. If the precision of 10^{-14} is used then the total number of possible values of x_0 that can be used as a part of the key is ≈ 6.28 x 10^{14}. Similarly, total number of possible values of y_0 that can be used as a part of the key is ≈ 6.28 x 10^{14}.As in the proposed encryption technique K can have any real value greater than 18.0 hence it has infinite number of possible values that can be used as a part of the key. The last part of the key is an integer N, which can have any value preferably greater than 100. Preferred value of N is between 100 and 1100. With this restriction, the total number of possible values of N that can be used as the part of key is 10^3. So, the complete key space for the proposed encryption/decryption technique is $(6.28)^3$ x 10^{45}, which is sufficient enough to resist the brute-force attack.

4 Conclusion

In this paper, an encryption cipher for video is proposed based on the substitution – diffusion architecture, which utilizes the chaotic standard and logistic maps. The initial conditions, system parameter of the chaotic standard map and number of iterations together constitute the effective secret key. The key can be refreshed at frequent intervals as decided between the sender and the receiver. An extensive security and performance analysis of the proposed encryption technique is carried out using various statistical analysis.

References

1. Socek, D., Furht, B.: New approaches to encryption and steganography for digital videos. Multimedia Systems 13(3), 191–204 (2007)
2. Menezes, A.J., Oorschot, P.C.V., Vanstone, S.A.: Handbook of applied cryptography. CRC Press, Boca Raton (1997)
3. Wu, C.-P., Kuo, C.-C.J.: Efficient multimedia encryption via entropy codec design. In: Security and Watermarking of Multimedia Contents, San Jose, California, USA, January 2001. Proceedings of SPIE, vol. 4314, pp. 128–138 (2001)
4. Wu, C.-P., Kuo, C.-C.J.: Design of integrated multimedia compression and encryption systems. IEEE Transactions on Multimedia 7(5), 828–839 (2005)
5. Fridrich, J.: Symmetric ciphers based on two-dimensional chaotic maps. Int. J. Bifurc. Chaos 8(6), 1259–1284 (1998)
6. Mao, Y., Chen, G., Lian, S.: A novel fast image encryption scheme based on 3D chaotic Baker Maps. Int. J. Bifurc. Chaos 14(10), 3613–3624 (2004)
7. Patidar, V., Pareek, N.K.: A new substitution – diffusion based image cipher using chaotic standard and logistic maps. Commun. Nonlinear Science Numer. Simulat. 14, 3056–3075 (2009)

Optimizing the Hybrid Approach for Time Synchronization in Wireless Sensor Networks

Neeta S. Bosamiya[1] and Devesh C. Jinwala[2]

[1] Department of Computer Engineering,
Sarvajanik College of Engineering and Technology, Surat, India
neeta_danthara@lycos.com
[2] Department of Computer Science and Engineering,
S.V. National Institute of Technology, Ichchhanath, Surat, India
dcj@svnit.ac.in

Abstract. There are various approaches to achieve time synchronization in case of wireless sensor networks. Amongst them "sender to receiver" and "receiver to receiver" are the frequently used approaches for synchronizing time. Both the methodology has some drawbacks with respect to number of message exchanged for synchronization. To overcome those drawbacks Hybrid approach was introduced. Hybrid approach is efficient with respect to number of message exchanged compared to both methodology. In this paper Hybrid Approach is improved, to reduce the message communication that is required to synchronize time between the nodes in sensor network.

Keywords: Wireless sensor networks, Time Synchronization, Sender to Receiver Approach, Receiver to Receiver Approach.

1 Introduction

In case of distributed systems, there is no global clock or common memory. This poses serious problems to applications that depend on synchronized notion of time. Time Synchronization is crucial aspect of sensor networks. In this paper various methodologies for Time Synchronization is described. Hybrid Approach is also discussed along with its optimization with following objectives.

- Our proposed Optimized Hybrid Approach will reduce message communication and convergence time that is required for synchronizing time in the network.

This paper is organized as follows: Section 3 describes the widely used time synchronization protocols and their approaches. Section 4 is devoted to analysis of Hybrid Time Synchronization protocol. Section 5 proposes new approach of synchronizing time. Section 6 describes the implementation of new approach, its methodology, performance results and analysis.

2 Related Work

Although there are many protocols introduced for time synchronization on wireless sensor networks, most of them are not designed with focus on energy consumption.

V.V Das et al. (Eds.): BAIP 2010, CCIS 70, pp. 169–174, 2010.
© Springer-Verlag Berlin Heidelberg 2010

Energy consumption is very crucial parameter for power constrained sensor network. Bharath Sundararaman, Ugo Buy, and Ajay D. Kshemkalyani, wrote an excellent survey on Time Synchronization in Sensor Networks [4]. Robert Akl and Yanos Saravanos introduced Hybrid Energy-aware synchronization algorithm [1], their algorithm provided a new concept of combining the widely used approach for time synchronization. In this paper optimization to Hybrid Approach is proposed along with survey of existing research on time synchronization protocols and in doing so following contributions is made:

- Discussion regarding various methodologies for Time Synchronization.
- Optimization to Hybrid Approach is proposed with the aim to improve upon the existing limitation. Describe theoretical evaluation and analysis of optimized hybrid approach along with its performance results and implementation on TinyOS platform.

To the best of our knowledge, this is the first effort to improve upon the Hybrid Approach of time synchronization in wireless sensor networks.

3   Time Synchronization Protocols and Their Approaches

This section is devoted to discuss widely used synchronization protocols namely Time Synchronization Protocol for sensor Network (TSPN), Reference Broadcast protocol (RBS) and Hybrid Protocol.

3.1   Time Synchronization Protocol for Sensor Networks

TSPN protocol is based on "Sender to Receiver" approach, in this approach sender synchronizes with a receiver by transmitting the current clock values as timestamps. TSPN protocol works in two phase level discovery phase followed by synchronization phase.

3.2   Reference Broadcast Protocol

The Reference Broadcast Synchronization (RBS) protocol is based on "Receiver to Receiver" approach, in this approach receiver's exchange the time at which they receive the same message and compute their offset based on the difference in reception times.

3.3   Hybrid Protocol

Hybrid protocol is combination of sender to receiver and receiver to receiver approach. Time synchronization protocols based on both approaches have unique strengths when dealing with energy consumption. RBS is most effective in networks where transmitting sensors have few receivers, while TSPN excels when transmitters have many receivers. Hybrid protocol minimizes power regardless of the network's topology by choosing RBS or TSPN Synchronization based on the number of children nodes.

4   Theoretical Analysis of Hybrid Protocol

This section analyzes Hybrid protocol in terms of total message exchanged and looks upon on calculation of threshold value for number of child nodes.

4.1   Calculation of Threshold Value for Hybrid Protocol

The threshold value of receivers will decide upon TSPN and RBS protocol. To calculate the threshold value, It is assumed that the energy required to receive the message is usually half than the energy required to transmit. Messages that are transmitted (TX_{TSPN}), (TX_{RBS}) and received (RX_{TSPN}), (RX_{RBS}) for TSPN, RBS protocol is as follows [1].

$$TX_{TSPN} = n+1, RX_{TSPN} = 2n . \qquad (1)$$

$$TX_{RBS} = n, RX_{RBS} = n+ (n*(n-1))/2 = (n*n + n)/2 . \qquad (2)$$

Combining equation 1, 2 to calculate threshold value, where α is the ratio of reception to transmission power and n denotes number of child nodes. [1]

$$TX_{RBS} + \alpha * RX_{RBS} = TX_{TSPN} + \alpha * RX_{TSPN}.$$
$$(n-4) (n+1) = 0 . \qquad (3)$$

Equation 3 shows that the energies used by RBS and TSPN are equal for 4 receivers per transmitter, so the threshold value is set to 4. When there are fewer receivers than 4, RBS is more efficient otherwise TSPN synchronization is selected.

4.2   Analysis of Message Transmission for Hybrid Protocol

Hybrid algorithm is carried out in two phases, in the first phase a hierarchical tree structure is created along with calculation of child nodes. In the second phase synchronization is carried out either by RBS or TSPN protocol. Message transmission for synchronizing is the total number of message for synchronization (TSPN or RBS) + n + m, where n is maximum number of nodes and m is total child nodes per level.

5   Optimized Hybrid Protocol: New Approach

This section is devoted to discuss proposed new approach that improvises existing Hybrid Approach and Algorithm for Optimized Hybrid Protocol is also presented.

5.1   Optimized Hybrid Protocol and Analysis of Message Transmission

Hybrid algorithm has the overhead of creating tree structure, as second phase of synchronization is based on calculation of child nodes computed from the first phase. But if both phases are combined the message transmission will be reduced by n broadcast and m unicast messages. Where n denotes total number of nodes and m denotes child nodes for each level. The parent node will broadcast the flood packet. The child node on receiving the flood packet will set the level greater than parent and will send acknowledge with time stamp of child node. Parent will receive acknowledgement, while receiving the acknowledgement parent node counts number of child nodes and if they are less than threshold, it waits for a predefined time. If after expiration of time, acknowledgement is still less than threshold value it performs RBS synchronization between the child nodes otherwise TSPN synchronization.

5.2 Algorithm for Optimized Hybrid Protocol

```
1. Set num_receivers to 0
2. If current_node is root node
   -Broadcast flood_sync packet with level no. and time
3. Else If current_node receives flood_sync packet
   -Set parent of current_node to source of broadcast
   -Set current_node level to parent's node level + 1
   -Rebroadcast flood_sync request with current_node
    ID,timestamp and level
   -Broadcast ack_flood_sync packet with current_node ID
    and local timestamps
   -Ignore subsequent flood_sync packets
4. Else If current_node receives ack_flood_sync_packet
   -Increment num_receivers
  5. If num_receivers greater then threshold value
     -Send acknowledgement for ack_flood_sync with
      timestamp of receiving, sending the ack_flood_sync
    6. Else If
       For each receiver
       -Record local time of reception for flood_sync packet
       -Broadcast observation_packet
      -Receive observation_packet from other receivers
       Endif
       Endif
```

6   Implementation

6.1   Methodology

Optimized Hybrid Protocol is implemented on TinyOS 1.x platform. TinyOS has a component-based programming model, provided by nesC language. The simulator used on TinyOS platform is TOSSIM. The testing of simulation is carried out using total nodes as three and above to check the selection of TSPN, RBS Synchronization.

6.2   Simulation and Tools Employed

TOSSIM is used to for simulation and code is deployed on mica2 sensor nodes with help of Avrora. The simulation is carried out with a single parent node and three or more child nodes. The call graph for our implementation is as shown in Figure 1.

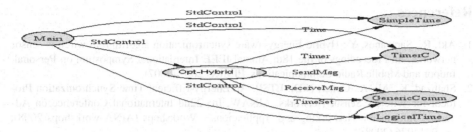

Fig. 1. Call graph for Simulation of optimized Hybrid Protocol

6.3 Performance Results and Analysis

Test application opt-hybrid was implemented for single hop communication. The below table provides the analysis of number of message that are transferred between the parent and child node. The value of child node for first table is four and for the next table it is less than the threshold value. For child node equal or more than threshold it is proved that total number of message transferred gets reduced to almost half when TSPN protocol is followed and In case of child node less than threshold value one broadcast message at each parent node is saved.

Table 1. Comparison of Message Transmitted for Hybrid and Optimized Hybrid Protocol for Four Child Nodes and TSPN Protocol

Type of node	Protocol	Hybrid		Optimized Hybrid Protocol	
		Broadcast	Unicast	Broadcast	Unicast
Parent Node	TSPN	2	4	1	4
Four Child nodes	TSPN	-	8	-	4

Table 2. Comparison of Message Transmitted for Hybrid and Optimized Hybrid Protocol for Three Child nodes and RBS Protocol

Type of node	Protocol	Hybrid		Optimized Hybrid Protocol	
		Broadcast	Unicast	Broadcast	Unicast
Parent Node	RBS	2	-	1	-
Three Child nodes	RBS	3	3	3	3

7 Conclusion

All Time synchronization protocols rely on some sort of message exchange between nodes. The number of message exchanged to achieve synchronization can be considered as crucial parameter to analyze any protocol. Converge time and consumption of power can be reduced with our proposed Optimized Hybrid Protocol. In our simulation it is proved that the message transfer gets reduced by n + m, here n denotes number of total nodes and m denotes number of child nodes per level.

References

1. Akl, R., Saravanos, Y.: Hybrid Energy-aware synchronization algorithm in wireless sensor networks. In: Proceedings of the 18th Annual IEEE International Symposium on Personal, Indoor and Mobile Radio Communications, PIMRC 2007 (2007)
2. Shahzad, K., Ali, A., Gohar, N.D.: ETSP: An Energy-Efficient Time Synchronization Protocol for Wireless Sensor Networks, AINAW. In: 22nd International Conference on Advanced Information Networking and Applications - Workshops (AINA workshops 2008), pp. 971–976 (2008)
3. Sun, Y., Qian, J., Wu, J.: Hybrid Energy-Aware Time Synchronization Protocol for WSNs in Coal Mine. In: Proceeding of IEEE Information Acquisition. ICIA 2007, pp. 436–441 (2007)
4. Sundararaman, B., Buy, U., Kshemkalyani, A.D.: Clock Synchronization for Wireless Sensor Networks: A Survey, Department of Computer Science, University of Illinois at Chicago, March 22 (2005)
5. Sivrikaya, F., Yener, B.: Time Synchronization in Sensor Networks: A Survey. IEEE Network 18(4), 45–50 (2004)
6. He, L.-M.: Time Synchronization Based on Spanning Tree for Wireless Sensor Networks. In: IEEE Wireless 4th International Conference on Communications, Networking and Mobile Computing, WiCOM 2008, October 12-14 (2008)
7. TinyOS tutorials
8. Levis, P., Lee, N.: TOSSIM: A Simulator for TinyOS Networks (2003),
   http://www.cs.berkeley.edu/~pal/pubs/nido.pdf

Tracking Based Secure AODV Routing Protocol

Parma Nand[1,*], S.C. Sharma[2], and Rani Astya[3]

[1] Doctoral Candidate, Wireless Computing Research Lab., DPT, IIT Roorkee, India
astya2005@gmail.com, astyadpt@iitr.ernet.ac.in
[2] Associate Professor, Wireless Computing Research Lab., DPT, IIT Roorkee, India
scs60fpt@iitr.ernet.in
[3] Assistant Professor. IILM-CET Greater Noida,
astyarani@gmail.com

Abstract. Adhoc networks are dynamic infrastructure-less network system in which nodes can communicate with each other freely. It is very different from normal network and thus prone to different kinds of attack. This makes security concerns very important. This paper proposes security improvements over the existing AODV protocol for attack detection and building up proposed Tracking based credence computation (TCV) to improve network security. When a malicious node is judged as an attacker by the credence mechanism, the improved security routing protocol will implement re-routing to isolate the attacker from the network. This algorithm includes the prompt alarm about the behavior of a malicious node to help in taking quick action against them.

Keywords: Multi-hop, MANET, attack, security, behavior.

1 Introduction

A multi-hop mobile ad-hoc network is a set of mobile nodes which communicate over radio and do not need any infrastructure. These self organized networks are very flexible and suitable for several types of applications, as they allow the establishment of temporary communication without any pre installed infrastructure. Beside the disaster and military application domain, the mobile ad-hoc networks are increasing deployed commercially e.g. multimedia applications. The security [1, 2, 7, 8, 10] is one of the major concerns of MANET because of its complexity and changing network topology. Different types of internal or external attacks are possible. This paper proposes a tracking based security protocol for an on-demand ad-hoc routing algorithm for prompt attack detection and protection against it. Subsequently, it presents analysis to show its suitability for security of MANET.

2 Related Works

Some of the existing secure routing protocols for MANETs are explored in this section. Jia, J. Wu, and Y. He [11] has used credential value (CV) based computation

---

* Corresponding author.

V. V Das et al. (Eds.): BAIP 2010, CCIS 70, pp. 175–180, 2010.

for security and analysis of misbehaving nodes. It has given very good work to detect illegitimate node and secure the network. G.Acs [12] has proposed a new secure routing protocol, called endairA. It was inspired by Ariadne protocol but it has opted for an authentication of the RREP message, contrary to Ariadne, which uses RREQ message for authentication. Marti [13] has proposed mechanisms for detecting and avoiding node failing to route packets, which apply to source routing protocols.

3   AODV Routing Protocol [3]

Ad-hoc On Demand Distance Vector(AODV) has been considered as one of the most popular and promising on-demand routing protocols, which has been standardized by IETF and attracts many concerns because of its lower network overhead and algorithm complexity. The routing of AODV protocol consists of two phases:

    i) Route discovery   ii) Route maintenance.

3.1 Route Discovery

A node wishing to communicate with another node first seeks for a route in its routing table. If it finds node, the communication starts immediately, otherwise the node initiates a *route discovery* phase. The route discovery process consists of a route-request message (RREQ) which is broadcasted. If a node has a valid route to the destination, it replies to the route-request with a route-reply (RREP) message. Additionally, the replying node creates a so called *reverse route* entry in its routing table which contains the address of the source node, the number of hops to the source, and the next hop's address.

3.2 Route Maintenance

It is performed by the source node and can be subdivided into: i) source node moves: source node initiates a new route discovery process, ii) destination or an intermediate node moves: a route error message (RERR) is sent to the source node. Intermediate nodes receiving a RERR update their routing table by setting the distance of the destination to infinity. If the source node receives a RERR it will initiate a new route discovery. To prevent global broadcast messages AODV introduces a local connectivity management by periodical exchanges of so called HELLO messages.

4   Security Problems in AODV Protocol

In this protocol each internal node on the route doesn't need to store all the routing information in its routing table. Though this increases its efficiency but this gives chance to malicious nodes to threat the security. The security attacks [4, 5, 9] of AODV take benefit of this procedure. Some of attacks are:

    i. Black Hole Attack   ii. Routing Table Overflow Attack (RTO)
   iii. Network Segmentation Attack. (a) Fabricating RERR Packet Attack.
                                        (b) Interrupting Routing Attack.

5   Proposed Tracking Based Credence Computation Algorithm

Credence mechanism proposed by Jia et.al. [11] has been used to improve security of the existing AODV protocol. The tracking based credence system tracks the behavior of node and records the number of times node misbehaves. This algorithm includes the prompt alarm about the behavior of a malicious node to help in taking quick action against them.

5.1   A Security Mechanism Built on AODV Protocol

The security features of the AODV protocol are analyzed & further a tracking based credence computation to enhance security of this protocol is proposed. In order to provide secure and reliable packet routing network services, nodes firstly assume the route with high credence value. In figure 1, as S wants to send packets to D, the number of hops is 2 when B as the next hop, the number of hops is 3 when C as the next hop, and 4 when C, F, E are the next hops. S will then compare the credence value of B and C. If C has higher credence value, S may choose C as the next hop ignoring its more hops.

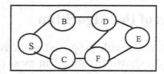

Fig. 1. Data forwarding based on the credence value

5.2   Credence Mechanism Built on AODV Protocol

Credence is just a credit measurement of entities in the network where credit is a belief that the entities will behave without malicious intent and a belief that the whole system will resist malicious manipulation.

The credence mechanism is mainly used to prevent the security threats brought by malicious nodes, especially selfish nodes. The main goals are as follows.

1.   Offering reliable information to decide whether a node is trustful.
2.   Encouraging cooperation among nodes.

Th.e reported work [11] does not take into account malicious behavioral history of the node while calculating credence value. In the proposed work it is taken heavily into account by reducing credence value exponentially.

5.2.1   Tracking Based Malicious Behavior Credence Computation
R_m denotes the credence value of a node which is under supervision for malicious behavior, in which m means the number of behaviors of node.

a) If legitimate behavior is exhibited credence value is increased by ΔR.

b) If illegitimate behavior is exhibited, this credence category evaluates whether an entity has malicious behavior. It is tracked and recorded. Correspondingly, the credence value is decreased exponentially in accordance to its history. The node's credence value is reduced as described below depending on whether its work was satisfactory ($R_m>0$) or not ($R_m<0$). The behavior of entity is tracked as.

$$R_{m+1} = \begin{cases} R_m + \Delta R & \text{when entity has legitimate behavior} \\ R_m/2^i - \Delta R, \quad R_m>0 & \text{when entity has illegitimate behavior(++i)} \\ R_m - 2^j \times \Delta R, \quad R_m<0 & \text{when entity has illegitimate behavior(++j)} \end{cases}$$

Where i, j (initially 0) tracks how many times an entity has illegitimate behavior. For every illegitimate behavior i or j is incremented by 1 to reach threshold of declaring malicious behavior promptly.

If the entity starts attacking after number of legitimate behaviors and attaining full trust then heavy penalty is imposed on it as per its past behavior. It decreases the credence value to reach threshold faster to detect malicious node promptly.

5.2.2 Detection and Removal of Node
Once a node reaches a threshold (depending on application) limit and found by a node. This node declares it a malicious node to all entity in the network system. This procedure led to remove an illegitimate node out of the routing system.

6 Results and Analysis of the Algorithm

The detection of a malicious node with proposed work is comparatively faster than the one recorded [11] work. As shown in table 2 in most of the cases it is founded to be faster by 30% or more depending on the value of ΔR and R_m. The better performance is shown by this algorithm with the higher value of R_m, (more legitimate behavior more value of R_m). For $R_m >0$ the performance is shown here in fig. 2 to 5 with different values of ΔR. The curve indicated by TCV (Tracking based Credential Computation) is the performance of proposed work and the curve shown by CV(Credential Computation) is the recorded one.

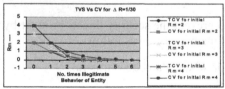

Fig. 2. Performance of TCV for $\Delta R=1/30$ & $R_m=2,3,4$

Fig. 3. Performance of TCV for $\Delta R=1/14$ & $R_m=2,3,4$

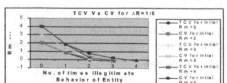

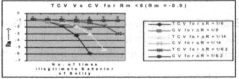

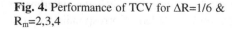

Fig. 4. Performance of TCV for $\Delta R=1/6$ & $R_m=2,3,4$

Fig. 5. Performance of TCV for $\Delta R=1/6,1/14,$ $1/62$ & $R_m=-0.9$

The figure 5 shows the performance of the algorithm when $R_m<0$ ($R_m=0.9$) and the value of ΔR varying as 1/6, 1/14, 1/62 and correspondingly these are shown in table 2.

Table 1. Perform of TCV in % for Rm>0

Rm ΔR	$R_m=2$	$R_m=3$	$R_m=4$
ΔR=1/6	0	25	25
ΔR=1/14	25	40	40
ΔR=1/30	20	33	33
ΔR=1/62	33	43	43
ΔR=1/126	43	50	50

Table 2. TCV vs CV for ΔR=1/6

i	ΔR=1/6		ΔR=1/14		ΔR=1/62	
	TCV	CV	TCV	CV	TCV	CV
0	-0.9	-0.9	-0.9	-0.9	-0.9	-0.9
1	-1.23	-1.233	-1.042	-1.043	-0.9323	-0.932
2	-1.9	-1.5667	-1.328	-1.186	-0.9968	-0.965
3	-3.23	-1.9	-1.9	-1.329	-1.1258	-0.997
4	-5.9	-2.2333	-3.042	-1.471	-1.3839	-1.029

7 Conclusions

In this paper security issue in the context of malicious behavior is analyzed with AODV protocol. With the tracking based credence computation system malicious nodes inside or outside can be detected easily and promptly as shown if fig. 3 to 6. As shown in these scenarios with different ΔR the detection is prompt and more than 30% for smaller ΔR. The table 1 analyzes the algorithm for Rm>0 and table 2 does it for $R_m<0$ ($R_m=0.9$) with different ΔR. In all the cases the proposed algorithm can detects and rules out malicious nodes faster and will improve the QoS of routing.

Future work includes extensive performance analysis of the proposed protocol with very large number of nodes using ns2 simulation software.

References

1. Yang, H.: Security in Mobile Adhoc Networks: Challenges and Solutions. IEEE Wireless Communications 11, 38–47 (2004)
2. Papadimitos, P., Hass, Z.: Secure Routing for Mobile Adhoc Networks. In: CNDS (2002), http://wnl.ece.cornell.edu/Publications/cnds02.pdf
3. Perkins, C.E., Royer, E.M., Das, S.R.: Ad-hoc On-Demand Distance Vector Routing (AODV) [EB/OL] (November 2002), http://www.ietf.org/internet-drafts/draft-ietf-manet-aodv-12.txt
4. Hu, Y.-C., Perrig, A., Johnson, D.B.: Ariadne: A Secure On-Demand Routing Protocol for Ad hoc Networks. In: Proceedings of the MobiCom 2002, Atlanta, Georgia, USA, September 23-28 (2002)
5. Habib, A., Hafeeda, M.H., Bhargava, B.: Detecting Service Violation and DoS Attacks. In: Proceedings of Network and Distributed System Security Symposium, NDSS (2003)
6. Hu, Y.-C., Johnson, D.B., Perrig, A.: SEAD: Secure Efficient Distance Vector Routing for Mobile Wireless Ad Hoc Networks. In: Proceedings of the 4th IEEE Workshop on Mobile Computing Systems & Applications(WMCSA 2002), June 2002, pp. 3–13. IEEE, Calicoon (2002)
7. Sanzgiri, K., Dahill, B.: A Secure Routing Protocol for Ad Hoc Networks. In: IEEE International Conference on Network Protocols (IC2 NP), Paris, France (2002)

8. Papadimitratos, Z.J.H.: Secure Routing for Mobile Ad Hoc Networks. In: Proceedings of SCS Communication Networks and Distributed Systems Modeling and Simulation Conference, San Antonio, USA (2002)

9. Royer, E.M., Toh, C.K.: A Review of Current Routing Protocols for Ad Hoc Mobile Wireless Networks. IEEE Personal Communications (4), 46–55 (1999)

10. Hu, Y., Perrig, A., Johnson, D.: Ariadne: A Secure On-demand Routing Protocol for Ad Hoc Networks. In: ACM MOBICOM 2002 (2002)

11. Jia, J.W., He, Y.: A Security Enhanced AODV Routing Protocol. In: Kreczmar, A., Mirkowska, G. (eds.) MFCS 1989. LNCS, vol. 379, pp. 298–307. Springer, Heidelberg (1989)

12. Acs, G., Buttyan, L., Vazda, I.: Provably Secure On-Demand Source Routing in Mobile Adhoc Networks, Technical report (March 2005)

13. Marti, S., Giuli, T., Lai, K.: Mitigating Routing Misbehavior in Mobile Adhoc Networks. In: 6th annual ACM/IEEE International Conference on Mobile Computing and Networking 2000 (2000)

Study of Visitor Behavior by Web Usage Mining

V.V.R. Maheswara Rao[1], V. Valli Kumari[2], and K.V.S.V.N. Raju[2]

[1] Professor, Department of Computer Applications,
Shri Vishnu Engineering College for Women, Bhimavaram, W.G.Dt, Andhra Pradesh, India
mahesh_vvr@yahoo.com
[2] Professor, Department of Computer Science & Systems Engineering,
College of Engineering, Andhra University, Visakhapatnam, Andhra Pradesh, India
vallikumari@gmail.com, kvsvn.raju@gmail.com

Abstract. Web usage mining focuses on discovering the potential knowledge from the browsing patterns of users and to find the correlation between the pages on analysis. With exponential growth of web log, the conventional data mining techniques were proved to be inefficient, as they need to be re-executed every time. As web log is incremental in nature, it is necessary for web miners to use incremental mining techniques to extract the usage patterns and study the visiting characteristics of user. The data on the web log is heterogeneous and non scalable, hence we require an improved algorithm which reduces the computing cost significantly.

This paper discusses an algorithm to suit for continuously growing web log, based on association rule mining with incremental technique. The algorithm is proved to be more efficient as it avoids the generation of candidates, reduces the number of scans and allows interactive mining with different supports. To validate the efficiency of proposed algorithm, several experiments were conducted and results proven this are claimed.

Keywords: Incremental Frequent Pattern Tree, Total Site Reach, Stickiness.

1 Introduction

The World Wide Web is fertile ground for web mining techniques. When users visit the web pages, the web servers accumulate and record the abundant data, which is structurally complex, non scalable and exponentially growing in nature. The web mining includes Web Content Mining, Web Structure Mining and Web Usage Mining. Web Usage Mining is a special kind of web mining, which can discover the knowledge in the hidden browsing patterns and analyses the visiting characteristics of the user.

Web usage mining is a complete process that includes various stages of data mining cycle, including Data Preprocessing, Pattern Discovery & Pattern Analysis. Initially, the web log is preprocessed to clean, integrate and transform into a common log. Later, Data mining techniques are applied to discover the interesting characteristics in the hidden patterns. Pattern Analysis is the final stage of web usage mining which can validate interested patterns from the output of pattern discovery.

V. V Das et al. (Eds.): BAIP 2010, CCIS 70, pp. 181–187, 2010.

Association rule mining techniques can be used to discover correlation between pages found in a web log. Association rules are often sought for very large datasets and efficient algorithms are highly valued. Association rule mining is an iterative process, thus, the existing mining techniques have the limitations like, multiple scans of transactional Data base, huge number of candidate generation and burden of calculating the support. In addition to the above, different combinations of frequent pages with different supports are often required obtaining satisfactory results.

Typical Web log will grow rapidly in the short time, and some of the web data may be antiquated or supported. The user behavior may be changed with the rapid growth of web logs. Therefore, one must re-discover the user behavior from the updated web logs using incremental mining. The essence of incremental mining is that it utilizes the previous mining results and finds new patterns from the inserted or deleted part of the web logs such that the mining time can be reduced. As web log is incremental and distributed in nature, most web servers maintain a common web log, which consists of IP Address of user, Date and Time of request, URL of the page, Protocol, size of the page and so on.

This paper introduces an Incremental Frequent Pattern Tree to store user-specific browsing path information in a condensed way. Incremental mining techniques emerged to avoid algorithm re-execution and to update mining results when incremental data is added or old data is removed, ensuring a better performance in the web mining process and discovers interesting patterns in an effective manner. This algorithm minimizes the number of scans of web log, avoids generation of candidates. In addition, this algorithm interactively mines the data for different supports with a single scan of database and allows addition / deletion of new click streams in a finest granularity.

The rest of this paper is organized as follows. Section 2 introduces recent researchers' related work. Section3 describes proposed work. In next section 4, we expressed the study of theoretical analysis. In section 5, the experimental analysis of proposed work is shown. Finally in section 6 we mention the conclusions.

2   Related Work

Many of the previous authors concentrated on I/O cost. Most of the works in the literature do not suitable for dynamically changing web log scenario.

A number of Apriori-based algorithms [1, 2 and 3] have been proposed to improve the performance by addressing issues related to the I/O cost. Han et al. [5] proposed a data structure, frequent pattern tree that allows mining of frequent itemsets without generating candidates. A new data structure called H-struct [6] was introduced to deal with sparse data solely. Most of the researches focused on Full Scan algorithm and Selective Scan algorithm [9] etc. Show-Jane Yen and his colleagues [11] introduced an Incremental data mining algorithm for discovering web traversal patterns.

To discover useful patterns one has to concentrate on structurally complex and exponential growth of web log scenario along with I/O cost.

3 Proposed Work

Web usage mining is a complete process, integrating various stages of data mining cycle, including web log Preprocessing, Pattern Discovery & Pattern Analysis as shown in figure 1. For any web mining technique, initially the preparation of suitable source data is an important task since the characteristic sources of web log are distributed and structurally complex. On applying a comprehensive algorithm on a web log one can get a formatted log which consists of unique sessions and respective pages. Later all the data mining techniques can be applied on preprocessed web log. Pattern analysis is a final stage of web usage mining, which can validate the discovered patterns and identifies interested unique patterns.

3.1 Pattern Discovery

As web log is incremental in nature, to discover hidden patterns in preprocessed web log frequently accessed together by a unique user using association rule based on incremental mining. The discovery of hidden pattern is computationally intensive procedure in the dynamic web log scenario. This paper proposes a novel data structure incremental frequent pattern Tree (IFP-Tree) which can reduce computational cost significantly. It avoids the generation of candidates, reduces number of scans and allows interactive mining.

3.1.1 Definition and Concept of IFP-Tree
The IFP-Tree is used to keep track of patterns identified during the web usage mining process. It takes preprocessed and formatted web log as input. The IFP-Tree builds on divide and conquers strategy. It retains associated pages information and frequency of pages at each node except the root node with a single scan on web log. The IFP-Tree structure is suitable for interactive frequent pattern mining.

3.1.2 Representation of IFP-Tree
The IFP-Tree is encouraging the interactive mining one has to navigate from any node to any other node and also its size grows dynamically, hence linked list representation is followed. It consists of root node, which is assigned by null value and all other nodes including intermediate and leaf nodes, holds the information of associated pages and respective frequencies as integers.

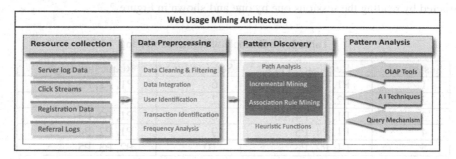

Fig. 1. Web Usage Mining architecture

3.1.3 Construction of IFP-Tree

The IFP-Tree can be constructed based on recursive procedure using formatted log as input. On reading the first session, repeatedly new nodes are created and assigned with respective page numbers with their frequencies till the end of the pages in that session. On reading new session first page is compared with the previously created immediate nodes of the root node. If it is found to be the same, the frequency of the matched node is updated and moved to the next node or new node that depends on the next page in the same session. The above step is repeated till the end of the formatted log. Traversal of the tree starts from root node to the desired node for interactive mining.

3.1.4 Algorithm of IFP-Tree

AddNewNode(TN,PS)
Step 1: while LS do
Step 2: If PS $\neq \varphi$ then
Step 3: PP $\leftarrow$ first page of PP
Step 4: while last page in PS do
Step 5: if PP $\notin$ TN.CN then
Step 6: TN.CN $\leftarrow$ New TN(PP,TN)
Step 7: end if
Step 8: TN.CN(PP).frequency ++
Step 9: AddNewNode(TN.CN(PP), PS)
Step 10: PP $\leftarrow$ next page in PS
Step 11: end of while
Step 12: else
Step 13: return
Step 14: end if
Step 15: PS $\leftarrow$ next session
Step 16: end of while

Where TN: Root Node, CN: Child Node, PS: Present Session, LS: Last Session, PP: Present Page and LP: Last Page. The above recursive procedure is used in construction of IFP-Tree.

3.1.5 Example of IFP-Tree

An example of formatted web log as shown in Table 1 is taken as input, a tree is constructed by reading the sessions one by one and shown in Figure 2.

Table 1. An Example of formatted web log

Session Id	Requested Page	Session Id	Requested Page
1	P1, P2	6	P1, P2, P3, P4
2	P2, P3, P4	7	P1
3	P1, P3, P4, P5	8	P1, P2, P3
4	P1, P4, P5	9	P1, P2, P4
5	P1, P2, P3	10	P2, P3, P5

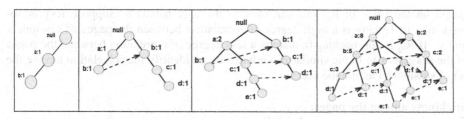

Fig. 2. After reading the session id = 1, 2, 3 and 10

3.1.6 Maintenance of IFP-Tree

The IFP-Tree structure is more convenient to update incrementally. However, in addition, depending on the applications, one can apply a minimum support or to limit the size of the tree. To do so, two possible methods are proposed. Method I: An effective approach for limiting the size of the IFP-Tree is to set a maximum number of nodes and prune it. Method II: One can apply a minimum support and insert only supported sessions into the tree. If the data do not change drastically, the size of the tree will remain reasonably small.

3.2 Pattern Analysis

The IFP-Tree discovered pages must be validated to eliminate irrelevant pages and extract interesting pages. In the present paper, we wish to find out a) Mathematical relationship among sessions of the same browser b) Stickiness among the frequently visited pages together.

Mathematical relationship among the sessions:
To identify the user behavior, it is essential to study the relationship among the set of sessions of the same user. This can be incorporated with a simple correlated technique. Let us defined the set D as data generated by N unique users from formatted web log,

$$D = \{D_i \,/\, i = 1, 2, ..., N\} \tag{1}$$

Where D_i is a session set of ith user, $1 \leq i \leq N$

$$\text{For each } D_i = \{S_{ij} \,/\, j = 1, 2, ..., M\} \tag{2}$$

Where S_{ij} is j^{th} session of ith user, $1 \leq j \leq M$. Hence an ith user may consist of finite multiple sessions. In any session the user may browse a set of pages,

$$S_{ji} = \{P_{ijk} \,/\, k = 1, 2, ..., L\} \tag{3}$$

Where P_{ijk} is k^{th} page of jth session of ith user. Let P_{ixk} and P_{iyk} be the set of pages of Xth and Y^{th} sessions browsed by i^{th} user. R_{xy} denotes the relationship between the sessions x,y and is defined as,

$$R_{xy} = \frac{Cov(x, y)}{\sigma x \sigma y} \tag{4}$$

Based on the value of R_{xy} one can identify the user behavior. Suppose Rxy is approaching to 1, there is a high degree of correlation between the pages of sessions x and y. If R_{xy} is approaching 0, there is a less degree of correlation between the pages of the sessions x,y. In the similar procedure we can identify the correlation among the set of sessions of an unique user.

Stickiness among the pages:
The stickiness can be expressed as follows:

$$\text{Stickiness,} \quad S = F * D * TSR \tag{5}$$

Where S = Stickiness, F = Frequency, D = Duration and TSR = Total Site Reach

$$F = \frac{\text{Number of visits in time period T}}{\text{Number of Unique users who visited in T}} \tag{6}$$

$$D = \frac{\text{Total amount of time spent viewing all pages}}{\text{Number of visits in time period T}} \tag{7}$$

$$TSR = \frac{\text{Number of unique users who visited in T}}{\text{Total number of unique users}} \tag{8}$$

Therefore,

$$S = \frac{\text{Total amount of time spent in viewing all pages}}{\text{Total number of unique users}} \tag{9}$$

4 Theoretical Study

The size of an IFP-Tree depends on the number of nodes in it, and the memory requirement of a tree node depends on the platform used to implement and run the program. For a 4-byte representation of integers and reference pointers one can get (3 + c) * 4 bytes, where c is the number of child nodes. That is, for a tree with n nodes approximately n * 4 * 4 bytes are needed, since in a tree the number of children references are equal to the number of nodes. Additionally, 4 bytes for each leaf node has to be counted, since they contain a null reference as children and possibly some platform-dependent overhead. Taking an average number of 180 nodes per tree, it takes approximately 3 Kbytes. For 20,000 Users, it is still needs only 40 Mbytes.

5 Experimental Analysis

The server side web log data is experimented over a period of six months. The memory usage of IFP-Tree is relatively decreased when compared with referred algorithms. For 20,000 users it is occupying only 40 MB. The CPU usage of IFP-Tree is almost twice the Cached Apriori and 40% betterment is observed when compared with other techniques. The results are shown in Figure 3 and Figure 4.

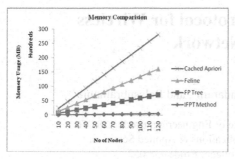

Fig. 3. Memory comparison

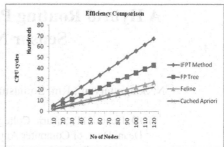

Fig. 4. Efficiency comparison

6 Conclusions

When users browse web pages, they leave lot of information in the log. By analyzing this information one can understand the behavior of the user. The present proposed novel data structure, IFP-Tree can handle the rapidly growing log data. There are many advantages with IFP-Tree. 1) Once the tree is built, it allows interactive mining with different supports. 2) It limits the number of scans of database to one. 3) It eliminates the generation of candidates. 4) It limits the size of the tree by removing the outdated instances. 5) It is a simple, effective and easy to apply to any application.

References

1. Savasere, A., Omiecinski, E., Navathe, S.: An Efficient Algorithm for Mining Association Rules in Large Databases. In: Proceedings of the VLDB Conference (1995)
2. Agrawal, R., Srikant, R.: Fast algorithms for mining association rules. VLDB, 487–499 (1994)
3. Brin, S., Motwani, R., Ullman Jeffrey, D., Shalom, T.: Dynamic itemset counting and implication rules for market basket data. In: SIGMOD (1997)
4. Han, J., Pei, J., Yin, Y.: Mining Frequent Patterns without Candidate Generation. In: SIGMOD, pp. 1–12 (2000)
5. Pei, J., Han, J., Nishio, S., Tang, S., Yang, D.: H-Mine: Hyper-Structure Mining of Frequent Patterns in Large Databases. In: Proc. 2001 Int. Conf. on Data Mining (2001)
6. Chen, M.S., Huang, X.M., Lin, I.Y.: Capturing User Access Patterns in the Web for Data Mining. In: Proceedings of the IEEE International Conference on Tools with Artificial Intelligence, pp. 345–348 (1999)
7. Brown, C.M., Danzig, B.B., Hardy, D., Manber, U., Schwartz, M.F.: The harvest information discovery and access system. In: Proc. 2nd International World Wide Web Conference (1994)
8. Frakes, W.B., Baeza-Yates, R.: Infomation Retrieval Data Structures and Algorithms. Prentice Hall, Englewood Cliffs (1992)

A Hybrid Routing Protocol for Wireless Sensor Network

N. Sengottaiyan[1], Rm. Somasundaram[2], and Balasubramanie[3]

[1] HOD, Dept of IT, Sasurie College of Engineering, Erode 638 056
[2] Dean, Dept of Computer Applications & Applied Sciences,
Nandha Engineering, College, Erode 638 052
[3] Head CSE (PG II) Kongu Engineering College, Perundurai 638 052
nsriram3999@yahoo.co.in

Abstract. Routing protocols in wireless ad-hoc networks are not well suited for Wireless Sensor Networks as they have huge number of nodes, densely deployed and limited power processing and storage. Energy consumption of sensor nodes and their lifetime has become the major issues of Wireless Sensor Networks. This paper aims at building up of hybrid routing protocol based on PROUD and LEACH in Wireless Sensor Networks. For randomly generated nodes with different energy levels, cluster heads are chosen. Every other common node chooses its own cluster heads based on the available cluster choices and thus forming clusters. Cluster heads get sensed data from the common nodes and they send their aggregated data to the Base station for monitoring. So, node to node communication happens through cluster heads. Only cluster heads spend their energy for long range data transmission and thus avoiding energy consumption of other nodes. This procedure of head selection and cluster formation distributes the energy consumption among the nodes thus maximizing the lifetime of Wireless Sensor Networks by extending the life of the nodes. The proposed approach has been justified with results.

Keywords: Wireless Sensor Networks, cluster head, common node, energy consumption, cluster formation.

1 Introduction

A wireless sensor network (WSN) is a wireless network consisting of spatially distributed autonomous devices using sensors to cooperatively monitor physical or environmental conditions, such as temperature, sound, vibration, pressure, motion or pollutants, at different locations [5]. The development of wireless sensor networks was originally motivated by military applications such as battlefield surveillance. In addition to one or more sensors, each node in a sensor network is typically equipped with a radio transceiver or other wireless communications device, a small microcontroller, and an energy source, usually a battery. A sensor network normally constitutes a wireless ad-hoc network, meaning that each sensor supports a multi-hop routing algorithm.

V. V Das et al. (Eds.): BAIP 2010, CCIS 70, pp. 188–193, 2010.

2 Constraints of Sensor Nodes

The inherent properties of sensor networks differentiate them from traditional distributed systems. Hardware Characteristics of MICA is Mote Processor 4Mhz, 8bit MCU (ATMEL), Storage 512KB, Radio 916Mhz Radio, Communication Range 100 ft.

Limited power. Currently, the energy of most sensor nodes is supplied by ordinary batteries (such as MICA motes). We need to consider energy usage as an important factor for both application designs and system evaluations.

High communication cost. Power consumption is dominated by radio communication. In order to conserve the limited power, communication utilization needs to be optimized.

Low computation capability. Even though each sensor node is a micro-processor, the processing speed is much slower than the modern computers. For example, MICA modes use ATMEL processor with clock rate 4Mhz. Hence the sensor node can not process very complex tasks.

Uncertainty. Readings of the sensor nodes may contain errors, which could result from environmental noises, the inherent precision of the sensors themselves. Thus average values should be considered instead of individual readings.

Low bandwidth. In sensor networks, sensor nodes use radio (wireless) to communicate with each other. Since the bandwidth of wireless is very low, it is necessary to decrease the number and the size of messages. Due to these properties, existing techniques developed for traditional distributed systems can not be applied to sensor networks directly.

3 Existing Protocols

3.1 AODV

Ad hoc On-Demand Distance Vector (AODV) Routing is a routing protocol for mobile ad hoc networks (MANETs) and other wireless ad-hoc networks. It is jointly developed in Nokia Research Center of University of California, Santa Barbara and University of Cincinnati by C. Perkins and S. Das. AODV is capable of both unicast and multicast routing. It is a reactive routing protocol, meaning that it establishes a route to a destination only on demand[4]. AODV is, as the name indicates, a distance-vector routing protocol. AODV avoids the *counting-to-infinity* problem of other distance-vector protocols by using sequence numbers on route updates, a technique pioneered by DSDV[2].

3.2 LEACH

Low Energy Adaptive Clustering Hierarchy ("LEACH") is a TDMA-based MAC protocol which is integrated with clustering and a simple routing protocol in wireless sensor networks (WSNs). The goal of LEACH is to provide data aggregation for sensor networks while providing energy efficient communication that does not predictably deplete some nodes more than others[1]. LEACH is a hierarchical protocol in which most nodes transmit to cluster heads, and the cluster heads aggregate and compress the data and forward it to the base station[8].

3.3 DSDV

Destination-Sequenced Distance-Vector Routing (DSDV) is a table-driven routing scheme for ad hoc mobile networks based on the Bellman-Ford algorithm. The main contribution of the algorithm was to solve the Routing Loop problem. Each entry in the routing table contains a sequence number, the sequence numbers are generally even if a link is present; else, an odd number is used. The number is generated by the destination, and the emitter needs to send out the next update with this number[2].

3.4 DSR

Dynamic Source Routing (DSR) is a routing protocol for wireless mesh networks. It is similar to AODV in that it forms a route on-demand when a transmitting computer requests one. However, it uses source routing instead of relying on the routing table at each intermediate device. Many successive refinements have been made to DSR, including DSRFLOW. To accomplish source routing, the routed packets contain the address of each device the packet will traverse. This may result in high overhead for long paths or large addresses, like IPv6. To avoid using source routing, DSR optionally defines a flow id option that allows packets to be forwarded on a hop-by-hop basis. The two phases are Route Discovery and Route Maintenance. The Route Discovery Phase is initiated to determine the most viable route.

3.5 TORA

The Temporally-Ordered Routing Algorithm (TORA) is an algorithm for routing data across Wireless Mesh Networks or Mobile ad-hoc networks. It was developed by Vincent Park at the University of Maryland and the Naval Research Laboratory. [3] Park has patented his work, and it was licensed by Nova Engineering, who are marketing a wireless router product based on Parks algorithm.

4 Proposed Approach

Proposed Hybrid Algorithm. The approach is designed considering the energy factors into account [6] [7]. The proposed method provides communication by managing energy across the sensor nodes using cluster heads [8]. For input, nodes are placed according to the coordinates specified in the scenario file and the following steps are involved.

1. At the start of simulation, energy of all nodes are compared and threshold is set so that there exist at least 10 % of nodes with energy beyond the threshold. Such nodes are elected as cluster heads.
2. These elected cluster heads sends cluster advertisement (Broadcast) message.
3. At this point of time, energy required for transmission is calculated and current energy level is maintained.
4. Nodes which are not elected as cluster heads as a result of step 1 are set to receive these cluster advertisements. Here also there is consumption of energy as nodes receive data. So consumed energy is calculated and current energy levels of nodes are maintained.
5. When a node receives more than one advertisement message it sends JOIN REQUEST to the nearest cluster.
6. In the mean time based on the dissemination type nodes generate sensor data and energy required for sensing is calculated.
7. Based on the disseminating interval node (sensing circuit) goes to sleep mode. Therefore for all of the events triggered by the nodes, energy consumptions are estimated.
8. Once it joins any cluster it sends the aggregated data to base station through its cluster head. Suppose if a node didn't get an advertisement message and generated more than one data then it assumes that no cluster heads are nearer to it and tries to send data directly to base station by broadcast.
9. Cluster heads also generates sensor data and they too send it to base station directly if it is nearer to it else, it sends to all other nearer cluster heads.

5 Results

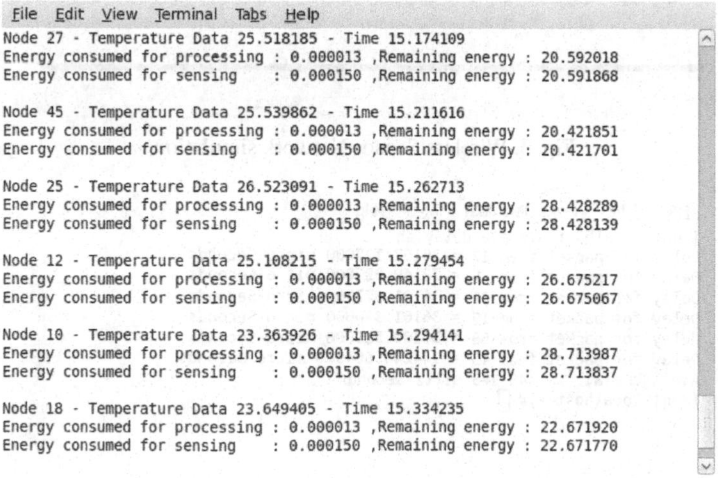

Fig. 1. Terminal Output on execution of Shell script

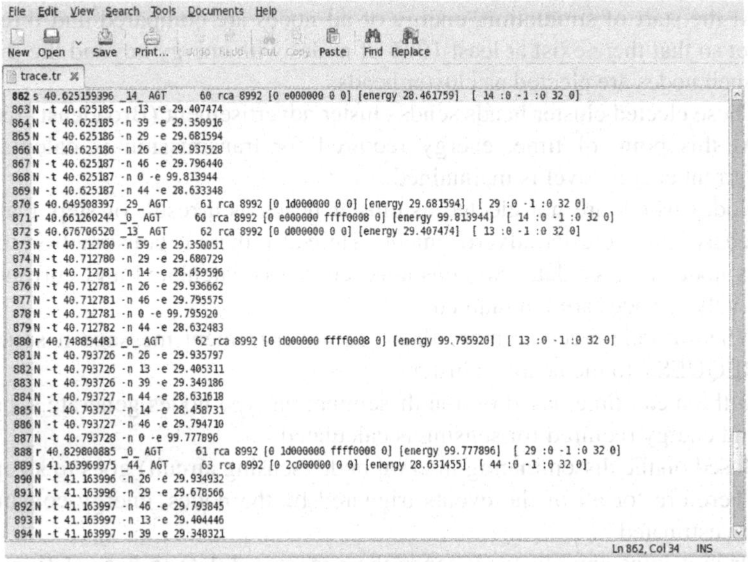

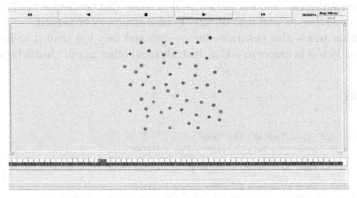

Fig. 2. Trace File

Fig. 3. Wireless Sensor Network simulation

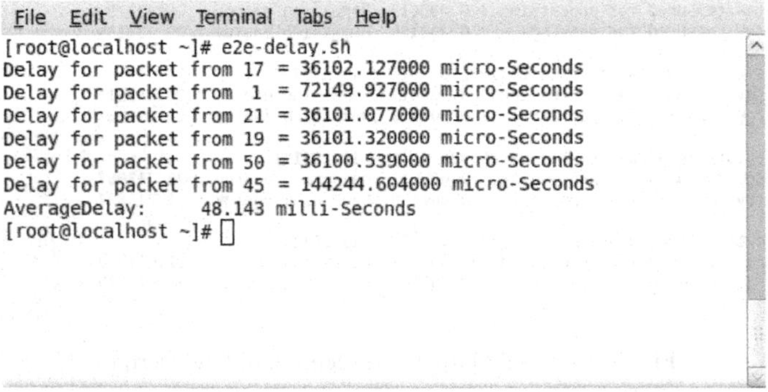

```
File  Edit  View  Terminal  Tabs  Help
[root@localhost ~]# e2e-delay.sh
Delay for packet from 17 = 36102.127000 micro-Seconds
Delay for packet from  1 = 72149.927000 micro-Seconds
Delay for packet from 21 = 36101.077000 micro-Seconds
Delay for packet from 19 = 36101.320000 micro-Seconds
Delay for packet from 50 = 36100.539000 micro-Seconds
Delay for packet from 45 = 144244.604000 micro-Seconds
AverageDelay:     48.143 milli-Seconds
[root@localhost ~]#
```

Fig. 4. End to End Delay calculation

6 Conclusion

Energy consumption is one of the important factors of Wireless Sensor Networks which has been taken care of in an effective way to extend the lifetime of Wireless Sensor Network in the proposed algorithm. The end to end delay factor has improved using the proposed approach. This approach can be further extended with implementation of mobile actuators, with larger buffer than regular nodes, instead of cluster heads to collect data from desired clusters effectively based on PROUD design and present it to Base Station. This greatly helps in achieving maximal performance and minimal energy dissipation for the same sensor nodes.

References

1. Xiangning, F., Yulin, S.: Improvement on LEACH Protocol of Wireless Sensor Network. In: International Conference on Sensor Technologies and Applications, SensorComm., Southeast Univ., Nanjing (2007)
2. IEEE Computer Society: An Efficient DSDV Routing Protocol for Wireless Mobile Ad Hoc Networks and its Performance Comparison. In: Second UKSIM European Symposium on Computer Modeling and Simulation (2008)
3. Amer, S.H., Hamilton, J.A.: DSR and TORA in Fixed and Mobile Wireless Networks. ACM, New York (2008)
4. Directional AODV Routing Protocol for Wireless Mesh Networks, Personal, Indoor and Mobile Radio Communications. In: IEEE 18th International Symposium, PIMRC (2007)
5. Wireless sensor networks: a new regime for time synchronization. ACM SIGCOMM Computer Communication Review (2003)
6. An architecture for energy management in wireless sensor networks. ACM SIGBED Review 4(3) (2007)
7. Distributed energy management algorithm for large-scale wireless sensor networks. In: International Symposium on Mobile Ad Hoc Networking & Computing, Proceedings of the 8th ACM international symposium on Mobile ad hoc networking and computing (2007)
8. Chi, S., Guizani, M., Sharif, H.: Adaptive clustering in wireless sensor networks by mining sensor energy data. ACM, New York (2007)

Efficient Group Key Distribution Mechanism for Dynamic Groups Using Public Key Broadcast Ring

D.V. Naga Raju[1], V. Valli Kumari[2], and K.V.S.V.N. Raju[2]

[1] Shri Vishnu Engineering College for Women, Bhimavaram, India
[2] College of Engineering, Andhra University, Visakhapatnam, India
{nagudatla,vallikumari,kvsvn.raju}@gmail.com

Abstract. Present day advancements in the Internet technologies, especially the increase of bandwidth are definitely encouraging environment for new developments like conferencing, interactive gaming etc. Maintaining security is a critical issue in these group oriented applications. The entry and eviction of the members are the main criteria to change the group key, known as re-keying. Since re-keying is the frequently performed activity during a communication, the group key updating needs to be done in a scalable and efficient manner. This paper proposes two novel ideas: i) Group communication using public key broadcast ring and ii) Region based group communication, for efficient and scalable rekeying. These techniques show their performance in terms of no single point of failure, no need of secure channel establishment, minimum key maintenance at each member, effective bandwidth utilization and minimum computation overhead.

Keywords: Rekeying, Scalability, Broadcast, Group communication.

1 Introduction

The revolutionary developments in Internet technologies which are highly dependent on effective network management techniques need effective and secure transmission algorithms. Up gradation and improving accessibility are the demanding requisites of present technological advancements. The increased bandwidth is encouraging people for the development of new services like secure video conferencing, interactive gaming, stock quotes distribution etc, which are based on group communication model.

Network resources can be best utilized with multicasting for group communication. Providing security is a challenging issue with the dynamic nature of the membership in any group communication model. The activity of key refreshment must be performed very often to maintain the forward and backward secrecy. Forward secrecy in the sense, a member who comes out of the group should not be able to decrypt the future communications. Backward secrecy means when a member newly joins a group should not be allowed to know the old messages. Forward and backward secrecies can be achieved by refreshing the group key.

V. V Das et al. (Eds.): BAIP 2010, CCIS 70, pp. 194–201, 2010.

2 Related Work

Sandro Rafaeli et al [6], Yacine Challal et al [7] conducted an excellent survey group key management protocols. C. K. Wong, M. Gouda, and S. S. Lam [1] proposed Logical Key Hierarchy (LKH). Each node is associated with a KEK (Key Encryption Key) and the members occupy leaf nodes. Each member knows all the KEKs corresponding to the nodes in the path from its leaf to the root. The key corresponding to the root of the tree is the TEK (Traffic Encryption Key). For a balanced binary tree, each member stores at most $1+\log_2 n$ keys. LKH suffers from a single point of failure. Inoue and kuroda [3] proposed FDLKH, in which they used the concept of LKH without any central server. Rakesh Bobba,Himamshu Khurana [2] proposed DLPKH: Distributed Logical Public Key Hierarchy. DLPKH used public key trees which suffer from a high computational overhead. Moreover DLPKH reveals the private keys of ancestor nodes to the respective members. Many of the earlier schemes [1], [2], [3], [4], [5] uses the tree hierarchy for the distribution of the key material to the group. The number of keys maintained at each member, number of key updates, communication overhead increases with the height of the tree.

3 Notations and Terminology

Mi	Member occupies the position i (i=1, 2, 3…)
PK, SK	Public Key and Private Key associated with a member
PK^I, SK^I	updated Public and Private Keys
E (K, X)	Encryption of data X using a key K
GK	Group key
GC	Group controller
SGC	Sub-group controller
DH	Diffie-Hellman key exchange protocol
n	Number of members in a group
SGC_n	Total Number of SGCs
p, g	ElGmal group parameters

4 Group Communication Using Public Key Broadcast Ring

This section describes the basic principle and assumptions of group key management protocol based on public key ring. The proposed scheme assumes a unidirectional logical broadcast ring. There is a group controller (GC, a trusted third party) for the entire group. The scheme uses public key cryptosystem. The public key of the group controller is made public. The GC will maintain the count of the number of members in the ring.

Each member occupies a position in the ring. Each member possesses its own private and public key and also a group key. Each member knows the public keys of its successor and predecessor. Each member also maintains its position (distance from GC) in the ring. This scheme takes the share of a member known as sponsor in the group key generation. The members change their private and public keys using the equations.

$$\text{New public key} = \text{old Public key} \times g^{newGK} \mod p \qquad (1)$$

$$\text{New private key} = \text{old Private Key} + \text{new GK} \mod p \qquad (2)$$

4.1 Join Protocol

When a member wants to join, it sends a join request to the GC encrypted with the public key of the GC. The join request includes the public key of the joining member. The insertion point is always the predecessor of the GC. The sponsor is the member who is the predecessor of the group controller before the join event is happened. For the group size of one, the new member and the GC will exchange the group key using the Diffie-Hellman key exchange algorithm. For group size greater than one, the sponsor and the GC, exchange the new group key using Diffie-Hellman key exchange algorithm. The GC broadcasts the new group key encrypted with the old group key. All the members except the new member get the new group key. The GC also sends to the joining member i) new group key encrypted with the public key of the new member ii) updated public keys of the predecessor (sponsor) and the GC (became the successor for the new member) encrypted with the public key of the new member iii) the new members position. The GC also sends the public key of the new member to the sponsor encrypted with the sponsor's public key. Now all the members get the new group key and update their key pair and the public keys of the successor and predecessor using the equations (1) and (2).

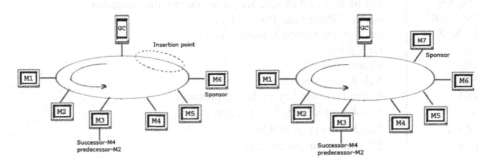

Fig. 1. Ring before join   **Fig. 2.** Ring after join

Suppose a new member wants to join the group. It sends a join request to the GC encrypted with the public key of the GC. The insertion point is between the GC and M6. The sponsor is M6. The new member is given a position seven and become M7. The GC and sponsor (M6) exchange the new group key using DH algorithm. The GC encrypts the new group key with the old group key and broadcast it. The GC also encrypts the new group key and the updated public keys of the predecessor (M6, for new member) and the GC (became the successor for the new member) encrypted with the public key of the new member.

GC →G : E (Old GK, new GK); GC →M7: E (PK of M7, (PK^I of M6, PK^I of GC, new GK))
GC →M6: E (PK of M6, PK of M7)

4.2 Leave Protocol

When a member wants to leave it broadcasts the leave request along with its position in the ring (distance from the GC). The leaving member also broadcasts the public keys of its successor encrypted with the public key of the predecessor and public key of the predecessor encrypted with public key of the successor. The predecessor of the leaving member becomes the sponsor.

Different scenarios of leave: i) If the leaving member position is odd, then all the members (if any) who occupy the odd positions in the ring will send their private keys to the GC (trusted third party). ii) If the leaving member position is even, then all the members (if any) who occupy the even positions in the ring will send their private keys to the GC. iii) If the leaving member is odd and if there exists only one member (even) between the leaving member and the GC this even member sends its public key to the GC encrypted with the GC public key. iv) If the leaving member is even and if there exist only one member (odd) between the leaving member and the GC, then this odd member sends its public key to the GC encrypted with the GC public key. The sponsor will not send its private key to the GC. The GC and the sponsor will exchange the new GK using DH algorithm.

The GC encrypts the new GK with the keys of the responded members. The successor and predecessor of the leaving member will update their public and private key pairs using the equations (1) and (2). All the existing members whose position is less than that of the leaving member will not change their position. All the existing members whose position is greater than that of the leaving member will change their position decrementing by one. After getting the new group key all the existing members update their key pair as well as their successor and predecessor's public keys using the equations (1) and (2).

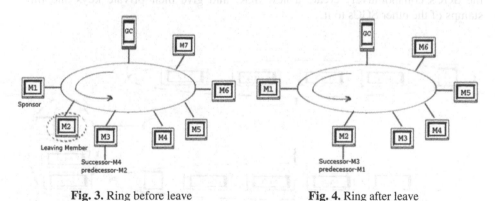

Fig. 3. Ring before leave   **Fig. 4.** Ring after leave

Suppose M2 wants to leave. It sends a leave request containing its position (2 in this case, even position). The leaving member also broadcasts the public key of M3 encrypted with the public key of M1and public key of M1 encrypted with the public key of the M3. Now M1changes its new successor (M3) public key at the same time M3 also change its new predecessor (M1) public key. Now all the members who occupied even positions (M4, M6) will send their private keys to the group controller encrypted with the public key of the GC. GC and sponsor (M1) get new GK using DH algorithm.

GC will send the new group key encrypted with the private keys it receives during the leave phase. All the members will change their positions. The members update the public keys of their successor and predecessor using the equations (1) and (2).

- M2→M3: E (PK of M3, PK of M1)   • M2→M1: E (PK of M1, PK of M3)
- M4→GC: E (PK of GC, SK of M4)   • M6→GC: E (PK of GC, SK of M6)
- GC→G : E (SK of M4, new GK)   • GC→G : E (SK of M6, new GK)

5 Region Based Group Communication

This section discusses the principle and assumption of Region Based Group Communication (Idea-2). In this scheme the entire group is divided into regions. Each region has one Sub Group Controller, SGC and is responsible for that region. Each region has certain capacity. With out loss of generality we assume that the capacity of the region is four. Each member holds the public keys of its successor and predecessor along with its own public and private key and a group key. Each member also knows the public key of the SGC to which it belongs. Each SGC maintains the private keys of the other SGCs and also the group key. Each member maintains the count of the number of members available in its own region. Each SGC maintains the time stamp which tells the time of join of this SGC in the ring. Each SGC also maintains the time stamps of other SGC. The region where there is a room, announces its public key along with the region ID. Two or more regions may also announce their public key at the same time. It is the user choice to choose the region. When there is a need of creation of another region (when there is no room in the existing regions) all the SGCs collaboratively create a new SGC and give their private keys and time stamps of the other SGCs to it.

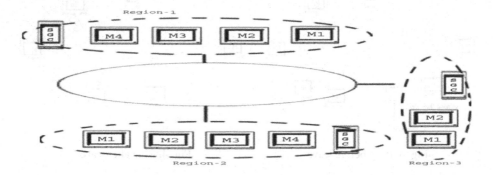

Fig. 5. Region based broadcast ring

5.1 Join Protocol

When a member wants to join a particular region, it encrypts its public key with the public key of the region in which he wants to join. The join protocol is similar to the one we discussed in the section 4.1. After exchanging the new group key with the sponsor the corresponding SGC encrypts the new GK with the old GK and broadcasts it to the entire group. All the members and other SGCs will get the new group key.

5.2 Leave Protocol

When a member wants to leave, it sends a request to its own SGC. The leave request includes the position of the leaving member in the same region, the region ID and also the count of the number of members available in its own region. The other SGCs will remove the entry of the corresponding SGC whose count is zero (after leave). This leave protocol is similar to the previous leave protocol discussed in section 4.2. The sponsor and the SGC use DH for getting the GK. The SGC encrypts the new GK with the private keys of the responded members and also with the private key of the other SGCs it had.

Special case of leave: If only one member is available in a region and if this member wants to leave, it announces its own region id and the number of members available in its own region (one before leave). All the other SGCs will remove the corresponding entry from their data base. A senior SGC (whose time stamp value is higher) will takes the responsibility of generating the new group key and broadcasts the new group key encrypted with the private keys of the other SGCs it had.

6 Analysis

6.1 Cost of Join

Scheme	Entity	DH	Encs	Decrs
Proposed scheme-1	GC	1	3	1
	Sponsor	1	-	1
	New member	-	1	1
	Other members	-	-	1
Proposed scheme-2	Main SGC	1	$3+SGC_{n-1}$	1
	Other SGC	-	-	1
	Sponsor	1		-
	New member	-	1	1
	Other members	-	-	1
FDLKH (Dedicated)	New member	l	-	-
	Other Member	-	-	2
	per Captain	1	1	$(l-1)/2$
FDLKH (Distributed)	New member	1	-	$l-1$
	Other Member	-	-	2
	per Captain□	$(2l-1)/ll$	$(2l-2)/l$	$(l-1)(l-2)/2l$
LKH	Key server	-	$2l$	-
	New member	-	-	1
	Per member	-	-	2

6.2 Cost of Leave

Scheme	Entity	DH	Encs	Decrs
Proposed scheme-1	GC	1	$(n/2)-1$	$(n/2)-1$
	Sponsor(predecessor)	1	-	2
	leaving member	-	-	-
	Successor	-	-	2
	*Other members	-	-	1
Proposed scheme-2	Main SGC	1	$(n/2)-1$	$(n/2)-1$
	Other SGCs	-	-	1
	Sponsor(predecessor)	1	-	2
	leaving member	-	-	1
	Successor	-	-	2
	*Other members	-	-	1
FDLKH (dedicated)	leaving member	-	-	-
	Other Member	-	-	2
	per Captain	1	1	$(l-2)/2$
	Buddy Captain	$l-1$	$l-2$	-
FDLKH (Distributed)	Leaving member	-	-	-
	Other Member	-	-	2
	per Captain	$(2l-2)/l$	$(2l-3)/l$	$(l-1)(l-2)/2l$
LKH	Key server	-	-	-
	New member	-	-	2
	Per member	-	$2l$	-

6.3 Number of Keys at Each Member

S.No	Protocol	Keys
1	Proposed scheme-1	6(constant)
2	Proposed scheme-2	6(constant)
3	FDLKH	l
4	LKH	$l+1$

7 Conclusion

Security maintenance is a critical issue with any group key management protocols. The frequent join and leaves are the main criteria for switching the re-keying process. Earlier several tree based hierarchal protocols were developed but the key maintenance at each member, communication overhead and number of rekey messages increase with respect to the height of the tree. The schemes proposed in this paper use the concept of broadcast ring. The key maintenance by each member, communication overhead is less with the proposed scheme.

References

1. Wong, C.K., Gouda, M., Lam, S.S.: Secure Group Communications Using Key Graphs. IEEE/ACM Transactions on Networking 8(1), 16–30 (2000)
2. Bobba, R., Khurana, H.: DLPKH: Distributed Logical Public Key Hierarchy. In: McDaniel, P., Gupta, S.K. (eds.) ICISS 2007. LNCS, vol. 4812, pp. 110–127. Springer, Heidelberg (2007)

3. Inoue, D., Kuroda, M.: FDLKH: Fully Decentralized Key Management scheme on a Logical Key Hierarchy. In: Jakobsson, M., Yung, M., Zhou, J. (eds.) ACNS 2004. LNCS, vol. 3089, pp. 339–354. Springer, Heidelberg (2004)
4. McGrew, Sherman: Key Establishment in Large Dynamic Groups using One-way Function Trees. IEEE Transactions on Software Engineering 29(5)
5. Ma, C., Ao, J.: Group Rekeying Approach for Group Communication. Information Technology Journal 7(7), 1081–1084 (2008)
6. Rafaeli, S., Hutchison, D.: A survey of key management for secure group communication. ACM Comput. Survey 35(3), 309–329 (2003)
7. Challal, Y., Bouabdallah, A., Seba, H.: A taxonomy of Group Key Management Protocols: Issues and Solutions. Proceedings of World Academy of Science, Engineering and Technology 6 (June 2005), ISSN 1307-6884

Investigation on Effectiveness of Simulation Results for Wireless Sensor Networks

A.K. Dwivedi[1], V.K. Patle[1], and O.P. Vyas[2]

[1] School of Studies in Computer Science & I.T.,
Pandit Ravishankar Shukla University, Raipur (C.G.), India-492010
{anuj.ku.dwivedi,patlevinod}@gmail.com
[2] Indian Institute of Information Technology, Allahabad (IIIT-A),
Deoghat, Jhalwa, Allahabad, U.P., India-211012
dropvyas@gmail.com

Abstract. For research experiments, simulators can be used to get easier access to fine grained results than corresponding real world experiments. One problem with simulators is that it is hard to show that a simulation experiment corresponds well with a similar real world experiment. The objective of this contribution is to investigate the effectiveness of simulation results for Wireless Sensor Networks (WSNs). For such purpose, a detail survey on simulators has been made and it has been found that there are 44 different simulators or simulation frameworks in existence, they are either adjusted or developed specifically for wireless sensor networks. Secondly, with the help of experimental results it is to highlighted, that there is an impact of operating system architectures on simulation results of routing mechanism used in WSNs. And finally our focus is on some factors that influences simulation results for WSNs.

Keywords: Wireless Sensor Networks, Operating System Architectures, Routing Mechanisms, Simulation.

1 Introduction

Wireless Sensor Networks (WSNs) employ a large number of miniature disposable autonomous devices known as sensor nodes to form the network without the aid of any established infrastructure. In a wireless sensor system, the individual nodes are capable of sensing their environments, processing the information locally, or sending it to one or more collection points through a wireless link. Deploying real WSNs testbed provides a realistic testing environment, and allows users to get more accurate test results. However, deploying real testbed is highly constrained by the available budget for research institutes when the test needs a large scale WSNs environment, thus use of simulators is a better option. Simulation is a powerful technique for studying the behavior of networks (it may be WSNs also) before implementing the real one. The aim of any simulator is to accurately model and predict the real physical conditions. Many published papers contain results only based on experimental simulation process. Researchers and developers of WSNs are provided with information on feasibility and reflectivity crucial to the

V. V Das et al. (Eds.): BAIP 2010, CCIS 70, pp. 202–208, 2010.

implementation of the system prior to investing significant time and money. Since with WSNs, hardware may have to be purchased in large quantities and at high cost. Even with readily available wireless sensor nodes, testing the network in the desired environment can be a costlier, time consuming and difficult task. Simulation-based testing can help to indicate whether or not these time and monetary investments are wise. Selecting an appropriate simulator for research is a challenging task. Simulator should enable the definition of different network nodes, network topologies, communication scenarios, and of course routing protocols. Also it should enable to simulate and measurement of different significant performance meters, like latency, power consumption, load balancing etc. using known mathematical formulas.

2 Problem Formation

After studying and reviewing a number of research papers it has been found that most research papers are based on simulation results, which are a type of comparative study of routing protocols on various factors which is mostly based on scenario conditions, energy efficiency, security, QoS etc. Through this contribution objective is to explore the effectiveness of simulation results for WSNs. For achieving desired objective, first a detail survey on simulators has been made, with presenting highly summarized pros and cons of each simulator or simulation framework with respect to WSNs. Secondly evaluating the impact of operating system architecture on simulation results of routing mechanisms used in WSNs. For such purpose two popular wireless sensor node's operating systems has been chosen, namely TinyOS and Contiki in term of their use on sensor nodes, as well as both have different architecture and having inbuilt simulation environments support namely TOSSIM and COOJA respectively. With TinyOS and Contiki, two popular traditional operating systems MS Windows XP and Turbo Linux has been selected, which have different design architectures on which they are built. For Windows XP, GlomoSIM simulator has been selected and for Turbo Linux, MannaSim and GlomoSIM has been selected, to get the experimental results. Finally some focus has been made on other common issues that make question marks on the effectiveness of simulation results for WSNs.

3 Simulators for Wireless Sensor Networks

Since, a simulator is a software tool that imitates selected parts of the behavior of the real world and is normally used as a tool for research and development. Depending on the intended usage of the simulator, different parts of the real-world system are modeled and imitated. The parts that are modeled can also be of varying abstraction level. A wireless sensor network simulator imitates the wireless network media - the air - and the nodes in the network. Some sensor network simulators have a detailed model of the wireless media including effects of obstacles between nodes, while other simulators have a more abstract model. Wireless Sensor Network Simulators can be categories as [1]:

3.1 Generic Network Simulators

Generic network simulators simulate systems with a focus on networking aspects. The user of the simulator typically writes the simulation application in a high level language different from the one used for the real sensor network. Since the focus of the simulation is on networking the simulator typically provides detailed simulation of the radio medium, but less detailed simulation of the nodes.

3.2 Code Level Simulators

Code level simulators use the same code in simulation as in real sensor network nodes. The code is compiled for the machine that is running the simulator, typically a PC workstation that is magnitudes faster than the sensor node. Typically code level simulators are operating system specific since they need to replace driver code for the sensors and radio chips available on the node with driver code that instead have hooks into the simulator.

3.3 Firmware Level Simulators

These types of simulators are based on emulation of the sensor nodes and the software that runs in the simulator is the actual firmware that can be deployed in the real sensor network. This approach gives the highest level of detail in the simulation and enables accurate execution statistics. This type of simulation provides emulation of microprocessor, radio chip and other peripherals and simulation of radio medium. Due to the high level of detail provided by firmware level simulators, they are usually slower than code level or generic network simulators.

Several simulators and simulation frameworks exist that are either adjusted or developed specifically for wireless sensor networks. An extensive survey has been made on simulators especially useful for WSNs; here is the list of 44 simulators and simulation frameworks for WSNs: Network Simulator (NS), Mannasim (NS-2 Extension for WSNs), TOSSIM, TOSSF, PowerTOSSIM, ATEMU, COOJA, GloMoSim (Global Mobile Information Systems Simulation), QualNet, SENSE, VisualSENSE, AlgoSenSim, Georgia Tech Network Simulator (GTNetS), OMNet++, Castalia, J-Sim (formerly JavaSim), JiST/SWANS (Java in Simulation Time/ Scalable Wireless Ad hoc Network Simulator), JiST/SWANS++, Avrora, Sidh, Prowler, (J)Prowler, LecsSim, OPNET, SENS, EmStar/Em*, EmTOS, SenQ, SIDnet-SWANS, SensorSim, Shawn, SSFNet (Scalable Simulation Framework), Atarraya, NetTopo, WSNet + WSim, WiseNet, SimGate, SimSync, SNetSim, SensorMaker, TRMSim-WSN, *PAWiS*, OLIMPO and DiSenS (Distributed SENsor network Simulation).

4 Evaluating Impact of O.S. Architectures on Simulation Results

The below given table presents summarized information related to operating systems used by us for our experimental purposes.

Table 1. Operating Systems, their supported platforms and architecture

S. No.	Operating System and Type	Supported Platforms	Operating System Architecture
1.	TinyOS (Sensor Node OS)	BTnode, EyesIF X v1, EyesIF X v2, IMote, IMote 1.0, IMote 2.0, Iris, KMote, Mica, Mica2, MicaZ, Rene, SenseNode, TelosB, T-Mote Sky, Shimmer	Monolithic
2.	Contiki (Sensor Node OS)	T-Mote Sky, TelosB, avr MCU, MSP430 MCU, x86, 6502	Modular (Micro)
3.	Windows XP (Traditional OS)	Personal Computers, including home and business desktops, notebook computers, and media centers.	Hybrid (Macro)
4.	Turbolinux10 (Traditional OS)	Personal Computers, including home and business desktops, notebook computers, and media centers.	Monolithic

4.1 Experimental Result-1

Number of Sensor Nodes :   25
Routing Protocol   :   AODV
Simulation Time   :   15 Minutes (900 Seconds)

Operating System	Simulator with OS	Total Packet Sent	Total Packet Received
Sensor Node OS	COOJA with Contiki	275525	260612
	TOSSIM with TinyOS	230612	205236
Traditional OS for PC	GlomoSim on Microsoft Windows XP	77824	3072
	GlomoSim on Turbolinux10	82782	4381
	MannaSim on Turbolinux10	1453543	913666

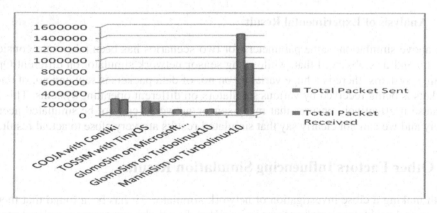

Fig. 1. Graphical representation of experimental result-1

4.2 Experimental Result-2

Number of Sensor Nodes   :   50
Routing Protocol   :   AODV
Simulation Time   :   10 Minutes (600 Seconds)

Operating System	Simulator with OS	Total Packet Sent	Total Packet Received
Sensor Node OS	COOJA with Contiki	495945	481732
	TOSSIM with TinyOS	392040	369426
Traditional OS for PC	GlomoSim on Microsoft Windows XP	124518	17236
	GlomoSim on Turbolinux10	151493	8456
	MannaSim on Turbolinux10	2775801	1604239

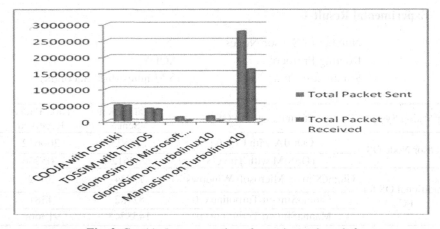

Fig. 2. Graphical representation of experimental result-2

4.3 Analysis of Experimental Result

For above simulation, same parameters for two scenarios has been taken into consideration and it is observed that, while using sensor network simulator on different Operating Systems, there is a huge variation on no. of data packets is sent and no. of data packets is being received by various simulators on different operating systems. This is because it effectively ensures that many sensor networks can not be simulated accurately and we can not clearly say that simulated results are very close to actual result.

5   Other Factors Influencing Simulation Results

With making a close investigation of network simulators, it has been found that there are several problems in order to use a simulator directly because most simulator users do not need to know how the simulator's core (kernel) works. According to our study these are the some factors that really influence the simulation results: The first one is that all of cases simulators use a simulated clock, which advances in constant increments of time. Constant increment of time is decided by time stamp of the earliest event. So we must replace simulation clock with real system clock; the second one is that all simulators has its own protocol stack in its core (kernel) called simulator protocol stack. There are several problems in order to use a simulator protocol stack as a real network protocol stack, such as most of the simulators have various redundant protocols at various levels of simulator protocol stack to support other types of networks for example TCP/IP based networks, Wireless Mesh Networks, Mobile Ad hoc Networks etc. The simulator also includes different radio, mobility, and propagation models. So according to our view these unnecessary redundant components must be removed in order to use a simulator protocol stack as a real protocol stack for WSNs; the third one is that all simulators have its own architecture and design objectives. We have not evaluated but we can say that these factors could also influences the simulation results.

6 Conclusion

The objectives of this paper were to prove the effectiveness of simulation results for wireless sensor networks. In this research contribution, first a detail survey on simulators and simulation frameworks has been made and it has been observed that most one are either adjusted or developed specifically for wireless sensor networks. Secondly, we highlight the impact of operating system architectures on simulation results of routing mechanism used in WSNs with the help of experimental results and it has been observed that for the same scenario conditions and parameters, while using sensor network simulator on different Operating System, there is a huge variation on no. of data packets is sent and no. of data packets is being received by various simulators on different operating systems. And finally, this contribution is focused on factors that really influences simulation results for WSNs such as simulators uses a simulated clock, which advances in constant increments of time, simulators has its own protocol stack in its core (kernel) called simulator protocol stack, and all simulators have its own architecture and design objectives.

References

1. Eriksson, J.: Detailed Simulation of Heterogeneous Wireless Sensor Networks. Dissertation for the degree of Licentiate of Philosophy in Computer Science at Uppsala University, Sweden (2009), ISSN 1404-5117
2. Dunkels, A., Gronvall, B., Voigt, T.: Contiki - a Lightweight and Flexible Operating System for Tiny Networked Sensors. In: 1st IEEE Workshop on Embedded Networked Sensors (2004)
3. Mannasim Simulator Information, http://www.mannasim.dcc.ufmg.br
4. UC Berkeley TOSSIM Information,
   http://www.cs.berkeley.edu/~pal/research/tossim.html
5. Glomosim's Academic Ver. 2.0, http://pcl.cs.ucla.edu/projects/glomosim/academic/register.html
6. Lessmann, J., Janacik, P., Lachev, L., Orfanus, D.: Comparative Study of Wireless Network Simulators. In: 7th International Conference on Networking-ICN 2008, pp. 517–523 (2008)

7. Varshney, M., Xu, D., Srivastava, M., Bagrodia, R.: SenQ: a Scalable Simulation and Emulation Environment For Sensor Networks. In: 6th International Conference on Information Processing in Sensor Networks, Cambridge, Massachusetts, USA (2007)
8. Girod, L., Ramanathan, N., Elson, J., Stathopoulos, L.T.M., Estrin, D.: Emstar- A Software Environment for Developing and Deploying Heterogeneous Sensor-Actuator Networks. ACM Transactions on Sensor Networks (TOSN) 3(3), 13 (2007)
9. Ghica, O.C., Trajcevski, G., Scheuermann, P., Bischof, Z., Valtchanov, N.: SIDnet-SWANS: A Simulator and Integrated Development Platform for Sensor Networks Applications. In: 6th ACM conference on Embedded network sensor systems, Raleigh, NC, USA (2008)
10. Titzer, B.L., Lee, D.K., Palsberg, J.: Avrora- Scalable Sensor Network Simulation with Precise Timing. In: 4th International Symposium on Information Processing in Sensor Networks, Los Angeles, California (2005)
11. Sundresh, S., Kim, W., Agha, G.: SENS - A Sensor, Environment and Network Simulator. In: 37th Annual Symposium on Simulation, p. 221 (2004)
12. Wen, Y., Gurun, S., Chohan, N., Wolski, R., Krintz, C.: Accurate and Scalable Simulation of Network of Heterogeneous Sensor Devices. Journal of Signal Processing Systems 50(2), 115–136 (2008)
13. Fekete, Kroller, S.P., Fischer, A., Pfisterer, S., Braunschweig, D.: Shawn-The Fast, Highly Customizable Sensor Network Simulator. In: 4th International Conference on Networked Sensing Systems. IEEE Xplore (2007), ISBN: 1-4244-1231-5
14. Shu, L., Hauswirth, M., Zhang, Y., Mao, S., Xiong, N., Chen, J.: NetTopo-A Framework of Simulation and Visualization for Wireless Sensor Networks. Submitted to ACM/Springer Mobile Networks and Applications-MONET (2009)
15. Fraboulet, A., Chelius, G., Fleury, E.: Worldsens-Development and Prototyping Tools for Application Specific Wireless Sensors Networks. In: 6th International Conference on Information Processing in Sensor Networks, Cambridge, USA (2007)
16. Wen, Y., Gurun, S., Chohan, N., Wolski, R., Krintz, C.: SimGate-Full-System, Cycle-Close Simulation of the Stargate Sensor Network Intermediate Node. In: International Conference on Architectures, Modeling and Simulation IC-SAMOS. IEEE Xplore (2006)
17. Xu, C., Zhao, L., Xu, Y., Li, X.: Time Synchronization Simulator and Its Application. In: 1st IEEE Conference on Industrial Electronics and Applications (2006), ISBN: 0-7803-9513-1
18. Yi, S., Min, H., Cho, Y., Hong, J.: SensorMaker: A Wireless Sensor Network Simulator for Scalable and Fine-Grained Instrumentation. In: Book-Computational Science and Its Applications. Springer, Heidelberg (2008)
19. Gómez, F., Martínez, G.: TRMSim-WSN, Trust and Reputation Models Simulator for Wireless Sensor Networks. In: IEEE International Conference on Communications, Germany (2009)
20. Polley, J., Blazakis, D., McGee, J., Rusk, D., Baras, J.S., Karir, M.: ATEMU- A Fine-Grained Sensor Network Simulator. In: 1st Annual IEEE Communications Society Conference on Sensor and Ad Hoc Communications and Networks (SECON 2004), Santa Clara, Calif., USA, pp. 145–152 (2004)
21. Weber, D., Glaser, J., Mahlknecht, S.: Discrete Event Simulation Framework for Power Aware Wireless Sensor Networks. In: 5th IEEE International Conference on Industrial Informatics (2007)
22. Barbancho, J., Molina, F.J., León, C., Ropero, J., Barbancho, A.: OLIMPO-An Ad-Hoc Wireless Sensor Network Simulator for Optimal SCADA-Applications. In: Communication Systems and Networks (CSN), Marbella, Spain (2004)
23. Wen, Y., Wolski, R., Moore, G.: DiSenS-Scalable Distributed Sensor Network Simulation. UCSB Computer Science Technical Report, University of California (2005)

A Novel Multipath Routing Scheme in Mobile Adhoc Networks

N. Jaisankar[1], R. Saravanan[2], and K. Durai Swamy[3]

[1,2] School of Computer Science and Engineering, VIT University, Vellore, India
[3] K.S.R.C.T., Tiruchengodu, India
{njaisankar,rsaravanan}@vit.ac.in, deanac@ksrct.ac.in

Abstract. Mobile adhoc network is a set of mobie devices that can communicate with each other without infrastructure. The reactive protocols use a flood-based discovery mechanism to find routes when required. Since each route discovery incurs high overhead and latency, the frequency of route discoveries must be kept low for on-demand protocols to be effective. Multipath on-demand routing protocols can achieve better performance and scalability because in the single route discovery process it will find out the several routes. This paper proposed a novel multipath routing scheme which is used to reduce the routing overhead by using derived paths. The multipath routing scheme calculates fail-safe multiple routes and gives all the in between nodes of the prime path with several paths to target node. Simulations show that the performance of proposed approach is better than the conventional AODV.

Keywords: MANET, Multipath routing, AODV, Primary path; derived path.

1 Introduction

Mobile Ad hoc Networks (MANETs) are formed by wireless hosts which may be mobile and opeate without pre-existing infrastructure. In MANET, nodes are act as a router. The mobile nodes may send packets to many in between nodes to reach the destination. In that case, each node acts as a router for forwarding packets to the next hop node. Mobile adhoc networks have less battery power, dynamic topology. So the routing protocols are designed to adopt the dynamic nature and pesist to sustain the link between the hosts even if the breakage in the paths.

The objective of the paper is to build up several routes in order to get better scalability. Spontaneously, finding the several routes in a single route discovery from source to destination decreases the routing overhead. In the multipath routing, if the prime path fails owing to mobility of the node or battery down, the derived paths can be used to send the packets to the target node.It evades the additional oberhead produced by new route discovery. When the route breaks are high in the large networks, these multiple paths are more useful.

While the sending node wants to send the data to target node and it does not have suitable path to the target node, the sending node initiate the timer and transmit the route request packet to the target node with unique route request ID. As soon as the sending node receives reply form the target node, it revises its routing table and launches the

V. V Das et al. (Eds.): BAIP 2010, CCIS 70, pp. 209–216, 2010.
© Springer-Verlag Berlin Heidelberg 2010

sending packet. If the timer expires in the middle, the sending node increases the route request ID and starts a fresh request to the target node. By using the several paths in the multipath routing, high thoughput and load balancing can be achived.

The rest of the paper is organized as follows. In section 2, surveys of the previous works have been given. In section 3, we present the proposed framework. Then in section 4, we describe the simulation results and performance evaluation metrics. Finally, we conclude in section 5.

2 Related Works

In this study we have given a brief review of routing protocols which is for multipath routing. In most cases the ability of creating multiple routes from a source to a destination is used to provide a backup route. When the primary route fails to deliver the packets in some way, the backup is used. This provides a better fault tolerance and efficient recovery from route failures. Multiple paths can also provide load balancing and route failure protection by distributing traffic among a set of paths. Multiple paths between a source and a destination can be disjoint in two ways: (a) link-disjoint paths and (b) node-disjoint paths. There is no common node in the node disjoint paths whereas there is no common link in the link-disjoint pahts.

Sung-Ju Lee and Mario Gerla proposed AODV-BR [2] routing protocol. The AODV-BR protocol uses the route discovery process as AODV [1]. While a sending node needs a route to a target node, and there is no route to that target node in its route cache, it searches a route by flooding a route request (RREQ) packet. Each of these packets has a unique ID so intermediate nodes can detect and drop duplicates. When an intermediate node receives a RREQ, it records the previous hop and the sending node information and then floods the packet or launce a route reply (RREP) packet back to the sending node if a route to the preferred destination is identified. The target node launches a RREP via the chosen route while it gets the first RREQ or later RREQs that navigated an improved route (with fewer hops).

Mahesh K. Marina Samir R. Das proposed AOMDV [3] routing protocol. Like AODV-BR, the AOMDV uses the basic AODV route construction process. In this protocol some extensions are made to create multiple loop-free, link-disjoint paths. The basic plan in AOMDV is to calculate several paths in path discovery. It consists of two components: (i) a path revise rule to set up and sustain several loop-free rouets at all nodes.

S.Lee and Mario Gerla proposed SMR [4] protocol. It provides way of determining maximally disjoint paths. Paths are maximally disjoint when they are node disjoint, but when there are no node-disjoint paths available, the protocol minimizes the number of common nodes. Multiple routes are discovered on demand, one of which is the route with the minimum delay. The routes established by the protocol are not necessarily equal in length.

To overcome the drawbacks of the shortest path routing protocols, investigators have proposed multipath routing. Multipath routing protocols recommend for MANET can be categorized as (a) delay aware multipath routing protocols, (b) trustworthy multipath routing protocols, (c) less overhead multipath routing protocols, (d) energy saving multipath routing protocols and (e) hybrid multipath routing protocols.

Delay aware multipath routing protocols suggestd in [5], [6], [7]), select the several paths so that the total delay and performance of a network is get better. Reliable multipath routing protocols suggested in [8], [9] sustain dependable data transfer between a sending node and the target node. Energy saving multipath routing protocols recommended in Dulman et al. [10] makes best use of the network life by using energy efficient route selection. Hybrid multipath routing protocols suggested in Wang et al. [11] employ both the shortest path and the multipath algorithms to fit in the improvements of both algorithms.

3 Proposed Architecture

A novel multipath routing scheme called Multipath on-demand Routing (MORT) has been proposed in this paper to reduce the route breakage overhead. It presents several paths on the in-between nodes on the prime path to target along with source node. Prime path is the foremost path obtain by the sending node subsequent to initiating the route discovery, which is generally the shortest path. The further route discovery when the prime path fails and decrease the route error packet broadcasted while route break discovery.

In the multipath routing protocols the superior performance can be attained by keeping more than one possible path. Because of the advantage of network redundancy, reduce congestion, and address QoS issues, the multipath routing in the wired networks has been proposed. Finding the several paths in mobile adhoc networks takes the advantages of achieving lower delay, increased fault tolerance, lower power consumption, and high security. The numerous link breaks occurs in mobile adhoc networks due to node mobility. So the perodic route request packet should be broadcasted to find out the route which leads a higher routing overhead and route establishment delay. The main advantage of finding multiple paths using multipath routing is even the prime path fails the packet can be transmitted in the path without waiting for the new dicovery of the route.

In the simulation, the proposed scheme is used to compute fail-safe multiple routes between source and destination pair and to maintain them in a route table as backup routes for data transmission. This task is achieved by extending the structure of route reply packet and the route table. This module extends the RREP control packet with additional fields. The RREQ packet structure is similar to AODV. Also creates two different tables Request Received Table and Route Table. Request Received Table entry is used for sending the RREP back to the source. Route Table maintains multiple route entries in a single discovery.

In the proposed scheme, each node maintains trust table in which the trust value of the path is stored. Each node monitors its neighbour's node. If the node successfully delivers the packet, then the trust value is increased. Otherwise, trust value is decreased. When a source node receives the route reply packet from the destination, it calculates the trust value of all the nodes in the path. The highest trust value path can be considered as most suitable path for safe transfer of packets.

RREQ packet creation
This packet is created based on the IETF format specification. The fields are:

PacketType: To identify the type of packet, SrcAddr: The node address which generates RREQ, SrcSeqN: Sequence number of source node, BcastId: Request Id of RREQ, DestAdd: Destination node address, Dest SeqNo: Sequence number of destination node, Hopcount: Number of hops from source.

RREP packet creation
The RREP packet is created with three additional fields. The format of RREP is:

PacketType: To identify the type of packet, SrcAdd: The node address which generates RREQ, DestAdd: Destination node address, Repgen: Address of the node which generates the RREP, Mulrep: Is a Boolean value. Set TRUE for the first Reply, Nodelist: List of node address which relayed the RREQ, Hopcount: Number of hops to reach the source node, trust table-trust value of the path.

RERR packet creation
PacketType: To identify the type of packet, NodeAddr: Address of node where link failure is occurred.

Route Request Table creation
LastHopAddress: The node which relayed the RREQ packet, Hopcount : Number of hops traversed from source.

Route Table creation
DestAddr: Address of the destination Node, RouteList: This filed holds multiple routes with the following values: nexthop, hopcount, lifetime, and fullpath. PrecurList: Holds list of nodes that relayed a RREQ packet.

The overall operation of the proposed scheme has been explained below.

Route discovery process
For finding the route from source node to target node, the source node relays an RREQ packet to its neighbours. The in-between node receives the packet and stores the node IP address in the route request table for sending the reply packet. When the in-between nodes get the route request packet next time, it will check the node's IP address with the table. If it is any match, then that particular packet would be discarded else stores a node details into the request received table. After storing the node details it checks for route to a destination is exist in its routing table. If this check is passed then creates a RREP and send to the source using request received table entry. If not it re-broadcasts the RREQ packet by incrementing the hopcount. When a RREQ is received by destination node itself it stores the node address which relayed the RREQ in the request received table and creates a RREP, updates its routing table and send the RREP to its upstream nodes using request received table information.

Route repley process
If any in-between nodes receive the route request packet will send unicast route reply packet back. So the source node gets several unicasts reply. The target node sends the

route reply packet to source node for the first arrived route request packet to set up the prime path. The target node creates the route reply packet based on the route reply extension fileds for the arrival of the delayed route request packet. The maximum number of route reply packet generated by the destination is based on the MAX_REPLY field. The in-between nodes get the first route request packet will be forwarded to its neighbouring node based on the reuest received table which is used to set up the reverse route to source and revise the routing table. By using the node list, the routing loop can be eliminated easily. If any node gets the delayed route reply packet, it revises the routing table like the route request extension by rejecting the route reply packet. The prime path can be set up by the source node which receives the first route reply packet. The source node formed the remaining secondary paths by receiving the subsequent route reply packets. Once the prime path is established, the data transfer commenced.

Route error process

The route breakage can be identified when a node does not get HELLO packets from the neighboring nodes. When the backup routes are not in neighboring node, the node nullify the routing table and locate the predecessor lists to transmit the route error packet to its neighboring nodes. If not, the nodes alter the existing route into backup route immediately. The eliminating the further route discovery leads to lessening of packet delay and the total number of routing packets in the networks. When the link failure detected by using HELLO packets, the node can revise the backup route exiration timer and broaden its life cycle.

4 Simulation Results

Experimental setup

The proposed multi path routing scheme has been implemented using the Global Mobile Information System Simulator library. The simulation environment consists of different number of nodes in a rectangular region of varying size. The nodes are randomly placed in the region and each of them has a radio range of 150 meters. Five sessions of Constant Bit Rate flows are developed for data transmission. The random waypoint model is chosen as the node mobility model. Simulation time is 300 seconds. Each scenario is simulated five times and an average is taken for the performance analysis. For the node mobility, random waypoint model has been chosen. All data packets are 512 bytes. The following metrics used to analyze the scalability and performance of AODV for 100 to 1000 nodes. Between randomly picked source-destination pairs, five CBR sessions have been produced. In order to analyze the performance of the proposed scheme, it is evaluated against the three matrices namely: Throughput, Control Packets and End-to-End Delivery Ratio.

Network Throughput

Network throughput can be calculated based on the ratio of the number of packets actually arrived at the target node to the number of packets sent by the source node. The nework thoughput can be directly controlled by the packet loss. This is origined by networks failure or disobliging behavior.

End-to-end delay
End-to-end delay can be calculated based on the average delay between the transfer-ring of data packet by the CBR and its reception at the corresponding CBR.

In order to evaluate and compare the performance of proposed scheme, a most widely used unipath on demand protocol AODV is chosen. The performance of the AODV is evaluated using three metrics. Throughput, delay, overhead by varying node speed.

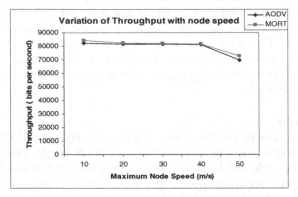

Fig. 1. Variation of throughput with node speed

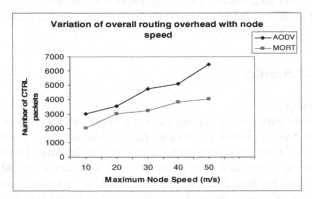

Fig. 2. Variation of routing overhead with node speed

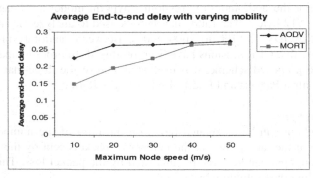

Fig. 3. Variation of packet transmission delay with node speed

Figure 1, 2 and 3 shows the throughput, routing overhead, packet transmission comparison of proposed scheme (MORT) and AODV by varying node speed. When the node mobility increases, the protocol acts like anticipated. Overhead in the routing and the packet dropping increases with node mobility due to large route breakage during the mobility. The proposed scheme attains progress over AODV caused by usage of derived paths.The routing overhads are increased heavily in AODV when node mobility. The proposed schme also improves its performance than the conventional AODV owing to handling of fail-safe multiple paths to restore path breakage.

5 Conclusions

This proposed a novel multipath routing scheme to get better scalability and secured path. At the same time, finding several paths in a single path discovery decreased the overhead on routing. Also, multipath routing provides load balancing and decreases the path finding process again and again. This can be considered as main benefits of the multipath routing.Finding the multiple paths involved with every other's transmissions and rate of penetrating for suitable multiple paths is generally superior than the single path. In future, we are planning to develop the security protocol in the multipath routing for safe routing.

References

1. Perkins, C.E., Royer, E.M.: Ad-hoc On-Demand Distance Vector Routing scalability. Mobile computing and communication Review 1(2) (2002)
2. Lee, S.J., Gerla, M.: AODV-BR: Backup Routing in ad hoc networks. In: IEEE Wireless Communications and Networking Conference WCNC, September 2000, vol. 3, pp. 1311–1316 (2000)
3. Marina, M.K., Das, S.R.: AOMDV: On-demand Multipath Distance Vector Routing in Ad Hoc Networks. ACM SIGMOBILE Mobile Computing and Communications Review 6(3), 92–93 (2002)
4. Lee, S.-J., Gerla, M.: Split Multipath Routing with Maximally Disjoint Paths in Ad hoc Networks. In: Proceedings of IEEE International Conference on Communications (June 2001)
5. Lim, H., Xu, K., Gerla, M.: TCP performance over multipath routing in mobile ad hoc networks. In: IEEE international conference on communication (ICC), vol. 2, pp. 1064–1068 (2003)
6. Liang, Q., Ren, Q.: Energy and mobility aware geographical multipath routing for wireless sensor networks. In: Proceedings of the IEEE wireless communications and networking conference, March 2005, vol. 3, pp. 1867–1871 (2005)
7. Jing, F., Bhuvaneswaran, R.S., Katayama, Y., Takahashi, N.: A multipath on-demand routing with path selection probabilities for mobile ad hoc networks. In: Proceedings of the international conference on wireless communications, networking and mobile computing 2005, vol. 2, pp. 1145–1148 (2005)
8. Tsirigos, A., Haas, Z.J., Tabrizi, S.S.: Multipath routing in mobile ad hoc networks or how to route in the presence of frequent topology changes. In: Proceedings of the military communications conference, Vienna, Virginia, October 2001, vol. 2, pp. 878–883 (2001)

9. Yao, Z., Jiang, J., Fan, P., Cao, Z., Vok, L.: A neighbor table based multipath routing in ad hoc networks. In: 57th IEEE semiannual vehicular technology conference, April 2003, vol. 3, pp. 1739–1743 (2000)
10. Dulman, S., Wu, J., Havinga, P.: An energy efficient multipath routing algorithm for wireless sensor networks. In: Proceedings of the 6th international symposium on autonomous decentralized systems with an emphasis on advanced distributed transportation systems, Pisa, Italy (April 2003)
11. Wang, L., Jang, S., Lee, T.-Y.: Redundant source routing for real-time services in ad hoc networks. In: Proceedings of IEEE international conference on mobile ad hoc and sensor systems conference, Washington, DC (November 2005)

A Novel Security Approach for Detecting Black Hole Attack in MANET

N. Jaisankar[1], R. Saravanan[2], and K. Durai Swamy[3]

[1,2] School of Computer Science and Engineering, VIT University, Vellore, India
[3] K.S.R.C.T., Tiruchengodu, India
{njaisankar,rsaravanan}@vit.ac.in, deanac@ksrct.ac.in

Abstract. A mobile ad hoc network (MANETs) consists of a group of mobile nodes which are connected by wireless links. The peculiar characteristics of MANET like open medium, high dynamic nature of the network lead to various attacks which partition or destroy entire network. A black hole attack can be working in opposition to routing in mobile adhoc networks. A black hole node is a malicious node which sends the fake reply for route requests and drops the packets. In this paper, a novel approach is proposed to detect blackhole nodes in the MANET. Our solutions find out the safe route between sending node and receiving node. The simulations show that the proposed approach is efficient than normal AODV when the black hole attack is present with high packet delivery and less packet drop.

Keywords: mobile adhoc networks, blackhole attack, AODV, routing protocol.

1 Introduction

An ad-hoc network is a multi-hop wireless network where all nodes are connected with each other without any centralized infrastructure. Each node acts not only as a host but also as a router. The receiving node is not in the transmission range, the sending node relaying packets for other node. Routing is the heart of the network. The main goal of the routing protocol is to establish and maintain the route thus avoiding stale routes and delay due to link breaks and failures.

The attacks in mobile ad hoc networks are classified into two types. They are active attacks and passive attacks. Mobile adhoc networks are highly vulnerable to active attacks. These include modification of data, deleting the content, dropping the packets, replication of the data. Some of the attacks that can be easily performed over mobile adhoc networks are blackhole attack, warmhole attack, rushing attack, spoofing, routing table overflow. Among the above mentioned attacks, black hole attack shows great impact on the performance of the network.

The following problems may occur in the AODV protocol. The misbehaving nodes may perform harmful operations by not following the protocol.

1. Masquerade as a source node S by falsifying a RREQ
2. When forwarding a RREQ, decrease the hop count field
3. Masquerade as a destination node D by falsifying a RREP

V. V Das et al. (Eds.): BAIP 2010, CCIS 70, pp. 217–223, 2010.
© Springer-Verlag Berlin Heidelberg 2010

So, this type of attack should be detected and removed from the network efficiently thereby establishing safe routes.The black hole attacks show great impact on the on-demand distance vector routing protocol (AODV). This paper aims to detect black hole attacks in AODV routing protocol.

The rest of the paper is organized as follows. In section 2, surveys of the previous works have been given. In section 3, we present the proposed framework. Then in section 4, we describe the simulation results and performance evaluation metrics. Finally, we conclude in section 5.

2 Related Works

In this section, we presented a survey of some of the approaches to solve the problem of routing misbehavior in ad hoc networks. Satoshi Kurosawa1, Hidehisa Nakayama, Nei Kato, Abbas Jamalipour, and Yoshiaki Nemoto's [1], proposed an anomaly detection scheme using dynamic training method in which the training data is updated at regular time intervals. According to V Sankaranarayanan and Latha Tamilselvan [2], they projected a technique that source will verfiy the reply packet coming from various nearest nodes to wait and check the replies from all the neighboring nodes to discover best possible and secure route. M. A. Shurman, S. M. Yoo, and S. Park [3] proposed a method where a source node verifies the authenticity of the node which sends the first RREP to it.The verification is done by checking the next hop fields of two or more replies from neighboring nodes. The request originator waits for two or more RREP packets.

S. Ramaswamy, H. Fu, M. Sreekantaradhya, J. Dixon, K. Nygard[4] proposed a solution that contain a data routing information table where 1 stands for 'true' and 0 for 'false'. Whenever a RREP is received a cross check is done to verify whether the reply is from a legitimate node or not. According to H. Deng, W. Li, and D. P. Agrawal [5], the method requires the intermediate node to send next hop information along with the RREP. Whenever the RREP is received by source node, it launches an additional request to next hop node to check if it is any route to intermediate and destination node. The receiving node replies to the further request with the check result. Based on the check result the source node verifies the route. But, his solution cannot identify the cooperative black hole attack nodes.

B. Han, and M. Shin, [6] proposed a method that requires intermediate nodes to launch path cinfirmation request to its next hop node to target node. The next hop node verifies its cache for taget node. When the next hop node has a route to the target node, it launches rroute confirmation reply to source node. The source node judges the path in RREP by matching it with the path in RREP route confirmation reply. This operation is carried along with the routing protocol. This increases the routing overhead which results in performance degradation of MANET which is a bandwidth constrained.

Animesh Patcha and Amitabh Mishra [7], proposed a solution in which the nodes in the network are classified as trusted nodes and ordinary nodes. Nodes which are in network when the network is formed are identified as trusted nodes. Nodes which join the network later are identified as ordinary nodes. To be identified as trusted nodes, ordinary nodes have to prove their trustworthiness. The trusted nodes are assumed to be not malicious and selfish. But, this classification of trusted nodes and ordinary nodes is hard to choose from network. According to Marti, Giuli et al [8], they proposed two techniques Watchdog and Pathrater to increase the performance of the ad hoc networks by detecting and isolating the nodes which agree to forward the packets but do not. Watchdog is used to detect malicious nodes and Pathrater is used to avoid the path which rated below a threshold value. But, these techniques fail to detect collusion among nodes, receiver collisions, false misbehavior, partial dropping and limited transmission power.

3 Proposed Approach

The proposed approach is consists of two parts, namely detection and reaction. The first part of the design includes detection of malicious nodes, which lead to the black hole attack by using the same routing protocol. The black hole node answers to all the requests claiming that it has the route to destination just at one hop away from the source. If the malicious reply arrives at the source node ahead of the respond from destination node, then the path is falsified. The malicious node is able to come between the communicating nodes. Once it enters between the two communicating parties, it can do anything with packets passing through it. Dropping the packets leads to DoS attacks and on the other hand using its position on the path directs to man in the middle attack. Our proposed mechanism is based on promiscuous mode to detect the malicious node. The detecting node calculates the ratio of number of packets dropped to total number of packets forwarded successfully. This ratio is checked with the threshold value to detect any malicious behavior. If any misbehavior is found, the detecting node avoids the misbehaviour node. Using simulations we evaluate the performance metrics such as packet throughput, end to end delay and routing control overhead. The final step our design includes the response to the black hole attack node. The second part is used to isolate the blackhole node from the network and improve the performance.

When a node requires a path to launch the packets to target node, initially it floods a route request packet. The RREQ packets flood over the network. The intermediate node receives the route request packet and if it has a route to destination, then it send the unicast route reply packet back to the source node. If not, it forwards the route request packet to other neighbouring nodes. The destination sequence number in the routing table is compared with the route request packet. If it is less, then the node forwards the packet to the neighbouring nodes, otherwise it represents the fresh route to the destination. When any node discovers the link breakage, then the nodes send the route error packet to all the remaining nodes. The performance of the network can be evaluated without black hole attack.

When the malicious node gets a request for a path to the destination node, the malious node advertises a false reply message which indicates the shortest route to the destination. If the false reply reached the source before actual reply arrived, then the particular route is forged by the black hole node. Once it is enter ito the network, it can do some harmful operations like modfiying packet, dropping the packet it receives etc. In this paper we proposed a novel security approach for detecting black hole nodes. In this approach, each node maintains the packet forwarding table for detecting attacks.

We added a field"next_hop" in the AODV route reply packet structure. The next hop information is collected from the route reply packet. In our approach, before sending the data packet, the first arrival of the packet with shortest route sent by the intermediate node has been checked. The route availability from the intermediate node to the destination node has been checked by the next hop node. If there is no route, then the intermediate node is identified as malicious node.

Furhter to detect the other harmful operations performed by the misbehaving node in the network, each node maintains a blackhole identification table (BIT) of neighbour node to keep tracks of the packets received, sent and modified. The fields in this table are < source, target, current_node_ID, Packet_received_count (PRC), Packet_forwarded_count (PFC), Packet modified count (PMC)>. Each node collects the blackhole identiifcation table from its neighbour. Initially the count value is set to zero. If the node successfully receives the packet, forwards or modifies the packet, the corresponding count value is incremented by one. A node is received the packet succesfflly many times but it is not forwarded to the neighbouring nodes means that particular node is considered as malicious. Each node overhears the neighbouring node transmission in the promiscous mode. Also every node maintains a buffer for storing packet contents tempororily. When the node A forwards the packet to the next node B, the node A copied the contents of the packet and monitors the neighbouring node B's behavior. The farwarded packet of node B is compared with the node A's buffer contents. If any devaition occurs, the PMC value is incremented by one. The following procedure is used to detect the harmful operations performed by the blackhole node or malicious node.

If (PRC – PFC) = 0, there is no packet dropping.
Else if
  PD= (PRC – PFC) > 0, or (PRC-PFC) < 0, then there is packet dropping (PD).
If PD > PREDETERMINED_THESHOLD_VALUE, then the particular node is identified as malicious.
If PMC > 0, then the particular node is identified as malicious.

In this way, packet dropping and packet modification attacks created by the black hole nodes can be detected efficiently.

The second part of the design is used to isolate the blackhole node from the network and improve the performance. Each node mantains isolation table(IT) in which the blackhole node ID is stored. Then the ID is braodcasted to all the nodes in the network. When the malicious node comes in the network for the participation next time, it can be eliminated by checking the isolation table.

4   Simulations and Discussion

In this section, the performance of the proposed framework has been evaluated through extensive simulations. The proposed framework is implemented in NS-2 simulator. Here the simulations take place in a 500 by 500 meter flat space filled with a scattering of 15 mobile nodes. In our simulation, the channel capacity of mobile hosts is set to the same value: 2 Mbps modified AODV protocol. All nodes have the same transmission range of 250 metres.The physical   layer and the 802.11 MAC layers used are included in the CMU wireless extension to ns. The simulation parameters are given in table 1.

Table 1. Simulation Parameters

Simulator	Ns-2(ver.2.33)
Simulation time	500(s)
Number of mobile nodes	50
Data payload	512 bytes
Transmission Range	250m
Routing Protocol	AODV
Maximum Bandwidth	2Mbps
Traffic	Constant bit rate
Maximum Speed	5 m/s

The following performance metrics has been analyzed. The packet delivery ratio can be calculated as the ratio of number of received packets by the number of sending packets from the source. The end-to-end delay will be more in the proposed approach beacause the node takes time to detect and isolate malicious nodes.Performance metrics was determined for the wireless network with and without black hole attack.

A. Packet Delivery Ratio
As it can be seen from the figure 1, in the proposed approach, the packet delivery ratio is more compared to BlackAODV.

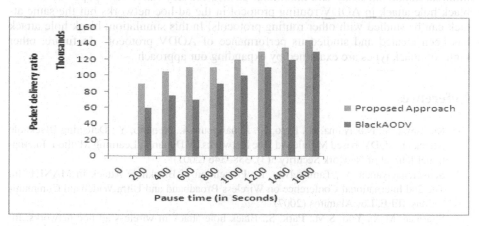

Fig. 1. Packet Delivery Ratio

B. Number of Packets Dropped

From the figure 2, it can be examined that, the number of packets dropped in the proposed approach is less when compared to the blackhole AODV.

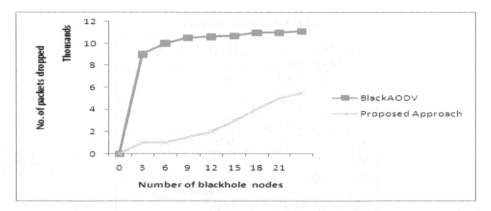

Fig. 2. Number of packets dropped Vs Number of blackhole nodes

5   Conclusion

In this paper, black hole attack is analyzed that can easily be deployed against a MANET and proposed a feasible solution for it in the AODV protocol. Upon detecting a misbehaving node, the detecting node tries to avoid the misbehaving node. Through simulation, the metrics evaluated are packets throughput and routing control overhead. The simulation shows that the proposed solution to the protocol provides better performance than the conventional AODV in the presence of Black holes with minimal additional delay and maximum packet delivery ratio. This paper deals with black hole attack in AODV routing protocol in the ad-hoc networks but the same attack can be studied with other routing protocols. In this simulation, black hole attack has been created and studied its performance of AODV protocol. In future, other kinds of attack types are examined by expanding our approach.

References

1. Kurosawa, S., Nakayama, H., Kato, N., Jamalipour, A., Nemoto, Y.: Detecting Blackhole Attack on AODV-based Mobile Ad Hoc Networks by Dynamic Learning Method. International Journal of Network Security 5(3), 338–346 (2007)
2. Sankaranarayanan, V., Tamilselvan, L.: Prevention of Blackhole Attack in MANET. In: The 2nd International Conference on Wireless Broadband and Ultra Wideband Communications. IEEE, Los Alamitos (2007)
3. Shurman, M.A., Yoo, S.M., Park, S.: Black hole attack in wireless ad hoc networks. In: ACM 42nd Southeast Conference (ACMSE 2004), April 2004, pp. 96–97 (2004)
4. Ramaswamy, S., Fu, H., Sreekantaradhya, M., Dixon, J., Nygard, K.: Prevention of Cooperative Black Hole Attack in Wireless Ad Hoc Networks. In: Proceedings of the International Conference on Wireless Networks (June 2003)

5. Deng, H., Li, W., Agrawal, D.P.: Routing security in ad hoc networks. IEEE Communications Magazine 40(10), 70–75 (2002)
6. Lee, S., Han, B., Shin, M.: Robust routing in wireless ad hoc networks. In: ICPP Workshops, p. 73 (2002)
7. Patcha, A., Mishra, A.: Collaborative Security Architecture for Black Hole Attack Prevention in Mobile Ad Hoc Networks. IEEE, Los Alamitos (2006)
8. Marti, S., Giuli, T.J., Lai, K., Baker, M.: Mitigating routing misbehavior in mobile ad hoc networks. In: 6th MobiCom, Boston, Massachusetts (August 2000)
9. Ramaswami, S.S., Upadhyaya, S.: Smart Handling of Colluding Black Hole Attacks in MANETs and Wireless Sensor Networks using Multipath Routing. In: Workshop on Information Assurance Proceedings. IEEE, Los Alamitos (2006)
10. Sun, B., Guan, Y., Chen, J., Pooch, U.W.: Detecting Black-hole Attack in Mobile Ad Hoc Networks. In: EPMCC. IEEE, Los Alamitos (2003)

NEEMON Algorithm Based on Data Locality for Priority Based Dynamic Load Balancing in Distributed Database

Neera Batra[1] and A.K. Kapil[2]

[1] Dept. of Computer Science & Engineering,
[2] Institute of Computer Technology & BusinessManagement,
M. M. Engineering College, Mullana-133203, Haryana, India
batraneera1@gmail.com, anil_kdk@yahoo.com

Abstract. A load balancing scheme comprises of three phases: information collection, decision making based on information and data migration. In distributed database, it is important to take data locality into account, since they have big impact on the communication requirements. Several techniques are proposed for balancing the load in homogeneous applications but still some improvement in terms of efficiency is required. In this paper, we present a load balancing architecture that can deal with homogeneous applications in distributed database [3] more efficiently. In our proposed architecture, memory utilization based priority method is used and data locality is also taken into consideration along with process waiting time and data transmission time. We have developed a load balancing algorithm which balances the load on different nodes working in homogeneous environment in a fragmented distributed database.

Keywords: Distributed database, load Balancer, Priority, CPU utilization, Memory Utilization.

1 Introduction

With the development of new technologies, the computing problems we need to solve have become more complicated and larger in size. This has leaded us to move towards deploying distributed systems to resolve our problems. The goal is attainable by partitioning problems into executable processes that can be executed on a single node. Load balancing is the process of improving the performance of a parallel and distributed system through a redistribution of load among the processors [2]. By applying suitable load balancing policies [1], [5] in distributed systems can affect directly the system's performance as each node has own processing power and system resources.

1.1 What Is Load Balancing?

Load balancing or load distribution [6] refers to the general practice of evenly distributing a load. Load balancing is the process by which inbound internet protocol (IP) traffic can be distributed across multiple servers. Typically, two or more web servers

V. V Das et al. (Eds.): BAIP 2010, CCIS 70, pp. 224–232, 2010.
© Springer-Verlag Berlin Heidelberg 2010

are employed in a load balancing scheme. In case, one of the servers begins to get overloaded, the requests are forwarded to another server. Load balancing brings down the service time by allowing multiple servers to handle the requests. This service time is reduced by using a load balancer to identify which server has the appropriate availability to receive the traffic.

It can be thought of as "distributed scheduling" [4] which deals with distribution of processes among processors connected by a network and handles issues such as deciding which process should be handled by a given processor.

2 Literature Survey

In this section, we describe several algorithms, each suitable for a different type of task which have been implemented. In chunk scheduling or self scheduling [8], Factoring [7] takes into account both the number of tasks in the queue and the number of processors used by the application.

One another algorithm called Self-Training Algorithm for load balancing in cluster computing uses load information including CPU load, memory usage and network traffic to decide the load of each node and combines this information with properties of each job, including CPU bound, memory bound and I/O bound features that are extracted from the previous runs of these jobs.

Tapering [10] selects a chunk size based on the distribution of the observed task execution time. Tapering has been implemented on a distributed memory system. In the gradient model [9], a "node load potential" field is established over the nodes, and newly created tasks drift to the node with the global minimum value through the potential field.

In this paper, an algorithm based upon hybrid technique of load balancing has been proposed which uses priority policy which is based on memory utilization of nodes with global task queue in distributed database homogeneous applications to improve CPU utilization as compared to above said policies of load balancing.

3 Proposed Model

In our proposed model, the system consists of a set of compute nodes and a global task scheduler. The task scheduler collects status information from the nodes and assigns task based on this information

In this system, we are using Priority based process load balancer that is responsible for the overall load balancing strategy which is based on "Less Memory Usage Higher Priority and Higher Memory Usage Less Priority" policy. A compute node includes data migration if data is not available at that particular node and data transmission time for data migration to remote node is less than process waiting time at local node and also provides this status to global task scheduler and application code. We will show how priority based technique is useful in load balancing in distributed database with higher CPU utilization as compared to the existing systems. We will compute the performance using **NEEMON** algorithm.

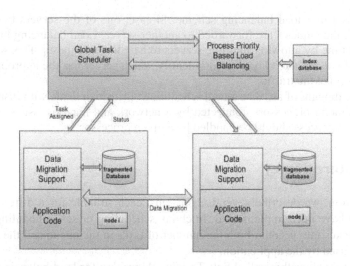

Fig. 1. Proposed Model of Priority Based Load Balancing

4 Implementation

Different nodes are already executing different tasks or workloads given to them by server which are being assigned to them randomly and dynamically depending upon the availability of the node at that instance of time. When load balancing algorithm is implemented, server decides about the next job to be given to which node, depending upon the current memory usage of that node because many processes are already running on that node. Same way, status of current memory utilization of all the nodes are known and the node having minimum memory utilization is chosen as the next node to which the next job is to be assigned. So, depending upon memory utilization, a node with lowest memory utilization at that particular instance of time, is given the highest priority amongst all the other nodes and a highest priority number is assigned to it. In the same fashion, all the other nodes are assigned priority numbers, with the maximum memory utilizing node having lowest priority number in the list of client nodes.

Server maintains a table (table1) which keeps details about the each node i.e. node IP address, no. of jobs running concurrently, memory used, free memory available, no. of data items accessible at each node. It also maintains an index table of data items which are accessible at each node. Each client node maintains a table (table 2) which stores information about each data item accessible at that node and maintains all the records of these particular data items.

Table 1. At Server side: Details about all nodes

Seq. No.	Node ID	No. of Job running	Memory	Free memory	No. of data items at each node

Table 2. At client side: Details about all data items stored at each node

Node ID	Data item ID	Data type1	Data type2	Data type3

Priority set at each node keeps on changing depending upon memory usage and jobs finished, periodically. Updates are being made in table 1 at the server, so that the current status of highest priority node is readily available for new job assignment.

Process:
In proposed algorithm, when a new request arrives at the server, it firstly checks for nodes which are having requested data available locally. Then the priority p[i] assigned to the node[i] where data is available locally is checked to get the information about the memory usage, free memory available at that node. The priority level is checked against a minimum priority level assumed which is a threshold value(α) and node with priority level less than threshold value(α) are considered overloaded. So, if the priority level of selected node p[i] where data is available locally is above the threshold value (α), then new process is assigned to that node even if it is not the highest priority node available. But if priority level of that node is less than the threshold value (α), then there are two considerations:

1. A new node with higher priority i.e. the node with priority no. p[α +1] is selected for job assignment
2. The process waiting time (t_w) at local node i and data transmission time (t_d) per hop from local node i with priority no. p[i] to new selected remote node with priority no. p[α +1] is calculated.

The new selected node is the first node having the priority level above the threshold value i.e. a node with priority no. p[α+1] so as to reduce the distance between data migrating node and data receiving node in order to reduce the transmission cost incurred to the minimum. The new selected node is efficient in executing the new job assigned because it's priority is above the threshold value (α), but now it is also a remote node where data is not available locally, so the required data need to be transmitted to node with priority no[α +1] which increases the data transmission time depending upon the no. of hops covered to transmit the data to destination node. **NEEMON** algorithm works based on mathematical complexities which are as follows:

If L is the load to be given to the node
$t_{p[i]}$ – processing time of node i
t_d – data transmission time per hop
n – No. of hops
Then $T_{pt} = L \ (n*t_d + t_{p[i]})$, where T_{pt} - total processing time taken by a node
AtLocalnode:
Since $t_d = 0$ i.e. data transmission time = 0 because data is available locally at that node. So, $T_{pt} = L \ (n*t_d + t_{p[i]} + t_w)$
Whereas waiting time is concerned, there are two considerations:

1. In case of high priority local node, waiting time is 0 because enough memory is available for new job execution.

$$T_{pt} = L (0 + t_{p[i]} + t_w)$$
$$= L (0 + tp[i] + 0)$$
$$= L (tp[i])$$

2. If the local node is low priority node, then waiting time need to be taken into consideration.

$$T_{pt} = L (0 + t_{p[i]} + t_w)$$
$$= L (t_{p[i]} + t_w)$$

Now even if data is available locally but if node is already over loaded, it may take more time to process that new job than if the same job has been executed at a remote node. Since this new job may have to wait for long in the waiting queue of the local node. So, a threshold value is decided based on the fact that for how long a new job should remain in waiting queue at a local node called as β.

If $t_w > \beta$ then
    If $t_w > t_d$ then
      Data migrated to remote node
    Else
      Job is kept in waiting queue at local node
  Else
    Job is kept in waiting queue at local node

If the waiting time[t_w] at local node exceeds β ,then it is better to migrate this new job to a new remote node of higher priority with the condition that data transmission time[t_d] to remote node is less than waiting time [t_w] at local node So here two conditions are checked. First waiting time at local node is checked against a threshold value β, so that a process doesn't not block for longer and if the waiting time for process at local node is greater than threshold value β, then waiting time is checked against data transmission time to remote node. If the waiting time is less then data transmission time , the process is still made to wait in waiting queue of local node but if the data transmission time is less than waiting time, then data is migrated from local node to the higher priority chosen node for process execution at remote node.

AtRemoteNode:
At remote node, depending upon the distance between data migrating node p[i] and the remote node chosen for execution of new load assignment i.e. a node with priority no. p[α +1], data transmission rate[t_d] is calculated per hop. Then according to number of hops covered to transfer the data, total data transmission time [n*t_d] is calculated where n is no. of hops.

T_d – data transmission time for one hop
t_p – processing time
t_w – waiting time
n – no. of hops
$T_{pt} = L (nt_d + t_p + t_w)$,
At remote node, $t_w = 0$, So,$T_{pt} = L (nt_d + t_p + 0)$

NEEMON Algorithm

1. For new request
   a. Check for node having data.
   b. Check the priority level (p[i]) of node having data.
   c. Set threshold value α for priority level for each node.
   d. At local node i, Priority level is checked
   > If (p[i] > α)
   >> New job is assigned to that ith node.
   >
   > Else if (p[i] < α)
   > {
   >> p[α +1] node is selected
   >> Set threshold value β for waiting time t_w at local node
   >> I. If $t_w > \beta$ then
   >>> If $t_w > t_d$ then
   >>>> Data migrated to remote node
   >>> Else
   >>>> Job is kept in waiting queue at local node
   >>> Else
   >>>> Job is kept in waiting queue at local node
   >> II. If $t_w < \beta$
   >>> New job assigned to p[i] node and sent to waiting queue

5 Performance

In this section, performance results for the dynamic load balancing architecture described in this paper are shown. The performance is evaluated using three measures: 1) CPU utilization w.r.t. no. of processes before load balancing and after load balancing. 2) Time taken at each node for task execution using priority load balancing and without load balancing. 3) decision of data migration based on comparison between data transmission time and process waiting time.

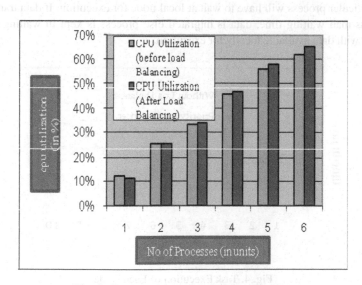

Fig. 2. Comparative study of CPU utilization

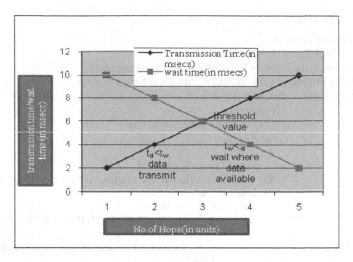

Fig. 3. Decision based on comparison between Data transmission time and process waiting time

Figure 2 shows CPU utilization with respect to no. of processes. In the beginning, when load balancing is yet to be implemented, different nodes are running different processes. So, memory available at each node is not known in advance. But as the no. of processes increases and they are allocated to different nodes based on load balancing criteria specified, CPU utilization increases gradually by almost 3% as shown in the figure.

Figure 3 shows that decision taken about whether the data should be migrated to a remote node or the process should be executed at the local node instead of migrating the data to a remote node, depends on the time taken for data migration as well as waiting time, a particular process will have to wait at local node for execution. If data transmission time is less than waiting time, data is migrated else process is kept in waiting queue of local node with data available locally for execution.

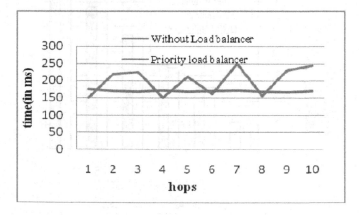

Fig. 4. Task Execution of Each Node

In figure 3, two equations are shown:

$$1) \quad t_d < t_w \qquad 2) \; t_w < t_d$$

Figure 4 shows time taken at each hop for process execution. It varies at each hop, depending upon the waiting time each process has to wait for execution, time taken to execute process, memory available etc. But when load balancing algorithm is implemented, time taken at each hop for process execution is almost constant. In other words, this algorithm increases the efficiency of each particular node in terms of CPU utilization and execution time.

6 Conclusion and Future Work

We described a new load balancing architecture that applies to a wide range of applications. Our architecture simplifies the task of developing load balancers that take into account data locality and priority for applications with homogeneous tasks. **NEEMON** algorithm works for a fragmented database where data migration takes place when the memory available at local node is not enough for process execution or the waiting time for the process is more than the execution time at a remote node. This algorithm works better in terms of memory usage and CPU utilization.

Further work is needed in several areas. First, the proposed architecture has to be evaluated using more complex applications and larger systems. Second, the current algorithm works for homogeneous systems using client server architecture. It can be made to work for peer-to-peer networking in heterogeneous systems also. Thirdly, priority can be set based upon CPU utilization along with memory usage.

References

1. Sharma, S., Singh, S., Sharma, M.: Performance Analysis of Load Balancing Algorithms. World Academy of Science, Engineering and Technology (PWASET) 28, 208–267 (2008)
2. Hamam, Y., Hindi, K.S.: Assignment of program modules to processors: A simulated annealing approach. European Journal of Operational Research 122(2), 509–513 (2008)
3. Amiri, A.: A Coordinated Planning Model for the Design of a Distributed Database System. Information Sciences 164, 229–245 (2004)
4. Li, W., Altintas, K., Kantarcıolu, M.: On Demand Synchronization and Load Distribution for Database Grid-Based Web Applications. Data and Knowledge Engineering 51(3), 295–323 (2004)
5. Yoshida, M., Sakamoto, K.: Code Migration Control in Large Scale Loosely Coupled Distributed Systems. In: Proceedings of the 4th International Conference on Mobile Technology, Applications and Systems, Singapore, September 2007, vol. 65, pp. 345–455 (2007)
6. Markatos, E.P., LeBlanc, T.J.: Load Balancing vs. Shared-Memory Multiprocessors. In: 21th International Conference on Parallel Processing, August 1992, vol. 22, pp. 234–345 (1992)
7. Hummel, S.F., Schonberg, E., Flynn, L.E.: Factoring: A Practical and Robust Method for Scheduling Parallel Loops. In: IEEE Supercomputing 1991, Albuquerque, vol. 1, pp. 610–619 (November 1991)

8. Kruskal, C., Weiss, A.: Allocating Independent Subtasks on Parallel Processors. IEEE Transaction on Software Engineering, SE-10, 10 (October 1985)
9. Lin, F.C.H., Keller, R.M.: The Gradient model load balancing method. IEEE Transaction on Software Engineering, SE-13 1, 32–38 (1987)
10. Lucco, S.: A Dynamic Scheduling Method for Irregular Parallel Programs. In: SIGPLAN 1992 Conference on Programming Language Design and Implementation, June 1992, vol. 2, pp. 200–211. ACM, San Francisco (1992)

A Secure e-Shopping Using Voice Ordering

Saroj Kumar Panigrahy, Debasish Jena, and Sanjay Kumar Jena

Department of Computer Science & Engineering,
National Institute of Technology Rourkela, 769 008, Odisha, India
skp.nitrkl@gmail.com, debasishjena@hotmail.com, skjena@nitrkl.ac.in

Abstract. Internet connectivity can offer enormous advantages, however security needs to be a major consideration when planning an Internet connection. There are significant security risks associated with
the Internet that often are not obvious to new (and existing) users. In
particular, intruder activities as well as vulnerabilities that could assist
intruder activity are widespread. Intruder activity is difficult to predict
and at times can be difficult to discover and correct. Many organizations
already have lost productive time and money in dealing with intruder
activity; some organizations have had their reputations suffer as a result
of intruder activity at their sites being publicized. This paper proposes
a secure method of e-shopping using Pocket PCs through voice ordering.

Keywords: e-shopping, security, speech recognition, RSA, .Net.

1 Introduction

With the start of design of website, the first and foremost thing the webmaster
is worried is about its security. But astonishingly most of the sites, around 90%
of the mass, have such a poor security system, that they can be hacked even by
a novice hacker, for this reason only security analysts evolved. The first thing
that takes fancy of a hacker or a security analyst is open ports. The more open
ports are there in a web server, the more prone is that server to a security
breach. The next thing that comes into mind is its mailing system. The kind of
system used in a site lets hacker to find possible flaws and exploit them such
as spamming, spoofing and the like. The next thing is to exploit the hardware
flaws, like routers, gateways etc. This is a serious issue that a webmaster should
look into.

Recent developments in ASP.NET where the computer uses one of the senses
of human beings, the speech sense, due to which, we can make the computer
speak and also a conversation can take place between a user and the computer.
Another development is the Mobile development or Call management controls.
This is highly useful for our Shopping management System. This is an advantage
for houses where the internet connection is not available. So the user can send
message from any mobile to the mobile which is placed in the Shopping Mall. The
user can ask for any information she needs. This gives the complete information
of the requested message to the user.

V.V Das et al. (Eds.): BAIP 2010, CCIS 70, pp. 233–237, 2010.
© Springer-Verlag Berlin Heidelberg 2010

The rest of the paper is organized as follows. Section 2 describes the design and implementation of the proposed method. A brief description of mobile services is explained in Section 3. Finally, the Section 4 describes the concluding remarks.

2   Design and Implementation

Our paper is mainly focused on secure e-shopping. The security that we have implemented is the password encryption and credit card validation. Another special feature that have been implemented in our secure e-shopping is voice ordering components. Each of these security criteria are explained below in greater details.

2.1   Credit Card Validation

The main aim of validating credit card numbers is that no unauthorized user accesses others card and all its substitutes involved with it. This unauthorized access can lead to loss of money and even huge theft using others credit card number. A typical e-business processing system is shown in Fig. 1. As a part of this web form, we wanted to include support to check that users had entered a card number, expiration date etc., and then wanted to extend it further to include support for checking that the card number was valid before issuing a request to the payment gateway's server. This is the result, a drop-in replacement for any of the other validation controls. The card system is implemented using the Luhn's Formula. The working of Luhn's formula together with its usage in creating a valid credit card number is given below [1].

1. ***Double the value of alternating digits***: The first step is to double each of the alternating digits in the number. But the trick is to start with the second digit from the right and work backwards. Say we have a credit card number 1234 5678 1234 5670. We'll start with the second rightmost number 7, double it, and then do the same for every other digit as follows.
   1234 5678 1234 5670

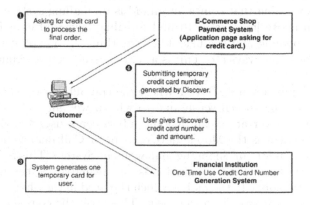

Fig. 1. A typical e-business processing system

This will give us the following values.

$7 \times 2 = 14$, $5 \times 2 = 10$, $3 \times 2 = 6$, ..., etc.

2. **Add the separate digits of all the products:** Now we will separate the digits of all the products, and come up with a final sum.

$(1 + 4) + (1 + 0) + 6 + 2 + (1 + 4) + (1 + 0) + 6 + 2 = 28$

3. **Add the unaffected digits:** Now we'll go back to the original number and add all the digits that we didn't double. We'll still start from the right, but this time we'll start from the rightmost number.

1234 5678 1234 5670

$0 + 6 + 4 + 2 + 8 + 6 + 4 + 2 = 32$

4. **Add the results and divide by 10:** Finally, we'll add both the results and divide the answer by 10.

$28 + 32 = 60$

60 is evenly divided by 10, so the credit card number is well formed and ready for further processing.

The design of our credit card validation first checks the credit card validity using the Luhn's Formula. It also takes into account the valid duration of the card. The amount to be credited is also taken into account. After this the details are submitted to the server which checks it using the Luhn's formula.

2.2 Password Encryption

For our password encryption we have taken use of the public key algorithm, where two keys are used for both encryption and decryption. Here we make use of the public key encryption algorithm called as RSA algorithm [2].

The password encryption has been designed as follows. It entitles the user to enter her name for checking the validity of the user by comparing the user name from the database. The encryption process takes place at the back end.

2.3 Voice Ordering Components

Voice can be used in personal communication systems [3]. In this voice ordering, any customer who logs into the website will be guided by a voice which tells them various aspects of shopping in the Shopping Mall. This voice also guides through the entire process of buying things, the various models that are available in each and every item. This voice will also tell whether an item is available or not. The Fig. 2 illustrates the process of recognizing the voice.

The voice that we speak through the microphone is captured. Then a sound wave is generated and the sound card which is available converts that particular signal into a digital signal, which again is converted into words inside the speech recognition engine. The resulting output from the speech-aware application is the output. The of design of speech recognition is shown in Fig. 3. The different buttons on the right of the figure explains the various buttons involved in generating a correct request. The semantic map button is used to compare the signal with the corresponding request. The other buttons are used in converting the words into the electrifying signal, which is finally converted to the requested word.

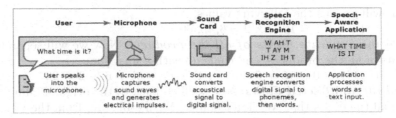

Fig. 2. Process of voice recognition

Fig. 3. Design of speech recognition system

3   Mobile Services

In this scenario, client is the Microsoft Pocket Internet Explorer with the Speech
Add-in installed. ASP.NET speech-enabled Web application pages reside on the
Web server, along with the application grammars, and a configuration file containing the URL to the Speech Server that performs speech processing [4, 5].

When the user enters a URL on Pocket PC, the Web server opens the application's default *.aspx* page. The Web server also sends the URL pointing to
Speech Server. The page that the Web server sends contains HTML, SALT, and
JScript. When the user taps a speech-enabled HTML element and talks, Pocket
PC sends the audio to Speech Server. Along with the compressed audio, Pocket
PC sends either an inline recognition grammar or a pointer to the location of
an externally-stored recognition grammar that is bound to that speech-enabled
element. If the recognition grammar is an inline grammar, Speech Server loads
the grammar and performs speech recognition. If the grammar is an externally-
stored grammar, Speech Server first downloads a copy of the grammar, loads the
grammar, and then performs speech recognition.

After the recognition finishes, Speech Server sends Semantic Markup Language (SML) output to the Pocket PC along with audio for prompts if the
application dialogue flow requires the application to play a prompt. The Pocket
PC client parses the SML output, and populates the speech-enabled HTML element with the semantic value to which it is bound, and plays any prompts
that Speech Server sends. The Fig. 4 shows the process of interfacing between a
computer and mobile.

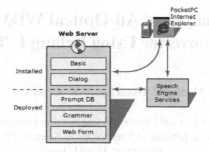

Fig. 4. The mobile and computer interfacing

4 Conclusion

Speech recognition is the latest kind in the market which will play a very important role in the future. We actually run a windows service which will scan for speech. The voice is scanned using microphone. If the voice is below a certain threshold or if a sudden voice is found, then the voice is discarded without compromising for a valid command. Since we have speaker detection, we can fix the commands for a specific speaker.

The above system can be further extended to mobile phones so that they can be accessed over a WAP enabled phone. This reduces the stress of the customer who doesn't have any access to internet. Accessing through mobile phones also enables the customer to get the same response as by accessing through internet.

References

1. Childs, L.N.: A Concrete Introduction to Higher Algebra. Springer, Heidelberg (2008)
2. Stallings, W.: Cryptography and Network Security: Principles and Practices, 3rd edn. Pearson Education, London (2003)
3. Burstein, A., Stolzle, A., Brodersen, R.: Using speech recognition in a personal communications system. In: IEEE International Conference on Communications, ICC 1992, Conference record, SUPERCOMM/ICC 1992, Discovering a New World of Communications, June 1992, vol. 3, pp. 1717–1721 (1992)
4. Evjen, B., Beres, J., et al.: Visual Basic. Net Programming Bible. Wiley, Chichester (2002)
5. Holzner, S.: Visual Basic.net Programming Little Black Book. Wiley Dreamtech, Chichester (2005)

Performance Analysis of All-Optical WDM Network with Wavelength Converter Using Erlang C Traffic Model

Manoj Kr. Dutta and V.K. Chaubey

Electrical and Electronics Engineering Department,
Birla Institute of Technology & Science, Pilani
Rajasthan -333031, India
mkdutta@bits-pilani.ac.in

Abstract. In this paper we have analyzed the performance of an all-optical WDM network for different parameters, such as number of channels, number of wavelengths associated, number of hops between source to destination etc. To establish a light path between two nodes wavelength continuity is a big constraint and to avoid this problem either wavelength converter or optical delay line or both may be used. Wavelength converter will convert the wavelength of the incoming signal into a desired wavelength at the output and the optical delay line will hold the incoming signal for a certain time. In this paper we considered that the network is equipped with wavelength converter and the traffic through the network is Erlang-C type. A mathematical model for the same has been devised and its performance has been analyzed with an investigation on collective impacts of various traffic parameters on transmission.

Keywords: Wavelength converter, WDM network, RWA, Blocking probability, Erlang Traffic, Hops.

1 Introduction

Wavelength division multiplexing (WDM) is an effective technique to make full use of the large amount of bandwidth in optical fibers to meet the bandwidth requirement of applications. It is generally believed that optical wavelength division multiplexing (WDM) networks are realized for building up of the backbone network. A WDM optical network consists of a set of optical fibers connected by switching nodes. There are multiple wavelengths available in each fiber, which provide a large transmission bandwidth. However, this feature also makes the network management problem more complicated [1].

Wavelength-routed networks are attractive for realizing the next generation wide-area networks since they offer a data transmission scheme for WDM all-optical networks [2-3]. In wavelength-routed networks, data is transferred on lightpaths. A lightpath is an optical path established between the source and the destination node. When a connection request arrives, a lightpath is set up. This involves routing and signaling to reserve a wavelength on each link along the path selected [4]. The benefit of wavelength-routed networks is the ability to more fully utilize the bandwidth of

V. V Das et al. (Eds.): BAIP 2010, CCIS 70, pp. 238–244, 2010.
© Springer-Verlag Berlin Heidelberg 2010

optical fibers since they do not require processing, buffering, and opto-electronic-optic conversions at intermediate nodes. It also allows the same fiber to carry many signals independently as long as each uses a different wavelength, known as routing and wavelength assignment (RWA) problem [5]. Calls are additionally subjected to the wavelength continuity constraint, which requires that a call use the same wave-length on all hops, maintaining this condition is difficult unless wavelength conversion is available at intermediate nodes. If full conversion is available at all nodes, the WDM network is equivalent to a circuit switched network; however, the high cost of wavelength converters often makes it desirable to keep the amount of conversion used in the network to a minimum [6].

There are few ways to classify WDM networks. Based on the wavelength conversion capability of the nodes, a WDM network can be classified as non-wave-length continuous (NWC), wavelength continuous (WC) or partial wavelength conversion (PWC) WDM. In an NWC network, each node is equipped with the full number of wavelength converters and each has the full range wavelength conversion capability. Unlike the NWC WDM network, there is no wavelength converter in the WC-WDM network. Therefore, the same wavelength has to be used in all the hops of a light-path from the source node to the destination node. PWC is an alternative that has been proposed as an alternative because of the high cost of wavelength converters. In this kind of network, each node only has limited wavelength conversion capability [7-9]. A partial wavelength conversion network, in which the wavelength converters in each node are shared by different links [10].

In the present paper we have considered an appropriate model of WDM optical network using wavelength converters [11] and we have estimated its traffic performance under Erlang-C traffic. The particular situation we considered here can be described like, one access station A requests a session to station B over some path of a mesh network and there are H hops (fibers) from A to B on this path. We consider networks where each session requires a full wavelength of bandwidth and there are F available wavelengths. For simplicity, we assume that A and B are not currently active at the time of the session request; however, our techniques can be easily generalized. Therefore, there are no busy wavelengths on the access or exit fiber and, in particular, a session cannot enter the requested path at node H + 1. However, sessions may enter or exit the path at each of the first H intermediate nodes, provided that no two sessions on the same fiber use the same wavelength. Any session which uses at least one of the H fibers on any wavelength is termed an interfering session. With wavelength changers at every node, this is a conventional circuit-switched network. In this case, the request between A and B is blocked only if one of the H fibers is full, (a fiber is full when it is supporting F sessions on different wavelengths).

This model intends to follow a wavelength reservation protocol which facilitates reservation of a particular wavelength from the source node itself, thus annulling possibility of wavelength conversion. Though under heavy traffic conditions, it is difficult to always reserve a particular wavelength before packet transmission this brings in the necessity for wavelength conversion. To cope up with such scenarios when there are no particular wavelength available at all nodes, we have considered a wavelength assignment scheme [4]. This scheme uses a center wavelength for a long hops connection and edge wavelength for short hops connection, each connection request is assigned to wavelength according to its hop number. Evidently, the noise and delay introduced by multiple channels accumulate to deteriorate the SNR in multiplexed optical networks. Therefore, the objective should be to transfer information over an optical network with minimum number of wavelength conversions. In fact, the network performs satisfactorily below a number of wavelength conversions [12-13]. Further, dispersion, attenuation and cross-talk characteristics of the multiplexed channels ensure that all the channels are not equally efficient. Legal and operational constraints also make the traffic distribution in the channels non-uniform. Even there is a specific band of wavelengths over which the transmission of packets is efficient. Moreover, practical wavelength converters also have few constraints.

2 Mathematical Model

In order to evaluate the performance of the proposed WDM optical network we need to derive the probabilistic evaluation of the present WDM network contain M number of output channels. Erlang C formula is derived from assumption that a queue is used a queue is used to hold all request calls which cannot be immediately assigned a channel. The Erlang C formula is given by

$$P_c[Call\ Delayed\quad] = \frac{\rho^M}{\rho^M + M\,!(1-\frac{\rho}{M})\sum_{i=0}^{M}\frac{\rho^i}{i!}} \qquad (1)$$

and the blocking probability is given by

$$P_C = \frac{\rho^M}{\rho^M + M\,!(1-\frac{\rho}{M})\sum_{i=0}^{M}\frac{\rho^i}{i!}} * \exp\frac{-(M-\rho)}{H}t \qquad (2)$$

where, ρ is the incoming traffic , t is the delay time and H is the average duration of the call.

Now let us consider the network with wavelength converters which is shown in fig. 1. The probability P_c that the session request between Node 1 to Node 3 is given by equation 2. As shown in [11] a measure of the benefit of wavelength converters can be expressed in terms of the increase in the gain of the network for the same blocking probability. Gain of a network can be defined as the ratio of the achievable utilization for a given blocking probability in networks with wavelength converters and without converters.

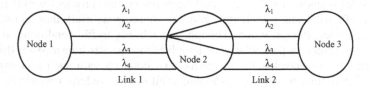

Fig. 1. Wavelength conversion at node 2

Increase in the gain G can be written as

$$G = \frac{[1 - (1 - \frac{\rho^M}{\rho^M + M!(1 - \frac{\rho}{M})\sum_{i=0}^{M} \frac{\rho^i}{i!}} * \exp \frac{-(M-\rho)}{H} t)^{1/H}]^{1/F}}{1 - (1 - (\frac{\rho^M}{\rho^M + M!(1 - \frac{\rho}{M})\sum_{i=0}^{M} \frac{\rho^i}{i!}} * \exp \frac{-(M-\rho)}{H} t)^{1/F})^{1/H}} \qquad (3)$$

$$G \approx H^{[1-(1/F)]} \frac{(\frac{\rho^M}{\rho^M + M!(1 - \frac{\rho}{M})\sum_{i=0}^{M} \frac{\rho^i}{i!}} * \exp \frac{-(M-\rho)}{H} t)^{1/F}}{-\ln[1 - (\frac{\rho^M}{\rho^M + M!(1 - \frac{\rho}{M})\sum_{i=0}^{M} \frac{\rho^i}{i!}} * \exp \frac{-(M-\rho)}{H} t)^{1/F}]} \qquad (4)$$

These equations have been used in blocking probability and gain calculation for different network parameters in the MATLAB environment under the appropriate node and traffic assumptions.

3 Simulation and Results

The simulations are carried out for a general optical switching configuration for a generic traffic with specific node architecture, having variable traffic routing factor. Here we have analyzed the network performance for various parameters like different incoming traffic rate, different numbers of available output channels and the effect of hop number on the network gain. The variation in blocking probability of the network for incoming traffic of 3,5 and 7 Erlang have been shown in fig 2, 3 and 4 respectively. Here we see that the blocking probability increases exponentially with increasing incoming traffic.

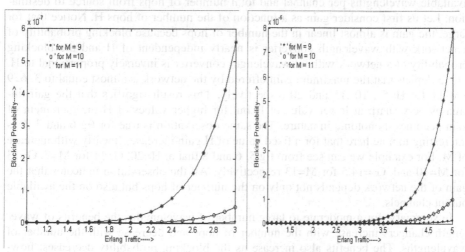

Fig. 2. Blocking Probability vs Traffic Arrival Rate for maximum 3 Erlang Traffic

Fig. 3. Blocking Probability vs Traffic Arrival Rate for maximum 5 Erlang Traffic

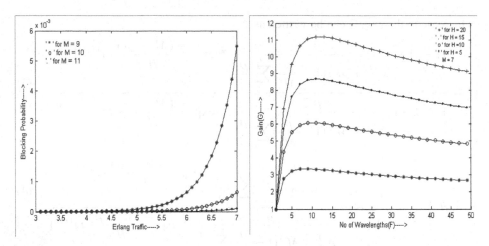

Fig. 4. Blocking Probability vs Traffic Arrival **Fig. 5.** Network Gain vs No. of wavelengths
Rate for maximum 7 Erlang Traffic

The change of blocking probability is more significant for less number of available output channels. It is interesting to note here that the blocking probability changes almost linearly with the increment of incoming traffic. For example we can consider the network with available output channels equal to 9. In this case blocking probability of the network reaches to 5.5×10^{-7}, 8×10^{-5} and 6×10^{-3} for 3, 5 and 7 Erlang of incoming traffic respectively. This result reveals that the blocking probability of a network is more dependent on the number of available output channels than the incoming traffic rate.

Fig. 5, 6 and 7 shows how the gain of the network is dependent on number of the available wavelengths per channel and total number of hops from source to destination. Let us first consider gain as a function of the number of hops H. Notice that for large, the gain is almost linear in the number of hops because blocking probability of a network with wavelength converter is nearly independent of H and the blocking probability of a network without wavelength converter is inversely proportional to H. Fig. 5 depicts that the maximum gain offered by the network is almost equal to 3, 6, 9 and 11 for H=5, 10, 15 and 20 respectively. This result signifies that the gain increases very sharp at lower value of H but for higher values of H the increment of gain becomes monotonic in nature. The same observation is true for fig 6 and 7. It is interesting to note here that for a fixed value of H gain increases linearly with increase of M. For example we can see from fig 5, 6 and 8 that at H=20, G=11 for M=7, G=13 for M=10 and, G =14.5 for M=13 respectively. All the observation indicates that the gain of the network depends not only on the number of hops but also on the available output channels.

In summary, for a moderate to large number of wavelengths, the benefits of wavelength changers increase with the number of hops and decrease with the number of wavelengths. The benefits also increase as the blocking probability decreases; however the effect is small as long as blocking probability is small.

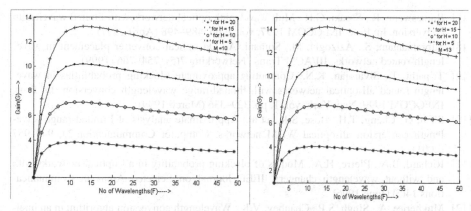

Fig. 6. Network Gain vs No. of wavelengths   **Fig. 7.** Network Gain vs No. of wavelengths

4 Conclusion

We have analyzed traffic performance of an Optical WDM network with wavelength converter under Erlang C traffic condition. Traffic parameters like number of output channels, number of wavelengths and number of hops, are considered. The traffic response found from this simulation is very close to the expected theoretical results. Performance of the network has shown large dependency on the number of output channels and hops. Qualitative studies have been performed in due consideration of traffic parameter values used in practical purpose and all simulations have been carried out using MATLAB tools and libraries. The analysis presented here is useful to predict the traffic throughput range of an all-optical WDM network with wavelength converter and relevant design parameters.

References

[1] Qiwu, W., Xianwei, Z., Jianping, W., Zhizhong, Y., Lin, L.: Multicast routing and wavelength assignment with delay constraint in WDM networks with sparse wavelength conversions. Springer Science + Business Media, LLC (2009)

[2] Chlamtac, I., Ganz, A., Karm, G.: Lightpath communications: An approach to high bandwidth optical WAN's. IEEE Transaction on Communications 49(7), 1171–1182 (1992)

[3] Chu, X., Li, B., Imrich, C.: Wavelength converter placement under different RWAalgorithms in wavelength-routed all-optical networks. IEEE Transaction on Communications 51(4), 607–617 (2003)

[4] Shimizu, S., Arakawa, Y., Yamanaka, N.: A wavelength assignment scheme for WDM Networks with Limited Range Wavelength Converters. In: IEEE ICC (2006)

[5] Chen, L.-W., Modiano, E.: Efficient Routing and Wavelength Assignment for Reconfigurable WDM Networks with Wavelength Converters. In: IEEE INFOCOM (2003)

[6] Kundu, R., Chaubey, V.K.: Analysis of optical WDM Network Topologies with Application of LRWC Under Symmectric Erlang –C Traffic. Springer Science + Business Media, B.V (2008)

[7] Ramaswami, R., Sasaki, G.H.: Multiwavelength optical networkswith limited wavelength conversion. In: Proc. INFOCOM 1997, vol. 2, pp. 489–498 (April 1997)

[8] Subramaniam, S., Azizoglu, M., Somani, A.: On optical converter placement in wavelength-routed networks. III/ACM Trans., Networking 7(5), 754–766 (1999)

[9] Tripathi, T., Sivarajan, K.N.: Computing approximate blocking probabilities in wavelength routed all-optical networks with limited-range wavelength conversion. In: Proc. INFOCOM 1999, New York, vol. 1, pp. 329–336 (March 1999)

[10] Shen, G., Cheng, T.H., Bose, S.K., et al.: Approximate analysis of Limited-range wavelength conversion all-optical WDM networks. Computer Communication 24, 949–957 (2001)

[11] Richard, B.A., Pierre, H.A.: Models of blocking probability in all-optical networks with and without wavelength changers. IEEE Journal on Selected Areas in Communications 14(5) (June 1996)

[12] Mukherjee, A., Singh, S.P., Chaubey, V.K.: Wavelength conversion algorithm in an intelligent optical network from a multi-layered approach. Journal of Optical Networks (OSA) 3(5), 354–362 (2004)

[13] Dutta, M.K., Chaubey, V.K.: Optical Network Traffic Control Algorithm under Variable Loop Delay: A Simulation Approach. Int. J. Communications, Network and System Sciences 7, 651–655 (2009)

A Concurrent Synchronization Model for Distributed Multimedia Systems

Janani Arthanari [1] and A. Kannan [2]

[1] Research Scholar, Department of Computer Science and Engineering,
Anna University, Chennai, India
janani.arthanari@gmail.com
[2] Professor, Department of Computer Science and Engineering,
Anna University, Chennai, India
kannan@annauniv.edu

Abstract. In this paper, a new architectural framework called CSMDM (Concurrent Synchronization Integrated Synchronization Model) for concurrency control and multimedia synchronization has been proposed and implemented that enables mapping active synchronization requirements to active multimedia databases. The main advantage of this work is the integration of concurrency control protocol with intelligent synchronization requirements and hence it is capable of achieving a high performance during transaction processing. A new locking protocol named Concurrent Secure two phase locking protocol has been proposed in this paper in order to enable better concurrency control during online transactions.

Keywords: CSMDM model, Multimedia Synchronization Manager, CS2PL protocol, SMIL.

1 Introduction

Creating innovative multimedia presentation is one of the challenging tasks. In relational databases, concurrency control and locking mechanisms are used for sharing of data among users. Hence, it is necessary to develop an intelligent database management system that can provide conventional database features as well as multimedia synchronization.

In this paper, a new architectural framework called CSMDM (Concurrent Synchronization Multimedia Database Model) for concurrency control and multimedia synchronization has been proposed and implemented that enables effective mapping of active synchronization requirements in multimedia databases using active rules.

2 Related Works

There are many works on multimedia databases, synchronization and concurrency control that are available in the literature. Multimedia Presentations were modeled to handle backward and skip interactions [3]. Synchronization rules were extracted

V. V Das et al. (Eds.): BAIP 2010, CCIS 70, pp. 245–249, 2010.
© Springer-Verlag Berlin Heidelberg 2010

explicitly from the user specification rules using Allen's [1] interval algebra operators. Moreover, synchronization rules can be deduced implicitly from explicit synchronization rules [2]. ECA rules can be deployed in the form of Synchronization rules so as to efficiently manage presentations [4]. To achieve concurrency control during multimedia transactions, many concurrency control protocols were proposed [5]. In this work, a new secure two phase locking protocol is proposed that aids a better concurrency control especially during online transactions.

3   System Architecture

The architecture of the proposed system, called CSMDM is shown in Fig. 1. CSMDM consists of two tiers namely Multimedia Presentation Manager and Multimedia Database Manager.

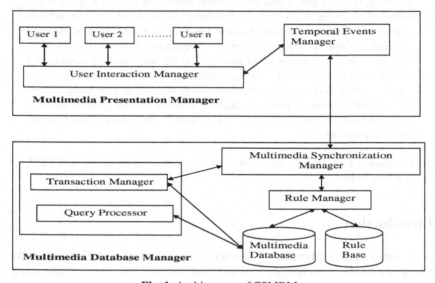

Fig. 1. Architecture of CSMDM

3.1   Multimedia Synchronization and Concurrency Control

In CSMDM, the multimedia database is designed such that synchronization is handled within the database. The complexity of the synchronization structure is simplified in using additional set of controllers. Moreover, a new concurrency control protocol called Concurrent Secure Two phase locking protocol has been proposed which modifies the features of Secure Two phase locking protocol.

4   Implementation and Results

In CSMDM, a synchronization model has been designed and the synchronization specifications are handled within the database. In this work, Receiver Controller and

Action (RCA) model is used to execute the ECA rules. Each controller has a Composite Condition Expression (CCE), and a CCE may be represented as a binary tree of conditions where leaf nodes are conditions (receivers or the direction) and internal nodes are binary operators like (AND, OR). Moreover, each CCE has one direction condition and has at least one receiver. Let L_{ci} be the number of leaf nodes containing receivers in the CCE of controller C_i. Let $L_c = \sum_{i=1}^{n} L_{C_i}$ denote the total number of leaf nodes containing receivers in CCES of all controllers. When the controller is notified, it checks the status of the receivers. Since the composite condition expression is a binary tree, the total number of internal nodes is $N_{C_i} = L_{C_i} - 1$ for CCE of controller C_i. Let $N_c = \sum_{i=1}^{n} N_{C_i}$ denote the total number of internal nodes in cces of all controllers. The number of triggers for a presentation in CSMDM model is denoted by

$$T_{db} = R + 3 * N_c + C + A . \tag{1}$$

where R, C, A are the set of receivers, controllers and actors respectively. N_c is the total number of internal nodes. The reason that CSMDM has $3 * N_c$ is the additional set of controllers being used to simplify synchronization structure.

The Concurrent Secure two phase locking protocol releases both write and read locks applied by a transaction based on priority level of users. For users of higher priority locks are released only when the transaction commits. For low priority users locks are released even if the transaction is partially committed. The Concurrent Secure two phase locking protocol has two phases: Growing phase and Shrinking phase. In growing phase there are certain changes made to the Secure two phase locking Protocol.

4.1 Results

The analysis on the time to notify the database is shown in Figure 2. From the graph, it can be seen that the average time to notify the database is 52ms in Pressbase. However, in CSMDM the average time to notify the database is only 48ms.

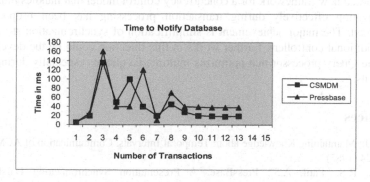

Fig. 2. Time to Notify the Database on Event Occurrence

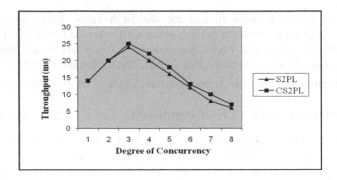

Fig. 3. Throughput Curves with 1 CPU and 2 Disks

In this work, comparative study between the performance of Secure two phase locking protocol and the Concurrent Secure two phase locking protocol was also carried out. The size of database is taken to be small enough to observe frequent conflicts. The throughput is used as the performance metric. Figure 3 shows the throughput measure with 1 CPU and 2 disks. The performance gain of the system rises to about 20% when concurrency control is being employed.

4.2 User Interactions

In CSMDM, multimedia specification is expressed using SMIL and synchronization rules. CSMDM have implemented a process that takes SMIL expressions and generates the forward synchronization rules. CSMDM is capable of handling backward and skip operations since we have adopted a model proposed by Aygun [3] which helps to manage backward and skip interactions using synchronization rules provided by them and the new temporal rules proposed in this work. This model deduces the relationship automatically for the backward presentation without any additional specification. The skip functionality is handled by using comprehensive timeline.

5 Conclusions and Future Enhancements

In this work, a new framework for a concurrency control model that handles multimedia synchronization effectively during transaction processing has been proposed and implemented. The major achievement is simplification of synchronization structure by adding additional controllers. Further works in this direction could be the development of separate Query processor that optimizes multimedia queries especially during online transactions.

References

1. Allen, J.: Maintaining Knowledge about Temporal Intervals. Communication of ACM 26(11), 823–824 (1983)
2. Aygun, R.S., Patil, A.S.: PressBase: A Presentation Synchronization Database for Distributed Multimedia Systems. IEEE Transactions on Multimedia 8(2), 289–296 (2006)

3. Aygun, R.S., Zhang, A.: Management of Backward Skip Interactions using Synchronization Rules. In: IEEE International Conference on Integrated Design and Process Technology, pp. 1–19. IEEE Press, New York (2002)
4. Aygun, R.S., Zhang, A.: SyncRuler- A Flexible Synchronization Model using Model Checking. IEEE Transactions on Knowledge Data Engineering 17(12), 1706–1720 (2005)
5. David, R., Son, S.: Secure Two Phase Locking Protocol. In: Proceedings of IEEE symposium on Reliable Distributed Systems, pp. 123–135. IEEE Press, New York (1993)

Secure QoS Enabled On-Demand Link-State Multipath Routing in MANETS

Rajneesh Gujral[1] and Anil Kapil[2]

[1] Assoc. Professor, Computer Engineering Department, M. M. Engineering College,
M. M. University, Ambala, India
rgujral77@yahoo.com
[2] Professor, M. M. Institute of Computer Technology and Business Management,
M. M. University, Ambala, India
anil_kdk@yahoo.com

Abstract. Mobile ad hoc networks (MANETS) are self-created and self organized by a collection of mobile nodes, interconnected by multi-hop wireless paths in a strictly peer to peer fashion. In MANETS the link bandwidth is limited and to provide Quality of Service (QoS) in term of bandwidth, security for soft real time processing services is very difficult. In this paper, we propose a secure QoS enabled on-demand link-state multipath routing mechanism that reactively collect link-state information from source to destination in order to dynamically construct a flow network, then the QoS enabled multipath routes between source & destination are detected by destination node under the CDMA-over-TDMA channel model of MAC layer, which collectively satisfy required bandwidth and security services during route discovery process (node authentication, secure route establishment, secure data communication). Our mechanism uses symmetric key cryptography and a one-way HMAC based key chain for broadcast node authentication (i.e.TESLA), so that any altering of route discovery packet (i.e. Qo.S route request (QRREQ) packet and QoS route reply (QRREP) is immediately detected).The proposed mechanism has better call acceptance rate in ad hoc wireless networks, where finding a single path satisfying all the QoS requirements is very difficult.

Keywords: QoS, MANET, Security, Multipath.

1 Introduction

Mobile ad hoc networks (MANETS) are self-created and self organized by a collection of mobile nodes, interconnected by multi-hop wireless paths in a strictly peer to peer fashion [1]. The nodes in the network may move and radio propagation conditions may change at any time. In ad hoc wireless networks, the QoS requirements are more influenced by the resources of the nodes, some of the resource constraints are battery charge, processing power and buffer space. The goal of QoS provisioning is to achieve a more deterministic network behaviors, so that information carried by the network can be better delivered and network resources can be better utilized. The QoS parameters differ from application to application.

V. V Das et al. (Eds.): BAIP 2010, CCIS 70, pp. 250–257, 2010.
© Springer-Verlag Berlin Heidelberg 2010

After receiving a QoS service request from the user, the first task is to find a suitable loop-free path from the source to the destination that will have the necessary resource available to meet the QoS requirements of the desired service. This process is known as QoS routing .A number of protocols has been proposed for QoS routing in ad hoc networks [2-7]. As designed, these QoS routing protocols are intended for operation in a trusted environment in which all nodes are honest, and they do not consider the disruptions that can be caused by a malicious attacker sending arbitrary (e.g. forged) routing packets. So it is highly important to secure the routing protocol. If the routing protocol can be subverted and messages can be altered in transit, then no amount of security on the data packets at the upper layers can mitigate threats. Recently, several secure QoS enabled MANET routing protocols have been proposed [8-12]. In this paper, we proposed a secure QoS enabled on-demand link-state multipath routing mechanism that use symmetric key cryptography approach & HMAC (Hash- based Message Authentication Code) key based chaining for broadcast node authentication (TESLA), so that any altering QRREQ message & QRREP is immediately detected. The rest of paper is organized as follow. In section 2, we describe related work, Section 3 describes the working of proposed mechanism and section 4 concludes the paper.

2   Related Works

The increase in multimedia, military application traffic has led to extensive research focused on achieving QoS guarantees in current networks. Early works on QoS provision in MANETS concentrated on achieve required Bandwidth. Initially, a ticket based QoS routing protocol is proposed in which the bandwidth of a link can be determined independently of its neighboring links [2].Another a less stronger CDMA-over-TDMA channel model is assumed in [3] to develop QoS routing in a MANETS where the use of a time slot on a link is only dependent on the status of its one-hop neighboring links. Another protocol the trigger-based (on demand) distributed QoS routing (TDR) protocol [4] was proposed by De et al. for supporting real-time applications in ad hoc wireless networks. Another protocol BR (Bandwidth Reservation) Protocol consists of an end-to-end bandwidth calculation algorithm to inform the source node of the available bandwidth to any destination in the Ad hoc networks, a bandwidth reservation algorithm to reserve a sufficient number of free slots for QoS flow. Another protocol OQR (on-demand QoS routing) protocol to guarantee bandwidth for real time applications. Since routing is on-demand in nature, there is no need to exchange control information periodically and maintain routing tables at each node. Similar to the bandwidth routing (BR) protocol, the network is time-slotted and bandwidth is the key QoS parameter [5]. Another Protocol On-demand Node-Disjoint Multipath routing protocol (NDMR) allows the establishment of multiple paths between a single source and destination node. It is also beneficial to avoid traffic congestion and frequent link break in communication because of the mobility of nodes. The important components of the protocol, such as path accumulation, decreasing routing overhead and selection node-disjoint paths, are explain [6].

Another protocol A Swarm Intelligent Multi-path Routing for multimedia Traffic over Mobile ad hoc networks was proposed to predict the significant traffic problems such as packet losses, transmission delayed, delay variation etc in real time[7].

3 The Proposed Mechanism

The proposed mechanism searches for multiple paths which collectively satisfy the required bandwidth requirement X. The original bandwidth requirement is split in to sub-bandwidth requirements. A mobile node in the network knows the bandwidth available to each of its neighbors. When the source node requires a QoS session with bandwidth X to the destination node, it floods QRREQ packet in the network. To make sure that the destination is receiving route request from claimed source without any modification in en route, it is necessary to embed security during flooding of QRREQ packets. In this paper to implement this mechanism, the process is divided into five phases.

- Secure broadcasting QRREQ Packets.
- Unipath Discovery Operations perform by Destination Node
- Multipath Discovery Operation perform by Destination Node
- Secure Unicasting QREEP packets to Source Node.
- Multipaths Route Maintenance

3.1 Secure Broadcasting QRREQ Packets

In this phase firstly we describe the QRREQ packet forwarding process. When the source node requires a QoS session with bandwidth X to the destination, it floods a QRREQ. Each packet records the path history and all link state information along it route. A QRREQ packet contains the fields $\{S_{id}, D_{id}, N_h, F_{ts}, X, TTL\}$ with their description shown in table 1.

The source node floods a $QRREQ$ $\{S_{id}, D_{id}, N_h = \{S\}, F_{ts} = \{\phi\}, X, TTL\}$ packet in the network toward the destination D. If the given Bandwidth requirement is X then all intermediate nodes receiving a QRREQ packet will perform the following function.

Step 1: Node N checks the node history N_h field of the $QRREQ$ packet for its address. If it is present, the node discards this QRREQ packet.

Step 2: Otherwise, node N decrements TTL by one. If TTL counts down to zero, it discards this QRREQ packet. Node N adds itself into the node history field, appends the free time-slots of the link between itself and the last node recorded in the node history field, into the free time-slot list field and then rebroadcasts this QRREQ packet. Destination eventually received many different QRREQ packets from source. Destination will re-configure the network topology and all of corresponding free time-slot information. The following Six QRREQ packets are collected by Destination D in figure 1 from taking different routes from figure 2.

Table 1. List of Abbreviations

S_{id}	Source node ID
D_{id}	Destination node ID
N_h	Node history fields records the path from source to the current transversed node.
F_{ts}	Free time slot list field contains a list of free time-slots, which each one record a free time slots among the current traversed node and last node recording in the field
X	Bandwidth requirements
TTL	Field limits the hop length of search path
H(X)	Hash of message X with any hashing algorithms for e.g. MD5,SHA-1 etc.
K_A, K_B	TESLA key of node A and B
K_{SD}	Symmetric key between node S and D
A→*	Node A local broadcasting Message

To embed security during route discovery process for source routing protocol of MANETS, the main challenge is to ensure that each intermediate node cannot remove or add extra node in existing nodes in the node history (N_h) field of QRREQ packet. The basic technique is to attach a per-hop authenticator for the source routing forwarder list so that any altering of the list can be immediately detected. So in this paper we used well-known one-way hash function H which authenticates the contents in the chain and $HMAC_{K_{SD}}(S, D)$ authenticates the source to destination relation. The following QEEEQ messages are routed from source S to destination D for path (S, A, B, D).

Step 1: Source S generates $P_S = (QRREQS, D, X, TTL)$ and M_S i.e. $HMAC$ of P_S with symmetric key K_{SD} ,then local broadcast (P_S, M_S) on ad hoc network.

1 QRREQ {$S,D,\{S,A,B,D\},[2,5,9,10],[1,5,8,9],[1,6,8,9],X,TTL$}

2 QRREQ {$S,D,\{S,E,F,D\},[2,3,5,7,9],[3,5,9],[6,8,9],X,TTL$}

3 QRREQ {$S,D,\{S,A,C,B,D\},[2,5,9,10],[2,4,5,8,9],[5,6,8,9],[1,6,8,9],X,TTL$}

4 QRREQ {$S,D,\{S,A,C,F,D\},[2,5,9,10],[2,4,5,8,9],[5,6,8,9],[6,8,9],X,TTL$}

5 QRREQ {$S,D,\{S,E,C,B,D\},[2,3,5,7,9],[2,5,9],[5,6,8,9],[1,6,8,9],X,TTL$}

6 QRREQ {$S,D,\{S,E,C,F,D\},[2,3,5,7,9],[2,5,9],[5,6,8,9],[6,8,9],X,TTL$}

Fig. 1. Show QRREQ Packets form S to D   **Fig. 2.** Show Ad hoc Network Topology

Step 2: For authenticate the contents in the chain, the intermediate node A calculate h_A i.e. hash of (M_S, A) with hashing algorithm H and for authenticate source to destination relations, it find chain of HMAC codes. So far, node A generated P_A and calculates M_A (i.e. MAC code of P_A with node TESLA key K_A) and broadcasted it locally. This process is followed by all the intermediates node of given path (S, A, B, D) as shown below.

S	:	$P_S = (QRREQ, S, D, X, TTL), M_S = HMAC_{K_{SD}}(P_S)$
S→*	:	(P_S, M_S)
A	:	$h_A = H(A, M_S), P_A = (QRREQ, S, D, [A], h_A, [], a, X, TTL),$
		$M_A = HMAC_{K_A}(P_A)$
A→*	:	(P_A, M_A)
B	:	$h_B = H(B, h_A), P_B = (QRREQ, S, D, [A, B], h_B, [M_A], a, b, X, TTL),$
		$M_B = HMAC_{K_B}(P_B)$
B→*	:	(P_B, M_B)

Step 3: Destination node D recomputed h'_B (i.e. $h'_B = H(B,(H(A,HMAC_{K_{SD}}(P_s)))))$ from the P_B. If $h'_B = h_B$ it verifies that no node modification is done during en-route phase.

3.2 Unipath Discovery Operations Perform by Destination Node

In this section, we describe a unipath discovery operation (i.e., path bandwidth calculation algorithm) does not follow the traditional hop-by-hop approach to determine the end-to-end path bandwidth X. The unipath discovery operation determines its maximum path bandwidth by constructing a least-cost-first reservation tree T_{LCF}. Before constructing T_{LCF}, a time-slot reservation tree T is constructed. A time-slot reservation tree T is constructed by the breadth-first-search approach as follows. Given a path{S, A, B, D}, let the root of T be represented as abc, where a represents the bandwidth i.e. set of free-slots of link (S, A) and b represents the bandwidth of link (A, B).Let _ab_ denote the time-slots that are reserved on links _a_ and _b_. Child nodes of root are _abc_ and _abc_ which form the first level of tree T. The tree T recursively expands all child nodes of each node on each level of tree T, and follow the same rules as that of the first level of tree T until the leaf nodes are reached. Each path from root to the leaf nodes gives a time-slot reservation pattern. This pattern is used to reserve time-slot from the source to the destination node. To reduce the time needed to search a path satisfying a given bandwidth requirement X, a least-cost-first time–slot reservation tree T_{LCF} is constructed from the time-slot reservation tree T as follow. To obtain the T_{LCF}, the child nodes on each level of tree T are sorted in ascending order from left to right by using the number of reserved time-slots on them. All T and T_{LCF} trees diagram of the figure 2 are shown below in figure 3(a-f).

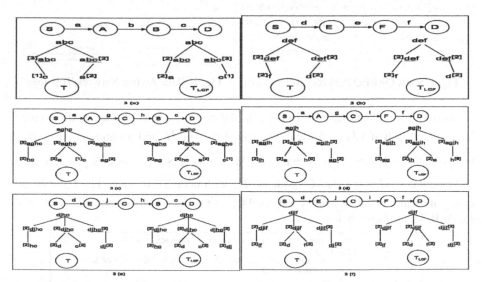

Fig. 3 (a-f). Shows T and T_{LCF} trees for all paths from Source S to Destination D

3.3 Multipath Discovery Operation Perform by Destination

An unipath discovery operation is performed on phase 3.2.Our multipath discovery operation is to sequentially exploit multiple unipaths such that the total sum of path bandwidths fulfills the original path bandwidth X. A centralized algorithm is proposed in the destination to determine the multipaths.Given the path bandwidth is X, the multi-path discovery algorithm is formally given as follow.

Step 1: Let $Bandwidth\_sum$ denote the total sum of multiple unipaths. Initially, we set $Bandwidth\_sum = 0$;

Step 2: An unipath discovery procedure is applied in destination to search all the T_{LCF} trees using depth-first search technique and to find a new QoS path from source to destination having a maximal path bandwidth. If there is more than one path satisfying the maximum bandwidth b, then chooses a path having minimum hop count. Let $Bandwidth\_sum = Bandwidth\_sum + b$, apply the same unipath discovery procedure until $Bandwidth\_sum \geq X$. For e.g. by taking network topology of Figure 2 with bandwidth requirement is 4. The following QoS enabled paths are chosen by destination using unipath discovery procedure satisfying the required bandwidth X=4 as shown in Figure 4 and Figure 5.

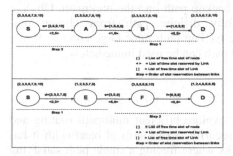 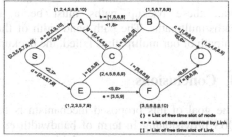

Fig. 4. Show unipaths found by multipath discovery algorithm

Fig. 5. Shows the QoS enabled multipath in Ad hoc network that satisfies the Bandwidth X=4

3.4 Secure Unicasting QRREP Packets to Source Node

Step 1: Destination node D generates reply packet $P_D = \{(QRREP, D, S, [A, B],$ $[M_A, M_B], X, TTL)\}$. It contains the following fields (destination id, source id, node history, MAC codes of all the intermediate nodes, Bandwidth requirement and TTL field), $R_P = HMAC_{K_{SD}}[abc, a]$ (which contain encrypted reservation pattern of chosen path) and $M_D = HMAC_{K_{SD}}(P_D)$ (which contain MAC code of P_D with symmetric key K_{SD}). After the destination D determines a multipath, it initiates a secure

QRREP packet unicast to source node S. So in the ad hoc network of Figure 2, the following QoS enabled multipaths (S, A, B, D) and (S, E, F, D) are selected. The following process is followed by destination D to unicast secure QRREP on path (S, A, B, D).

Step 2: Every intermediate node receives the packet and adds their TESLA key (i.e. the key that is used during QRREQ to find the chain of MAC codes).

$$D : P_D = \{(QRREP, D, S, [A, B], [M_A, M_B], X, TTL)\},$$
$$R_P = HMAC_{K_{SD}}[abc, a], M_D = HMAC_{K_{SD}}(P_D)$$

$$D \rightarrow B : (P_D, R_P, M_D, [])$$

$$B \rightarrow A : (P_D, R_P, M_D, [K_B])$$

$$A \rightarrow S : (P_D, R_P, M_D, [K_B, K_A])$$

Step 3: Source node S can recomputed M'_D from received P_D. If $M'_D = M_D$ then there is no modification in en-route and source & destination relation is confirmed. So with the same process destination node D send secure QRREP packet to source S through all the other selected QoS enabled paths.

3.5 Multipaths Route Maintenance

The multipath maintenance presented herein to provide a single-path tolerant capability. This multipath maintenance is to add a backup path into the multipath. Observe that, these backup paths must be a fully disjoint path from chosen unipaths/multipaths. The path bandwidth of the backup path must large enough, if any unipath of our multipath is failed, the backup path can be used immediately.

4 Conclusions

The goal of this proposed mechanism is to explore efficient multipath routing and QoS provisioning in term of bandwidth & security. So in term of bandwidth it has better call acceptance rate in Ad hoc networks where finding a single path satisfying all the QoS requirements is very difficult. But the overhead of maintaining and repairing paths is very high as compared to traditional routing protocols. For secure route discovery, we use symmetric key cryptography & HMAC chaining approach for authenticating source and destination relation and no modification is done during en-route process. This mechanism offers detection of several malicious behaviors and robustness under most of routing attacks (e.g. spoofing, modification, fabrication, routing loops and Denial of service Attacks), while minimizing the cryptographic computational overhead.

References

[1] Pitt, J., Venkatarram, P., Mamdani, A.: QoS Management in MANETS Using Norm-Governed Agent Societies. In: Dikenelli, O., Gleizes, M.-P., Ricci, A. (eds.) ESAW 2005. LNCS (LNAI), vol. 3963, pp. 221–240. Springer, Heidelberg (2006)
[2] Chen, S., Nahrstedt, K.: Distributed Quality-of Service Routing in Ad hoc Networks. IEEE Journal on Selected Areas in Communications 17(8), 1488–1504 (1999)

[3] Lin, C.R.: On-Demand QoS Routing in Multihop Mobile Networks. In: Proceedings of IEEE INFOCOM 2001, pp. 1735–1744 (April 2001)

[4] De, S., Das, S.K., Wu, H., Qiao, C.: Trigger-BasedDistributed QoS Routing in Mobile Ad hoc Networks. ACM SIGMOBILE Mobile Computing and Communications Review 6(3), 22–34 (2002)

[5] Lin, C.R.: On –Demand QoS Routing in Multi-Hop Mobile Networks. In: Proceedings of IEEE INFOCOM 2001, vol. 3, pp. 1735–1744 (April 2001)

[6] Li, X.: Multipath Routing and QoS Provisioning in Mobile Ad hoc Network. PhD. Thesis, Dept. of Electronics Engineering, Queen Mary, University of London (April 2006)

[7] Ziane, S., Mellouk, A.: A Swarm Intelligent Multi-path Routing for Multimedia Traffic over Mobile Ad hoc Networks. In: Proceeding of Q2SWinet 2005, Montreal, Quebec, Canda, pp. 55–62 (October 2005)

[8] Bucciol, P., Li, F.Y., Fragoulis, N., De Martin, H.C.: Hierarchical and QoS-Aware Routing in Multihop Wireless Mesh Networks. Springer, London (2009)

[9] Hu, Y.-C., Johnson, D.B.: Securing Quality-of-Service Route Discovery in On-Demand Routing for Ad hoc Networks. In: Proceedings of SANS 2004, Washington, USA, pp. 106–117 (October 2004)

[10] Crepeau, C., Davis, C.R., Maheswaran, M.: A secure MANET routing Protocol with resilience against Byzantine behaviors of malicious or selfish nodes. In: Proceeding of 21st IEEE International conference on Advanced Information Networking and Applications Workshops AINAW 2007, Canda (2007)

[11] Krichene, N., Boudriga, N.: On a QoS Intrusion Tolerant Routing protocol in Ad hoc networks. In: Al agha, K. (ed.) International Federation for Information Processing (IFIP), Ad hoc Networking, vol. 212, pp. 29–46. Springer, Boston (2006)

[12] Toubiana, V., Labiod, H.: ASMA: Toward Adaptive Secured Multipath in MANETS. In: Pujolle, G. (ed.) IFIP International Federation For Information Processing, Mobile and Wireless Communication Networks, vol. 211, pp. 175–185. Springer, Boston (2006)

A Novel Approach for Building a Dynamically Reconfigurable Trustworthy Distributed System

Shakti Mishra, D.S. Kushwaha, and A.K. Misra

CSED, Motilal Nehru National Institute of Technology, Allahabad
{shaktimishra,dsk,akm}@mnnit.ac.in

Abstract. Trust management systems are the robust architectural frameworks for allowing authorization to resources of a distributed computing environment that could be cluster and grid based extendible to peer to peer paradigm. A policy driven methodology is adopted in cluster based architecture in order to provide control to remotely accessible resources. The interaction between nodes and resource allocation with trustworthiness dimensions is a central challenge in building a trustworthy distributed system. By imposing authentication procedure in a cluster, nodes can grant access to their critical resources to each other thus forming a trusted relationship. This work addresses the crucial issue of forming a trusted cluster of distributed entities in order to facilitate resource sharing and load balancing. Experimental results show that the communication cost of establishing trust among entities in terms of number of message exchange by our approach is reduced by 11–18% with comparable memory consumption.

Keywords: Trust, Load Balancing, Authentication, Process Migration Server.

1 Introduction

Distributed environment provide open access to resource and information, but offer few security mechanisms to protect them. One solution is to deploy traditional cryptographic techniques [3]. Distributed architectures are highly dynamic and volatile in nature; single authorization based on identity of a user is not a flexible approach [2]. The coordination among distributed entities is fragile and can easily be damaged by selfish behaviors, malicious attacks and even unintentional misconfigurations [1]. Wu et. Al. [5] proposes Trusted Cluster Computing (TCC) to automatically construct user trustable cluster computing environment. Deqing Zou et. Al. [6] propose an automated trusted negotiation architecture which the authors call the virtual automated trust negotiation (VATN) to centralize automated trust negotiation policies. The trusted intermediaries [7] are the systems which authenticate clients and servers such as the Certificate Authorities in public key based systems and KDC in Kerberos. A decentralize approach [3] is used to establish trust in the information provided by specific nodes in a distributed infrastructure based on the reputation of the nodes. An agent based approach [8] envisages on-line and off-line monitoring in order to analyze users' activity but the authors have not considered

V. V Das et al. (Eds.): BAIP 2010, CCIS 70, pp. 258–262, 2010.

the level of trust at the time of joining the nodes. Sun et. Al [4] addresses various dynamic properties of trust and trust models. The problem associated with their approach is that a chain of recommendation leads to single point crash failure.

Based on the previous researches, we find that a comprehensive approach for trustworthiness in cluster based distributed systems for load balancing is needed to address the following issues:

- Single tier identity based authorization
- Multiple entities participating for a single operation
- Determination of trust when a node joins a cluster
- Periodic identification of malicious nodes based on activities performed.

2 Proposed Approach

This work addresses the issue of building trust among the distributed entities of cluster.

2.1 TrustProb: A Measure of Trust

Our proposed trust management framework is based on measurement of trust probability. As per the work carried out in [10], it is proposed that probability based mechanism can be used to measure the trust value of each node. We propose that the value of trust at each node can be quantified by assigning a trust probability (TrustProb). This trust value lies between 0 and 1.

2.2 Trust Scale and Classification of Nodes

Before assigning TrustProb to each node, we can draw a Trust Scale based on TrustProb as in Fig. 1.

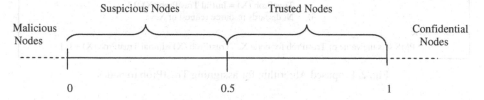

Fig. 1. Trust Scale based on TrustProb and classification of nodes

2.3 Trust Management Framework for Load Balancing

The central coordinator Process Migration Server (PMS) [9, 10] is responsible for updating the value of TrustProb for each node. Each node is required to register itself to the PMS via registration module. The node authentication module (NAM) grants session_id to each node and maintains NAM table which includes the entries as Node_id, Resource_id, and Node_Session_id. This table is sent to migration module of PMS for further updation. As nodes initiate sharing and demanding resources for load balancing, the migration module adds TrustProb to NAM.

2.4 Our Proposed Trust Building Approach

A cluster comprises of various nodes. As a new node X joins the cluster and its initial TrustProb is set to 0 by migration module. Now, this node X sends a request for a resource R to PMS via migration module. This module sends back the list of nodes owning resource R with their TrustProb to X. X selects a node on the basis of the highest value of TrustProb, say a trusted node N_1, from given list and sends its process directly to node N_1. Since, a newly joined node can be potentially harmful; Node N_1 scans the codes sent by X through security utility.

---

1. A new node X wants to join the cluster. Set Initial TrustProb=0 for newly joining nodes.
2. If new node X request for resource <R_r „CPU, Memory, Network Bandwidth> to PMS
    a. PMS returns the list of designated nodes equipped with requested resource to X.
    b. X selects one node (say N_1) from the list and migrates its process to N_1.
    c. N_1 scans the code of X by security utility routine.
        i. If found "OK", allocate resource to X.
            1. Send Code Found "No Error" message to PMS (migration module).
            2. PMS sets the value of TrustProb for node X, TrustProb (X) =Initial TrustProb +0.1
            3. N_1 sends the Execution Result back to X.
            4. X scans the Execution result.
                a. If found "OK",
                    X sends Result Found "No Error" message to PMS.
                    PMS sets the value of TrustProb for node N_1 TrustProb (N_1) = TrustProb (N_1) +0.1
                b. Else
                    X sends Result Found "Error" message to PMS.
                    PMS sets the value of TrustProb for Node N_1, TrustProb (N_1) = TrustProb (N_1) -0.1
        ii. Else
            1. N_1 sends Code Found "Error" message to PMS.
            2. PMS sets the value of TrustProb for node X, TrustProb (X) = Initial TrustProb (X)-0.1
            3. N_1 discards resource request of X.
3. Else
    PMS sets the value of TrustProb for node X, TrustProb (X) =Initial TrustProb (X) + 0.1

Fig. 2. Proposed Algorithm for assigning TrustProb to nodes

3 Simulation and Results

We compared the performance of our proposed approach with previous approaches. The set of experimental results were average values of 10 iterations. In order to analyze, the efficiency and scalability of proposed algorithm, the server performance has been recorded in terms of memory consumption, communication cost in terms of number of message exchange and number of threads.

Figure 3 shows the number of threads required on server. Figure 4 indicates the communication cost of incurring trust among entities in terms on number of message exchanged.

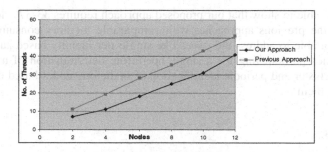

Fig. 3. No. of Threads (Y-axis) on the server (Our approach vs. previous approach)

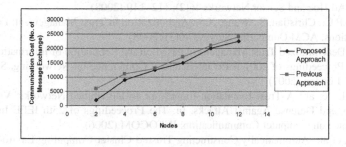

Fig. 4. Communication Cost (*in terms of no. of message exchange*) on the server

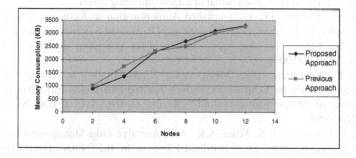

Fig. 5. Memory Consumption (*in KB*) on the server (Our approach vs. previous approach)

4 Conclusion

The interaction between nodes and resource allocation with trustworthiness dimensions is a central challenge in building a trusted distributed system. We have made an attempt to design a policy driven methodology in order to dynamically scan the activities of the nodes thereby assigning the trust probability. This in turn provides control to remotely accessible resources in cluster based architecture. Experimental results show that the communication cost of establishing trust among entities in terms of number of message exchange by our approach is reduced by 11–18%. The implementation includes the Node Authentication Module table with trust probability.

We have been able to show that our proposed approach requires 33-37% lesser no. of threads than the previous approaches with comparable memory consumption. This work has been able to address the issues like single tier identity based authorization, multiple entities participating for a single operation, determination of trust when a node joins a cluster and periodic identification of malicious nodes based on activities performed by them.

References

1. Sun, Y., Han, Z., Ray Liu, K.J.: Defense of Trust Management Vulnerabilities in Distributed Networks. IEEE Communications Magazine, Feature Topic on Security in Mobile Ad Hoc and Sensor Networks 46(2), 112–119 (2008)
2. Chapin, P.C., Christian, S., Wang, X.S.: Authorization in Trust Management: Features and Foundations. ACM Computing Surveys 40(3) (2008)
3. Yu, Z.: Decentralized Trust Management based on the Reputation of Information Sources. In: The Proceedings of 2007 IEEE International Conference on Networking, Sensing and Control, London (2007)
4. Sun, Y.L., et al.: A Trust Evaluation framework in Distributed Networks: Vulnerability Analysis and Defense Against Attacks. In: The Proceedings of 25th IEEE International Conference on Computer Communication: INFOCOM (2006)
5. Wu, Y., et al.: Automatically Constructing Trusted Cluster Computing Environment. The Journal of Supercomputing (July 2009)
6. Zou, D., et al.: Building an Automated Trust Negotiation Architecture in Virtual Computing Environment. The Journal of Supercomputing (2009)
7. Sirbu, M.A., Chuang, J.C.-I.: Distributed Authentication in Kerberos using Public Key Cryptography. In: Symposium on Network and Distributed System Security, p. 134 (1997)
8. Skakun, S., Kussul, N.: An Agent Approach for providing Security in Distributed Systems: TCSET (2006)
9. Mishra, S., Kushwaha, D.S., Misra, A.K.: Jingle-Mingle: A Hybrid Reliable load Balancing approach for Load Balancing in a Trusted Distributed Environment. In: IEEE Proceedings of 5th International Joint Conference on INC, IMS & IDC, NCM 2009, pp. 117–122 (2009)
10. Mishra, S., Kushwaha, D.S., Misra, A.K.: A Cooperative Trust Management framework for Load Balancing in Cluster based Distributed System. In: IEEE International Conference on Recent Trends in Telecommunication, Information and Computing (accepted, 2010)

An Improved Three Pattern Huffman Compression Algorithm for Medical Images in Telemedicine

Divya Mohandass[1] and J. Janet[2]

[1] Research Scholar, St.Peter's University, Avadi, India
[2] Veltech Dr.RR. & Dr.SR Technical University, Chennai, India
divya.skrec@gmail.com, janetjude1@rediffmail.com

Abstract. The objective of this paper is to effectively improve the existing Huffman lossless compression algorithm and to evaluate its performance on various types of medical imaging data like CT, MRI, Ultrasound, and X-ray images. Huffman Algorithm is a statistical coding technique. It is technically simple to implement for both the purposes of encoding and decoding .In this paper, a pattern finder component is proposed, which determines the best component and the most frequent occurring pattern in the image to be transmitted via the telemedicine network. The best pattern will be an input to the encoder and the output of the encoder would be the compressed image and the footer information. The footer information comprises of the data which were compressed and needs to be inserted at the decoder component. The proposed pattern replacement greatly enhances the performance in terms of improved compression ratios over the existing system. It is aptly applicable for data transfer where bandwidth should be at an optimal level. The present work yields 4-5% improved compression ratio, thereby permitting reduced traffic on the telemedicine network.

Keywords: Huffman compression, Pattern finder, Lossless compression, Telemedicine.

1 Introduction

Telemedicine aims at providing reliable and quality health care for continuous diagnosis, providing patient care and treatment at an affordable cost [1] [2]. Despite several advantages, compression efficiency is one major threat for effective data transfer. Compression is a process used to reduce the physical size of the information, which in turn, results in minimum space usage. The time taken for transmission and the bandwidth on a network are also reduced [3]. The current work deals with the compression of medical images and concepts of developing a compression algorithm whose efficiency surpasses the existing system by achieving better compression ratios.

2 Related Work

Medical images used at medical facilities are now commonly digitalized due to corresponding advances in Information Technology. CT (Computed Tomography) or MRI

V.V Das et al. (Eds.): BAIP 2010, CCIS 70, pp. 263–268, 2010.
© Springer-Verlag Berlin Heidelberg 2010

(Magnetic Resonance Image) generates digitalized signals by its own, and diagnostic images from legacy devices can be digitalized by film scanner. They are one of the most important means for diagnosis and for controlling the therapeutic action.

The past two decades witnessed a number of image compression algorithms [4] [5]. Based on the ability of reconstruction from the compressed images, they could be broadly categorized into lossless and lossy compression .The medical fraternity primarily relied on lossless compression schemes to maintain the integrity of data [6].

Huffman coding is an entropy encoding algorithm used for lossless data compression [7]. Variable length code table is used for encoding a source symbol such as a character in a file. The variable-length code table has been derived in a particular way, based on the estimated probability of occurrence for each possible value of the source symbol.

Huffman coding uses a specific method for choosing the representation for each symbol, resulting in a code. It is also known as prefix-free codes, which means that, the bit string representing some particular symbol is never a prefix of the bit string representing any other symbol. The most common characters use shorter strings of bits. Huffman was able to design the most efficient compression method .No other mapping of individual source symbols to unique strings of bits will produce a smaller average output size when the actual symbol frequencies agree with those used to create the code.

For a set of symbols with a uniform probability distribution and a number of members which is a power of two, Huffman coding is equivalent to simple binary block encoding, e.g., ASCII coding. Huffman coding is a widespread method for creating prefix codes.

The goal of this work is to present a new method for lossless compression of medical images. It is based on Huffman compression. The 3-pattern Huffman compression is expected to give improved compression ratios than the existing system.

3   Materials and Methods

The proposed three pattern compression algorithm based on the Huffman compression algorithm [8] uses a new concept named the pattern finder. The basic steps involved in a Huffman coding technique are

  a) Histogram the residual image.
  b) Combine two bins of the lowest value until there is only one bin left and build
     a coding tree.
  c) The residual image is encoded and the coding tree is saved with the encoded
     values.

The operation of the pattern finder is to find the best pattern. The best pattern is the most frequently occurring pattern. Therefore the best pattern will also be an input to the encoder. The output of the encoder will be the code together with the footer information [9].

The effect of this research on the outlook of information technology is to develop data delivery systems where communication bandwidth should be optimal. The compressed medical image in the existing 2-pattern Huffman algorithm, displays low image

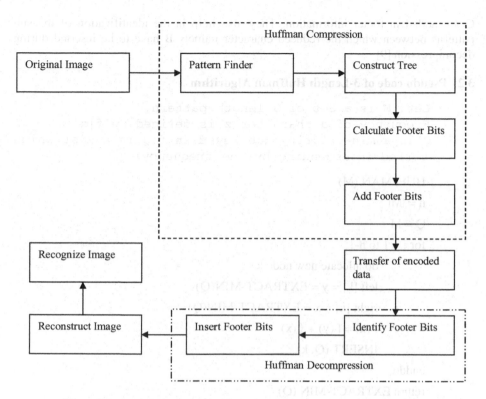

Fig. 1. Proposed system for improved three pattern Huffman compression

quality as compared to the 3-pattern Huffman algorithm. In this paper, a 3-pattern Huffman compression algorithm with better compression ratio and with no compromise in the quality of the image is proposed.

The Pattern Finder step further includes checking for three best patterns. The three patterns are replaced with a single set of footer information [9]. The proposed system is shown in Figure 1.

3.1 Pattern Finder

The idea is based on the redundant nature of the character or signals in the data. Consider for example a 3-length pattern commonly occurring in text files say ABC. We can also encounter its sub pattern of length 2(i.e.) AC. So we encode all the ABC patterns as AC in the corresponding compressed version. To differentiate between ABCs and ACs in order to bring out the exact original file on decoding, the concept of a new feature called Footer information is introduced. Through this footer information bits we add 1s to indicate the presence of B in ABCs and 0s to denote the absence of B in the sub patterns ACs. These bits are added at the end of the compressed file after coding other characters in the file. These extra sets of bits are called *footer bits*, as they resemble footer note of a word document that is added at the end of the page. To identify the start of footer bits from the normal compressed bits, the codes for first and third characters found in the pattern being selected are added. The codes of A and

C are added in footer information. They also help in the identification of the sub patterns between which the reduced character namely B have to be inserted during decompression [9].

3.2 Pseudo code of 3-Length Huffman Algorithm

```
Let, M is a Set of 3 length pattern.
Frequency of a character z is defined by f|z|
Q is a min-priority que keyed on f(Q is a list which
sorted in ascending by the frequency)
```

HUFFMAN (M)

n = |M|

Q = M

for i = 1 to n-1

      do allocate new node k

      left [k] = y = EXTRACT-MIN(Q)

      right [k] = x = EXTRACT-MIN(Q)

      f (k) = f (y) + f (x)

      INSERT (Q, k)

enddo

return EXTRACT-MIN (Q)

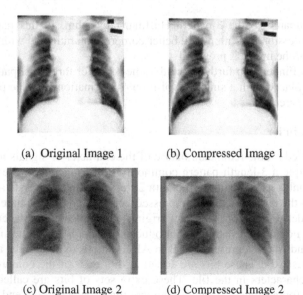

(a) Original Image 1   (b) Compressed Image 1

(c) Original Image 2   (d) Compressed Image 2

Fig. 2. (a) Original Image 1 (b) Compressed Image1(c) Original Image 2 (d) Compressed Image 2

4 Experimental Results and Discussion

The image set used in this study consisted of 20 digital posterior anterior chest radiographs obtained from different patients. A commercial detector system was used to obtain the images. The images selected for this investigation included studies in men and women with pneumonia, pulmonary nodules, and interstitial lung disease.

Output parameters like compression ratio are determined by the efficiency of system.

% of compression ratio = (Original file size) – (Compressed file size) / (Original file size) x100.

Original image 1 is a scan image of the chest. The original size of the image occupies 451308 bytes. The proposed 3-pattern Huffman compression algorithm is applied. The size of the compressed image is reduced to 17094 bytes, thereby achieving a compression ratio of 26.4%. The results obtained from the above sample test images are given in Table 1.

Table 1. 3-Pattern Huffman Compression Results

Image	Raw Image(bytes)	Compressed Image(bytes)	Compression Ratio %
Original Image1	451308	17094	26.4
Original Image2	513216	37588	13.65

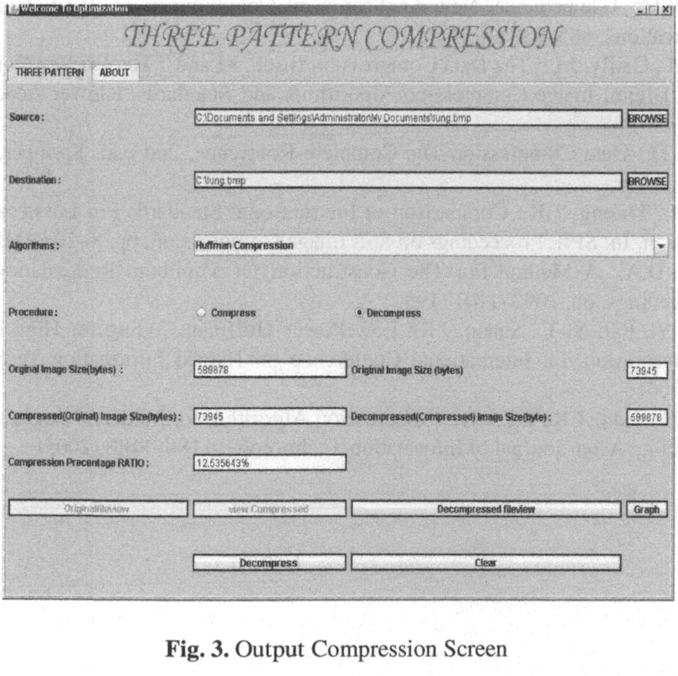

Fig. 3. Output Compression Screen

Experimental results obtained from the proposed 3-pattern compression algorithm were encouraging. The average telecommunication and storage costs are cut to 1/3 compared to old fashioned plain systems. After testing the algorithm on a reduced set of images we have opened the possibility to apply the same to different models and different medical images. On decompression, the file regains its original image with file size to be 451308 bytes. The same applies to image 2.The chest X ray image occupies 513216 bytes. The size of the image is reduced to 37588 bytes on applying the 3-pattern Huffman compression algorithm. A compression ratio of 13.65% is achieved. The Output screenshot is shown in Figure 3.

5 Conclusion

This paper focuses on the 3-pattern Huffman Algorithm for various types of medical images.

Experimental results reveal that the proposed method show superior results. Improved compression ratios are obtained without any loss of information. In future, compression ratio can be improved and more efficiency is to be verified by enhancing the existing 3 pattern to 4-pattern replacement. We are currently working on a hybrid compression method which could be tested on different categories of medical images.

References

1. Moghadas, A., Jamshidi, M., Shaderam, M.: Telemedicine in a Health Care System. In: Automation Congress WAC, pp. 1–6 (2008)
2. Holzer, W.H.: Telemedicine: New Application of Communications. IEEE Transactions on Communications, 685–688 (1974)
3. Nelson, M., Gailly, J.L.: The Data Compression Book. M and T Books, NewYork (1995)
4. Kou, W.: Digital Image Compression Algorithms and Standards. Kluwer Academic Press, Boston (1995)
5. Salomon, D.: Data Compression-The Complete Reference, 2nd edn. Springer, Heidelberg (2001)
6. Arps, R.B., Truong, T.K.: Comparison of International Standards For Lossless Still Image Compression. In: SPIE Proceedings on Still Image Compression, pp. 8–20 (1995)
7. Huffman, D.A.: A Method For The Construction Of Minimum Redundancy Codes. In: IRE Proceedings, pp. 1098–1101 (1952)
8. Chen, C.-Y., Pai, Y.-T., Shanq, J.R.: Low Power Huffman Coding for High Performance Data Transmission. In: International Conference on Hybrid Information Technology, pp. 71–77 (2006)
9. Janet, J., Natesan, T.R.: Effective Compression Algorithm for Medical Images as an Aid To Telemedicine. Asian Journal of Information Technology, 1180–1186 (2005)

Encryption Algorithm for Block Ciphers Based on Programmable Cellular Automata

Abhishek Ray and Debasis Das

School of Computer Engineering, KIIT University, Bhubaneswar-751024
ar_mmclub@yahoo.com, deba16@gmail.com

Abstract. A Cellular Automata (CA) is a computing model of complex System using simple rule. In this paper the problem space is divided into number of cell and each cell can be one or several final state. Cells are affected by neighbor's with the application of simple rule. This paper deals with the Cellular Automata in cryptography for a class of Block Ciphers through a new block encryption algorithm based on programmable cellular automata. The proposed algorithm belongs to the class of symmetric key systems.

Keywords: Cellular Automata, Programmable Cellular Automata, Cryptography, Block Ciphers.

1 Introduction

The popularity of Cellular Automata [2] can be traced to their simplicity and are used for the modeling of complex system using simple rule [1]. This can be viewed as a simple model of a spatially extended decentralized system made up of a number of individual components, called as cell. The communication between cells is performed using simple rules. Each individual cell is in a specific state, which changes over time depending on the state of its local neighbors. The overall structure can be viewed as parallel processing device. The state of each cell is updated simultaneously at discrete time based on the states in the neighborhood at the preceding time step.

The block encryption algorithm used to compute the next cell state based on CA local rules. The local rules are classified based on existing catagories [3,5,6]. A CA is called Programmable CA if it employs some control signal.

The main aspects of information security [4] due to rapid Information Technology application in various fields are privacy, data integrity, authentication, and non-repudiation. Encryption and decryption are two complementary operations satisfying the demand of privacy. Cryptographic techniques are divided into two categories [4] symmetric key and public key. There are two classes of symmetric key encryption schemes [4] block ciphers and stream ciphers. This paper deals with symmetric key block ciphers and consider both issues of encryption and decryption. CA has been used so far in both symmetric key and public key cryptography. CA based public cipher was proposed by Guan [7]. Security of block encryption algorithm was based on difficulty of solving a system of nonlinear polynomial equations. Stream CA based encryption algorithm was first proposed by Wolfram [8]. The idea was to use CA as a

V.V Das et al. (Eds.): BAIP 2010, CCIS 70, pp. 269–275, 2010.

pseudo-random number generator (PRNG). The Generated sequence was combined using XOR operation with the plain text. The result of that operation formed the cipher text. The secret key was the initial state of CA. In the decryption process some pseudo-random sequence needed to be regenerated using the secret key and then combined with the cipher text.

2 Survey of Existing Encryption Algorithm

2.1 Motivation

The IDEA encryption algorithm uses the 64 bit plain text and 128 bit key. The AES encryption algorithm is based on 128 bit plain text and 256 bit key block. By increasing both plain text size and key size in the different block cipher algorithm, the security as well as the cost will increase but encryption or decryption system slows down increasing the complexity of the circuit. This paper deals with the symmetric key based block encryption algorithm to reduce the circuit complexity.

As CA uses simple rule for modeling complex system the selection of rule configuration will reduce the circuit complexity. The block encryption algorithm is chosen to be cellular automata based because CA achieves higher parallelism and simplify the implementation.

2.2 Encryption Algorithm Based on PCA

The Encryption method is proposed in this paper based on programmable CA. The block diagram of PCA encryption systems is presented in Fig-1. The rules specify the evolution of the CA from the neighborhood configuration to the next state and these are presented in Table-1.

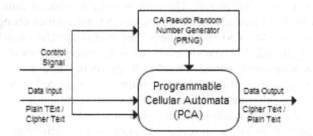

Fig. 1. Block Diagram of PCA Encrytion System

The corresponding combinational logic of rules 90 and 150 for CA can be expressed as follows:

$$Rule90 : a_i(t+1) = a_{i-1}(t) \oplus a_{i+1}(t) \tag{1}$$

$$Rule150 : a_i(t+1) = a_{i-1}(t) \oplus a_i(t) \oplus a_{i+1}(t) \tag{2}$$

Table 1. The rules that updated the next state of the CA cells

Rule	111	110	101	100	011	010	001	000
90	0	1	0	1	1	0	1	0
150	1	0	0	1	0	1	1	0
153	1	0	0	1	1	0	0	1
102	0	1	1	0	0	1	1	0
195	1	1	0	0	0	0	1	1
51	0	0	1	1	0	0	1	1
60	0	0	1	1	1	1	0	0

The simple CA is used to provide real time keys for the block cipher. The operation of the simple CA can be represented by the state transition graph.

Each node of the transition graph represents one of the possible states of the CA. The directed edges of the graph correspond to a single time step transition of the automata.

If we consider a 4 bit hybrid CA under the null boundary condition the rule vector is (90, 150, 90, 150). The transition graph is shown in Fig-2.

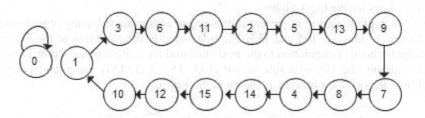

Fig. 2. The state transition diagram of a maximal length group

The combinational logic of rules 153, 102, 195, 51 and 60 [1] for the programmable CA can be expressed as follows:

$$Rule153 : a_i(t+1) = a_i(t) \oplus a_{i+1}(t) \tag{3}$$

$$Rule102 : a_i(t+1) = a_i(t) \oplus a_{i+1}(t) \tag{4}$$

$$Rule195 : a_i(t+1) = a_{i-1}(t) \oplus a_i(t) \tag{5}$$

$$Rule60 : a_i(t+1) = a_{i-1}(t) \oplus a_i(t) \tag{6}$$

$$Rule51 : a_i(t+1) = \neg a_i(t) \tag{7}$$

The rules 153, 195, 51, 60, 102, 204 are used in the block chipper [4] scheme.

Algorithm 1: Null boundary State Transition for CA:
Input : Rule Vector Size (n) and CA State Size
Output : State Transition Diagram for CA
Step 1 : Enter The Initial State of CA
Step 2 : Convert decimal value to binary and store in an Array
Step 3 : for j=1 to 2^n,
Step 4 : for i=1 to n
Step 5 : Apply the corresponding rule on the i^{th}Cell
Step 6 : Store the next state value
Step 7 : Convert binary to decimal value
Step 8 : End of loop2
Step 9 : End of loop1
Step 10 : Stop.

3 Proposed Model Based on PCA for Encryption

The rule combination for the programmable CA is based on elementary CA. So, the output of the simple CA is applied on the control signals of the pro- grammable CA. The proposed encryption system is realized using the combina- tion of two CA. One is elementary CA and the other is programmable CA. This PCA is used to provide real time keys for the block cipher.

The encryption algorithm present in this paper is constructed using programmable CA based on rules 51, 195 and 153. The rules specify the evolution of the CA from the neighborhood configuration to the next state and these are represented in Table 1.

Considering the CA with rule vector (153, 153, 153, 153) under null boundary condition, the cycle is obtained as shown in the Fig-3.

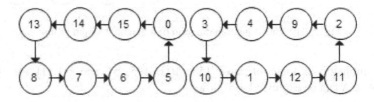

Fig. 3. The state transition diagram of a non maximal length group

In Fig-3, the CA has two equal length cycles and each cycle has a cycle length 8, which is a basic requirement of the enciphering process.

Algorithm 2: Enciphering and Deciphering Process
Input : Given Plain Text/Cipher Text
Output : Cipher Text/Plain Text
Step 1 : Create State Transition Diagram of Cycle length using rule vector and apply
         the Corresponding rule.
Step 2 : Insert the value of plain text into original state of CA.
Step 3 : If it is goes to its immediate state after four cycles then
Step 4 : Plain Text is enciphered into cipher text.

Step 5 : Else After running another four cycle the immediate state return back to its original state.

Step 6 : The cipher text is deciphered into plain text.

A circuit with two control signals C1 and C2 are shown in Fig-4. When C1 is logic 0 then rule 51 is applied to the cell. When C1 is logic 1 and C2 is logic 0 then the cell is configure with rule 195. When C1 and C2 are both logic 1 then the cell configure with rule 153.

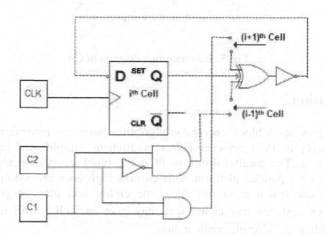

Fig. 4. PCA Structure with rule 51, 153 & 195

Considering the CA with rule vector (51, 51, 195, 153) under null boundary conditions, we obtain the cycle as shown in the Fig-5.

Table 2. Selection of rule 51, 195, 153

C1	C2	Rules Applied
0	0	51
0	1	51
1	0	195
1	1	153

Cellular Automata used for modeling of complex system using simple rule. The selection of rule configuration reduce the circuit complexity. Block Encryption Algorithm are chosen PCA because reduce the circuit complexity. So, the diagram is not complex in Fig-4 and the corresponding truth table is simple in Table 2.

In Fig-5 the CA has four equal length cycles, each cycle has a cycle length 4. Considering this PCA as an enciphering function and defining a plaintext as its original state it goes to its immediate state after two cycles which is enciphering process. After running another two cycles, the immediate state returns back to its original state which deciphers cipher text into plain text ensuring deciphering process.

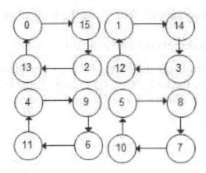

Fig. 5. State transition diagram of CA

4 Conclusion

This paper presents a block encryption algorithm based on programmable cellular automata theory as PCA achieves higher parallelism, simplify the implementation with cheap cost. The parallel nature of PCA the block encryption algorithm to be implemented on a parallel platform. This ensures high encryption/decryption speed. In the PCA encryption algorithm, the same cipher text may be generated from different plain text and any cipher text may give as well to different plain text depending different PCA rule configuration.

References

[1] Wolfram, S.: A new kind of science. Wolfram Media, Inc., Champaign (2002)
[2] Adamatzky, A., Alonso-Sanz, R., Lawniczak, A., Martinez, G.J., Morita, K.: In: Worsch, T. (ed.) AUTOMATA-2008 Theory and Application of Cellular Automata (2008)
[3] Kahata, A.: Cryptography and Network Security, 2nd edn. Tata Mc-graw hill, New York (2008)
[4] Stallings, W.: Cryptography and Network Security, 3rd edn. Prentice-Hall, Englewood Cliffs (2003)
[5] Seredynski, M., Bouvary, P.: Block Cipher Based on Reversible Cellular Automata. New Generation Computing 23, 245–258 (2005)
[6] Kundu, A., Pal, A.R., Sarkar, T., Banarjee, M., Guha, S.K., Mukhopadhayay, D.: Comparative Study on Null Boundary and Periodic Boundary Neighbourhood Mulriple Attractor Cellular Automata for Classification. In: IEEE 2008 (2008)
[7] Guan, P.: Cellular Automaton Public Key Cryptosystem. Complex system 1, 51–56 (1987)
[8] Wolfram, S.: Cryptography with cellular Automata, pp. 429–432. Springer, Heidelberg (1985)
[9] Tripathy, S., Nandi, S.: LCASE: Lightweight Cellular Au- tomata Based on Symmetric Key Encryption. International Journal of Network Security 8(2), 243–252 (2009)

[10] Pal Chaudhuri, P., Roy Chowdhury, D., Nandi, S., Chattopadhyay, S.: Additive Cellular Automata Theory and Applications, vol. 1. IEEE Computer Society Press, USA (1997)

[11] Ganguly, N.: Cellular Automata Evolution: Theory and Applications in Pattern Classification. PhD thesis, B. E. College (2003)

[12] Anghelescu, P., Ionita, S., Safron, E.: Block Encryption Using Hybrid Additive Cellular Automata. In: 7th International conference on Hybrid Intelligent Systems, IEEE 2007 (2007)

Performance Analysis of Reactive Routing Protocols with OSPF for IEEE 802.11s Wireless Mesh Network

Dhaval K. Patel[1], S.K. Shah[2], and Minesh P. Thaker[3]

[1,3] Lecturer, V.T Patel Department of Electronics and Communication,
Charotar University of Science and Technology, Changa, Guj, India
dhavalpatel.ec@ecchanga.ac.in, mineshthaker.ec@ecchanga.ac.in
[2] Professor, Electrical Engineering Department, Faculty of Technology & Engineering,
M. S. University of Baroda, Kalabhavan, Vadodara, Guj, India
skshsh-eed@msubaroda.ac.in

Abstract. WMNs are dynamically self-organizing; self-configuring and self-healing in nature to maintain the communication with neighbors in the network. Routing protocols in WMN protocols requires different metrics as compared to ad-hoc network. A performance analysis is done on reactive routing protocols to verify the suitability of reactive routing protocols over WMN under IEEE 802.11s. The suitability of Ad Hoc On-Demand Distance Vector (AODV) and Dynamic MANET On-demand (DYMO) routing protocol are compared with OSPF (Open shortest path first) is explored.

Keywords: Wireless Mesh Network (WMN), Routing Protocols, AODV, DYMO, Qualnet.

1 IEEE 802.11s Mesh Network Architecture

Wireless Mesh Network (WMN) has emerged as important architectures for the future wireless communications [1, 2, 3]. The WLAN Mesh architecture comprises the different IEEE 802.11 based elements like Mesh Points (MP), Wireless Distribution System (WDS) which is a collection of MPs, Mesh Access Point (MAP), Mesh Portals (MPP) and different type of STA (stations) which may be mobile or stationary. The proposed architecture of mesh network IEEE 802.11s draft as shown in Fig.1.

The Station (STA) is a node that requests services but neither forward frames nor participates in path discovery mechanisms. The formation and operation of the mesh cloud can be handled by different MP connected with each other. Mesh Access Point (MAP) which is an MP who has attached with access point (AP). It provides services to the stations. Mesh Portal Point (MPP) acts as a bridge or gateway between the mesh cloud and external net. The doted lines represent the mesh network itself (mesh cloud) in which other non-802.11s nodes may participate indirectly (solid lines) connecting to mesh nodes extended with access point functionalities (MAPs).

V.V Das et al. (Eds.): BAIP 2010, CCIS 70, pp. 276–280, 2010.

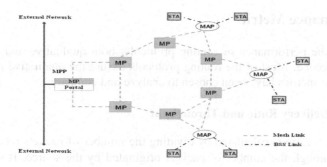

Fig. 1. IEEE 802.11s meshed WLAN Mesh architecture

A description of un-optimized Link state routing protocol as OSPF and reactive routing protocols as AODV and DYMO is covered in section 2, while the performance metric are covered in Section 3. Comparative Simulation result of these protocols is covered in Section 4, which leads to expedite standardization of 802.11s as in [4, 5, 6].

2 Protocol Description

2.1 AODV (Ad hoc On-demand Distance Vector)

AODV algorithm is inspired from the Bellman-Ford algorithm like DSDV. The principal change is to be On Demand. The node is requesting a route for a packet, a "ROUTE REQUEST" packet will be sent to the direct neighbor. If a neighbor has a route corresponding to the request, a packet "ROUTE REPLY" will be returned, otherwise, each neighbor will forward the "ROUTE REQUEST" to their own neighbors. Process continues until a route has been found. A "ROUTE ERROR" packet is unicast to all previous forwarders and to the sender of the packet if link is broken as described in [7, 8].

2.2 DYMO (Dynamic MANET On-demand)

The Dynamic MANET On-demand (DYMO) protocol is a reactive routing protocol and improvement over the AODV protocol. DYMO routing protocol enables reactive, multi hop unicast routing between participating DYMO routers. The basic operations of the DYMO protocol are route discovery and route maintenance as described in [9, 10].

2.3 OSPF (Open Shortest Path First)

OSPF is a very comprehensive and complex routing protocol, and has implemented several extensions to adapt to different network types [11]. OSPF is a link-state (LS) routing protocol. Each router running OSPF maintains a database describing the Autonomous System's (AS) topology. The database is referred to as the Link-State database (LS-database) from the LS-database each router constructs a tree of shortest path to the rest of the network with itself as a root [12, 13].

3 Performance Metric

To evaluate the performance of routing protocols, both qualitative and quantitative metrics are needed. Most of the routing protocols ensure the qualitative metrics. The following four metrics have been chosen to analyze and compare.

3.1 Packet Delivery Ratio and Throughput

Packet delivery ratio is calculated by dividing the number of packets received by the destination through the number of packets originated by the source. It specifies the packet loss rate, which limits the maximum throughput of the network. Throughput is the average number of messages successfully delivered per unit time. Better the delivery ratio, the more complete and correct is the routing protocol.

3.2 End-to-End Delay and Average Jitter

End-to-end delay represents the average data delay an application or a user experiences when transmitting data. The end to end delay shows the suitability of the protocol for these applications. Jitter is the time variation of a characteristic of the latency packets at the destination.

4 Simulation Environment and Results

The network was designed carefully which is facilitate to appraise and vary the impact of node density (STA), with DYMO. The Qualnet Simulator which has a scalable network libraries and gives accurate and efficient execution [14, 15] was used Simulations were carried out with different STA connected with MAPs and MPs of mesh architecture.

Table 1. Different parameters for IEEE 802.11s mesh network simulation

STA Density Variations	traffic flow (CBR)	terrain	path loss model	Data rate	Mobility Model	Network Protocol	channel frequency
0-100	512 bytes	1500m X 1500m	two ray	2mbps	Random Waypoint	IPv4	2.4 GHz

The performance of AODV was very good in all network sizes. AODV and DYMO protocols perform relatively well in small networks (i.e. 5-20 STA), when only few hops need to be taken to reach the destination node. At medium range with 25 STAs DYMO's performance is an increase in terms of throughput and PDR both but exponentially decay as numbers of STAs increases. Fig. 3 indicates that throughput for both the protocols is similar in low density networks, but as density increases, AODV

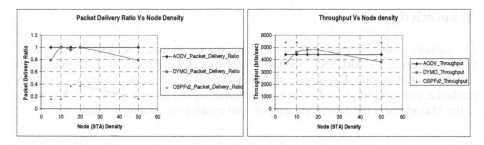

Fig. 2. PDR   **Fig. 3.** Throughput

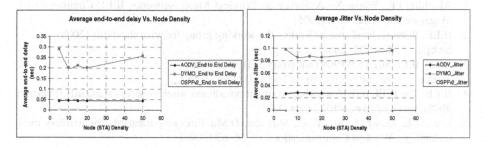

Fig. 4. Average End to End Delay   **Fig. 5.** Average Jitter

outperforms than the DYMO. Exponential drop in AODV suggests that as the network size grows, AODV manages to deliver the packets with reliability greater than 95%. Form Fig 4 and Fig 5, it may be concluded that AODV has the lowest average end-to-end delay and jitter compared with DYMO has significantly high average end-to-end delay and jitter.

OSPF is a typical representative of link state routing protocols. It can be easily observed that due to its mentioned property average end-to-end delay and jitter both are very less compared to AODV and DYMO. With increase in node intensities, delay in AODV explodes and is very unstable and OSPF maintains the delay experienced by the packets in a relatively low level. However, Fig 2 and Fig. 3 suggest that OSPF has worst PDR as compared to DYMO and AODV, so when high PDR is desirable OSPF may not be used.

5 Conclusion

With simulations it is found that with the increase in density of the network the end-to-end delay for DYMO protocol increased. AODV is a good performer in both low and high dense networks as compared to DYMO and OSPF with respect to PDR and throughput. AODV has relatively higher packet delivery ratio and throughput, but OSPF achieves low end-to-end delay and jitter. OSPF needs relatively much time to converge, as messages are transmitted from one node to another. This may introduce instability, particularly when nodes are also moving.

Acknowledgement

The authors wish to thank Research paper review committee, Faculty of Technology and Engineering, CHARUSAT, and Dr. Y. P. Kosta, Dean-Faculty of Technology and Engineering, Charotar University of Science and Technology, Changa for their guidance, encouragement and support in undertaking the present work. Special thanks to the Management for their moral support and continuous encouragement.

References

1. Akyildiz, I.F., Wang, X.: A Survey on Wireless Mesh Networks. IEEE Communication Magazine 43(9), S23–S30 (2005)
2. IEEE. Wireless local area networks - the working group for wlan standards (2008), http://ieee802.org/11/
3. IEEE. IEEE 802.15 WPAN task group 5, TG5 (2003), http://www.ieee802.org/15/pub/TG5.html
4. IEEE. The IEEE 802.16 working group on broadband wireless access standards (February 2008), http://ieee802.org/16/
5. Lee, M.J., Zheng, J., Ko, Y.-B., Shrestha, D.M.: Emerging standards for wireless mesh technology. Wireless Communications 13, 56–63 (2006)
6. Max, S., Zhao, R., Denteneer, D., Berlemann, L., Hiertz, G.R.: Principles of IEEE802.11s. In: Proceedings of 16th International Conference on Computer Communications and Networks, ICCCN 2007, August 13-16, pp. 1002–1007. IEEE, Los Alamitos (2007)
7. Perkins, C.E., Royer, E.M.: Adhoc on-demand distance vector routing. In: Proceedings of the 2nd IEEE Workshop on Mobile Computing Systems and Applications (WMCSA), pp. 90–100 (1991)
8. Das, S.R., Perkins, C.E., Royer, E.M.: Performance Comparison of Two On-Demand Routing protocols for Ad Hoc Networks. In: Proceedings, FOCOM 2000, Tel-Aviv, Israel (March 2000)
9. Nacher, M., et al.: Multipath Extensions to the DYMO routing protocol. In: Proceedings of the 9th International Conference on Mobile and Wireless Communications Networks, Cork, Ireland, September 19-21. IEEE, Los Alamitos (2007)
10. Chakeres, I.D., Perkins, C.E.: Dynamic MANET On demand (DYMO) Routing, Internet-Draft (July 2007), http://www.ietf.org/internetdrafts/draft-ietf-manet-dymo-10.txt
11. http://www.ietf.org/rfc/rfc1583.txt
12. http://www.cisco.com/univercd/cc/td/doc/cisintwk/ito_doc/ospf.htm
13. http://www.ietf.org/rfc/rfc2178.txt
14. Scalable Network Technologies, "Qualnet simulator," SoftwarePackage (2003), http://www.qualnet.com
15. The software, http://www.scalablenetworks.com

Quality of Service On-demand Power Aware Routing Algorithm for Wireless Sensor Networks

Deepali Virmani[1] and Satbir Jain[2]

B5/107 Mayur Apartment, Sector 9, Rohini, Delhi, India
deepalivirmani@gmail.com

Abstract. Wireless Sensor networks are non-infrastructure networks which consist of mobile sensor nodes. Since the mobile nodes have limited battery power, it is very important to use energy efficiently in sensor networks. In order to maximize the lifetime of sensor networks, traffic should be sent via a route that can avoid nodes with low energy thereby minimizing the total transmission power. In addition, considering that the nodes of sensor networks are mobile, on-demand routing protocols are preferred for sensor networks. In this paper, we propose a novel on-demand power aware routing algorithm supporting quality of service called QDPRA. QDPRA prolongs its network lifetime by compromising between minimum energy consumption and fair energy consumption without additional control packets. QDPRA also improves its data packet delivery ratio, minimizes delay and maximizes throughput of the network.

Keywords: SPIN, LEACH, DDiff, RTREQ, RTREP, QDPRA.

1 Introduction

A sensor network is a collection of wireless sensor nodes that come together to form a self-organizing network without any support from the existing fixed communication infrastructure. In such a network, each device plays the role of a router and has limited battery energy. Thus, it is widely accepted that conventional routing protocols are not appropriate for sensor networks and consequently, the design of routing protocols for such networks is a challenging issue taking power factor into consideration. The physical layer can save energy by adapting transmission power according to the distance between nodes. At the data link layer, energy conservation can be achieved by sleep mode operation. The purpose of on demand power-aware routing protocols is to maximize the network Lifetime and minimize energy consumption by only transmitting message when there is demand of that message (Sleep and Wake technology). The network lifetime is defined as the time when a node runs out of its own battery power for the first time [1]. If a node stops its operation, it can result in network partitioning and interrupt communication. Minimizing the total energy consumption tends to favor min-hop routes. However, if the min-hop routes repeatedly include the same node, the node will exhaust its energy much earlier than the other nodes and the network lifetime will decrease.

V.V Das et al. (Eds.): BAIP 2010, CCIS 70, pp. 281–289, 2010.
© Springer-Verlag Berlin Heidelberg 2010

This paper proposes an on-demand power-aware routing algorithm supporting quality of service called QDPRA (Quality of Service On-Demand Power Aware Routing Algorithm). Our proposed routing algorithm balances between minimum transmission energy consumption and fair node energy consumption in a distributed manner.

The rest of the paper is organized as follows. Section 2 reviews typical routing algorithms and discusses the pros and cons from the viewpoint of the network lifetime. In Section 3, we present our proposed power-aware routing algorithm in detail. Section 4 describes the simulation results and performance comparison. Finally, we conclude this paper in Section 5.

2   Overview of Routing Algorithms

2.1 Sensor Protocols for Information via Negotiation (SPIN)

Heinzelman et.al. in [2] and [3] proposed a family of adaptive protocols called Sensor Protocols for Information via Negotiation (SPIN) that disseminates all the information at each node to every node in the network assuming that all nodes in the network are potential base-stations. One of the advantages of SPIN is that topological changes are localized since each node needs to know only its single-hop neighbors. SPIN provides much energy savings than flooding and meta- data negotiation almost halves the redundant data.

2.2 Low-Energy Adaptive Clustering Hierarchy (LEACH)

LEACH is a clustering-based protocol that minimizes energy dissipation in sensor networks [4]. LEACH randomly selects sensor nodes as cluster heads, so the high energy dissipation in communicating with the base station is spread to all sensor nodes in the sensor network. However, data collection is centralized and is performed periodically. Therefore, this protocol is most appropriate when there is a need for constant monitoring by the sensor network. LEACH can suffer from the clustering overhead, which may result in extra power depletion.

2.3 Directed Diffusion (DDiff)

In [5], C. Intanagonwiwat et al. proposed a popular data aggregation paradigm for WSNs, called directed diffusion. Directed diffusion is a data-centric (DC) and application- aware paradigm in the sense that all data generated by sensor nodes is named by attribute-value pairs. The main idea of the DC paradigm is to combine the data coming from different sources and combines them by eliminating redundancy, minimizing the number of transmissions; thus saving network energy and prolonging its lifetime. But still power consumption is high .

Therefore we propose an algorithm that tries to prolong the network lifetime by compromising between minimum energy consumption and fair energy consumption without additional control packets. QDPRA also improves its data packet delivery ratio, minimizes delay and maximizes throughput of the network.

3 Quality of Service On-demand Power Aware Routing Algorithm (QDPRA)

3.1 Basic Idea

Generally in on-demand routing protocols [6] and [7], the source floods an RTREQ (Route-Request) packet to search a path from source to destination. The destination node receives the RTREQ packet and unicasts an RTREP (Route-reply) packet to the source to set up a path. Likewise, our proposed QDPRA is an on-demand algorithm. QDPRA doesn't use additional control packets to acquire necessary information for power aware routing but utilizes RTREQ packets which are already used in on-demand routing protocols. QDPRA only requires the average residual battery level of the entire network, which can be obtained without any control packets other than RTREQ packets. In our proposed algorithm, intermediate nodes control the rebroadcast time of the RTREQ packet, where retransmission time is proportional to the ratio of average residual battery power of the entire network to its own residual battery power. In other words, nodes with relatively larger battery energy will rebroadcast RTREQ packets earlier. Because on-demand routing protocols drop duplicate RTREQ packets without rebroadcasting them, QDPRA can set up the route composed of the nodes with relatively high battery power.

3.2 Average Residual Battery Power Estimation

Basically the nodes use their residual battery power for the rebroadcast time of RTREQ packets. If the time is determined only by the nodes absolute residual battery power, then the retransmission time will increase as time passes by. Therefore, the relative measure should be used. As a relative measure, we used the average residual batter power of the entire network. The exact value of this average power can be acquired by periodic control packets, but using periodic control packets isn't an on-demand method and it also consumes more energy.

To estimate the average energy, our proposed algorithm uses only RTREQ packets that are already used in on-demand routing. For this end, AR and NR fields are added to the packet header, where AR is the average residual battery power of the nodes on the path and NR is the number of hops that the RTREQ packet has passed. The mechanism to obtain the estimated average value is as follows.

1. First, the source records its own battery power to the AR field, and sets the NR to 1, and broadcasts the RTREQ packet.
2. Assume that a node x has received an RTREQ packet, and the node x's residual batter power is BP_x and the AR value of the RTREQ packet is AR_{old}. Then the average residual battery power, AR_{new}, of new route that includes the node x is as following

$$AR_{new} = \frac{AR_{old} \times NR + BP_x}{NR + 1} \tag{1}$$

Before the node $x3$ rebroadcasts the packet, it updates AR to AR_{new} and increases the value of NR by one.

This step is not executed for duplicate RTREQ packets.

3. Whenever a node x receives an RTREQ packet, it calculates the average residual battery power of the network by the following equation.

$$AEr_{new} = (1 - \beta) AEr_{old} + \beta AR_{old} \qquad (2)$$

where β is the weighting factor of the moving average. The β is set to 0.75 in our simulations.

3.3 Rebroadcast Time Control

A node x determines its rebroadcast time T_R as follows.

$$T_R = D_T \times \left(\frac{AEr}{BP_x} \right) \qquad (3)$$

is the estimated average power, BP_x is its own residual power, and D_T is a constant to scale the retransmission time. According to equation (3), if the residual battery power Bp_x is smaller than the average network residual power AEr, then the retransmission time D_T will be longer, and if BP_x is larger then vice versa. So if the individual battery power BP_x is larger than the average, then the node x would tend to be selected as a member of the route, which results in fair energy consumption among the nodes. When the residual battery power variation is small, most nodes have a similar retransmission time. In that cast, the route with a smaller hop count will be selected. This shows that QDPRA compromises between the min-hop path and the fair energy consumption path.

3.4 Delay Metric

Each node includes in the *Hello* message, during the neighbor discovery performed by the QDPRA, the creation time of this message. When a neighbor node receives this message, it calculates the difference between such a time and the current time, which represents the *MD* (Measured Delay) .This delay, includes the queuing time, the transmission time, the collision avoidance time and the control overhead time. Otherwise, the measurement of the one-way delay avoids the increase of traffic load at adding acknowledgment messages to the QDPRA protocol. Average Delay (*AD*) is calculated as follows.

$$AD = \gamma \times AD + (1 - \gamma) MD \qquad (4)$$

Where γ is the delay parameter and γ is set to 0.5 in our simulations.

3.5 Bandwidth Metric

A flow is formed by the packets with the same pair of source and destination. When a data flow takes a path P, it interacts with other flows in the near neighborhood of the nodes which compose P. The principle in a wired network is simpler because flows interact only between each other, when they go through the same link. Moreover, nodes can reserve bandwidth. The higher bandwidth used by flows is the higher performance of the algorithm. The saturate bandwidth B_{sat} [8] is the minimum bandwidth on a link when all the flows of this link have the same bandwidth. It can be represented on a graph (G, V) by the function:

$$\forall (A_x, A_{x+1}) \in V \quad B_{sat} = \min \left\{ \frac{b_{x,y+1}}{Nf_x} \right\} \tag{5}$$

Where $b_{x,y+1}$ is the bandwidth of link (A_x, A_{x+1}) and Nf=$_x$ is the number of flows on this link. Highest saturate bandwidth can be calculated by the formula:

$$B_{sat} \max = \max \left(Bsat^{R_1}, \ldots, Bsat^{R_n} \right) \tag{6}$$

Where $R_1, \ldots\ldots, R_n$ are all possible loop free routing links for a given network and B_{sat}^{Rz} is the saturate bandwidth yielded by the algorithm. The algorithm which returns B_{sat}max is optimal . So the problem is to find the saturate bandwidth.

In wireless network, collisions may interfere with packet transmissions. Moreover, it is difficult to reserve a part of bandwidth. Many algorithms use the TDMA access method to reserve a bandwidth part on a shared channel. However, nodes need to be synchronized [9]. We modify the definition of the saturate bandwidth so that the network collisions are taken into account. As a consequence, the saturate bandwidth can be represented in a graph (G, V) by:

$$\forall (A_x, A_{x+1}) \in V \quad B_{sat} = \min \left(\frac{\min (SP_x, SP_{x+1}) - B_{coll}}{Nf_x} \right) \tag{7}$$

Where SP_x is the speed of the node interface x and Nf_x is the number of flow of the link. (x, x+1) .B_{coll} is the bandwidth with collision on this link. is necessary to calculate the number of packets transmitted by the link layer. In [9] a method to calculate the time for a collision-free packet transmission is given. So the bandwidth seen by one packet of M bits can be calculated as

$$B_{packet} = \frac{M}{(T_{TT} + T_{CAT} + T_{CDT} + T_{COT}) \times RT + \sum_{n=1}^{RT} T_{BT_n}} \tag{8}$$

Where T_{TT} is the packet transmission time, T_{CAT} is the Collision Avoidance phase time, T_{CDT} is the collision detection time, T_{COT} is the Control Overhead time (e.g. RTS, CTS, etc.), RT the number of necessary transmissions, T_{TBn} is the Backoff time for nth retransmission. Then we derive the bandwidth with collisions for each packet P as follows:

$$B_{coll}(P) = \frac{M_P}{(T_{TT} + T_{CAT} + T_{CDT} + T_{COT}) \times (RT_p - 1) + \sum_{n=1}^{RT} T_{BT_n}} \quad if \ RT_P > 1 \tag{9}$$

$$B_{coll}(P) = 0 \quad if \quad RT_p = 1 \tag{10}$$

The increase of the saturate bandwidth involves an increase of the flow path bandwidth. The only increase of the bandwidth does not imply all the time an increase of the saturate bandwidth. so we use a weight function($W(p)$) in our proposed routing algorithm to give a path with the highest bandwidth. Finally, for a path $p = (v_1, \ldots\ldots, v_n)$ the weight function is:

$$W(p) = \frac{\sum_{x=1}^{n=1} \frac{x}{B_{x,y+1}}}{1 - \max\left(\frac{B_{coll}^2}{B_{1,2}}, \ldots\ldots, \frac{B_{coll}^n}{B_{n-1,n}}\right)} \tag{11}$$

Our weight function is asymmetric i.e. for two paths P and P' with $w(P) \leq w(P')$, a path P'' can exist and breaks the order relation so $w(P',P'') \leq w(P,P'')$.

4 Simulations

We used J-Sim (Java simulator supporting wireless networks) to compare the performance of QDPRA with that of existing power-aware routing algorithms SPIN, LEACH, DDiff.

4.1 Simulation Model

In all simulations, the same topology is used, where 100 nodes are uniformly distributed and nodes are 150m apart. The initial energy of all the nodes is 0.3J. The transmission power is 250mW and the receiving power is 150mW. A node waits a maximum pause time of 500 seconds. The traffic is CBR. The data packet length is 500 bytes. Each node pauses for 70 seconds and moves to a random position at the maximum speed of 2m/s (average 1m/s).

4.2 Results

4.2.1 Network Lifetime
Figure 1 shows the number of nodes that run out of their battery power as a function of time. If the slope is small, it means that the variation of the lifetime of the nodes is large. That is, the use of batteries is unfair. On the contrary, if the slope is steep, it means that the battery power of the nodes has been fairly used.

Comparing the network lifetime of each algorithm, the SPIN had the shortest lifetime of 52 seconds. SPIN routing also had the smallest slope, which means the energy was consumed unfairly among the nodes. Although LEACH extended the network lifetime to approximately 78 seconds by using battery power evenly among the nodes, the lifetime extension wasn't so good since it tended to select long paths

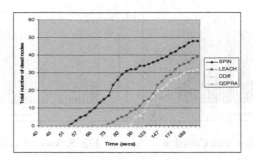

Fig. 1. Expiration Sequence of nodes

with many hops to guarantee fairness. DDiff minimized the network energy consumption and extended its network lifetime to 93 seconds. As DDiff used additional control packets, the network lifetime didn't increase dramatically compared to SPIN. QDPRA showed better performance than the others. The network lifetime increased to 128 seconds which is about 2.5 times longer than that of SPIN routing. The network lifetime is about 1.4 times longer than that of DDiff. This improvement is due to the fair energy consumption without additional control packets.

4.2.2 Delivery Ratio
Figure 2 shows a comparison of the delivery ratio among power-aware routing algorithms. We can see that the better power-aware routing algorithms also have a better delivery ratio. QDPRA showed the highest delivery ratio of about 95% with the increasing number of nodes, which is approximately 13% higher than that of SPIN and approximately 7% higher than that of DDiff. The delivery ratio is increased because residual battery power are excluded from the route in power-aware routing algorithms.

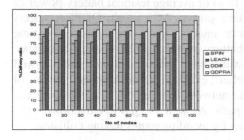

Fig. 2. % Delivery Ratio   **Fig. 3.** Saturate Bandwidth

4.2.3 Saturate Bandwidth
In figure 3, we show the saturate bandwidth according to the number of flows in network of 10 nodes. The saturate bandwidth decreases with the increase of the number of flows, because when the number of flows grows the saturate link is crossed by a higher number of flows. As compared with previous algorithms our proposed algorithm shows most promising results but maximizing the bandwidth utilization.

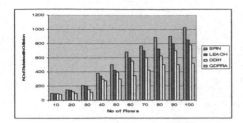 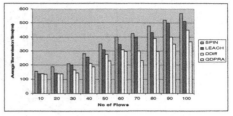

Fig. 4. Packets with Collision   **Fig. 5.** Average Transmission Time

4.2.4 Packets with Collision

The analysis of simulation traces in figure 4 shows that our algorithm chooses paths with few collisions than those chosen by SPIN, LEACH and DDiff. The reason is that the path doesn't change, except when a link is down.

4.2.5 Average Delay

Figures 5 depicts an improvement of average transmission time i.e. the complete time between a data packet leaves the sender node and arrives in the destination node. As expected, the average transmission time is reduced in QDPRA , minimizing the average delay and a gain of 17% is achieved.

5 Conclusion

In this paper, we proposed a new power-aware routing algorithm called QDPRA. QDPRA is an on-demand routing protocol which sets its route in a distributed manner. QDPRA only requires average residual battery level of the entire network, which can be obtained without other control packets except for RTREQ packets. When RTREQ packets are broadcasted, the rebroadcast time is determined by the amount of time which is proportional to the ratio of average residual battery power of the entire network to its own residual battery power. As a result, QDPRA selects nodes that have relatively abundant battery energy. Since the rebroadcast time dynamically varies according to residual battery power, QDPRA keeps a balance between min-hop routing and fair battery consumption. The simulation results showed several advantages of QDPRA over other existing algorithms in terms of performance. QDPRA not only prolongs the network lifetime but also improves the delivery ratio by selecting a more reliable path. As well as QDPRA maximizes the bandwidth utilization and minimizes the delay by avoiding routes having collision.

References

1. Li, Q., Aslam, J., Rus, D.: Online Power-aware Routing in Wireless Ad-Hoc Networks. In: MOBICOM, New York, pp. 303–309 (2001)
2. Heinzelman, W., Kulik, J., Balakrishnan, H.: Adaptive Protocols for Information Dissemination in Wireless Sensor Networks. In: 5th ACM/IEEE Mobicom Conference (MobiCom 1999), Seattle, WA, August 1999, pp. 174–185 (1999)

3. Kulik, J., Heinzelman, W.R., Balakrishnan, H.: Negotiation-based protocols for disseminating information in wireless sensor networks. Wireless Networks 8, 169–185 (2002)
4. Subramanian, L., Katz, R.H.: An Architecture for Building Self Configurable Systems. In: IEEE/ACM Workshop on Mobile Ad Hoc Networking and Computing, Boston, MA, August 2005, pp. 45–51 (2005)
5. Intanagonwiwat, C., Govindan, R., Estrin, D.: Directed diffusion: a scalable and robust communication paradigm for sensor networks. In: ACM MobiCom 2005, Boston, MA, pp. 56–67 (2000)
6. Johnson, D., Maltz, D.: Dynamic Source Routing Ad Hoc Wireless Networks. Mobile Computing (1996)
7. Perkins, C., Royer, E.: Ad-hoc On-Demand Distance Vector Routing. In: 2nd IEEE Workshop on Mobile Computing, Systems and Applications, pp. 78–85 (1999)
8. Wang, J., Nahrstedt, K.: Hop-by-Hop Routing Algorithm for Premium-class Traffic in Diffuser Networks. In: INFOCOM 2002, pp. 23–39 (2002)
9. Elson, J., Romer, K.: Wireless Sensor Networks: A New Regime for Time Synchronization. ACM Computer Communication Review (CCR) 33(1), 149–154 (2003)

A Cryptographic Approach to Defend against IP Spoofing

Mangalam Ravi, S. Narasimman, G.K. Arun Kumar, and D. Karthikeyan

Department of Information Technology, Anna University, Chennai
mangalan@gmail.com, narasi.mit@gmail.com,
arun.theprofessional@gmail.com,
karthik88foru@gmail.com

Abstract. IP spoofing has often been exploited by Distributed Denial of Service (DDoS) attacks to: 1) conceal flooding sources and dilute localities in flooding traffic, and 2) coax legitimate hosts into becoming reflectors, redirecting and amplifying flooding traffic. Thus, the ability to filter spoofed IP packets near victim servers is essential to their own protection and prevention of becoming involuntary DoS reflectors. Our scheme is based on a firewall that can distinguish the attack packets (containing spoofed source addresses) from the packets sent by legitimate users, and thus filters out most of the attack packets before they reach the victim. We estimate that an implementation of this scheme would require the cooperation of only about 20% of the Internet routers in the marking process. The scheme allows the firewall system to configure itself based on the normal traffic of a Web server, so that the occurrence of an attack can be quickly and precisely detected. By this cryptographic approach, we aim at combining both the existing approaches namely, Victim Based and Router Based approaches against IP spoofing thereby enhancing the speed of detection and prevention of IP spoofed packed.

Keywords: Distributed denial-of-service attacks, firewall, IP address spoofing, packet filtering.

1 Introduction

Today, the Internet is an essential part of our everyday life and many important and crucial services like banking, shopping, transport, health, and communication are partly or completely dependent on the Internet. The incidents which has raised the most concern in recent years are the denial-of-service (DoS) attacks whose sole purpose is to reduce or eliminate the availability of a service provided over the Internet, to its legitimate users. This is achieved either by exploiting the vulnerabilities in the software, network protocols, or operation systems, or by exhausting the consumable resources such as the bandwidth, computational time and memory of the victim .These types of attack work by sending a large number of packets to the target, so that some critical resources of the victim are exhausted and the victim can no longer communicate with other users, for which ip spoofing is most popular tool. Packets sent using the IP protocol include the IP address of the sending

V.V Das et al. (Eds.): BAIP 2010, CCIS 70, pp. 290–296, 2010.

host. The recipient directs replies to the sender using this source address. However, the correctness of this address is not verified by the protocol. This implies that an attacker could forge the source address to be any he desires. This is a well-known problem and has been well described in all but a few rare cases, sending spoofed packets is done for illegitimate purposes.

2 Related Work

2.1 Probabilistic Packet Marking

Probabilistic Packet Marking (PPM) is a marking technique, in which the routers insert path information into the Identification field of IP header in each packet with certain probability, such that the victim can reconstruct the attack path using these markings and thus track down the sources of offending packets. Peng et al. proposed to reduce the number of packets needed for the attack path reconstruction in PPM, by dynamically changing the marking probability of a router according to its location in the path. If each router marks packets with a fixed probability, the victim needs to wait for the packets marked by the routers farther away from it, which are relatively fewer. Therefore, the farther a router is to the victim, the higher the marking probability should be.

2.2 Deterministic Packet Marking

Belenky and Ansari proposed a deterministic marking approach (DPM), in which only the address of the first ingress interface a packet enters instead of the full path the packet passes (as used in PPM) is encoded into the packet.

2.3 Neighbor Stranger Discrimination (NSD)

Neighbor Stranger Discrimination (NSD) approach, NSD routers perform signing and filtering functions besides routing. It divides the whole network into neighbors and strangers. If the packets from a network reach the NSD router directly without passing through other NSD routers, this network is a neighbor network. Two NSD routers are neighbor routers to each other if the packets sending between them do not transit other NSD routers. Therefore, a packet received by an NSD router must either from a neighbor networks, or from a neighbor router. Each NSD router keeps an IP addresses list of its neighbor networks and a signatures list of its neighbor routers. If a packet satisfies neither of the two conditions, it is looked as illegitimate and dropped.

3 Existing Approaches for Detecting and Preventing IP Spoofed Attacks

Recent scheme for this purpose are based on packet marking scheme some popular schemes are as follows. For marking purpose, the 16-bit Identification field in IP header has been commonly employed as the marking space. The ID field is currently used to indicate IP fragments belonging to different packets, but only less than 0.25% of the packets on the Internet actually use this feature. Therefore, employment of ID-field as the marking space will not much affect the normal transmission of IP packets.

3.1 Stack Pi: New Packet Marking and Filtering

The Pi DDoS defense scheme is composed of a packet marking algorithm that encodes a complete *Path Identifier* (Pi) in each packet; and a packet filtering algorithm, that determines how a DDoS victim will use the markings of the packets it receives to identify and filter attack packets.Because each packet contains the complete path marking, and the marking for a path is unchanging, then the victim need only identify a single attack packet or flow in order to block all subsequent packets arriving from the same path, and presumably, from the same attacker.

Draw backs of stack pi

1. ID field of IP packet used as stack and overwritten after over flow.
2. No of router and No of packet required to detect and prevent spoofing is more.
3. Slow speed.

3.2 Marking-Based Detection and Filtering (MDADF)

Though source IP addresses can be spoofed by attackers, the path packets take to the destination are totally decided by the network topology and routers in the Internet. There-fore, the path a packet has taken can really show the source of it. The simplest way is to add all the routers' IP addresses into the packet. Since the length of a path is uncertain, it is difficult to reserve enough space in the packet. In order to avoid the increase in packet size, a router puts its IP address into the marking space of each packet it receives;if there is already a number in that space, it calculates the exclusive-or of its address with the previous value and puts the new value back. This method ensures that the marking does not change its length when a packet travels over the Internet.MDADF scheme has the following functions:

1. Distinguish and filter out spoofed packets by checking the marking of each packet using the Filter Table.
2. Detect the occurrence of DDoS attack, so that appropriate defensive measures can be taken before serious damage is caused.
3. Ensure that not many legitimate packets are dropped mistakenly, due to route changes on the Internet.

3.2.1 Marking Scheme

To make the marking scheme more effective, we let each router perform a Cyclic Shift Left(CSL) operation on the old marking Mold and compute the new marking as $M = CSL(Mold)\_MR$. In this way, the order of routers influence the final marking on a packet received by the firewall.

```
Marking procedure at router R (having IP address A):
k <- a 16-bit random number
M(R) <- k XOR h(A)
For each packet w
        If W.ID = 0 Then
            w.ID <- M(R)
Else
        M_old <- w.ID
        M_new <- M(R) XOR CSL(M_old)
        w.ID <- M_new
```

On employing this marking scheme, when a packet arrives at its destination, its marking depends only on the path it has traversed. If the source IP address of a packet is spoofed, this packet must have a marking that is different from that of a genuine packet coming from the same address. The spoofed packets can thus be easily identified and dropped by the filter, while the legitimate packets containing the correct markings are accepted.

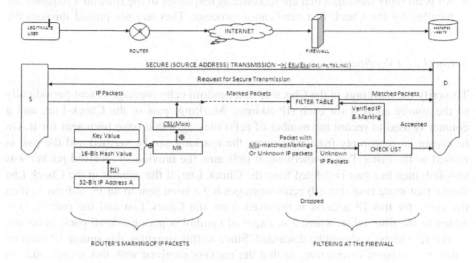

Fig. 1. The System Structure

3.2.2 Filtering Scheme

After the learning phase, the firewall begins to perform its normal filtering operations. To the packet from an IP address recorded in the Filter Table, it is accepted if it has a consistent marking; otherwise, it is dropped. Filtering scheme has following four steps:

1. Learning Phase

To distinguish the spoofed packets, the firewall needs to keep a record of the genuine markings. During normal time that no attacks are happening, the firewall can learn about the correct markings for packets sent from specific IP addresses. The (IP-address, Marking) pairs are stored in a Filter Table, which are later used to verify each incoming packet and filter-out the spoofed ones. The learning phase continues for a sufficient time to allow most of the filter table to be filled up. If the Filter Table gets full, any new entry to be added replaces the oldest one.

2. Normal Filtering Procedure

Any packet received by the firewall is judged by the filter according to the following rules

1. If the (IP-address, Marking) pair is same with one of the records in the Filter Table, the packet is received.

2. If the source IP address of the packet exists in the Filter Table, but the marking does not match, this packet is considered to be a spoofed packet and is dropped. TMC is incremented.
3. If the source IP address does not appear in the Filter Table, then this packet is accepted with a probability p. TMC is incremented.
4. If the TMC value exceeds the threshold, an attack is signaled.
5. All echo reply messages that are received as responses to the firewall's requests are handled by the Check List verification process. They are not passed through the filter.

3. Check List Verification

To verify the markings in the Check-List, a random echo message is sent periodically to the source address for each (IP-address, Marking) pair in the Check-List, and a counter is used to record the number of echo messages that have been sent for it. On receiving an echo reply from the source, the marking can be verified and the pair is moved to the Filter Table; otherwise, it indicates the previously received packet was spoofed, then this pair is deleted from the Check List. If the counter in the Check List shows that more than $d(= 10)$ echo messages have been sent to an IP address x, then the entry for this IP address is removed from the Check List and the pair (x,*) is added to the filter table, where * is a special symbol denoting that all packets having source IP address x should be discarded. Since in this situation, this source IP must be either non-existent or inactive, so that the packets received with this source address are coming from the attacker and need to be rejected.

4. Route Change Consideration

Though routes on the Internet are relatively stable, they are not invariable. Once the route between two hosts has changed, the packet received by the destination will have a different marking with the one stored in the Filter Table, so that it may be dropped according to our basic filtering scheme. Taking route changes into consideration, another counter called SMC is introduced, to count the number of mismatching packets for any IP address A. When the value of SMCA reaches a threshold , the entry (A, Marking) is copied to the Check List to test whether the route from this source has changed and SMCA is reset to zero. If the new marking is verified by the Check List verification process, the marking for this IP address is updated in the Filter Table. Otherwise, the original marking is preserved.

Drawback of the scheme

1. At each participant router it is required to mark all the packets and at each step due to this more time is required to detection and prevention.
2. Time in detecting the attack is varies with the number of attackers.
3. Requires at least 20% router participation continually.
4. Route change considerations invokes further overhead in the basic scheme itself .

4   Cryptographic Approach

With the help of cryptosystem we can enhance the speed of detection and prevention of IP spoofed packed. The new scheme can be implemented as below. Rather than doing the marking for each packet after confirmation of source validity, if further packet transmission is required, put it in secure transmission with cryptosystem. It would be more reliable if the Source address of the IP packet be encrypted.

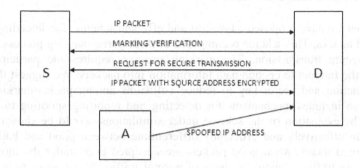

Fig. 2. Cryptosystem

4.1   Key Generation Algorithms

Setup algorithm: It takes a security parameter as input. It outputs a master public key PK and a master secret key msk.

Key-derivation algorithm: It takes as input the master secret key msk and an identity ID. Keys are generated in a hidden manner.

Encryption algorithm: It takes as input the master public key PK, an identity ID and a message m in some implicit message space; it outputs a ciphertext C.

Decryption algorithm: It takes as input an identity ID, an associated decryption key SK, and a ciphertext C. It outputs a message m.

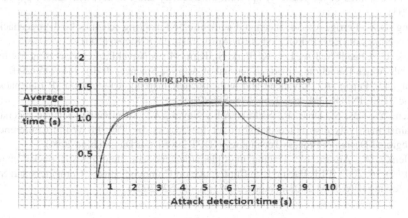

Fig. 3. Detection time Vs Transmission time

So we can say that following benefits can be achieved by proposed scheme.

1. High speed filtering of spoofed packet.
2. Enhancement in packet transmission.
3. Once secure transmission is established no role of participating router in filtering process.

5 Conclusion and Discussion

In this paper we have proposed a low-cost and efficient scheme, for defending against IP spoofed attacks, This scheme is composed of three parts: marking process, filtering process, secure transmission. The marking process requires the participation of routers in the Internet to encode path information into packets. We suggest the use of a hash function and secret key to reduce collisions among packet-markings. The scheme also includes mechanisms for detecting and reporting spoofing in a timely manner. The evaluation of the scheme under simulations, would be shown that our scheme can effectively and efficiently differentiate between good and bad packets under spoofed attack. Most good packets are accepted even under the most severe attack, whose traffic is about 10 times of normal traffic. At the same time, the bad packet acceptance ratio is maintained at a low level. The quick detection is valuable to the victim so that appropriate actions can be taken to minimize the damage caused by a IP spoofed attack.

References

1. Wang, H., Jin, C., Shin, K.G.: Defense against Spoofed IP Traffic using Hop Count Filtering. IEEE transactions on networking (February 2007)
2. Wang, W., Gombault, S.: Efficient Detection of DDoS Attacks with Important Attributes. ©2008 IEEE Transactions on Secure computing (2008)
3. Yaar, A.P., Song, D.: Pi: A path identification mechanism to defend against DDoS attacks. In: Proceedings of the IEEE Symposium on Security and Privacy, May 2003, pp. 93–109 (2003)
4. Song, D.X., Perrig, A.: Advanced and authenticated marking schemes for IP traceback. In: Proceedings of IEEE INFOCOM 2001, April 2001, pp. 878–886 (2001)
5. Beak, C., Chaudhry, J.A., Lee, K., Park, S., Kim, M.: A Novel Packet Marketing Method in DDoS Attack Detection. American Journal of Applied Sciences 4(10), 741–745 (2007)
6. Song, D., Perrig, A.: Advanced and authenticated marking schemes for IP traceback. In: Proc. IEEE INFOCOM, vol. 2, pp. 878–886 (2001)
7. Chen, Y., Das, S., Dhar, P., Saddik, A.E., Nayak, A.: An effective defence mechanism against massively distributed denial of service attacks. In: The 9th World Conference on Integrated Design & Process Technology (IDPT 2006), SanDiego (June 2006)
8. Belenky, A., Ansari, N.: Tracing multiple attackers with deterministic packet marking (DPM). In: 2003 IEEE Pacific Rim Conference on Communications, Computers and Signal Processing (PACRIM 2003), August 2003, pp. 49–52 (2003)

Multi-agent Based Network Performance Tuning in Grid

C. Valliyammai, S. Thamarai Selvi, R. Satheesh Kumar, E. Pradeep, and K. Naveen

Department of Information Technology, Anna University, Chennai
cva@annauniv.edu, stselvi@annauniv.edu,
satheesh.ravindranath@gmail.com, pradeepfree4u@gmail.com,
naveen19892000@gmail.com

Abstract. Grid environment is used for performing high-end computations with a large number of systems. The proposed work is to monitor the grid network with the help of mobile agents and tune the network metrics on performance degradation of the grid network. The grid network is monitored using the cost function to analyze the network performance in grid. Any degradation in the network performance is reflected by the cost function. The network parameter that has caused the degradation will then be identified through analyzing of each network metrics by the tuning manager. Then the network performance is tuned by tuning the degraded network metrics, which has high impact over it. Tuning is done based on changing the sending and receiving TCP socket buffer size of the compute nodes. It is also shown that the network monitoring is equally important as the resource metrics at the time of job submission in the grid network.

Keywords: Bandwidth delay product, Cost Function, Grid, Monitoring; Socket buffer size, Tuning, TCP Throughput.

1 Introduction

Grid environment is an extended distributed environment used for performing high-end computations with a large number of systems. Due to the diversity of computing resources in grid, there is a need of monitoring grid resources for its efficient utilization. Monitoring effectively leads to benefits like tuning the network metrics during the times of performance degradation of the grid application.

In order for information services to address the mentioned user needs, they must systematically collect information regarding the current and, sometimes, past status of grid resources and also the network metrics; a process known as *monitoring* [12]. There is a compulsive need for debugging the grid network when the performance of executing the submitted jobs drops down. Users of high-performance grid environment often observe degradation in the performance of the network in terms of low throughput or high latency. Regular monitoring of the grid setup helps in identifying the source for the performance problems [8]. Grid Monitoring helps in the Prediction and Tuning of the network metrics. This greatly helps the job submitters in the grid setup to know the duration of execution of their job.

V.V Das et al. (Eds.): BAIP 2010, CCIS 70, pp. 297–304, 2010.
© Springer-Verlag Berlin Heidelberg 2010

Similar to any other computational resources Grid resources can face unexpected performance issues [1]. The end users can cause unexpected performance problems during job submission at various hours of the day. This is because the usage pattern will not be the same when the users submit different jobs. So there is a need to find out what the problem is. The difficulty in finding out the problems is more challenging as grid environment consists of geographically distributed groups of people. [9]

2 Related Work

Network performance monitoring is very important in the operation of networks of significant size. This monitoring service acts as an aid to fault detection and performance evaluation [6]. Grid Monitoring Architecture involves formation of the cluster in a computational grid [12]. Debugging networks for efficiency is an essential step for those wishing to run data intensive applications [2]. Grid middleware and applications to make intelligent use of the network, optimizing their performance by adapting to changing network conditions (including the ability to be "self healing") [2]. Some of the factors affecting TCP throughputs are transfer size, maximum sender/receiver buffer size, path characteristics (RTT, loss rate, available bandwidth, nature of traffic etc)[3]. Grid network and monitoring system (GMMPro) is a network monitoring system for grid, which is based on SNMP [10].

The need for dynamic buffer sizing in high computational grid is frequent [4]. Different types of tools are used for monitoring of various network metrics. Kernel level tuning techniques such as auto-tuning[14] and dynamic right sizing (DRS)[18] which is either sender/receiver based flow control deals with end-end tuning [4].On comparison of various TCP buffer-tuning techniques in [5], some of the current tuning techniques are Manual tuning, PSC's Automatic TCP Buffer Tuning, Dynamic Right-Sizing (DRS), Linux 2.4 Auto-tuning, Enable tuning, NLANR's Auto-tuned FTP (in ncFTP) and LANL's DRS FTP (in wuFTP). In DRS, only end-end performance is considered and further it restricts itself to only single network metric. In Linux Auto tuning [17], initially during connection setup maximum of memory is allocated and wasted which is not actually required. With auto tuning, excessively large initial buffer waste the memory and can even affect the performance. [5]

3 System Design

3.1 Detailed System Design

Figure 1 shows a detailed architecture of our grid monitoring and tuning system. This figure shows two separate blocks of nodes namely the head node and the compute node (CE). *Sensors* deal with the collection of the network metrics from the CEs. Tools like Iperf [24], UDPMon [23], and TCPMon [22], Ping are used for collecting the network metrics between the head node and the compute node. *Local collector* collects the series of metrics data from the CEs using mobile agents. It stores the collected data into the local archive maintained in every CE. A *Local database* which stores the collected data from the monitoring tools on the local site (compute node).

This is stored for the later reference by the head node. *Data Accumulator* is responsible for gathering the data from multiple CEs in the cluster. It maintains a global archive that is accessible only by the head node. *Data Processor* renders the network data collected by sensors as valuable information about the network performance. It effectively computes the cost function of the grid setup with the help of elementary cost functions for each compute nodes. A *global database* collects data from the local archive, which is available in the compute nodes. This also stores the results of the cost function computations.

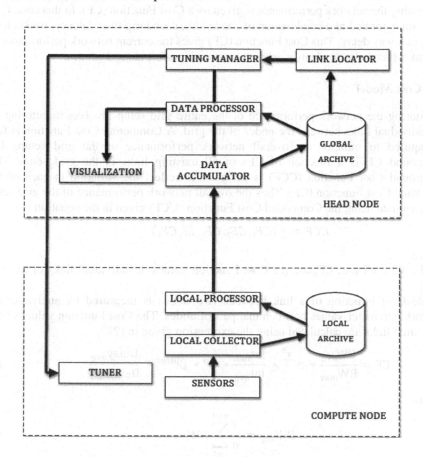

Fig. 1. Detailed view of the monitoring and tuning model

Link Locator analyses the Compound cost function and finds the corresponding link, which got deprecated in its performance. *Tuning Manager* analyses the metrics in the link, which has been identified by the *Link Locator* and diagnoses which network metric has got affected. Then it correspondingly sends the command to the *Tuner*. The *Tuner* which is available in the compute node changes the TCP socket buffer size of the compute node for bringing back the TCP throughput to the original level.

4 Implementation

4.1 Network Monitoring

Monitoring the grid network performance requires the analysis of various parameters like round trip time, latency, packet loss, etc. which varies frequently depending upon the real time network conditions across the links. These parameters individually won't determine the network performance accurately. The analysis of multiple metrics for monitoring the network performance is given by a Cost Function (CF). In this case, Cost Function is formed as a combination of bandwidth, round trip time, latency, packet loss, jitter, one-way delay. This Cost Function (CF) gives the current network performance of the link which helps to identify, when the network performance degrades.

4.2 Cost Model

Monitoring the network performance of the entire grid setup involves monitoring all the individual links between the nodes of the grid. A Compound Cost Function (CCF) is required to monitor the overall network performance of the grid setup. The Compound CF is a function of CFs of all existing links in the grid setup. This Compound Cost Function (CCF) is designed to reflect the variation in each of the individual Cost Function (CF). Thus the overall network performance of the grid setup is determined using the Compound Cost Function (CCF) given in the equation (1).

$$CCF = f\ (CF_1, CF_2, CF_3, \dots, CF_n) \tag{1}$$

Where,

CF$_1$, CF$_2$, CF$_3$, .., CF$_n$ are the Cost Function values of individual links of the grid setup.

The Cost Function of a link between two nodes is measured by analyzing the network parameter values between that pair of nodes. The Cost Function values of the individual links are calculated using the expression given in (2).

$$CF = \frac{BW_{avg}}{BW_{max}} * e^{-\frac{\tau^2}{2}} * \frac{lat_{min}}{lat_{avg}} * \alpha^p * \beta^{jitter} * \frac{Delay_{avg}}{Delay_{max}} \tag{2}$$

Where,

$$BW_{avg} = \frac{1}{n} \sum_{i=1}^{n-1} BW_i \tag{3}$$

$$Delay_{avg} = \frac{1}{l} \sum_{j=1}^{l-1} Delay_j \tag{4}$$

$$\tau = 1 - [RTT_{avg}/RTT_{max}] \tag{5}$$

$$RTT_{avg} = \frac{1}{l} \sum_{k=1}^{l-1} RTT_k \tag{6}$$

p = Packet loss rate.

i = Number of values taken for calculating the mean bandwidth.

j = Number of values taken for calculating the mean one-way delay.

k = Number of values taken for calculating the mean Round Trip Time (RTT).

α = Varies in interval [0, 1] and tuned to balance the dependency of packet loss rate.

β = Varies in interval [0, 1] and tuned to balance the dependency of jitter.

lat_{min}= Minimum latency between the corresponding pair of nodes.

lat_{avg}= Mean latency between the corresponding pair of nodes.

RTT_{max} = Maximum Round Trip Time between the corresponding pair of nodes.

BW_{max} = Maximum available bandwidth between the corresponding pair of nodes.

$Delay_{avg}$ = Mean one-way delay between the corresponding nodes.

$Delay_{max}$ = Maximum one-way delay between the corresponding nodes.

4.3 Network Performance Tuning

Bandwidth Delay Product

The network performance of the grid setup is improved by dynamically tuning the buffer size of the link which has degraded. The buffer size is set to an optimal value based on the values of average available bandwidth and delay. The optimal socket buffer size is twice the size of the bandwidth * delay product of the link [6].

$$Buffer\ capacity = 2 * BW * Delay \qquad (7)$$

Where,

BW = average available bandwidth.

Delay= delay between the head node and the compute node.

The TCP throughput increases by altering the send and receive socket buffer size of the compute nodes [19].

5 Results and Discussion

A grid network was formed with high computational jobs using Globus tool kit which acts as a middleware for developing the grids [25]. The monitored values will be stored in the local archive. The computed cost function is stored in the global archive which is present in the head node. The cost function gives an idea of the current network's performance. Tuning module is invoked when the cost function goes below a threshold value which is fixed according to our grid setup.

Figure 2 shows the variation of the cost function when the grid network is under load-free scenario which uses the Linux Auto Tuning .The graph has been plotted when the grid network is free without any job submission. The cost function plot is stable under load free state. In this case, if any Grid FTP is occurring it will affect the cost function's value to an extent. A Grid FTP was used for testing the performance of the grid network. As the network's performance degrades when the Grid FTP is occurring, the cost function's value also decreases. Hence, the network's performance degradation may be noticed if the cost function's value is lesser than the threshold set.

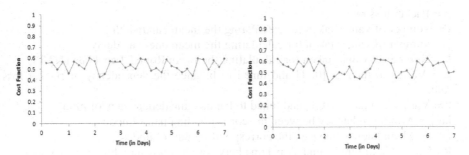

Fig. 2. Network performance without network load

Fig. 3. Network performance with network load and tuning

If the degrading metric is bandwidth or Delay, then the Bandwidth Delay product is used for tuning. The TCP's socket buffer sizes are altered such that it is always twice the Bandwidth Delay product. This buffer capacity is realized to be an optimum measurement for TCP data transfer. As Grid FTP also uses TCP for data transfer, it naturally brings up the performance of the Grid FTP. As identified in Figure 3, the graph has been plotted during Grid FTP transfer. Tuning has been performed at the point where the value goes beyond the threshold set in our grid environment.

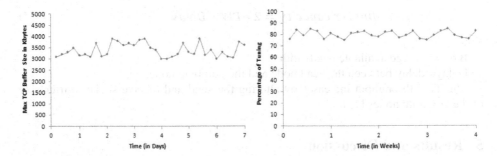

Fig. 4. TCP Socket Buffer Size Vs Time

Fig. 5. Percentage of Tuning Vs Time

Figure 4 shows the optimal size of the buffer capacity that has to be present while Grid FTP transfer is occurring. This naturally brings back the performance of the network which has previously degraded due to bandwidth and delay metrics. The performance of tuning in percentage is shown in figure 5 which was observed in weeks. From the experimental results, it was noted that only a slight overhead is available in our tuning model to run. But this is over-weighed by the tuning performance of the network. Figure 6 shows a three-dimensional plot of the number of applications and the maximum TCP socket buffer size with the percentage of efficiency. It was inferred that as the number of applications increase, the maximum buffer size also consistently increases, in turn all the applications to be executed efficiently in the grid network.

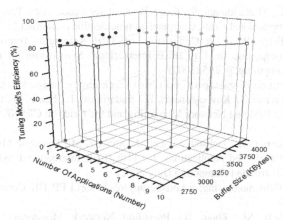

Fig. 6. Number of applications Vs Buffer Size

6 Conclusion

In this paper, the grid network monitoring and tuning is done using agent technology through deploying sensors. Agents provide improved automation and better fault tolerance to grid monitoring. The proposed framework can be improvised by imparting few extensions to support existing standards. The proposed tuning model improves the TCP throughput of the networks, which increases the grid network performance for efficient utilization of the grid resources. Considering network status for resource allocation, it increases the reliability of the submitted job being executed successfully and also increases the trust of the grid nodes for efficient utilization.

7 Future Work

The proposed system can be extended with additional network characteristics like router traffic and service availability. The number of mobile agents necessary for a particular grid environment with given nodes can be studied, analyzed and optimized further. The proposed system can be extended to support GGF standards and tested in significant grid test beds. The cost functions can act as decision-making rules for a resource broker to schedule the job in grid. The parameters that are considered for tuning can be increased.

References

1. Valliyammai, C., Thamarai Selvi, S., Santhana Kumar, M., Sathish Kumar, S., Suresh Kumar, R.: Network Performance monitoring using mobile agents in grid. In: IEEE International Advance Computing Conference (2009)
2. Leese, M., Tyer, R., Tasker, R.: Network Performance Monitoring for the Grid. In: UK e-Science, All Hands Meeting (2005), http://gridmon.dl.ac.uk/
3. He, Q., Dovrolis, C., Ammar, M.: On the Predictability of Large Transfer TCP Throughput. Computer Networks: The International Journal of Computer and Telecommunications Networking 51(14), 3959–3977 (2007)

4. Gardner, M.K., Thulasidasan, S., Feng, W.-c.: User-Space Auto-Tuning for TCP Flow Control in Computational Grids. Computer communications – Journal 27, 1364–1374 (2003)
5. Weigle, E., Feng, W.-c.: A Comparison of TCP Automatic Tuning Techniques for Distributed Computing. In: 11th IEEE International Symposium on High Performance Distributed Computing, p. 265 (2002)
6. TCP tuning, http://www.psc.edu/networking/projects/tcptune/
7. Coviello, T., Ferrari, T., Kavoussanakis, K., Kudarimoti, L., Leese, M., Phipps, A., Swany, M., Trew, A.S.: Bridging Network Monitoring and the Grid. In: CESNET Conference 2006 (2006)
8. Gunter, D., Tierney, B., Jackson, K., Lee, J., Stoufer, M.: Dynamic Monitoring of High-Performance Distributed Applications. In: 11th IEEE International Symposium on High Performance Distributed Computing (July 2002)
9. Millar, A.P.: Grid monitoring: a holistic approach. Grid PP UK Computing for Particle Physics (2006)
10. Wang, J., Zhou, M., Zhou, H.: Providing Network Monitoring Service for Grid Computing. In: Proceedings of the 10th IEEE International Workshop on Future Trends of Distributed Computing Systems, FTDCS 2004 (2004)
11. Cox, R.W.: NIfTI-1 Statistical Distributions: Descriptions and Sample C Functions
12. Zanikolas, S., Sakellariou, R.: A taxonomy of grid monitoring systems. Future Generation Computer Systems 21, 163–188 (2005)
13. TCP Auto Tuning, http://www.csm.ornl.gov/~dunigan/netperf/auto.html
14. Weigle, E., Feng, W.-c.: A Comparison of TCP Automatic Tuning Techniques for Distributed Computing. In: 11th IEEE International Symposium on in High Performance Distributed Computing
15. De Sarkar, A., Kundu, S., Mukherjee, N.: A Hierarchical Agent Framework for Tuning Application Performance in Grid Environment. In: IEEE Asia-Pacific Services Computing Conference (2007)
16. Hacker, T.J., Athey, B.D., Sommerfield, J., Walker, D.S.: Experiences Using Web100 for End-to-End Network Performance Tuning for Visible Human Testbeds
17. Prasad, R.S., Jain, M., Dovrolis, C.: Socket Buffer Auto-Sizing for High-Performance Data Transfers. Journal of Grid Computing 1(4), 361–376 (2003)
18. Gardner, K., Feng, W.-c., Fisk, M.: Dynamic Right-Sizing in FTP (drsFTP):Enhancing Grid Performance in User-Space. In: IEEE Symposium on High- Performance Distributed Computing,
19. Yoo, G.-c., Sim, E.-s., Kim, D., Byun, T., Kim, K.-h., Byun, O.-h.: An efficient TCP Buffer Tuning Technique based on packet loss ratio (TBT-PLR). In: Proceedings of the International Conference on Internet Computing, IC 2004, Las Vegas, Nevada, USA, June 21-24, vol. 1 (2004)
20. Jain, M., Dovrolis, C.: Ten fallacies and pitfalls on end-to-end available bandwidth estimation. In: Proceedings of the 4th ACM SIGCOMM conference on Internet measurement table of contents
21. Aglets, http://aglets.sourceforge.net/home.htm
22. TCPmon, http://www.hep.man.ac.uk/u/rich/Tools_Software/tcpmon.html
23. UDPmon, http://www.hep.man.ac.uk/u/rich/net/index.html
24. Iperf, http://www.noc.ucf.edu/Tools/Iperf/
25. Globus, http://www.globus.org

Finding Discriminative Weighted Sub-graphs to Identify Software Bugs

Saeed Parsa, Somaye Arabi, Neda Ebrahimi, and Mojtaba Vahidi-Asl

{Parsa,m_vahidi_asl}@iust.ac.ir,
{atarabi,n_ebrahimi}@comp.iust.ac.ir

Abstract. The aim has been to detect discriminative sub-graphs which are highly distinguishable between program failing and passing execution graphs resulted from different runs. In this paper, a novel approach to mine weighted-edge graphs is proposed. We also apply our efficient objective function to find most discriminative patterns between failing and passing graphs. To find bug relevant sub-graphs, a decision tree classifier is used to classify program failing and passing runs based on their discriminative sub-graphs. The experimental results on Siemens test suite reveal the effectiveness of the proposed approach specifically in finding multiple bugs. It also gives the debugger an infection path related to the discovered bug(s).

Keywords: Software Fault Localization, Discriminative Graph, Graph Mining, Execution Graphs, Decision Tree, Classification.

1 Introduction

Despite of many attempts to decrease the number of software bugs before its deployment, a major number of latent bugs still remain. The majority of latent bugs are occasional non-crashing ones, which do not reveal themselves, unless specific inputs are given to the program [7].

The logic structure of a program can be represented as a control flow graph, where each node represents a basic block of the program, a sequence of instructions which are executed sequentially, and each edge characterizes the possible control flow between blocks [7]. In each execution, a sub-structure of this graph is executed which could represent a faulty or successful path of the program. Therefore, each incorrect or correct execution of a program can be converted as a failing or passing execution graph, respectively. Instead of basic blocks, each node in an execution graph represents a branch statement, namely predicate [1]. Consider we have a number of failing and passing execution graphs constructed from program runs. The aim is to extract bug relevant sub-graphs by investigating the program's execution graphs. Bug relevant sub-graph(s) may help the debugger to easily detect the faulty program path(s) and fix the existing bugs. Since, a program may have many failing and passing execution graphs, an appropriate graph mining technique should be applied to find most discriminative sub-graphs. Furthermore, to find bug relevant sub-graphs among the extracted discriminative ones, we also require a suitable classification method [4].

V. V Das et al. (Eds.): BAIP 2010, CCIS 70, pp. 305–309, 2010.
© Springer-Verlag Berlin Heidelberg 2010

In summary, the following contributions have been made in this paper:

1. Each program run is considered as a weighted execution graph which holds the control flow among the program predicates during each execution.
2. A new objective function which considers edge weighted graphs for finding highly discriminative sub-graphs has been proposed.
3. A decision tree classifier has been applied to find those discriminative sub-graphs which highly discriminate failing runs from passing ones. These sub-graphs may contain the suspicious code related to the failure.

The remaining parts of this paper are organized as follows: the proposed graph mining approach for bug localization is explained in section two. Section three presents the experimental results on Siemens test suite. Finally, concluding remarks are described in section five.

2 Proposed Approach

The proposed fault localization approach contains four major phases: 1) Instrumentation 2) Constructing the execution graphs 3) Discriminative sub-graph detection and 4) Classification. The work flow diagram is illustrated in Figure 1. In the instrumentation phase, some extra code is injected before each predicate in the source code to build an instrumented version. In this section, we describe the phases two, three and four.

2.1 Building Weighted Execution Graphs

Each program execution sequence could be represented as a graph structure $G = (V, E)$. V and E are the set of graph nodes and edges, respectively. The sets V and E are described as:

$$V \subseteq \{p_1, p_2, ..., p_N\}$$
$$E = \{edg | edg = [id, w], id = (p_k, p_j), w \in Z^+\}$$

Each p_i is a predicate in the instrumented program P^*. id is an identifier for an edge which determines the two connected nodes and w is a positive integer number which determines the weight of an edge. The weight of an edge with id (p_k, p_j) is the number of occurrences of subsequence p_k, p_j in a specific execution [9].

2.2 Mining Discriminative Sub Graphs

After representing failing and passing executions of a program as a set G, we deal with the problem of finding discriminative sub-graphs from G. We use information gain as a criterion to evaluate the discriminability of sub-graphs.

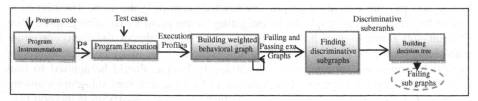

Fig. 1. The flow diagram of the proposed approach for detecting failing sub-graphs

Suppose that a sub graph g is given and that G is divided into two subsets g_G and $\bar{g}_G$ which consist of graphs including and not including g. The information gain of g is defined in relations (1) to (3):

$$Gain(g, G) = Ent(G) - \sum_{sub\_g \in \{g_G, \bar{g}_G\}} \frac{weighted\_f(Sub\_g)}{|G|} Ent(Sub\_g) \tag{1}$$

$$weighted\_f(g_G) = \{|\acute{g}_G| \in G : \forall \ [id, w] \in g, [id, \acute{w}] \in \acute{g}.w \le \acute{w}\} \tag{2}$$

$$weighted\_f(\bar{g}_G) = |G| - weighted\_f(g_G) \tag{3}$$

Where $weighted\_f(g_G)$ is the number of graphs in G containing weighted sub-graph g. The $Ent(G)$ and $Ent(sub\_g)$ are the entropies [6]:

$$Ent(G) = - \sum_{j \in \{fail, pass\}} \frac{|G_j|}{|G|} log_2 \frac{|G_j|}{|G|} \tag{4}$$

$$Ent(sub\_g) = - \sum_{j \in \{fail, pass\}} \frac{weighted\_f(sub\_g_j)}{weighted\_f(sub\_.g_G)} log_2 \frac{weighted\_f(sub\_g_j)}{weighted\_f(sub\_g_G)} \tag{5}$$

2.3 Pruning Strategies Based on the Upper-Bound of Information Gain

Cl-GBI [3] yields many sub-graphs that extending many of them do not increase the discrimination between failing and passing executions. If we know that for an extracted sub-graph, none of its super-graphs can give an information gain greater than a threshold, we could prune such a sub-graph [5]. The maximum estimated information gain for a weighted sub-graph g is the $max\_gain(g, G)$:

$$max\_gain(g, G) = max \ (max\_gain(g, G_{pass}), max\_gain(g, G_{fail})) \tag{6}$$

$$max\_gain(g, G_{pass}) = Ent(G) - \frac{|G - g_{G_{pass}}|}{|G|} Ent(G - g_{G_{pass}}) \tag{7}$$

$$max\_gain(g, G\_fail) = Ent(G) - |G - g\_(G\_fail)| / |G| \ Ent(G - g\_(G\_fail)) \tag{8}$$

The Algorithm 1 (*Gmine*) shows how to find discriminative weighted sub-graphs.

2.4 Applying Decision Tree for Isolating Discriminative Sub-graphs

In order to detect bug relevant part of the program, a decision tree classifier [10] has been used to classify all failing and passing execution graphs based on more discriminative sub-graphs in each level. The process of building proposed decision tree is described as follow:

1. Finding the most discriminative sub-graph, g, using *Gmine* algorithm in each level of the decision tree construction.
2. Dividing each node of the decision tree based on the existence/not existence of a subgraph g in G, into two groups: g_G and $\bar{g}_G$.
3. Repeating step 1 and 2 until each set of execution graphs in each decision tree leaf contains only passing executions or only failing executions.

If the two sibling leaves have different classes, failing and passing, then the parent node of them is considered as failure inducing sub-graph.

Algorithm 1. Gmine (G,g)

Input. A graph database = $\{(G_1, C_1), (G_2, C_2), ..., (G_m, C_m)\}$, A threshold of the upper-bound of information gain τ, k is a number for selecting high discriminative sub-graph.
Output. A discriminative sub-graph $disc\_g$;
0. $disc\_g = \emptyset, gain(disc_g, G) = -\infty$;
1. Extract all the sub-graphs consisting of two connected nodes in G and construct a set of sub-graphs D (called pseudo-nodes in CL-GBI algorithm. From the 2nd level on, only two connected nodes with at least one pseudo-node is selected as sub-graph.
2. (Pruning) For each sub-graph $g \in D$ calculate max_$gain(g, G)$ and delete g from set D if max_$gain(g, G) < \tau$.
3. For each remaining sub graph $g \in D$ calculate $gain(g, G)$.
4. Select k sub-graphs g from D such that $gain(g, G) > gain(disc_g, G)$ then update $disc\_g$ and $gain(disc_g, G)$.
5. Each remaining sub-graph g in D is restored as a new pseudo-node in all graphs containing g .A new name is assigned to each pseudo-node. Go back to Step 1

---

3   Experimental Results

In this section, the effectiveness of the proposed graph mining technique in fault localization has been evaluated. To achieve this, we use the Siemens suite, a well-known test suite, as the subject programs [8]. Siemens has 132 faulty versions of seven subject programs and each faulty version contains one manually injected fault.

For evaluating the effectiveness of a fault localization process, two criterions should be always considered: The number of detected faults and the amount of code that a user should inspect manually to find the main causes for the program failure. Figure 2 manifests the amount of code that should be scrutinized manually by the user in source code to find the main causes of failure compared with three well-known debugging techniques [1], [2]. Experimental results show that, the proposed approach could detect 86 bugs out of 132 ones. Figure 3 shows the number of faults that our approach has detected comparing with three different approaches described in [1][2].

In order to investigate the effectiveness of our approach, we integrated some faulty versions of programs together to make more complex bugs. The results of applying the proposed approach on such complex bugs are presented in Figure 4.

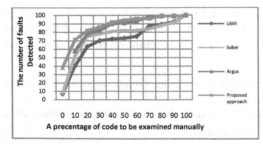

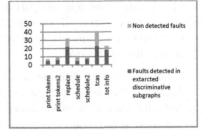

Fig. 2. The proposed approach compared with known statistical approaches on Siemens test suite

Fig. 3. The number of faults detected in each program of Siemens test suite

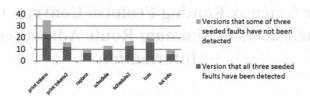

Fig. 4. The effectiveness of the proposed approach in finding multiple bugs in Siemens

4 Concluding Remarks

In this paper a novel approach based on graph mining for fault localization has been proposed. Instead of mining call graphs of a program, we extract an execution graph for each run of the program. Since the edges of the graphs are weighted, we propose a novel approach for mining such graphs. For finding bug relevant sub-graphs, we have classified failing and passing graphs by taking discriminative sub-graphs as features, using a decision tree classifier.

References

1. Arumuga Nainar, P., Chen, T., Rosin, J., Liblit, B.: Statistical debugging using compound Boolean predicates. In: International Symposium on Software Testing and Analysis, pp. 5–15. ACM Press, London (2007)
2. Fei, L., Lee, K., Li, F., Midkiff, S.P.: Argus: Online statistical bug detection. In: Baresi, L., Heckel, R. (eds.) FASE 2006. LNCS, vol. 3922, pp. 308–323. Springer, Heidelberg (2006)
3. Yan, X., Cheng, H., Han, J., Yu, P.: Mining Significant Graph Patterns by Leap Search. In: International Conference on Management of Data, pp. 433–444. ACM Press, Canada (2008)
4. Cheng, H., Lo, D., Zhou, Y., Wang, X.: Identifying Bug Signatures Using Discriminative Graph Mining. In: International Symptoms on Software Testing and Analysis, pp. 141–151. ACM Press, USA (2009)
5. Ohara, K., Hara, M., Takabayashi, K., Motoda, H.: Pruning Strategies Based on the Upper Bound of Information Gain for Discriminative Sub-graph Mining. In: Richards, D., Kang, B.-H. (eds.) PKAW 2008. LNCS, vol. 5465, pp. 50–60. Springer, Heidelberg (2009)
6. Cook, D., Holder, L.: Mining Graph Data. John Wiley and Sons, Chichester (2006)
7. Zeller, A.: Why Programs Fail: A Guide to Systematic Debugging. Morgan Kaufmann, San Francisco (2006)
8. Software-artifact infrastructure repository, http://sir.unl.edu/portal
9. Eichinger, F., Bohm, K., Huber, M.: Mining Edge-Weighted Call Graphs to Localize Software Bugs. In: Daelemans, W., Goethals, B., Morik, K. (eds.) ECML PKDD 2008, Part I. LNCS (LNAI), vol. 5211, pp. 333–348. Springer, Heidelberg (2008)
10. Tan, P., Steinbach, M., Kumar, V.: Introduction to Data Mining. Addison-Wesley Press, USA (2005)

Border Gateway Routing Protocol Convergence Time Analysis with Minimum Route Advertisement Information

Manoj V.N. Vadakkepalisseri[1] and K. Chandrashekaran[2]

[1] Department of Computer Science and Engineering,
Mekelle Institute of Technology,
Mekelle, Ethiopia, East Africa
manojvnv@gmail.com
[2] Department of Computer Engineering,
National Institute of Technology, Surathkal, India
kchnitk@gmail.com

Abstract. The Border Gateway Protocol (BGP) is the default routing protocol for the routing between autonomous systems in the Internet. BGP's convergence time is mainly dependent on the Minimum Route Advertisement Interval (MRAI) value, But the influence of this MRAI value on the router's resources is not yet understood well enough to improve the existing protocol implementation in terms of the specific aspects like CPU utilization, Memory requirement, Bandwidth utilization and convergence time. Therefore it has been analyzed to understand the relationship between the setting of Minimum route advertisement (MRAI) value and the resource requirement of BGP. This paper analyse the convergence times and number of exchanged updates to the different MRAI settings of BGP. In particular, the influence of the MRAI timer in the router CPU utilization, Bandwidth and Memory requirement, number of updates and convergence time is investigated. Designed an algorithm to enhance the convergence time of BGP by considering the minimum route advertisement interval time and reduce routing update overhead. And it shows enhancement of 17% of CPU utilization, 10% of Bandwidth, 10% of memory requirement and 14% of convergence time when compared with the existing system.

1 Introduction

Routing in the Internet is performed on two levels (intra-domain and inter-domain) implemented by two sets of protocols [13]. Interior gateway protocols (IGPs), such as Routing Information Protocol (RIP) etc., Exterior Gateway Protocols (EGPs), such as EGP and Border Gateway Protocol (BGP), route packets between Autonomous Systems (inter-domain). This paper focus on BGP, it performs interdomain routing in Transmission-Control Protocol/Internet Protocol (TCP/IP) networks. BGP is an Exterior Gateway Protocol (EGP), which performs routing between multiple autonomous systems or domains and exchanges routing and reachability information with other BGP systems. The primary function of a BGP system is to exchange network-reachability information, including information about the list of autonomous system

V.V Das et al. (Eds.): BAIP 2010, CCIS 70, pp. 310–319, 2010.

paths, with other BGP systems. BGP uses a single routing metric to determine the best path to a given network. This metric consists of an arbitrary unit number that specifies the degree of preference of a particular link. The BGP metric typically is assigned to each link by the network administrator. The value assigned to a link can be based on any number of criteria, including the number of autonomous systems through which the path passes stability, speed, delay, or cost.

The BGP routers have to gain knowledge about possible destinations. As long as the involved routers negotiate the new routes but try to route data on invalid or contradictory paths, data may never reach its destination. The time of unsettled path selection after a topology change is also called convergence time. Its duration is dependent on the Minimum Route Advertisement Interval Timer (MRAI) [13]. Its value has critical interest to the stability of the Internet. As the global Internet encompasses a huge number of computers, routing update is also big overhead. MRAI and Routing update values are the two main concern of this work.

When a BGP router first comes up on the Internet, either for the first time or after being turned off, it establishes connections with the other BGP routers with which it directly communicates. BGP neighbours exchange full routing information when the TCP connection between neighbours is first established. When changes to the routing table are detected, the BGP routers send to their neighbours only those routes that have changed. BGP routers do not send periodic routing updates, and BGP routing updates advertise only the optimal path to a destination network. BGP routers send and receive update messages to indicate a change in the preferred path to reach a computer with a given IP address. If the router decides to update its own routing tables because this new path is better, then it will subsequently propagate this information to all of the other neighbouring BGP routers to which it is connected, and they will in turn decide whether to update their own tables and propagate the information further. Routers that use BGP are called BGP speakers [7].

2   Exchange of Route Information and Route Processing in BGP

BGP speakers perform two tasks. The first task is forwarding of packets between end systems on the Internet [13]. For a router the destination of a packet is a network, rather than a single end system. Routers in their routing tables store only network addresses, called destination. One destination in a BGP routing table is represented by a pair consisting of an IP address prefix and the length of the prefix [13].

The second task of BGP speakers is maintaining information regarding routes (paths) from a particular speaker toward destinations in the Internet. The path contains a list of AS numbers, which describes all ASs which a packet has to traverse along the route to the destination. A BGP speaker may store multiple paths to each destination. Those paths are stored in a BGP routing table or RIB (Routing Information Base). The list of AS numbers in a path conveys more information than the distance use in traditional distance-vector protocols. It is used to prevent creation of routing information loops. That is also the reason why BGP is often called path-vector protocol, to distinguish it from distance-vector routing protocols. BGP uses the length of a path (the number of ASs in the path), as a distance metric.

BGP exchanges routing information only between peers, using four types of messages as stated above: open, update, notification, and keep-alive. There are two types of BGP peer sessions: external BGP (eBGP) for peers from different ASs and internal BGP (iBGP) for peers from the same AS. A BGP router may receive multiple paths to the same destination prefix from its eBGP and iBGP neighbors and put them in Adjacency RIB IN (Route Information Base in). Figure 1 shows the steps of BGP route processing. The router first applies import policies to filter out unwanted routes. The router then invokes a decision process by referring the BGP routing Algorithm to select exactly one best route for each destination prefix by comparing the new routes to all other known routes to the same destination. The router applies a sequence of steps to narrow the set of candidate routes to a single choice. The best route will be installed in the router's forwarding table or LOC-RIB (Local-RIB), while the unselected routes are remembered for backup purposes. Finally, the router applies export policies to manipulate attributes and decide whether to advertise the route to neighbouring ASs. If LOC-RIB is changed then the router generates updates for the Neighbour ASs. If the route is advertised, the router may modify some of the path attributes. It will at least add its own AS number to the AS path.

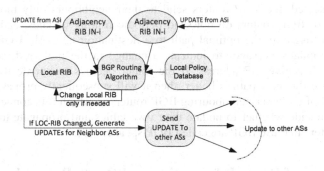

Fig. 1. BGP Route Processing

2.1 MRAI Timers

A BGP speaker may learn about a change of destination reachability from multiple peers. A BGP speaker selects the best route from all received routes. A BGP speaker may also receive a number of suboptimal routes before receiving the best route. A BGP speaker cannot wait indefinitely to receive the best route. Hence, it has to minimize the number of update messages and react in a timely manner to changes in the Internet topology. A solution, proposed in RFC 1771 [2], is rate limiting: it limits the frequency of route advertisements by imposing a minimal interval of time that should pass between two consecutive advertisements of the same destination sent from a BGP speaker to one of its peers. This interval is called the Minimal Route Advertisement Interval (MRAI) or the MRAI round. RFC 1771 [2] specifies the duration of an MRAI round to be 30s which is controlled by using MRAI timers. To avoid synchronization and possible peaks in the update messages distribution, RFC 1771 [2] proposes using values of MRAI multiply by a uniform jitter in the range 0.75-1. Nevertheless, the majority of BGP speakers in the Internet do not implement this MRAI modification [4]. RFC 1771 [2] proposes implementing per-peer, rather than per-destination, MRAI timers: one per-peer MRAI timer is associated with one peer. The timer is set when a route advertisement is sent to the corresponding peer, regardless of its destination.

A path in a network is defined in order to estimate time needed for a route advertisement to traverse a route between BGP speakers, A simple path p is a sequence of k nodes (u1,..., uk), such that each node is included in the path only once (a path cannot have loops) [4]. In the case of per-peer MRAI timers, time t(p) required for a route advertisement to traverse path p is:

$$t(p) \leq |p| . MRAI \tag{1}$$

Where |p| is the number of hops of path p. It is assumed that all BGP speakers have identical MRAI, i.e., it is not modified by a uniform jitter [13]. The maximal time that a route advertisement may be delayed in one BGP speaker is equal to MRAI [13] and, hence, the maximum time needed to reach consistency by a given network topology is as given in equation 1.

3 BGP Modified Distance Vector Algorithm

It is a modified distance vector algorithm referred to as a "Path Vector" algorithm that uses path information to avoid traditional distance vector problems. Each route within BGP pairs destination with path information to that destination. Path information (also known as AS_PATH information) is stored within the AS_PATH attribute in BGP. The path information assist BGP in detecting AS loops thereby allowing BGP speakers select loop free routes. BGP uses an incremental update strategy in order to conserve bandwidth and processing power. In addition to incremental updates, BGP has added the concept of route aggregation so that information about groups of destinations that use hierarchical address assignment (e.g., CIDR) may be aggregated and sent as a single Network Layer Reachability Information (NLRI) [2][7]. Routes learned via BGP have associated properties that are used to determine the best route to a destination when multiple paths exist to a particular destination. These properties are referred to as BGP attributes, and an understanding of how BGP attributes

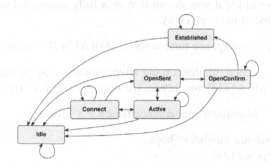

Fig. 2. BGP Finite State Machine

influence route selection is required for the design of robust networks. The attributes that BGP uses in the route selection process are Weight Attribute, Local Preference Attribute, Multi-Exit Discriminator Attribute, AS_path Attribute, and Next-Hop Attribute. In order to make decisions in its operations with other BGP peers, a BGP peer uses a simple finite state machine (FSM) that consists of six states: Idle, Connect, Active, OpenSent, OpenConfirm, and Established, Figure 2 [2].

4 BGP Performance Analysis Metrics

Link Bandwidth: If we denote the total number of routes in the Internet by N, the total path attributes (for all N routes) received from a peer as A, and assume that the networks are uniformly distributed among the autonomous systems, then the worst case amount of bandwidth consumed [2] during the initial exchange between a pair of BGP speakers is:

$$BW = O\,(N + A) \tag{2}$$

CPU Utilization: BGP's CPU utilization depends only on the stability of its network which relates to BGP in terms of BGP UPDATE message announcements. The processing delay of each message is estimated using a uniformly distributed random variable from the interval [Pmin, Pmax]. Commonly used values are Pmin = 0.01 s and Pmax = 0.1 s [1]. The average processing delay TBGProcess(p) for a group of N queued updates is [13]:

$$T_{BGPproces\sin g} = N * \left[\frac{P\max - P\min}{2} \right] \tag{3}$$

Memory requirements: If the total number of networks in the Internet by N, the BGP peers per network by P, the total number of unique AS paths as A then the worst case memory requirements (MR) can be expressed as

$$MR = O\,((N + A) * P) \tag{4}$$

Convergence time: In [3] it was shown that in a fully connected network, the lower bound on convergence time is given by

$$\text{Minimum convergence time } = (N\text{-}3)*MRAI \text{ in N node network} \tag{5}$$

The maximal convergence tim that a route advertisement may be delayed in one BGP speaker is equal to MRAI [13] and, hence, the upper bound for t (p) is:

$$\text{Maximum convergence time} = P \times MRAI \tag{6}$$

Where p is the maximum number of hops.
    Average convergence time

$$= \frac{(N - 3 + P) * MRAI}{2} \tag{7}$$

4.1 Performance Metrics Analysis for One Sample Topology

The Table 1 shows the performance metric for a given topology with 100,000 networks one node of that topology may send an update of 100,000 networks and 3,000 AS paths this update consumes 8.12Mbytes of memory, 0.406Mbytes of Bandwidth.

Table 1. Analysing BGP's Memory Requirements, Bandwidth, CPU Utilization and Convergence Time Based On the Size of the BGP RIB Table

Number of Networks	Number of ASs	BGP Peers per net	Memory Requirement	Bandwidth	CPU Utilization (Sec)	Convergence Time (MRAI= 20)
4000	100	6	97200	16200	180	79940
10000	300	10	406000	40600	450	199940
100000	3000	20	812000	406000	4500	1999940

5 Design of BGP with Minimum Convergence Time and Less Number of Updates

BGP Timing Algorithm

This algorithm is based on Figure 3 which uses for two routers which are peer to each other (R1 in AS1 with routing table RT1 and R2 in AS2 with routing table RT2) and one (R1) is sending update about network Z to the other router(R2).

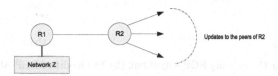

Fig. 3. Two ASs with two BGP enabled routers and one network Z

The Algorithm:
1. Check the Routing Table of R2 so that there is an entry in RT2 to network Z from R1
2. If no entry about network Z then first R2 compares the lengths of different AS from different peers and selects the best AS paths.
3. Then it checks the local policy database and if it passes the local policy R2 updates its LOC-RIB and sends an update immediately with MRAI=20 and restart the timer.
4. If R2 fails the local policy database it drops the packet.
5. If there is an entry then, check weather RT2's entry was originally from RT1 (in other word check if there is a previous routing update from that same router).
6. yes it is from RT1 then, check the timer weather it is expired
7. if expired send with MRAI = 30 timer and restart it
8. Else wait the left time.

9. else check if length of RT1 previous not equal to length of RT1 new ,leng(RT1previous) != leng(RT1new), and length of RT1 +1 less than length of RT2, leng(RT1) +1< leng(RT2)
10. if it satisfy the above then check the timer weather it is expired
11. if expired send the update with MRAI=20 timer and restart it
12. Else wait the left time.
13. if the update doesn't satisfy the 7ths step then drop the update

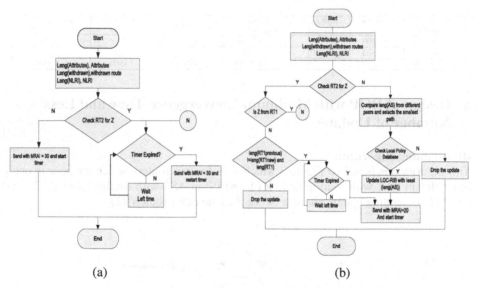

(a)   (b)

Fig. 4. (a) The existing BGP Algorithm; **(b)** The modified BGP Algorithm

6 Results and Discussion

We have used network simulator ns-2.27 [6] developed by the VINT research group at University of California at Berkeley and ns-BGP is an implementation of BGP-4 [8] in ns-2 network simulator.

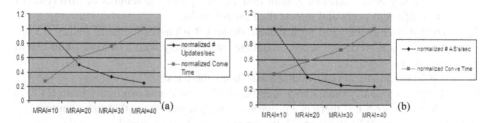

Fig. 5. (a) Convergence time vs. average number of updates for 11 nodes. **(b)** Convergence time vs. average number of autonomous systems for 11 nodes scenario.

BGP with modified MRAI values i.e., BGP MRAI 20 and 30, shows a slight improvement in the number of Ass send in the routing update than that of BGPMRAI 30.

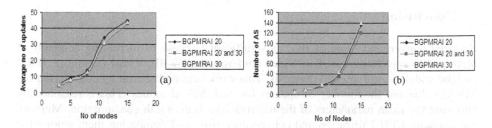

Fig. 6. (a) Average Number of AS comparison for BGP with MRAI 20, 20&30 and 30, **(b)** Average Number of update comparison for BGP with MRAI 20, 20&30, 30

The numbers of updates send for the case of BGPMRAI 20 and 30 shows lesser than that of BGPMRAI 20 and BGPMRAI 30 individually.

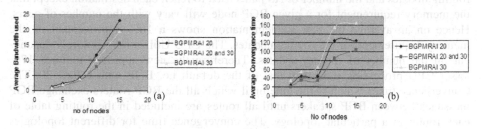

Fig. 7. (a) Bandwidth comparison for BGP with MRAI 20, 20&30, 30, 14 **(b)** Convergence time comparison for BGP with MRAI 20, 20&30, 30

From the results shown in the above figures we can ascertain, the number of AS number Attribute is increasing with increasing number of BGP nodes, we can also interpret that the number of AS is the same regardless of different MRAI values for less number of BGP nodes. The number of routing Update is becoming higher when the number of BGP nodes are increasing, especially for the MRAI =20 but for the case of MRAI =20&30 and 30 needs lesser number of updates to converge.

Since Bandwidth and Memory requirement are directly dependent on the values of Number of updates and Ass attribute we can see that BGP with MRAI =20 &30 needs lesser value of Bandwidth and Memory requirement. The CPU Utilization is entirely dependent on the number of Updates. Convergence time of BGP with MRAI= 20&30 is lesser than BGP with MRAI=30 and BGP with MRAI=20. It can be seen that the number of updates per second decreases when the value of MRAI value is increasing, but the convergence time increases when the MRAI value is increasing. Also we can notice that the optimal point between convergence time and Number of updates is around MRAI = 20 which we can get minimum Bandwidth, Memory requirement, CPU utilization with minimum Number of updates which leads to have minimum convergence time.

7 Conclusion

Reduced convergence time of BGP is significant because of increasing demands of high quality applications such as Video conferencing, VOIP, Video Gamming, IPTV and the widely use of internet demands. This work accomplished it by considering the MRAI value and the number of updates for each MRAI values. This is reasoned by choosing the main parameters of the network like Bandwidth consumption, Memory requirement, CPU Utilization and convergence time and comparing them among the existing and the modified system. The bandwidth used during routing update until the network is converged is directly dependent on the number of updates and AS attributes, so from the result it is evident that for different topology with different number of nodes the bandwidth used by BGP with MRAI 20 & 30 is 10% lesser than the existing routing protocol implementation i.e. BGP with MRAI 30. The Memory Requirement used by routing updates has also a direct relation with that of the number of routing updates and the number of AS paths used to reach each destination except that the memory requirement for a given BGP node will vary with the number of peers. Hence on an average the new implementation shows a 10% improvement on the memory requirement for the routing updates. The CPU Utilization is entirely dependent on the number of routing updates. Therefore the new approach requires 17% lesser CPU processing time than that of the default i.e. BGP with MRAI 30. The Convergence times which is the time until which all the BGP routers exchange BGP messages between BGP speakers until all routes are included in the routing table of each router in a particular topology. The convergence time for different topologies shows 14% lesser for the case of BGP with MRAI 20 &30 than the default value.

References

1. Labovitz, C., Wattenhofer, R., Venkatachary, S., Ahuja, A.: The impact of Internet policy and topology on delayed routing convergence. In: Proc. INFOCOM, Anchorage, AK, April 2001, pp. 537–546 (2001)
2. Rekhter, Y., Li, T.: A border gateway protocol 4 (BGP-4): IETF RFC 1771 (March 1995)
3. Sahoo, K., Kant, P.: Mohapatra: Improving BGP Convergence Delay for Large-Scale Failures, Dependable Systems and Networks (2006)
4. Hares, S., Retana, A.: BGP 4 implementation report, Internet Draft (October 2004), http://www.ietf.org/internet-drafts/draft-ietf-idr-bgp-implementation-02.txt/ (Last visited, December 2008)
5. The network simulator ns-2, http://www.isi.edu/nsnam/ns (Last visited, December 2008)
6. Zhang, B., University of California, Los Angeles, Massey, D., Colorado State University, Zhang, L., University of California, Los Angeles: Destination Reachability and BGP Convergence Time
7. Cisco Documentation: Using the Border Gateway Protocol for Interdomain Routing, http://www.cisco.com/univercd/cc/td/doc/cisintwk/ics/icsbgp4.htm (Last visited, December 2008)
8. Feng, T.D.: Implementation of BGP in a network simulator: M.Sc. Thesis, Simon Fraser University (April 2004)

9. Pei, D., Azuma, M., Nguyen, N., Chen, J., Massey, D., Zhang, L.: BGP-RCN: Improving BGP Convergence through Root Cause Notification, Technical Report TR-030047 UCLA Computer Science Department (October 31, 2003)
10. Bremler-Barr, A., Afek, Y., Schwarz, S.: Improved BGP convergence via ghost flushing. In: Proceedings of IEEE INFOCOM, San Francisco, CA (March 2003)
11. Sun, W., Mao, Z.M., Shin, K.G.: Differentiated BGP Update Processing for Improved Routing Convergence, Network Protocols (2006)
12. Bu, T., Gao, L., Towsley, D.: On routing table growth. In: Proc. of Global Internet Symposium, Taipei, Taiwan (November 2002)
13. Lasković, N., Trajković, L.: BGP with an adaptive minimal route advertisement interval. In: Proc. IPCCC 2006, Phoenix, AZ (April 2006) (to appear)
14. http://www.cisco.com/en/US/docs/internetworking/technology/handbook/bgp.html (Last visited, December 2008)

Design and Implementation of an Efficient Method for Certificate Path Verification in Hierarchical Public Key Infrastructures

Balachandra[1] and K.V. Prema[2]

[1] Department of Information and Communication Technology
[2] Department of Computer Science and Engineering
Manipal Institute of Technology,
Manipal, India, 576104
bala_muniyal@yahoo.com, prema.kv@manipal.edu

Abstract. In order to challenge the security threats for e-commerce and e-business transactions, robust and trustworthy security systems are required. Public Key Infrastructure (PKI) is a frame work on which the security services are established. Most of the business corporations deploy Hierarchical PKI as their security infrastructure, in which, certificate path is unidirectional, so certificate path development and validation is simple and straight forward. In this paper, we propose a novel method for certificate path verification in Hierarchical Public Key Infrastructures and compare the experimental results with the existing certificate Path verification methods.

Keywords: PKI, Certification Authority, Hierarchical PKI, Certificate path verification, Certificate path validation.

1 Introduction

Authentication of the users in e-commerce and e-business transactions is considered as a crucial operation, in which the participating users are challenged to prove their identity. This is commonly realized by means of a Public Key Infrastructure(PKI). A PKI is a set of hardware, software, people, policies, and procedures needed to create, manage, store, distribute, and revoke digital certificates[1]. In cryptography, a PKI is an arrangement that binds public keys with respective user identities by means of a Certification Authority (CA). The primary function of a PKI is to allow the distribution and use of public keys and certificates with security and integrity.

Different business corporations deploy different types of PKIs[2][3]. In Hierarchical PKI, certificate path is unidirectional, so certificate path development and validation is simple and straight forward. However, if the root CA is compromised, which is everyone's trust point, the security of the whole system is collapsed. Similarly, other types of PKIs also have their own advantages as well as disadvantages[4][5]. Considering that the scalability, simplicity and path verification are important issues in PKIs, our proposal is based on Hierarchical PKI. We propose

V.V Das et al. (Eds.): BAIP 2010, CCIS 70, pp. 320–324, 2010.
© Springer-Verlag Berlin Heidelberg 2010

an efficient method to verify certificates in Hierarchical PKI. We show that the time requirement for certificate path verification in the proposed method is very less compared to the existing solutions.

1.1 Hierarchical PKI Model

A PKI constructed with superior-subordinate CA relationships is called a Hierarchical PKI. A Hierarchical PKI, as depicted in Fig. 1, is one in which all of the subscribers / relying parties trust a single CA. This CA is called the Root CA. The Root CA certifies the public keys of subordinate CAs. These CAs certify their subscribers or may, in a large PKI, certify other CAs. Certificate path construction in a Hierarchical PKI is a straightforward process that simply requires the relying party to successively retrieve issuer certificates until a certificate is located that was issued by the trusted root. Hierarchical PKIs are scalable, certificate paths are easy to develop and are relatively short[6].

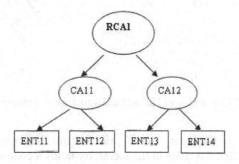

Fig. 1. Hierarchical PKI

2 Certificate Path

A Certificate path is an ordered sequence of certificates where the subject of each certificate in the path is the issuer of the next certificate in the path. A certificate path begins with a trust anchor certificate and ends with an end entity certificate. For example, in Fig.1, CA12 << ENT14 >>, RCA1 << CA12 >> is a valid path.

We can construct Certificate path in two ways:

i. Forward path construction in which the path is constructed from end entity certificate to the trust anchor certificate.

The Forward certificate path construction is a straightforward approach in which we start constructing the path from target certificate to the root certificate via the intermediate CAs' certificates.

ii. Reverse path construction in which the path is constructed from trust anchor certificate to end entity certificate.

Reverse path construction is not straightforward because it is difficult to determine the exact path from root CA to the target certificate directly. So we implement an algorithm suggested in[7]. The procedure is to transform Hierarchical PKI to a binary tree so that we can build the path without any ambiguity. A representation of a general (ordered) tree T is obtained by transforming T into a binary tree T'.

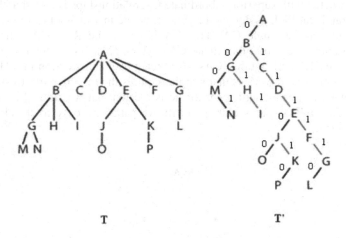

Fig. 2. Conversion of Hierarchical structure to a binary tree

As shown in Fig.2, in the binary tree T', the left link is labeled with bit 0 and the right link with bit 1. Each CA node in the hierarchy holds a codeword[7] consisting of the accumulated 0-1 sequence from the root to the target node in question. Each parent CA assigns to its subordinate CAs with its codeword plus a new distinguished code. The number of '0's in the codeword represents the level in the tree. Since the depth of the nodes increases after transforming the general tree to a binary tree, the path verification time also increases.

3 Proposed Method of Certificate Path Verification

In business transactions, the method of building a trusted path between the trusted anchor and target entity constructs a path as each certificate is retrieved from a repository via Lightweight Directory Access Protocol(LDAP)[8]. In the proposed method, the process of certificate path verification needs a local cache stored in the client environment, containing all certificates that constitute the path between the user's issuing CA and its hierarchy Root CA, including the latter.

Following are the high level set of instructions of the proposed method:

1. Retrieve the certificate of the user to be authenticated from the repository;
2. If the certificate path is found in the cache then validate the path and terminate the process;

3. If not, perform the following steps:
    (a) Determine the Distinguished Name(DN) of the certificate's issuing CA;
    (b) Retrieve the certificate of the issuing CA;
    (c) While(The certificate of the issuing CA is not self-signed)
        i. Validate the certificate and include it in the path
        ii. Retrieve the certificate of the issuing CA
    (d) If the certificate of the issuing CA is self-signed, announce successful construction of the path and store the path in the cache
    (e) If not, announce unsuccessful construction of the path and terminate the process.

4 Implementation and Experimental Results

4.1 Forward Vs. Reverse Path Construction

We have implemented the methods of Forward certificate path construction and Reverse path construction in Java with OpenSSL tool. It can be seen from Fig. 3 that, the time required for certificate path verification using Forward path construction method is less than that of the Reverse path construction method.

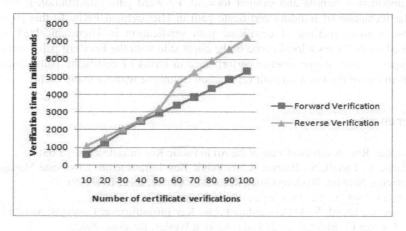

Fig. 3. Path Verification time with Forward and Reverse path constructions

4.2 Proposed Method of Certificate Path Verification

We have implemented the proposed method of path verification using Java with OpenSSL tool. Fig. 4 shows the comparison of Normal method(i.e. Path verification using forward path construction method) with the proposed method for different number of certificate verifications. We can observe that the verification time in the proposed method reduces significantly as compared to the normal method. As the cache hit increases, the proposed method gives significant improvement in terms of the path verification time.

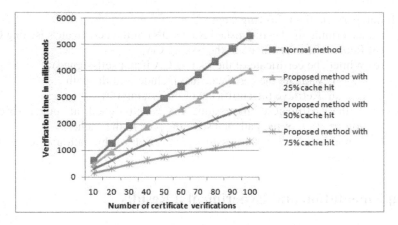

Fig. 4. Normal method vs. Proposed method with 25%, 50% and 75% cache hit

5 Conclusions

In Hierarchical PKI, certificate path is unidirectional, so certificate path development and validation is simple and straight forward. Forward path construction is the most popular technique of building certificate path in Hierarchical PKIs. In this paper, we propose a novel method of certificate path verification in Hierarchical PKIs. The proposed method uses a local cache in the client side with the Forward path verification technique, so that, it gives better performance in terms of certificate path verification time than that of the Forward path verification technique without using cache.

References

1. Mazaher, Roe: A survey of state of the Art in Public Key Infrastructure (2003)
2. Adams, S., Farrell, S.: Internet X.509 Public Key Infrastructure Certificate Management Protocols. Network Working Group Request for Comments 2510 (1999), http://www.ietf.org/rfc/rfc2510.txt
3. Adams, C., Lloyd, S.: Understanding Public Key Infrastructure: Concepts, Standards, and Deployment Considerations, 2nd edn. Addison Wesley, Reading (2003)
4. Satizbal, C., Hernndez-Serranoa, J., Forna, J., Peguerolesa, J.: Building a Virtual Hierarchy to Simplify Certification Path Discovery in Mobile Adhoc Networks. Journal of Computer Communications 30(7), 1498–1512 (2007)
5. Satizbal, C., Pez, R., Forn, J.: Building a Virtual Hierarchy for Managing Trust Relationships in a Hybrid Architecture. Journal of Computers 1(7) (October/November 2006)
6. Saxena, A.: Public Key Infrastructure Concepts, Design and Deployment, TMH (2004)
7. Huang, H.: On the Protection of Link State Routing and Discovery of PKI Certificate Chain in MANET, A Ph.D thesis submitted to the Graduate Faculty, North Carolina State University (2005)
8. Hodges, J., Morgan, R.: Lightweight Directory Access Protocol (v3): Technical Specification, RFC 3377 (September 2002)

Iris Recognition Technique Using Gaussian Pyramid Compression

G. Savithiri[1,*] and A. Murugan[2]

[1] Dept. of Computer Applications,
Velammal College of Management and Computer Studies, Chennai - 66, India
savithiri75@yahoo.co.in
[2] Dept. of Computer Science,
Dr. Ambedkar Govt Arts College, Vyasarpadi, Chennai - 39, India
amurugan1972@gmail.com

Abstract. Iris recognition is one of important biometric recognition approach in a human identification is becoming very active topic in research and practical application. In this paper, Gaussian pyramid compression technique is used to compress the eye image and this compressed eye is used for the localization of the inner and outer boundaries of the iris region. Located iris is extracted from the compressed eye image and after normalization and enhancement it is represented by a data set. With Gaussian pyramid compression improved matching performance is observed down to 0.25 bits/pixel (bpp), attributed to noise reduction without a significant loss of texture. To ensure that, the iris-matching algorithms are not degraded by image compression. The proposed method is evaluated using CASIA iris image database version 1.0 [7] and achieved high accuracy of 96%. Experimental results demonstrate that the proposed method can be used for human identification in an efficient manner.

Keywords: Iris recognition, Biometric, Gaussian, 1D-Log Gabor filter, Hamming Distance.

1 Introduction

A Biometric system is a pattern recognition system that determines the authenticity of an individual using some physical or behavior features. Biometrics based on the iris is among the most accurate existing techniques for human identification and verification. No two iris patterns are alike, even those of identical twins, even between the right and left eye of the same person [2]. From one year of age until death, the patterns of the iris are relatively constant over a person's life-time [2, 3].

With the growing employment of iris recognition systems and associated research to support this, the need for large databases of iris images is growing. If required storage space is not adequate for these images, compression is an alternative. It allows a reduction in the space needed to store these iris images, although it may be at a cost in some amount of information lost in the process. There are many loss-less

---

*Corresponding author.

V. V Das et al. (Eds.): BAIP 2010, CCIS 70, pp. 325–331, 2010.

compression algorithms available that work best on certain types of data, such as predictive coding for one dimensional data and string coding for text.

Among the various loss-less compression algorithms available today, achievable compression is of the order of 1.5:1 to 3:1. Alternatively, lossy codes can compress images further with varying degrees of loss. Pyramid compressions have demonstrated very good loss-less compression performance with most types of imaginery [13]. This consists of a set of low-pass or band-pass copies of an image, representing pattern information of a different scale.

In this paper, we investigate that the effect of gaussian pyramid compression on the ability of an iris recognition system to accurately identify individuals. The performance is evaluated by means of the change in the Hamming distances between Iris codes using an iris recognition implementation based on several algorithms including Libor Masek's algorithm [8]. We seek to compress the original images because it is the data that is valuable and serves as training and testing images for the development of new algorithms. Typically a database for an iris recognition system does not contain actual iris images, but rather it stores the compressed images stored as 512 bytes per eye. Compression has been investigated and used in some biometric applications such as the FBI standard for fingerprint compression [6] [7] using MPEG compression [9]-[10] for video that may be used in facial recognition applications. There have been some limited research in the area of iris image compression [9] but this was compression applied to Iris Codes, not iris images. Here, Gaussian pyramid compression is applied to the iris imagery itself.

This paper is organized as follows. In section 2, the iris preprocessing steps that include detailed introduction to iris compression, localization, normalization and enhancement are described; and also provide feature extraction. Section 3 discusses iris matching based on hamming distance. Experiments and results are reported in Section 4. Conclusion is drawn in Section 5.

2 Iris Recognition

2.1 Image Preprocessing

A good and clear image eliminates the process of noise removal and also helps in avoiding errors in calculation. In this stage, we transformed the images from RGB to gray level for further processing. Before extracting features from the original image, the image needs to be preprocessed to localize iris, normalize iris and reduce the influence of the factors such as brightness, non-uniform illumination, etc., such preprocessing is described in the following subsections.

1) Gaussian Pyramid compression: The original image is convolved with a Gaussian kernel. The resulting image is a low-pass filtered version of the original image.

Level 0 measures 255 by 255 pixels and each higher-level array is roughly half the dimension of its predecessor. Thus, level 2 measures just 64 by 64 pixels. We have selected the 2-by-2 patterns because it provides adequate filtering at low computational cost. The low-pass filter effect of the Gaussian pyramid, which is of the order of 1.7:1 for RGB image and 1.9:1 for gray image, is clearly shown in the Fig 1.

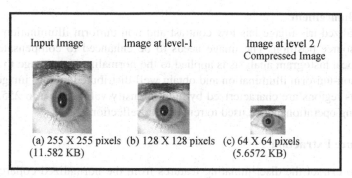

Fig. 1. Low pass filter effect of the Gaussian pyramid, which is of the order of 1.7:1 for RGB image and 1.9:1 for gray image

2) Iris localization: Before performing iris pattern matching, the image is compressed by Gaussian pyramid, and then the boundaries of the iris are to be located. Integro-differential operator is used for locating the inner and outer boundaries of iris as well as the upper and lower eyelids [1][2]. The operator computes the partial derivative of the average intensity of circle points with respect to increasing radius r. After convolving the operator with Gaussian kernel, the maximum difference between inner and outer circle will define the center and radius of the iris boundary. For upper and lower eyelids detection, the path of contour integration is modified from circular to parabolic curve. The operator is accurate because it searches over the image domain for the global maximum. It can compute faster because it uses the first derivative information.

3) Iris Normalization: Irises from different people may be captured in different size and even for the iris from the same person; the size may change because of the variation of the illumination and other factors. Such elastic deformations in iris texture affect the results of iris matching. For the purpose of achieving more accurate recognition results, the homogenous rubber sheet model devised by Daugman [1] used to remap each point within the iris region to a pair of polar co-ordinates (r, θ) where r is on the interval [0,1] and θ is the angle $[0,2\pi]$. The remapping of the iris region $I(x, y)$ from raw co-ordinates (x, y) to the doubly dimensionless non-concentric polar co-ordinate system (r, θ) can be represented as

$$(I(x(r, \theta), y(r, \theta)) \rightarrow I(r, \theta) \quad \text{with } x(r, \theta) = (1\text{-}r) \, x_p \, (\theta) + rx_1 \, (\theta)$$
$$y(r, \theta) = (1\text{-}r) \, y_p \, (\theta) + ry_1 \, (\theta)$$

where $I(x, y)$ is the iris region image (x, y) are the original Cartesian co-ordinates, (r,θ) are the corresponding normalized polar co-ordinates and x_p, y_p and x_1, y_1 are the co-ordinates of the pupil and iris boundaries along the θ direction. The rubber sheet model which takes into account pupil dilation and size inconsistencies in order to produce a normalized representation with constant dimensions.

4) Iris Enhancement
The normalized iris image has low contrast and non-uniform illumination caused by the light source position. The image needs to be enhanced to compensate for these factors. Local histogram analysis is applied to the normalized iris image to reduce the effect of non-uniform illumination and obtain well-distributed texture image [10][11]. Reflections regions are characterized by high intensity values close to 255. A simple thresholding operation can be used to remove the reflection noise.

2.2 Feature Extraction

In order to extract the discriminating features from the normalized collarette region, the normalized pattern is convolved with 1D Gabor wavelets [8]. Thus, feature encoding is implemented by first breaking the two-dimensional normalized iris pattern into one-dimensional wavelets and then these signals are convolved with 1D Gabor wavelet. The resulting phase information for both the real and imaginery response is quantized, generating a bit wise template. In this work, the angular and radial resolutions are set as 240 and 20 pixels, respectively. Two bits are used to represent the quantized phase information for each pixel. Therefore, the total size of the iris template is 9600 bits.

3 Template Matching

This test enables the comparison of two iris patterns. This test is based on the idea that the greater the Hamming distance between two Iris Codes A and B is defined as

$$HD = \frac{\left\| \left(\text{code A} \otimes \text{code B} \right) \cap \text{mask A} \cap \text{mask B} \right\|}{\left\| \text{mask A} \cap \text{mask B} \right\|}.$$

The $\otimes$ operator is the Boolean XOR operation to detect disagreement between the pairs of phase code bits in the two Iris Codes (code A and code B), and mask A and B identify the values in each Iris Code that are not corrupted by artifacts such as eyelids/eyelashes and specularities. The $\cap$ operator is the Boolean AND operator. The $\|.\|$ operator is used to sum the number of "1" bits within its argument. This method corrects for misalignments in the normalized iris pattern caused by rotational differences during imaging. From the calculated distance values, the lowest one is taken. This serves as a measure of recognition performance, as it is the fractional Hamming distance that determines if identification has been made. The decision of whether these two images belong to the same person depends upon the following result [2].

- If HD = 0.32 decide that it is a perfect match between two iris codes
- If HD < 0.32 decide that it is same iris
- If HD > 0.32 decide that it is different iris

Hamming distance of ≤ 0.32 allows identification with high confidence and used as a threshold for recognition. To derive the performance results, each original iris image was compared against ever other image in the database.

4 Experimental Results

Numbers of experiments were performed in order to evaluate the performance of the proposed method using Matlab 7.0 on an Intel Pentium IV 3.0GHz processor with 512MB memory.

4.1 CASIA Database

Experiments are conducted on CASIA iris database provided by the Chinese Academy of Sciences Institute of Automation [7] and 135 images are chosen for the experiments. Those 135 images are divided into 27 classes and each of them has 5 images. The first image from each class is selected to be the template. The remaining 4 images of each class are adopted as the test set.

4.2 Recognition Analysis

Fig 2 shows statistical distribution of Hamming distance between different and same iris feature vectors for both compressed and uncompressed iris. The y-axis and x-axis indicate the number of data samples and the Hamming distance respectively. It indicates that the Hamming distance is between 0.16 and 0.32 for the iris images from the same eye and between 0.33 and 0.55 for the iris images from different eyes. Table 1 shows the different Hamming distance to find the recognition rate of an iris. The correct recognition rate of this system is 96% when we use 27 classes (135 images). The graphical representation in Fig 3 shows the recognition rate according to the Hamming distance.

Fig 4(a) and 4(b) shows that the processing time of iris recognition is relatively lesser when compared to the existing method. From the experimental results, the proposed method shows an overall accuracy of 96%.

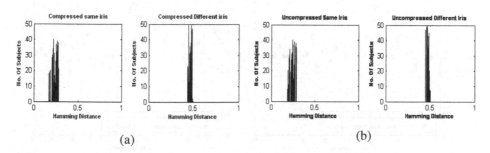

(a)   (b)

Fig. 2. (a) The distribution of hamming distance for compressed iris; (b) The distribution of hamming distance for different iris

Table 1. Recognition Rage According to the Hamming Distance

HD	Compressed (135 Images)	Compressed (%)	Uncompressed (135 Images)	Uncompressed (%)
0.28	128	95	125	92
0.29	130	96	126	93
0.30	130	96	126	93
0.31	130	96	127	94
0.32	130	96	127	94
0.33	130	96	129	96
0.34	130	96	131	97
0.35	131	97	131	97
0.36	132	98	131	97

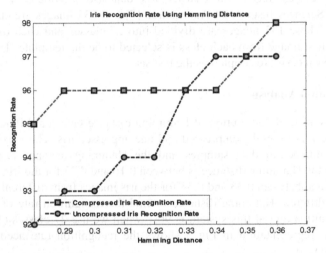

Fig. 3. Iris Recognition Rate using Hamming Distance

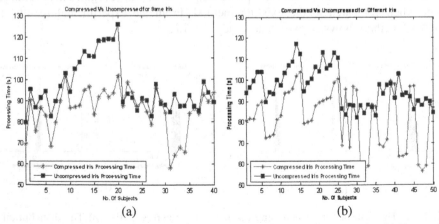

(a)   (b)

Fig. 4. (a) Processing Time of Compressed Vs Uncompressed for same Iris; (b) Processing Time of Compressed Vs Uncompressed for different Iris

5 Conclusions

Proposed iris recognition method is relatively simple and efficient against existing methods. We reached the correct segmentation for the pupil center and outer boundary radius and also average execution time for inner boundary detection was 0.016s, 0.031s for outer boundary detection and for matching was 0.016s using Matlab 7. From the experimental results, the proposed method shows an overall accuracy of 96%. The processing time of iris recognition is relatively lesser when compared to the existing method. It is noted that the result is not perfect due to low quality of the iris images. The iris region is occluded by eyelids and eyelashes. The experimental results show that the proposed approach has a good recognition performance and speed. This experiment is applicable to do experiments on a larger iris database in various environments for iris recognition system.

References

1. Daugman, J.: Complete Discrete 2-D Gabor Transforms by Neural Networks for Image Analysis and Compression. IEEE Transactions on Acoustics, Speech, and Signal Processing 36(7), 1169–1179 (1988)
2. Daugman, J.: How Iris Recognition Works,
   http://www.ncits.org/tc_home/m1htm/docs/m1020044.pdf
3. Daugman, J.: Biometric Personal Identification System Based on Iris Analysis, U.S.Patent No. 5,291,560 (March 1, 1994)
4. Brislawn, C.M.: The FBI Fingerprint Image Compression Specification. In: Topiwala, P.N. (ed.) Wavelet Image and Video Compression, ch. 16, pp. 271–288. Kluwer, Boston (1998) (invited book chapter)
5. Bradley, J.N., Brislawn, C.M.: Compression of fingerprint data using the wavelet vector quantization image compression algorithm., Los Alamos Nat'l La, Tech.Report LA-UR-92-1507, FBI report (April 1992)
6. Burt, P.J.: Fast filter transforms for image processing. Computer Graphics, Image Processing 16, 20–51 (1981)
7. CASIA iris image database, Institute of Automation, Chinese Academy of Sciences,
   http://www.sinobiometrics.com
8. Masek, L.: Recognition of Human Iris Patterns for Biometric Identification. M.Thesis, The University of Western Australia (2003),
   http://www.csse.uwa.edu.au/~pk/studentprojects/libor/
   LiborMasekThesis.pdf (March 26, 2005)
9. Daugman, J.: Face and gesture recognition: Overview. IEEE Transactions on Pattern Analysis and Machine Intelligence 19(7), 675–676 (1997)
10. Wang, H., Chang, S.F.: A Highly Efficient System for Automatic Face Region detection in MPEG video. IEEE Transactions on Circuits and Systems for Video Technology 7(4), 615–628 (1997)
11. Huang, J., Wang, Y., Tan, T., Cui, J.: A New Iris Segmentation Method for Recognition. In: Proceedings of the 17th International Conference on Pattern Recognition (2004)
12. Ma, L., Wang, Y., Tan, T.: Iris recognition using circular symmetric filters. In: International Conference on Pattern Recognition, vol. 2, pp. 414–417 (2002)
13. Burt, P.J., Adelson, E.H.: The Laplacian Pyramid as a Compact Image Code. IEEE Transactions on Communications 31(4) (April 1983)

Coverage of Access Points Using Particle Swarm Optimization in Indoor WLAN

Leena Arya[1], S.C. Sharma[2], and Millie Pant[3]

[1] Research Scholar, Electronics & Computer Engg. Discipline, DPT, IIT Roorkee
[2] Associate Professor, Electronics & Computer Engg. Discipline, DPT, IIT Roorkee
[3] Assistant Professor, Mathematics Discipline, DPT, IIT Roorkee
{Leenadpt,scs60fpt,millifpt}@iitr.ernet.in

Abstract. Wireless indoor positioning systems have become very popular and attractive in recent years. With the increasing use of mobile computing devices such as PDAs, laptops and an expansion of Wireless Local Area Networks, there is growing interest in optimizing the WLAN infrastructure, so as to increase productivity and efficiency in various colleges and office campuses with carrying out a cost effective infrastructure model. This paper describes an indoor propagation model, which can be used to predict the signal strength taking into consideration propagation path losses. In this paper we describe a mathematical model developed to find the optimal number of APs and their locations. To solve the problem, we use the Particle Swarm optimization.

Keywords: Wireless LAN, Access point, Path loss model, Particle Swarm Optimization.

1 Introduction

Wireless LAN (Wireless Local Area Network) is a computer network system that uses radio air interface for data transmission instead of conventional metallic or optical wire. Nowadays, several standards for WLAN air interface for various frequency bands exist. IEEE 802.11b is the most successful standard for WLANs in 2.45 GHz ISM band. This gives users the mobility to move around within a broad coverage area and still be connected to the network. WLAN networks have become very popular means for providing a wireless networking facility for home users, educational institutions, companies etc. due to their ease of installation and their high data rate provision, apart from providing, although limited, mobility to users. The basic structure of a WLAN is called a Basic Service Set (BSS) which comes in two categories: Infrastructure BSSs and Independent BSSs. These devices communicate with each other through the AP as shown in figure 1.In an independent BSSs (IBSS) stations communicate directly with each other and are usually composed of a small number of stations set up for a short period of time as shown in figure-2. Particle swarm optimization (PSO) is a kind of evolvement-computation technology based on the movement and intelligence of swarms was developed in 1995 by James Kennedy (social-psychologist) and Russell Eberhart

V. V Das et al. (Eds.): BAIP 2010, CCIS 70, pp. 332–336, 2010.

(electrical engineer). It uses a number of agents (particles) that constitute a swarm moving around in the search space looking for the best solution.

This paper is organized as follows: Notations are given in section 2. Section 3 presents the mathematical model description and path loss model. Section 4 shows the algorithm of the access point's calculation and flowchart. Section 5 presents the solution of the model. Finally, section 6 gives the conclusion.

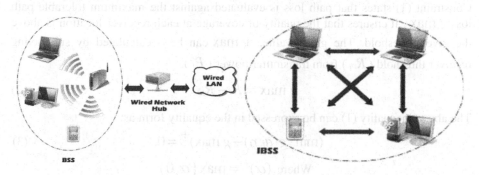

Fig. 1. Infrastructure Basic Service Set   **Fig. 2.** Independent Basic Service Set

2 General Notations

In this paper the following notations are used;

a_j	$j = 1 \dots N$	Access point (AP)
r_i	$i = 1 \dots M$	Receiver/user
$g(a_j, r_i)$		Path loss from i_{th} user to access point j
g max		Maximum tolerable path loss
P_t		Transmit power
P_r		Received power
R_{th}		Receive threshold
Ap		Position of AP

In the present analysis a_j represents the unknown coordinates of APs. Their number N is not known either. The coordinates of users r_i are assumed to be known and these users can be distributed in design area according to the design specifications. In the above analysis the distance function assumed to be Euclidean, hence on the plane, the distance (d) between an AP a_j and a receiver r_i is given by [2]:

$$d(a_j, r_i) = \sqrt{(r_i^1 - a_j^1)^2 + (r_i^2 - a_j^2)^2} \; .$$

Where $d(a_j, r_i)$ =Distance between AP and receiver, $a_j = a_j(a_j^1, a_j^2)$ and $r_i = r_i(r_i^1, r_i^2)$

3 Model Description

The aforementioned problem can be modeled as an optimization problem for which the objective function is to minimize the path loss. Mathematically it may be given as

$$\min g(a_j, r_i) \leq g \max \forall i = 1, ..., M . \tag{1}$$

Constraint (1) states that path loss is evaluated against the maximum tolerable path loss $g \max$. It ensures that the quality of coverage at each receiver location is above the given threshold. The given value, $g \max$ can be calculated by subtracting receiver threshold (R_{th}) from transmitter power (P_t).

$$g \max = P_t - R_{th} \tag{2}$$

The above inequality (1) can be expressed in the equality form as:

$$(\min_j g(a_j, r_i) - g \max)^+ = 0, \tag{3}$$

$$\text{Where } (\alpha)^+ = \max(\alpha, 0)$$

3.1 Path Loss Model

The power received by an antenna that is separated from the transmitting antenna by the distance d in free space is given by [2],[3]:

$$P_r(a_j, r_i) = \frac{P_t G_t G_r \lambda^2}{(4\pi)^2 d(a_j, r_i)^2} \tag{4}$$

where P_t is the transmitted power, G_t and G_r are the transmitter and receiver antenna gain, $\lambda = c/f$ is the wavelength of the carrier frequency, c is the speed of light (3×10^8 meter per second) and f is the frequency of radio carrier in hertz and d is the distance between transmitter and receiver. The path loss is measured in dB (decibels) and in free space environments, is given by [2], [3]:

$$g(a_j, r_i)[dB] = -10 \log \left[\frac{G_t G_r \lambda^2}{(4\pi)^2 d(a_j, r_i)^2} \right] .$$

This equation does not hold when points a_j and r_i are very close to each other. Therefore, large scale propagation models use a close–in distance, d_0 which is known as the received power reference distance point. Therefore, path losses at reference distance assuming transmit and receive antenna with unity gain as described in [2],[3] can be calculated

$$g(a_j, r_i) = g(d_0)[dB] = 20 \log \frac{4\pi d_0 f}{c} \tag{5}$$

Therefore, path loss function in free space at a distance greater than d_0 is given by

$$g(a_j, r_i)[dB] = g(d_o)[dB] + 10 \log \left(\frac{d(a_j, r_i)}{d_o} \right)^2. \tag{6}$$

4   Computational Steps for Access Point's Calculation

Initially set the number of APs to 1: $N = 1$; then the necessary number of APs is found through the following steps.

1) Solve the constraint condition of path loss for each receiver using equation (3);
2) Solve the power received by an antenna in free space using equation (4);
3) If the solution exists, then N is the desired number;
4) Otherwise, N is increased by 1: $N = N + 1$;
5) Go to step 1.

5   Solution of the Model

The standard powerful optimization techniques (Newton based, quasi-Newton methods, conjugate gradient search method, steepest descent method cannot be applied to the problem at hand because the function in the left hand side of (3) is nondifferentiable and nonconvex. Direct search methods are seem to be the best option but suitable for continuous functions only and the problem at hand is discontinuous. The discontinuity is because of a tiny change in the position of users or APs that can happen. We use the new Particle Swarm Optimization Algorithm (PSO). PSO is the only algorithm that does not implement the survival of the fittest and no crossover operation in PSO.

5.1   Operation of PSO

All particles in PSO are kept as members of the population through the course of the run.

The modification in the particle's position can be mathematically modeled according to the following equation:

$$V_i^{k+1} = wV_i^k + c_1 rand_1(...)x(pbest_i - s_i^k) + c_2 rand_2(...)x(gbest - s_i^k)v \tag{7}$$

V_i^k : Velocity of agent i at iteration k,

c_i : weighting factor,

$rand$: uniformly distributed random number
         between 0 and 1,

s_i^k : Current position of agent i at iteration k,

$pbest_i$: $pbest$ of agent i,

$gbest$: $gbest$ of the group.

The following weighting function is usually utilized in eq (7)

$$w = wMax - [(wMax - wMin) \times \max iter ..$$ (8)

where $wMax$ = initial weight,

$wMin$ = final weight,

$iter$ = current iteration number.

max $iter$ = maximum iteration number,

$$s_i^{k+1} = s_i^k + V_i^{k+1}$$ (9)

6 Conclusion

This paper investigates allocation problems with objective functions based on minimizing the average path loss received over the entire design area and maximum path loss received by any receiver. The algorithm described above used for finding the optimal placement of APs. To solve the problem we used the Particle Swarm Optimization. By Using the algorithm & efficiency of software the processing time of optimal placement of APs can be minimize. Further work will be extended to include obstacles in the mathematical model presented in this paper and test will be conducted.

References

1. Kobayashi, M., Haruyama, S., Kohno, R., Nakagawa, M.: Optimal Access Point Placement in simultaneous broadcast system using OFDM for indoor wireless LAN. In: IEEE symposium on PIMRC, vol. 1, pp. 200–204 (2000)
2. Kamenetsky, M., Unbehaun, M.: Coverage Planning for Outdoor Wireless LAN Systems. In: IEEE International Zurich Seminar on Broadband Communications, Sweden, pp. 49-1 – 49-6 (2002)
3. Kouhbor, S., Ugon, J., Kruger, A., Rubinov, A.: Optimal Placement of Access Point in WLAN Based on a New Algorithm. In: Proc. of the International Conference on Mobile Business, July 2005, pp. 592–598. IEEE/ICMB (2005)

Energy Conservation of Multicast Key Distribution in Mobile Adhoc Networks

Devaraju Suganya Devi[1] and Ganapathi Padmavathi[2]

[1] Sr.Lecturer, Department of Computer Applications,
SNR SONS College(Autonomous)
Coimbatore, Tamil Nadu, India
sugan.devil@gmail.com

[2] Prof and Head, Department of Computer Science,
Avinashilingam University for Women,
Coimbatore, Tamil Nadu, India
ganapathi.padmavathi@gmail.com

Abstract. Multicast communication in mobile adhoc networks is challenging due to its inherent characteristics of infrastructure-less architecture with lack of central authority, limited resources such as bandwidth, time, energy and power. Many emerging commercial and military applications require secure multicast communication in adhoc environments. Moreover, mobile nodes are often power constrained so that energy conservation is also an important issue on multicast key distribution. This paper evaluates the energy conservation of a new approach of multicast key distribution called cluster based multicast tree algorithm with multicast destination sequenced distance vector routing protocol to provide reliable and efficient energy conservation of multicast key distribution. Simulation results in NS_2 accurately predict the performance of proposed scheme in terms of energy consumption and end to end delay rate under varying network conditions.

Keywords: Mobile Adhoc Networks, Multicast, Key Distribution, Energy conservation.

1 Introduction

A MANET (Mobile Adhoc Network) is an autonomous collection of mobile users that offers infrastructure-free communication over a shared wireless medium. Multicasting is a fundamental communication paradigm for group-oriented communications such as video conferencing, discussion forums, frequent stock updates, pay per view programs, and advertising. The combination of an adhoc environment with multicast services [1, 2] induces new challenges towards the security infrastructure. The security services can be facilitated if group members share a common secret, which in turn makes key management a fundamental challenge in designing secure multicast and reliable group communication systems. Group confidentiality requires that only valid users could decrypt the multicast data.

V.V Das et al. (Eds.): BAIP 2010, CCIS 70, pp. 337–341, 2010.
© Springer-Verlag Berlin Heidelberg 2010

Most of these security services rely generally on encryption using Traffic Encryption Keys (TEKs). The Key management includes creating, distributing and updating the keys then it constitutes a basic block for secure multicast communication applications. If the membership changes are frequent, key management will require a large number of key exchanges per unit time in order to maintain both forward and backward secrecies.

To overcome these problems, several approaches propose a multicast group clustering. [3,4,5]. Clustering is dividing the multicast group into several sub-groups. Local controller (LC) manages each subgroup, which is responsible for local key management within the cluster. Moreover, few solutions for multicast clustering such as dynamic clustering did consider the energy and latency issues to achieve an efficient key distribution process, whereas energy and latency constitutes main issue in adhoc environments.

This paper proposes a cluster based multicast tree (CBMT) algorithm for secure multicast key distribution in mobile adhoc networks. Several methods applied in this paper are as follows:

1. MDSDV (Multicast Destination Sequenced Distance Vector)
2. MAC 802.11 for providing communication between nodes.
3. Channel bandwidth for minimization of congestion that occurs during transmission.
4. Multicast Congestion control mechanism to control flooding message.

Thus this new CBMT approach is an efficient dynamic clustering scheme using MDSDV routing protocol, which makes easy to elect the local controllers of the clusters and updates periodically as the node joins and leaves the cluster. The main objective of the paper is to present a new approach of clustering algorithm for efficient multicast key distribution in mobile adhoc network by overcoming issues of energy conservation and end to end delay of key distribution.

The remainder of this paper is structured as follows. Section 2 presents the related works about multicast clustering approaches. Section 3 describes the proposed CBMT for efficient multicast key distribution. Section 4 evaluates performance characteristics of cluster based multicast key distribution. Section 5 describes simulation results. Finally, Section 6 concludes the paper.

2   Related Work

Several Clustering approaches [3, 4, and 5] for securing multicast key distribution in adhoc networks have been proposed. They are basically classified into two main approaches. They are static clustering and dynamic clustering. In Static clustering approach, the multicast group is initially divided into several subgroups. Each subgroup shares a local session key managed by LC. Example: IOLUS [6] and DEP [3] belong to the category that is more scalable. Dynamic clustering approach aims to solve the "1 affect n" phenomenon. AKMP [4], SAKM [7] belong to this approach and are dedicated to wired networks. Enhanced BAAL [5] proposes dynamic clustering scheme for multicast key distribution in adhoc networks.

OMCT [8, 9] needs the geographical location information of all group members in the construction of the key distribution tree, which does not reflect the true connectivity between nodes. Based on the literature reviewed, OMCT is the efficient dynamic clustering approach for secure multicast distribution in mobile adhoc networks. However knowing the true connectivity between the nodes in mobile adhoc networks simplifies the key distribution phenomenon due to the node mobility. Hence the true node connectivity is taken into consideration for the cluster formation.

To overcome the above limitations another method called Optimized Multicast Cluster Tree with Multipoint Relays (OMCT with MPR) [10] is introduced which uses the information of Optimized Link State Routing Protocol (OLSR) to elect the LCs of the created clusters. OMCT with MPRs assumes that routing control messages have been exchanged before the key distribution. It does not acknowledge the transmission and results in retransmission which consumes more energy and unreliable key distribution for mobile adhoc networks.

The proposal of this paper is to present a new Cluster Based Multicast Tree (CBMT) approach for multicast key distribution. The LCs are elected easily using periodic updates of node join and leave information.

3   CBMT Algorithm

The main idea of CBMT is to use MDSDV routing protocol to elect the local controllers of the created clusters. The principles of the proposed clustering approach are described in steps as follows.

Step 1: Initially, the list of LCs contains only the source of the group GC, which collects all its 1-hop neighbors by MDSDV, and to elect LCs which are group members and which have child group members. The list of the current LC is collected.

Step 2: Traverse the list nodes, while there are group members not yet covered by LCs, and verify for each one if it is a group member and if it has child group members. In case of success, add the LC to the list of LCs, and withdraw from the list of group members. All the members reachable by this new LC will form a new cluster.

Step 3: If group members that exist and do not belong to the formed clusters then choose the nodes that have the maximum reachability to the others nodes in one hop from the remaining members. This reachability information is collected through the MDSDV routing protocol. However, the created clusters do not cover group members yet. Thus, nodes are selected as local controllers for the remaining group member.

4   Performance Evaluation

A Performance evaluation of CBMT for multicast key distribution is done in terms of QOS characteristics as performance metrics and simulated using NS2 simulation environment. The performance metrics are namely end to end delay in key distribution, energy conservation of multicast key distribution.

End to End Delay (TD): The average end to end delay of keys transmission from the source to the receivers. This metrics allows evaluating the average delay to forward a key from a LC to its cluster members.

Energy Conservation (E) is defined as the sum of units required to the keys transmission throughout the duration of simulation.

5 Simulation Results

This approach is simulated under Linux Fedora, using the network simulator NS2 version ns-allinone-2.33.

This section presents simulation results to compare the performance of end to end delay and energy consumption in CBMT and OMCT in varying density of cluster and network surface. The results of this simulation are presented in table 1.

Table 1. Simulation results

Surface	Nodes	End to end Delay (ms)		Energy (100 J)	
		CBMT	OMCT	CBMT	OMCT
1000	7	0.25	0.5	46	60
*	13	0.5	0.8	55	70
1000	28	0.58	1.2	58	79
1500	7	0.2	0.3	47	63
*	13	0.4	0.64	50	70
1500	28	0.6	0.89	58	86
2000	7	0.12	0.12	50	82
*	13	0.32	0.92	55	86
2000	28	0.51	1.00	60	90

This comparison table 1 show that the efficiency is improved by CBMT approach of multicast key distribution in terms of end to end delay of key distribution and energy conservation compared to the OMCT as shown in fig.1a and fig. 1b.

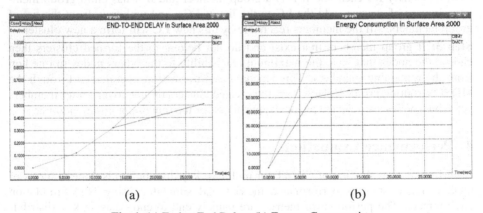

(a)   (b)

Fig. 1. (a) End to End Delay; (b) Energy Conservation

The end to end delay of key delivery and the energy conservation are better with this approach of CBMT. This is due to the fact that it sends acknowledgement for each transmission in order to reduce the retransmission. Hence it reduces end to end delay and energy conservation of multicast key distribution in CBMT compared to OMCT. Indeed, this approach divides the multicast group with the effective connectivity between nodes. It allows fast reaction to topology changes. This is due to the fact that it sends acknowledgement for each transmission in order to reduce the retransmission.

6 Conclusion

Secure multicast communication is a significant requirement in emerging applications in adhoc environments like military or public emergency network applications. Some of the existing algorithms like OMCT address the critical problems using clustering approach like energy and end to end delay issues. Therefore an attempt is made to reduce the energy and end to end delay using an algorithm called Cluster Based Multicast Tree algorithm for multicast key distribution. This algorithm uses MDSDV routing protocol for electing LCs. The proposed CBMT is tested and the entire experiments are conducted in a simulation environment using network simulator NS2 which accurately predict the performance of proposed scheme in terms of energy consumption and end to end delay rate under varying network conditions.

References

1. Chiang, T., Huang, Y.: Group keys and the multicast security in adhoc networks. In: Proc. IEEE International Conference on Parallel Processing, October 2003, pp. 385–390. IEEE press, Los Alamitos (2003)
2. Lazos, L., Poovendram, R.: Energy-Aware Secure Multicast Communication in AdHoc Networks Using Geographical Location Information. In: Proc.IEEE International Conference on Acoustics Speech and Signal Processing, April 2003, pp. 201–204 (2003)
3. Dondeti, L., Mukherjee, S., Samal, A.: Secure one-to many group communication sing dual encryption. In: IEEE sym. on Computers and Communications, July 1999, pp. 1–25 (1999)
4. Bettahar, H., Bouabdallah, A., Challal, Y.: An adaptive key management protocol for secure multicast. In: Proc. IEEE International Conference on Computer Communications and Networks, October 2002, pp. 190–195 (2002)
5. Bouassida, M., Chrisment, I., Festor, O.: An Enhanced Hybrid Key Management Protocol for Secure Multicast in AdHoc Networks. In: Mitrou, N.M., Kontovasilis, K., Rouskas, G.N., Iliadis, I., Merakos, L. (eds.) NETWORKING 2004. LNCS, vol. 3042, pp. 725–742. Springer, Heidelberg (2004)
6. Mittra, S.: Iolus: A framework for scalable secure multicasting. In: SIGCOMM, pp. 277–288 (1997)
7. Challal, Y., Bettahar, H., Bouabdallah, A.: SAKM: A Scalable and Adaptive Key Management Approach for Multicast Communications. ACM SIGCOMM Computer Communication Review, 55–70 (April 2004)
8. Bouassida, M., Chrisment, I., Festor, O.: Efficient Clustering for Multicast Key Distribution in MANETs. In: Boutaba, R., Almeroth, K.C., Puigjaner, R., Shen, S., Black, J.P. (eds.) NETWORKING 2005. LNCS, vol. 3462, pp. 138–153. Springer, Heidelberg (2005)
9. Bouassida, M., Chrisment, I., Festor, O.: Group Key Management in Manets. International Journal of Network Security, 67–79 (January 2008)
10. Bouassida, M., Chrisment, I., Festor, O.: Efficient group key management protocol in MANETs using multipoint relaying technique. In: Proc. IEEE International Conference on Networking, April 2006, p. 64 (2006)

An Optimal Trust Based Resource Allocation Mechanism for Cross Domain Grid

P. Varalakshmi, M. Nandini, K. Krithika, and R. Aarthi

Department of Information Technology, MIT, Anna University
varanip@gmail.com, nandini.mraman@gmail.com, kri1211@gmail.com,
aarthi_raj_88@yahoo.in

Abstract. Trust has been an essential quality factor in grid computing that has its influence in various other parameters like response time, throughput and resource utilization. This paper considers a method in which the factor "trust" is used in scheduling and resource allocation. Trust is calculated for both Service Provider and Client. In order to guarantee efficiency in resource allocation, a scheduling technique, which schedules the jobs according to the trust index of the Clients, is proposed. This optimal resource allocation scheme is implemented in a cross domain environment, that is, domains having different security mechanisms. The authentication is done using the signing of X.509 certificates. A common administrator is used between cross domains to provide interoperability. Both identity-based and reputation-based trusts are calculated for each entity. This ensures best service to customers. To overcome single point of failure, additional systems are provided that act as the administrator. A dynamic fault tolerance technique is proposed to guarantee successful execution of jobs in the event of resource failures.

Keywords: Grid Computing, Service Provider, Scheduling, Trust.

1 Introduction

Grid computing is a form of distributed computing that involves coordinating and sharing computing, application, data storage or network resources across dynamic and geographical disperse domains. Security in grids is challenging. In grid environment, job execution needs to invoke resources in different domains; hence the issue of trust is important. Trust is a complex subject relating to an entity's belief in reliability, trustfulness, and performance of another entity. In order to maintain the trust of a domain, the Service Provider (SP) trust alone, is not enough. Hence we have a broker. The domain can have a higher trust value only when all its entities have higher trust indices. Grid is actually composed of a number of security domains which deploy different security mechanisms. The problem of interoperability between these domains has to be considered. Trust between a Client and a SP is established based on identity and reputation. This identity-based trust model is concerned with verifying the authenticity of an entity and what it is authorized to do. The Clients who have had transactions with the SP provide feedback on the services provided by the Service Provider. The feedback received for SP from various Clients is aggregated over a period of time. This forms the reputation or trust index of that specific SP. When both

V.V Das et al. (Eds.): BAIP 2010, CCIS 70, pp. 342–348, 2010.
© Springer-Verlag Berlin Heidelberg 2010

identity and reputation are taken for trust calculation, there would be a consistency of services offered by the SP. There are certain jobs which specify a request for trust in its requirement. This request is called demand-for-trust. This is one issue that needs to be considered while scheduling of the jobs. Fault-tolerance is the property that enables a system to continue operating properly in the event of the failure of some of its components. Commonly utilized techniques for providing fault tolerance in grid systems are periodic job checkpointing and replication. But both techniques can delay job execution if inappropriate checkpointing intervals and replica numbers are chosen. A novel fault-tolerant algorithm combining checkpointing and replication is presented. This paper proposes a technique which best overcomes the above mentioned issues and evaluates trust for resource allocation and scheduling.

2 Related Work

Ezedin Barka et al[1] designed a role-based delegation model a federal method for authentication and authorization which is based on trust management and delegation [1], and proposes a model for interoperability in cross-domain grid. A decentralized automated trust negotiation framework, FORT [4] for establishing trust relationship between Service Provider and service requester in grids. Shangyuan Guan et al. [5] propose CASTTE which protects the sensitive services and identify bad services from good ones. Gabriel Queiroz Lana et al. [9] defines an approach that can be used in Grid Security systems to assist in issuing authorizations, in resource and service Management, and in decision-making processes. Yongsheng Hao et al. [13] propose a technique which calculates expectation trust and trust loss function before scheduling the jobs that arrive at the job queue. In fact, the essence of trust management is trust propagation, so a key feature of trust management is the support of delegation [3]. Maria Chtepe et al [6] proposed mean failure checkpointing where mean failure intervals of the resources are considered to examine the stability of the environment. But this has a clear disadvantage that the deviation of each resource from the mean value may differ much.

3 Trust Management

Trust Management is an important issue in a grid environment where Clients and SPs are distributed geographically across autonomous administrative domains. Traditional grids allocate resources based on the availability of SPs. Trust management architecture supports the choice of SPs based on their trust-indices maintained by Brokers. The selection criteria of the SPs is done by two steps: Trust Index Calculation and Trust Value Updation. SPs and Clients are distributed across these brokers, with each of these entities being associated with more than one broker. This improves redundancy of information maintained at broker's sites, thereby improving reliability, and eases network traffic while handling consumer requests and feedbacks. Trust-indices of brokers, SPs and Clients are updated dynamically after the completion of each transaction, enables Clients to receive quicker responses from brokers. Use of broker's and Client's feedback for the computation of trust-index has a positive impact on choosing a 'trust-worthy' SP. Trust index of SP is calculated based on the equation (1),

Trust index(T.I) of SPi=(feedback of Client/broker)/no of past transactions   (1)

The Client utilizes the services of the SP and at the end of the transaction provides a feedback to the broker. This feedback includes the Client's ID, SP's ID and the satis-faction-index for different parameters such as: Job completion time(p1), Job cost(p2) and Job satisfaction(p3). Different weights(w1,w2,w3) are assigned for these parame-ters. The satisfaction-index indicates the level of satisfaction achieved by the Client on the service provided by the SP. A value between 1 and 10 is used, with 10 indicat-ing 100% satisfaction and 1 indicating the lowest satisfaction. This is computed at the Client's site based by the broker who is associated with the selected SP. The broker also generates its feedback on the services provided by the SP by continuously moni-toring the job execution at SP's site. The broker compares his own feedback and the Client's feedback. If the Client's feedback deviates from the broker's feedback by more than a particular value(here the value is assumed as 5) then the Client's feed-back is considered as false and only the broker's feedback is updated. Consequently the false feedback count of the Client is updated. If on the other hand Client's feed-back does not deviate more than that value then the average of the feedback values of the Client and the broker is updated. The feedback from Client and SP is calculated based on equation (2),

$$feedback=(w1*p1)+(w2*p2)+(w3*p3)$$ (2)

The false feedback count is calculated and the Client (Ci) rank is computed based on equation (3),

Client rank(C.R) of C i=(no of false feed back counts)/no of past transactions   (3)

4   Trust Based Scheduling

In traditional grid, the jobs which require high quality trust may not be executed when they are allocated to low quality nodes. For this purpose scheduling of jobs is done based on trust too. Jobs are of two types that is jobs require trust and jobs that do not require trust. The first type of job is that which will have a mandatory trust require-ment when it submits job requirements. For this purpose a set of SPs is maintained along with trust values which has been computed based on previous transactions. A trust prediction function is also calculated. Then after each transaction feedback from Client and broker is collected and trust values of each SP is updated. When the jobs arrive, it is seen that if the job has specified a trust requirement. When there is a trust requirement, it is checked if there is a SP available with high trust index. If there is no such SP then the job is put in wait queue and the jobs that do not require trust can be executed in the mean time. The SPs i.e. the grid nodes available should increment their trust value in such a way that they are capable to execute the jobs in the waiting queue which has specified a trust requirement. We calculate the max expectation trust function value of every demand-for-trust jobs in Grid nodes, then map jobs and re-sources which has max expectation benefit. After that, we can update the trust func-tion and supervise the reliability of Grid node from the updated trust value. If the value is low, the node has to regain the trust value. If there is no job which can satisfy the trust requirement, then we schedule the jobs which have no trust requirement until a Grid node can provide reliable service number for that job.

4.1 Client Rank Based Scheduling

This paper considers the trust of the Client while scheduling jobs that has arrived in the job queue. Scheduling can be done taking into account various parameters such as arrival time, waiting time and so on. But here a method is proposed where scheduling is done based on the trust index of the Client. The Client's trust is evaluated at the end of each transaction. A rank for each Client is maintained based on its behavior that is the number of false feedbacks he gives after each transaction. When scheduling, the best SP is allocated as follows. When there are a set of Clients, the Clients are sorted based on their rank and the Client which is having the highest rank is allocated to the SP having the highest trust value. The Client which is having the highest trust value need not wait long. The average number of false feedbacks given by Clients is also found to decrement thereby making the domain more trustworthy.

4.2 Algorithm

1. Consider SPs=(SP1,SP2,SP3…SPi,..SPn) and Clients=(C1,C2,C3…..Ci,...Cn)
2. For each Client, get the required node count and memory and check if there is demand for trust in the request.
3. For each SP, the available node count and the available memory are determined.
4. Calculate the ranks of each SP based on previous transactions and retrieve the trust value from database based on equation (1).
5. Calculate the ranks of each Client based on previous behavior and also the number of false feedbacks given by that Client based on equation (2).
6. Jobs are matched according to node count and memory required and checks if there is a demand for trust specified in the request.
7. The Client Ci which is having the highest rank is selected.
8. If the SP does not have maximum trust value then the job is put in wait queue and jobs that do not require demand for trust are executed.
9. Allocate it to matched SPi which is having the highest trust index.
10. After job completion update $T.I$ and $C.R$.
11. The SPs need to increase their trust value to execute the jobs present in wait queue. Go to step 6.
12. End (when there are no jobs in wait queue)

5   Fault Tolerance Techniques

A grid is a distributed computational and storage environment often composed of heterogeneous autonomously managed subsystems. To avoid delays in job execution and ensuring good performance, fault tolerance should be taken into account.

5.1 Checkpointing

In Mean Failure Checkpointing, average failure intervals of the resources are considered. We enhance this method by Standard Deviation Checkpointing which measures the deviation of each resource from its stability. It uses RE_j (Remaining Execution time for job j) and SF_r (Standard deviation of the Failure intervals of resource r). By this method, active checkpointing method is done. Let the initial checkpointing interval be $I_j < \alpha * RE_j$ where α is a constant such that $\alpha < 1$ and $I_j > C$ where C is the time taken for checkpointing. Let MF_r be the the the mean of failure intervals of the resources, I_{jnew} is the new checkpointing interval and I_{jold} is the old checkpointing interval. After time t, a job requests for checkpointing, then if

$$RE_j < MF_r \ \& \ Sd_r < 5$$

the checkpointing interval I is changed as

$$I_{jnew} = I_{jold} + I_j$$

If even one of the equations is not satisfied, the interval is decreased as

$$I_{jnew} = I_{jold} - I_j \quad \text{such that} \quad I_{jnew} > C$$

Thus checkpointing interval is selected dynamically based on the standard deviation of the failure intervals of resources. Standard deviation shows how much variation there is from average. Standard Deviation when low indicates that the resources tend to be very stable, whereas when high indicates that the resources are very unstable. Thus overhead of checkpointing in stable environment is reduced and the method gives more accurate idea of resource failure in future.

5.2 Replication

Replication method implies making many replicas of the job and running in individual resources so that at least one replica of the job executes successfully in minimum time. The number of replicas depends upon the factors which are obtained from user. They are Rep_{min}(minimum job copies needed) and Rep_{max}(maximum job copies needed) and CL(CPU Limit). CL specifies the lower bound on the number of active free CPUs for replication to take place. Let n be the number of remaining jobs in the queue. Now the algorithm follows that:Given Rep_{min}, Rep_{max} and CL.

The CPU available(CA) is compared with CL.

If CA >= CL, select job with earlier time and give replicas rep<Rep_{max} such that n*2 is equal to the remaining resources other than allotted to the the first job. This ensures that at least one replica per job is activated. If CA<n, rep replicas of job j is taken and remaining resources are allotted to jobs in queue each until CA=0.

If 0<CA<CL, select job with earlier time and give replicas rep<Rep_{min} such that n*2 is equal to the remaining resources other than allotted to the the first job. If CA<n, replicas of job j is taken and remaining resources are allotted to jobs in queue each until CA=0. If CA=0, round is skipped. When one of the replicas finishes execution, all other replicas are cancelled. When load is decreased before execution gets completed, Rep_{max}-Rep_{min} replicas are activated. Since job queue length is also considered in this method, the first job is prevented from using all the resources for its own replicas and resources are left idle for the coming jobs too. Hence it avoids delayed copy problem. Since CA and CL are checked before replicating, ideal number of replicas is activated.

5.3 Combined Fault Tolerance Technique

Replication method is effective only when there are enough resources available for the replicas to execute. Replication is avoided during peak hours. At that time, it is efficient to use checkpointing. Hence system traffic is a critical factor in switching between the two techniques of fault tolerance. When the system is idle, checkpointing is cancelled and replication method is activated. When traffic rises and available number of resources reduces, replication is cancelled and the most completed replica is checkpointed while other replicas are cancelled and the process is repeated.

6 Performance

The performance of the algorithm with scheduling based on trust is measured by comparing it with the first-come-first-served scheduling. In the latter mechanism the jobs are scheduled as and when they come based on their arrival time. In this manner the jobs of Clients whose ranks are higher may have to wait for jobs of Clients whose ranks are lower. The correspondence between rank of Client and waiting time does not follow a linear pattern and it varies a lot. But in the former mechanism, higher ranked Clients will have lesser waiting time. Also more trustworthy Clients are allocated to more trustworthy SPs. Thus the trust provided is increased. The variation of the waiting times for jobs based on Client ranking for the two different algorithms is shown in the graph(Fig 1). The first-come-first-served scheduling shows the lack of correspondence between waiting time and rank of Clients. On the other hand in scheduling based on trust there is linear correspondence between the two.

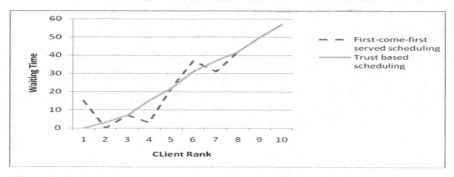

Fig. 1. Graph showing client rank versus waiting time for the two scheduling algorithms

7 Conclusion

In this paper a grid resource allocation mechanism between cross domain grids based on trust index of the SP is proposed. Trust management is done by using techniques of trust calculation and trust value updation. The scheduling of jobs is based on rank of the Client submitting the job calculated using its trust index. The trust index is determined using the average number of false feedback counts of the Client. Interoperability between the cross domain grids is provided by exchanging X.509 certificates which is facilitated by an administrator who is common to all domains. Fault tolerant mechanisms are implemented to take care of single point of failure of the common administrator. This paper provides better performance by using a trust based scheduling method and an improved interoperability mechanism.

References

1. Shen, S., Tang, S.: Cross-Domain Grid Authentication and Authorization Scheme Based on Trust Management and Delegation. In: 2008 IEEE, International Conference on Computational Intelligence and Security (2008)
2. Yu, Y., Tang, J., Hao, L., Dai, S., Wu, Y.: A Grid Trust Model Based on MADM Theory. In: Global Telecommunications Conference. IEEE GLOBECOM 2008. IEEE, Los Alamitos (2008)
3. Guan, S., Dong, X.: FORT: a Decentralized Automated Trust Negotiation Framework for Grids. IEEE, Los Alamitos (2008)
4. Guan, S., Dong, X., Mei, Y.: CASTTE: a Trust Management for Securing the Grid. In: The 10th IEEE International Conference on High Performance Computing and Communications (2008)
5. Chtepen, M., Claeys, F.H.A., Dhoedt, B., De Turck, F., Demeester, P., Vanrolleghem, P.A.: Adaptive Task Checkpointing and Replication: Toward Efficient Fault-Tolerant Grids. IEEE Transactions on Parallalel and Distributed Systems 20(2) (February 2009)
6. Lana, G.Q., Westphall, C.B.: User Maturity Based Trust Management for Grid Computing. In: Seventh International Conference on Networking. IEEE, Los Alamitos (2008)
7. Hao, Y., Xu, Y., Liu, G., Zhenkuan: An Expectation Trust Benefit Driven Algorithm for Resource Scheduling in Grid Computing. IEEE, Los Alamitos (2008)

Reactive Network Monitor for DDoS Attacks

P. Varalakshmi, P. Karthik Narayanan, M. Hariharan, P. Nagaraj, and K. Amritha

ddosreactivenetworkmonitor@gmail.com

Abstract. Distributed Denial of Service attacks has emerged as a prevalent way to take down servers imposing huge financial losses to companies. Only a few responses have been designed to actively respond to the attack traffic while the majority have been designed to trace or log attack traffic. The DDoS defence mechanism presented here is effective for the detection and mitigation of fast-changing attacks at the earliest. The system architecture usually consists of many routers attached with victim and the edge routers are having the hosts attached with them. This is the basic system architecture seen in the proposed simulation. Based on the packet loss statistical analysis the proposed system finds the router with the highest packet loss. The monitoring system then invokes the trace back approach and black hole filtering system. The edge router then finds the suspected hosts and traces the attacker meanwhile the victim is protected from any other attacks.

Keywords: Edge Router, Victim, Packet loss, Attack detector, Packet Processor, wired network topology, Trace back approach, Black hole filtering.

1 Introduction

A Distributed Denial-of-Service (DDoS) attack is one of the major threats in current computer networks. It is an attempt to make a computer resource unavailable to the intended users. One common method of attack involves saturating the target (victim) machine with external communications requests, such that it cannot respond to legitimate traffic, or responds so slowly as to be rendered effectively unavailable.

The proposed DDoS defense methodology which traces back the source based upon the packet arrival rate and the packet loss rate at each intermediate router. To ensure that the victim is not attacked during the trace back, black hole filtering is done at the intermediate router thereby mitigating the attack.

2 Related Work

The Proposed Defense methodology divided into three parts i.e Traffic Monitoring, Trace back and detection. Attack mitigation [5] schemes presents Attack Diagnosis (AD), a novel attack mitigation scheme that adopts a divide-and-conquer strategy. AD attack detection is performed near the victim host and packet filtering is executed close to the attack sources. DDoS Attack Trace back and Mitigation System [5] (DATMS) is proposed to trace the DDoS attack sources based on network performance monitoring by monitoring packet loss rate and packet arrival rate. Hop-Count

V.V Das et al. (Eds.): BAIP 2010, CCIS 70, pp. 349–355, 2010.
© Springer-Verlag Berlin Heidelberg 2010

Filtering (HCF) [3] which builds an accurate IP-to-hop-count (IP2HC) mapping table—to detect and discard spoofed IP packets as the attacker cannot falsify the number of hops an IP packet takes to reach its destination.. Information Gain and Chi-square methods are used to rank the importance of 41 attributes[2] extracted from the network traffic in which 9 attributes are important for detection. Payload Content based Network Anomaly Detection (PCNAD) [6] is a complete systems for payload based anomaly detection and CPP (Content based Payload Partitioning) technique which divides the payload into different partitions depending on content of payload. This system has two major components: Packet Profiler and PCNAD normally Detector. Black hole filtering is a flexible ISP Security tool that will route packets to Null0 (i.e. black holed). In networking, black holes refer to places in the network where incoming traffic is silently discarded (or "dropped"), without informing the source that the data did not reach its intended recipient and Black hole filtering refers specifically to dropping packets at the routing level, usually using a routing protocol to implement the filtering on several routers at once, often dynamically to respond quickly to distributed denial-of-service attacks.

3 Proposed Framework

The system architecture consists of many routers attached with victim and the edge routers are having the hosts attached with them. This is the basic system architecture in the proposed framework in which router and victim are the most important component in this architecture. The assumptions here are: Host based detection is considered where in the routers must know the victim. Since the packets from the victim to the hosts are legitimate packets, the flow considered in only from hosts to victim.

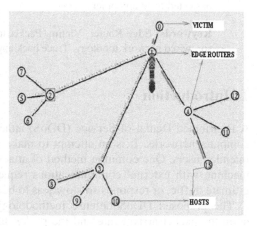

Fig. 1. Overall topology

3.1 Router Components

Statistical study should be performed for certain period of time in router component and that will be done by **pre-processor**. The pre-processor calculates the packet loss values through observation of the network for a finite period of time like average, highest and lowest packet loss. The average packet loss is the average of all the packet losses over the initial observation period. The highest and lowest packet loss is the highest and least number of packets lost at a particular time in that period of observation. **Routing table** stores information regarding the next hop to which a packet has to be forwarded based on the destination address of the packet. Any changes in the network are constantly noticed and will be updated in the routing table and then the flow of the packets takes place based on the information present in the routing table. **Packet Forwarder** forwards the packets to the next router as specified by the routing table. The updating of routing table is constantly looked upon by the system and then the forwarding of the packet is done. The pre-processor sends message to traffic analyzer present in the victim when Packet loss is greater than or equal to Highest Packet loss. The **Traffic monitor** module sends the same to the traffic analyzer present in the victim. Traffic analyzer then triggers trace back and filtering modules present in the victim. Traffic monitor then receives reply from traffic analyzer and changes the routing table entry to null zero database so that the packets are stored instead of forwarding to the victim. Also asks the null zero database to forward legitimate packets after getting messages from Attack detector.

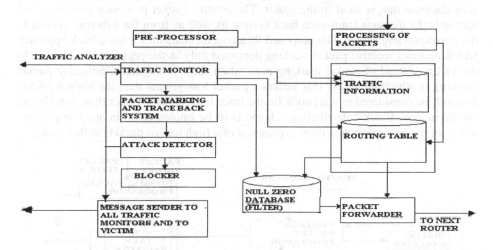

Fig. 2. Router Components

Packet marking and **traceback system** is used to identify the edge router associated with the attacker and they both receives the message from the traffic monitor through the control packet processor and triggers the trace back system in the router. They both starts processing from the router that experienced a packet loss greater than the highest packet loss. The interfaces of that router are individually monitored. If any interface connected has a high packet arrival rate, that router in turn performs the above mentioned steps. This is continued till the attacking host is identified. An **attack detector** present in the edge router identifies the suspected attacker associated with it. At the edge router, for each of the suspected attacker performs EX-OR of the payload of certain number of sequential packets. If EX-OR value is zero, then that should be an attacker and attack detector present in the edge router sends message to all Traffic Monitors and victim too and Finally triggers the blocker. **Blocker** present in the edge router blocks the messages of the attacking host that is identified using the trace back and filtering system. It is used to provide the reliable service to the other non-attacking nodes. The messages are initially stored by the filtering mechanism. Once the attacker is identified by the blocker then all the messages sent by that host are removed from the black hole database system and then the legitimate packet flow takes place effectively.

3.2 Victim Components

At the victim side the packets received are processed by data or **control packet processor** depending upon the type of the packet. An attack registry is maintained to load the different attacks that possibly occur. If any control message received by control packet processor from traffic monitor, it gives the details about attacker which is stored in attack registry and forwards message to traffic analyzer. **Traffic analyzer** triggers trace back and filtering modules. **Trace back system initiator** sends a message to router's Packet Marking Trace back system to initiate Packet marking and Trace back. **Filtering initiator** sends the message to Traffic Monitor of a router to change the next hop entry in the routing table where the destination is victim to null zero database that is local to the router. The control packet processor processes and forwards the message from trace-back system as well as from the Filtering system to the corresponding router. The proposed Reactive mechanism for trace-back approach which includes reactive packet marking deployed only in the presence of an attack to the victim instead of packet marking even when there is no attack. Selective packet marking in which the router that suffers a packet loss greater than the highest packet loss will be considered as start node for the trace back scheme rather than considering all the routers. Black hole filtering scheme is to be implemented in any router (anywhere in the network) when there is presence of a high loss of packets at that node.

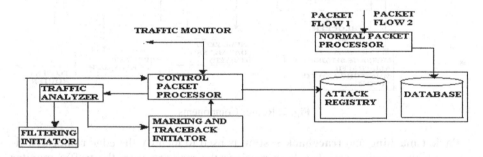

Fig. 3. Victim Components

4 Algorithm

Algorithm of how we implemented with the above considerations is given below:

- In the network, for each of the routers find their respective Packet loss such as : **Average** Packet Loss, **Highest** Packet Loss, **Lowest** Packet Loss
  This information is obtained through the statistical study about the Router's behavior in a network.
- The flow Monitor will constantly monitor the whole network and if for any router, its Packet Loss is $\geq$ Highest Packet Loss Send a SNMP message to the victim under attack.
- The victim then asks the attached edge router to start Trace back and packet marking scheme, to find the attacker in the network by tracing back from the router of initial interest and then the corresponding attacker is found out through trace back.

- Black hole filtering done to prevent the denial of the service to the valid users even at the instant of the attack and simultaneously the mitigation scheme is also enabled.
- Through the trace-back approach, the edge router corresponding to the attacker is determined.
- At the edge routers, for each of the suspected hosts, we consider their payload and then we perform EX-OR of the payload for certain number of sequential packets. If EX-OR value is 0 then that will be Attacker, Else that suspected one is a Normal user.
- After finding the attacker from step 5, the identity information about the attacker is given to the edge router regarding where the packet loss is high and who is connected with the victim server.
- The edge router then discards the messages from the respective attacking hosts.

5 Simulation Results

The proposed system is simulated using an network simulator (NS2) with the topology existing of 14 nodes as in Figure 1. The simulation that is developed is the overall flow of the reactive monitoring of the network at the event of any DDoS attack. Victim server, node 0, which suffers heavily in performance due to the attack. And it is connected with an edge router node 1. That edge router of the victim is connected to the respective edge routers that are connected with the hosts node 2,3,4 that are connected with the hosts of the network which are the nodes 5,6,7,8,9,10,11,12,13. Node 13 is taken as the attacker in term of frequency of sending the message and thus all the nodes will transmit their message and when 13 sends the message there will be loss of messages at the edge router of the victim and so the traceback is started from that router and the black hole filtering is initiated there so no further packets will be forwarded to the victim and only when the attacker is found out, the messages of the legitimate user will then be allowed.

Thus the black hole filtering and the traceback is performed and the malicious host that causes the attack is found and its link is broken. Here link connected to node13 is broken. The initial filtering and the traceback is started at the first node of 1 as it is the first node in this network that experiences more intensity in signal strength and hence has greater value than the link and hence the overflow occurs.

Another flow that performs the trace back mechanism of the proposed work is implemented. Here flow monitor is used for each of the links present in the network. The packet arrival rate value is set to a threshold and using this value, the attacker is determined by comparing that value with Threshold values at each point of the network. From the victim's edge router to those of the router present for the hosts, the value for threshold is 1000 and for the router to the host it is 10000. Any value if found to be greater than the above two values, then those nodes are susceptible to attack and we travel in their path to find the attacker and finally the attacking host is found out and displayed by the program with their source and destination port and address. Thus from this program the hosts that have the higher probability to be as an attacker can be found.

Table 1. Comparison of the performance factors with existent and proposed methodology

PARAMETER	EXISTENT METHOD	PROPOSED METHOD
Trace back Approach	**Proactive:** Packet marking is done always by the victim.	**Reactive:** Packet marking is started only when the Packet loss is high.
	Packet Marking is done for all routers involved	Packet Marking is done only from the routers which suffer from high Packet loss.
Black hole Filtering	**Destination based filtering:** Packet loss will be high. All legitimate as well as illegitimate packets are also filtered	The Black hole filtering deployed at any intermediate router or node so that the packet loss will be less.
	Source based filtering: Time to detect the source of the attacker is high, and in that, duration the victim may get affected.	Source need not be found out. Time of detecting the source is less and works best
Payload	Dependent on IP address and so they are Vulnerable to IP spoofing attacks	Independent on IP address. And EX-ORing on the payload on packets determines the attacker.

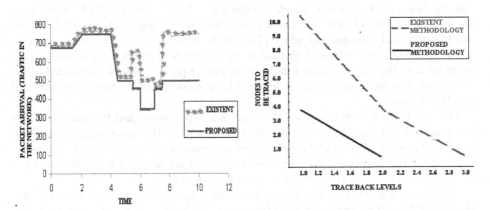

Graph 1: Comparison of Networks Traffic

Graph 2: Comparison of Nodes Traced Back with levels

Performance analysis is given below:

In Graph 1, Xaxis indicates Time and Yaxis indicates Network Traffic. Till the preprocessing time of 5 seconds both the graphs overlap. After that network traffic is less in the proposed system(blue) due to the black hole filtering which eliminates the excess of the illegitimate packets causing traffic(red).In Graph 2, X-axis indicates the levels in the network hierarchy and Y-axis indicates the number of nodes traced back. This Xgraph basically indicates that the overhead of traversing all the nodes has reduced in the proposed system(blue). Whereas existing system increases the nodes to be traversed thus increasing the overhead of monitoring (red).

6 Conclusion

The proposed DDoS defence methodology which traces back the source based upon the packet arrival rate and the packet loss rate at each intermediate router. To ensure that the victim is not attacked during the trace back, black hole filtering is done at the intermediate router thereby mitigating the attack. At the edge router, for each of the suspected attacker performs EX-OR of the payload of certain number of sequential packets. If the EX-OR value of two sequential packets are zero then the node is an attacker, else not an attacker. The system proves to be effective in detecting DDoS attacks by using the proposed detection and mitigation mechanisms.

References

1. Kim, Y., Lau, W.C., Chuah, M.C., Jonathan Chao, H.: PacketScore: Statistics-based Overload Control against Distributed Denial-of-Service Attacks. In: Proceedings of IEEE INFOCOM (2004)
2. Wang, W., Gombault, S.: Efficient Detection of DDoS Attacks with Important Attributes. IEEE Transactions on Secure Computing (2008)
3. Wang, H., Jin, C., Shin, K.G.: Defense against Spoofed IP Traffic using Hop Count Filtering. IEEE Transactions on Networking (February 2007)
4. Chen, Y., Hwang, K., Kuu, W.-S.: Collaborative Detection of DDoS Attacks over Multiple Network Domains. IEEE Transactions on Parallel and Distributed Systems, TPDS-0228-0806
5. Chen, R., Park, J.-M., Marchany, R.: A Divide-and-Conquer Strategy for Thwarting Distributed Denial-of-Service Attacks. IEEE Transactions on Parallel and Distributed Systems 18(5), 577–588 (2007)
6. Thorat, S.A., Khandelwal, A.K., Bruhadeshwar, B., Kishore, K.: Payload Content based Network Anomaly Detection. In: IEEE CADIWT (2008)

Statistical Method for English to Kannada Transliteration

P.J. Antony, V.P. Ajith, and K.P. Soman

CEN, Amrita University, Coimbatore, India
antonypjohn@gmail.com, {vp_ajith,kp_soman}@cb.amrita.edu

Abstract. Language transliteration is one of the important area in natural language processing. Machine Transliteration is the conversion of a character or word from one language to another without losing its phonological characteristics. It is an orthographical and phonetic converting process. Therefore, both grapheme and phoneme information should be considered. Accurate transliteration of named entities plays an important role in the performance of machine translation and cross-language information retrieval processes. The transliteration model must be design in such a way that the phonetic structure of words should be preserve as closely as possible. This paper address the problem of transliterating English to Kannada language using a publically available translation tool called Statistical Machine Translation (SMT).This transliteration technique was demonstrated for English to Kannada Transliteration and achieved exact Kannada transliterations for 89.27% of English names. The result of proposed model is compared with the SVM based transliteration system as well as Google Indic transliteration system.

Keywords: Transliteration, Kannada, SMT, GIZA++, MOSES.

1 Introduction

Machine transliteration is the practice of transcribing a character or word written in one alphabetical system into another alphabetical system. Most of the information in Internet is available in a selected number of languages. Indian languages have comparatively lesser amount of data available over the Internet. Many technical terms and proper names, such as personal, location and organization names, are translated from one language into another language with approximate phonetic equivalents. The phonetic translation from the native language to foreign language is defined as transliteration.

Machine transliteration can play an important role in natural language application such as information retrieval and machine translation, especially for handling proper nouns and technical terms, cross-language applications, data mining and information retrieval system. The Kannada language is the one of the four major Dravidian languages of South India. It is the state language of Karnataka and is spoken by about 20 million people. It has a long linguistic of about 1,500 years and had a continuous literature for over 1,200 years.

V.V Das et al. (Eds.): BAIP 2010, CCIS 70, pp. 356–362, 2010.
© Springer-Verlag Berlin Heidelberg 2010

2 Statistical Machine Translation

Statistical machine translation (SMT) is a tool mainly used for machine translation and contrasts with the rule-based approaches as well as with example based machine translation [4]. Translations are performed on the basis of statistical models whose parameters are derived from the analysis of bilingual text corpora. Generally, SMT systems are not tailored to any specific pair of languages.

3 Transliteration Procedure Using SMT

In the proposed method, English to Kannada transliteration is modelled as translation problem using SMT. The purpose of the statistical transliteration model is to find a transliteration of the source language word into a target language with a specific probability. The best transliteration is the word in the target language has the highest probability. The parameters of the models are automatically learned from a bilingual proper name list.

The statistical transliteration system requires three prime components, Language model, Transliteration model and Decoder. The transliteration model called n-grams transliteration model, describes the transformation rules. The open source tools SRILM and GIZA++ are used for creating language and transliteration model. Another tool called MOSES, a beam search decoder is used for English to Kannada transliteration. The model is evaluated using BLEU, an evaluator for machine translation commonly used evaluator for SMT.

Machine transliteration can be formalized by using the noisy channel method [6]. Under the noisy channel model, the transliteration problem is to find the most probable word 'Y' in the target language K for the given word 'X' in source language E that maximizes

$$P(Y/X) = P(X/Y) * P(Y)/P(X) . \tag{1}$$

where 'Y' is the most likely word for the given 'X'. $P(X)$ can be omitted since it is constant. The n-gram transliteration model can be built using n-gram statistics obtained by direct one to one mapping between the transliteration units of source language and target language words. The language model can be modeled using maximum likelihood estimation [8].

3.1 Language Model

Language modeling is the process of assigning probability to every unit of the text or word [8]. Given a word 'Y', the task is to compute $P(Y)$. For a word contains the sequence of alphabets $a_1, a_2, \ldots a_n$, $P(Y)$ can be written as

$$P(Y) = P (a_1, a_2 \ldots a_n) . \tag{2}$$

$$P(Y) = P(a_1) P(a_2/a_1) P(a_3/a_1 a_2) \ldots P(a_n/a_1 a_2 \ldots a_{n-1}) . \tag{3}$$

An alphabet can occur only in certain contexts in the history of words using which these probabilities can compute. In an n-gram model [7], the probability of an alphabet given all previous alphabets is approximated by the probability of the alphabet given the previous n-1 alphabets. The approximation works by assigning all contexts that agree in the last n-1 alphabets into one equivalence class. With n=2, the model is called the bigram model and n=3 gives the trigram model. n-gram probabilities can be directly computed from a corpus [6]. The bigram probabilities can be computed as

$$P(a_n/a_{n-1}) = \text{count}(a_{n-1}\, a_n) / \sum \text{count}(a_{n-1}\, a_n). \tag{4}$$

The above probability can be computed as

$$P(a_n/a_{n-1}) = \text{count}(a_{n-1}\, a_n) / \sum \text{count}(a_{n-1}). \tag{5}$$

The technique behind this model is called maximum likelihood estimation. Based on the maximum likelihood estimation technique, given a training corpus, the model is generated such that the probability is maximized.

3.2 Transliteration Model

The transliteration model is used to find the probability of the source language word 'X' given the transliteration 'Y', i.e. P(X/Y). The n-gram transliteration model uses data driven approach to generate probabilistic transformation rules. The value of P(X/Y) is estimated based on the n-gram statistics obtained by using one to one mapping between the transliteration units of the source language and target language words. An aligned parallel corpus of the source and target language words are used for training the transliteration model.

Giving a bilingual parallel corpus using an unsupervised learning algorithm called Expectation –Maximization algorithm, the transliteration probabilities are computed. The probability of 'X' given 'Y' denoted as P(X/Y) is calculated using the below formula:

$$P(X/Y) = \sum_M P(X, M/Y) = \sum_M P(X/M, Y)\, P(M/Y) \tag{6}$$

where 'M' is the match type defined as a pair of transliteration unit lengths for the source and target languages. When the summation criterion in P(X/Y) is approximated into maximization the computational complexity is reduced as below:

$$P(X/Y) \approx \text{Max} \sum_M P(X/M, Y)\, P(M/Y). \tag{7}$$

That is

$$P(X/Y) \approx \text{Max} \sum_M P(X/M, Y)\, P(M). \tag{8}$$

3.3 Decoder

The function of decoder is to generate the transliterated word in a target language for a given source input word. Using the learned parameters the decoder performs the transliteration using the trained model that is created already. The decoder uses the modified Viterbi and A* algorithms to search for highest probability transliteration that satisfies the condition

$$Y = \text{argmax}_M (P(X/Y)\, P(Y)). \tag{9}$$

4   English to Kannada Statistical Transliteration

Based on the methodology of SMT, the transliteration system for English language to Kannada language is developed. The Fig.1 shows the architecture of the Statistical Transliteration system for English language to Kannada language.

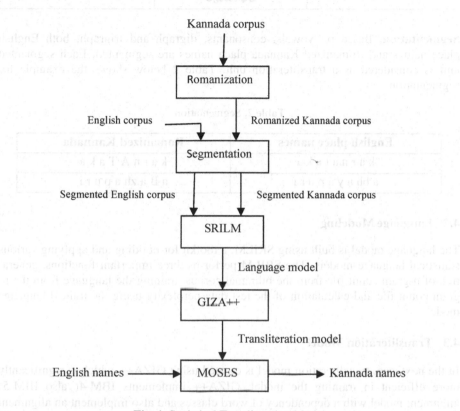

Fig. 1. Statistical Transliteration Model

4.1   Preprocessing

The training file is converted into a format required by SMT. The preprocessing phase consists of the following two steps: Romanization and Segmentation. The segmented bilingual corpus is used for training the proposed model. The sequence of steps in preprocessing is as follows.

Romanization. The following two tasks are performed during this step. All the English words (place names) are converted in to lowercase and then corresponding Kannada words. Using the mapping rules that defines English alphabet for each Kannada alphabet Romanize these Kannada words. The table 1 shows the example for Romanization.

Table 1. Romanization

English place names	Kannada	Romanized Kannada
karnataka	ಕರ್ನಾಟಕ	karnATaka
abhayapuri	ಅಭಯಪುರಿ	aBazhapuri

Segmentation. Based on vowels, consonants, digraph and trigraph, both English place names and Romanized Kannada place names are segmented. Each segmented unit is considered as a transliteration unit. Table 2 below shows the example for segmentation.

Table 2. Segmentation

English place names	Romanized Kannada
k a r n a t a k a	k a r n A T a k a
a bh a y a p u r i	a B a zh a p u r i

4.2 Language Modeling

The language model is built using SRILM, a toolkit for building and applying various statistical language models. The SRILM performs three important functions, generation of n-gram count file from the bilingual corpus, training the language from the n-gram count file and calculation of the test data perplexity using the trained language model.

4.3 Transliteration Model

In the next step, transliteration model is created using GIZA++ which is significantly more efficient in training the model. GIZA++ implements IBM-4(also IBM-5) alignment model with a dependency of word classes and also implement an alignment model based on HMM using Baum-Welch training and Forward-Backward algorithm. The transliteration of English to Kannada is performed with the decoder MOSES. MOSES trains automatically the transliteration models for any language pair based on the parallel corpus.

5   Evaluation and Results

The performance of the proposed statistical transliteration is evaluated with the evaluator tool called BLEU. The efficiency of the proposed model is evaluated by using a set of 1000 test names. Scores are calculated for individual transliterated segments, by comparing them with the set of good quality reference transliteration using BLEU. The scores are then averaged over the whole corpus to find an estimate of the transliteration's overall quality. The transliteration accuracy of our model is shown in table 3.

Table 3. SMT Transliteration Accuracy

Output	Accuracy
Top1	89.27%
Top2	91.88%
Top3	93.57%
Top4	95.61%
Top5	97.32%

6 Comparison with SVM and Google Indic -Transliteration Systems

The proposed model is compared with SVM(Support Vector Machine) based transliteration system developed using sequence labeling approach. SVM [2], [3] belongs to binary classifiers group. The SVM binary classifier predicts all possible class labels for a given sequence of source language alphabets and selects only the most probable class labels. The transliteration accuracy of SVM model is shown in table 4.

Table 4. SVM Transliteration Accuracy

Output	Accuracy
Top1	81.25%
Top2	85.88%
Top3	87.64%
Top4	89.11%
Top5	91.32%

The proposed model is also compared with publically available Google Indic transliteration system. From the results we observed that the overall accuracy for Google when transliterating Indian names and places was 69 % when considering the Top1 result. But the fact that the Google system is designed for general transliteration whereas the model presented here is trained exclusively for Indian names.

Table 5. Comparison with SVM and Google

English Names	Google Output	SVM Output	SMT Output
Raichur	ರೈಚುರ್	ರಾಯ್ಚ್ಚುರ್	ರಾಯ್ಚ್ಚುರ್
Kerala	ಕೇರಳ	ಕೇರಲ	ಕೇರಳ
Adesh	ಅದೆಷ	ಆದೇಶ್	ಆದೇಶ್
Adit	ಆಡಿಟ್	ಆದಿತ್	ಆದಿತ್

A sample of the test data used to compare the results of proposed Statistical model with that of SVM and Google Indic transliteration systems are shown in table 5.

7 Conclusion

In this paper we modeled the transliteration as statistical machine transliteration. The tools such SRILM, GIZA++, MOSES and BLEU have been used to creating the transliteration model. The framework based on data driven method and one to one mapping approach simplify the development procedure of transliteration system and facilities better improvement in transliteration accuracy when compared with that of other state-of-the-art machine learning algorithms. The model is trained on 40,000 words containing Indian place names. The model is evaluated by considering top5 transliterations. From the experiment we found that considering first five ranked transliteration result increase the overall transliteration accuracy in a great extent. We also compared the result with SVM and Google Indic transliteration systems and observed that the result obtained was much better. We hope this will be very useful in natural language application like bilingual machine translation and in many natural language processing areas.

References

1. Ganesh, S., Harsha, S., Pingali, P., Varma, V.: Statistical Transliteration for Cross Langauge Information Retrieval using HMM alignment and CRF. In: Proceedings of the 2nd workshop on Cross Lingual Information Access (CLIA). IIIT Hyderabad, India (2008)
2. Vijaya, M.S., Loganathan, R., Shivapratap, G., Ajith, V.P., Soman, K.P.: In: International Conference on Asian Language Processing, Thailand (November 2008)
3. Giménezand, J., Màrquez, L.: SVMTtool: Technical manual v1.3 (August 2006)
4. Vapnik, V.N.: Statistical Learning Theory. J.Wiley & Sons, Inc., New York (1998)
5. Cortes, C., Haffner, P., Mohri, M.: A Machine Learning Framework For Spoken-Dialog Classification: Springer Handbook on Speech Processing and Speech Communication (2008)
6. Ramanathan, A.: Statistical Machine Translation.: Ph.D. Seminar Report. IIT-Bombay, India (2008)
7. Jurafsky, D., Martin, J.H.: Speech and Language Processing- An Introduction to Natural Language Processing. In: Computational Linguistics and Speech Recognition, pp. 799–801. Prentice Hall, Englewood Cliffs (2000)
8. Koehn, P.: MOSES a Beam-Search Decoder for Factored Phrase-Based Statistical Machine Translation Models User Manual and Code Guide. University of Edinburg, UK (2009)

RIFMAS: River Flow Management System Using Wireless Sensing Agents

R.B. Patel[1], Deepika Jain[1], and Bhanu Kaushik[2]

[1] Dept of Computer Engineering, M. M. University, Mullana(Ambala), India
[2] Dept of Computer and Information Sciences, Northeastern University, Boston, MA, USA
deepikajain_dg@yahoo.co.in, {drrbpatel, bhanukaushik}@ieee.org

Abstract. Floods have always been a major cause of destruction from the past itself. In the manual river flow control system there is always a situation of the increasing or decreasing of the discharge available depending on the precipitation of the catchment region. In this article, with a blend of mobile agents (MAs), wireless sensor networks (WSNs) and intelligent systems we intend to formulate a new application to manage the water flow of a river by continuously monitoring the precipitation and correspondingly changing the position of the diversion head regulators (HR) of a barrage. Finally a global model of RIFMAS is also presented and it will be simulated in near future for its feasibility.

Keywords: Mobile Agent, RIFMAS, GIMAS, WSN.

1 Introduction

The growing need of automation and the application of the sensors in the real world have provided dynamicity to both the physical and the virtual world. This has in turn made the Wireless Sensor Networks (WSNs) and its application as the hottest topics of research in the current scenario. Small mobile sensing agents in a networking arrangement have made it possible to collect and estimate the data of the physical phenomenon with precision and accuracy which was however impossible or difficult to calibrate. Large scale WSNs [5] have bagged potential applications in a variety of virtual and physical world critical application scenarios including wild life tracking and battlefield surveillance, habitat monitoring, traffic monitoring and security applications, fire rescue applications, medical monitoring environmental monitoring [1][4], home security and industrial machine monitoring astronomical studies(Cloud monitoring Systems) [2-4]. These are the most powerful means of observing the variety of variations in the variety of events over a large period of time. In the architecture of WSN a large number of small and simple mobile sensing agents communicate over short-range wireless interfaces to deliver observations and stimuli to central location called sink (Base Station). This data is then acted upon by an intelligent system and can be worked upon accordingly. The WSN aim is to facilitate the human life by providing ubiquitous sensing, computing and communication capability which help in observing and interacting with the environment.

V.V Das et al. (Eds.): BAIP 2010, CCIS 70, pp. 363–368, 2010.

Floods have always been a major cause of destruction from the past itself. In the manual river flow control system there is always a situation of the increasing or decreasing of the discharge available depending on the precipitation of the catchment region.

This article presents a prototype called River Flow Management System (RIF-MAS) which is intended to make the flood management system automated adaptive and autonomous to support advanced management services of rainfall data and information mining in order to avoid floods. RIFMAS deploys the wireless sensing agents to make this process self-operational in nature so that the system in itself controls the movement of the HR depending on the estimated discharge. The information needed by the intelligent system is provided by sensor agents [6] despite the challenges in detecting the precipitation, monitoring, collection and calibration of the data, assessing and evaluation of discharge information, formulating meaningful user displays, and decision-making with emergency and alarm functionalities and form the mainstay for sensing as well as for the first stages of the processing hierarchy. This application of wireless sensor networks is expected to be a precursor of the modern day river monitoring and Flow control systems.

Rest of the paper is organized as follows. Section 2 highlights on Motivation and Related work. Section 3 presents System Architecture and Implementation of the System is given in Section 4. Future model of RIFMAS, i.e., GRIFMAS and its implementation is discussed in Section 5 & 6 respectively. Finally the article is concluded in Section 7.

2 Motivation and Related Works

In the modus operandi of the trivial river flow control systems we firstly measure the total precipitation at the various rain gauge centers. Secondly, based on these readings the discharge that flows out of the catchment is calculated [2] [3]. Thirdly, the time taken by the discharge to reach the HR of the barrage is calculated which is generally constant for a particular barrage setup and its catchment. Fourthly, as soon as the estimated discharge and the time is estimated this data is fed to the barrage section. Fifthly, as the data arrives the barrage is set in accordance to the provided values (manually). In [4] authors presented a River water-monitoring system for water pollution monitoring using sensing agents.

3 System Architecture

The System Architecture of RIFMAS {Fig. 1.} comprises the following.(a) Sensing Agent (NODE 1 to N): These are the MICA2 MOTE sensors by crossbow which are being deployed to measure the precipitation in the catchment region. These sensors are integrated with MAs. These MAs are used to measure the precipitation level in inches. MA carries these sensed data to the Data Collector (DC). (b) DATA COLLECTOR (DC): collects and assemble data and provides this data to the Data Processing and Management Unit (DPMU) using MAs. (DC could also be used as a server for maintaining the database of the rainfall data by the metrological department).

DC actually acts as a mediator between the DPMU and the Gate Manager (GM). DC works like sink. (c) Data Processing & Management Unit (DPMU): collects the data from the DC and calibrate it to Q_DISCHARGE and EST_TIME. The DPMU executes MAs [6] for calibration charts to estimate Q_DISCHARGE. The EST_TIME is generally constant for a particular catchment. The DPMU forwards a MA with estimated data back to the DC. (d) GATE MANAGER (GM): The DC sends the calibrated Q_DISCHARGE and EST_TIME to the GM. The GM takes Q_DISCHARGE as input and performs the following operation over it. Divide the Q_DISCHARGE into Q1_DISCHARGE, Q2_DISCHARGE, and QM_DISCHARGE in a predefined ratio. Calculate the Gate Openings for the divided data, i.e., Q1_HOPENING, Q2_HOPENING, and QM_HOPENING. Set the gates to these values so as the discharge reaches the gates and the gates should be set to receive that amount of discharge.

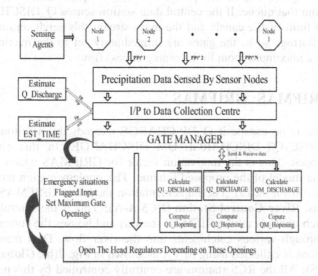

Fig. 1. System Architecture of RIFMAS

4 Implementation of RIFMAS

The data read from the sensor nodes is acted upon by an MA intelligent system, which in turn computes the relevant discharge, and using MA the data is transferred to the Barrage section, which operates accordingly. A brief discussion is as follows. The agents (node 1, node 2 . . . node N) correspond to the MOTES deployed for the sensing purposes. These agents are sensing the precipitations (PPt^n1, PPt^n2... PPt^nN) corresponding to each node. In the trivial system these are the rainfall gauging stations under the supervision of the Metrological Department which continuously monitor the rainfall and are fixed for a particular catchment as shown in Fig. 1. The data collected from the various gauging stations is reported to a main data station. This station estimates the Q_DISCHARGE and secondly EST_TIME for the discharge, i.e., the time to reach the HR which is generally constant for a particular barrage and a main data station. The estimated Q_DISCHARGE and EST_TIME are then reported to main data centre to the Barrage section using a MA. The data received is now acted upon by an intelligent calibrating agent (ICA) which decides Q1_DISCHARGE, Q2_DISCHARGE and QM_DISCHARGE depending upon the total capacities of the canals or in the same ratio. ICA also divides the received data as per the need of the application. Depending on the respective discharges Q1_DISCHARGE, Q2_DISCHARGE, and QM_DISCHARGE ICA computes the respective head movements, i.e., Q1_Hopening, Q2_Hopening, QM_HOPENING, respectively. Now when the discharges and the corresponding gate openings are calculated for the respective canals, the gates of the HR are set on the values decided earlier, i.e., Q1_Hopening, Q2_Hopening and QM_HOPENING. The data is collected at a clock of 15 minutes and depending on the pond level, Highest Flood Level and the Crest Level will adjust the Head Opening. The inputs are queued in a system queue and the Head regulator takes input from that queue. If the central data station senses Q_DISCHARGE above the maximum limit of the canals and the main stream this sends an emergency flag signal to the Barrage so as the gates are immediately set to the maximum value in order to allow a maximum room for incoming excess flow.

5 Global RIFMAS: GRIFMAS

In Fig. 1, there is no escape if Q_DISCHARGE exceeds the maximum value, i.e., Q1_DISCHARGE+Q2_DISCHARGE+QM_DISCHARGE. In this situation flood cannot be stopped. This is the motivation factor for GRIFMAS which is a futuristic implementation model of the proposed scheme. The implementation model of GRIFMAS is shown in Fig. 2 (a). The implementation model of GRIFMAS includes the following parts. **River Control Station (*RCS A-N*):** This is the central control for a particular which controls all the RIFMAS stations and houses the current data of water flowing through various catchments into the river flow. Data from each of the RIFMAS stations is collected using MA *A* as shown in Fig. 2(b). **Global Monitoring Station (GMS):** All the RCS stations are centrally controlled by this unit. GMS also

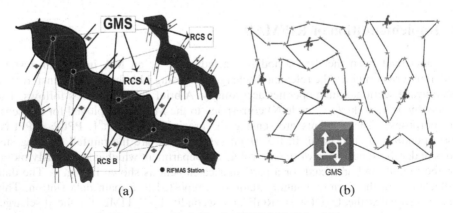

(a)   (b)

Fig. 2. Data Gathering in GRIFMAS Using MAs

receives any alarming signals from the RCS stations and in acknowledgement broadcasts an alarming signal to all the RCS sections. It also computes the best and the shortest path for the overflowing discharge. This information is again broadcasted to the respective RCS stations.

6 Implementation of GRIFMAS

All the RIFMAS stations are deployed at the various catchment regions. These RIFMAS stations are then in turn connected to the RCS stations which are actually deployed for each of the river. The RCS stations are updated through the information regularly about proper functioning of each RIFMAS station. As soon as any alarming value of discharge is estimated by any of the RIFMAS stations it reports this to its respective RCS center. On arrival of alarm RCS sends an emergency signal to the GMS. The GMS then broadcasts a packet to all RCS centers demanding the current status of each of the RCS centers and the RCS centers acknowledge this signal. With this collected data the GMS computes shortest path through all the catchment in the downstream to the catchment which issued alarming signal. This shortest path has the following features. (a) It includes the canals and streams which are in downstream only. (b) The path may include even those canals which are running to maximum capacity, i.e., we keep the amount of water added and taken out to be equal. (c) The path is found using a weighted graph so the cost factor is considered beforehand only. As soon as the graph is computed the emergency gates at each of the RIFMAS stations are set open. The system operates till stable values of precipitation are sensed by sensors at the RIFMAS stations.

7 Conclusion and Future Work

In this article we have presented a new design and implementation of multi-node wireless sensing agents, i.e., the RIFMAS to manage and control the flow of a river stream. The RIFMAS can also be deployed for the water distribution purposes. Extended model of RIFMAS is GRIFMAS. The safety and proper functioning of the sensor node in moist conditions are a primary cause of concern for the proper functioning of the proposed architecture. Battery backup of the sensing agent is another issue of concern. It is required to replace the sensors/battery at regular intervals of time. In future we are also aiming to devise a new prototype called VRIFMAS, i.e., Vigilant RIFMAS to keep a check on proper working of RIFMAS stations by the applying reverse engineering to the RIFMAS.

References

1. Steere, D.C., Baptista, A., McNamee, D., Pu, C., Walpole, J.: Research challenges in environmental observation and forecasting systems. In: Proceedings of the 6th Annual international Conference on Mobile Computing and Networking (MobiCom 2000), Boston, Massachusetts, USA, August 06 - 11, pp. 292–299 (2000)

2. Schreider, S.Y., Jakeman, A.J., Gallant, J., Merritt, W.S.: Prediction of monthly discharge in ungauged catchments under agricultural land use in the Upper Ping Basin, Northern Thailand, Integrated Catchment Assessment and Management (iCAM) Centre. Mathematics and Computers in Simulation 59(1-3), 19–33 (2002)
3. Blyth, E., Bell, V.: Links between river flow statistics and catchment characteristics: Implications for land surface schemes. In: Teuling, A.J., Leijnse, H., Troch, P.A., Sheffield, J., Wood, E.F. (eds.) Proceedings of the 2nd international CAHMDA workshop on: The Terrestria Water Cycle: Modelling and Data Assimilation Across Catchment Scales, Princeton, NJ, October 25-27, pp. 77–80 (2004)
4. Kotsilieris, T., Karetsos, G.T.: A mobile agent enabled wireless sensor network for river monitoring. In: Proceedings of The fourth international conference on Wireless and Mobile communications, Athens, July 27 -August 1, pp. 346–351 (2008)
5. Cheng, Z., Perillo, M.A., Heinzelman, W.B.: General Network Lifetime and Cost Models for Evaluating Sensor Network Deployment Strategies. IEEE Trans. Mob. Comput. (TMC) 7(4), 484–497 (2008)
6. Patel, R.B., Garg, K.: A New Paradigm for Mobile Agent Computing. WSEAS Transaction on Computers 1(3), 57–64 (2004)

Finite Element Approach to Radial Heat Flow in Human Dermal Tissues

Neha Jain

Department of mathematics, K.R. Mangalam School of Engineering & Technology,
New Delhi 110048
smile.jain@gmail.com

Abstract. The problem of heat migration through skin layers in human bodies are complex due to various physiological parameters. Such types of problems arise in the study of heat generation and migration through skin and sub- dermal tissue of human body. Structure and the function of the skin and blood circulation system in human body are described as *body core temperature is 37⁰C*. Thermo-genesis and Thermolysis are explained by *Stefan's law and cooling law*. The mathematical modeling of physiological heat transfer process in human body and analytical and discrete methods to solve the heat flow problem. The problem of temperature distribution in spherical tissue layers solve by the *finite element method*. Through the techniques *Variational finite element method, Galerkin method, Least square method*.

Keywords: Stefan's law, Cooling law, Finite element method, Heat flow problem.

1 Introduction

Here using the Finite element approaches to find the flow analysis in dermal tissues of skin in human body, that summarize in three sections. The first section deals with general description of physiological heat migration in living bodies. It also deals with the structure and function of the skin and blood flow in human body. The second section explains the mathematical modeling of physiological heat transfer process in human body and various methods to solve the heat flow problem. The third section of this work includes the finite solution method for the problem of temperature distribution in spherical tissue layers.

Various control process are taking place in a human or animal body such as fluid control, temperature control and water control etc. the study of these control process have proved to be of great use for clinical situation. One of the notable examples is of temperature control system, which is popularly known as temperature regulation system. A human body maintains its body core temperature at a constant temperature (37⁰C) by maintaining a balance between heat generation in the body and heat loss from the body. Heat generation in the living organism is either lost to the environment or stored in the body to maintain the body core temperature. Any abnormality in the physical and physiological conditions can disturb this thermal balance of the body with the environment. Thus study of temperature regulation system of human body

V.V Das et al. (Eds.): BAIP 2010, CCIS 70, pp. 369–375, 2010.

under normal and abnormal conditions is useful for various clinical situations as the quantity and type of abnormality can be corrected with its effect on the system.

Living organism consume food for their growth and to work. The food is converted into heat by various chemical process associated with breathing, digestion and physical efforts. The main factor of heat production is metabolism. Metabolism is the total collection of comical reactions (Anabolic and catabolic reaction) that occurs in the human body. Mechanism of heat loss (Thermolysis) heat is lost from the body by three channels; skin, lungs and excretion. The heat loss from the skin (surface of the body) occurs by:

(i)   Radiation (heat loss 60% by Stefan's law

$$H_r \propto (T_s^4 - T_a^4))$$

(ii)   Conduction (heat loss 3% from the surface of the body to the objects)

(iii) Convection (heat loss 12% by Cooling law

$$H_c = (T_s - T_a) ; (T_s > T_a))$$

(iv)   Evaporation (heat loss 25% by

$$He = LE)$$

Where H_r = heat loss due to radiation, T_s = temperature of body surface, T_a = temperature of body surrounding, H_e = heat loss by evaporation, Hc = heat loss by conduction, L = latent heat of water, E = rate of evaporation.

Here an equilibrium exist between thermo-genesis and Thermolysis by the equation

$$M \pm C \pm R - E = \pm S$$

where M: Metabolic heat production (positive), E: Heat loss by evaporation, C: Heat loss/gain by conduction and convection (positive or negative), R: heat loss/gain by radiation (positive or negative), S: Heat loss/gain from the surface of the body (positive or negative).

2 Structure of Skin

Skin is composed of two main layers; inner connective tissue called *dermis* and outer layer of epithelial layer called *epidermis* deep to the dermis lie a layer of loose irregular connective tissue called *subcutaneous tissue* this tissue mainly responsible for the temperature control and heat regulation in the body. Epidermis is the superficial layer consists of stratified type of epithelium. It is further divided into four layers; Stratum corneum, stratum lucidum, stratum granulosum, stratum germinativum. Dermis is made up of connective tissue and lies below the epidermal layer. Basically it is made up of oleaginous and elastic fibers which provide it with tensile strength. The superficial part of dermis is compact and the deeper part of dermis is composed of rather loose connective tissue and it filtrated with fat.

Functions of the skin are classified into seven terms these are:

(i)   *Protective function*: skin forms a protective coating of the body and thus acts as mechanical barrier against entry of bacteria etc. which cannot enter through the intact skin. It also protects the body tissues from thermal, chemical and mechanical injuries.

(ii) *Regulation of the body temperature*: skin is one of the major factors in regulating the body temperature through vasomotor mechanism. There is vasodilatation and vasoconstriction of skin blood vessels in hot and cold weather respectively. The importance of skin in temperature regulation can be appreciated from the fact that about 88% of heat loss in the body through the skin (by conduction, convection, radiation and evaporation), 6% heat lost by vapor evaporation through respiratory system, 4% lost in warming inspired air ingested food and 2% of heat is lost through feces and urine excretion.

(iii) *General sensation*: the skin serves as the medium for receiving the general sensation. Tough, pain, temperature etc. are sub served by the respective nerve endings present in the skin.

(iv) *Excretion*: through sweat and insensible perspiration salts and metabolites are excreted to some extent.

(v) *Water balance*: formation and evaporation of sweat is an important factor in the regulation of water balance of the body.

(vi) *Acid-base equilibrium:* sweating being acid reaction, a good amount of acid is excreted through it. In acidosis it become more acid and in this way helps to maintain a constant reaction in the body fluids.

(vii) *Storage function*: the dermis as well as subcutaneous tissue can store fats, water, salts, glucose and such other subcutaneous.

The blood circulation through the skin has to serve two major functions firstly, it supplies nutrition to the skin tissues and secondly it transfers heat from the body core to the skin surface i.e. regulation of the body temperature. The rate of blood flow in SST region is characterized by more frequent changes than perhaps any other region of the body. It is controlled by venous system which regulates the supply of blood, in accordance with the change in atmospheric temperature and metabolic activities in the tissue. When the skin is heated the blood vessels dilate until maximum vasodilatation has resulted. When the skin is exposed to cold, the blood vessels constrict more and more and at a temperature of about 13^0C they reach start dilating to head the living cells active in the peripheral region. At the minimum blood flows the insulation property of SST maximum.

3 Mathematical Background

The mathematical formulation of heat diffusion in solids is governed by the practical differential equation. If Q denotes the quantity of heat in a tissue element of volume V at time t. then $\partial Q / \partial t$ is assumed as the sum of rates of change due to perfusion p, diffusion d and metabolic heat generation m.

$$\partial Q / \partial t = (\partial Q / \partial t)p + (\partial Q / \partial t)d + (\partial Q / \partial t)m \dots\dots\dots \dots\dots\dots \dots\dots\dots \dots\dots\dots \dots(i)$$

Changing Q to concentration C of heat energy per unit volume by dividing equation (i) with ΔV, we have

$$\partial C / \partial t = (\partial C / \partial t)p + (\partial C / \partial t)d + (\partial C / \partial t)m \dots\dots\dots\dots\dots\dots\dots\dots\dots\dots\dots\dots\dots\dots\dots(ii)$$

The first term correspond to the heat supplied or heat removed through perfusion. It can be evaluate using Fick's perfusion principle according to which rate of change of concentration of heat Q in a tissue volume equals differences of heat via venous blood. Mathematically,

$$(\partial C / \partial t)p = \Delta FaCa - \Delta FvCv$$

Where Fa is sum of rate of blood flow in all arterioles intersecting ΔV and Ca is arteriole heat energy per unit volume of blood and similar operational definitions apply to ΔFv and Cv.

Defining further tissue perfusion rate per unit volume as Φa and Φv respectively, we obtain

$$\Phi a = \Delta Fa / \Delta V, \quad \Phi v = \Delta Fv / \Delta V$$
$$\therefore \ (\partial C / \partial t)p = \Phi aCa - \Phi vCv$$

Moreover, since thermal energy per unit volume at any instant $= \rho CT$

Where ρ = Density of the mass

C = Specific heat of blood

T = Absolute temperature

We get,

$$(\partial C / \partial t)p = \rho \, bCb \, (\Phi aTa - \Phi vTv) \dots\dots\dots\dots\dots\dots \text{(iii)}$$

The second term of right hand side in equation (ii) corresponds to conduction. According to Fourier's law of heat from high temperature to law temperature and the quantity of heat passing through a plan is proportional to the area and the temperature gradient.

Let A denotes the area of surface in the body perpendicular to the X- direction and let grad T be the temperature gradient at any point of S. then the magnitude of grad T is $\partial T / \partial X$. The rate Q at which the heat flows across S is proportion to A and to $\partial T / \partial X$ i.e.

$$Q \propto A \partial T / \partial X$$
$$Q = - KA(\partial T / \partial X)x = -f(x)$$

Where K is the constant of proportionality is called the thermal conductivity of the medium and the minus sign indicates that heat flows in the direction of decreasing temperature.

Also at a distance $(x + \delta x)$

$$Q = - KA(\partial T / \partial X)(x + \delta x) = -f(x + \delta x)$$

Hence the rate of change of heat,

$$\partial Q / \partial t = -f(x) + f(x + \delta x)$$

$$\partial (MCT) / \partial t = -f(x) + f(x + \delta x)$$

$$MC\partial T / \partial t = -f(x) + f(x + \delta x)$$

Since $\rho = M/V$ then $M = \rho V$

$$\rho V \delta x C \partial T / \partial t = -f(x) + f(x + \delta x) \quad\text{................(iv)}$$

Expanding by Taylor's Series, we get from equation (iv)

$$\rho C \partial T / \partial t = \delta / \delta x (K \partial T / \partial x)$$
$$\rho C \partial T / \partial t = div(KgradT)$$

Hence

$$(\partial C / \partial t)d = div(KgradT) \quad\text{................   ....(v)}$$

The third term of the equation (ii) corresponds to the effect of metabolism is

$$(\partial C / \partial t)m = S \quad\text{................   ....(vi)}$$

Where equation (vi) is the variable metabolic heat generation per unit volume of tissue. Also the concentration of the thermal energy per unit volume C is given by $C = \rho cT$

Substituting the values from (iii), (v), (vi) in equation (ii) we get,

$$(\partial C / \partial t)d = div(KgradT) + mbCb(Tb - T) + S... \quad\text{............(viii)}$$

Where $\Phi a = \Phi v = \Phi$ and $\Phi \rho b = mb$ and mb = Blood mass perfusion rate per unit volume. This equation designated as Heat Transfer Equation.

4 Numerical Solution of the Problem

We have developed a three layered finite element to find the temperature profiles in skin and sub dermal tissues and we divide the region into three natural layers namely epidermis, dermis and sub dermal tissues. We use the partial differential equation (viii) for one dimensional which is given by

$$pc(\partial \theta / \partial t) = div(Kgrad\theta) + mbCb(\theta b - \theta) + S \quad\text{...................(ix)}$$

Then the cylindrical equation from the equation (ix) in steady state case is the

$$1/r * d/dr(kd \theta /dr) + M(\theta b - \theta) + S = 0 \quad\text{................................(x)}$$

Using the Euler Lagrange equation (x) transformed into the following variation form

$$I = (1/2) \int_{a3}^{a0} [Kr(d\theta / dr)^2 + Mr(\theta b - \theta)^2 - 2Sr\theta \quad\text{......................(xi)}$$

Where θ = temperature at the time t at the point r

θb = Temperature of heat flowing inside the body
K = Thermal conductivity
M = Rate of blood mass flow
S = Rate of metabolic heat generation

We assume that θ_0, θ_1, θ_2 be the temperature at the epidermis, dermis and subcutaneous tissues layers respectively. Lets denote the thickness of epidermis, dermis and subcutaneous tissues by (a0 –a1), (a1 – a2), (a2 – a3) respectively according to our assumptions the boundary and interface condition, thickness are in epidermis (a1 < r < ao), in dermis (a2 < r < a1), subcutaneous (a3 < r < a2) after solving the integration of equation (xi) we get

$I_1 = X_0(\theta_0 - \theta_1)^2 + [h/2(\theta_0 - \theta_a)^2 + LE\theta_0]$,

$I_2 = X1(\theta_1 - \theta_2)^2 + X_2 + X_3\ \theta_1^2 + X_4\theta_2^2 + X_5\theta_1\theta_2 + X_6\theta_1 + X_7\theta_2$
$\quad + X_8(\theta_1 - \theta_2)^2 + X_9(\theta_1 - \theta_2) + X_{10}\theta_1^2 + X_{11}\theta_1\theta_2 + X_{12}\theta_1\theta_2 + X_{13}\theta_2^2$
$\quad + X_{14}\theta_1 + X_{15}\theta_2 + X_{16}(\theta_1 - \theta_2)$

$I_3 = G1(\theta_2 - \theta_3)^2 + G_2 + G_3\theta_2^2 + G_4\theta_3^2 + G_5\theta_3\theta_2 + G_6\theta_2 + G_7\theta_3 + G_8(\theta_2 - \theta_3)^2$
$\quad + G_9(\theta_2 - \theta_3) + G_{10}\theta_2^2 + G_{11}\theta_3\theta_2 + G_{12}\theta_3\theta_2 + G_{13}\theta_3^2 + G_{14}\theta_2 + G_{15}\theta_2$
$\quad + G_{16}(\theta_2 - \theta_3)$

Where I_1, I_2, I_3 are solution at epidermis, dermis and subcutaneous tissue layers and X_0, X_1, X_2, X_3.....................X_{16}, G_1, G2, G $_3$, G $_4$, ...G $_{16}$ are physical and physiological constants.

Hence $I = I_1 + I_2 + I_3$, therefore

$$\partial I/\partial\theta i = (\partial I1/\partial\theta i) + (\partial I2/\partial\theta i) + (\partial I3/\partial\theta i) \text{ where } i = 0, 1, 2$$

After solving, we get the values of θ_0, θ_1, θ_2 temperatures of epidermis, dermis and subcutaneous tissues layers respectively are

$$\theta_2 = [\alpha_3\beta_1\gamma_1 - \alpha_1\beta_4\gamma_1 + \alpha_1\gamma_3 + \beta_1\gamma_3] / (\alpha_1\beta_3\gamma_1 - \alpha_1\beta_2\gamma_1 + \alpha_2\beta_1\gamma_2)$$
$$\theta_1 = (\alpha_1\beta_3\gamma_3\gamma_1 + \alpha_1\beta_2\gamma_3\gamma_1 + \alpha_2\beta_1\gamma_3\gamma_2 - \alpha_3\beta_1\gamma_2\gamma_1 + \alpha_1\beta_4\gamma_2\gamma_1 - \alpha_1\gamma_3\gamma_2 - \beta_1\gamma_3\gamma_2) / (\alpha_1\beta_3\gamma_1^2 - \alpha_1\beta_2\gamma_1^2 + \alpha_2\beta_1\gamma_2\gamma_1)$$
$$\theta_0 = [-(\alpha_3 + \beta_4) - \beta_3\theta_2 - (\alpha_2 + \beta_2)\theta_1] / (\alpha_1 + \beta_1)$$

5   Numerical Result and Discussion

The numerical result have been obtained using the following values of physical and physiological constants

$K_1 = 0.030$ cal/cm- min deg c
$K_2 = 0.045$ cal/cm- min deg c
$K_3 = 0.060$ cal/cm- min deg c
$L = 579$ cal / gm
$h = 0.009$ cal / cm^2 –min deg c
$\theta_b = 37^0$c $= \theta_3$
$a_0 = 6.5$, a1 = 6, a2 = 5, a3 = 4

Then the result table as follows:

Atmospheric temperature θ^0c	S cal/cm-min deg c	M cal/cm-min deg c	E Gm / cm^2 – min deg c	θ_2	θ_1	θ_0
15	0.0357	0.003	0	36.23	35.66	34.73
23	0.018	0.018	0	34.05	34.0	33.73
33	0.0341	0.133	0.0334	34.0	35.05	36.0

6 Conclusion

We consider steady state temperature distribution in skin and sub dermal tissue in a cylindrical tissue of a human body. The whole SST region is composed of three natural layers, epidermis, dermis and subcutaneous tissues. Subcutaneous tissues play an important role in the temperature regulation in the human body being the surface of interaction between human body and atmosphere (37^0c). Finite element approach help to prepare modeling for heat flow problem. Fick's perfusion principle, Fourier's law and metabolic heat generation are important factors to solve the heat flow problem by Euler Lagrange method then only we can generate important information regarding thermoregulation and radial heat flow in human dermal tissues.

Acknowledgement

I am grateful to my respected guide Dr. R. K. Shrivastave, HOD SMMRS Govt. Science College Gwalior to guide me on this work and would like to pay thanks to my colleagues and my husband to support me. At the last but not least, I am thankful to The Association of Computer, Electronics and Electrical Engineers (ACEEE) to promote me.

References

[1] Henriques, F.C., Moritz, A.R.: Studies of Thermal injury. The American Journal of Pathology 23, 531–549 (1947)
[2] Pardasani, K.R., Saxena, V.P.: Exact Solution to Temperature Distribution Problem in Annular Skin Llayers. Bull. Calcutta Math. Soc. 81, 1–8 (1989)
[3] Steady – State radial Heat Flow in Skin and Underlying Tissues Layers of Spherical Regions of Human or Animal Body
[4] Verma, T.: A Mathematics Study of Temperature Profiles in Human Dermal Parts with Bums and Other Abnormalities (1995)
[5] Structure of Human Skin, http://www.google.com

An Efficient Auction Based Ticket Booking Scheme for Indian Cinemas

Sajal Mukhopadhyay[1], Roshan Kumar Singh[1], D. Ghosh[1], Jaya Bhattacharjee[2],
and Nivedita Mukherjee[1]

[1] NIT, Durgapur, Durgapur-9, West Bengal, India
[2] Mallabhum Institute of Technology, Bishnupur-2, West Bengal, India
{sajmure,singh.roshan08,jayabesu,nivedita211}@gmail.com,
profdg@yahoo.com

Abstract. Indian film industry is one of the biggest in the world. A considerable number of movies out of the all movies released in a year are considered as hit movies. In a cinema hall k tickets are available and for a hit movie more than k people give demand for a ticket to watch the movie. To earn more profit in that environment, in this paper an auction based truthful mechanism is proposed for selling all the tickets of the cinema hall and it is shown that our auction based scheme is significantly better than the existing scheme in terms of the total income earned per annum. Our scheme could be applied on any film industry.

Keywords: VCG Mechanisms, Multiunit Auction.

1 Introduction

In a cinema hall k tickets are available and n number of people (where $k < n$) come on each day to watch the hit movie. To earn more profit in that environment, in this paper an auction based VCG Mechanisms [1],[4],[5] for multiunit auction is proposed for selling all the tickets of the cinema hall and it is shown that our auction based scheme is significantly better than the existing scheme in terms of the total income earned per annum. Auction theory has been in use for quite a long time since its first introduction by Vickery in 1961 [2]. For selling a single item through auction, the VCG mechanisms are adopted by eBay, one of the largest on-line shopping website [1], [14]. When government is under taking a public project, where public interest is sought for, VCG mechanism is utilized for maximizing the social welfare [1], [2]. Procuring a path in a communication network where each link is assumed as a player with some positive cost if that link is used for carrying some message, VCG mechanism could be used in Maximizing social welfare [1],[14]. If in a carton k ice creams are there and those are demanded by n number of buyers (where $k < n$), could be modeled by VCG based multi-unit auction and its on-line version where n buyers arrive and departs dynamically is also addressed in [1]. An interesting application of VCG based Multiunit auction for earning more profit for Indian Railways is addressed in [15]. Here in our paper, VCG based multi-unit auction mechanism is applied in selling k tickets when those k tickets are demanded by n buyers (where $k < n$) and this is exactly the situation when hit movies are released in cinema halls. Our rest

V. V Das et al. (Eds.): BAIP 2010, CCIS 70, pp. 376–381, 2010.
© Springer-Verlag Berlin Heidelberg 2010

of the paper is organized as follows. In section 2 interesting result of VCG mechanism and multi-unit auction are discussed, which is the main motivation of adopting our scheme. In section 3 our scheme is proposed. In section 4 we have shown the result of our experimentation and simulation of the scheme. In section 5 some social issues that may arise on implementation of this scheme have been highlighted. Section 6 deals with conclusion and further research.

2 VCG Mechanisms and Multi-unit Auction

2.1 VCG Mechanisms

Arguably the most important positive result in mechanism design is what is usually called Vickery-Clarke-Groves (VCG) mechanism [4], [5]. It is a sealed bid auction. The important property of the VCG mechanism is that it is truthful [4], [5]. In algorithmic game theoretic literature bidders are also termed as agents in a more generalized term. So in our subsequent discussion bidders and agents will be used interchangeably. Our paper will be based on the concepts of multiunit VCG mechanisms which are addressed later in detail. For further reference of VCG mechanisms and multiunit auction see [1], [4], [5], [15].

2.2 Multi-unit Auction

"Allocation Problem", which addresses the issue of allocating "resources" among the different possible users of these resources. This problem has been in the center stage in computer science and economics. An auction of a single item may be viewed as a simple abstraction of this question: we have a single indivisible resource, and two (or more) player desire using it- who should get it? This simple and general abstraction plays a central role in mechanism design theory. Instead of single item if we consider multiple items (say m items) to be allocated to several users (say n users) the problem of allocation of the items become combinatorial in nature. The problem is formalized as: There is a set of m indivisible items that are concurrently auctioned among n bidders. The problem of combinatorial auction has been studied in [8], [9], [10]. Due to The hardness of the problem some approximation schemes have been proposed [13].

Multiunit auction is a special case of combinatorial auction where k identical units of some good are sold in an auction (where k< n). Here n are the number of bidders. In a generalized case bidders may be interested in more than a single-unit and have a different value for each number of units obtained. The next level of sophistication comes when the items in the auction are heterogeneous, and valuations can give a different value to each combination of items which is already termed as combinatorial auction. In the simple case each bidder is interested in only a single unit. In this case $|S|$ the number of bidders gets a single item that (such that S is equal to k) is exactly equal to k. Let us denote the set of n bidders by I .In this case the number of possible outcomes or social choices $A = \{S - win| S \subset I, |S| = k\}$, and each bidder's valuation v_i gives some fixed value v^* if I gets an item, i.e. $v_i(S) = v^*$ if $i \in S$ and $v_i(S) = 0$. Maximizing social welfare means allocating the items to the k highest bidders, and in the VCG mechanism with the Clarke's pivot rule, each of them should pay the $k + 1^{st}$ highest offered price. Losers pay 0.

3 Our Scheme

Indian film industry produces films in several regional languages as well as national language (Hindi). A considerable number of movies out of the all movies released in a year are considered as hit movies. These hit movies are usually shown in the Cinema Halls for more than two weeks. Here the hit movies not only for the films based on Hindi language but also the films based on regional languages are considered. There is a huge rush for watching the hit movies released throughout the year and throughout India where ever they are released. The existing scheme for purchasing the ticket for a movie is to go to the cinema hall and purchase the ticket from a counter standing in the queue or can be booked through Internet. There is a fixed amount charged for each of the ticket sold. Usually several categories of tickets are available based on the comfort provided in the cinema halls. Usually there are j numbers of categories. Each category is denoted by c_j, where i = 1, 2,..., j and j is a constant could have a maximum value of 4. In our auction based scheme bids are taken from the movie-goer for different categories separately.

In the existing scheme tickets are sold on a first-come-first-serve basis when movie-goers line-up in the ticket counters or book through Internet. But from our experience it is seen that there is a huge demand for the tickets for a hit movie. And people in urgent need of a ticket are ready to pay extra amount to get it. In that situation, to earn a more profit, it is obvious to use the auction based VCG mechanism which not only gives a benefit for each ticket but it will also help to reveal the true willingness of anybody trying to purchase a ticket in terms of the money he or she actually wants to spend. This case is exactly matching the scheme of multiunit auction stated in section 2. In our scheme for booking a seat in a cinema hall demand for a ticket is given by the agents either standing in a queue in front of the ticket counter or through Internet. However one can give demand for several tickets in different categories. There are k_i seat available for each category c_i and there are n_i movie-goer try to get the k_i tickets (where $k_i < n_i$). In the present scheme the tickets are sold in the first-come-first-serve manner and each buyer of the ticket is charged a fixed amount of money. However for different categories different fixed price is charged. In the present ticket booking scheme a fixed price is charged for each ticket being sold. In our auction based scheme this fixed price is utilized as the base price that is no movie-goer can bid a lower value than this. The introduction of the base price is to ensure the fact that owner of the cinema hall will not lose any money in terms of their total income from the current existing scheme.

Here in our scheme every movie-goer wants to watch the hit movie will bid for a ticket and bids are accepted as and when they come. The bids to be given in each category c_i will have to be specified by each bidder. The bids are allowed up to half an hour before the schedule movie-show time. Immediately after that, the bids are processed and result may be displayed via Internet and in the respective booking center. In our algorithm, first all the bidders according to their bid price are sorted for the respective category c_i. Then k_i highest bidders are allocated the tickets with a payment of k_i+1st bidder's bid price which follows the multi-unit VCG Mechanisms, where k_i is the total number of seats available in that category. For the hit movies all the tickets are sold out, so the number of bidders will be more than k_i. Here we wait for the allocation until the closing time of the auction. This idea we now represent in the algorithm stated below:

1. Sort the bids according to the bid price for the respective category c_i.
2. Allocate the tickets to the k_i highest bidders, where k_i is the total number of seats available in that category.
3. For payment function: Each bidder, getting a ticket, will pay the value of the k_i+1st bidder's bid price.

The overall time complexity of our algorithm could be given as follows: Sorting the list takes $\Theta(nlgn)$. Allocation of tickets take $\Theta(k)$, Where $(k < n)$.Calculation of the bidder's payment takes $\Theta(k)$. So over all time complexity is $\Theta(nlgn)$ as the number of categories are constant.

4 Experiment

Our scheme is tested by simulating the auction scenario through a program written in C language by considering the number of tickets purchased by the movie-goer and the total earnings of the owner of the cinema hall based on fixed and auction based price. In the x-axis we have taken the different values of k and in the y-axis we have shown the total earning for the existing scheme as well as for the auction based scheme in terms of Indian currency (Rupees) which is abbreviated as Rs. The total income has been calculated combining all the income from the different categories with the formula $\sum_{i=1}^{j} K_i$, where K_i is the income earned from the category c_i .The income shown here is the per day income. The graph obtained through this simulation is shown in fig.1 which evidently shows that if auction based scheme is introduced, there will be a large gain altogether. If in each of the cinema hall there is on and average, say, P_i amount of total earning increased if we introduce auction-based scheme, then the total earning increased will be equal to $\sum_{i=1}^{m} P_i$, where m is the number of hit movies shown in a cinema hall. If each Pi on an average is, say, Rs. 50000 then altogether

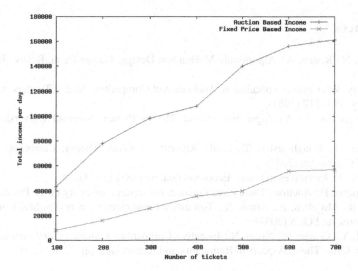

Fig. 1. Simulation result

we could have Rs. 500000 of total earnings increased per annum, when m is 10. If there are 5000 cinema halls in India which are located in big towns , then per annum the profit is 500000*5000 = Rs.2500000000 that is 2.5 billion which is a big amount for Indian cinema industries. If this scheme is adopted, after the release of a movie more money could be demanded from the cinema halls if they are interested for that movie for their respective cinema hall.

5 Social Issues

In our scheme there is a possibility that the price of tickets may inflate above the budget of the middle-class people. So to address this issue a small percentage of the tickets could be excluded from the auction-based scheme and they could be sold at a nominal fixed price on a first-come-first-serve basis to the middle to lower-middle-class people.

6 Conclusion

Our auction based ticket booking scheme for the Indian cinema hall could be applied on any film industry and a huge profit could be earned. In our scheme the auction is closed half an hour before the schedule movie-show time. But a person coming to the cinema hall for watching the movie may have to travel a long distance before reaching there. But if the auction is closed before half an hour of the schedule movie-show time, and if the information of the allocation of the tickets are sent via Mobile service or is displayed via Internet half an hour may not be sufficient. Our future works will be concentrated on that to make it more convenient for the movie-goer so that they could have a choice to wait for a certain time and after that they could stop bidding.

References

1. Nisan, N., Ronen, A.: Algorithmic Mechanism Design. Games Econ. Behav. 35, 166–196 (2001)
2. Vickery, W.: Counter Speculation, Auctions and Competitive Sealed Tenders. J. Economic Theory, 187–217 (1961)
3. Roughgarden, T.: An Algorithmic Game Theory Primer. Stanford University, Stanford (2008)
4. Nishan, N., Roughgarden, T., et al.: Algorithmic Game Theory. Cambridge University Press, Cambridge (2007)
5. Groves, T.: Incentives in teams. Econometrica, 617–631 (1973)
6. Klemperer, P.: Auctions Theory and Practice. Princeton University Press, Princeton (2004)
7. Lavi, R., Mu'alem, A., Nisan, N.: Towards a Characterization of Truthful Combinatorial Auctions. In: FOCS (2003)
8. Bartal, Y., Gonen, R., Nisan, N.: Incentive Compatible Multiunit Combinatorial Auction. In: 9th Conf. Theor. Aspects of Rationality and Knowledge, pp. 72–87 (2003)

9. Cramton, P., Shoham, Y., Steinberg, R. (eds.): Combinatorial Auctions. MIT Press, Cambridge (2006)
10. Ausubel, L.M.: An Efficient Dynamic Auction for Heterogeneous Commodities. Amer. Econ. Rev. 96(3), 602–629 (2006)
11. http://en.wikipedia.org/wiki/Bollywood
12. http://www.time.com/time/magazine/article/0,9171,985129,00.html
13. Briest, P., Krysta, P., Vocking, B.: Approximation Techniques for Utilitarian Mechanism Design. In: The 37th ACM Symp. Theor. Comp., pp. 39–48 (2005)
14. Dütting, P., Geiger, A.: Algorithmic Mechanism Design. Seminar Report (May 9, 2007)
15. Mukhopadhyay, S., Mukherjee, N., Bhattacharjee, J., Ghosh, D., et al.: An Efficient Auction Based TATKAL Scheme for Indian Railways. In: 2010 International Conference on Innovative Computing and Communication and 2010 Asia- Pacific Conference on Information Technology and Ocean Engineering (CICC-ITOE 2010) (January 2010) (to be published)

Supervised Learning Approach for Predicting the Quality of Cotton Using WEKA

M. Selvanayaki, M.S. Vijaya, K.S. Jamuna, and S. Karpagavalli

PSGR Krishnammal College for Women
Coimbatore – 641 004, India
{msvijaya,ksjamuna,karpagam}@grgsact.com

Abstract. Cotton is the world's most important natural fibre used in Textile manufacturing. Cotton fiber is processed into yarn and fabric. Yarn strength depends extremely on the quality of cotton. The physical characteristics such as fiber length, length distribution, trash value, color grade, strength, shape, tenacity, density, moisture absorption, dimensional stability, resistance, thermal reaction, count, etc., contributes to the quality of cotton. Hence determining the quality of cotton accurately is an essential task to make better raw material choices in textile industry which in turn will support better buying and selling decisions. In this work, cotton quality prediction is modeled as classification task and implemented using supervised learning algorithms namely Multilayer Perceptron, Naive Bayes, J48 Decision tree, k-nearest neighbor in WEKA environment on the cotton quality assessment dataset. The classification models have been trained using the data collected from a spinning mill. The prediction accuracy of the classifiers is evaluated using 10-fold cross validation and the results are compared. It is observed that the model based on decision tree classifier produces high predictive accuracy compared to other models.

Keywords: Machine learning Techniques, Multilayer Perceptron, Naïve Bayes, J48, k-Nearest Neighbor.

1 Introduction

Cotton is the most commonly used textile fiber in the world. Its current market share is 56 percent for all fibers used for apparel and home furnishings. Cotton fiber is spun into yarn before being woven or knitted into fabric. The quality of the cotton fibre is determined by three factors, namely, the color of cotton, purity (the absence of foreign matter) and quality of the ginning process, and the length of fibers.

The color of cotton fibres is primarily determined by conditions of temperature and/or humidity, cotton lint exposure to sunlight, and cotton varieties. Fibre length is defined as the average length of the longer one-half of the fibres (upper half mean length) [1]. Length uniformity or uniformity ratio is determined as a ratio between the mean length and the upper half mean length of the fibers and is expressed as a percentage. Fiber strength is measured in grams per denier. Micronaire measurements reflect fiber fineness and maturity. A constant mass 2.34 grams of cotton fibers is compressed into a space of known volume and air permeability measurements of this

V.V Das et al. (Eds.): BAIP 2010, CCIS 70, pp. 382–384, 2010.

compressed sample are taken. These, when converted to appropriate number, denote Micronaire values [2]. A trash measurement describes the amount of non-lint materials in the fiber. Trash content is highly correlated to leaf grade of the sample. There are seven leaf grades ranging from #1 to #7 and a lower grade #8.

United States Department of Agriculture (USDA) classification specifically identifies the characteristics of fiber length, length uniformity, strength, Micronaire, color, preparation, leaf and extraneous matter. This work concentrates on the physical properties of cotton for prediction by employing machine learning techniques.

Machine learning provides methods techniques and tools, which help to learn automatically, and to make accurate predictions based on past observations. Machine learning is popularly being used in areas of business like data analysis, financial analysis, stock market forecast and so on. The supervised learning techniques namely k-nearest neighbor, Multilayer Perceptron, Naïve Bayes Classifier, Decision tree induction have been used to learn and build the classification models.

2 Experimental Setup

The data set with 12 different features was collected from a private spinning mill. The training was carried out with 14325 instances. The predominant features that decide the quality of cotton include span length (mm), uniformity ratio%, strength (g/tex), micronarie, lint, trash, invisible loss, maturity coefficient. As the quality of the cotton has to be predicted, Quality_Indicator is selected as the class label. The instances in the dataset pertaining to the three quality measures of cotton are labeled as Low (L), Medium (M) and High (H).   Using WEKA [3], a software environment for machine learning, independent models have been trained for predicting the cotton quality. The performance of the classifiers is evaluated and the results are analyzed. The 10-fold cross validation has been applied to test the performance of the four models on cotton data.

3 Results and Discussion

The statistical results of the experiments are summarized in Table 1. The performances of the four models are evaluated based on the three criteria, the prediction accuracy, learning time and error rate.

The prediction accuracy of the four models is shown in Fig 1. J48 algorithm shows the higher accuracy than the other models. The accuracy rate of the Naive bayes model is comparatively very low. The learning time of the four schemes under consideration are shown in Fig. 2. Multilayer perceptron consumes more time to build the model. The Naïve Bayes classifier and KNN learn more rapidly for the given dataset. The error rate for J48 is insignificant thereby indicating higher accuracy than the other models. The Multilayer perceptron model produces higher error rate than the other machine learning algorithms employed in this work.

Table 1. Predictive Performance of the Classifiers

Evaluation Criteria	J48	NB	MLP	NN
Kappa Statistics	0.9827	0.2841	0.8524	0.9827
Mean Absolute Error	0.0048	0.2487	0.0167	0.0042
Root Mean Squared Error	0.0491	0.4305	0.0094	0.0463
Relative Absolute Error	2.3237%	121.52%	8.1462%	2.0594%
Root Relative Squared Error	15.352%	134.59%	31.074%	14.464%
Time to build the model (sec)	0.3	0.17	226.58	0.8
Correctly classified instance	14239	8871	13726	14239
Incorrectly classified instance	76	5444	589	76
Prediction Accuracy	99.46%	61.97%	95.88%	99.46%

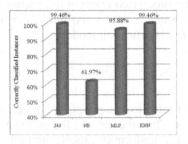

Fig. 1. Prediction Accuracy   Fig. 2. Learning Time

4 Conclusion

In this work, cotton quality prediction is modeled as classification task and four supervised machine learning schemes namely K-Nearest Neighbor, Multilayer Perceptron, Naïve Bayes Classifier, Decision tree induction have been applied on the cotton
data in order to learn and predict the quality of cotton. The independent trained models are generated and their performance has been evaluated based on their predictive
accuracy and ease of learning. The results indicate that the J48 classifier outperforms
other classifiers.

References

1. Lawrence, H.S.: Cotton's Importance in the Textile Industry. In: Symposium, Lima, Peru
   (1998)
2. Gordon Cook, J.: Handbook of Textile Fibers, Part I. Natural Fibers. Merrow Publishing
   Co. Ltd. (1968)
3. Witten, I.H., Frank, E.: Data Mining – Practical Machine Learning Tools and Techniques,
   2nd edn. Elsevier, Amsterdam (2005)

Music-Inspired Optimization Algorithm: Harmony-Tabu for Document Retrieval Using Relevance Feedback

K. Latha[1] and R. Manivelu[2]

[1] Computer Science Department, Anna University Tiruchirappalli,
Tiruchirappalli, India (South)
erklatha@gmail.com
[2] Information Technology Department, Thiagarajar College of Engineering,
Madurai-15, India (South)
manivelu@tce.edu

Abstract. In this paper a novel hybrid Harmony Clustering with Tabu Search (TS) has been proposed to achieve better document retrieval. Experimental results on TREC dataset reveal that the proposed algorithm can find better results. Finally Relevance Feedback mechanisms such as Term Feedback, Cluster Feedback and Term Cluster Feedback are used to further improve the performance of the retrieved results.

Keywords: Harmony Search, Tabu, meta-heuristic algorithm, Relevance Feedback, Term Feedback, Cluster Feedback, Term-Cluster Feedback.

1 Introduction

Initially Latent Semantic Indexing (LSI) can be used for representing documents which overcomes the problems of lexical matching. In this paper, a new algorithm called, Harmony K-means clustering which combines the power of the Harmony with the speed of a K-means. TS [2] have been customized for retrieval purpose and Relevance feedback [4] for improving retrieval performance.

2 The Basic Harmony Search (HS) Clustering Algorithm

In music the harmony [1] is improved time after time, likewise in HS the solution vector is improved iteration by iteration. K-means clustering procedure uses the randomly generated seeds as the initial cluster's centroid and refines its position in each iteration. Let us consider each cluster centroid be a decision variable; so each row of Harmony memory (HM), which contains K decision variables, represents one possible solution for clustering. A New Harmony vector is improvised by following three rules (1) Random selection, (2) HM consideration, and (3) Pitch adjustment.

3 Tabu Search for Retrieval

The principle of Tabu search [2] is to pursue local search whenever a local optimum is encountered. **Intensification** is used for enlargement of the neighborhood.

V.V Das et al. (Eds.): BAIP 2010, CCIS 70, pp. 385–387, 2010.

Diversification is to restrict search to a limited portion of the solution space. An **aspiration criterion** is used to allow certain move which is forbidden by Tabu.

4 Harmony Tabu Algorithm

Initialize each cluster C_i to contain k different document vectors as the initial cluster centroids. For each cluster a).assign each document vector in the document set to the closest centroid vector. Recalculate the cluster centroid $cent_i$. b).compute the fitness of the cluster. The set of clusters C_i are given as input and the best clusters are retrieved by the Harmony approach and are given to Tabu. When length reaches certain size of Tabu, it is freed from it and the process continues until termination criteria are met.

5 Relevance Feedback and Query Expansion

The Relevance feedback [4] is used to improve effectiveness of the returned results. Term feedback (TFB) cause undesired effects when irrelevant terms occur along with relevant ones. Cluster Feed Back (CFB) assigns weights to unchecked terms when they are judged as relevant, but it does not distinguish which terms in a cluster are presented. Therefore, we try to combine the two methods and call it as TCFB.

6 Empirical Results

The OHSUMED data set (16,140 query-document pairs) has been used for experiments. In Table 1 the results of proposed approach are significantly high. After user feedback, the feedback algorithms are applied to estimate updated query models, which are then iterated. In Table 2, TCFB3C (3 clusters) achieve a highest results improvement in MAP (Mean Average Precision). Both CFB3C and CFB5C perform better than TFB. Table 3 shows the performance varying with the presentation terms. Table 4 shows that when the Clarification forms contain more clusters, fewer are checked terms, relevant terms and relevant checked terms. There seems to be a trade-off between increasing topic diversity by clustering and losing extra relevant terms.

Table 1. Comparison of the performance measures

Methods	Metric	@10	@20	@30
	Precision	0.6	0.5	0.46
Hybrid	Recall	0.23	0.38	0.53
	MAP	0.59	0.5830	0.563
	Precision	0.3	0.25	0.23
Harmonic	Recall	0.115	0.1923	0.269
	MAP	0.3871	0.3656	0.3368
	Precision	0.4	0.3	0.26
Tabu	Recall	0.15	0.23	0.34
	MAP	0.5332	0.4816	0.4321

Table 2. Retrieval performance for term and cluster feedback methods and CF types

	TFB 1C	TFB 3C	TFB 5C	CFB 1C	CFB 3C	CFB 5C	TCFB 1C	TCFB 3C	TCFB 5C
MAP	0.793	0.750	0.736	0.827	0.806	0.776	0.853	0.834	0.809
P@30	0.817	0.769	0.751	0.843	0.817	0.794	0.874	0.848	0.825

Table 3. MAP variation with the number of presented terms (TFB and CFB)

#Terms	TFB 1C	TFB 3C	TFB 5C	CFB 1C	CFB 3C	CFB 5C	TCFB 1C	TCFB 3C	TCFB 5C
5	0.744	0.720	0.685	0.795	0.785	0.745	0.831	0.806	0.759
10	0.751	0.726	0.692	0.799	0.788	0.749	0.834	0.817	0.762
15	0.766	0.733	0.699	0.807	0.792	0.754	0.838	0.825	0.789
20	0.780	0.743	0.725	0.817	0.798	0.760	0.846	0.829	0.791
25	0.788	0.745	0.729	0.822	0.801	0.768	0.851	0.831	0.803
30	0.793	0.750	0.736	0.827	0.806	0.776	0.853	0.834	0.809

Table 4. Term Selection statistics

CF TYPE	1x 30	3x10	5x6
#Checked Terms	11	9	8
#rel terms	13	12	12
#checked rel terms	7	6	5
Precision	0.63	0.66	0.62
Recall	0.53	0.5	0.41

7 Conclusion

Our experimental results showed that the proposed Harmony-Tabu algorithm produces better solutions for document retrieval. The results of the hybridized methods are the initial seeds for the relevance feedback [4] approaches. We found the best-performing algorithm to be TCFB, compared to TFB and CFB. To extend our work, the framework can be designed with concept-based features.

References

1. Mahdavi, M., Fesanghari, M., Damangir, E.: An improved harmony search algorithm for solving optimization problems. Appl. Math. Comput. (2006)
2. Sadan, K.-K.: Multi-objective tabu search using a multinomial probability mass function. J. operational Research 169 (2006)
3. Hersh, W., Buckley, C., Leone, T.J., Hick-man, D.: OHSUMED: an interactive retrieval evaluation and new large text collection for research. In: SIGIR (1994)
4. Spink: Term relevance feedback and query expansion: relation to design. In: Proceedings of the 17th annual international ACM SIGIR conference on research and development in information retrieval, pp. 81–90 (1994)

Challenges in Segmentation of Text in Handwritten Gurmukhi Script

K. Sharma Rajiv[1] and S. Dhiman Amardeep[2]

[1] SMCA, Thapar University, Patiala, Punjab, India
rajiv.patiala@gmail.com
[2] UCoE, Punjabi University Patiala, Punjab, India
amardeep_dhiman@yahoo.com

Abstract. The scanned image of the text is not of any use for user, because that image is not editable. One can not make any change if required to the scanned document. This provides a food for thought for the theory of optical character recognition (OCR). OCR is nothing but character recognition of a segmented part of the scanned image. Therefore the segmented part of the image would be such that it should provide a close relation to the character to be recognised. Hence segmentation plays an important role in the OCR process. There are problems in segmentation process, but the degree of the problems varies from script to script, that is, the problem set for segmentation of the text written in a particular script may differ than the problem set for the text written in other scripts. The characteristics of the script, plays a significant role in deciding the segmentation points. The present study is an effort to find these problems especially for the segmentation of text in Gurmukhi scripts – typed and handwritten.

Keywords: OCR, Segmentation, Characteristics, Gurmukhi, Handwritten, Style.

1 Introduction

The objective of automatic document processing is to recognise text, graphics and pictures in digital images and extract the intended information, as would a human. Textual and graphical are two categories of document processing dealing, respectively, with the text and the graphics components of a document image. Textual processing includes

- Determine the skew (any tilt at which the document may have been scanned);
- Finding columns, paragraphs, text lines and words;
- Performing optical character recognition.

In most OCR systems, character recognition is performed on individual characters. Character segmentation is a technique, which partitions images of lines or words into individual characters. It is an operation that seeks to decompose an image of a sequence of character into sub-images of individual symbols. So this is one of the decision processes for optical character recognition system. Its decision, that a pattern

V.V Das et al. (Eds.): BAIP 2010, CCIS 70, pp. 388–392, 2010.

isolated from the image is that of character (or other identifiable unit), can be right or wrong. Character segmentation is all too often ignored in the research community, yet broken and touching characters are responsible for the majority errors in automatic reading of both machine and hand – printed text.

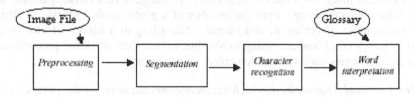

Fig. 1. Steps in Word Interpretation

Character segmentation is fundamental to character recognition approaches, which rely on isolated characters. It is a critical step because incorrectly segmented characters are not likely to be correctly recognised. The present study is related to Gurmukhi, one of the Indian scripts, so it would be appropriate to discuss the properties of Gurmukhi script first.

2   Gurumukhi Script and Its Charaterstics

In Gurumukhi Script, alphabet system consists of basic characters (which are actually vowel and consonant characters), as well as compound characters formed by combining two or more basic characters. The shape of a compound character is usually more complex than the constituent basic characters. In Gurmukhi, it is to be noted that many characters of the alphabet system have a horizontal line at the upper part, which we are referring as *head-line*. A line of Gurmukhi script can be partitioned into three horizontal zones namely, higher zone, heart zone and lower zone. Consonants are generally present in the heart zone. These zones are shown in Figure 2. The higher and lower zones may contain parts of vowel modifiers and diacritical markers.

Fig. 2. a) Higher zone from line number 1 to 2, b) Heart Zone from line number 3 to 4, c) Lower zone from line number 4 to 5

Gurmukhi script alphabet consists of 41 consonants and 12 vowels. Besides these, some characters, in the form of half characters, are present in the feet of characters. Writing style is from left to right. Like English, the concept of upper or lowercase characters is not used in Gurmikhi. Most of the characters contain a horizontal line at the upper of the heart zone. This line is the headline. The characters in a word are connected through the headline along with some symbols as i, I, A etc.

3 Segmentation: Significance in Recognition Process

Segmentation is the process of separating out the individual character, which make up a word. With reference to segmentation, we are to follow the step (given starting point in a document image) – Find the next character image. Extract distinguishing attributes of the character image. Find the member of a given symbol set whose attributes best match those of the input, and output. According to a survey of vast literature done by Casey *et. al.* and according to Shridhar *et. al.*, there are three pure elementary strategies for segmentation. The elementary strategies are:

The Classical Approach, in which segmentations are done on the points identified based on character-like properties. This process of cutting up the image into meaningful components is called *dissection*.

Recognition Based Segmentation, in which the segmenting system searches the image for components that match classes in alphabet stored in database.

Cut Classification Methods, in which the segmenting system seeks to recognize words as a whole, thus avoiding the need to segment into characters.

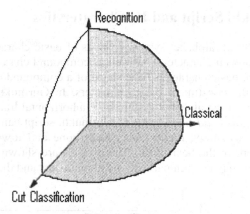

Fig. 3. A Three D space representing the strategies of segmentation

There are many strategies for segmentation, which are combinations of one or more of above three *pure* ones i. e. hybrid approaches that are the weighted combination of these three elementary approaches. These three strategies can be shown to occupy orthogonal axes. Hybrid methods can be represented as weighted combinations of these lying at points in the intervening space.

4 Challenges in Segmenting Handwritten Gurmukhi Scripts

Although segmentation is a straightforward task when dealing with typewritten or well-written characters, it can be quite difficult when the words are handwritten. The main reason for this difficulty is that the handwritten characters often overlap and, in some cases, may be disjointed. Also, the wide variations in handwriting styles make it very difficult to make generalizations for making segmentation heuristics. But for a symbol in Gurmukhi script, the same pixel values in horizontal direction might be shared by two or more characters/symbols of same word. This adds to the complication of segmentation problem in Gurmukhi script.

Uniformly spaced characters in which each character occupies an invisible box that is of the same width as the boxes for all the other characters in the face. Well-separated and unbroken characters in proportional spacing, in which character occupy different amounts of horizontal space, depending on their shapes. Broken characters can be considered as different characters having more than one component. Touching characters can be taken as one character in a single connected component. The letters in cursive writing are often connected. This connectivity creates problem for segmentation process. Overlapping can be there. The individual letters in a cursive word are often written so as to be unidentifiable as isolated characters. The variance in writing style, because of variation in writing style of individuals, it is very difficult to make segmentation decision. In a handwritten document, different written character may vary in size, even if they are present in the same line. There is no predefined font type for characters in handwritten documents. Unlike typed document, the ink used to write character may be spread in different densities. In the handwritten, or even typed document, if text line is slanting then it is difficult to segment. Wrong segmenting point may result a bad output as shown in Figure 4.

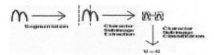

Fig. 4. Incorrect Segmentation of Any character

5 Conclusion

In the end one can say that segmentation is the backbone of optical character recognition process. If the output of the segmentation process is wrong then one can not expect a correct recognition of character. For a particular script, if OCR is to be developed then one has to study the characteristics of that particular script so that these characteristics can be exploited for segmentation process. From the discussion so far, one can draw conclusion that segmentation is difficult as well as critical phase of OCR. It is difficult even for typed text but that can be handled in better way as compared to handwritten text. The situation becomes grim for handwritten texts written in scripts which are two dimensional in nature and in which the character in a word share same pixel value in horizontal direction. As most of the Indian scripts support compound characters formed by combining two or more basic characters, it is really difficult to handle such characters while going through segmentation process. So one has to develop a hybrid approach, which may depend upon classical as well as recognition based approach, to have correct segmentation.

References

1. Yi, L.: Machine Printed Character Segmentation – an Overview. Pattern Recognition 28, 67–80 (1995)
2. Giovanni, S., Edward, C.: External word segmentation of off – line handwritten text lines. Pattern Recognition 27(1), 41–52 (1994)
3. Su, L., Shridhar, M., Ahmad, M.: Segmentation of touching characters in printed document recognition. Pattern Recognition 22(6), 825–840 (1994)
4. Casy, R.G., Lecolinet, E.: A survey of methods and strategies in character segmentation. IEEE PAMI 18, 690–706 (1996)
5. Lu, Y., Shridhar, M.: Character segmentation in handwritten words – an overview. Pattern Recognition 29, 77–96 (1996)
6. Messelodi, S., Modena, C.M.: Context driven text segmentation and recognition. Pattern Recognition Letters 17, 47–56 (1996)
7. Lehal, G.S., Singh, C.: A Gurmukhi Script Recognition System. In: 15th International Conference on Pattern Recognition (ICPR 2000), vol. 2, p. 2557 (2000)
8. Sharma Rajiv, K., Singh, A.: Segmentation of Handwritten Text in Gurmukhi Script. International Journal of Computer Science and Security 2(3) (2008)
9. Grau, V., et al.: Hierarchical image segmentation using a correspondence with a tree model. Pattern Recognition 34, 47–59 (2004)
10. Plamondon, R., Sargur Srihari, N.: On – Line and Off – Line Handwritting Recognition: A Comprehensive Survey. IEEE Transaction on Pattern Analysis and Machine Intelligence 22(1) (2000)

Exploring the Contrasts of VoIP Phone Services

Bala Dhandayuthapani Veerasamy

Department of Computing, College of Engineering, Mekelle University, Ethiopia
dhanssoft@gmail.com

Abstract. A Voice over Internet Protocol (VoIP) is a protocol for transporting voice conversations across a data network. It is an emergent trend on Information and Communication Technology (ICT). This paper consist of connectivity, equipment, provider, cost factors, voice quality and phone book are the exploring contrasts among VoIP phone services that assist people to prefer VoIP phone services.

Keywords: Analog Terminal Adapter, Integrated Services Digital Network, Public Switched Telephone Network, Voice over Internet Protocol, Wireless Fidelity.

1 Introduction

Public Switched Telephone Network (PSTN) [1] is reachable by dialling a number. Instances on interconnection with PSTN is inappropriate, people have an expectation to reach the world at large. Integrated Services Digital Network (ISDN) [1] is a digital network, which divides a line into multiple channels to place simultaneous calls. VoIP services [1] receive real telephone number, with the area code that depends upon VoIP providers. They will route calls over VoIP infrastructure over the PSTN. If you place call to different countries/states/cities, it can be worthwhile at the same rate as local calls.

2 Types of Telephones Used in VoIP

2.1 VoIP Hard Phones

VoIP hard phone [1] can be seen, touched and linked with network cable. The RJ-45 connector on hard phone is an Ethernet port used to communicates over network with other IP based device on network. This phone includes server that keep tracks of everybody's telephone number, voice mail and gateway to PSTN for off-net calling, and router establishing connection to other VoIP phones on the network on-net calling.

2.2 VoIP Soft Phones

If computer is connected to a network using TCP/IP, you have the capability to run a VoIP soft phone [1]. Soft phones are software's, which enables us to do everything through computer. To dial a number on soft phone, you can either use mouse or keyboard.

V.V Das et al. (Eds.): BAIP 2010, CCIS 70, pp. 393–395, 2010.

2.3 VoIP Wireless Phones

VoIP wireless phones [1] will have a limited range and are strictly tied to corporate networks. One thing to watch for in IP wireless phones is whether they are WiSIP (Wireless Session Initiation Protocol) compatible or not. If they are, the phones can include quite a few features not normally available, such as the ability to connect WiFi (Wireless Fidelity) networks.

3 VoIP Phone Services

3.1 Internet VoIP Phone Services

Internet VoIP phone services [2] can provide phone services over the Internet. In home, you would have Analog Terminal Adapter (ATA), which enable phone hand-sets to work with digital VoIP. VoIP provider has softswitch, which acts like central office to route calls to/from phones. There are subscriber databases, voice-mail servers and gateway to the public switched telephone network for off-net calls. This call originates or terminates on a different network than the broadband phone service provider's. A phone number assigned will be assigned for dialing that almost identical to PSTN. AT & T CallVantage, EarthLink trueVoice, Verizon Voicewing are example for Internet VoIP service providers.

3.2 Cable VoIP Phone Services

Cable VoIP services [2] are replacement for PSTN line. Broadband cable modem usually serves dual role, also acting as terminal adapter. An Internet VoIP provider has softswitch, which acts like central office to route calls to/from phones. There are subscriber database, voice-mail server and gateway to PSTN for off-net calls. This call originates or terminates on different network than the cable VoIP service providers. A phone number assigned will be assigned for dialing that almost identical to PSTN. Cablevision Optimum Voice, Charter Telephone and Cox Digital Telephone are example for cable VoIP provides in USA.

3.3 VoIP Chat Services

VoIP chat services [2] works like Instant Messaging (IM) software's that are often referred as PC-to-PC calling. The terminal adapter function is provided by a desktop or laptop computer. Broadband Internet access provides connection to VoIP chat provider. Google Talk, MSN Messenger, Skype, Yahoo Messenger are example of VoIP Chat services.

4 Contrasts of VoIP Phone Services

Table 1 shows the contrasts among VoIP phone services, which include connectivity, equipment, provider, cost factors, voice quality and phone book. This assists people to prefer VoIP phone services.

Table 1. Contrasts of VoIP Phone Services

Contrasts	Internet VoIP	Cable VoIP	VoIP chat
Connectivity	Works similarly to a PSTN line and uses existing handsets.	Works similarly to a PSTN line and uses existing handsets.	Available anywhere you take laptop.
	Can be added as an alternative line to a primary PSTN line.	Can be added as a cable (TV) line to a primary PSTN line.	Requires Internet connection to place phone calls.
Equipments	Terminal adapter used (Analog Terminal Adapter - ATA).	Broadband cable modem usually serves instead of terminal adapter.	Terminal adapter function is provided by a desktop or laptop.
Providers	Choose from a number of providers.	Limited choice of providers.	Choose from a number of providers.
Cost factors	Cost is low.	Cost is low.	Cost is free or cheap.
Voice Quality	Voice quality can be affected by traffic.	Voice quality can be very high.	Voice quality varies from good to poor.
Phone Book	Can often keep existing phone number.	Can often keep existing phone number.	Can often keep existing conduct list.

5 Conclusion

ICT is a growing recent technology, which offers wide scope of providing connection to communication. One of the top most technologies includes VoIP. This paper emphasizes three types of phones and services. As a result of the exploring contrasts, people can prefer the VoIP phone services with no trouble.

References

1. Kelly, T., Peterson, D.: VoIP for Dummies, pp. 141–152. Wiley Publishing Inc., Chichester (2005)
2. Doherty, J., Anderson, N.: Internet Phone Services Simplified. Cisco Press (2006)

Performance Comparision of FSR, LAR1 and LANMAR Routing Protocols in MANET'S

Shaily Mittal[1] and Prabhjot Kaur[2]

[1] Dept. of Computer Science,
Institute of Technology and Management, Gurgaon
shally@itmindia.edu
[2] Dept. of Electronics & Communication,
Institute of Technology and Management, Gurgaon
Prabhjotkaur@itmindia.edu

Abstract. This paper aims to compare performance of some routing protocols for Mobile Ad-Hoc networks (MANET's). A Mobile Ad-Hoc Network (MANET) is a collection of wireless mobile nodes forming a temporary network without using any centralized access point, infrastructure, or centralized administration. To establish a data transmission between two nodes, typically multiple hops are required due to the limited transmission range. Mobility of the different nodes makes the situation even more complicated. Multiple routing protocols especially for these conditions have been developed during the last years, to find optimized routes from a source to some destination. This paper presents performance evaluation of three different routing protocols i.e. LANMAR, LAR1 and Fisheye in variable pause times. Performance evaluation of these three protocols is based on Average end to end delay, TTL based hop count and Packet delivery ratio.

Keywords: MANETS, LANMAR, LAR1, Fisheye.

1 Introduction

A routing protocol is a protocol that specifies how routers communicate with each other, disseminating information that enables them to select routes between any two nodes on a computer network, the choice of the router. Each router has a priori knowledge only of networks attached to it directly. A routing protocol shares this information first among immediate neighbors, and then throughout the network. This way, routers gain knowledge of the topology of the network. An ad hoc routing protocol is a convention, or standard to decide route for packets between computing devices in a network. MANET routing protocols are broadly divided into two categories [2] i.e. Unicast and Multicast protocols. Unicast protocols send messages to single host in a network while multicast protocols send messages to a group of nodes in a network. Various unicast routing protocols for Ad- hoc networks are AODV, CGSR, DSDV, DSR, Fisheye, LANMAR, LAR1, OLSR, WRP, ZRP etc. MRMP, OBAMP, MOLSR, DCMP and ADMR are multicast MANET protocols. In this paper we are using Fisheye, LANMAR and LAR1 i.e. unicast routing protocols for their performance comparison. We have taken these protocols as these are not evaluated earlier for such comparisons.

V.V Das et al. (Eds.): BAIP 2010, CCIS 70, pp. 396–400, 2010.

An earlier protocol performance comparison was carried out by Guangyu Pei *et all* in [10], who conducted experiments with Ad hoc On-Demand Vector routing (AODV), Fisheye, Dynamic MANET On-demand (DYMO), Source Tree Adaptive Routing (STAR) protocol, Routing Information Protocol (RIP), Bellman Ford, LandMark Ad hoc Routing protocol (LANMAR) and Location Aided Routing protocol (LAR). The Bellman- Ford routing protocol shows highest throughput and RIP, STAR, Fisheye and LANMAR protocols showed a dip at a node density of 50. This simulation experiment showed that AODV, Dymo and Bellman ford protocols are having higher end to end delays than others, indicating that the speed of simulation in large scale networks will be affected, whereas LANMAR and RIP shows the considerable amount of delay in scaled up environment.

Performance comparison of AODV, DSR, FSR and LANMAR is presented by M. Gerla *et all* in [11]. According to their simulation results LANMAR outperforms FSR under all delay and throughput measures. Moreover, LANMAR provides a dramatic reduction in route table storage overhead with respect to FSR. Their results shows when the number of communication pairs increases, AODV and DSR will generate considerable routing overhead. Because of this increase in routing O/H, the performance of both AODV and DSR is worse than LANMAR for medium to high traffic loads.

In the last few years, there are several researches have evaluated the performance of routing protocols for mobile Ad- Hoc network as a function of mobility rate and pause time using ns2(network simulator 2)[9] . There are lesser evaluations available using Qualnet simulator [1] which is commercially available and faster than ns2 [3]. We are using Qualnet simulator for comparison evaluation of *LANMAR, LAR1 and Fisheye*.

The rest of the paper is organized as follows: Section 2 describes three concerned protocols in detail i.e. Fisheye, LANMAR and LAR1. Section 3 describes the simulation environment, parameters evaluated and simulation results. Lastly work is concluded in section 4.

2 Preliminaries

2.1 FSR

Fisheye State Routing (FSR) [4] generates accurate routing decisions by taking advantage of the global network information. Fisheye Routing determines routing decisions using a table-driven routing mechanism similar to link state. The table-driven ad hoc routing approach uses a connectionless approach of forwarding packets, with no regard to when and how frequently such routes are desired. It relies on an underlying routing table update mechanism that involves the constant propagation of routing information.

2.2 LANMAR

The Landmark Ad-hoc Routing Protocol (LANMAR) [5] combines the features of FSR and landmark routing. LANMAR assumes that the large scale ad hoc network is grouped into logical subnets in which the members have a commonality of interests and are likely to move as a "group". LANMAR uses the notion of landmarks to keep track of such logical subnets[6]. Each logical group has one node serving as landmark. The route to a landmark is propagated throughout the network using a Distance Vector mechanism [11].

2.3 LAR1

The goal of Location-Aided Routing (LAR)[7] is to reduce the routing overhead by the use of location information. LAR protocol uses the GPS (Global Positioning System) to get location information of mobile hosts. In the LAR routing technique,[8] route request and route reply packets similar to DSR and AODV are being proposed.

3 Performance Evaluation

We carried out simulations on Qualnet simulator. The simulation parameters are summarized in the table 1. We designed the network using Random waypoint model with different pause times. We are compiling the results using 15 simulations and the application traffic between the randomly chosen source and destination is CBR traffic. The metrics used to measure the performance of protocols are average end to end delay, average TTL based hop count and packet delivery ratio.

Average End to End Delay

End-to-end delay indicates duration for a packet to travel from the CBR source to the application layer of the destination. According to results obtained in figure1 (a) Fisheye shows minimum end to end delay of 0.01 s and almost remains constant irrespective of pause time. Similar is the case with LANMAR protocol which shows a slight higher delay in comparison with FSR. LAR1 shows worst performance with highest end to delay of 0.12 s and minimum delay of 0.08 s.

Table 1. Parameters for simulation evaluation

No. of nodes	50
Dimension of space	1500 X 1500 m
Minimum velocity(v min)	0 m/sec
Maximum velocity (v max)	20 m/sec
Simulation Time	180s
Item size	512 bytes
Source data pattern	4 packets / sec
Pause time	30s,60s,90s, 120s,150s

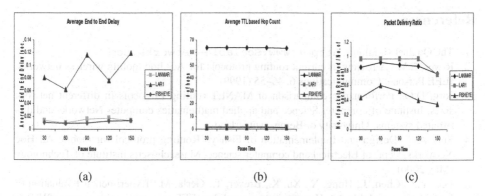

Fig. 1. Simulation results of FSR, LANMAR and LAR1

TTL based average hop count

Hop count is the number of hops a packet took to reach its destination. The results for TTL based hop count in figure 1(b) shows three protocols have a constant hop count irrespective of the pause time. With the increase of pause time it remains constant. LANMAR have highest hop count of 64 hops while FSR and LAR1 require less number of hops of 2hops and 1hop respectively. The plotted graph shows that hop count is independent of pause time as 15 simulations with different source and destination pairs show same value.

Packet Delivery Ratio

Packet delivery ratio is calculated by dividing the number of packets received by the destination through the number of packets originated by the source. As shown in figure 1(c) protocols show similar behavior of decrease in delivery ratio with increase in pause time. LAR1 describes best results with highest delivery ratio approaching near to 100% while FSR performs worst with lowest delivery ratio of 30%. LANMAR delivers almost 80% of packets from source to destination.

4 Conclusion

In this paper, a performance comparison of three different routing protocols i.e.FSR, LANMAR, and LAR1 for mobile Ad-hoc networks is presented as a function of pause time. Three performance metrics used to compare protocols are average end to end delay; average TTL based hop count and packet delivery ratio. FSR performs best in measuring end to end delay and TTL based hop count having minimum values of these two parameters. LAR1 performs best in case of packet delivery ratio with almost 100% delivery ratio. Hence, in case packet delivery ratio is of high concern, LAR1 is the best protocol to suit this requirement. In future, this work may be extended for analyzing the behavior of these protocols in heterogeneous networks with many more metrics for evaluation.

References

1. The Qualnet simulator, http://www.Scalable-Networks.com
2. Royer, E.M.: A review of current routing protocols for Ad- hoc mobile wireless networks. IEEE Personal Communications 6, 46–55 (1999)
3. Jorg, D.O.: Performance comparison of MANET routing Protocols in different network sizes, Institute of computer Science and applied mathematics computer Networks and distributed systems. University of Berne, switzerland
4. Sun, A.C.: Design and Implementation of Fisheye Routing protocol for mobile Ad Hoc Networks, Dept. of Electrical and computer science, Massachusetts institute of Technology (May 2000)
5. Lee, Y.Z., Chen, J., Hong, X., Xu, K., Breyer, T., Gerla, M.: Experimental Evaluation of LANMAR, a scalable Ad- Hoc routing protocol. In: IEEE communications society/WCNC 2005, University of California, Los Angles (2005)
6. Pei, G., Gerla, M., Hong, X.: LANMAR: Landmark Routing for Large Scale Wireless Ad-Hoc Networks with Group Mobility. In: Proceedings of IEEE/ACM MobiHOC 2000, Boston, MA, August 2000, pp. 11–18 (2000)
7. Performance Evaluation of Secure on-Demand Routing Protocols for Mobile Ad-hoc Networks, Junaid Arshad Mohammad Ajmal Azad FAS, IIUI Pakistan FAS, IIUI Pakistan. In: 15th IEEE International Conference on Network Protocols, Beijing, China (2007)
8. Kurkowski, S., Navidi, W., Camp, T.: Discovering Variables that Affect MANET Protocol Performance. In: Global Telecommunications Conference. GLOBECOM 2007, Air Force Inst. of Technol., Wright Patterson, November 26-30. IEEE, Los Alamitos (2007)
9. Boomarani Malany, A., Sarma Dhulipala, V.R., Chandrasekaran, M.: Throughput and Delay Comparison of MANET Routing Protocols. Int. J. Open Problems Compt. Math. 2(3) (September 2009) ISSN 1998-6262
10. Pei, G., Gerla, M., Hong, X.: Landmark Routing for Large Scale Wireless Ad Hoc Networks with Group Mobility, Computer Science Department, University of California
11. Gerla, M., Hong, X., Pei, G.: Landmark Routing for Large Ad Hoc Wireless Networks. In: Proceeding of IEEE GLOBECOM 2000, San Francisco, CA (November 2000)

Impact Factor of E - Learning: Using Secondary Education Case Study

Tamanna Siddiqui and Munior Ahmad Wani

Department of Computer Science, Jamia Hamdard, New Delhi
tsiddiqui@jamiahamdard.ac.in, muneer.wani@gmail.com

Abstract. With a firm belief that technology-enabled learning can truly nullify social and economic boundaries, the concept of E-Learning has helped many students to achieve their dreams. These diverse operations are testament to the firm focus and dedication towards spreading quality Education. The use of audio visual technology is increasing with exponential rates in major Indian cities. In this paper, we have proposed Impact factor to calculate the academic perform-ance of the students, of those schools where E–Learning technology has already been introduced. Experiments have been performed on past three years academic data to show the overall impact of E – Learning in Secondary Education.

Keywords: E-Learning, MIMEO, Interactive Board, Z – Test, Secondary Education Case Study.

1 Introduction

Audio Visual teaching methods have always been appealing to the students. Due to the changing nature of technology, electronic portfolios are often believed to be an ideal replacement for paper based ones. Yet, this process is not without challenges. More often than not, such projects are initiated in a top-down manner, but fail to gain program-wide adoption.[5] Rural areas are picturesque but often have a lack of ac-cess to education and training facilities. E-Learning provides a mechanism to bridge this gap. The Analytical view of E-Learning framework provides live interactive training and a social environment for the participants to cooperate and learn.[8]

1.1 Content Development

The Content support division has been chosen specifically for their long years of academic and industry-related experience [2]. The instructional material is generated after a long process of research, which relies on best practices and proven educational techniques. Leading and experienced educationalists, research associates, faculty, content developers and animators form this team. Their commitment to ensuring qual-ity education to students across the country is also reflected. Hughes, the global leader in online education has taken an initiative to provide Digital Compressed Satellite Services (DCSS) for the Government Education and Training Network (GETN) in United States and shall be ready for execution by 2012 [4]. This effort is through the U.S. General Services Administration's SATCOM-II vehicle and is anticipated to be a multi-million dollar effort.

V.V Das et al. (Eds.): BAIP 2010, CCIS 70, pp. 401–404, 2010.
© Springer-Verlag Berlin Heidelberg 2010

1.2 MIMEO Technology

It's a collection of hardware that attaches to any standard whiteboard and captures all the scribbling for posterity. The mimeo capture bar sticks to the whiteboard using suction cups. There is also an LED (Light emitting diodes) that indicates if we have a good connection to the computer. Before we start using MIMEO technology for teaching purposes, we need to specify the coordinates of the white board so that MIMEO recognizes the field of capturing events. Than the touch with the interactive pen on the white board is recognized as an event by MIMEO and accordingly operations are carried out by the computer connected to it.

2 Proposed Work

1. To collect data of ten secondary schools three years prior and three years after the use of e-learning technology.
2. To calculate Z-Test on the data.
3. If we are able to find out that Null hypothesis is rejected in every school, we will have authentic results to improve and expand this technology in all secondary schools.

3 Experiment

Secondary Education case study:

Sample Data

S. No	%age		S.No	%age		S.No	%age	
	After	Before		After	Before		After	Before
1	74.56	70.3	11	73.33	65.66	21	89.95	86.44
2	78.43	72.5	12	58.25	51.33	22	89.33	85.33
3	60.56	61.3	13	65.33	56.44	23	75.33	63.25
4	62.45	58.5	14	68.45	62.33	24	69.55	65.45
5	85.5	80.4	15	67.55	61.5	25	89.44	85.33
6	68.45	60.3	16	78.33	70.2	26	60.44	58.2
7	72.33	66.3	17	70.33	72.45	27	80.5	75
8	78.65	72.5	18	89.25	82.25	28	88.33	87.66
9	60.05	56.3	19	65.44	61.25	29	88.25	84.33
10	82.35	78.8	20	81.44	82.35	30	69.67	71.25

A sample of 30 students was taken where their percentage was collected before and after the introduction of E – Learning technology in St. Joseph's Higher Secondary school. The following statistical tests   (Mean, Standard Deviation & Z – Tests) were applied to verify whether the increase in the percentage was significant after the E – Learning technology was introduced.

Formulas used:

$$Z_{Value} = \frac{(X_1 - X_2) - (\mu_1 - \mu_2)}{S.E_{(X1 - X2)}} \dots\dots\dots\dots\dots\dots\dots\dots\dots\dots(1)$$

Where:

X_1 : Mean of Sample-1.
X_2 : Mean of Sample-2.
μ_1 : Population mean after E - Learning.
μ_2 : Population mean before E- Learning.

$$S.E_{(Standard\ Error)} = \frac{(S1)^2}{N_1} + \frac{(S2)^2}{N_2} \dots\dots\dots\dots\dots\dots\dots\dots\dots(2)$$

Where,

S_1 : Standard deviation after E-Learning.
S_2 : Standard deviation before E-Learning.
N_1 : Sample size taken after E - Learning
N_2 : Sample size taken before E – Learning.
H_0 : $\mu_1 = \mu_2$ (Null Hypothesis)
H1 : $\mu_1 = \mu_2$ (Alternate Hypothesis)

Data	
Hypothesized Difference	0
Level of Significance	0.05
Population 1 Sample (After E - Learning technology)	
Sample Size	30
Sample Mean	74.7273
Population Standard Deviation	10.1064
Population 2 Sample(Before E - Learning technology)	
Sample Size	30
Sample Mean	70.175
Population Standard Deviation	10.5965
Intermediate Calculations	
Difference in Sample Means	4.55233
Standard Error of the Difference in Means	2.67348
Z-Test Statistic	1.70277
Upper-Tail Test	
Upper Critical Value	1.64485
p-Value	0.04431
Reject the null hypothesis	

Results: Z – Test Value = 1.70277, and the upper critical value at 5% significance (95% confidence) = 1.64485, so that means Null Hypothesis is rejected. Since Null hypothesis has been rejected this means that the introduction of E – Learning technology has been improving the academic performance of the students.

4 Conclusion

We shall be able to design new streaming/ buffering methods so that our online sessions run successfully without snags or failures and with low bandwidth constraints. We shall try to design a proper plan for the updation of E content servers after every week without any delay in teaching learning processes. A technology of lecture recording also needs to be emphasized so that same recorded lectures can be delivered at other dispersed places across the globe.

5 Future Scope

Many companies, which are into this business, are planning to expand it more by introducing M-Learning (Mobile Learning) rather than E – Learning (as it is only in school). M-Learning will revolutionize the whole concept of audio – visual teaching if given a 3G bandwidth exposure. Many algorithms can be developed for the searching of required content with cell phones. A new data model could be proposed for the storage of M content (Animations etc).

References

[1] Education observer. BGS International School inaugurates first State-of- the-art comprehensive ICT education solution for schools from NIIT eGURU, Bangalore (August 5, 2008)
[2] Everonn web portal, http://www.everonn.com
[3] Green, B.: Techno Literacy Program, Printed in Australia (2008)
[4] Hughes to provide distance learning network for GETN, http://digitalsignagetoday.com
[5] Zumbach, J.: Information Technology in Childhood Education AnnualISSN 1522-8185, vol. 2004(1). Association for the Advancement of Computing in Education (AACE), University of Heidelberg, Germany (2004)
[6] Beckerman, A.: Information Technology in Childhood Education Annual ISSN 1522-8185, vol. 2004(1), Leonard Fontana, Broward Community College, USA; Nova Southeastern University, USA (2004)
[7] Bijlani, K., Pai, C., Bijlani, B.: World Conference on Educational Multimedia, Hypermedia and Tele communications (EDMEDIA), Honolulu, HI, USA, June 22. AACE, Amrita University, India (2009)
[8] Bijlani, K., Pai, C., Bijlani, B.: World Conference on Educational Multimedia, Hypermedia and Tele communications (EDMEDIA), Honolulu, HI, USA, June 22. AACE, Amrita University, India (2009)

Annotating Indian Tribal Medicinal Documents Using Semi Automatically Extracted Ontology

Sanchit Gupta, Himanshu Gahlot, Varun Gupta, and Banshi Dhar Chaudhary

Department of Computer Science and Engineering,
MNNIT Allahabad, India
{sanchit.gupta210,himanshu.gahlot86, varuninmnnit}@gmail.com,
bdc@mnnit.ac.in

Abstract. Indian Tribal Medicinal Documents date back to around 1920's and has not been explored much before. This paper attempts to structure these documents by extracting their ontology semi automatically and help in their annotations with the ontological concepts. It outlines our work in finding specific medical or tribal terms in such documents. It describes a two way annotation system through which experts can annotate the documents with the ontology concepts and also expand and refine the ontology with the new concepts. The results show that the system has high performance across documents with different concept densities.

Keywords: Indian Tribal Medicinal Plants, Ontology Extraction, Annotation, OntoLT, Stanford Parser.

1 Introduction

In the past few decades researchers have turned to semi automatic ontology extraction and annotation to help structure the vast information present in the form of text [1]. These systems are able to extract ontology to an extent after which its manual construction becomes quite easy [2]. Indian Tribal Medicinal Documents date back to around 1920s and have not been explored much before. These documents can be structured by:

- Constructing their ontology automatically using OntoLt [3], a java based Protégé plug-in for automatic ontology extraction.
- Providing a platform for experts in the annotation of documents with the ontological concepts, all the while refining and enhancing the ontology with new concepts.
- Providing a platform for a normal user to view the documents, annotated by experts.

Indian Tribal Medicinal Documents are available only as hard copy. These documents were scanned, converted to text format and manually corrected, and thus made usable to the computer. These documents had to be converted to a linguistically (e.g. POS tags, morphological inflection and decomposition) and semantically (e.g. clause consisting of a predicate with its arguments and adjuncts) annotated XML format [4]

V.V Das et al. (Eds.): BAIP 2010, CCIS 70, pp. 405–410, 2010.

before tools such as OntoLT could be deployed for ontology generation. Such a tool for generating this XML format was not available. The tool was built using Stanford Parser, through which not only the linguistic but also the underlying structure can be captured. We have named this system OntoAnnot.

The remainder of this paper is structured as follows: Section 2 describes the annotation system and ontology extraction module. Section 3 outlines the results of our experiments carried out over 6 different documents. Finally section 4 provides conclusion and directions for future work.

2   The OntoAnnot System

The OntoAnnot system consists of the following two modules:

- Ontology Extraction module.
- Annotation Module.

The document to be annotated is loaded in both these modules. In the Annotation System the document is presented to the user for annotation. The user can view previous annotations and may add new annotations. The Ontology Extractor builds the ontology for this document, which can be used by the user to annotate documents.

2.1   Ontology Extraction Module

The Ontology Extraction module accepts a text document as input and semi automatically extracts its ontology. The flow diagram of this module is shown in Figure. 1.

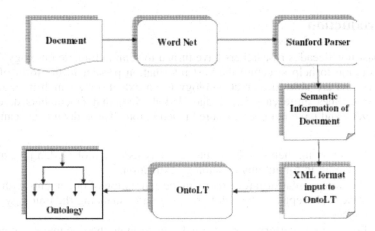

Fig. 1. Ontology Extraction Module of OntoAnnot

In order to construct an accurate ontology the corpus needs to be refined to include only those sentences that contained the tribal medicinal terms. These words were identified using Wordnet[5].The whole document was first tagged with part of speech information using Stanford P.O.S Tagger and then identified nouns (NN,NP,NNP,NNS) were fed to the Wordnet. Those words, which were not found in Wordnet were supposed to be the tribal medical terms. The accuracy of the process was very high and we were able to extract almost all sentences containing tribal medical terms. This method improved the extracted ontology since it removed those sentences, which did not contain terms related to our domain.

This refined document is then parsed using Stanford Parser [6]. Stanford parser provides various linguistic information about the sentences like POS tags(for example nouns, verbs, adjectives, adverbs etc.), phrases(Noun phrase , verb phrase, adjective phrase etc), dependency structure(head modifier and head compliments)[7]. With this information triplets [8] (Subject, Object, and Predicate) can be extracted from sentences. The whole information can then be used to construct the XML file which is the required input format for OntoLT. OntoLT then constructs the ontology using this XML file in the owl format. The expert can then modify the ontology by adding missing concepts or deleting the wrong ones.

2.2 Annotation Module

This module deals with annotation of documents. Its design consists of three interfaces:

- File Viewing
- Annotating
- Ontology Viewing

A File Viewer Window enables browsing and loading the document in OntoAnnot. If the document already contains some annotations then these are highlighted in yellow as shown in Figure. 2. If the file has not been annotated before then it is displayed in the text area without highlighting. The annotations are stored, in the xml format, on a server, in accordance with the Annotea protocol. [9].

To make annotations the user has to select the text in the File Viewer Window and request Annotation. This pops up the Annotation Window, which provides options for

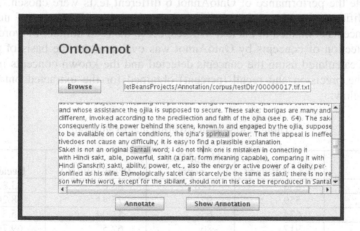

Fig. 2. The File Viewer Window of the Annotation module

making and saving new annotations. The Annotation Types displayed in this window remain the same as those in Amaya 10.0 [10] with the flexibility of adding a new type. The user can either choose the already provided annotation types for example Comment, Example, and Explanation etc. or may choose a new type. If he chooses the new type then he needs to type in the name of this annotation. The expert or user can then type in the actual annotation in the Text Area provided. The expert might want to annotate some text with a concept of the same domain. In this case he can download the ontology of the concerned domain from a central repository of the ontologies. This would enable the concepts to be displayed in the ontology window from where user can select the appropriate concept. An expert can also edit the existing ontology by adding the concepts and relations or description not present in the existing ontology.

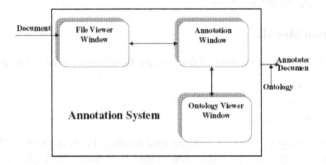

Fig. 3. Annotation System of OntoAnnot

3   Experimental Evaluation and Results

To evaluate the performance of OntoAnnot 6 different texts were chosen. The texts were of different lengths and had different concept densities (ratio of number of known concepts contained in the text with respect to the total number of words).

The detection of concepts by OntoAnnot was evaluated on the basis of precision and recall calculated using the concepts detected and the known concepts in the test corpus. The precision and recall (percent) obtained for the extracted ontology are reported below:

Table 1. Results of Experimental Evaluation

File#	No. of Words	No. of Concepts	Precision (%)	Recall (%)
File 1	838	146	83.03	93.83
File 2	559	92	77.41	78.26
File 3	634	65	51.04	75.38
File 4	917	86	62.5	69.76
File 5	1273	40	53.52	95
File 6	825	72	87.5	92.22

The overall Precision of the tested corpus was 70.88%.

On an analysis of the accuracies obtained we found that files 3 and 5 contained mostly a few word sentences (two or three worded). Also in such cases most of the medical concepts were two-worded which led to a low identification accuracy and hence to a lower precision in these files.

The overall Recall of the Tested corpus was 85.03%.

The inconsistencies in the recall rate of these files are less and the extracted ontology seems quite satisfactory with an accuracy of 85.03%.By plotting the F measure (Harmonic mean of precision and recall) along with the percentile of the concept density (assuming the 0.17 of file number 1 as 100) we see that the performance of the OntoAnnot remains satisfactorily above 60% for all different concept densities. This is shown in Figure 4.

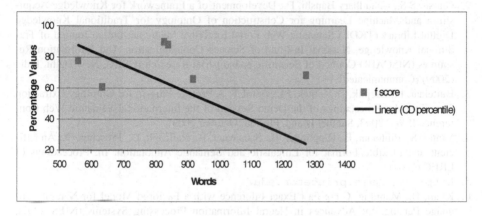

Fig. 4. Plot of F measure against number of words in the text

4 Future Work

This paper has presented a fully functional annotating system which generates ontology semi-automatically. The users can then work on this ontology and refine it according to their needs.

Future work that could be incorporated in OntoAnnot will focus on

- Integration of linguistic annotation over a web service
- Integration of an information extraction approach for ontology population (identifying class instances)
- Definition and implementation of an evaluation platform to evaluate extracted ontology in a quantitative (technical performance) and qualitative (user satisfaction) way.

A number of different methods for text-based ontology extraction and learning have developed over recent years. However, in order to compare the performance of OntoAnnot with these and other methods, a proper evaluation framework needs to be set up. Currently it is very hard to compare methods and approaches, due to the lack of a shared understanding of the task at hand.

Future work will therefore be concerned also with a contribution towards the development of such a shared understanding and an appropriate evaluation framework accordingly.

Acknowledgements. Assistance from lab members at CSE, IITB, Mumbai in completion of this paper is hereby acknowledged.

References

1. Maedche, A., Staab, S.: Semi-automatic Engineering of Ontologies from Text. In: Proceedings of the 12th International Conference on Software Engineering and Knowledge Engineering (2000)
2. Ghosh, S.S., Chaudhary Banshi, D.: Development of a Framework for Knowledge Acquisition and Machine Learning for Construction of Ontology for Traditional Knowledge Digital Library (TKDL) Semantic Web Portal for Tribal Medicine, Indian Journal of Traditional Knowledge, National Institute of Science Communication And Information Resources (NISCAIR) Council of Scientific & Industrial Research (CSIR), New Delhi, India (2009) (Communicated)
3. Buitelaar, P., Olejnik, D., Sintek, M.: OntoLT: A Protégé Plug-In for Ontology Extraction from Text. In: Proceedings of the Demo Session of the International Semantic Web Conference ISWC 2003, Sanibel Island, Florida (October 2003)
4. Vintar, Š., Buitelaar, P., Ripplinger, B., Sacaleanu, B., Raileanu, D., Prescher, D.: An Efficient and Flexible Format for Linguistic and Semantic Annotation. In: Proceedings of LREC (2002)
5. http://wordnet.princeton.edu/
6. Klein, D., Manning, C.D.: Fast Exact Inference with a Factored Model for Natural Language Parsing. In: Advances in Neural Information Processing Systems (NIPS 2002), vol. 15, pp. 3–10. MIT Press, Cambridge (2003)
7. Klein, D., Manning, C.D.: Accurate Unlexicalized Parsing. In: Proceedings of the 41st Meeting of the Association for Computational Linguistics, pp. 423–430 (2003)
8. Rusu, D., Dali, L., Fortuna, B., Grobelnik, M., Mladenić, D.: Triplet Extraction from Sentences. Ljubljana: 2007. In: Proceedings of the 10th International Multiconference Information Society IS 2007, vol. A, pp. 218–222 (2007)
9. http://www.w3.org/2002/12/AnnoteaProtocol-20021219
10. http://www.w3.org/Amaya/

A Comparative Study of Feature Extraction Approaches for an Efficient Iris Recognition System

Chandrashekar M. Patil[1] and Sudarshan Patilkulkarni[2]

[1] Research Scholar, JSS Research Foundation,
Department of Electronics and Communication, Mysore, India
patilcm@gmail.com
[2] Assistant Professor, Department of Electronics and Communication,
SJ College of Engineering, Mysore, India
pk.sudarshan@gmail.com

Abstract. A wide variety of biometrics based tools are under development to meet the challenges in security in the existing complex scenario. Among these, iris pattern based identification is the most promising for its stability, reliability, uniqueness, noninvasiveness and immunity from duplication. Hence the iris identification technique has become hot research point in the past several years. This paper compares recognition rates, speed and other efficiency parameters resulting from three iris feature extraction algorithms that use statistical measures, lifting wavelet transform (LWT), and Gray-Level Co-occurrence Matrix (GLCM) respectively. Experimental results show that while LWT provides higher recognition rate, GLCM approach offers reduction in computation time with a small compromise in recognition rate. It also demonstrates that statistical measures is the most economical when recognition requirement is crucial.

Keywords: Iris Recognition, Texture analysis, Statistical Measures, Lifting Wavelet Transform, GLCM.

1 Introduction

Iris provides outstanding recognition performance when used as a Biometric. It provides a great uniqueness among people including twins. Compared with other biometrics, iris is more stable and reliable for identification. In this paper, iris recognition system was implemented by composing the following five steps. The first step consists of iris image preprocessing, where the pictures' size and type are manipulated in order to be able to process them subsequently. Once the preprocessing step is achieved, it is necessary to extract features and redundant ones are eliminated. Finally, we compare the coded image with the already coded iris in order to find a match an impostor. These procedures can be viewed as depicted in Fig. 1.

The first promising results in iris recognition can be traced to combined efforts of Flom, Safir and Daugman in 1992 [1]. Later, similar efforts were reported by Wildes, Boles and Sanchez-Reillo, whose methods differed both in the iris feature representation (iris signature) and pattern matching algorithms. The solution proposed by Wildes [2] uses Hough transform for iris localization by modeling eyelids with parabolic curves. The prototype of Boles [3] on the other hand, works based on a one-texture coding.

V.V Das et al. (Eds.): BAIP 2010, CCIS 70, pp. 411–416, 2010.
© Springer-Verlag Berlin Heidelberg 2010

Noh et al. [7] use the composition of multi-resolution analysis and principle component analysis of the texture. A comparison with the results of some of these techniques with those using techniques of authors of this paper will be presented in end.

2 Proposed Methodology

The first phase of the iris recognition method is to collect a large database consisting of several iris images from various individuals. The image is then subjected to various pre-processing stages to reduce the noise and specular reflections as much as possible to improve the quality of the image. Then the iris is extracted from the eye image i.e. disturbing features like eyelids and eyelashes are eliminated to the maximum possible extent and then process of normalize is carried out.The main contribution of this paper is at the feature extraction and selection which will be now explained in detail.

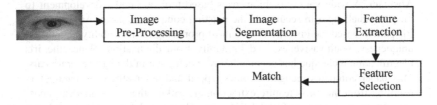

Fig. 1. Flow chart of our methodology

3 Feature Extraction

Feature extraction is a key process where the two dimensional image is converted to a set of mathematical parameters. The iris contains important unique features, such as stripes, freckles, coronas, etc. These features are collectively refereed to as the texture of the iris.Only the significant features of the iris must be encoded so that comparisons between templates can be made. These features are extracted and selected by using various algorithms.

3.1 Statistical Measures

Following statistical features are considered in this paper for iris recognition process: mean median, mode, standard deviation, and variance.

$$x_k = \Sigma(R1 + R2) \tag{1}$$

$$mean = \frac{\sum_{k=1}^{n} x_k}{n} \tag{2}$$

$$\text{Variance}: s^2 = \frac{\sum_{k=1}^{n}(x_k - \overline{x})^2}{n-1} \tag{3}$$

$$\text{Standard Deviation}: s = \sqrt{\frac{\sum_{k=1}^{n}(x_k - \overline{x})^2}{n-1}} \tag{4}$$

$$\text{Feature Vector}: \vec{F}_c = (x^c, m^c, y^c, s^c, d^c, ...) \tag{5}$$

x^c = mean, m^c = median, y^c = mode, s^c = standard deviation, d^c = variance

3.2 Lifting Wavelet Transforms

Thus, lifting scheme contains three [8] steps to decompose signal, that is,Split, Predict and Update. The original signal is $s[n]$. It is transformed into approximated signal $c[n]$ in high frequency and detail signal $d[n]$ in low frequency.

$$\text{Split}: \begin{array}{l} s_e[n] = s[2n] \\ s_o[n] = s[2n+1] \end{array} \tag{6}$$

$$\text{Predict}: d[n] = s_o[n] - P(s_e)[n] \tag{7}$$

$$\text{Update}: c[n] = s_e[n] + U(d)[n] \tag{8}$$

For the feature extraction purpose, only the coarse or approximation coefficients (those of $c[n]$) are of interest. If there are 2^n data elements, the first step of the forward transform will produce 2^{n-1} approximation coefficients. In case of an image of size N× M, at the Kth level coarse approximation component will get reduced to $(N/2)^k \times (M/2)^k$. In the proposed approach the original masked image is resized to [256, 256] and then 6th level coefficients were obtained by increasing the frequency. After sixth level image size becomes too small to be useful.

3.3 Grey Level Co-occurrence Matrix(GLCM)

GLCM(gray-level co-occurrence matrix),also known as the gray-level spatial dependence matrix is a statistical measure used to characterize the texture of an image by calculating how often pairs of pixel, with specific values and in a specified spatial relationship occur in an image and then by extracting statistical measures from this matrix. The statistics are calculated from these GLCMs and then subtracting the database GLCM with input GLCM then the threshold value is to be set for the comparison of database image with respect to input image. The statistical parameters that can be derived for GLCM are contrast, entropy, energy, homogeneity and Dissimilarity.

$$Contrast = \sum_{i,j=0}^{N-1} P_{i,j}(i-j)^2 \tag{9}$$

$$Entropy = \sum_{i,j=0}^{N-1} P_{i,j}(-\ln P_{i,j}) \tag{10}$$

$$Energy = \sum_{i} \sum_{j} p(i,j)^2 \tag{11}$$

$$Homogenity = \sum_{i,j=0}^{N-1} \frac{P_{i,j}}{1+(i-j)^2} \tag{12}$$

$$Dissimilarity = \sum_{i,j=0}^{N-1} P_{i,j} |i-j| \tag{13}$$

4 Matching

In order to make the decision of acceptance or refusal, a distance is calculated to measure the closeness of match. The extracted features of the iris are compared with distance between the feature vectors of two iris images. The following distance measures have been considered and maximum of the distance between iris images of the same person in the database is considered as the threshold.

4.1 Euclidean Measures

Euclidean Measures: The Euclidean distance is one way of defining the closeness of match between two iris feature templates. It is calculated by measuring the norm between two vectors X and Y respectively of two images under consideration.

$$EM1 = \sqrt{(y1-x1)^2 + (y2-y1)^2 + \dots} \tag{14}$$

$$ED = \min(FI, FD)$$

Where FI, FD are the feature vector of the input image and feature vector of the database image.

4.2 Separable Power

$$d = \frac{|\mu_1 - \mu_2|}{\sqrt{\dfrac{\sigma_1^2 + \sigma_2^2}{2}}} \tag{15}$$

Where $\mu 1$ and $\sigma 1$ are the mean and standard deviation of the distance of the codes belonging to the same person, and $\mu 2$ and $\sigma 2$ are the mean and standard deviation of the distance of the codes belonging to different persons.

4.3 Distance Threshold

Distance Threshold: It is defined as the square of the difference between the threshold maximum value of input image (Max_1) and database image (Max_2) of the 6th level decomposition:

$$DT = \{Max(\max\_1 - \max\_2)\}^2. \tag{16}$$

5 Experimental Results

To evaluate the performance of the proposed system, extensive experiments were performed. Iris images are obtained from CASIA version II iris image database consisting of 750 images. These iris images are from non-ideal conditions with noise thrown in. The choice of this particular database is intentional in order to test the robustness of our algorithm. The experiments were done using MATLAB® and tested our algorithm on 750 images, and we obtained an average correct recognition rate 98.91%.The proposed method achieved up to 99.78%(Refer Table 2).

Table 1. Runtime Results for Iris Recognition

Algorithm	Feature vector Length(Bits)	Localization (Sec)	Feature Extraction (msec)	Comparison (msec)	Total Time (sec)
Daugman	2048	8.7	682.5	54	9.436
Wildes	87	8.3	210	401	8.911
Our proposed methods					
Statistical measures	10	1.42	3698	10	5.218
Lifting wavelet transform	16	1.42	3762	42	5.224
GLCM	12	1.42	3532	25	5.202

Table 2. Comparison of recognition rate

Methodology	Recognition rate
Daugman	99.37%
Boles	92.61%
Li Ma	94.33%
Y.Wang	97.25%
Our proposed methods	
Statistical measures	99.38%
Lifting wavelet transform	99.78%
GLCM	99.57%

6 Conclusion

In this paper, the performance of Iris recognition system by using statistical measure, Lifting wavelet transforms and Gray-Level Co-occurrence Matrix for detecting singularities to extract features and capable of comparing two eye images was investigated. While LWT approach provides higher recognition rate, it is relatively slow when feature vectors using GLCM are used. Statistical measures approach uses feature vector of least size while providing significantly higher recognition rate, if not as high as more complex approaches of LWT and GLCM. Results of this investigation will guide the designers towards improving their iris recognition system depending on their application and cost specifications.

References

1. http://www.cl.cam.ac.uk/users/jgd1000/history.html (2003)
2. Wildes, R.: Iris Recognition: An Emerging Biometric Technology. Proceeding of IEEE 85(9), 1348–1363 (1997)
3. Boles, W., Boashah, B.: A Human Identification Technique Using Images of the Iris and Wavelet Transform. IEEE Trans. on Signal Processing 46, 1185–1188 (1998)
4. Daugman, J.: Biometric Personal Identification System Based on iris analysis, U.S. Patent No. 5, pp. 264–271, March 1 (1994)
5. Daugman, J., Downing, C.: Epigenetic Randomness, Complexity, and Singularity of Human Iris Patterns. Proceedings of the Royal Society, Biological Sciences 268, 1737–1740 (2001)
6. Lim, S., Lee, K., Byeon, O., Kim, T.: Efficient iris recognition through improvement of feature vector and classifier. Electronics and Telecommunication Research Instuitute journal 23(2) (June 2001)
7. Noh, S., Pae, K., Lee, C., Kim, J.: Multiresolution Independent Component Analysis for Iris Identification. In: The 2002 International Technical Conference on Circuits/Systems, Computers and Communications, Phuket, Tailand (July 2002)
8. Uytterhoven, G., Roose, D., Bultheel, A.: Integer wavelet transforms using the Lifting Scheme. Proc. Circuits Systems Communications and Computers 1, 6251–6253 (1999)

Binary Data Compression Using Medial Axis Transform Algorithm

Jagadish H. Pujar[1] and Pallavi S. Gurjal[2]

[1] Faculty, Department of EEE, B V B College of Engg. & Tech., Hubli, India
jhpujar@bvb.edu
[2] Student, Department of EEE, B V B College of Engg. & Tech., Hubli, India
pallavigurjal@yahoo.co.in

Abstract. The amount of data associated with visual information is so large that its storage would require enormous capacity. Implementation of any picture archiving and communication system (PACS) requires a discussion of how to deal with the large quantities of data that must be transmitted and stored. Even before PACS, we engineers have made an attempt in developing encoding schemes that reduced the apparent size of images to reduce the demands placed on transmission and storage devices. In this work, image compression is achieved by taking the Medial axis transform of the binary image.

Keywords: Binary images, Compression, Distance transform, Medial axis transform, Redundancy.

1 Introduction

A digital image obtained by sampling and quantizing a continuous tone picture requires an enormous storage. To transmit such an image over a 28.8 Kbps modem would take almost 4 minutes. The purpose for image compression is to reduce the amount of data required for representing sampled digital images and therefore reduce the cost for storage and transmission.

1.1 Data Redundancy

A common characteristic of most images is that the neighboring pixels are correlated and therefore contain redundant information. The foremost task then is to find less correlated representation of the image. Two fundamental components of compression are redundancy and irrelevancy reduction.

- **a.** Redundancies reduction aims at removing duplication from the signal source (image/video).
- **b.** Irrelevancy reduction omits parts of the signal that will not be noticed by the signal receiver, namely the Human Visual System.

1.2 Medial Axis Transform

Medial axis transform technique is one of the image representation schemes for binary images. The medial axis transform (*MAT*) is a shape model that represents an

V. V Das et al. (Eds.): BAIP 2010, CCIS 70, pp. 417–419, 2010.

object by the set of maximal balls that are completely contained within the object. This technique not only reduces the space but also preserves the topological relationship.[3]

2 Review of Medial Axis Transform

The definition of medial axis transform was given by Blum in 1967.The medial axis transform (MAT) is a process for reducing foreground regions in a binary image to a skeletal remnant that largely preserves the extent and connectivity of the original region while throwing away most of the original foreground pixels.

2.1 Generation of Medial Axis Transform

This involves two steps via, a distance transform is taken .it can be either by chessboard distance transform method or by city block distance transform method. Based on the method we can derive the medial axis transform by applying conditions depending on the method used to obtain the distance transform. [4]

3 Implementation of Proposed Algorithm

3.1 Distance Transform Algorithm

Input: binary Image
Output: distance transformed (chessboard)

Step 1: Store the input image in two dimensional arrays.

Step 2: Perform from left to right A [I,J]=distances in increasing order.

Step 3: Perform from right to left A [I,J]=distances in decreasing order.

Step 4: compute the minimum of above two matrices and call it A1

Step 5: repeat steps 2, 3, 4 from top to bottom and minimum of this is A2

Step 6: obtain minimum of A1 and A2, which is distance transformed output.

3.2 Medial Axis Transform

Input: distance transformed (chessboard)
Output: Medial axis Transform

Step 1: compare A [I, J] with its four neighbors to obtain city block medial axis transform

Step 2: compare A [I, J] with its eight neighbors to obtain chessboard medial axis transform

4   Results and Conclusion

The result obtained with city block method has used 20 bits to represent the image which was originally with 100 bits. Thus with this we get a compression ratio of 0.2.Similarly the result obtained with chessboard distance transform used only 4 bits to represent the same input image. Thus compression ratio would be 0.04.A comparative analysis of the two methods considering their output compression ratio, we can say that compression using chessboard medial axis transform is more efficient.

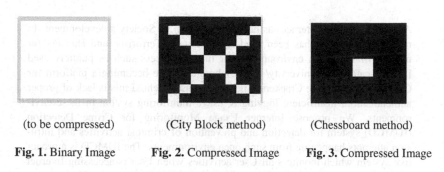

(to be compressed)   (City Block method)   (Chessboard method)

Fig. 1. Binary Image   **Fig. 2.** Compressed Image   **Fig. 3.** Compressed Image

References

1. Aswatha Kumar, M.: Medial Circle and medial Sphere representation of binary images, Ph.D.Thesis, Indian Institute of Technology, Kharagpu-721, 302 (August 1995)
2. Brandt, J.W., Jain, A., Algazi, V.R.: Medial axis representation and encoding a second documents. Journals of visual communication and image representation 2(2), 55–65 (1991)
3. Xia, Y.: Skeletonization Via the realization of the Fire Front Propagation and Extinction in Digital Binary Shapes. IEEE Transactions on pattern analysis and machine intelligence 11(10), 1076–1085
4. Y.-h. Lee, S.-J.: Horng. The chessboard distance transform and medial axis transform are interchangeable
5. Gonzalez, R.C., Woods, R.E.: Digital Image Processing. Addison Wesley, Reading (1992)
6. Gonzalez, R., Woods, R.: Digital image processing, 2nd edn., pp. 567–612. Prentice-Hall Inc., Englewood Cliffs (2002)

Internet Usage Monitoring for Crime Detection

Sandeep A. Thorat[1] and Samadhan R. Manore[2]

[1] Computer Science Department, RIT Sakharale, Sangli, India
[2] Computer Science Department, NDMVPS KADGP College, Nashik, India

Abstract. Though Internet has huge contribution to Society's development; In recent time Internet has been used by Criminals, Terrorists, and Hackers for mal-activities. Open environments for Internet access such as publicly used Internet café's and university/school laboratories are becoming a platform for Criminals and newbie Crackers. The major reason behind this is lack of proper authentication, insufficient logging & usage monitoring system in these environments. We propose Internet Usage Monitoring for Crime Detection (IUMCD) system for detection and prevention of criminal activities and intrusion attempts happening from such open environments. The IUMCD is a proactive system which monitors all User activities when User is accessing Internet from an open environment. We observed that IUMCD system is able to detect and report many different types of Criminal activities and Intrusion attempts while maintaining User's private information inaccessible to others.

1 IUMCD Architecture and Working

The IUMCD system has three major components Monitor, Agent and Central coordinator. The Monitor and Agent are deployed in an open environment (like Internet Café's, Universities) whereas Central Coordinator is deployed on publicly available web server. As shown in Figure 1 the Monitor system is deployed on proxy server which is connected to MODEM or Internet Gateway. The Internet access on other machines is via proxy server. The Agent's are present on each individual hosts in network used to access Internet.

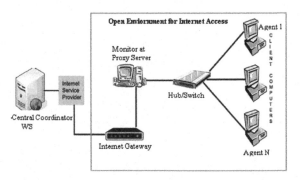

Fig. 1. IUMCD System Architecture

V. V Das et al. (Eds.): BAIP 2010, CCIS 70, pp. 420–423, 2010.
© Springer-Verlag Berlin Heidelberg 2010

1.1 IUMCD Monitor

The IUMCD Monitor authenticates the User who is interested to access Internet using an Agent machine. In open environments like Internet Café's unknown users are accessing Internet hence we do not implement password based mechanism for authentication. Rather the system accepts and keeps the User information in database for future digital forensic purpose. The User information is verified by Internet Café's owner or school/university laboratory In-charge. The detailed log record of User's Internet access is also stored in *User-Info*; it contains all details of activities initiated by the User while accessing Internet. The *User-Info* also includes the sensitivity score which shows sensitivity level of User's activities across the Internet.

$$User - info = \left\langle \begin{array}{l} UID, UserName, Address, Phone, IDCard, Photo, \\ SensitivityScore, DetailedLogR\,e\,cord \end{array} \right\rangle$$

1.2 IUMCD Agent

The Agent software which is deployed at individual hosts in network allows unknown users Internet access after proper authentication is done. For authentication the Agent takes User's information (name, address, and phone) along with scanned copy of Photo Identity proof and a photo snap using Web Camera. The Agent monitors different activities initiated by User while accessing Internet and creates User profile depending on same. The following criteria's are taken into consideration while monitoring User's activity. Each activity has a sensitivity level; depending on these activities the sensitivity level of User's profile is computed. The criteria's are -: Web sites visited by User, Malware existence on the system, E-mail Contents, Communication in Instant Messaging.

1.3 IUMCD Central Coordinator

The IUMCD Central coordinator is deployed at publicly available web server. The main functionality of Central coordinator is accepting very sensitive User profiles from the Monitors. If very sensitive information is found in the profile then the Administrator generates alerts to authorities like Police officer, Owner of Internet Café' depending on sensitivity of User profile.

2 Experimental Observations

Presently we have deployed IUMCD system in 15 open environments used for Internet access; 9 are Internet Café's and 6 are school/university laboratories. The IUMCD system is running in these places since last 6 months. The threshold and sensitivity score values set are mentioned next-, $TH_{CC} = 4$ (User profile is sent from the Monitor to Central Coordinator after crossing TH_{CC}), $sVal_{kwd} = 0.2$ (sensitivity score value for blocked keyword), $sVal_{bl} = 1$ (sensitivity score value for blocked URL), $sVal_{ml} = 1$ (sensitivity

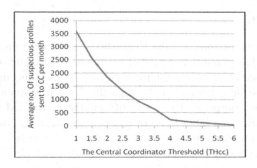

Fig. 2. Average % of mal-activities correctly detected for different values of TH_{CC}

score value for malware existence). These threshold values are fixed after experimental analysis of the system for various different values of TH_{CC}.

3   Conclusion

In this paper we purposed the IUMCD system which is helpful for prevention and detection of mal activities in open environments used to access Internet. The IUMCD system guarantees User authentication and monitoring of all User activities across the Internet; this is beneficial for digital forensics. The proposed system immediately sends alert messages to Central Coordinator on detection of suspicious activities by the User. This helps in taking immediate actions against such attempts. Thus the IUMCD system helps Internet café's owners, university laboratory administrators for prevention and early detection of criminal activities happening from their backyard.

References

[1] Qi, F., Tang, Z., Wang, G.: Attacks vs. Countermeasures of SSL Protected Trust Model. In: ICYCS 2008, pp. 1986–1991 (2008)

[2] Markendahl, J.: Analysis of Customer Relations For Public Internet Access in The Local Environment. Special Session paper The 18th Annual IEEE International Symposium on Personal, Indoor and Mobile Radio Communications, PIMRC 2007 (2007)

[3] Navajas, J.F., Viruete Navarro, E.A., Ruiz, I.M.: On-line Internet Access Estimation Tool: EQoSIM. In: EUROCON 2005, pp. 1163–1166 (2005)

[4] Doja, M.N., Kumar, N.: Image Authentication Schemes against Key-Logger Spyware. In: SNPD 2008, pp. 574–579 (2008)

[5] Do, T.D., Hui, S.C.: Web Mining for Cyber Monitoring and Filtering. In: Proceedings of the 2004 IEEE Conference on Cybernetics and Intelligent Systems, Singapore, December 1-3, pp. 399–404 (2004)

[6] Deri, L., Suin, S.: Practical network security: experiences with ntop. Computer Networks 34(6), 873–880 (2000)

[7] Chan, W.C.: Globalization of Internet Access. In: Proceedings of The IEEE International Conference on Industrial Technology, pp. 485–488 (1996)

[8] Lizcano, P.J., Azcorra, A., Solé-Pareta, J., Domingo-Pascual, J., Alvarez-Campana, M.: MEHARI: a system for analyzing the use of the internet services. Computer Networks 31(21), 2293–2307 (1999)

[9] Appenzeller, G., Roussopoulos, M., Baker, M.: User-Friendly Access Control for Public Network Ports. In: INFOCOM 1999, pp. 699–707 (1999)

Spectral Fluctuation Analysis for Audio Compression Using Adaptive Wavelet Decomposition

S. Gunasekaran and K. Revathy

Department of Computer Science,
University of Kerala,
Trivandrum, India
yesgunaa@gmail.com, revathy_srp@yahoo.com

Abstract. This paper discusses the design and implementation of a spectral fluctuation analysis based lossy audio coding scheme. We present a simple lossy audio codec, composed of an adaptive wavelet decomposition filter, a modified psycho-acoustic model, an intra-channel de-correlation block followed by quantization and coding block. The intra-channel de-correlation block does the spectral fluctuation analysis to find the successive frames found to be similar and de-correlates it and codes. A Modified psychoacoustic model with simplified masking model was designed to fit this system. The evaluation of the system was done by using European Broadcasting Union – Sound Quality Assessment Material (EBU-SQAM) stereo wave files. Experimental results show the compression ratios achieved and subjective quality evaluation report.

Keywords: EBU-SQAM: European Broadcasting Union – Sound Quality Assessment Material, NMR: Noise-to-Masking Ratio, WFB: Wavelet Filter Bank, STFT: Short-Term Fourier Transform.

1 Introduction

Lossy compression of audio aims to reduce the bandwidth or memory required to transmit or store the original audio signal, with the bit rate determined by the required fidelity for the application. The many forms of audio compression techniques differ in the trade-offs between encoder and decoder complexity, the compressed audio quality, and the amount of data compression.

In our proposed System, the audio signal was divided into overlapping frames of length 2048 samples and Hann windowed. The time-frequency analysis was done with an adaptive wavelet decomposition and reconstruction filter of Daubechies 10 wavelet. A 2048-point complex-FFT was performed to do the psychoacoustic analysis. The psychoacoustic model was simplified with the perceptual threshold for each sub-band of the wavelet filter bank. We have evaluated the spectral fluctuation analysis based audio coding system by using EBU-SQAM two channel audio files [3]. In listening experiments, this system has shown fairly good quality audio at low bit rate cases.

The rest of this paper is organized as follows. The perceptual audio codec blocks such as psycho acoustic model, bit allocation and quantization are reviewed in section

V. V Das et al. (Eds.): BAIP 2010, CCIS 70, pp. 424–429, 2010.

two. In section three, we discuss about adaptive Wavelet decomposition filter chosen for our proposed system. The spectral fluctuation analysis for intra-channel audio de-correlation is described in section four. The experiments described in section five and shows the subjective listening test scores and listeners comments. Finally, section six concludes the paper.

2 Perceptual Audio Coding

Most of the perceptual audio codecs uses a complex-FFT to decompose the input signal into spectral components. The auditory masking threshold is calculated using the signal spectrum. The transform coefficients are quantized and coded using the masking threshold. Figure.1 shows block diagram of the proposed perceptual audio codec using Wavelet sub-band filter. This chapter describes different blocks of perceptual audio codec.

Psychoacoustic Model: Auditory perception is based on a critical band analysis in the inner ear. Masking is a perceptual weakness of the ear that occurs whenever the presence of a strong audio signal makes a spectral neighbourhood of weaker audio signals within the critical band imperceptible. Scharf measured the bandwidth of critical bands as a function of their centre frequency [5]. While attempting to represent the inner ear as a discrete set of non-overlapping auditory filters, he determined that 25 critical bands were sufficient to represent the audible frequency range of the ear.

In general psychoacoustic models can be broadly divided into three categories, physiological models, excitation pattern models, and masking pattern models. Masking pattern models were found to be the most popular among the three due to the reasonable trade-off that it offers in terms of complexity and accuracy. The idea suggested in this paper is to use a simplified masking pattern model. This is achieved by using subbands that resemble the critical bands of the auditory system to optimize the masking threshold. The concept is of using a spreading function that describes the noise-masking property and compute the masking threshold in each subband of the wavelet decomposition structure.

Bit Allocation: Information bits are allocated to frequency bands such that a distortion criterion is optimized. An adaptive bit assignment is used so that the spectrum of quantization noise is shaped to be less audible than a noise spectrum

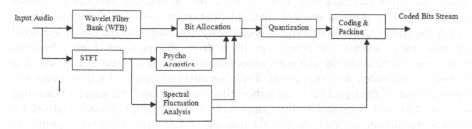

Fig. 1. Block diagram of the proposed audio coding method

evenly distributed without shaping. The process is known as spectral noise shaping, under the constraint that the total number of bits is fixed.

Two categories of distortion measures, perceptual and non-perceptual, are used to shape the audible noise. In the perceptual approach, the quantization noise spectrum is shaped in parallel with the masking threshold curve. NMR (Noise-to-Masking Ratio), among others, is an example distortion measure. The non-perceptual approach employs criteria such as the noise power above the masking threshold.

Quantization: A vector quantizer is a mapping from a vector to a finite set of points, called codewords. By exploiting the correlation among the vector components, vector quantization achieves a bit-rate performance advantage over scalar quantization, at the expense of complexity and computation power when searching for the matched codeword in a large codebook. For this reason, the Non linear vector quantizer was considered most appropriate and has been selected for our proposed system.

3 Wavelet Filter Bank

The Wavelet Filter Bank (WFB) is a filter bank that offers a great deal of flexibility in terms of the choice of the basis filter and the decomposition tree structure. Additionally, the WFB offers a variety of ways of handling boundary artifacts in the context of block processing.

In our proposed system the WFB was based on a fixed 29-band critical band resolution tree structure and an adaptive basis filter. The filter selection was done by computing the bitrate required for perceptual transparency with each filter from a library of basis filters, and choosing the filter that provided the best performance. The filter library was limited to wavelets with the maximum number of vanishing moments. Filters with the maximum number of vanishing moments were indicated as being "near optimal" among different classes of filters. Boundary artifacts were minimized by dividing the audio signal into overlapping frames, weighted by a hanning window with an overlap of 128 samples.

4 Spectral Fluctuation Analysis

For a given time instance, removing intra-channel redundancy would result in a significant bandwidth reduction. This can be done via Spectral fluctuation analysis based redundancy removal method. Spectral fluctuation analysis is to measure how rapidly the power spectrum of a signal is changing, by comparing the power spectrum for one frame against the power spectrum from the previous frame. Spectral fluctuation can be analyzed with a magnitude-based method, a phase-deviation-based method or a complex domain method. These methods make use of a time-frequency representation of the signal based on a short time Fourier transform using a Hamming window. The idea suggested in this paper is to use a complex domain method for spectral fluctuation analysis. Amplitude and phase has been considered jointly to analyse the behaviour by calculating the expected amplitude and phase of the current frame, based on the previous frame.

5 System Implementation

In our proposed system, the elimination of data redundancy is obtained by replacing wavelet filter bank sub-band coefficients with zeros when the spectral fluctuation for that bark-band falls below the specified threshold. Such zeroed spectral coefficients of that bark-band can be reconstructed in the decoder side using the respective values from the previously decoded data frame. The threshold was computed using an iterative method.

The proposed system can be briefly described by the following steps.

a) For the input vector x, the spectral domain coefficients X are obtained using the STFT.
b) A Complex Spectral Fluctuation analysis (CSF) module defines the status of each bark-band/frame as was defined in the previous paragraph.
c) The psychoacoustic masking function is estimated according to the decision taken in step-b, in order to define the allocation of bits and the noise shaping.
d) A non-linear vector quantizer is used to map the wavelet sub-band coefficients to the corresponding quantized data.
e) The quantized values are coded and the header data is included and transmitted to the receiver.

The decoder has a simpler structure compared to the encoder. One bit flag per bark-band is transmitted as side information allows the discrimination of the reconstruction type of the processed bark-band.

6 Experiments and Results

We have implemented the proposed coder in Matlab. The source code was written for flexible experimentation and not optimized for execution speed. The basic audio coding blocks including the psychoacoustic model, filter bank (Wavelet), quantization and coding, are still adopted. Furthermore, an intra-channel redundancy removal block was added to construct the proposed audio codec. Two kinds of experimental results are shown in this section. They are results measured by compression ratio achieved and results measured in subjective metric, i.e. listening test score. Table-1 shows the experimental results of compression ratio achieved for EBU-SQAM test material using the proposed audio coding method.

Subjective evaluation is the ultimate method for assessing the quality of audio signals. In order to confirm the advantage of the proposed algorithm, a formal subjective listening test was conducted in an audio lab to compare the coding performance of the proposed audio coding algorithm. Expert group of listeners participated in the listening test.

Table 1. Results: Compression Achieved

S.No	EBU-SQAM Stream Name	Compression Achieved
1	bass47_11.wav	10.08
2	gspi35_11.wav	32.22
3	gspi35_21.wav	21.19
4	harp40_11.wav	10.51
5	horn23_21.wav	13.24
6	quar48_11.wav	7.65
7	sopr44_11.wav	12.78
8	trpt21_21.wav	13.06
9	vioo10_21.wav	7.88
	Overall	**14.29**

Table 2. Results: Subjective Listening test

S.No	Stream Name	Avg Listener Score	Listener's Comments
1	bass47_11.wav	4	
2	gspi35_11.wav	3.3	musical noise present
3	gspi35_21.wav	3.8	residual noise
4	harp40_11.wav	4.2	static towards the end
5	horn23_21.wav	4.5	
6	quar48_11.wav	4	slight distortion
7	sopr44_11.wav	4.2	slight distortion
8	trpt21_21.wav	3.8	transients affected
9	vioo10_21.wav	3.9	harmonic distortion
	Overall	**3.96**	

During the Listening test, for each test sound clips, subjects listened to two versions of the same sound clips, i.e. the original one followed by the processed one, subjects were allowed to listen to these files as many times as possible until they were comfortable to give scores to the two processed sound files for each test material. The five-grade impairment scale was adopted in the grading procedure and utilized for final data analysis. Audio files selected for listening test only contains short durations, i.e. 20 to 30 seconds long. Table-2 shows the score given to each test material coded during the listening test for EBU-SQAM audio materials.

7 Conclusion and Future Work

The proposed spectral fluctuation based audio coding method aims at lowering the bitrate requirements of wavelet-based perceptual audio coders, by reducing the perceptual entropy of such data. This reduction is achieved by utilizing the temporal stationarity of audio signals and by detecting and coding only the audible differences between data frames. The decoding process of our method employs the subband coefficients from the previous reference frames, kept in a buffer, in order to reconstruct frames of small perceptual significance. According to the tests conducted, it was found that the proposed method achieved an average improvement of approximately 14.3% in audio data compression in addition to existing techniques. These results are encouraging, given that the proposed method introduces a novel approach in the utilization of the signal's stationarity and can be further improved in terms of both compression gain and signal quality. Additional work must be undertaken to improve the proposed method, mainly with respect to the optimal selection of bark-bands for the choice of subband coefficient substitution in the stationary segments of the audio signals. In this way, it may be possible to reduce the overall coding error rate (audible artifacts), using the well-established perceptual criteria.

References

1. Sinha, D., Tewfik, A.: Low Bit Rate Transparent Audio Compression using Adapted Wavelets. IEEE Trans. ASSP 41(12) (December 1993)
2. Srinivasan, P., Jamieson, L.H.: High Quality Audio Compression Using an Adaptive Wavelet Packet Decomposition and Psychoacoustic Modeling. IEEE Transactions on Signal Processing 46(4) (April 1998)
3. European Broadcasting Union – Tech 3253 - SQAM Sound Quality Assessment Material, http://www.ebu.ch/en/technical/publications/tech3000_series/tech3253/index.php
4. Klapuri, A.: Sound onset detection by applying psychoacoustic knowledge. In: Proc. IEEE Int. Conf. Acoust., Speech, and Sig. Proc., Phoenix, Arizona (1999)
5. Scharf, B.: Critical bands. In: Tobias, J. (ed.) Foundations of Modern Auditory Theory. Academic Press, London (1970)
6. Strang, G., Nguyen, T.: Wavelets and Filter banks. Wellesley-Cambridge, Wellesley (1996)
7. Sodagar, I., Nayebi, K., Barnwell, T.: Time-varying filter banks and wavelets. IEEE Trans. Signal Processing 42, 2983–2996 (1994)
8. Karam, J., Saad, R.: The Effect of Different compression schemes on speech signals. International Journal of Biomedical Sciences 1(4), 230–234
9. International Telecommunication Union, Method for Objective Measurements of Perceived Audio Quality, ITU-R Recommendation BS.1387 (July 1999)
10. ISO/IEC JTC1/SC29/WG11 14496-3 (1997)
11. Gersho, A., Gray, R.: Vector Quantization and Signal Compression. Kluwer Academic Publishers, Dordrecht (1992)

Defending against Node Misbehavior to Discover Secure Route in OLSR

Sanjeev Rana and Anil Kapil

[1] Assoc. Professor, Computer Engineering Department, M. M. Engineering College,
M. M. University, Ambala, India
sanjeevrana@rediffmail.com
[2] Professor, M.M. Institute of Computer Technology and Business Management,
M. M. University, Ambala, India
anil_kdk@yahoo.com

Abstract. OLSR is one of the efficient routing protocols for MANETs, which is identified by IETF and assumes that all nodes are trusted. However, the OLSR is known to be vulnerable to various kinds of malicious attacks in hostile environment. In this paper, we propose a new security enhancement mechanism by adding security features to the existing the OLSR protocol. The security features included are based on authentication checks of information injected into the network, mutual authentication between two nodes as well as more advanced techniques such as authentic route confirmation ticket which regulates the behavior of nodes to prevent from internal attacks i.e. node misbehavior attack. The main contribution of our approach is to allow only legitimate nodes to participate to establish secure route rather than trying to detect adversary nodes after their involvement in the routing protocol.

Keywords: Authentication, MANETs, OLSR, Security.

1 Introduction

Currently OLSR [1] is known to be vulnerable to various kinds of internal and external attacks i.e. identity spoofing, link spoofing, replay attacks, wormhole attacks. Recently, several researches have appeared [2-8] in order to counter against these kinds of attacks. In [2], a fully distributed certificate authority based on threshold cryptography is proposed. In [3],[4] the uses of timestamps are proposed in order to counter against replay attacks. The authors of [5] also proposed the use of signature to ensure authentication in order to prevent identity spoofing attacks. In [6], [7], the author proposed a simple mechanism to detect the link withholding and misrelay launched by MPR nodes based on overhearing of traffic generated by one-hop neighbors. The authors of [8] proposed intrusion detection scheme to detect the misbehavior in OLSR on intrinsic properties of OLSR messages. However, their approach could not detect the link spoofing attack where a malicious node advertises fake links in HELLO message. Although they can solve some of the problems, still the issues of link spoofing, DoS, wormhole attacks are not totally solved. In this paper, we propose a new security enhancement mechanism allow only legitimate

V. V Das et al. (Eds.): BAIP 2010, CCIS 70, pp. 430–436, 2010.
© Springer-Verlag Berlin Heidelberg 2010

nodes to participate to establish secure route rather than trying to detect adversary nodes after their involvement in the routing protocol.

2 The Proposed Security Enhancement Mechanism

The Security Enhancement Mechanism consists of number of modules which are designed to address various internal and external threats in the network. We are motivated by secure neighbor's discovery mechanism for mutual authentication. The misbehaviors and false link information generated by compromised node can be prevented using the authentic route confirmation module. An offline certification authority is assumed to distribute keys and certificates in the network.

2.1 Message Authentication

There are two types of fields in the control messages that is mutable and non-mutable. Thus, different criteria will be used to ensure the authentication and integrity of mutable and non-mutable fields of control message.

- For non-mutable field, we use digital signature using hash function
- For mutable field, hash chaining method will be used

Sender first calculates the message digest of all non-mutable fields only. Then sender signed the message digest using its private key. Now, the signed message digest will be attached with the control message. Receivers can verify the authentication of the message with signer's public key. For mutable field, we use the hash chain concept to ensure about integrity and authentication of message by adding some extra fields Nonce, HASH_HOP in the OLSR packet. When a node generates a new control packet, it performs the following steps:

Step 1: Generates a large random number say 'Nonce'.
Step 2: Calculate the hash on 'Nonce' as many times as the value of TTL.

$Hash \_ Hop = H^{TTL} (Nonce)$

Step 3: Calculate the Signature of all non-mutable fields as described earlier:

$Signature = sign (H (All \_ non \_ mutable \_ Attributes))$

Every time a node receives an OLSR packet, it performs following operation:

Step 1: First, we verify about mutable fields that $H^{TTL - HC} (Nonce) = Hash \_ Hop$

If value does not match then discard the packets. Second, verify the packet's signature for non-mutable fields, if it does not match then again discard the packets.
Step 2: If both steps are successful, then perform following operation:

$TTL=TTL-1 \quad HC=HC+1 \quad Nonce = H (Nonce)$.

Thus, this mechanism provide source authentication and protect integrity of packets during transmission and enable receiver to validate the received packets.

2.2 Mutual Authentication

We propose a simple and efficient algorithm to authenticate two nodes each other.

Step 1: Node A introduces itself to node B using its certificate. $A \rightarrow B : C_A$

Step 2: Node B introduces itself to Node A and also sends a challenge (Nonce) signed using public key K_A^+ of Node A. $B \rightarrow A : C_B \parallel \{N_B\} K_A^+$

Step 3: Node A receives the above message and gets N_B, Node A sends its challenge N_A to Node B and also add the reply of B challenge. $A \rightarrow B : \{N_A, N_B\} K_B^+$

Step 4: Node B decrypt the message, N_B shows that this message is the response of previous message and also verify that this message is originated by Node A. Node B prepares the response of Challenge of Node A. $B \rightarrow A : (N_A) K_A^+$ Node A will decrypt the message and ensure that this message is the response of previous challenge and it is originated from Node B.

2.3 Authentic Route Confirmation

The basic idea of authentic route confirmation module is that a node must provide a piece of information which regulates its behavior. This requirement can be achieved using digital signature of link information between two nodes. First, two nodes verify each other identity using mutual authentication process, then, they generate a authentic route confirmation ticket (ARCT) in the format of $[ID_A, ID_B, C_B, \{ID_A \parallel T_1\} K_B^-]$. This ticket can be read as "Node A ensures that it can route to Node B and Node B approves the claim of node A". Thus, a remote node is able to verify the claim of node A by evaluating the ticket of node A.

2.4 Timestamp Exchange Mechanism

A common problem in distributed systems with non-secure communication channels is that, even assuming a signature is checked, replay of previously transmitted messages is possible by an intruder Thus, we proposed a new timestamp exchange protocol with three steps which is derived with a slight variation over the Needham-Schroeder public key protocol [9] as follows.

Step 1: At time t_0 node A send message to node B.

$$A \rightarrow B : \{A \parallel T_A(t_0)\} K_A^-$$

Step 2: At time $t_1 > t_0$, node B has received the message from node A and sends a reply to node A. $B \rightarrow A : \{B \parallel T_B(t_1) \parallel A \parallel T_A(t_0)\} K_B^-$

Step 3: At time $t_2 > t_1$, node A has received the message from node B and sends a reply to node A. $A \rightarrow B : \{A \parallel T_A(t_2) \parallel B \parallel T_B(t_1)\} K_A^-$. Thus, node A and node B have knowledge about relatively recent values of each other respective timestamps.

3 OLSR with Security Enhancement Mechanism

OLSR reduces the control traffic overhead by using Multipoint Relays (MPR). A MPR is a node's one-hop neighbor which has been chosen to forward packets. Instead of pure flooding of the network, packets are forwarded by a node's MPR. OLSR uses

HELLO and Topology Control (TC) messages to discover and then disseminate link state information throughout the network. Individual nodes use this topology information to compute next hop destination for all nodes in the network using shortest hop forwarding paths. Our mechanism extended the HELLO and TC messages to carry additional information to make the route secure.

1. Hello message Extension
2. TC message Extension

3.1 HELLO Message Extension

In OLSR, many attacks, i.e. wormhole attack, occurs due to wrong selection of two-hop neighbors. Thus, two-hop neighbors selection or MPR set selection must be done after mutual authentication and authentic route confirmation ticket process between two nodes. This will ensure that only legitimates or trusted nodes will be involved during secure route establishment. The format of modified HELLO message with extension is shown in figure 1. After the standard message header, digital signature that guards the entire message (non-mutable attribute). The HASH_HOP, Nonce fields are included to guard mutable fields in the message. Timestamp is included in the message to foil replay attacks. Different information may be appended after each neighbor interface address, depending on the authentication state that is indicated by the stat field. The Option field indicates what contents are included: this can be handshake, identity certificate or ARCT. If node A wishes to authenticate node B then it follows all the steps of mutual authentication between two nodes as shown in figure 2.

Fig. 1. HELLO Message Extension Format   Fig. 2. TC Message Extension Format

After nodes authentication, they exchange an ARCT as the proof of their relationship. ARCT is appended in the HELLO message. Both nodes verify the link status by validating their ARCTs. MPR selection will be calculated after verification success.

3.2 TC Message Extension

In security enhancement mechanism, TC messages will also carry node identity certificate and authenticate route confirmation ticket. The format of TC extension message is shown in figure2 is similar to HELLO messages but with different contents of the authentication field. A remote node performs the following steps to construct a secure routing table by receiving the TC message with ARCTs.

Step 1: Receiver authenticates the mutable and non-mutable fields. The message will be discarded if the authentication fails.

Step 2: Check the validity of each ARCT, the neighbor who is confirmed to have authentic ink to the originator will be marked as pending in the topology table. This is because the originator itself may not be reachable. The neighbor with invalid ARCT will be discarded.

Step 3: If the TC message originator address is found in the routing table, all verified neighbors in the TC message will be added in the routing table otherwise they must wait till originator is reachable.

Step 4: Each reachable address has a valid time in the topology map, which is determined by the ARCT. The valid time must be updated for every new ARCT received. If the valid time for an address is expired, the node is considered unreachable and will be removed from the routing table.

4 Performance Evaluation of OLSR with Security Enhancement Mechanism

In this section, we evaluate security aspects of our proposed security enhancement mechanism compared to standard OLSR protocol. The following attacks with their countermeasures are addressed in next section.

4.1 Security Analysis

Incorrect Hello message generation: A misbehaving node X may send hello messages on behalf of node C as shown in figure3. Subsequently, node A and node B may announce reachability to node C through their HELLO and TC messages. Furthermore, Node X may choose MPRs from among its neighbors, signaling this selection while pretending to have the identity of node C. therefore, the chosen MPRs will advertise in their TC messages that they provide a last-hop to node C. Conflicting routes to node C, with possible connectivity loss, may result from this. Our mechanism can foil this attack using authentic route confirmation module. ARCT thwarts such misbehavior by requesting timestamped signature from all the neighbors, which requires a node to be in contact with advertised neighbors to acquire such information.

Message Modification: A malicious node may modify the passed-on messages and cause connectivity lost and conflicting routes. For example, the advertised neighbor sequence number attack , where an attacker can modify the ANSN field of the TC messages to a large value, so that any further message from the same originator will be dropped due to the loop free mechanism. Our security enhancement mechanism can detect any change occur in the messages during transmission and ensure the message integrity because of digital signature attached in the messages for non-mutable fields and hash chaining for mutable fields.

Wormhole Attack: The wormhole attack is quite severe, and consists in recording traffic from one region of the network and replaying it "as is" in a different region.

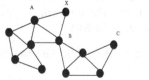

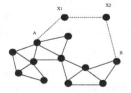

Fig. 3. Node X sends HELLO messages pretending to be node C   **Fig. 4.** A. wormhole created by intruder node X   **Fig. 5.** A wormhole created by two colluding nodes X1 & X2

An extraneous A—B link can be artificially created by an intruder node X by wormholing control messages between A and B as shown in figure4 and figure5. The created link is at mercy of the attacker. Our security enhancement mechanism prevent from wormhole attack using mutual authentication and ARCT. Node A can detect either node B is actually one-hop neighbor or artificially created neighbor, by an intruder using wormhole attack, using ARCT. Node A demand ARCT from Node B which was assumed to be created earlier after the mutual authentication process and also signed by node A private key. As node B is not a genuine one-hop neighbor, so it cannot produce ARCT to node A. thus, node A can detect this is not an authentic one-hop neighbor and will not add it in its one-hop neighbor list.

Denial of Service Attack (DoS): An attacker could for instance transmit thousand of timestamp exchange challenge messages within a short period of time, all aimed at the same host. This would cause the receiving host to generate and transmit signed replies to all the challenges. This DoS attack can be prevented with the uses of timers. New timers will be started for every first challenge generated by different nodes. After than, any new received challenge from the same host, while the timer has not timed out, are discarded. Further, due to signing of the challenge messages, an attacker cannot spoof the sender address of challenge messages.

MPR selector isolation: If a node is selected by its neighbour as MPR, this node is responsible for advertising MPR selector's information and forwarding message to this neighbour. However, a malicious node may isolate its MPR selector neighbour by not including it in the control messages. Such violation can be regulated with the slight variation in ARCT. After two nodes establish connection, they exchange route confirmation ticket. Instead signing link status itself, the node signs for all neighbors of the other node i.e. include all identity addresses from the other node's HELLO messages. Under this rule, a node must include all connected neighbors addresses in its control message to assure the ARCT can be verified properly.

5 Conclusions

In this paper, we propose a security mechanism which not only defend external attack but also prevent many internal attacks, i.e. wormhole attack, link spoofing, by regulating the behavior of internal nodes using ARCTs. We have applied the proposed security mechanism to the OLSR routing protocol, which ensures secure routing using only the routes which include verified nodes. Within the authentic route confirmation and key distribution module, there is currently a substantial amount of overhead added, which may result in scalability problem in large and dense network environments. In future work, we plan to search for signature schemes that can reduce the overhead and computation time.

References

[1] Clausen, T., Jacquet, P. (eds.): Optimized Link State Routing protocol (OLSR), RFC 3626, Experimental (October 2003)
[2] Dhillon, D., Randhawa, T.S., Wang, M., Lamont, L.: Implementing a fully distributed certificate authority in an OLSR MANET. In: IEEE WCNC 2004, Atlanta, Georgia, USA, pp. 1976–1986 (2003)

[3] Adjih, C., Raffo, D., Muhlethaler, P.: Attack against OLSR: Distributed Key Management for security. In: 2nd OLSR interop/ Workshop, France, July 28-29 (2005)

[4] Raffo, D.: Security Schemes for OLSR protocol in Ad hoc Network, Ph.D thesis, Universite Paris (2005)

[5] Kannhavong, B., Nakayama, H., Kato, N., Jamalipour, A., Nemoto, Y.: Analysis of Node Isolation Attack against OLSR-based Mobile Ad Hoc Network. In: 7th International Symposium on Computer Networks (ISCN), Istabul, Turkey, June 2006, pp. 30–35 (2006)

[6] Dhillon, D., Zhu, J., Richards, J., Randhawa, T.: Implementation and Evaluation of an IDS to safeguard OLSR integrity in MANETs. In: IWCMC 2006 (2006)

[7] Adjih, C., Raffo, D., Muhlethaler, P.: Attack against OLSR: Distributed Key Management for security. In: 2nd OLSR interop/ Workshop, France, July 28-29 (2005)

[8] Wang, M., Lamont, L., Mason, P., Gorlatova, M.: An Effective Intrusion Detection approach for OLSR MANET protocol. In: 1st IEEE ICNP workshop on Secure Network Protocols, NPSec 2005 (2005)

[9] Needham, R.M., Schroeder, M.D.: Using Encryption for Authentication in Large Networks of Computers. Communication of the ACM 21(12), 993–999 (1978)

SIMBIC: SIMilarity Based BIClustering of Expression Data

J. Bagyamani[1] and K. Thangavel[2]

[1] Department of Computer Science, Government Arts College, Dharmapuri, 636 705,
TamilNadu, India
bagya.gac@gmail.com
[2] Department of Computer Science, Periyar University, Salem, 636 011,
TamilNadu, India
drktvelu@yahoo.com

Abstract. With the advent of the "Age of Genomics", generation, accumulation and analysis of gene expression datasets that contain expression levels of thousands of genes across different experimental conditions is emerging. Analysis of gene expression data is used in many areas including drug discovery and clinical applications. This proposed biclustering algorithm extracts maximum similarity bicluster using multiple node deletion method after applying feature selection. Experimental results show the effectiveness of the proposed algorithm.

Keywords: Data mining, gene expression data, biclustering, feature selection, multiple node deletion.

1 Introduction

Biclustering is a data mining technique which allows simultaneous clustering of rows and columns of a matrix. These biclusters provide hidden information about the main biological processes associated to various physiological states. Gene expression is the conversion of information encoded in a gene. It plays a vital role in cell differentiation, development and pathological behavior. They serve as valuable clues to understand the genetic behaviors. A cluster is a set of objects with similar values over the entire set of attributes whereas a bicluster can be composed of objects that are similar over only a subset of attributes.

This paper is organized as follows: Section 2 details the background study and related works. Section 3 explains the proposed algorithm. Section 4 provides the experimental analysis and conclusion is presented in Section 5.

2 Background

Biclusters were identified using the following methods of biclustering algorithms [5]. Getz et al., (2000)[2] used Iterative Row and Column Method in Coupled Two-Way Clustering (CTWC). Hartigan JA (1972)[3] identified biclusters based on Divide and Conquer method. Cheng and Church (2000)[1] and Liu (2007)[4] in Randomized

V. V Das et al. (Eds.): BAIP 2010, CCIS 70, pp. 437–441, 2010.
© Springer-Verlag Berlin Heidelberg 2010

Maximum Similarity Bicluster Extension (RMSBE) applied greedy iterative search methods that optimizes the given criteria namely Mean Squared Residue (MSR) score and similarity score of a bicluster respectively. Ron Shamir (2005) proposed Statistical-Algorithmic Method for Bicluster Analysis (SAMBA) based on exhaustive bicluster enumeration method.

2.1 Problem Statement

A gene expression matrix A of size m x n where each element a_{ij} represents the expression level of gene 'i' under condition 'j' is considered. Biclustering identification is to find $A_{IJ} = (I ; J)$ denotes the sub-matrix A_{IJ} of A that contains only the elements a_{ij} belonging to the sub-matrix with set of rows I and set of columns J.

3   Proposed Work

3.1 Feature Selection

In order to reduce the dimensionality of the data, feature selection for unsupervised data by Varshavsky [6], was applied and features were sorted based on entropy value. Let s_j be the singular values of the matrix A, N, the total number of attributes and E denote dataset entropy defined by

$$E = \frac{1}{\log N} * \sum_{j=1}^{j=N} V_j \log(V_j) \qquad \text{where } V_j = \frac{s_j^2}{\sum_k s_k^2} \qquad (1)$$

This entropy varies between 0 and 1. Features were sorted based on entropy values and N/2 features were selected.

3.2 Reference Genes and Reference Conditions

Let i* which has specific functional importance in the Gene Ontology (GO) be a reference gene and j* chosen from the selected 'N/2' features of the expression data be the reference condition. Similarity score between genes and similarity score for a bicluster were calculated as in Liu[4]. The parameters, minimum number of rows (m_r) and minimum number of conditions (m_c) specify the stopping criteria.

SIMBIC Algorithm : (*Constant bicluster*)

Input:1. Gene expression matrix A(I, J).
    2. Parameters $\alpha = 0.2$, $\beta = 0.2$, $\gamma = 0.9$, $m_r = 1$, $m_c = 1$.
    3. Reference gene i* and reference condition j*.

Output: a significant bicluster.
    1. Consider A(I, J) as a bicluster and compute S(I, J) as in Liu [4].
    2. Do steps 3 to 7   for all rows 'i' and n/2 columns 'j' until $m_r <= 1$ & $m_c <= 1$.
    3. Compute sim-row $S(i, J) = \sum_{j \in J} s_{ij}$ and sim-col $S(I, j) = \sum_{i \in I} s_{ij}$.
    4. Compute min S(i, J) and min S(I, j) and compute min { min(S(i, J') , min S(I', j)}.

5. If this minimum is min(S(i, J')) remove **all** those rows corresponding to the minimum from A(I,J) to get A(I',J) else remove **all** those columns corresponding to the minimum from A(I, J) to get A(I, J').

6. Update A(I, J) = A(I', J) or A(I, J) = A(I, J') and S(I, J) = S(I', J) or S(I, J) = S(I, J').

7. Compute the similarity of bicluster.

8. Extract the bicluster with maximum similarity.

Additive biclusters were identified by applying constant bicluster method to B(I, J) = $[b_{ij}]$, where b_{ij} = aij - (a_{ij*} - a_{i*j*}). An O*ptimal bicluster* with more number of rows can be arrived by applying node addition algorithm which includes all rows 'i' that satisfy $s(i,J') \geq \gamma |J'|$.

4 Experimental Analysis

4.1 Performance of the Proposed Algorithm

The efficiency of the proposed algorithm was tested for the benchmark datasets (i)Yeast Saccharomyces Cerevisiae dataset (ii) Breast cancer dataset (iii) Colon cancer dataset. The performance of the algorithm was validated using the MSR and the Average Correlation Variation (ACV). For each bicluster, MSR and ACV were computed using

$$MSR = (1/ m_*n) * \Sigma \Sigma (r_{ij})^2 \qquad (2)$$

where r_{ij} = a_{ij} - μ_{ik} - μ_{jk} + μ_k, μ_{ik} is the row mean, μ_{jk} is the column mean and μ_k is the mean of the bicluster and

$$ACV = max \left\{ \frac{\sum_{i=1}^m \sum_{j=1}^m |crow_{ij}| - m}{m^2 - m}, \frac{\sum_{i=1}^n \sum_{j=1}^n |ccol_{pq}| - n}{n^2 - n} \right\} \qquad (3)$$

where $crow_{ij}$ is the correlation coefficient between rows i and j and $ccol_{pq}$ is the correlation coefficient between columns p and q. ACV approaching 1 denote a significant bicluster.

4.2 Merits of SIMBIC over RMSBE

SIMBIC extracts bicluster in which similarity and size of bicluster was maintained as in RMSBE.

RMSBE	SIMBIC
1. Every gene was considered as a reference gene i*.	1. Only functionally important genes were reference genes.
2. Every condition was considered as a reference column j*.	2. Only selected (N/2) conditions were set as reference column j*.
3. Number of iterations is m+n-2.	3. Number of iterations is very less.
4. Use of Single Node Deletion method.	4. Use of Multiple Node Deletion method.
5. More time to required to extract one bicluster.	5. Less time required to extract one bicluster.

Table 1. Performance Analysis

i*	j*	RMSBE			SIMBIC		
		No. of Iterations	Time in seconds	Size of bicluster	No. of Iterations	Time in seconds	Size of bicluster
288	14	2899	105.8	19 x 14	**251**	4.5	19 x 14
133	10	2899	106.2	29 x 15	**217**	3.7	29 x 15
374	1	2899	105.7	27 x 16	**298**	5.2	27 x 16
93	16	2899	105.7	13 x 11	**159**	3.2	13 x 11

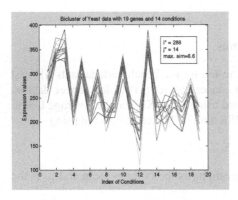

Fig.1. Bicluster plot of yeast data   **Fig. 2.** Bicluster plot of breast cancer data

Comparison of number of iterations and the time required for identifying a maximum similarity bicluster for corresponding i* and j* of Yeast Saccharomyces Cerevisiae dataset was represented in Table 1.

Bicluster of Yeast dataset with i* chosen as 288 (gene ID 'YBR198C' which has the functional importance of SLIK (SAGA like) complex) and j*=14 was shown in Fig. 1. This maximum similarity bicluster has MSR 5.3994e+004 and ACV 0.9224. Bicluster of breast cancer data with 26 genes and 25 conditions with MSR 6.7765e+005 and ACV 0.7180 was shown in Fig. 2. It was also observed that the maximum similarity bicluster for a specific reference gene (i*) occurs in any of the (N/2) selected features j*.

5 Conclusion

This proposed algorithm identifies maximum similarity biclusters of gene expression data. The multiple node deletion method based on similarity score applied on the extracted features makes the algorithm more efficient.

Acknowledgment. The first author acknowledges the *UGC, SERO, Hyderabad* to carry out this research under FIP. The second author acknowledges the *UGC, New Delhi* for financial assistance under major research project grant No. F-34-105/2008.

References

[1] Cheng, Y., Church, G.M.: Biclustering of expression data. In: Proceedings of 8th International Conference on Intelligent Systems for Molecular Biology, ISMB 2000 Proceedings, pp. 93–103 (2000)

[2] Getz, G., Levine, E., Domany, E.: Coupled two-way clustering analysis of gene microarray data. Proceedings of the Natural Academy of Sciences USA 97(22), 12079–12084 (2000)

[3] Hartigan, J.A.: Direct clustering of a data matrix. Journal of the American Statistical Association Statistical Assoc. (JASA) 67(337), 123–129 (1972)

[4] Liu, X., Liu, L.W.X.: Computing maximum similarity biclusters of gene expression data. Bioinformatics 23(1), 50–56 (2007)

[5] Madeira, S.C., Oliveira, A.L.: Biclustering algorithms for biological data analysis: a survey. IEEE/ACM Transactions on Computational Biology and Bioinformatics 1(1), 24–45 (2004)

[6] Varshavsky, R., Gottlieb, A., Linial, M., Horn, D.: Novel Unsupervised Feature Filtering of Biological Data. Bioinformatics 22(14), 507–513 (2006)

An Efficient and Cost Effective Multilayer Peer to Peer Distributed Database Model for Mobile E-Polling System

Neera Batra and A.K. Kapil

[1] Dept. of Computer Science & Engineering,
M.M. University Campus, Mullana, Distt. Ambala, Haryana, India 133203
batraneera1@gmail.com
[2] Institute of computer technology & Business Management, M.M. Engineering College,
Mullana-133203, Haryana, India
anil_kdk@yahoo.com

Abstract. At present, there are two ways of vote casting: either through Paper-Ballot system or through Electronic Voting Machine (EVM). Both these methods do not ensure integrity, secrecy, accuracy, authentication and flexibility. We proposed a network efficient, cost effective multilayer peer to peer distributed model for E-Polling System which resolves the above mentioned problems in an effective way.

Keywords: E-Polling, mobile booths, multilayer, peer to peer, distributed database.

1 Introduction

Various models proposed for electronic voting system [3], [2] can be categorized under two broad names [4]. One is electronic voting (e-Voting), which is less complex but voters are limited to polling stations only. Second is internet voting, which is voting on internet without limiting the people to the polling stations but it is more complex, needs higher security. In this paper, we proposed an architecture which combines the plus points of both the architectures and reduces the consumption of resources like disk space and communication cost, traffic bottlenecks etc.

1.1 Architecture Overview

We have a multilayer system consisting of peer systems arranged logically in hierarchical fashion (as shown in Fig. 1) providing the system its scalability and communication efficiency. Top layer contains the main database containing information of voters and of candidates who will compete in the elections. At the time of elections, a copy of these databases is divided into fragments and transferred to the state servers at layer 2 which are linked together through a dedicated communication channel thus giving rise to a virtual or 'hybrid' peer to peer system where each state server maintains the data related to that particular state. State servers further fragment the copies of their databases and send them to district servers at layer 4. Now these district

V.V Das et al. (Eds.): BAIP 2010, CCIS 70, pp. 442–445, 2010.
© Springer-Verlag Berlin Heidelberg 2010

servers send all data to the cluster heads of the clusters connected to them at layer 5. These cluster heads then transfer the data to all the clients active in their clusters. An intermediate layer is maintained between the state level and district level layer i.e. state cache server layer which maintains two index tables: First index table contains information about location of the databases maintained at each state. Second index table contains the information about location of database of each district which comes under that state. This voting system is very reliable, flexible and scalable with the assumption that it is failure free. In fig. 1, notions used are as: *MS*-Main server BS-Backup server *SS*-State server *CS*-Cache server DS-District server *CH*-Cluster head *DMB*-District mobile booth *DFB*-District fixed booth *VMB*-Village mobile booth *VFB*-Village fixed booth.

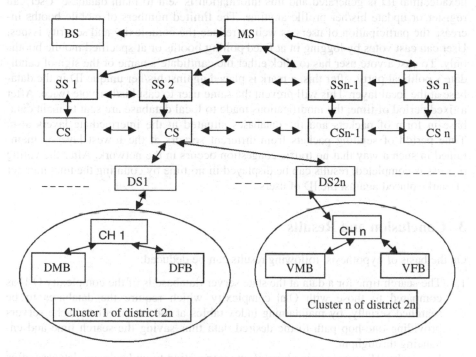

Fig. 1. Architecture of proposed model

COUNTRY CODE	STATE CODE	DISTRICT CODE	VILLAGE CODE	PERSONAL CODE	SOURCE OF DATA
1-256	1-256	1-256	1-256	1-268435456	MAXIMUM RANGE
1A	C4	D3	B6	90A54D3	HEXADECIMAL ID
8 BIT	8 BIT	8 BIT	8 BIT	28 BIT	SIZE OF ID

Fig. 2. Format of 15-digit hexadecimal ID

2 ID Scheme and Its Working

In this proposed architecture, each layer maintains its own system ID. Each user has 15-digit Hexadecimal ID. In this format(fig. 2) ,first 2-digit represent a country code, next 2-digit for state, next 2-digit for district, next 2-digit for village and last 7-digits for representing the user's personal ID. The format enables to identify uniquely a total population of 268435456 in village or in district. Thus, by using this assumption more than 10^{12} million users can be uniquely identified, which is quite a good assumption to manage a whole world population. This unique ID is made available to each layer in the system. To get the unique 15-digits hexadecimal ID, every user has to fill online form at district level or village level. After submission of the form, unique hexadecimal ID is generated and this information is sent to main database. User can register or update his/her profile anytime. The limited numbers of mobile booths increase the participation of users as well as reduce the complexity and security issues. User can cast votes by logging in at fixed polling booths or at specified mobile booths only. To cast a vote user has to click either the candidate's name or the sign of candidate's political party, after this, a mark is placed against his/her unique ID in the database at the local layer. This will prevent the same user to cast his/her vote twice. After a fixed period of time, the modifications made to local database are sent to main database in form of packets and the databases situated at the intermediate layers also. Time period of sending packets from different servers at the lowest layer is maintained in such a way that no traffic congestion occurs in the network. After the voting process is completed, results can be displayed in no time by counting the total number of marks placed against the ID of users..

3 Conclusion and Results

On the basis of hypothesis, following results can be deduced:

1. The search time for a data at the state server database is of the complexity $O|1|$ as compared to those with $O|n|$ complexity which require the databases to be searched serially, by maintaining index tables at the intermediate cache servers providing one-hop path to the desired data thus saving the search time and enhancing throughput.

2. If we take PT as processing time of one transaction to update main database after fixed intervals.

$$PT = UT + AT + WT \tag{1}$$

Where UT is time taken to update database at topmost layer and AT is time taken to send acknowledgment back to the lowest layer. In our hypothesis, WT (waiting time for each transaction) is 0 as each server does its transaction on its turn only after fixed interval. So processing time will remain constant. We consider one another constant factor ND (network delay) which depends upon the execution environment in which proposed model works. Finally, Total Processing Time for m^{th} transaction as TPT(m).

$$TPT\ m\ = ND + PT \tag{2}$$

As ND and PT are constant, so the total processing time will remain constant as the time goes on. We have assumed no work failure in our hypothesis as shown in fig. 3.

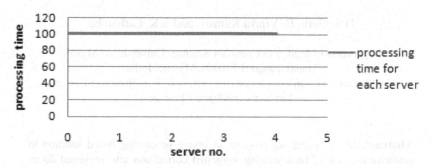

Fig. 3. Processing time of different servers

References

1. Vaid, R., Patel, R.B.: A 7-Layer Model For Modernizing The World: A Step Towards A Hi-Tech World. In: Proceedings of International Conference on Advances in Recent Technologies in Communication and Computing. IEEE Computer Society, Los Alamitos (2009)
2. Kohno, T., Stubblefield, A., Ribin, A.D., Wallach, D.S.: Analysis of an Electronic Voting System, pp. 27–40. IEEE Computer Society, Los Alamitos (2004)
3. Vora, P.L., Bucholz, R., Chaum, D., Dill, D.L., Jefferson, D., Jones, D.W., Lattin, W., Rubin, A.D., Shamos, M.I., Yung, M.: Evaluation of voting systems. Communications of ACM 47 (November 2004)
4. Lai, J.-Y., Lin, C.-F., Yang, C.-H.: Design and Implementation of Electronic Voting System with Contactless IC cards

Automatic Incorporation of Corrections into Reviewed Documents

D.S. Guru, B. Vijaya Kumari, and S.K. Lathamba

Department of Studies in Computer Science, University of Mysore
Manasagangotri-570006, Mysore, India
dsg@compsci.uni-mysore.ac.in, viji.mys@gmail.com,
lathask.ms@gmail.com

Abstract. In this paper we propose an image processing based solution to automate the task of incorporating suggested corrections into reviewed documents. The proposed method extracts the symbols put in by a reviewer on a hard copy and then recognizes the symbols to understand their meanings. The recognition is achieved by the use of centroidal profile features. A software package is developed to incorporate the corrections into the soft copy by identifying the positions of symbols (in the hard copy). Several experiments have been conducted to demonstrate the feasibility of the proposed methodology. Experimental results have demonstrated that the proposed method can withstand minor deformation and orientation and in addition, it is capable of handling joined symbols.

Keywords: Document correction, Centroidal method, Feature extraction, Euclidean distance, handwritten symbol recognition.

1 Introduction

It is practiced that printed documents (Research articles, Project reports/proposals, Business letters, Assignments etc.,) are submitted to a person (reviewer) for the evaluation. While evaluating a document, the reviewer suggests the correction by marking on the document using some standard symbols. Some of the symbols being generally used are given in Table 1 along with their meanings. To incorporate the suggested modifications the soft copy of the document needs to be edited. Editing involves insertions, deletions, swapping of two, and/or some recommendations to change, character/words/lines/paragraphs. The process of reviewing and incorporating corrections is repeated for many times to get an error free and well organized document.

Documents may under go several iterations of editing before it attains a final version. If bundle of documents are to be edited, then it is difficult to incorporate corrections manually as a person has to concentrate on locating corrections. Then there may be chances of missing of these corrections. And the person has to aware of all standard symbols used by reviewer to indicate corrections. After identifying the corrections he has to incorporate these reviewed corrections in their appropriate positions. Automatic incorporation of corrections can overcome these aforementioned problems

V.V Das et al. (Eds.): BAIP 2010, CCIS 70, pp. 446–451, 2010.

in addition to making the process efficient. Here the 'automatic incorporation of corrections' is defined as the process of editing a document by a computer itself without intervention of human beings.

Only one work has been reported in this direction by Jyothi et al., (2007) [1]. However, they have focused on theoretical aspects and general frame work of the system. They have used filters and pixel density to recognition of symbols.

This paper presents a methodology to recognize complex symbols(Table 1) and also joined symbols. Symbols may get joined while reviewer correcting the document, either vertically or horizontally. The proposed system is robust to recognize scaled, deformed and complex symbols also. The experiments conducted show that the performance of handwritten symbol recognition gains 86.53% accuracy and the recognition of joined symbols gains the accuracy of 72.66% on a database of size 90 documents with 23 different symbols.

The rest of the paper is organized as follows. The proposed methodology is presented in section 2. Section 3 gives the experimental results. Further conclusion is given along with future works in section 4.

2 Proposed Methodology

This section presents in detail the proposed method of editing a soft copy of a reviewed document automatically.

A marked document containing several symbols conveying suggested corrections is scanned and fed into the system. The system extracts all handwritten symbols/corrections from the scanned document image using image processing techniques. In case of joined symbols, the system separates those into individual symbols. Then system recognizes the symbols using centroidal method to incorporate corrections in their appropriate positions. These positions are found using a profiling method. The recognized symbols/corrections and their corresponding positions are then fed into a visual basic application. This application is designed such that it incorporates corrections automatically into the soft copy of the document at appropriate positions.

The reviewed document is scanned in color-tone with 300dpi resolution and stored as JPEG format. Then it is converted into two-tone format and stored as BMP file. Handwritten symbols are extracted from the reviewed document by image subtraction, which finds the difference between the original document and the reviewed document. The resultant image contains symbols extracted. Figure 1 shows the reviewed document and extracted symbols.

The binary image of the extracted symbols may be broken because of low resolution or due to overlapping of symbols with the printed characters of the reviewed document. Therefore, to obtain continuous connected components, the extracted symbols are first dilated to fill the breakages and the dilated symbols are then skeletonized to bring them into a pixel thickness.

If two or more symbols are very close to each other then the symbols may get joined because of dilation process. In some cases symbols are joined by reviewer himself, as shown in the Fig 1, posing a problem during classification of symbols. To avoid this problem, joined symbols are identified using line and symbol bounds and then they are separated by the use of vertical and horizontal profilings.

Table 1. Few symbols and their meanings

Symbol	Meaning	Symbol	Meaning
	Line swapping		Word deletion
	Paragraph swapping		Word deletion
	Character deletion		Space between characters
	Word Deletion		Word swapping

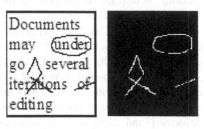

Fig. 1. (a) reviewed document (b) symbols extracted and separated

Number of symbols extracted conveys the number of editions required in the soft copy of the document. As our main focus is on building up an automatic system for incorporation of corrections suggested by the reviewer into a reviewed document, we just adopt here the existing yet simple method of recognizing symbols by concentrating more on integrating various necessary image processing techniques together to accomplish the task. The features are extracted for these symbols using the centroidal method [4]. A symbol is bound minimally and its centroid is computed. Then the bound symbol is divided into a desired number of sub blocks and for each sub block the centroid is computed. The Euclidean distances are measured from the centroid of each block to the centroid of the symbol which gives a feature vector representing a symbol. Likewise, the feature vectors are extracted for all samples of all symbols. This feature matrix serves as a knowledge base for later usage during recognition.

For an instance, in order to recognize the symbol denoting deletion, the symbol is minimally bounded (Fig 2(a)) and centroid is computed. Then the symbol is divided into 7 × 7 blocks (Fig 2(b)) and centroid for each sub block is computed. Euclidean distance (Fig 2(c)) is measured from the centroid of each block to the centroid of the bound symbol. This process is applied for each sample of deletion symbol and can get feature matrix of that symbol.

The test symbol is recognized by matching the feature vector of the test symbol with that of the symbols present in the knowledge base. This matching process is carried out by taking the difference between the feature vector of a test symbol and feature vectors of all symbols using the equation (1).

$$D_{(p,\,k)} = \sum_{i=1}^{m} \text{dist}\,(f_k^i, f_q^i) \qquad p = 1,2,3,\ldots\ldots\ldots 23 \qquad \text{For each } p,\; k = 1, 2, 3 \ldots n \qquad (1)$$

Where, p is the number of distinct symbols (Table 1) present in the database, f_k^i is the ith feature of kth database symbol, f_q^i is the ith feature of test symbol, n is the total number of samples for each symbols present in the database, m is the total number of feature values of each sample (number of blocks).

Finally the test symbol is recognized as that symbol (in the database) which has the minimum distance with the test symbol.

After recognition, corrections are incorporated at appropriate positions in the soft copy. In order to find the positions of symbols where corrections are to be incorporated, the document is segmented into paragraphs, lines, words and characters [2]. Then we found symbol bounds, word bounds, line bounds and character bounds. By using all these information positions of symbols are computed.

The Visual Basic application uses the information about the symbols (operations: deletion, insertion, etc.., and their positions) in the reviewed document. Then corresponding editing is performed in the electronic document. The overall architecture of the proposed system is shown in Fig 3.

3 Experimental Results

An extensive experiment has been conducted on various documents containing well separated and also joined symbols. We validate this work on a large number of documents marked with different symbols (Table 1). 60 documents were considered with slightly deformed and complex symbols and 30 documents were considered with joined symbols. These documents were collected from research scholars and teachers. Going through these corrected documents, 23 symbols which are widely used by the reviewers are tabulated in Table 1. For each symbol 100 samples are taken. Therefore, 2300 symbols are present in the database, out of which few sample symbols are tabulated in Table 2.

For the database, containing 23 different symbols each with 100 samples, feature vectors are generated using centroidal method. Then test symbol is recognized by the use of knowledge base as explained in section 2. Few results of symbol recognition along with their positions are shown in Table 3.

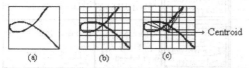

→ Centroid

(a)   (b)   (c)

Fig. 2. (a) A symbol with minimum bounding rectangle (b)the symbol is divided into 7x7 blocks (c)the Euclidean0020distance measured from the centroids of each block to the centroid of the symbol

Table 2. Example 4 different symbols each with 5 samples

Category	1	2	3	4	5
Question mark					
Corrections					
Line swapping					
Word deletion					

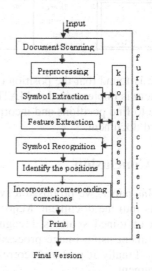

Fig. 3. Architecture of the proposed system

It is very clear from the results that our system has shown a good performance for on all documents containing all the categories of symbols. We were able to achieve 100% accuracy in categorizing symbols such as question mark, word deletion, space between characters, full stop, open and closed parenthesis/ bracket. But this method has a reduced accuracy in categorizing symbols such as insert a word, line swapping, open and closed flower bracket, character deletion. Therefore, the overall performance of handwritten symbol recognition gains 86.53%. The system in addition could withstand the minor deformations and orientations.

In an experiment on separating joined symbols we considered 30 documents. It shows 100% accuracy in the recognition of word deletion (i.e., ×, α) and word swapping after separating the joined symbols. The rest of the symbols have more than 50% recognition accuracy. This is because during separation process there may be a lose of certain parts of symbols making classification task itself difficult. This reduces the accuracy of joined symbol recognition. Therefore, the overall performance of the joined symbol recognition is 72.66%. Few results of recognition of joined symbols are shown in Table 4.

Table 3. Results obtained on parts of two documents

Input Document	Obtained Results	
	Symbol	Position
Major parts of this method) are: symbols extraction,	Word swapping	Line 2, swap word4 and 5
	Space between characters	Line3, space between charater 28 and 29
Separation of joined symbol, recognizes the handwritten	Word deletion	Line 2. word 4
	Word deletion	Line 3, word 5
	Character deletion	Line 4, character 45

Table 4. Results of joined symbol on parts of two documents

Input Document	Obtained Results	
	Symbol	Position
Major parts of this method are: symbols extraction,	Character deletion	Line 1, character 7
	Word deletion	Line 2, word 3
Separation of joined symbol, recognizes the handwritten	Character deletion	Line 2, character 19
	Word deletion	Line 3, word 5

It is found that the position computation for all symbols is accurate. The proposed system is implemented in MATLAB. The Visual Basic application is used as an interface to find positions and incorporate symbol information while editing the Microsoft word document.

4 Conclusion

In this paper, we proposed a system for automating the task of incorporating corrections into the document. Major stages of this system are: symbol extraction, separation of joined symbols, recognizing the handwritten symbols on a hard copy of a document using image processing techniques and position computation of the symbols. Finally it performs corresponding changes/corrections in the soft copy of the document.

We have made a successful attempt to explore the applicability of image processing techniques in document editing process. The success of the current work has motivated us to continue towards a scalable product taking into account even incorporation of handwritten sentences by the use of OCR technology, as our future work.

References

[1] Kiranagi, J.B., Kiranagi, B.B., Guru, D.S.: Automation of Document Editing - A Vision based approach. In: International Conference on Computational Intelligence and Multimedia Application (ICCIMA), vol. 299, pp. 453–457 (2007)

[2] Tripathy, N., Pal, U.: Handwriting Segmentation of Unconstrained Oriya text. Sadhana 31, Part 6, 755–769 (2006)

[3] Sharma, N., Pal, U., Kimura, F.: Recognition of Handwritten Kannada Numerals, pp. 133–136. IEEE, Los Alamitos

Performance Comparison of Multicast Routing Protocols for MANETs

Maya Mohan and S. Mary Saira Bhanu

Department of Computer Science and Engineering, National Institute of Technology,
Tiruchirappalli, India
mayajeevan@gmail.com, msb@nitt.edu

Abstract. Mobile Ad-hoc Network (MANET) is a dynamic network of self controlled mobile nodes without any centralized coordinator or wired infrastructure. The physical measures adopted in wired networks are less efficient for wireless networks. The leading challenges of wireless networks are battery power, bandwidth and mobility. The best way of overcoming these challenges in wireless networks is through efficient routing protocols. Multicast is transferring data from a single source to a group of destinations identified by a single address. This paper compares three multicast routing protocol and finding the optimal one which will perform in a better way against the major challenges.

Keywords: Multicast, MANETs, Routing.

1 Introduction

A MANET is a collection of wireless mobile nodes that forms dynamic networks without any centralized coordinator. Multicasting is the best one for group communication. The paper is aiming to find an optimal multicast routing protocol for MANET based on the performance in terms of power consumption, packet delivery and throughput and makes it enable to handle the major challenges. The protocols under consideration are OPHMR [1] (Optimized Polymorphic Hybrid Multicast Routing protocol), CAMP [2] (Core Assisted Mesh Protocol) and ODMRP [3] (On Demand Multicast Routing Protocol).All the three protocols follow mesh topology. OPHMR is of type hybrid and CAMP is a proactive protocol, whereas ODMRP is a type of reactive protocol.

2 Related Work

The protocol such as Distance Vector Multicast Routing Protocol will perform flooding of data packets whereas Forwarding Group Multicast Protocol performs flooding of control packets. Protocols such as CBT follow tree topology leads to drop of packets when link fails.

V.V Das et al. (Eds.): BAIP 2010, CCIS 70, pp. 452–454, 2010.
© Springer-Verlag Berlin Heidelberg 2010

3 Operational Principles of OPHMR, CAMP and ODMRP

3.1 OPHMR

The routes are maintained by the hard state (Reactive) approach. The working of the protocol is based on four threshold values. Two power thresholds (P_TH1 and P_TH2), one vicinity density threshold (V_TH) and one mobility density threshold (M_TH). Based on these threshold values it will switch to four modes (proactive mode1, proactive mode2, proactive ready mode and reactive mode) of operation and the Change of mode will be updated with neighbors.

Table 1. Group management of CAMP, ODMRP and OPHMR

Proto-col	GROUP MANAGEMENT		
	Group Join		Group Disjoin
	Join Request	Join Response	
CAMP	if core is reachable & neighbors are not members of the desired group then send a join request to the core else broadcast the join request if any one neighbor is a member then announces its membership by updates	ACK will send to the joining node via intermediate nodes	Issuing Quit Message
ODMRP	Floods the join query and waits for response	Modify the Multicast Routing Table(MRT) and send the reply	Automatic deletion if time out
OPHMR	**Proactive mode or PRM mode** if nodes ∈ NT (Neighbor routing Table) then unicast the join_req to them else broadcast join_req **Reactive mode-** Floods the join_req	**Proactive mode or PRM mode or Reactive** Modify the MRT and send the reply	Automatic deletion if time out

3.2 CAMP

The routes are maintained by the hard state approach (reactive). Packets from any source in the group are forwarded along the Reverse Shortest Path (RSP) to each source in the multicast group. CAMP uses cores only to limit the traffic needed for a router to join a multicast group. Core failures do not stop packet forwarding. CAMP assumes the availability of routing information from a unicast routing protocol.

3.3 ODMRP

ODMRP follows the multicast scheme and only subsets of nodes forward the packets via flooding. It applies on-demand procedures to dynamically build routes and maintain multicast group membership. It has also unicast routing capability.

Table.1 dictates the group management performed in CAMP, ODMRP and OPHMR.

4 Simulation Results

The simulation of CAMP, ODMRP and OPHMR were implemented using the Glo-mosim Simulator. The assumptions are timeset - 10 seconds, terrain-area - 500mX500m, radio propagation range - 250m and channel capacity - 2Mbps. The simulation results obtained are shown in the figures below and OPHMR shows a better performance than ODMRP and CAMP except throughput.

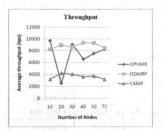
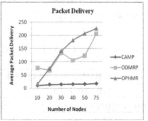
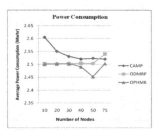

Fig. 1. Throughput   **Fig. 2.** Packet Delivery   **Fig. 3.** Power Consumption

5 Conclusion

The overhead caused due to the group communication has to be controlled by using efficient multicast routing protocol. The performance evaluation results show that OPHMR is having a better performance over ODMRP and CAMP.

References

1. Mnaouer, A.B., Chen, L., Foh, C.H., Tantra, J.W.: OPHMR:An Optimized Polymorphic Hybrid Multicast Routing Protocol for MANET. IEEE Transactions on Mobile Computing (5) (May 2007)
2. Garcia-Luna-Aceves, J.J.: A Multicast Routing Protocol for Ad-Hoc Networks (CAMP). IEEE INFOCOM 1999 2, 784–792 (1999)
3. Clausen, T., Jacquet, P.: Optimized Link State Routing Protocol, Internet Draft, draft-ietf-manet-olsr-11.txt (January 2003)

Traffic Aware LSP Selection Method in MPLS Networks

Ravindra Kumar Singh[1], Kanak Saxena[1], and Reena Singh[2]

[1] Samrat Ashok Technological Institute, Vidisha, M.P., India
[2] IIT Madras, Chennai, Tamil Nadu, India
{singh.ravindrakumar,kanak.saxena,reena.cs}@gmail.com

Abstract. In Multi-protocol Label Switching (MPLS) networks, selecting LSP pair i.e. both upward and downward LSP is practically beneficial, but before that we should assure that the selection does not contribute to network congestion and packet losses and at the same time it should increase the efficiency of network. In this paper we propose a new algorithm for an optimum LSP pair selection from multiple parallel LSP pairs. It minimizes the probability of network congestion, packet loss and request loss by selecting the LSP which is lightly loaded and possess upward and downward bandwidth proportional to the service request.

Keywords: LSP pair, Multi-protocol Label Switching.

1 Introduction

In MPLS networks there are multiple LSPs established between ingress LSR and egress LSR for making the network reliable, efficient, congestion free, etc. For every request it is usually beneficial to establish both upward and downward LSPs at the same time for performing various management and design tasks with ease [1].

In this paper we propose an approach to select an LSP pair among parallel LSP pairs with the aim to minimize total bandwidth used and other desirable requirements as probability of congestion, packet loss and request loss.

2 Related Work

Our work is closely related to that of Kuribayashi and Tsumura in [1] where they have proposed two algorithms for LSP pair selection among parallel LSPs. Their work tries to minimize the service request loss probability. It considers permissible delay by the service request and avoids the dead lock state where we have the required upward and downward bandwidth to fulfill a request but in different LSP pairs. But it does not provide adequate measures to avoid congestion by distributing the load among different parallel LSP pairs. We here alter their algorithm and introduce the traffic aware congestion avoidance concept to their work. Zenghua Zhao. et al in [2] present a heuristic state dependent load balancing based on delay. The delay itself cannot reveal the correct network congestion state since it varies according to the speed of

V.V Das et al. (Eds.): BAIP 2010, CCIS 70, pp. 455–457, 2010.

the network [3]. Moreover they have not approached the selection of LSP pair. He. et al in [3] proposed state-dependent adaptive load balancing taking with the help of queuing delay and packet loss probability in the networks. They have also worked on unidirectional LSPs and did not approach the overall bandwidth reduction.

3 Proposed LSP Selection Method

Our work enhances the model presented in [1] so we follow its conventions through-out this paper. Suppose there are multiple LSPs between a pair of ingress and egress LSRs such that each LSP pair has different route and further that the bandwidth of upward and downward LSP in a pair may not be same. For an optimized and efficient LSP selection algorithm, following problems should be solved.

a. The algorithm should be simple with minimal complexity.
b. It should reduce the service request loss probability and the possibility of situation in which we have the requested upward and downward bandwidth, but in different LSP pairs, so the request can not be fulfilled and leads to a dead lock state.
c. It should reduce the total bandwidth required by balancing the load and should not contribute in network congestion.

Our algorithm solves the above problems. Let Xu and Xd be the maximum upward and downward bandwidth of an LSP pair and Yu and Yd be the requested service upward and downward bandwidth. Let $Zu= Yu-Yd$ and $Zd=Yd-Yu$

Algorithm for LSP pair selection

```
Step 1:  Select an LSP pair amongst the parallel LSP pairs
         in round robin fashion.
Step 2:  IF (Zu is positive) then
              IF¹ (Zu <= Xd-Xu) then
                   IF (Yu >= Xu and Yd >= Xd) then GOTO step 4
              ELSE GOTO step 1
         ELSE GOTO step 1
         ELSE GOTO step 3
Step 3:  IF (Zd is positive) then
              IF¹ (Zd <= Xu-Xd) then
                   IF (Yu >= Xu and Yd >= Xd) then GOTO step 4
              ELSE GOTO step 1
         ELSE GOTO step 1
         ELSE GOTO step 4
Step 4:  Check the LSP pair for the packet loss
         probability and packet queuing delay. If they are
         less than the threshold values then assign LSP to
         the service request else GOTO step 1.
```

In the first step we select a LSP pair in round robin fashion. Selecting each LSP in round robin fashion and comparing its attributes with all others' increases the complexity of algorithm as done in [1]. It is better to select an LSP, analyze it for its suitability

---

[1] This IF with its ELSE statement can be removed for relaxing the constraints.

and allocate or reject it. In this way the first problem i.e. complexity is solved. Step 2 and 3 solve next problem. In these steps we check whether the difference between upward and downward bandwidth of service request is less than or equal to that between downward and upward bandwidth of maximum available bandwidth of the selected LSP. This would not let the situation of second problem to arise. For instance, suppose we have a service request of upward and downward bandwidth of 20 and 40 respectively then by this step the LSP pair having upward and downward bandwidth of 80 and 100 respectively will get preference than the pair having 100 and 80 as the upward and downward bandwidth. The remaining bandwidth in former case will be 60 and 60 while in latter case it will be 80 and 40 thereby leading to situation of problem 'b'.

After this, it is checked whether the upward and downward bandwidth of LSP is greater than or equal to the service request. Step 4 takes care of last problem. The ingress LSR periodically updates itself of the status of LSPs established by sending packets with time stamp for finding queuing delay and flood of packets for calculating the packet loss in the network [3]. Moreover some service requests also mention their required delay. If the service request does not mention delay constraint then only packet loss probability needs to be checked and it should be allocated the path with maximum delay so that paths with less delay remain for future requests. Thus this algorithm does not select the LSP with congestion.

After n iterations which is equal to the number of LSPs, the IF statement with footnote can be removed with its corresponding ELSE to reduce the constraints. If an LSP pair is not allocated in next n iterations then the request is rejected.

4 Conclusion and Future Work

This study addresses the problem of LSP pair selection among multiple parallel LSP pairs between same ingress and egress LSR. A simple iterative algorithm involving trivial arithmetic calculations at each step is proposed. This is expected to minimize the total bandwidth required taking care of the congestion control and efficiency in the network. For future work we would investigate this work using simulations.

References

1. Kuribayashi, S.-i., Tsumura, S.: Optimal LSP selection method in MPLS networks. In: IEEE Pacific Rim Conference on Communications, Computers and Signal Processing (2007)
2. Zhao, Z., et al.: Flow-level multipath load balancing in MPLS network. In: Proceedings of IEEE international conference on communications (June 2004)
3. He, X., Tang, H., Zhu, M., Chu, Q.: Flow-level based adaptive load balancing in MPLS networks. In: Fourth International Conference on Communications and Networking in China, ChinaCOM 2009 (2009)

Context-Aware Intrusion Detection in Mobile Ad-Hoc Networks

R.S. Ambili Chandran and S. Mary Saira Bhanu

Department of Computer Science and Engineering, National Institute of Technology,
Tiruchirappalli, India
ambily0123@gmail.com, msb@nitt.edu

Abstract. Security issues in MANETs (Mobile Ad-hoc Networks) cannot be solved by conventional intrusion detection techniques since they have relied on monitoring traffic at switches, gateways, and routers. Due to the mobility of nodes and the higher rate of interaction of nodes, MANETs needs to have an intrusion detection system which allows the node to react according to the context. A monitor placing algorithm is considered which will try to reduce the overhead of using more memory and at the same time maximize the detection of any threat in the system. The monitoring policy repository building is done by a probability based Bayesian approach which helps the intrusion detection system (IDS) to adapt to the context.

Keywords: Context-awareness, Intrusion detection, MANETs.

1 Introduction

The advent of improved communication and mobility of the communicating nodes have also given way for more security challenges. The mobility of nodes and the increased interaction between the nodes made it difficult to stick to one normal behavior pattern of the system. Context-awareness in mobile environment is adaptation to the current situation of the user. The goal is to support the user without too much interaction with a computing device.

2 Background and Motivation

There are several works regarding the context-aware intrusion detection system in ubiquitous computing environment. The generic architecting framework for adaptive context-aware intrusion detection system is proposed in [1]. The proposed approach on [2],[3] have considered distributed and co-operative intrusion detection architectures. The Bayesian algorithm suggested in [4] is used as the learning algorithm to filter the junks in emails. In our work, we have consolidated the co-operative architecture with adaptive learning algorithm to provide an efficient context-aware intrusion detection policy.

V.V Das et al. (Eds.): BAIP 2010, CCIS 70, pp. 458–460, 2010.
© Springer-Verlag Berlin Heidelberg 2010

3 Adaptive Context-Aware Intrusion Detection

The intrusion detection system works as follows. Monitor is selected among a set of nodes which will be having a learning repository. All the nodes other than the monitor will be having a minimum level of intrusion detection i.e., filtering and will also check for flooding attack. If filtering fails, data is sent to the monitor for further analysis. Fig. 1 shows the schematic of the IDS for monitor / non-monitor nodes.

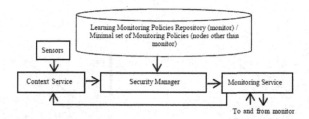

Fig. 1. IDS schematic diagram for monitor / nodes other than monitor

The monitor uses an adaptive learning algorithm in which probability of the data to be valid is calculated by considering the occurrence of the data in the past. For learning, the Bayesian algorithm is used. The algorithm needs a token dictionary. The dictionary will be containing the basic patterns which are needed in the current context and their corresponding count of valid and invalid matches. The total number of valid and invalid message count is also stored in the monitor's database.

3.1 Experimental Results

Adaptive context aware intrusion detection system is implemented using Glomosim. We have considered 20 nodes with FTP application running. All the nodes are assumed to be moving randomly using the random waypoint algorithm. The data got at the destination is checked with minimum filter and will be sent to the monitor if it fails validating. The network is divided into square areas and the node which is having the minimum distance from the center of the square is set as the monitor. Let 'n' be the node and 'n_x' and 'n_y', 'X' and 'Y' be the x and y coordinates of node as well as the center position of the area considered. Then position of monitor node 'm' is calculated as min [abs $(X-n_x)$ + abs$(Y-n_y)$]. The monitor will start learning and updates the database using Bayesian algorithm by checking the data. Initially the database in the monitor will be having a set of predefined values same as that of the other nodes. The database will also have the information about the number of valid and invalid messages it have got. Let "CD" represent the context related data. The probability of validity of the message is calculated as given in Fig.2.

When the nodes send message for validation to the monitor, it will calculate the values and decide whether the message is valid and also updates its database with the new values it have got from the new message. The limited filtering in each of the nodes help to reduce the network overhead up to some extent and the saving of data only in the monitor reduces the overhead of using large memory in each of the nodes.

ALL (No. of all messages) = valid msg count + invalid msg count
P (CD|msg is invalid) = for all matched data (N1 value of the current CD/invalid msg)
P (CD|msg is valid) = for all matched word (N2 value of the current CD/valid msg)
P (msg in invalid) = invalid msg count/Entire msg count
P (msg is valid) = valid msg count/Entire msg count
P (msg is invalid|CD) = P (msg is invalid) * P (CD|msg is invalid)
P (msg is valid|CD) = P (msg is valid) * P (CD|msg is valid)

Fig. 2. Steps involved in calculating validity of message

Whenever the monitor goes out of the area, the database will be handed over to the new monitor.

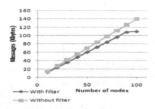
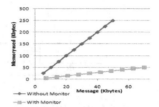

Fig. 3. N/w overhead vs. number of nodes   **Fig. 4.** N/w overhead vs. memory overhead

The network overhead with respect to the increased number of nodes with and without filter is shown in Fig.3. We have assumed that two messages among ten messages will be invalid one of which is resolvable at the node itself with the minimum filter. The network overhead with respect to memory used with and without monitor is shown in Fig. 4. We have made the assumption that five nodes are present and among five messages received, two messages are invalid of which one is resolvable at the node itself with the minimum filter.

4 Conclusion and Future Work

The algorithm will provide better utilization of resources which is very sensitive in the case of MANETs. The algorithm can be improved by selecting the monitor based on prediction of its mobility.

References

1. Saidane, A.: A Reliable Context-Aware Intrusion Tolerant System. In: Meersman, R., Tari, Z., Herrero, P., et al. (eds.) OTM-WS 2007, Part II. LNCS, vol. 4806, pp. 1062–1070. Springer, Heidelberg (2007)
2. Zhang, Y., Lee, W., Huang, Y.: Intrusion detection techniques for mobile wireless networks. A CM MONET Journal, 3 (2003)
3. Zhou, B., Shi, Q., Merabti, M.: Intrusion Detection in Pervasive Networks Based on a Chi-Square Statistic Test. In: 30th Annual International Computer Software and Applications Conference, COMPSAC 2006, 3 pages (2006)
4. Sahami, M., Dumais, S., Heckerman, D., Horvitz, E.: A Bayesian Approach to Filtering Junk E-Mail. In: AAAI 1998 Workshop on Learning for Text Categorization (1998)

Energy and Fault Aware Management Framework for Wireless Sensor Network

V.R. Sarma Dhulipala[1], V. Aarthy[2], and RM. Chandrasekaran[3]

[1] Lecturer (Physics), Center for Convergence of Technologies/Anna University
Tiruchirapalli, TamilNadu, India
[2] Student, Anna University Tiruchirapalli, TamilNadu, India
[3] Registrar, Anna University Tiruchirapalli, TamilNadu, India
{dvrsarma,aarthyvetharathinam}@gmail.com
aurmc@hotmail.com

Abstract. Wireless Sensor Networks (WSN) is a collection of numerous tiny sensor nodes which are randomly deployed in distributed environment. The reliability of WSN is affected by faults that may occur due to various reasons. The Fault Tolerance is the key factor for distributed sensor application. The main objective of this paper is to create an algorithm for fault tolerance. According to the network environment changes, this algorithm guarantees reliability. Our paper also gives out a framework which can be a solution for various faults occurring in WSN environment.

Keywords: Wireless Sensor Networks, Fault Tolerance, Framework.

1 Introduction

A wireless sensor network is a self-organizing system, comprised of numerous tiny sensor nodes that are scattered in a sensor field [1]. It monitors the performance and environmental conditions such as temperature, pressure, motion, etc [2]. Data are communicated through Base Station. Mostly sensors are battery operated and posses limited computing and communication capabilities. Sensors networks are failure-prone [3]. Realizing a fault-tolerant operation is critical to the success of a WSN. Fault tolerance is the main factors that are influencing the sensor networks [4]. It is the ability of the system to sustain functionalities without any disturbances or interruptions. Fault, it may be expected or unexpected by the system engineer and the nodes. Apply the algorithm needed to maintain a fault -tolerant environment, eliminate its effect and runback to its normal operating conditions. The reliability or Fault-tolerance (F(t)) of sensor nodes is given by, Using poison distribution,

$$F(t) = \exp{(\lambda * t)} \tag{1}$$

Where, λ -> Failure rate of a sensor node & t -> time period.

V.V Das et al. (Eds.): BAIP 2010, CCIS 70, pp. 461–464, 2010.

2 Fault Tolerant Framework

In wireless sensor networks, failures may occur due to various reasons. Assumes the main three possible failures are lack of power, loss of data and hardware failures [5] are shown in Fig. 1. Sensors may fail due to depletion of batteries or destruction by an external event. Second are link failures, results partitions and changes in a network. The last failure is hardware failure; it is unpredictable or otherwise replaces the faulty position/ components into new one. The Lack Of Power (LOP) Algorithm proposes to tolerate the fault of power lagging. Checking the battery level of the sensor nodes and act accordingly. The Loss Of Data Algorithm (LOD) tells to avoid or prevent the data loss. Single node or link failure leads to miss behavior or missing reports of the sensor nodes. This two are predicted and we can reduce and tolerate the faults.

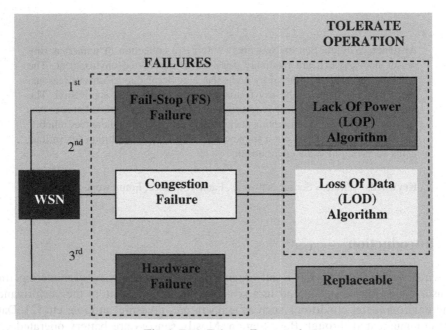

Fig. 1. Fault Tolerant Framework

3 Lack of Power (LOP) and Loss of Data (LOD) Algorithms

In existing fault tolerance framework, analysis and recovered their result using CRAFT (Checkpoint/Recovery-bAsed scheme for Fault Tolerance) algorithm. CRAFT is fully based on clear out the faults and increase the performance of the networks. The main idea of CRAFT is to tolerate the possible as well as the predict-able faults. Data collection and dissemination are essential one in WSN. This paper proposes and deals a fault in different environmental conditions. The fail-stop failure and congestion failure are the main possible failures in wireless sensor networks and it is predictable by the system engineer. The LOP and LOD algorithms gives the good result for this type of failures. The following algorithm clearly explains about the way of flowing and how the sensor nodes tolerate the fault and runback into normal working conditions [6]. In this paper, introduces a new term called Sensor Head (S_h). Sensor Head/Cluster head acts like a Base station [7]. 'S_h' check and update the nodes and report to the base station. The control of congestion algorithm increases the network efficiency, improves the channel quality and reduces the energy consumption [8], [9] & [10]. Energy consumption is the main criteria in wireless sensor networks. By proper utilization of energy, lack of power gets minimized. Each node knows the remaining percentage power of its battery. The variable 'n' is the number of nodes that is assigned by the system engineer. LOP and LOD algorithms are explained as follows.

Step 1: Assumes symbols for each variable and assign a name for it.

Step 2: Each sensor knows the remaining power of its battery level.

Step 3: Let the power of the sensor nodes be 'P'
The remaining power of the sensor be 'S'
T1, T2, T3 are the assigned symbols for variable conditions.

Where, T1 = (3/4)th of the power
T2 = (2/4)th of the power
T3 = (1/4)th of the power

Step 4: If(S >= T1)
Sensor act as an operational sensor

Step 5: If(S >= T2)
Sensor cannot be a sink

Step 6: If(S >= T3)
Sensor handover to another node depend upon the condition
Check the highest energy level of neighbor sensors.
Continue the Looping conditions of i=1; i>=n; and increment the value of 'i' till the condition gets TRUE.

Where, i=Variable (default assigned value)
n=Number of nodes in the sensor field or assigned by the System Engineer

Step 7: If all conditions are not satisfied, it will give the default answer Ie. Sensor is going to be die.

Step 1: Consider the total number of nodes in the terrain, both static and mobility.

Step 2: Checking the power level of the sensor nodes.

Step 3: Choose the highest energy sensor nodes as Cluster Head /Sensor-Head.

Step 4: Sensor-Head (S_h) updates the state of the sensor nodes and report to the higher order node (Base Station).

Step 5: If (STATE == IDLE)
Check the battery level conditions.
If it is satisfied, routing the packets to the sink.
If not, S_h chooses the next node depending upon the condition.

Step 6: If (STATE == SLEEP)
S_h activate the node and sending the packets to the end user.

Step 7: If any fault occur, S_h gives the IP address of the faulty node to the Base Station.

Step 8: Sensor-Head (S_h) allocate the channel, create a path and routing the packets to the sink successfully.

Step 9: If S_h drains all energy, before it dies. It chooses another head and broadcast to all another nodes

4 Results and Conclusion

The LOP and LOD are checked out using high-level language. The proposed algorithm gives a best performance for selected fault tolerant constraints like throughput and average end to end delay of the network. Sensors are managed and recovered by a sensor heads. Power lagging and data loss are occurred due to the sudden environmental changes. It is unavoidable but it is tolerated by the sensor nodes. Our approach enables fault tolerance in the system by performing periodic checks.

5 Future Work

In the future, we plan to have a detailed study and implementation of our framework and algorithms proposed. We also plan to implement this work using hardware set up with the help of TinyOS.

References

1. Saleh, I., El-Sayed, H., Eltoweissy, M.: A Fault Tolerance Management Framework for Wireless Sensor Networks. IEEE Explore (2006)
2. Akyildiz, I.F., Sanakarasubramaniam, W.S., Cayirci, E.: Wireless Sensor Networks. Computer Networks (38), 393–422 (2002)
3. Paradis, L., Han, Q., IEEE: A Survey of Fault Management in Wireless Sensor Networks. Journal of Network and Systems Management 15(2), 171–190 (2007)
4. Koushanfar, F., Potkonjak, M., Sangiovanni-Vincentelli, A.: Fault Tolerance in Wireless Sensor Networks
5. Yen, I.-L., Ahmed, I., Jagannath, R., Kundu, S.: Implementation of a Customizable Fault Tolerance Framework. In: IEEE Explore TX, Texas Univ., Dallas, April 20-22, pp. 230–239 (1998)
6. Han, X., Cao, X., Lloyd, E.L., Shen, C.-C.: Fault Tolerant Relay Node Placement in Heterogeneous Wireless Sensor Networks. In: IEEE Infocom 2007 (2007)
7. Sivaraman, R., Sarma Dhulipala, V.R., Aarthy, V., Kavitha, K.: Energy Comparison and Analysis for Cluster-based Environment in Wireless Sensor Networks. In: IJRT, pp. 89–91.
8. De Cicco, L., Mascolo, S., Palmisano, V.: A Mathematical Model of the Skype VoIP Congestion Control Algorithm. In: 47th IEEE Conference on Decision and Control Cancun., Mexico, December 9-11, pp. 1410–1415 (2008)
9. Hao, B., Sen, A., Shen, B.H.: A New Metric for Fault-Tolerance in Sensor Networks, pp. 289–290. ACM, New York (2004)
10. Zhao, J., Govindan, R.: Understanding packet delivery performance in dense Wireless Sensor Networks. In: Proceedings of ACM Sensys (2003)

An Image Index Model for Retrieval

B. Janet, A.V. Reddy, and S. Domnic

Department of Computer Applications, National Institute of Technology,
Trichirappalli – 620015
{janet,reddy,domnic}@nitt.edu

Abstract. An image index model has been proposed that will help in the retrieval of images based on query by example. It is based on Vector Quantization (VQ). VQ represents the similarity of the images based on the codebook that is used for compression. An index is constructed based on the encoding distortion (ED) values using the Terrier Direct Index. It is found that some image transformations do not have any impact on the ED values and the retrieval accuracy is higher, efficient and faster. It can be combined with the cube index model for text documents to give a single structure for facilitating both image and text retrieval.

Keywords: Image Retrieval, Vector Quantization, Indexing method, Content based image retrieval, Text Mining.

1 Introduction

In an age of Information explosion, we are starved for knowledge. With the advent of the internet, web pages with both text and image data has to be searched to satisfy the information need of the user. Content based retrieval has become the need of the hour. An index [1] is a data structure with its own set of algorithms for insertion, maintenance and search that identifies the position at which the indexed values occur. In the context of a textual database, an index categorizes which document contains which words. In the context of an image database, an index categorizes which image contains which features [2].

1.1 Motivation

Image has always been represented as a feature vector. Features of an image that are represented as a set of values have been difficult to be represented in an index. There is also the problem of a large number of dimensions [2]. VQ [3] represents the image as a set of code vectors in a code book. It calculates a distortion value for each image by comparing the code book values such that similar images have smaller distortion while dissimilar images have larger distortion values [4]. This helps us to represent the image with the distortion as a single value that represents the image. An index of the distortion values of the images for each codebook that is generated for individual images has been used as an image index to facilitate retrieval of the images.

V.V Das et al. (Eds.): BAIP 2010, CCIS 70, pp. 465–467, 2010.

2 Vector Quantization Based Image Index

Vector Quantization is a lossy encoding method. It is used to quantize and compress the feature vectors of an image. An image is blocked into N, k- dimensional image vectors. A code book C with M code vectors is built. It is encoded by assigning to each source vector x, a code vector y in C following the nearest-neighbor mapping:

$$Q(x) = y_i \text{ only if } d(x, y_i) <= d(x, y_j) \text{ for all } j \neq i, \qquad (1)$$

Where d(x,y) is the distortion function between two vectors taken as $d(x,y) \equiv \|x - y\|^2$.

Schaefer [4] uses a separate codebook for each image as its feature. To determine the image similarity based on distortion distance, codebooks of images are directly compared and the distance noted. There are encoding distortion distance [5] and Modified Hausdorff Distance [5] that is used to calculate the image similarity. We have considered the encoding distortion only, to be represented in the image index based on which the images are retrieved.

To determine the image similarity, encoding distortion (ED) value is calculated by comparing the image codebooks and stored as an image index using Terrier [6] Direct Index structure. Terrier is the Terabyte Retriever version 2.1 developed by University of Glasgow - Department of Computing Science, Information Retrieval Group. The open source version of Terrier is written in Java.

The Image is first resized into a fixed size to reduce the Index size and processing. It is transformed into the 8-bit gray scale image. The pixel values of the image are grouped into blocks of fixed size. Then the code book of the image is calculated. It is stored into a modified direct index structure using Terrier to enable the ED calculation.

Direct index for an image consist of the image identifier and the code vector values for that image stored in the modified direct index structure.

The Document Index stores the Image information such as the Image identifier, Image title, path and offset of the Image codebook information in the direct file.

The Image index is created by calculating the ED of one image, for all the codebooks of the other images. This distortion value is stored in image index as a single value D.

Consider an image I that is to be indexed. If there are 3 other images to be indexed, then each of the codebook C is used on I to find the ED values and they are stored in the index as shown in Fig. 1. The Terrier direct index is modified to store the ED values for each image. When an image is added to the database, its codebook value is added to the index and the encoding distortion value calculated for all the other images.

Fig. 1. Image Index Structure

If the query image exists in the Index, then the ED values are obtained and sorted to get the lowest distortion that is most similar to the image, ordered in ascending order.

If the query image does not exist, then it has to be encoded and the ED calculated for all the codebook values found in the direct index. Then the ED values are sorted and the result shows the images that are similar to the query.

3 Experimental Results and Evaluation

Terrier 2.1 is modified to implement an image direct and document index in Pentium 4 processor with 3.2 GHz and 1 GB RAM. To test the index, a sample of the database due to Wang, Li, Wiederhold [7] is used. Retrieval effectiveness is evaluated using two standard quantities: precision and recall. For a given query, let a be the number of relevant images that are retrieved, b, the number of irrelevant items, c, the number of relevant items that are not retrieved. Then Precision = fraction of the images retrieved that are relevant = a/(a+b) and Recall = fraction of the relevant images that are retrieved = a/(a+c). For image retrieval, the average recall is found to be 0.8 and the average precision is found to be 0.6. Some image transformations do not affect the ED values like flip, cut, resize, skew and rotate.

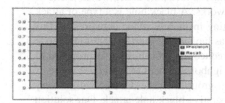   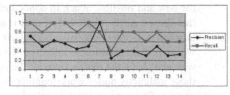

Fig. 2. Precision and Recall Curves   **Fig. 3.** Average Precision vs. Recall

4 Conclusions and Future Work

An Image Index structure using VQ method is proposed for images. It considers the complete image. The encoding distortion of each individual image is obtained and the values stored in the index. The lowest distortion gives the best match for the image. This method will help in creating a common index structure to represent both text and image. It is created using Terrier and tested with the image database and found to be efficient. The Text index and the Image index have to be combined to be represented as a single structure for the web documents that contain both images and text.

References

1. Frakes, W.B., Yates, R.B.: Information Retrieval Data Structures and Algorithms. Pearson, London (2008)
2. Jaiwei, H., Kamber, M.: Data Mining Concepts and Techniques. Elsevier, Morgan Kaufmann Publishers (2006)
3. Gray, R.M.: Vector quantization. IEEE Acoustics, speech and Signal Processing Magazine, 4–29 (1984)
4. Schaefer, G.: Compressed Domain Image Retrieval by Comparing VQ Codebooks. In: Proceedings of the SPIE Visual Communications and Image Processing, vol. 4671, pp. 959–966 (2002)
5. Daptardar Ajay, H., Storer James, A.: Content Based Image Retrieval via Vector Quantization. In: Bebis, G., Boyle, R., Koracin, D., Parvin, B. (eds.) ISVC 2005. LNCS, vol. 3804, pp. 502–509. Springer, Heidelberg (2005)
6. Terrier 2.1, http://ir.dcs.gla.ac.uk/terrier/
7. http://wang.ist.psu.edu/docs/related/

Trust Based Strategy to Resist Collaborative Blackhole Attack in Manet

N. Bhalaji[1], Alok V. Kanakeri[2], Krishna P. Chaitanya[2], and A. Shanmugam[3]

[1] Research scholar Anna University Coimbatore & Member ACEEE
[2] PG Scholars, School of Engineering, Vels University
[3] Principal, Bannari Amman Institute of Technology, Sathy

Abstract. This paper analyses the cooperative black hole attack which is one of the new and possible attack in adhoc networks. A black hole is a type of attack that can be easily employed against routing in mobile adhoc networks. In this attack a malicious node advertises itself as having the shortest path to the node whose packets it wants to intercept. To reduce the probability it is proposed to wait and check the replies from all the neighboring nodes to find a safe route. If these malicious nodes work together as a group then the damage will be very serious. This type of attack is called cooperative black hole attack. Our solution discovers the secure route between source and destination by identifying and isolating cooperative black hole nodes. In this paper, via simulation, we evaluate the proposed solution and compare it with other existing solutions in terms of throughput, Packet delivery ratio and latency. We have conducted extensive experiments using the network simulator-2 to validate our research.

Keywords: Secured Routing, Blackhole attack, Cooperative Blackhole attack, DSR, Malicious nodes, Mobile adhoc network.

1 Introduction

A Mobile Ad-hoc Network [1] is a self-configuring network of mobile routers (and associated hosts) connected by wireless links—the union of which form an arbitrary topology. The routers are free to move randomly and organize themselves arbitrarily; thus, the network's wireless topology may change rapidly and unpredictably. MANETs are usually set up in situations of emergency for temporary operations or simply if there are no resources to set up elaborate networks. In this paper we attempt to analyze threats faced by the DSR protocol [2] in ad hoc network environment and provide a classification of the various security mechanisms.

1.1 Blackhole and Cooperative Blackhole Attack

A black hole attack [3] is a kind of denial of service attack where a malicious node can attract all packets by falsely claiming a fresh route to the destination and absorb them without forwarding them to the destination. It is a type of attack in which black-hole nodes act in a group [4] [5]. For example when multiple black hole nodes are

V.V Das et al. (Eds.): BAIP 2010, CCIS 70, pp. 468–474, 2010.

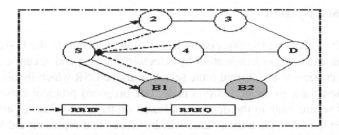

acting in coordination with each other, the first black hole node B1 refers to the one of its team mates B2 in the next hop.

2 Related Work

Secure ad hoc routing protocol has been proposed as a technique to enhance the security in MANET. In [6], Hu et al. proposed a common key encryption system for Dynamic Source Routing (DSR) [2]. In Secure AODV (SAODV) [7][8][9] and Secure Efficient Ad hoc Distance vector routing protocol (SEAD) [10], secure routing protocol using hash functions have been proposed. In [11], Authenticated Routing for Ad hoc Networks (ARAN), an AODV-based secure routing protocol using public key encryption system is proposed. Hu and Perrig [12] survey the weakness and strength of various secure routing protocols. The above mentioned secure protocols can only guard against external attacks. However, for the internal attacks coming from compromised hosts could still have severe impacts on network performance and its connectivity. Therefore, detecting the internal attack launching from these compromised hosts is indispensable. In [13], Deng et al. proposed a solution for individual black holes. But they have not considered the cooperative black hole attacks. According to their solution, information about the next hop to destination should be included in the RREP packet when any intermediate node replies for RREQ. Then the source node sends a further request (FREQ) to next hop of replied node and asks about the replied node and route to the destination. By using this method we can identify trustworthiness of the replied node only if the next hop is trusted. In [15], Yin et al. proposed a solution to defending against black hole attacks in wireless sensor networks. The scenario that they considered in sensor networks is quite different than MANETs. They consider the static sensor network with manually deployed cluster heads. Hesiri Weerasinghe and Huirong Fu [16] simulated the algorithm proposed by [5] with several changes to improve the accuracy of preventing cooperative black hole attacks and to improve the efficiency of the process. They also simulated AODV [17] and the solution proposed by [5] and compared them with [13]. In this scheme proposed solution is applied over the Dynamic Source Routing protocol and the over head of FREQ and FREP is not required as routing will be done based on the trust value of the nodes.

3 Proposed System

The purpose of applying the association based route selection to the DSR protocol is to fortify the existing implementation by selecting the best and securest route in the network. In contrast to the current route selection in the DSR which involves selection of the shortest route to the destination node, our proposed protocol choose the most reliable and secure route to the destination based on the trust values of all nodes. For each node in the network, a trust value will be stored that represent the value of the trustiness to each of its neighbor nodes. This trust value will be adjusted based on the experiences [17] [18] that the node has with its neighbor nodes. In our proposed scheme we classify the Association among the nodes and their neighboring nodes in to three types [19] as below. In an adhoc network the Association between any node x and node y will be determined as Unknown, Known, Companion.

3.1 Association Estimator Technique

The Association status [20] which we discussed in the previous section depends up on the trust value and threshold values. The trust values are calculated based on the following parameters of the nodes. We propose a very simple equation for the calculation of trust value.

$T = tanh \ (R1+R2+A)$

Where
T = Trust value,
$R1$= Ratio between the number of packets actually forwarded and number of packets to be forwarded, $R2$ = Ratio between total number of packets that are received by node and node should forward and the total number of packets sent by node's 1-hop neighborhood and are not destined for another neighbor or to itself. (If the denominator is not zero and $R2 = 1$), A = Acknowledgement bit. (0 or 1).

The threshold trust level for an unknown node to become a known to its neighbor is represented by T_K and the threshold trust level for a known node to become a Companion of its neighbor is denoted by Tc. The Threshold parameters are design parameters. There is a tradeoff between offering good security in adhoc networks and overall throughput of the network. Hence, choosing an optimal value is crucial for the good functioning of the network. When any node wishes to send messages to a distant node, its sends the RREQ o all the neighboring nodes. The RREP obtained from its neighbor is sorted by trust ratings. The source selects the most trusted path. If its one hop neighbor node is a Companion, then that path is chosen for message transfer. If its one-hop neighbor node is a known, and if the one hop neighbor of the second best path is a companion choose C. Thus the black hole nodes will be identified as unknown in both the hops and were not given preference in the route selection.

4 Results

Simulation is carried out in the cooperative black Hole attack Scenario for three sources and three destinations. Results have been observed for the parameters [21] Throughput, Latency, Packet Delivery Ratio and. Again Simulation is carried out in the same cooperative black hole environment for the same three paths with the association table (proposed system). The simulation is being implemented in the network Simulator-2 [22], a simulator for mobile adhoc networks. The simulation parameters are provided in Table 1.

Table 1. Simulation parameters

Parameter	Value
Application traffic	CBR
Radio range	250 m
Packet size	512 bytes
Pause time for nodes	50 s
Simulation time	200 s
Number of nodes	30
Area	1000 m * 1000 m

Results have been taken for same parameters as mentioned above. Comparing these two sets of systemic graphs, following results have been achieved which proves the efficiency of our system. Throughput and Packet Delivery Ratio in our system is higher. But the Latency is little bit higher than the existing DSR system because of the implementation of the trust evaluation mechanism in the proposed system.

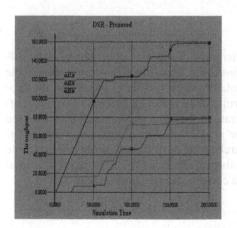 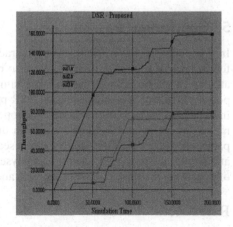

Fig. 1. Comparison of Throughput

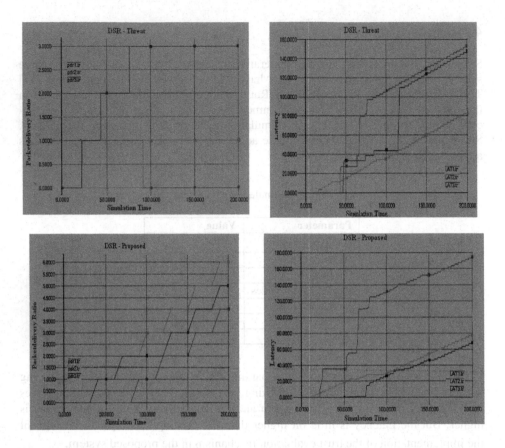

Fig. 2. Comparison of Packet Delivery ratio   **Fig. 3.** Comparison of Latency

5 Conclusion

In this paper we have discussed the characteristics of mobile adhoc network and different type of routing protocols. We also discussed about the Cooperative Blackhole attacks. With the help of the Network simulator we were able to prove that the proposed scheme of Association based DSR protocol increases the security level of routing and also encourages the nodes to cooperate in the adhoc structure. It identifies the malicious nodes and isolates them from the active data forwarding and routing. The paper represents the first step of our research to analyse the cooperative black hole attack over the proposed scheme to analyse its performance. The next step will consist of analyzing the protocol over Greyhole and cooperative greyhole attacks.

References

[1] Siva Ram Murthy, C., Manoj, B.S.: Ad Hoc Wireless Networks: Architectures and Protocols. Prentice Hall, Englewood Cliffs (2004)
[2] Johnson, D.B., Maltz, D.A.: Dynamic Source Routing in Adhoc wireless networking. Mobile Computing 353, 153–181 (1996)

[3] Papadimitratos, P., Haas, Z.J.: Securing the Internet Routing Infrastructure. IEEE Communications 10(40), 60–68 (2002)

[4] Hod, B.: Cooperative and Reliable Packet- Forwarding On top of AODV (2005),
http://www.cs.huji.ac.il/~dolev/pubs/reliable-aodv.pdf

[5] Ramaswamy, S., Fu, H., Sreekantaradhya, M., Dixon, J., Nygard, K.: Prevention of Cooperative Black Hole Attack in Wireless AdHoc Networks (2003),
http://www.cs.ndsu.nodak.edu/~nygard/research/
BlackHoleMANET.pdf

[6] Hu, Y.C., Perrig, A., Johnson, D.B.: Ariadne: A secure on-demand routing protocol for ad hoc networks. In: Eighth Annual International Conference on Mobile Computing and Networking (Mobi-Com 2002), September 2002, pp. 12–23 (2002)

[7] Zapata, M.G.: Secure Ad hoc On-Demand Distance Vector (SAODV) Routing. IETF Internet Draft, draft-guerrero-manet-saodv-00.txt (2001)

[8] Zapata, M.G.: Secure Ad hoc On-Demand Distance Vector Routing. ACM SIGMOBILE Mobile Computing and Communications Review 6(3), 106–107 (2002)

[9] Zapata, M.G., Asokan, N.: Securing Ad hoc Routing Protocols. In: International Conference on Mobile Computing and Networking, Atlanta, GA, USA, pp. 1–10 (2002)

[10] Hu, Y.C., Johnson, D.B., Perrig, A.: SEAD: Secure efficient distance vector routing for mobile wireless ad hoc networks. In: The 4th IEEE Workshop on Mobile Computing Systems & Applications, June 2002, pp. 3–13 (2002)

[11] Sanzgiri, K., Dahill, B., Levine, B.N., Shields, C., Belding-Royer, E.M.: A Secure Routing Protocol for Ad Hoc Networks. In: 10th IEEE International Conference on Network Protocols (ICNP 2002), Paris, France, pp. 78–89 (2002)

[12] Hu, Y.C., Perrig, A.: A survey of secure wireless ad hoc routing. IEEE Security & Privacy Magazine 2(3), 28–39 (2004)

[13] Deng, H., Li, W., Agrawal, D.P.: Routing Security in Wireless Ad Hoc Network. IEEE Communications Magazines 40(10) (October 2002)

[14] Weerasinghe,]., Fu, H.: Preventing Cooperative Black Hole Attacks in Mobile Ad Hoc Networks: Simulation Implementation and Evaluation. International Journal of Software Engineering and Its Applications 2(3), 39–54 (2008)

[15] Perkins, C.E., Royer, E.M.: Ad hoc on demand distance vector routing. In: Proceedings of IEEE Workshop on Mobile computing systems and Applications 1999, pp. 90–100 (February 1999)

[16] Buchegger, S., Le Boudec, J.-Y.: Nodes Bearing Grudges: Towards Routing Security, Fairness and robustness in Mobile ad hoc networks. In: Proceedings of the Tenth Euromicro Workshop on Parallel, Distributed and Network–based processing, Canary Islands, Spain, January 2002, pp. 403–410. IEEE Computer Society, Los Alamitos (2002)

[17] Marti, S., Giuli, T.J., Lai, K., Baker, M.: Mitigating routing misbehaviour in Mobile ad hoc networks. In: Proceedings of MOBICOM 2000, pp. 255–265 (2000)

[18] Buchegger, S., Boudec, J.-Y.L.: Performance Analysis of the CONFIDANT Protocol. Cooperation of Nodes - Fairness in Dynamic Ad-hoc Networks. Technical Report (IC/2002/01), EPFL I&C, Lausanne, January 21 (2002)

[19] Buchegger, S., Boudec, J.Y.L.: Performance analysis of the CONFIDANT protocol. In: Proceedings of the 3rd ACM international symposium on Mobile ad hocnetworking & computing, Lausanne, Switzerland, June 2002, pp. 226–236 (2002)

[20] Bhalaji, N., Shanmugam, A.: Association between nodes to Combat Blackhole attack in DSR based MANET. In: Proceedings of Sixth IEEE-IFIP International conference on WOCN, Egypt (2009) ISBN: 978-1-4244-4704-6, doi:10.1109/WOCN.2009.5010579

[21] Broch, J., Johnson, D., Maltz, D., Hu, Y., Jetcheva, J.: A Performance Comparison of Multihop Wireless Ad Hoc Networking Protocols. In: Proceedings of 4th ACM/IEEE International Conference on Mobile Computing and Networking (1998)

[22] Fall, K., Varadhan, K.: The ns manual,
    http://www.isi.edu/nsnam/ns/doc/index.html

Extended Finite State Machine Model-Based Regression Test Suite Reduction Using Dynamic Interaction Patterns

S. Selvakumar[1], M.R.C. Dinesh[1], C. Dhineshkumar[1], and N. Ramaraj[2]

[1] Department of Information Technology, Thiagarajar College of Engineering,
Madurai, India
[2] Department of Computer Science & Engineering, G.K.M college of Engineering,
Chennai, India
ssit@tce.edu, {dinesh.mrc,dhineshjim2006}@gmail.com,
prof.ramaraj@yahoo.co.in

Abstract. An EFSM (Extended Finite State Machine) model-based regression test suite (RTS) reduction method based on dynamic dependence analysis is proposed. Our approach automatically identifies the difference between the original model and the modified model as a set of elementary model modifications. This proposed method reduces the size of a given RTS by examining the various interaction patterns covered by each test case in the given RTS.

Keywords: Regression testing, Extended finite state machine, Control dependence, Data dependence, Regression test suite reduction.

1 Introduction

Regression testing is the process of validating the modified software to increase our confidence that the changed parts of the software behave as intended and that the unchanged parts of the software have not been adversely affected by the modifications [5]. In this paper, we present a novel approach of model-based regression test reduction(Dynamic Dependence Graph) that uses EFSM model dependence analysis to reduce a given regression test suite. This approach overcomes the drawback of the Static Dependence Graph [1] by considering all the interaction patterns instead of ignoring the patterns of the same dependencies between transitions which occur during the traversal of the model in the iterative manner. Our initial experience shows that this approach may significantly reduce the size.

2 The EFSM Model

The model based regression testing techniques use only a modified system model in which the modified elements(states and transitions) are tested using selective test generation techniques, i.e., each regression test case contains a modified model element. An EFSM is a 5-tuple (S, I, O, V, T) where

V.V Das et al. (Eds.): BAIP 2010, CCIS 70, pp. 475–481, 2010.

i)   S is a nonempty finite set of states with two states designated as Start and Exit states of the EFSM
ii) I is a nonempty finite set of input interactions
iii) O is a nonempty finite set of output interactions
iv) V is the nonempty finite set of all variables which is the union of set of all local variables and set of all interaction parameters
v)   T is a nonempty finite set of transitions

An EFSM model consists of states and the transitions between them. EFSM models are graphically represented as nodes and transitions as direct edges between states. A transition has the following elements namely 1.) an event, 2.) a condition, and 3.) a sequence of actions. A simplified EFSM model of a global banking system is shown in the Figure 1.

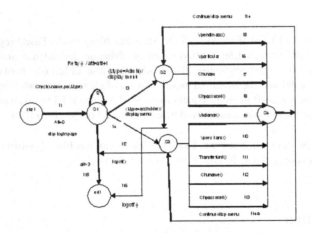

Fig. 1. EFSM for Global Banking System

The EFSM model shown in the Figure 1 will be used as a running example throughout this paper. Since transitions represent active elements of the EFSM model, we concentrate on their modifications rather than those on the states. In an EFSM model, data and control dependences may exist between transitions. These dependencies are identified using the Dependence Analysis.

A. Data Dependence

Data Dependence captures the notion that one transition defines a value for a variable and the same or some other transition may potentially use this value [3].

B. Control Dependence

The concept of Control dependence in the EFSM exists between transitions and captures the notion that one transition may affect traversal of another transition. Control between transitions can be defined in terms of the concept of post-dominance.

C. Static Dependence Graph

Static Dependence Graph (SDG) graphically represents the Data Dependencies (DDs) and Control Dependencies (CDs) in an EFSM. Here the nodes represent the transitions and the directed arcs represent the Data and Control Dependencies.

Drawbacks

Test reduction using Static Interaction Patterns is appropriate in the initial stages of testing, when a relatively small number of high quality tests are supposed to be used. However, test reduction using Static Interaction Patterns ignores repetitions of the same dependencies (interactions) between transitions. Therefore, we present test reduction using more sophisticated interaction patterns that take into account repetition of the same interactions. This leads our approach to the Dynamic Interaction Patterns.

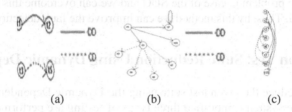

(a)   (b)   (c)

Fig. 2. (a) Data and Control Dependencies; (b) Static Dependence Graph; (c) Dynamic Dependence graph

D. Dynamic EFSM Dependencies

Our approach works as follows: Given a test (sequence of transitions), during traversal each traversed transition is represented as a node in the dynamic EFSM dependence graph, and each identified data or control dependence is represented by an arc between corresponding transitions. This process results in a dynamic EFSM dependence graph. In the next step, all the dependencies in the dynamic EFSM dependence graph that influence the transition(s) under test are identified by traversing backwards from the transition(s) under test and marking all traversed dependencies. All unmarked dependencies are removed from the dynamic dependence graph. The resulting dynamic EFSM dependence sub-graph is referred to as a Dynamic Interaction Pattern, where data and control dependencies represent interactions between transitions. Let us consider the following two tests:

    Test 1: t1 t2 t2 t2 t3 t5 t14 t6 t14
    Test 2: t1 t2 t2 t2 t2 t3 t5 t14 t6 t14

A Static Dependence Graph is represented for the above two tests in Figure 3a. Here both the tests provide the same interaction patterns even though the test suites are different. So, we will remove one of them in case of the Static Dependence Graphs(SDG). A Dynamic Dependence Graph is represented for the same two tests in Figure 3b.

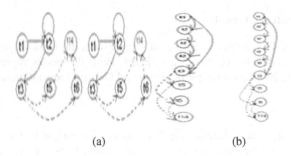

(a)   (b)

Fig. 3. (a) Static Dependence Graph for the above two tests; (b) Dynamic Dependence Graph for the above two tests

Here the interaction patterns differ from each other and hence we should not ignore them. This is the problem in case of the SDG and we can overcome this drawback by our concept of DDG. Thus, by this method we can improve the fault detection capability.

3   Regression Test Suite Reduction Using Dynamic Dependencies

Our goal is to reduce the given test suite using the Dynamic Dependencies. In general, when a software system is modified three types of testing are performed:(I) testing the affect of the model on the modification (modified part of the model), (2) testing the affect of the modification on the remaining part of the system model, and (3) testing side affects caused by the modification. If the same interaction pattern of a certain type is computed for two different tests for an elementary modification, these tests are considered equivalent, with respect to the elementary modification and the interaction pattern.

A. Testing the Addition of a Transition

When a transition is added, three types of testing needs to be performed: (I) testing the affect of the model on the added transition, (2) testing the affect of the added transition on the model, and (3) testing the side effects introduced by the added transition. During the traversal of a test, data and control dependencies that occur during the traversal of the test are identified and marked in the EFSM Dynamic Dependence Graph. In the next step all the unmarked dependencies are removed from the graph. Then all the dependencies in the dependence sub-graph that affect the added transitions are identified by traversing backwards from the added transition and marking all traversed dependencies. All unmarked dependencies are removed from the dependence sub-graph.

i) Testing the Affect of the Model on the Added Transition
Consider the model shown in the Figure 1 where balance/display() transaction has been added to the Banking system and represented by the transition t18.

Eg: TEST 1: t1 t3 t5 t14 t6 t14 t7 t14 t8 t14 t8 t4 t18 t14 t16
TEST 2: t1 t3 t5 t14 t6 t14 t7 t14 t8 t14 t8 t4 t18 t14 t14 t16

Both the tests result in the same Dynamic interaction patterns as shown in the Figure 4a, and hence these two tests are equivalent with respect to the affecting interaction pattern.

ii) Testing the affect on the added transition on the model

Two tests are equal, with respect to the affected interaction pattern, if both tests have the same interaction patterns. These two tests result in the same affected Dynamic interaction pattern as shown in the Figure 4b.

iii) Testing side-effects introduced by the added transition

Two tests are equivalent, with respect to the side-effect interaction pattern, if both tests result in the same side interaction pattern. Side-affect dynamic interaction pattern is shown in Figure 4c.

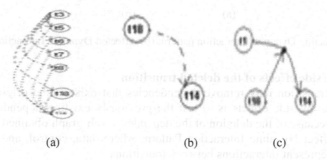

(a)   (b)   (c)

Fig. 4. (a) Affecting Dynamic Interaction Pattern; (b) Affected Dynamic Interaction Pattern; (c) Side-Effect Dynamic Interaction Pattern

B Testing the Deletion of a Transition

Consider the Banking system shown in the Figure 1. The vparticular acc() transaction is deleted from the original model, resulting in the model shown in the Figure 1. The deleted transition t6 is represented in the dashed arrow in the Figure 1. The deleted transition is represented by an empty transition t19 in the state s2. Testing the newly added transition t19 will result in a single test because all the patterns for testing t19 are empty.

i)Testing the Affect of the Model on the Deleted Transition

Deletion of a transition can cause elimination of dependencies associated with the deleted transition where the deleted transition was dependent on another transition. For example, there exists ghost dependence between transitions t3 and t6 in the modified model of Figure 4a.

     Test 1: t1 t3 t7 t19 t14 t16,
     Test 2: t1 t3 t7 t14 t18 t14 t16

Both these tests result in the same affecting Dynamic interaction pattern as shown in the Figure 5a. Therefore these two tests are equivalent with respect to the affecting Dynamic pattern.

ii) Testing the Affect of the Deleted Transition on the Model

The affected interaction pattern for the following test is shown in the Figure 5b.Both these tests result in the same affecting Dynamic interaction pattern as shown in the Figure 5b. Therefore these two tests are equivalent with respect to the affected Dynamic pattern.

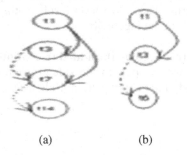

(a)   (b)

Fig. 5. (a) Affecting Dynamic Interaction pattern; (b) Affected Dynamic Interaction Pattern

iii) Testing the side effects of the deleted transition

Deletion of a transition may remove dependencies that exist in the original model. The goal of testing side effects is to test the previously existing dependencies that cease to exist because of the deletion of the dependence sub-graph obtained is referred to as a Side-Effect Dynamic Interaction Pattern, where data, control, and activation dependencies represent interactions between transitions.

4   Regression Test Suite Reduction

For each regression test 3*N interaction patterns are computed where N is the number of elementary modifications. A reduced test suite has the following property: For every test in the reduced test suite, there exists an interaction pattern p associated with an elementary modification m such that, all the remaining tests in the reduced test suite do not have pattern p associated with modification m. The problem of test reduction is to find a test suite that satisfies the properties of the reduced test suite. There may be many test suites that satisfy the properties of the reduced test suite but our aim is to identify a test suite of a minimum size that satisfies the properties of the reduced test suite.

5   Performance Analysis

Here we have compared the HGS algorithm with our proposed approach and the comparisons are showed in the Figures 6a, 6b and 6c. Based on the initial experimentation with our presented approach, we observed that the Regression TSR using Dynamic Dependencies have not only reduced the test suites but also improved the fault detection capability when compared to the Static Dependencies.

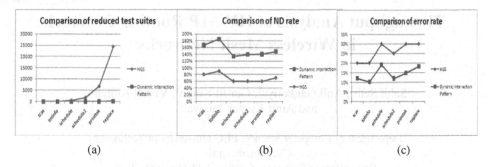

Fig. 6. (a) Comparison of reduced test suites; (b) Comparison of ND rate; (c) Comparison of error rate

6 Conclusion

In this paper, we have presented a novel approach of Regression TSR using Dynamic Dependency Graph. Using the Dynamic Dependencies, we considered all the possible test cases with their interaction patterns. Then we analyzed each and every test cases and removed the test cases having the same interaction patterns similar to another test case. Finally, we formed a Reduced Test Suite with the remaining test cases and then we tested our application our Reduced Tested Suite. The results we obtained showed that our method had a high fault detection capability than the previous methods.

References

[1] Vaysburg, B., Tahat, L., Korel, B.: Dependence Analysis in Reduction of Requirement Based Test Suites. In: Proceedings of IEEE International Symposium on Software Testing and Analysis (ISSTA), Rome, Italy (2002)
[2] Korel, B., Tahat, L.H., Vaysburg, B.: Model-based regression test reduction using dependence analysis. In: Proceedings of ICSM 2002, Montréal, Canada, October 3-6 (2002)
[3] Tahat, L.H., Bader, A., Vaysburg, B., Korel, B.: Requirement- based automated black box test generation. In: Proceedings of COMPSAC 2001, Chicago,USA, October 8-12 (2001)
[4] Rothermel, G., Harrold, M.: A Safe, Efficient Regression Test Selection Technique. ACM Transactions on Software Engineering and Methodology 6, 173–210 (1997)
[5] Gupta, R., Harrold, M.J., Soffa, M.L.: An approach to regression testing using slicing, pp. 299–308. IEEE Computer Society Press, Washington (1992)

Throughput Analysis of HWMP Routing Protocol in Wireless Mesh Networks

Sahil Seth[1], Anil Gankotiya[1], Gurdit Singh[1], Vishal Kumar[2],
and Amit Kumar Jaiswal[2]

[1] Department of Computer Science, PEC University of Technology,
Chandigarh, India
[2] Department of Computer Science, NIT Hamirpur, India
{sahilseth,anilgankotiya,gurditsingh}@ieee.org,
{kumarvishalji,ashuamit.akj}@gmail.com

Abstract. To become independent of backbone networks leading to cheap deployments, the traditional single-hop approach needs to be replaced by Wireless Mesh Networks (WMNs). Wireless Mesh Networks is cost-effective alternative to wireless local area networks. Due to multi hop networking, WMN requires multi hop routing protocol. Mostly the nature of data is from client to gateway and vice versa. So, according to IEEE 802.11s Draft 3.0, HWMP routing protocol is adopted. In this paper, we analyzed the throughput of HWMP protocol with increase in number of nodes and increase in size of packets using simulation model.

Keywords: Multi Hop Routing, Multi Hop Networking, Throughput Analysis, HWMP.

1 Introduction

Wireless networks provide unprecedented freedom and mobility for a growing number of laptop and PDA users who no longer need wires to stay connected with their workplace and the Internet. Mesh networking overcomes the biggest problem remaining in wireless communications: the wires. Wireless Mesh networks are an emerging technology towards cheap deployment [2].

Wireless mesh network often consists of mesh clients, mesh routers and gateways. The mesh clients are often laptops, cell phones and other wireless devices while the mesh routers forward traffic to and from the gateways which may but need not connect to the Internet. The coverage area of the radio nodes working as a single network is sometimes called a mesh cloud. A mesh network is reliable and offers redundancy [3] [4] [5]. When one node can no longer operate, the rest of the nodes can still communicate with each other, directly or through one or more intermediate nodes.

In Wireless mesh networks mostly the nature of the traffic is from client to Gateway and vice versa. According to IEEE Draft 3.0 released in 2009 [1], HWMP routing protocol is adopted and RA-AODV has been eliminated. HWMP combines the flexibility of on-demand routing with proactive topology tree extensions.

V.V Das et al. (Eds.): BAIP 2010, CCIS 70, pp. 482–484, 2010.

2   Scenario Description

We implemented the scenario in qualnet 4.5. To analyze the throughput with increase in number of nodes. Firstly, Scenario run with 25 nodes having three CBR applications with packet size 256 bytes. Secondly, scenario run with 50 nodes. Thirdly, scenario run with 100 nodes and so on with 150 and 200 nodes respectively with 256 bytes. To analyze throughput with increase in size of packets, scenario with 25 nodes firstly runs with 256 byte packet size, secondly runs with 512 byte and so on with 1024, 2048 and 4096 bytes.

Table 1. Description about scenario with 25 nodes

NODE NUMBER	TYPE
1	Mesh portal
2	Mesh access point
3	Mesh access point
4	Mesh access point
5-25	Mobile nodes
9,15,17,19,22,24	Nodes with CBR Application

3   Results

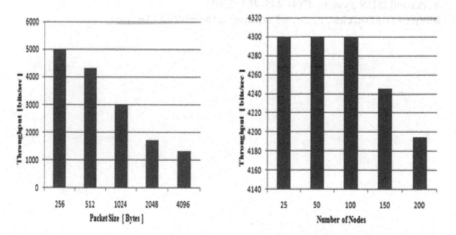

Fig. 1. (Left) Throughput Vs Packet Size, (right) Throughput Vs number of nodes

4   Conclusion

In this paper, we have analyzed the throughput of HWMP routing protocol in wireless mesh networks using simulation model of HWMP routing protocol. Throughput analyzed with increase in number of nodes and with increase in packet size. The result section showed us degradation in throughput. Hence, there is a requirement of scalable routing protocol in wireless mesh networks.

Acknowledgement

This work was done as collaborative work at Cyber Security Research Center, situated at PEC University of Technology, Chandigarh with support from Department of Computer Science, NIT Hamirpur and PEC University of Technology. The authors would like to thank Government of India, Ministry of Communications and Information Technology, Department of Information Technology, New Delhi, for funding the Project *"Investigate, Explore & Implement security aspects in existing protocols in Wireless Mesh Network",* under which this work has been done.

References

1. IEEE 802.11s Draft 3.0 released in 2009 (2009)
2. Hertz, G.R., Max, S., Weiß, E., Berlemann, L., Denteneer, D., Mangold, S.: Mesh Technology enabling Ubiquitous Wireless Networks. In: Proceedings of the 2nd Annual International Wireless Internet Conference (WICON 2006), August 2-5, p. 11. ACM, Boston (2006) (invited paper), http://www.comnets.rwth-aachen.de
3. Akyildiz, I.F., Wang, X.: A survey on wireless mesh networks. IEEE Communications Magazine 43(9), S23–S30 (2005)
4. Akyildiz, I.F., Wang, X., Wang, W.: Wireless mesh networks: a survey. Computer Networks and ISDN Systems 47(4), 445–487 (2005)
5. http://networks.rice.edu/papers/mesh80211s.pdf

Separation of Machine Printed Roman and Gurmukhi Script Words

Dharamveer Sharma

Department of Computer Science, Punjabi University, Patiala, Punjab, India
dveer72@hotmail.com

Abstract. In a multi-lingual country like India, a document may contain more than one script forms. For such a document, it is necessary to separate different script forms before feeding them to OCRs of respective scripts. In the work presented in this paper, a successful attempt has been made to identify the script at the word level in a bilingual document containing Roman and Gurmukhi scripts. The technique presented here can separate English and Punjabi words present in a single document. In this approach English and Punjabi words are separated using certain features of Gurmukhi and Roman script. Words with various font styles and sizes have been used for the testing of the proposed algorithms and the results are quite encouraging. The system has an overall accuracy of 98.78% of identification.

Keywords: OCR, Multilingual OCR, Machine Printed, Gurmukhi Script, Roman Script, Bi-lingual.

1 Introduction

Identification of the script of the text in multi-script documents is one of the important steps in the design of an OCR system. Identification of the script is one of the challenging tasks facing a designer of an OCR system. Script identification makes the task of analysis and recognition of the text easier by suitably selecting the modalities of OCR. A few results have already been reported in the literature, identifying the scripts in a multi-lingual and multi-script document dealing with Roman and other Oriental scripts such as Chinese, Korean and Japanese. A few attempts have also been made to isolate and identify the scripts of the texts in the case of multi-script Indian documents. In our work, a successful attempt has been made to identify the script, at the word level, in a bilingual document containing Roman and Gurmukhi scripts.

The bilingual document may be printed in one of the official Indian language like Hindi (Devnagari), Punjabi (Gurmukhi) and English (Roman). In the present work the project main concern will be on separating Gurmukhi and Roman script words from printed document. However, the system will be, with minor or no modifications, suitable to some other Indian scripts which have structural features similar to Gurmukhi e.g. Devnagari, Bangla and Gujrati.

In some scripts (like Devnagari, Gurmukhi, Bangla and Gujrati etc) many characters have a horizontal line at the upper part. This line is called head-line. When two or

V.V Das et al. (Eds.): BAIP 2010, CCIS 70, pp. 485–490, 2010.

more characters sit side by side to form a word the head-line portions touch one another and generate a long head-line which is used as a feature to isolate one word from text line.

English script is distinguished by the absence of this head-line feature. These features help us to separate Gurmukhi script words from the Roman script words. This paper has been organized into 6 sections. Section 2 discusses related work, section 3 contains proposed technique. Results, discussions and conclusions are given in section 4 and section 5 contains references.

2 Related Work

Pal and Chaudhuri [4,5,6] in their papers explained schemes of automatic word separation of different scripts namely Roman, Bangla and Devnagari from a single document.

Ahmed M. Elgammal and M.A. Ismail [7] in their paper addresses the problem of language identification for documents printed in hybrid Arabic/ English languages. Proposed techniques address the languages identification problem on the word level and on text line levels. Because of the many differences between Arabic and English text styles, character recognition methods differ in the way they handle text in these two languages.

There are two basic approaches for document analysis [8]; top down approach and bottom up approach. In the top down approach, starting with the scanned page, the page is segmented into large blocks which are then classified to text blocks, Figures, tables, etc. Text blocks are then resegmented into text lines and then into words and characters. In the bottom up approach, black pixels are grouped into small components (character size). These components are combined to form words and then text lines and paragraphs. Language identification is performed on word level, i.e., after extracting tokens corresponding to words, these tokens are passed to a language identification process to label them either Arabic or English.

Character segmentation strategies are divided into two categories [9].

a) Explicit Segmentation: In this strategy, the segments are identified based on "character-like" properties. The process of cutting up the image into meaningful components is given a special name: *dissection*. Dissection is a process that analyzes an image without using a specific class of shape information.

b) Implicit Segmentation: This segmentation strategy is based on recognition. It searches the image for components that match predefined classes. In this approach, two classes of methods can be employed: 1) methods that make some search process and 2) methods that segment a feature representation of the image [9]. The first class attempts to segment words into letters or other units without use of feature-based dissection algorithms. Rather, the image is divided systematically into many overlapping pieces without regard to content. Conceptually, these methods originate from schemes developed for the recognition of machine-printed words [10]. The second class of methods segments the image implicitly by classification of subsets of spatial features collected from the image as a whole.

3   Proposed Technique

The proposed technique is based on the following assumptions:

(i)   The image is noise and skew free.
(ii) In a word, inter-character gap should be nearly uniform otherwise it may give wrong results and accuracy may decrease.
(iii) No Punjabi word should have upper headline pixels less than horizontal threshold i.e. 77%.

The target of segmentation is to get each word and decide which word is Punjabi one, which is English one. Segmentation includes line and words segmentation. The algorithm includes three steps, in first step line segmentation is performed and in second segmentation step the words blocks are detected. Each block may correspond to a single word. The third step is used to identify the words whether they are Gurmukhi or English words.

3.1   Line Segmentation

According to the horizontal and vertical projections, a line block that contains the characters is candidates for regions that will be extracted. As a result, a series of line blocks in a document are identified, the general information of current text line, i.e., height and the width will be obtained. In pre-segmentation it is not known whether the current line is purely composed of English or Punjabi characters. The procedure to segment line uses the horizontal projection of a line. In this step the document is scanned in horizontal direction from left to right and each line's first and last black pixel is marked as top and bottom of the line and the line length is also checked by evaluating black pixel found at minimum position along y axis and at maximum location along y axis as shown in the figure 1 below.

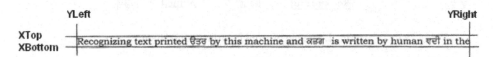

Fig. 1. Sample 1 of segmented line

After line segmenting the document is divided into lines as shown in figure 2:

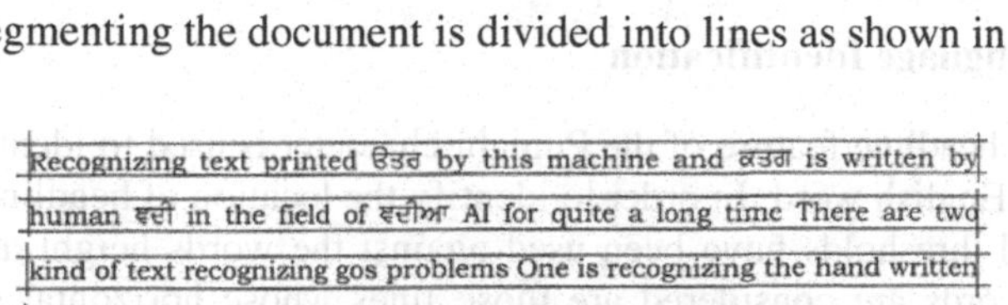

Recognizing text printed ਉਤਰ by this machine and ਕਤਰ is written by
human ਵਦੀ in the field of ਵਦੀਆ AI for quite a long time There are two
kind of text recognizing gos problems One is recognizing the hand written
languages which is handwritten ਪਤਰ ਵਦੀਆ text recognizing and the
printed character recognizing, which is optical character

Fig. 2. Result of line segmentation

3.2 Word Segmentation

Vertical projections on a text line found are considered in this segmentation step. According to the projections, a line block that contains the words is regions that are to extract. As a result, a series of word blocks are identified in a document; the general information of current text line is used to perform this step. The procedure for segment words uses the vertical projections on a line. In this step the lines extracted are scanned in vertical direction from bottom to top and here inter word gap is considered for word segmentation lines first and last black pixel scanned vertically is marked and stored yleft and yright vectors in a word segmentation. Here the word gap threshold considered is around 5 if there is vertical line gap greater then equal to 5 vertical lines then word coordinates are preserved as in figure 3.

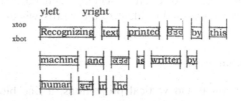

Fig. 3. Example of word segmentation

3.3 Word Coordinates Updation

In this step the word coordinates are updated and actual word bounding blocks are considered. It is shown in the figure 4 below.

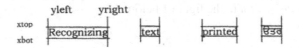

Fig. 4. Sample of word coordinates updation

In the word "text" the word height is considered of the line height, which is more than the actual word height.

3.4 Word Language Identification

In this step the headline feature of the Punjabi character is used to identify the Punjabi word from the English word. In order to identify the location of headlines the horizontal and vertical thresholds have been used against the words height and length. The headlines of words are considered are those lines whose horizontal projections are greater than or equal to 77% of word length, which has been proved by experimentation. If word starts from y1 and ends at y2 then horizontal threshold will be equal to 77% of (y2-y1). For each line a vertical threshold of 35% of the word height has been considered to find out the headline location. If word starts from XTop and ends at XBottom then vertical threshold will be equal to 35% of (XBottom-XTop). Then those words which falls under the category described above are identified as Punjabi words and others are English words.

4 Results and Discussions

The system has been tested on binary files at 100, 200 and 300 dpi resolution images. Following results have been obtained by inputting a binary image obtained by scanning the document at a resolution of 300 dpi (figure 5). The input document is assumed to contain only text and is thus free from graphics figures, maps and tables. To identify the textual blocks of interest, the binary document is first segmented into lines and then into words which is discussed above in line segmentation and word segmentation.

This ਇਹ is ਇਕ a sample ਨਮੂਨਾ text ਲੇਖ for testing ਹੈ ਜਿਸ ਨਾਲ multilingual script ਅਸੀਂ ਆਪਣਾ ਪ੍ਰੋਗਰਾਮ identifier and ਟੈਸਟ ਕਰਾਂਗੇ separator. ਇਹ ਪ੍ਰੋਗਰਾਮ ਦੇ ਭਿਨੰ ਭਿੰਨ ਸਕਰਿਪਟਾਂ ਨੂੰ ਅਲਗਾ ਅਲਗਾ ਕਰ ਦਿੰਦਾ ਹੈ। This has been developed as a research project for award of M.Tech. thesis.

Fig. 5. Sample document Punjabi words found

The results of segmentation and separation of words of Gurmukhi and Roman scripts are given in figure 6.

ਇਹ ਇਕ ਨਮੂਨਾ ਲੇਖ ਹੈ ਜਿਸ ਨਾਲ ਅਸੀਂ ਆਪਣਾ ਪ੍ਰੋਗਰਾਮ ਟੈਸ
ਕਰਾਂਗੇ ਇਹ ਪ੍ਰੋਗਰਾਮ ਦੇ ਭਿਨੰ ਭਿੰਨ ਸਕਰਿਪਟਾਂ ਨੂੰ ਅਲਗਾ ਅਲ
ਕਰ ਦਿੰਦਾ ਹੈ।
24 Punjabi words found

This is a sample text for testing multilingual script identifier and separator. This has been developed as a research project for award of M.Tech. thesis.
25 English words found

Fig. 6. Output of Punjabi words of sample document Image

A simple and efficient projection profile method has been proposed based on which words of two scripts i.e. Roman and Gurmukhi are identified. Bilingual document is first segmented for lines and than words are extracted from segmented lines. From these extracted words distinctive features of Gurmukhi and Roman scripts are searched. Distinctive features like presence of head-line in Gurmukhi script and its absence in Roman script which is tested using horizontal projection profile.

References

1. Lehal, G.S., Singh, C.: A Gurmukhi script recognition system. In: Proc. 15th ICPR, Barcelona, Spain, vol. 2, pp. 557–560. IEEE Computer Society Press, California (2000)
2. Dhanya, D., Ramakrishan, A.G., Pati, P.B.: Language identification in printed bilingual documents. Sadhana 27(1), 73–82 (2002)

3. Peake, G.S., Tan, T.N.: Script and Language Identification from Document Images. In: Workshop on Document Image Analysis (DIA 1997), pp. 10–17 (1997)
4. Chaudhary, B.B., Pal, U.: Skew angle detection of digitized Indian script documents. IEEE Trans. PAMI 19, 182–186 (1997)
5. Pal, U., Chaudhuri, B.B.: Automatic identification of English, Chinese, Arabic, Devnagari and Bangla script line. In: Proc. 6th ICDAR, September 10-13, pp. 790–794 (2001)
6. Pal, U., Chaudhuri, B.B.: Script line separation from Indian multi-script documents. In: Proc. 5th ICDAR, Banglore, India, pp. 406–409 (1999)
7. Elgammal, A., Ismail, M.A.: Techniques for Language Identification for Hybrid Arabic-English Document Images. In: Proc. 6th ICDAR, Seattle, Washington, U.S.A., September 10-13, pp. 1100–1104 (2001)
8. Casey, R.G., Wong, K.Y.: Document-analysis systems and techniques. In: Kasturi, R., Trivedi, M.M. (eds.) Image Analysis Applications, pp. 1–36. Marcel Dekker, New York (1990)
9. Casey, R.G., Lecolinet, E.: A survey of methods and strategies in character segmentation. IEEE Trans. PAMI 18, 690–706 (1996)
10. Casey, R.G., Nagy, G.: Recursive segmentation and classification of composite patterns. In: Proc. 6th ICPR, München, Germany, pp. 1023–1031 (1982)

FPGA Implementation of AES Co-processor in Counter Mode

Balwinder Singh[1], Harpreet Kaur[2], and Himanshu Monga[3]

[1] Department of VLSI & Embedded Division, CDAC, Mohali, India
[2,3] Department of Electronics and Communication Engineering,
RBIEBT, Mohali, India
balwinder@cdacmaohali.in

Abstract. In many applications strong security and high speed performance is required. For this purpose, DES and AES techniques are usually chosen, but these results in the lowering of security strength and less throughput. This paper presents the design FPGA implementation of AES processor in Counter Mode for 256 bits. In this work, the encryption rate is 52.6124 G bits /sec and memory efficiency is 1.565 with the key length of 256 bits. HDL simulations, verifications and implementations are done on Spartran 3, vertex 2 and vertex E devices.

Keywords: AES (Advance Encryption Standard), FPGA (Field Programmable Gate Array), ECB (Electronic Codebook), CTR mode (Counter Mode).

1 Introduction

Information security is a fundamental requirement for an operational information society. Cryptography is an art and science of hiding data, plays a central role in achieving information security. It has become a fundamental part of communication and commercial applications in the Internet as well as in many other digital applications. Cryptography is deployed with cryptographic algorithms, mathematical functions for hiding messages and retrieving hidden messages.

AES is short for Advanced Encryption Standard and is a United States encryption standard defined in Federal Information Processing Standard (FIPS) 192, published in November 2001. It was ratified as a federal standard in May 2002. AES is the most recent of the four current algorithms approved for federal us in the United States.[1]AES is an algorithm for performing encryption and decryption, which is a series of well-defined steps that can be followed as a procedure. Plain text original information is encrypted as cipher text. The cipher text message contains all the information of the plaintext message, but it is not readable by a human or computer without decrypt mechanism as shown in Fig.1.

The AES encryption algorithm is a block cipher that uses an encryption key and a several rounds of encryption. A block cipher is an encryption algorithm that works on a single block of data at a time. In the case of standard AES encryption the block is 128 bits, or 16 bytes, in length. The term "rounds" refers to the way in which the encryption algorithm mixes the data re-encrypting it ten to fourteen times depending on the length of the key.

V.V Das et al. (Eds.): BAIP 2010, CCIS 70, pp. 491–496, 2010.
© Springer-Verlag Berlin Heidelberg 2010

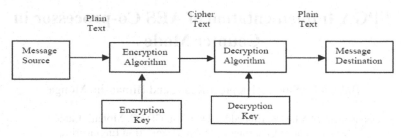

Fig. 1. Basic Cryptography Process

There are different methods of using keys with the AES encryption method. These different methods are called modes of operation. The National Institute of Standards and Technology (NIST) [4] defines six modes of operation that can be used with AES encryption: Electronic code book (ECB), Cipher block chaining (CBC), Counter (CTR), Cipher feed back (CFB), Output feed back (OFB), Galois Counter Mode (GCM). Each mode uses AES in a different way. For example, ECB encrypts each block of data independently .CTR mode encrypts a 256-bit counter and then adds that value to the data to encrypt it.

The remaining paper is organized as follows: In section 2 lists previous work on the AES algorithms implementation. Section 3 discusses AES algorithms in counter mode implementation on FPGA. Section 4 presents the results and discussion and section 5 concludes the Paper.

2 Previous Work

D. Canright (2005) has implemented an S-Box algorithm using only logic. This provided small cost area for algorithm implementation over LUT implementation in FPGA. This S-Box is implemented for both encryption and decryption operations and compares their area ratio, speed with LUT implementation [5].Jingmei Liu et al. (2005) have discussed the algebraic expression of AES S-box in terms low in complexity. In this paper, AES S-box is improved, and increases its algebraic expression terms to 255. The improved AES can not only greatly avoid vulnerability of only 9 terms in AES S-box algebraic expression, but also has a good performance of other algebraic properties [6].Yongzhi Fu et al. (2005) have proposed a design that extremely high performance counter mode AES processor designed on Xilinx Virtex2 FPGAs. They have explored several techniques for implementation and optimization of the AES-Rijndael algorithm on reconfigurable platforms. [8]. M.Dworkin (2001) has discussed that NIST PUB-800-38A provided the detail operation of Block Cipher Modes and Methods and Techniques which are used in AES Rijndael algorithm implementation in ECB, CBC, OBC, CTR modes [7].

Bo Yang et al. (2001) proposed a design for fully pipelined high speed hardware architecture for Galois/Counter Mode of Operation (GCM) by analyzing the data dependencies in the GCM algorithm at the architecture level that GCM encryption circuit and GCM authentication circuit have similar critical path delays resulting in an efficient pipeline structure [9].W. Diffie et al. (1979) have introduced Cryptography principles and different types of algorithm for security according to their uses. DES, 3DES, AES, MD5 are mainly used in secure information transmission [10].

3   Present Work

Designing AES co-processor in counter mode has avoided the problem of ECB (ECB is a mode of operation for a block cipher, with the characteristic that each possible block of plaintext has a defined corresponding cipher (text value) which would reveal pattern information of plain text. It is processed by encrypt the counter value with key K and exclusive OR the output with the plain text to get the cipher text, where AES algorithm is used in counter mode operation for 128 bit plain text and key text is varying from 128 to 256 bits with 128 bit counter text. It's provided strong security and high throughput without using AES decryption algorithm. By applying only AES encryption algorithm in CTR mode with parallel pipeline process-reducing area and increase speed of operation of encryption and decryption.

3.1   AES Algorithm Module in Counter Mode

In AES algorithm, four basic transformations are performed. First, we apply 128 bit input data to store in input register, take its SubBytes transformation by using S-box values and then ShiftRows transformation and then apply Mixcolumns transformation. Finally Xoring with round key values and save output data at output register. The procedure of counter mode operation is given in Fig 2. Decrypt procedure takes the same process to cover the plain text back from the cipher text. Since only the forward cipher is needed, the implementation of the inverse cipher is unnecessary. Ciphers are simplified with identical structure for encipher and decipher process. The transformation of a counter value have no dependencies with previous output, thus pipelining can be fully used. Counter mode has the advantage of no padding overhead, which is required for ECB, CBC, and CFB modes when the size of the data is not a multiple of block length. In cipher text errors situations, CBC and CFB mode will pass the error down to the following blocks, but Counter mode can restrict the error to that specific block. Therefore, in the case of extremely high throughput implementations, counter mode is the most suited.

Counter mode have special security requirement. The same counter value and key should not be used to encrypt more than one block of data. If that happened, the plain text information will be revealed by exclusive OR the two cipher text, which equals to exclusive OR of the two plain text. Especially in the case that one of the plain text is already known, the other one can be easily recovered by exclusive OR the known plain text to the output of the XORed cipher text. To avoid such problem, we have divided the 128-bit counter into 3 parts, shown in Fig 3.

The counter consists of a 40-bit cipher ID, a 48-bit key counter, and a 40-bit block counter. For each cipher, there is a specified cipher ID. The number of Cipher IDs is abundant. The key counter increases when a new key has been updated. In the situation that the key updates for a thousand times a minute, it will need thirty thousand years to use up the key counter space.

For each key there can be up to 16TB encrypted without refreshment of a new key. If the block counter is used out, the key counter will be increased to avoid the use of same key with same counter value. In this way, our design has guaranteed that there will be no same key and counter value pairs are used for more than once.

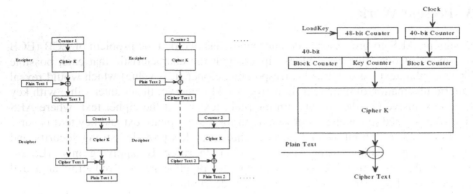

Fig. 2. Counter Mode Operation of AES Algorithm   **Fig. 3.** Counter Value Generation

4   Results and Discussion

The design of AES co-processor in counter mode is implemented using VHDL. Synthesis process has performed using Xilinx tools. The Technology mapping has chosen in this project from Spartan 3E (xc3s1600), Vertex 2P and vertex the synthesized schematic is also simulated to ensure the synthesized design functions. The simulation results are shown in fig 4 and comparison of three devices is given in terms of throughput CLBs used and Max frequency used in fig 5.

For key size of 256 bit …..key len=10

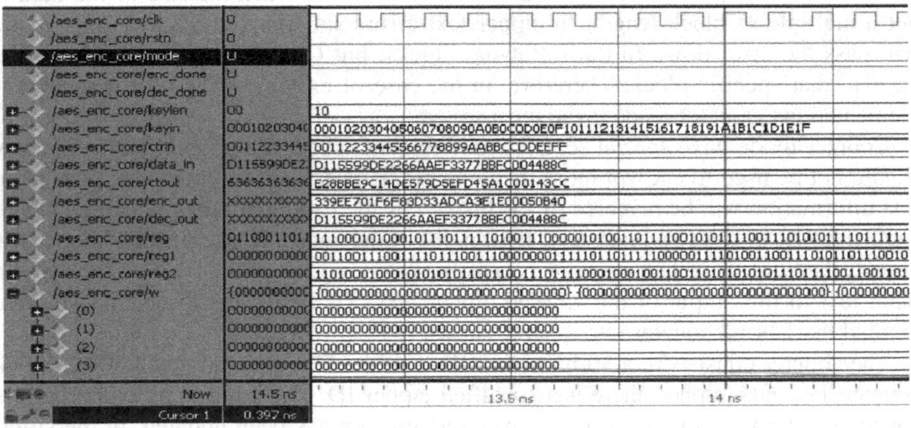

Fig. 4. Simulation results of AES CTR co-processor with Key size=256 bit

Encryption / Decryption operations with key size of 128 bits to 192, 256 bits, where plain text data_in having size of 128 bits and counter value ctr_in having size of 128 bits which is unique for the all operations. First of all, all inputs are feeded and the select the key len size according to key size and simulate the code and obtain the value of ctr_out. For encryption process, select mode =1 then encryption algorithm is performed and obtained the enc_out value of 128 bits which is the again used during decryption process, where mode=0 select for decryption process and obtained the value of dec_out of 128 bits.

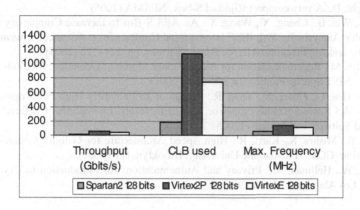

Fig. 5. Throughput versus Device Utilization

5 Conclusion

The proposed architecture uses non-feedback logic for Counter mode operation. We perform both the encryption and decryption operations, with data block and counter block equal to 128 bits with key size of 256 bits by using only encryption flow of AES algorithm for designing of the proposed architecture. The complexity of the decryption lies in the inverse Mix Column operation and the key scheduling for decryption requires more number of cycles than encryption because it has the over-head of pre-scheduling to generate the last round key, which is avoided in CTR mode by using only AES encryption algorithm. We obtained a VLSI realization, which per-forms the encryption at a rate of 52.6124 Gbits/sec and memory efficiency of 1.565 with the key length of 256 bits. In the proposed architecture, the standard round is duplicated for 13 (Nr -1) times followed by the final round. These rounds are cas-caded by using the pipelining registers. Using this architecture 14 blocks of data can be transformed at the same time, which results in high throughput.

References

1. Gaj, K., Chodowiec, P.: FPGA and ASIC Implementations of AES 235-294 FPGA and ASIC Implementations of AES. In: Cryptographic Engineering, pp. 235–294. Springer, US (2008)
2. Saggese, G.P., Mazzeo, A., Mazzocca, N., Strollo, A.G.M.: An FPGA-based performance analysis of the unrolling, tiling, and pipelining of the AES algorithm. In: Y. K. Cheung, P., Constantinides, G.A. (eds.) FPL 2003. LNCS, vol. 2778, pp. 292–302. Springer, Heidel-berg (2003)

3. Pramstaller, N., Wolkerstorfer, J.: A universal and efficient AES co-processor for field programmable logic arrays. In: Becker, J., Platzner, M., Vernalde, S. (eds.) FPL 2004. LNCS, vol. 3203, pp. 565–574. Springer, Heidelberg (2004)
4. National Institute of Standards and Technology (NIST), Advanced Encryption Standard, Federal information Processing Standards Publications 197 (FIPS197) (November 2001)
5. Canright, D.: A very compact Rijndael S-box, NPSMA (2005)
6. Liu, J., Wei, B., Cheng, X., Wang, X.: An AES S-Box to Increase Complexity and Cryptographic Analysis. In: 19th IEEE International Conference on Advanced Information Networking and Applications (AINA), Taipei, Taiwan, pp. 724–728 (2005)
7. Dworkin, M.: Recommendation for Block Cipher Modes of Operation: Methods and Techniques, NIST Special Publication 800-38A (2001)
8. Fu, Y., Hao, L., Zhang, X., Yang, R.: Design of an Extremely High Performance Counter Mode AES Reconfigurable Processor. In: IEEE Second International Conference on Embedded Software and Systems (2005)
9. Yang, B., Mishra, S., Karri, R.: High Speed Architecture for Galois / Counter Mode of Operation (GCM), Polytechnic University, Brooklyn, NY (2001)
10. Diffie, W., Hellman, M.: Privacy and Authentication: An Introduction to Cryptography. IEEE, Los Alamitos (March 1979)

Detecting Plagiarism in Text Documents

Shanmugasundaram Hariharan[1], Sirajudeen Kamal[2], Abdul Vadud Mohamed Faisal[2],
Sheik Mohamed Azharudheen[2], and Bhaskaran Raman[2]

[1] Assistant Professor, Department of Information Technology
B.S. Abdur Rahman University, Chennai-48, Tamilnadu, India
[2] Student, Department of Information Technology
B.S. Abdur Rahman University, Chennai-48, Tamilnadu, India
{mailtos.hariharan,kamal66077,ramancre}@gmail.com,
{azhar_cres,bruce_faisal}@yahoo.com

Abstract. Plagiarism aims at identifying the amount of information that is copied or reproduced in modified representation of original documents. This is quiet common among students, researchers and academicians that leads to a kind of unrecognizing. Though there exits some commercial tools to detect plagiarism, still plagiarism is tricky and quiet challenging task due to abundant information available online. Commercially existing softwares adopt methods like paraphrasing, sentence matching or keyword matching. This paper focuses its attention on identifying some key parameters that would help to identify plagiarism in a better manner and to report plagiarism in an effective way. The result seems to be promising and have further scope in detecting the plagiarism.

Keywords: Plagiarism, similarity metric, paraphrasing, sentence matching.

1 Introduction

Plagiarism defined as the use or close imitation of language and thoughts of another author and the representing them as their one's work. Plagiarism affects the education quality of the students and there by reduce the economic status of the country which is done by techniques like paraphrasing or similarities between keywords and verbatim overlaps, change of sentences from one form to another form [7]. Internet has changed the student's life and also has changed their learning style. It allows the student to deeper the approach towards learning and making their task easier. Detecting plagiarism in a mass of students is difficult and also they are expensive too. Hence automated tools like Beagle were created [10] that work on the basis of similar text that matches, automated computer algorithms [8, 9] were proposed for automatic plagiarism detection. Students do learn the art of cheating and in common practice these plagiarism methods are hard to identify. Some of these methods includes copying of textual information, paraphrasing (representing same content in different words), using content without reference to original work, artistic (presenting same work using different forms),code plagiarism, misinformation of references (adding reference to incorrect or non existing source)[5].

V.V Das et al. (Eds.): BAIP 2010, CCIS 70, pp. 497–500, 2010.
© Springer-Verlag Berlin Heidelberg 2010

2   Related Works

Dominic Keuskamp et al. [1] examined how well text-matching software can contribute to the academic language and learning in developing integrity among students. This software generates the report which contains the percentage of text that matches with the source document with percentage of matching text shown as highlights. Benno Stein et al [2] presented a workshop on topic plagiarism analysis, authorship identification, and high similarity search. They prefer similarity based metric to detect plagiarism. The authors distinguished between the corpus based approach and the intrinsic analysis. They also check the suspicious document against the original document. Hybrid plagiarism detection approach using diagonal line and simplified Smith-Waterman algorithm is also considered as a classical tool in identifying similarities [4].

Romans Lukashenko et al. [5] have mainly focused on the corpus used, as it is needed to assign numeric value, so called, similarity score to each document. These obtained score is used for contents analysis either based on semantics or statistical approach. The advancement in information technologies made huge amount of data to be gathered in the internet at a rapid speed [6]. People use search engines to find what they need in order to solve the data overloading problem. Plagiarist can be reassembled, grabbed and redistributed without much difficulty. As a prelude an intelligent system to reduce the misapplication of search engines was also developed. Suspicious documents were tested by collaboration with plagiarism detection system and search engines. The extracted text segments are given different priorities with a proper design and pattern.

3   Experimental Section

The corpus for detecting plagiarism was collected from set of 120 students, spitted into 40 groups from various departments like Electrical, Electronics, Mechanical, Computer Science, Information Technology and Civil engineering. There were 414 words, 33 sentences and 9 words in a sentence on an average for the corpus constituted. The proposed system design performs the following tasks.

- Tokenization of documents into sentence format.
- Preprocessing of documents by removal of stop words & stemming [3].
- Measuring the similarity of each sentence using cosine metric[3]
- Detecting plagiarism among sentences.

We focus on comparing our approach with that of article checker. Commercial tools do search for the exact words or sentences online. If those words are not available, they fail report plagiarism. We made a study pertaining to assignments collected by the students and asked them even to quote the exact reference from which they have copied. All these data's were stored in the warehouse and retrieved for processing. We could find that by significantly removing the stop words and applying stemming, we would identify plagiarism in a better way. Table 1 presents a sample sentence pairs showing the original and plagiarized sentence. The percentage of plagiarism detected is also reported. Our approach forms the term frequency table and measures the relevancy among sentences using the cosine metric, which is used as default standard for measuring content relevancy in Vector Space model. Please note this value is obtained after preprocessing. Based on the term frequency table obtained, the cosine similarity value is 0.89 (i.e. 22/ 24.64).

Table 1. Plagiarism detected using commercial tool and our approach

Original sentence: In electrical engineering and computer science, image processing is any form of signal processing for which the input is an image, such as photographs or frames of video; the output of image processing can be either an image or a set of characteristics or parameters related to the image. **Plagiarised sentence:** Image processing is modifying the input image such as photographs or frames of video to image or a set of characteristics or parameters related to the image. Reference source:http://en.wikipedia.org/wiki/Image_processing	Article Checker	Our Approach
	19%	89.28%

4 Conclusion and Future Improvements

The proposed algorithm focuses on to preprocess the documents effectively and then identifies plagiarism in a better way as compared to commercial Article checker tool. When the content is represented as non textual forms like tables, forms or as images, we do not report such plagiarism which is left for future extensions. Improper editing of reference and detecting plagiarism from it is also left for future work.

References

1. Keuskamp, D., Sliuzas, R.: Plagiarism prevention or detection? The contribution of text-matching software to education about academic integrity. Student Learning Centre, Flinders University, Adelaide SA 5001, Australia, pp. 91–99 (2007)
2. Stein, B., Koppel, M.: Plagiarism Analysis, Authorship Identification and Near-Duplicate Detection. ACM SIGIR Forum 41(2), 68–71 (2007)
3. Hariharan, S., Srinivasan, R.: A Comparison of Similarity Measures for Text Documents. J. Information & Knowledge Management 7(1), 1–8 (2008)
4. Su, Z., Ahn, B.R., Eom, K.O., Kang, M.K., Kim, J.P., Kim, M.K.: Plagiarism Detection Using the Levenshtein Distance and Smith-Waterman Algorithm. In: Proceedings of Intetnational Conference on Innovative Computing Information and Control, ICICIC 2008 (2008)
5. Lukashenko, R., Graudina, V., Grundspenkis, J.: Computer-Based Plagiarism Detection Methods and Tools: An Overview. In: Proceedings of International Conference on Computer Systems and Technologies - CompSysTech 2007, pp. IIIA.18-1– IIIA.18-6 (2007)
6. Liu, Y.T., Zhang, H.R., Chen, T.W., Teng, W.G.: Extending Web Search for Online Plagiarism Detection. In: Proceedings of International Conference on Information Reuse and Integration, pp. 164–169 (2007)

7. Uzuner, O., Katz, B., Nahnsen, T.: Using Syntactic Information to Identify Plagiarism. Massachusetts Institute of Technology Computer Science and Artificial Intelligence Laboratory Cambridge, pp. 37–44 (2005)
8. Parker, A., James Hamblen, O.: Computer Algorithms for Plagiarism Detection, pp. 94–99 (1989)
9. Engels, S., Lakshmanan, V., Craig, M.: Plagiarism Detection Using Feature-Based Neural Networks (2007)
10. Adeva, J.J.G., Carroll, N.L., Calvo, R.A.: Applying Plagiarism Detection to Engineering Education. School of Electrical and Information Engineering, University of Sydney (2006)

Hiding Relevant Information in an Image

Madhusmita Das[1] and Mahamaya Mohanty[2]

[1] Department of Information Technology
KIST, Bhubaneswar
smita.madhusmita@gmail.com
[2] School of Computer Engineering
KIIT University, Bhubaneswar
mahamayamohanty@yahoo.co.in

Abstract. Data transmission is a vital issue for modern communication systems and for this security is highly required. Cryptography changes the message such that even if it is overheard by a third party, it would be unintelligible. Steganography, on the other hand, involves hiding message in such a way that the casual observer should not be able to detect the hidden information. Seemingly meaningless data can contain complex details, maps, or text. Steganography is often combined with cryptography to provide an additional layer of security.

Keywords: Steganography, Cryptography, Plain text, Cipher Text, Asymmetric Key, Symmetric Key.

1 Introduction

The security of the transformation of hidden data can be obtained by two ways: encryption and steganography. A combination of the two techniques can be used to increase the data security. In encryption, the message is changed in such a way so that no data can be disclosed if it is received by an attacker whereas in steganography, the secret message is embedded into an image often called cover image, and then sent to the receiver who extracts the secret message from the cover message. The visibility of this image should not be distinguishable from the cover image, so that it almost becomes impossible for the attacker to discover any embedded message. There are many techniques for encrypting data, which vary in their security, robustness, performance and so on. Also, there are many ways for embedding a message into another one. The most popular one is embedding a message into a colored image using LSB. In this method the data is being hidden in the least significant bit of each pixel in the cover image. This paper presents a new scheme for embedding bits and the algorithm is based on the number of occurrences of 0s & 1s in bit stream of data as well as the number of occurrences of 0s and 1s in last 4 bit of blue pixel in a binary image file that need to be modified to hide the data successfully.

2 Problem Statement

We have considered two groups named as Group 1 and Group 2. In Group 2 all its members are expected to be the enemies to Group 1. Let's consider A and B are two

V.V Das et al. (Eds.): BAIP 2010, CCIS 70, pp. 501–504, 2010.
© Springer-Verlag Berlin Heidelberg 2010

friends where A belongs to Group 1 and B belongs to Group 2. A sends a secrete message through a named image to B. The image is a message for Group 2 which can be read by any of its members, but the secrete message that is within the image is read only by B, who is friend of A. In this problem scenario, we consider there exit 3 databases where the first database contain the names of all the original images.2nd Database contain the name of all original images which are attached with secret message i.e the 2nd Database contain the name of embedded image. The 3rd Database contain both plain images as well as embedded images (image+ secrete message).When Group 1 send an image name to Group 2, all members of Group 1 can read the same image name from 1st Database. But B, who is the friend of A can read a new image name in which the image is attached with a secret message, this new image name is available in 2nd Database. As A and B are friends, they share an algorithm to map 1st Database image name to 2nd Database image name. The 2nd Database image name can be read only by B, So B can only find out the secret message. The third data base contain both the plain image as well as embedded image.B can map the image name which is retrieve from the 2nd Database to the embedded image of 3rd Database, but A can map the image name of 1st Database to the plain image of the 3rd Database.

2.1 Proposed Algorithm(Modulus 11) for Cryptography

In our proposed scenario, except the person who required to receive the secrete message, no one else can receive the image along with embedded secrete message. All the person receive only the original images, which doesn't contain any secret message. Here if it is suspected that communication of secret message is going on, then a comparison will be done with the sent image and received image, but in this scenario both the sent image and received images are same. The actual receipt ant of the secrete message maps the original sent image name to the new image name, where the new image contain the secrete message.

The following algorithm is used for cryptographic purpose. Here one image name is encoded into another name.

Step-1: An image of certain name is taken. The name of the image is stored in the first data base is converted to its ASCII form or decimal value. i.e known as code.

Step-2: Multiply 2 with the ASCII value of the last significant character, the character to its left by 3, the character to its left by 4 and so on. Add the products (the digits 2,3,4 etc, with which we multiply the ASCII value of the name called weights).After the addition of the products the result is known as weighted sum.

Step-3: Divide the weighted sum of digits by 11.

Step-4: Shift the each character of the name by(11-reminder) to the down, This is the new image name to be used.

2.2 Proposed Embedding Algorithm

Step 1: Preparing container or cover image: Read the 24 bit colour image, which will be use as a cover or container image to hide the secret message. From the cover image read the RGB colour of each pixel. Read the last bit of each pixel i.e from RGB (8+8+8)bits-read the blue colour's 8 bits i.e the last 8 bits of the pixel's colour. Embedded zeros in the last 4 bit of the 8 bit blue pixel.Repeat this for 2 x size of data times. Use two adjacent pixel to hide one character.

Step 2: Preparing secret text message: A terminating character(for e.g '\0',','.') must be attached with the secret message. This terminating character may be chosen by the sender. This terminating character can not be a part of data file. Convert each character of the secret message including terminating character to decimal number and then convert the decimal number to binary number i.e each character is represented in the form of o's and 1's. Take the 4 least significant bits alone of the character; i.e perform AND operation with 15 and the 4 upper significant bits alone of the character; i.e perform right shift operation by 4.

(Number)10 AND (15)10 = (Number)2 AND (0000 1111)2 and (Number)10 Shift to right by 4.

Step 3: Preparing Stego image: From the cover image, Read the RGB colour of each pixel.Now add the secret message which we prepare in step 2 to the cover image by applying OR operation. i.e embedded the data bit(4 bit) to the last 4 bit of the colour blue, of the pixel. Now write the above pixel to stego image. Repeat this until all the data bits embedded in the pixel of stego image.

Step 4: After completion of embedding of data, write the rest pixel to stego image file as it is in cover image.

2.3 Proposed Extraction Algorithm

Step 1: Open the stego image file in read mode and read each pixel of the stego image file.

Step 2: Take two adjacent pixels from the stego image to reconstruct a single character and shift the first pixel's 8 bit of colour blue by 4 to left.

Step 3: Perform AND operation with 15 to the second pixel's 8 bit of colour blue. i.e (8 bit of colour blue)2 AND (00001111)2

Step 4: Add the result of step 4 and step 5 together and we get the binary vale of the first character i.e actually ASCII value of the character and repeat until decimal value of terminating character's ASCII is found.

3 Conclusion

The above proposed algorithms has the advantages of minimal change is permitted in Stego Image and normal human beings' eyes cannot catch any difference. This new algorithm does not need any secret key. The ratio of hiding secrete message size to carrier size is more in comparison to other method. Furthermore the encoded message can be easily recovered and even altered by a 3rd party. It would appear that is good method of steganography due to its tremendous information capacity. Using the proposed method we can exchange secret messages over public channel in a safe way. We can conclude that the suitability of steganography as a tool to conceal highly sensitive information has been discussed by using a new methodology This suggests that an image containing encrypted data can be transmitted to anybody any where across the world in a complete secured form. Downloading such image and using it for many a times will not permit any unauthorized person to share the hidden information. Thus, a new technique has been proposed to hide data in a binary image. The used algorithm is secure and the hidden information is quite invisible. The future Scopes aims in distributing the information in the image randomly where a random generator can generate the location of the letter randomly and can increase further security to data hide. Statistical analysis of 0s and 1s can be applied block by block on data bit stream to make the algorithm more complex and we can achieve a new methodology to hide data in a more secured way.

References

[1] Petitcalas, F.A.P., Anderson, R.J., Kuhn, M.G.: Information Hiding –A Survey. Proceedings of the IEEE Special Issue on Protection of Multimedia Content 87(7), 1062–1078 (1999)
[2] Van Schyndel, R.G., Tirkel, A.Z., Osborne, C.F.: A Digital Watermark. In: Proceedings of IEEE International conference in image processing 1994, Austin,TX, vol. II, pp. 86–90 (1994), doi:10.1109/ICIP 1994.413536
[3] Bender, W., Gruhl, D., Morimoto, N., Lu, A.: Techniques for Data Hiding. IBM Systems Journal 35(3-4), 313–336 (1996)
[4] Yuan Chen, Y., Kuang Pan, H., Chee-Tseng, Y.: A Secure Data Hiding Scheme for Two color Images. In: Proceedings of the Fifth IEEE Symposium on Computer and Communication, ISCC 2000, p. 750 (2000) ISBN: 0-7695-0722-0
[5] Wu, M., Tang, E., Liu, B.: Data Hiding in Digital Binary Image. In: 2000 IEEE International Conference on Multimedia and Expo., New York City, NY, USA, July 30-August 2, vol. 1, pp. 393–396 (2000)
[6] Pan, H.-K., Chen, Y.-Y., Tseng, Y.-C.: A Secure Data Hiding Scheme for Two-ColorImages. In: Fifth IEEE Symposium on Computers and Communications, Antibes-Juan LesPins, France, July 3-6, p. 750 (2000)

Knowledge Discovery from Web Usage Data: A Survey of Web Usage Pre-processing Techniques

G. Shiva Prasad, N.V. Subba Reddy, and U. Dinesh Acharya

Department of Computer Science and Engineering,
Manipal Institute of Technology, Manipal-576 104
shiva.prasad@manipal.edu

Abstract. Knowledge discovery from Web Usage Data has become very critical in order to understand and better serve the needs of Web based applications. Web usage mining consists of three phases, namely preprocessing, pattern discovery and pattern analysis. A survey of Web Usage Preprocessing techniques is presented in this paper.

Keywords: Web Usage Data, Web Usage Mining, Web Usage Pre-Processing.

1 Introduction

Web-based organizations generate large volumes of data in their day-to-day activities and collected in server access logs in an unstructured format. Web usage mining is the application of data mining techniques to discover usage patterns from Web data, in order to understand and better serve the needs of Web-based applications. Web Usage mining contains three steps [1]: *Preprocessing*, *Pattern Discovery* and *Pattern Analysis*. Web Usage Preprocessing is usually complex and critical [2] to the successful extraction of useful patterns from the log files. Purpose of the pre-processing is to offer a structural, reliable and integrated data source for pattern discovery. The raw log files are cleansed, formatted, and then grouped into meaningful sessions before being utilized by web usage analysis.

2 Pre-processing Steps

A line in a Web server log represents the request made to the server and usually in Common Log Format (CLF) contains: Host, Client id, User login, Date and time of Request, HTTP Request, Status, Page size, Referrer and User agent.

The Web Usage Pre-processing phase mainly consists of the following steps: Data cleaning, User identification, User session identification, Path completion and Transaction Identification.

2.1 Data Cleaning

Data cleaning is the first step performed in the pre-processing of web usage mining. Appropriate cleaning of the data set has profound effects on the performance of web usage mining. The procedures of data cleaning are as follows:

V.V Das et al. (Eds.): BAIP 2010, CCIS 70, pp. 505–507, 2010.

De-Spidering the Web Log File: The access records generated by search engines should be identified and removed from the web log file. Methods based on heuristics and on classification techniques are proposed in [3][4].

Page Extension Exploration and Filtering: The requests for image files and other irrelevant files associated with requests for a particular page are filtered out from the web log file by exploring the page extensions in the web log file [2].

Additional Steps: In addition, Variable Extraction, Time stamp Creation and Inclusion of successful explicit user requests are employed in [2]. A generalized algorithm for data cleaning is presented in [5].

2.2 User Identification

The goal of this step is to identify each distinct user, a very complex task. A profiler using Java based remote agent, requiring user's cooperation, is proposed in [6]. In [1], heuristic based methods employing IP address, User Agent and Referring URL are presented. One heuristic uses IP address in conjunction with the User Agent, while the other, uses access log in conjunction with referrer log and site topology. Generalized user identification algorithms are proposed in [5][7]. As learners must login using their unique ID, user identification in e-learning context, is a straightforward problem [8].

2.3 User Session Identification

Session Identification is the process of segmenting the access log of each user into individual access sessions. For logs that span long periods of time, it is very likely that users will visit the Web site more than once. For session identification, following strategies are usually considered [2]: Two time-oriented heuristics and one navigation-oriented heuristic. Discovered from empirical findings, a 30-min threshold for total session duration has been recommended and used in many applications [9]. A 30-minute timeout to start a new session is adopted in [8]. This heuristic is not necessarily true in the online learning context since learners can wander in other sites gathering relevant information while their access session at the e-learning site is still on hold.

2.4 Path Completion and Transaction Identification

Path Completion refers to inclusion of important page access records that are missing in the access log due to browser and proxy server caching. Methods that try to overcome this problem include the use of cookies, cache busting, and explicit user registration. None of these methods are without serious drawbacks. Heuristic methods based on referrer log and site topology are employed in [1].

The goal of transaction identification is to create meaningful clusters of references for each user. This can be achieved by the following divide transaction identification approaches [2]: In *Maximal Forward Reference*, each transaction is defined to be the set of pages in the path from the first page in a user session up to the page before a backward reference is made. An algorithm for finding the maximal forward reference is proposed in [1]. In *Reference Length*, based on the amount of time a user spends on a page, the page is classified as an auxiliary or content page for that user. If the time spent on a resource is long enough, the resource is considered as a content one, otherwise an auxiliary reference [1]. The *Time Window approach* partitions a user session into time intervals no larger than a specified parameter. This strategy is normally combined with the previous ones.

3 Conclusion

This paper presents a survey of the specialized Web Usage Preprocessing methods for handling web log data. The techniques and methods used in each individual task are also presented in great details. Each task relies heavily on each other. In practical application, some of the tasks are carried out together and do not distinguish with each other very clearly. Moreover, for specific mining applications, the procedures of preprocessing may be of a little variation.

References

1. Cooley, R., Mobasher, B., Srivastava, J.: Data Preparation for Mining World Wide Web Browsing Patterns. Journal of Knowledge and Information Systems 1 (1999)
2. Das, R., Turkoglu, I.: Creating meaningful data from web logs for improving the impressiveness of a website by using path analysis method. Expert Systems with Applications 36(3), 6635–6644 (2009)
3. Berendt, B., Spiliopoulou, M.: Analyzing navigation behavior in Web sites integrating multiple information systems. VLDB Journal 9(1), 56–75 (2000)
4. Tan, P.-N., Kumar, V.: Modeling of Web Robot Navigational Patterns. In: WebKDD 2000, Second International Workshop (2000)
5. Arumugam, G., Suguna, S.: Predictive prefetching framework based on New Preprocessing Algorithms Towards Latency Reduction. Asian Journal of Information Technology 7, 87–99 (2008)
6. Shahabi, C., Zarkesh, A.M., Adibi, J., Shah, V.: Knowledge Discovery from Users Webpage Navigation. In: Proceeding 7th International Workshop on Research Issues in Data Engineering, pp. 20–29 (1997)
7. Huiying, Z., Wei, L.: An Intelligent Algorithm of Data Preprocessing in Web Usage mining. In: 5th World Congress on Intelligent Control and Automation, pp. 3119–3123 (2004)
8. Ba-omar, H., Petrounias, I., Anwar, F.: A Framework for Using Web Usage Mining to Personalise E-learning. In: 7th IEEE International Conference on Advanced Learning Technologies, pp. 937–938 (2007)
9. Spiliopoulou, M., Mobasher, B., Berendt, B., Nakagawa, M.: A framework for Evaluation of Session Reconstruction Heuristic in Web Usage Analysis. INFORMS: Journal on Computing 15(2), 171–190 (2003)

Context-Aware System Using .NET Approach

Arun Mishra[*], Bikash Tiwari, J.S.R. Kartik, and Arun Kumar Misra

Computer Science and Engineering Department,
Motilal Nehru National Institute of Technology, Allahabad, India
{rcs0802,it078038,it078015,akm}@mnnit.ac.in

Abstract. In context-aware system, components are dynamically adapted without requiring system to restart, in response to all possible changes in the execution environment. Existing approaches to make such a system more vigorous and safe, are both brittle and time intense. A approach has been devised for dynamic adaptation, to automate the component integration process at runtime by accessing the equivalent component from a set of diversified components. The .NET technology allows developers to adapt run-time component by specifying assertions on the component's services and also allows performing comparison of these assertions. These assertions will help us to compute metadata for each component in the repository. This metadata-driven component selection is an efficient and promising mechanism. In this paper, we describe the mechanism for component adaptation using .NET approach, by considering a system in dynamic context having proxy switcher and network switcher components.

Keywords: Services, Metadata, Adaptation, Context-aware, Dynamic.

1 Introduction

In context-aware system where several changes can occurs in their execution environment, system has to specify a response to all possible changes in the environment and may cause reduction of system performance. This kind of system achieves its goal by unlimited availability of resources. This method imposes strong synchronization requisites on system components, and these requisites may cause degradation in system performance to unacceptable levels [1]. In our work, we introduce an approach that automates the component selection and integration process. To automate the component assessment procedure, we present a technique that makes our system smart one. All this is done by using metadata, called numerical metadata. Our model compares behavioral aspect of the components of the system against the behavioral aspects of the components which are in the repository and calculates the numerical metadata for the repository's components with reference of their matching behavior with the required component. This assessment is achieved by deriving Abstract

---

[*] Please note that the LNCS Editorial assumes that all authors have used the western naming convention, with given names preceding surnames. This determines the structure of the names in the running heads and the author index.

V.V Das et al. (Eds.): BAIP 2010, CCIS 70, pp. 508–513, 2010.
© Springer-Verlag Berlin Heidelberg 2010

Syntax Trees (AST) which we used for arranging the constraint expressions (assertions) to simplify the behavior analysis [2]. The result of comparison is captured in numerical metadata corresponding to each component presents in the repository. On the basis of numerical metadata, our architecture finds out which is the most suitable component for integration.

The rest of the paper is organized as follows: Section 2 describes the methodology for component assessment. Section 3 provides metadata-driven solution for component integration using .NET approach. Section 4 gives an example of dynamic adaptation, finally the conclusions and possible future work.

2 Component Assessment on the Basis of Metadata

Our approach uses the concept of sufficient accuracy rather than absolute correctness [3] and such system should make every effort to maintain their normal operating behavior by using best available alternate component for required one. The alternate component detection in terms of component behavior is based on component structure; that structure must include signature of required services, pre-post assertions to abstract out the hidden behavior of the services and the order in which the services are invoked in a component [4]. With the help of reflection mechanism of .NET framework we can access the signature of services and easily can detect equivalency in number of parameter in corresponding operations, types of their parameters and their corresponding return type. To match the behavior of corresponding components, there is need to prove similarity in pre and post assertions of respective components services. For that we have used the concept of numerical metadata whose computation is based on the assertions of the services of component, the exact way to compute the numerical metadata is covered in a previous work [5]. In that procedure we have presented a basic tree equivalency algorithm to compare among assertions. This algorithm uses the Abstract Syntax Tree structure to represent the assertions. To find the exact assertion matches, exact tree matches are required. This procedure has been explained in our previous work [5].

3 Component Assessment Using .NET Approach

In .NET we can add assertion as metadata on the member of the component by annotating them with so-called attribute specifications. An attribute specification consists of a type name which names an attribute class, plus an argument list consisting of literal expressions. The type name and the literal value are stored in the assembly by the programming language compiler (e.g. C #, VB).At run-time, this information is used by the CLR (middleware service of .NET framework) to create an instance of the named attribute class. The CLR and the application itself can retrieve the instances associated with an element, and act upon them [6]. In example, section 4 of this paper, we have discussed implementation level details for attribute specification.

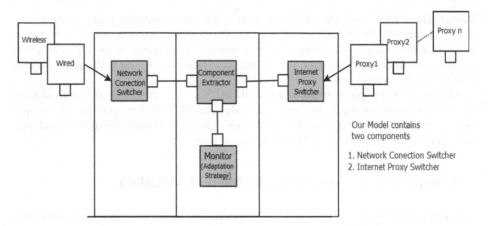

Fig. 1. Framework for the Dynamic Assimilation of Internet Proxy Switcher and Network Connection Switcher

4 Run-Time Adaptations: An Example

Consider, for instance an application, Internet browser running in a system. Several changes can occur in the work environment. For example, the proxy server, through which the internet connection is available, may fail or work for a period without wired connection i.e. for this period, network connection is available through wireless access point. To adapt these changes, the application might switch to another available proxy server or switch to wireless access point. So, when such changes occur application should adapt accordingly.

We are putting forward a dynamic adaptive system which involves two components designed to detect two types of failure in the system, Internet proxy failure and Network connection failure. Detection of point of failure in Internet browser is based on hierarchical dependency of components (from top to bottom in hierarchical order each component depends on its predecessor). In our system, Network connection failure precedes Internet proxy failure. So, firstly, network connection is checked for point of failure and then Internet Proxy is checked. After detection of fault, it searches for the best suitable alternative component for the failed component and integrate it in order to revitalize the system. Selection of alternate component at run-time is done with the help of .NET services such as Custom attribute [6] and Reflection [7].

Fig. 1 shows the system's component framework, for the dynamic assimilation of Internet proxy switcher and Network connection switcher, using a notation like UML 2.0.

The system framework is composed of three segments

- Component switcher(After detection of fault, system may adapt either Network connection switcher or Internet proxy switcher)
- Monitor (BHO)
- Component extractor

4.1 Component Switcher

Our system has two main components one is Internet proxy switcher and other is Network connection switcher. When changes occurs in the application running context, system adapt corresponding component to minimize the impact of changes on the system. Example, Network connection switcher replaces failed network connection with alternate network connection i.e. when wired network connection fails, wireless network is connected. Internet proxy switcher sets working internet proxy server IP (proxy that gives reply on pinging it) in internet explorer by replacing the failed internet proxy IP. To abstract the hidden behavior of components, we add metadata in the form of pre-assertion and post-assertion on each component. Custom attribute service provided by Microsoft's .NET technology used to attach pre-assertion and post- assertion to each component in the component assembly [6].

For Proxy switcher component, following methods contains pre-assertion and post-assertion.

```
Public class proxy_switcher
{Pre-assertion ("=(( IPAddress.TryParse(IP, outip)), true
)")]
//A function which set the poxy IP, takes IP address as
input. So, Pre-assertion checks the validity of IPAdress
[Post-assertion("=((Ping.Send(ip,1000, buffer, null)).
status), true ")]
// For the same function Post-assertion checks if the IP
address on ping gives success, with the help of send
function of Ping class.
public static void Set_Proxy(IPAddress ip);}
```

proxy_switcher component is loaded from component assembly when the current proxy set in internet explorer fails. The Set_Proxy (void Set_Proxy(IPAdress ip)) function is called, it pings the available internet proxies and select the first found IP address of proxy server(Proxy server IP that gives reply on pinging it)[8].

For network switcher component, following are the pre-assertion and post-assertion

```
public class Network_switcher
{ //Checks if the Wireless networks (Access points) are
available by counting the available access points
 [Pre-assertion(">(WirelesszeroConfigNetworkInterface.
PreferredAccessPoints.Count),0)")]
//Connection is established with the access point.
[Post-assertion("=(WirelesszeroConfigNetworkInterface.
connectToPreferedNetwork(apName),true )")] }
```

Network_switcher component is loaded from component assembly when the current wired Network connection fails. Wireless function (void wireles ()) is called and it connects to available wireless network (Access point). We used WirelessZeroConfigNetworkInterface present in OpenNet Class Framework (OpenNETCF.Net 2.3) provided by Microsoft to connect to nearby points [9].

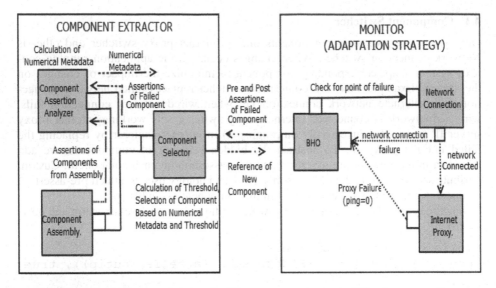

Fig. 2. Architecture framework of Component extractor and Monitor segment

4.2 Monitor

In our system monitoring is done by BHO (Browser Helper Object) attached to Internet explorer. BHO is a DLL module designed as a plug-in for Microsoft's Internet explorer web browser to provide added functionality [10]. Some of the additional functionalities provided by BHO are detection of browser's typical events, such as Go-Back, Go-Forward, and Document Complete and access to browsers menu and toolbar [11]. We are using Document Complete event of BHO in our application to detect the failure of Internet browser.BHO checks the components in the order of their hierarchical dependency (Network connection failure component first and Internet proxy failure next) i.e. BHO played a major role in deciding adaptation strategy. Whenever it encounters failure, it passes the pre-assertion and post-assertion of failed component to Component Extractor segment of our framework. Fig. 2 shows framework architecture of Monitor segment (BHO) and Component extractor segment.

4.3 Component Extractor

This segment gets the pre-assertion and post-assertion of the failed component from Monitor. It extracts the suitable alternate component (with the help of attribute services and reflection mechanism in .NET) form the assembly by comparing its pre-assertion and post-assertion with the respective failed one. Component selector obtains the pre-assertion and post-assertion of failed component from the monitor. It extracts all the components from component assembly and provides each component's pre-assertion and post-assertion to the compare module. Analyzer module compares the pre-assertion and post-assertion of the services and finds matches. This work is done according to the component assessment technique in section 2 of this paper. The coordination between Component extractor and Monitor segment is shown in Fig. 2.

5 Conclusion

Each individual aspect of our approach is allowed for improvements in configurability and usability of context-aware system. An interesting feature of our approach is the easy determination of alternate component with the help of metadata from the large set of diversified components. Our approach has the benefit of optimizing any self-adaptive system by automation of the assessment of required component and their integration process at run-time. It takes the advantages of Abstract Syntax Tree to get the arranged assertion's expressions to reduce the complexity in component analysis. This approach is pervasive, in a sense that, it applies to all components of a large system. We have developed a dynamic adaptive system using .Net services which provides a clear view of how the .NET services are used in dynamic modification of the system. We have not discussed intermediate state transfer during the replacement of components. In future we plan to update this model to transfer the states from the replaced to the inserted component. So far we have given our attention to run-time component assessment and integration. We also see the opportunities to improve consistency process for the self adaptive system. Thus, future work also concerns the validation of the approach on large-scale systems.

References

1. Diaconescu, A., Murphy, J.: A Framework for Using Component Redundancy for self-Optimizing and self-Healing Component Based Systems. In: WADS workshop, ICSE 2003, Hilton Portland, Oregon, USA, May 3-10 (2003)
2. Baxter, I., Yahin, A., Moura, L., Sang'Anna, M., Bier, L.: Clone Detection Using Abstract Syntax Trees. In: ICSM 1998, Bethesda, Maryland, March 1998, pp. 368–377 (1998)
3. Shaw, M.: Self-healing: Softening precision to avoid brittleness. In: Proceedings of the First ACM SIGSOFT Workshop on Self-Healing Systems, pp. 111–113 (2002)
4. Flores, A., Gracia, I., Polo, M.: Net Approach to Run-Time component Integration. In: Proceedings of the Third Latin American Web Congress, p. 45. IEEE Computer Society, Los Alamitos (2005)
5. Mishra, A., Misra, A.K.: Component Assessment and Proactive Model for Support of Dynamic Integration in Self Adaptive System. ACM SIGSOFT (SEN) 34(4), 1–9 (2009)
6. Accessing Attributes With Reflection (C# Programming Guide),
   http://msdn.microsoft.com/en-us/library/z919e8tw.aspx
   (accessed: September 20, 2009)
7. MethodBase...Invoke Method, http://msdn.microsoft.com/en-us/library/
   system.reflection.methodbase.invoke.aspx (accessed: October 20, 2009)
8. Tool to Automatically Set Internet Explorer Proxy, http://blogs.msdn.com/
   irenak/archive/2008/12/16/sysk-366-tool-to-automatically-set-
   internet-explorer-proxy.aspx (accessed: October 18, 2009)
9. WirelessZeroConfigNetworkInterface Class, http://www.opennetcf.com/library/
   sdf/html/6bf65eb2-2530-7129-a1a2-d859cf2c156e.htm
10. Browser Helper Objects: The Browser the Way You Want it,
    http://msdn.microsoft.com/en-us/library/bb250436VS.85.aspx
    (accessed: October 5, 2009)
11. Building Browser Helper Objects with Visual Studio 2005,
    http://msdn.microsoft.com/en-us/library/bb250489VS.85.aspx
    (accessed: October 5, 2009)

Genetic Audio Watermarking

Mazdak Zamani, Azizah Bt Abdul Manaf, Rabiah Bt Ahmad, Farhang Jaryani,
Saman Shojae Chaeikar, and Hossein Rouhani Zeidanloo

Universiti Teknologi Malaysia, 54100 Kuala Lumpur, Malaysia
{azizah07,rabiah}@citycampus.utm.my,
{mazdak_zamani,fjaryani,saman_shoja}@yahoo.com,
h_rouhani@hotmail.com

Abstract. This paper presents a novel, principled approach to resolve the re-
mained problems of substitution technique of audio watermarking. Using the
proposed genetic algorithm, message bits are embedded into multiple, vague
and higher LSB layers, resulting in increased robustness. Substitution techniques have naturally high capacity, but two major problems, having low robustness and transparency, negate the advantage. The robustness specially
would be increased against those intentional attacks which try to reveal the hidden message and also some unintentional attacks like noise addition as well.

Keywords: Data hiding, substitution techniques, audio watermarking, artificial
intelligence, genetic algorithm.

1 Introduction

During the early to mid-1990s, digital watermarking attracted the attention of a significant number of researchers after several early works that may also be classified as
such [1]. Since then the number of publications has increased exponentially to several
hundred per year. It started from simple approaches presenting the basic principles to
sophisticated algorithms using results from communication theory and applying them
to the watermarking problem [2,5].

Digital watermarking has been proposed as a new, alternative method to enforce
the intellectual property rights and protect digital media from tampering. It involves
embedding into a host signal a perceptually transparent digital signature, carrying a
message about the host signal in order to "mark" its ownership. The digital signature
is called the digital watermark. The digital watermark contains data that can be used
in various applications, including digital rights management, broadcast monitoring
and tamper proofing. Although perceptually transparent, the existence of the watermark is indicated when watermarked media is passed through an appropriate watermark detector [4].

2 Why Still Substitution Techniques of Audio Watermarking

The theory of substitution technique is that simply replacing either a bit or a few bits
in each sample will not be noticeable to the human eye or ear depending on the type

V.V Das et al. (Eds.): BAIP 2010, CCIS 70, pp. 514–517, 2010.

of file. This method has high embedding capacity (41,000 bps) but it is the least robust. It exploits the absolute threshold of hearing but is susceptible to attacks.

The obvious advantage of the substitution technique, the reason for choosing this
technique, is a very high capacity for hiding a message; the use of only one LSB of
the host audio sample gives a capacity of 44.1 kbps. Obviously, the capacity of substitution techniques is not comparable with the capacity of other more robust techniques
like spread spectrum technique that is highly robust but has a negligible embedding
capacity (4 bps) [3].

3   Problems of Substitution Techniques of Audio Watermarking

Like all multimedia data hiding techniques, audio watermarking has to satisfy three
basic requirements. They are perceptual transparency, capacity of hidden data and
robustness. Noticeably, the main problem of audio substitution watermarking algorithm is considerably low robustness.

There are two types of attacks to watermarking and therefore there are two type of
robustness. One type of attacks tries to reveal the hidden message and another type
tries to destroy the hidden message. Substitution techniques are vulnerable against
both types of attacks. The adversary who tries to reveal the hidden message must
understand which bits are modified. Since substitution techniques usually modify the
bits of lower layers in the samples -LSBs, it is easy to reveal the hidden message if
the low transparency causes suspicious.

Also, these attacks can be categorized in another way: Intentional attacks and unintentional attacks. Unintentional attacks like transition distortions could destroy the
hidden message if is embedded in the bits of lower layers in the samples -LSBs.

As a result, this paper briefly addresses following problems of substitution techniques of audio watermarking:

- Having low robustness against attacks which try to reveal the hidden message
- Having low robustness against distortions with high average power

4   The Solution

Accordingly, there are two following solutions for mentioned problems:

- *The solution for first problem:* Making more difficult discovering which bites are
  embedded by modifying the bits else than LSBs in samples, and selecting the
  samples to modify privately-not all samples
- *The solution for second problem:* Embedding the message bits in deeper layers
  and other bits alteration to decrease the amount of the error

To integrate these two solutions, "embedding the message bits in deeper layers" that is a
part of second solution also can satisfy "modifying the bits else than LSBs in samples"
of second solution. In addition, when we try to satisfy "other bits alteration to decrease
the amount of the error" of second solution, if we ignore the samples which are not
adjustable, also "selecting not all samples" of first solution will be satisfied.

Thus, intelligent algorithm will try to embed the message bits in the deeper layers of samples and alter other bits to decrease the error and if alteration is not possible for any samples it will ignore them.

It is clear that the main part of this scenario is bit alteration that it should be done by intelligent algorithms which use either genetic algorithms or a symbolic AI system.

5 Genetic Algorithm Approach

As Figure 1 shows, there are four main steps in this algorithm that are explained below.

Alteration: At the first step, message bits substitute with the target bits of samples. Target bits are those bits which place at the layer that we want to alter. This is done by a simple substitution that does not need adjustability of result be measured.

Modification: In fact this step is the most important and essential part of algorithm. All results and achievements that we expect are depending on this step. Efficient and intelligent algorithms are useful here. In this stage a genetic algorithm tries to decrease the amount of error and improve the transparency so that each sample is like a chromosome and each bit of a sample is like a gene. First generation or first parents consist of original sample and altered sampled. Fitness may be determined by a function which calculates the error. It is clear, the most transparent sample pattern should be measured fittest. It must be considered that in crossover and mutation the place of target bit should not be changed.

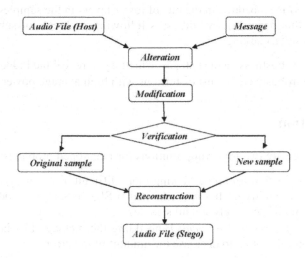

Fig. 1. Approach Diagram

Verification: In fact this stage is quality controller. What the algorithm could have done is already done, and now the outcome must be verified. If the difference between original sample and new sample is acceptable and reasonable, the new sample will be accepted; otherwise it will be rejected and original sample will be used in reconstructing the new audio file instead of that.

Reconstruction: The last step is new audio file creation. This is done sample by sample. There are two states at the input of this step. Either modified sample is input or the original sample that is the same with host audio file. It is why we can claim the algorithm does not alter all samples or predictable samples. That means whether which sample will be used and modified is depending on the status of samples (Environment) and the decision of intelligent algorithm.

6 Conclusions

A new approach is proposed to resolve two problems of substitution technique of audio watermarking. First problem is having low robustness against attacks which try to reveal the hidden message and second one is having low robustness against distortions with high average power. Using the proposed genetic algorithm, message bits could be embedded into multiple, vague and deeper layers to achieve higher capacity and robustness.

Acknowledgments. This work is part of a project supported by the Ministry of Science, Technology and Innovation of Malaysia whose title is "Development of Digital Audio Information Hiding Systems   For High-Embedding-Capacity Applications" (01-01-06-SF0524).

References

1. Cvejic, N., Seppänen, T.: Increasing the capacity of LSB based audio steganography. In: Proc. 5th IEEE International Workshop on Multimedia Signal Processing, St. Thomas, VI, December 2002, pp. 336–338 (2002)
2. Alvaro, M., Guillermo, S., Gadiel, S.: Is Image Steganography Natural? IEEE Transactions on Image Processing 14(12) (December 2005)
3. Huang, H.-C., Pan, J.S., Huang, Y.H., Wang, F.H., Huang, K.C.: Progressive Watermarking Techniques with Genetic Algorithms. Circuits Systems and Signal Processing 26(5), 671–687 (2007)
4. Kuo, S., Johnston, J., Turin, W., Quackenbush, S.: Covert audio watermarking using perceptually tuned signal independent multiband phase modulation. In: Proc. IEEE International Conference on Acoustics, Speech, and Signal Processing, Orlando, FL, pp. 1753–1756 (2002)
5. Huang, D., Yeo, T.: Robust and inaudible multi-echo audio watermarking. In: Proc. IEEE Pacific-Rim Conference on Multimedia, Taipei, China, pp. 615–622 (2002)

Effective BST Approach to Find Underflow Condition in Interval Trees Using Augmented Data Structure

Keyur N. Upadhyay[1], Hemant D. Vasava[2], and Viral V. Kapadia[2]

[1] Lecturer, CE Dept., Sardar Vallabhbhai Institute Of Technology
[2] Lecturer, CP Dept., B.V.M. Engg. College, Vallabh Vidyanagar
mailtokeyur@gmail.com, hemantdvasava@yahoo.co.in,
kapadia_viral2005@yahoo.co.in

Abstract. In many trivial or complex situation augmentation of a data structure would required. To solve real world complex problem augmentation of data structure is must by creating entirely new data structure using existing data structure by adding some additional information like Minimum, Maximum, Successor, and Predecessor in it. Augmentation of data structure is not that much straightforward. This approach is developed with respect to existing data structure of BST (Binary Search Tree) and some additional information. So, in this attempt we presented BST as underlying data structure for interval tree, which leads to easy implementation, reduced searching complexity and less memory requirement.

Keywords: Binary Search Tree (BST).

1 Introduction

For solving various engineering problems it is enough and sufficient to use existing data structure. In such situation we can use data structure such as a binary search tree, a linked list or a hash table. But in many complex engineering problems these are not sufficient to achieve desired outcomes. So, it requires creating an entirely new data type of data structure for implementation. More often it is sufficient to augment an existing data structure by storing additional information like Minimum, Maximum, Successor, and Predecessor in it. *Traditionally an **Interval tree** is a **red black tree*** that maintains a dynamic set of elements with each element x containing an interval $int[x]$ and the key of x is a low endpoint of interval, $low[int[x]]$. $high[int[x]]$ is the high endpoint of interval. Traditional interval tree underlying red black tree of height n node takes O (log n) interval search time in any case. By augmenting BST as underlying data structure to interval tree takes searching time O(log n) either an overlapping found or O(1) if not found. So, it becomes easy to solve complex problems, reduce searching complexity and there is no need of memory to store color value for each node as compared to traditional tree.

2 Traditional BST Approach

If the tree is a linear chain of n nodes, however, the same operations takes O (n) worst-case time. If we repeatedly insert a sorted sequence of values to form a BST,

V.V Das et al. (Eds.): BAIP 2010, CCIS 70, pp. 518–520, 2010.
© Springer-Verlag Berlin Heidelberg 2010

we obtain a completely skewed BST. The height of such a tree is $n - 1$ if the tree has n nodes. Thus, the worst case complexity of searching or inserting an element into a BST having n nodes is $O(n)$[3].

3 Traditional Interval Tree [1]

A *closed interval* is an ordered pair of real numbers [$t1$, $t2$], with $t1 \leq t2$. The interval [$t1$, $t2$] represents the set $\{t \_ R : t1 \leq t \leq t2\}$. *Open* and *half-open* intervals omit both or one of the endpoints from the set, respectively. We are assuming that intervals are closed; extending the results to open and half-open intervals is conceptually straightforward.

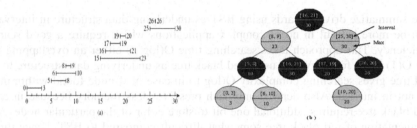

(a)   (b)

4 Modification Suggested for Underflow Condition in Interval Trees

Data structure augmentation steps to develop new approach are defined as below.

1. Underlying Data Structure
We have chosen a BST in which each node x contains an interval $int[x]$ and the key of x is the low endpoint, $low[int[x]]$, of the interval. $high[int[x]]$ is the high endpoint of interval.

2. Additional Information
In addition to the intervals , each node x contains a value $min[x]$ and $max[x]$, which is the minimum and maximum value of any interval stored in the sub tree rooted at x.

3. Maintaining the Information
We must verify that searching can be performed in $O(\lg n)$ or $O(1)$ time on an interval tree of n nodes. We also need to determine $min[x]$ and $max[x]$ for given interval $int[x]$. The *min* and *max* values of node x's children:

$min[x] = \min(low[int[x]], min[left[x]], min[right[x]])$.
$max[x] = \max(high[int[x]], max[left[x]], max[right[x]])$.

4. Developing New Operations
The INTERVAL-SEARCH(T, x) new operation which finds a node in tree T whose interval overlaps interval. If there is no interval that overlaps x in the tree, a pointer to the sentinel $nil[T]$ is returned.

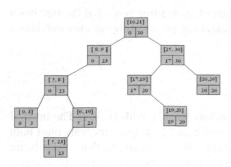

INTERVAL-SEARCH procedure gives complexity $O(1)$. Because for that key element it start comparison with min and max values stored at the root x to downward. If that key element is out of range then searching complexity will be $O(1)$ because we do not need to traverse bottom if node is out of range. Where in case of traditional interval tree it will traverse up to leaves so complexity will be $O(\lg n)$ if element is not in given tree.

5 Conclusion

We summarize drive towards using BST as underlying data structure in interval tree can be more helpful in no of complex applications which require a good searching efficiency. This approach takes searching time O(log n) either an overlapping found or O(1) if not found. While using red black tree as underlying data structure to interval tree gives searching complexity O(log n) in case of if node found within interval or not in interval. Also derived approach preserves less memory because in case of red black tree requires additional one bit to store color of the particular node. As implementation of red black tree somewhat difficult compared to BST, hence this will makes implementation easy.

References

1. Coreman, T.H., Leiserson, C.E., Rivest, R.L., Stein, C.: Introduction to Algorithm. Prentice Hall India PHI
2. http://www.cs.rochester.edu/~gildea/csc282/slides/ C14-augmenting.pdf
3. Binary Search tree, IISc Banglore, http://lcm.csa.iisc.ernet.in/dsa/node91.html
4. The Binary Search Tree Property, CSC 378 tutorial: School of Computing, Queen's University, Canada K7L 3N6, http://research.cs.queensu.ca/~jstewart/applets/ bst/bst-property.html
5. Interval Trees, Winter 1997 Class Notes for 308-251B, McGill University, Quebec, Canada (1997), http://cg.scs.carleton.ca/~luc/1997notes/topic20/#interval

Natural Disaster Impact Assessment Using Genetic Algorithm

N. Bhalaji and Nandini Sundara Raman

Member ACEEE

Abstract. Earthquake Impact Assessment using Genetic Algorithm' aims at estimating the damage caused by an Earthquake. When the epicenter is specified, the application estimates the casualties and the type of infrastructure damaged. For Tsunami, the application calculates the tsunami arrival time and lists the tsunami characteristics. There is no system yet that predicts Earthquake damage based on Genetic algorithm. However there are several systems that use the ground vibrations and seismic data to predict the earthquake which has proven inadequate in more occasions than one. Although predicting an earthquake might be out of scope for us, but in this endeavor we can make software, which estimates the damages the earthquake causes and help the authorities concerned to take the appropriate mitigation measures.

Keywords: Earth quake, Impact assessment, tsunami, genetic algorithm, damage estimation.

1 Introduction

Our system uses the latest advancement in computers i.e. Genetic Algorithm which makes the prediction and estimation of the Damages more reliable than what the current systems can provide. By using genetic algorithms the application optimizes to make the damage prediction more accurate and reliable. The current application domain is restricted to south-east Asia. The application uses databases concerning land and sea. Both the databases have been constructed to comprehensively cover the characteristics of regions. The Earthquake characteristics like Magnitude, Energy etc. have also been taken into account. The algorithm is built in such a way that it uses random selection, single point crossover at random points. The mutation probability used is 0.1 and it runs for ten generations. The assumptions we make are the Seismic waves travels for longer distance and the Tsunami is assumed to occur only if the earthquake magnitude is seven or above on Richer scale.

1.1 Genetic Algorithm

Genetic algorithm [1] [2] is based on Darwin's theory of the survival of the fittest. It simulates the actual process in nature to optimize the given solution. The genetic algorithm performs a parallel, non-comprehensive search for the global maximum of the graph. The search is not precise meaning that there is no guarantee that the global maximum will be found. However, the result should be a good approximation of the

V.V Das et al. (Eds.): BAIP 2010, CCIS 70, pp. 521–526, 2010.
© Springer-Verlag Berlin Heidelberg 2010

maximum value. Genetic algorithms are excellent for quickly finding an approximate global maximum or minimum value. They exploit the domain space with mutation and exploit good results with selection and crossover. The two major problems with creating genetic algorithms are in converting a problem domain into genes (bit patterns) and creating an effective evaluation function. For many problems the answers will be obvious, but for many others it is non-trivial. Four operations are applied to every generation of chromosome evaluation, selection, crossover, and mutation. These operations are modeled after the evolutionary process of organisms in nature.

2 Earth Quake

Earthquake is the shaking of the Earth's surface caused by rapid movement of the Earth's rocky outer layer. Earthquakes occur when energy stored within the Earth, usually in the form of strain in rocks, suddenly releases. This energy is transmitted to the surface of the Earth by earthquake waves.

The destruction an earthquake [3][4]causes depends on its magnitude and duration, or the amount of shaking that occurs. A structure's design and the materials used in its construction also affect the amount of damage the structure incurs. Earthquakes vary from small, imperceptible shaking to large shocks felt over thousands of kilometers. Earthquakes can deform the ground, collapse buildings and structures, create tsunamis (large sea waves) and also cause loss of several lives. Earthquakes, or seismic tremors, occur at a rate of several hundred per day around the world. A worldwide network of seismographs (machines that record movements of the Earth) detects about 1 million small earthquakes per year.

2.1 Tsunami

Tsunami is a Japanese word with the English translation, "harbor wave." In the past, tsunamis were sometimes referred to as "tidal waves" by the general public and as Seismic sea waves by the scientific community and both are misnomers. Although a tsunami's impact upon a coastline is dependent upon the tidal level at the time a tsunami strikes, tsunamis are unrelated to the tides. Tides result from the imbalanced, extraterrestrial, gravitational influences of the moon, sun, and planets. "Seismic" implies an earthquake-related generation mechanism, but a tsunami can also be caused by a non-seismic event, such as a landslide or meteorite impact.

Generally, once the water has been pushed upward, gravity acts on it, forcing the energy out horizontally along the surface of the water. It's sort of the same ripple effect you get from throwing a pebble in the water, but in reverse - The energy is generated by a force moving out of rather than into the water. The energy then moves through the depths of the water and away from the initial disturbance. This tremendous force created by the seismic disturbance generates the tsunami's incredible speed. The actual speed of the tsunami is calculated by measuring [5] the water depth at a point in time when the tsunami passes by.

3 Proposed System

The application estimates the amount of damage that is caused by an Earthquake using Genetic Algorithm (GA) and was created using Java JDK 1.3. GA consists of a number of Chromosomes which represents the information of the given problem. The chromosomes undergo Crossover and mutation. Crossover produces new offspring's which are evaluated by the fitness function and only the fittest chromosomes are carried forward to the next generation. This way we get the best chromosomes towards the end which is the best solution to the given problem. The chromosomes in the GA contain ten fields namely Seismicity, Population density, Altitude, Rock characteristics, Faults, Plate Tectonics, Infrastructure, Volcanoes, Dams and Sea nearby which describe the characteristics of a given place and is stored and retrieved from the corresponding tables stored in Microsoft Access 2003 database. A random population of chromosomes is generated for the selected place and the nearby places which undergo Crossover and Mutation to produce the fittest chromosomes in the end which best withstand the given Earthquake. The fitness function consists of the Earthquake attributes namely Magnitude, Energy, Acceleration, Epicentral Distance and Up-throw. The Fitness function evaluates the Chromosomes and only allows the fittest Chromosomes to be carried forward to the next generation. So optimization takes place at each step and the solution gets better after each generation. The Epicenter of the Earthquake is given as input to the application. It then locates the nearby places, as the consequence of any Earthquake is felt over a large area. Then the place characteristics are extracted and the chromosome is constructed. A random population of chromosomes is fed to GA. Higher the value of a chromosome, the more chance it has to survive the given Earthquake. This value depends on a given place and its characteristics. The output consists of the damage figures [6] like the estimated killed, estimated injured and the type of infrastructure damaged. It also lists the optimum characteristics a place should have to survive the earthquake. The history of earthquakes in the region and the earthquake preparedness are displayed. The application also has a feature of Tsunami. When an epicenter in sea is selected, it locates the nearby countries and points out the Tsunami wave arrival time and the save time when Tsunami warning system like DART is installed. This gives us an idea of how much time one will get to escape before the Tsunami strikes the coast. It also lists the Tsunami facts, its characteristics and the history of Tsunami.

Genetic Algorithm: Pseudo Code

```
// start with an initial time
   t: = 0;
// initialize a usually random population of
   individuals Initpopulation P (t);
//A maximum of 120 Chromosomes are generated
// evaluate fitness of all initial individuals
of population
         Evaluate      P
            (t); do
   // select a sub-population for offspring
            production P' := selectparents P (t);
```

```
// Crossover the "genes" according to the crossover
point selected
              Crossover  P'  (t);
  // perturb the mated population
              stochastically mutate P' (t);
              // evaluate its new
              fitness evaluate P' (t);
// select the survivors from actual fitness and replace
              P: = replacement P,P' (t);
          // increase the time counter
              t: = t + 1;
// test for termination criterion (time, fitness, etc.)
```

4 Sample Input and Output

Tsunami Computation steps

From the selected sea as epicenter, the nearby countries and their corresponding distances from the epicenter are retrieved from the database. The Tsunami arrival time is computed using the following formula:

$$t = \text{Square root } (g \times d) \tag{1}$$

Where

t = tsunami speed in meters per second
g = acceleration of gravity (32 feet/10 meters per second/per
second) d = quantity of water depth
Assuming constant depth and highest Tsunami speed, the arrival time is calculate.

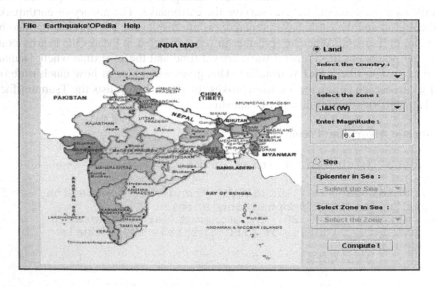

Fig. 1. Input Screen

Input Screen: The Input Screen has two sections. One is the Earthquake section and the other is the Tsunami section. For an Earthquake, the Country and its corresponding state/zone should be selected in the lower drop-down list. The magnitude entered should be a value between 4 and 11 and then the 'Compute' button should be clicked. The Asia image will be displayed on the left to aid the user to select the exact epicenter. India image will open when India, Nepal, Bhutan or Bangladesh is selected.

Computation Screen: A computation box will appear after you click the Compute button. User should wait till it finishes. The buttons on the window will be activated once the computation is over. In case of Earthquake, the 'view damage' button can be clicked to see the output.

Output in the default browser: The output for both the Earthquake and Tsunami will be displayed in the user's default browser. After viewing the results, the user can close the browser and continue to use the application.

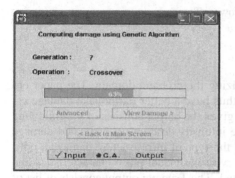
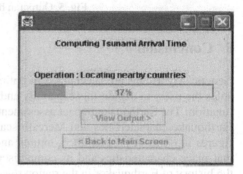

Fig. 2. Processing Screen: GA Computation   **Fig. 3.** Tsunami arrival computation

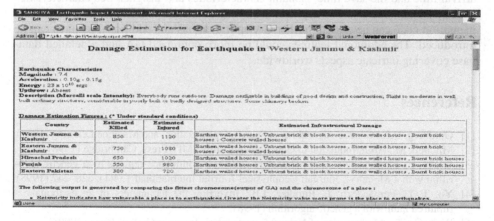

Fig. 4. Output in Browser: Earthquake

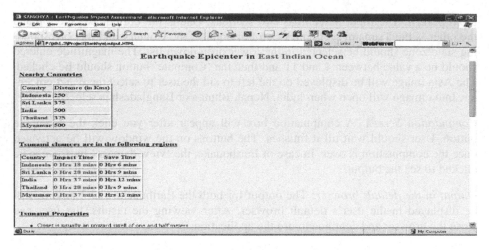

Fig. 5. Output in browser Tsunami

5 Conclusion

Genetic Algorithms are specialized in optimizing the problem domain. The paper enables the users to exploit this capability and thus have a better Earthquake damage estimation. The Earthquake impact assessment gives the output consists of the following Earthquake characteristics and Mercalli scale intensity description, estimated damage figures in terms of people killed, injured and the type of infrastructure damaged, optimal place characteristics and its comparison with individual place characteristics and the history of Earthquakes in the region selected. The Tsunami output consists of list of nearby countries and their corresponding distances from the epicenter, tsunami wave arrival time and the save time, tsunami characteristics and insights, Sea characteristics and the tsunami history. The application has a user friendly interface where the implementation code can be reused, further GA optimizations and additional features can be introduced. The additional features could be more optimized GA and a detailed database covering intricate aspects worldwide.

References

[1] Goldberg, D.E.: Genetic Algorithms in Search, Optimization, and Machine Learning (1989)
[2] Mitchell, M.: An Introduction to Genetic Algorithms. MIT Press, Cambridge (1998)
[3] Šílený, J.: Earthquake source parameters and their confidence regions by a genetic algorithm with a'Memory'. Journal: Geophysical Journal International 134(1), 228–242 (1998)
[4] Yu, T.-T., Fernàndezb, J., Rundlec, J.B.: Inverting the parameters of an earthquake - ruptured fault with a genetic algorithm (1998)
[5] Woo, G.: The Mathematics of Natural Catastrophes. Imperial College Press (1999)
[6] Shaw, R. (ed.): Disaster Prevention and Management. International Journal Recovery from the Indian Ocean tsunami disaster, 15.1 (2006)

An Approach to Enhance Security Environment Based on SIFT Feature Extraction and Matching to Iris Recognition

C.M. Patil[1] and Sudarshan Patilkulkarni[2]

[1] Research Scholar, JSS Research Foundation,
Department of Electronics and Communication, Mysore, India
patilcm@gmail.com
[2] Assistant Professor, Department of Electronics and Communication,
SJ College of Engineering, Mysore, India
pk.sudarshan@gmail.com

Abstract. With growing emphasis on human identification, iris recognition has recently received increasing attention. Iris feature extraction is the crucial stage of the whole iris recognition process. Through analyzing iris feature extraction and matching method, iris features are not consistent because most feature extraction techniques are sensitive to the variations of captured image data. In this paper we use the Scale Invariant Feature Transformation (SIFT) for recognition using iris images which is invariant to image scaling and rotation. We extract the characteristic SIFT feature points which shows the higher feasibility in the iris feature extraction and matching process.

Keywords: Scale Invariant Feature Transformation (SIFT), Iris Recognition, Texture Analysis.

1 Introduction

Iris recognition is a new technology in the field of biometric feature recognition and has many merits. The conventional iris patterns are randomly generated after almost three months of birth and it is reported that they are not changed all the life long. Also it is non contact method and user's refusal feeling is small compared to other contact method such as fingerprint and hand vessel recognition. The diagram of typical iris recognition system is shown in Fig 1. Which includes the image acquisition, iris segmentation, polar transformation, feature extraction, template generation and matching.

2 Proposed Approach

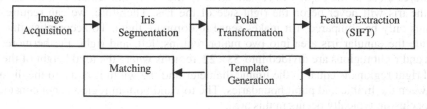

Fig. 1. Proposed Methodology for Iris Recognition System

V.V Das et al. (Eds.): BAIP 2010, CCIS 70, pp. 527–530, 2010.

2.1 Iris Segmentation and Polar Transformation

In this phase the iris is extracted from the eye image i.e. disturbing features like eye-lids & eyelashes are eliminated to the maximum possible extent and then process of normalization is carried out. Fig 2 shows the original image, its inner and outer boundary and then converting in terms of polar transformation to extract the features.

(i)   (ii)   (iii)

Fig. 2. (i) Original Image. (ii) Inner and Outer Boundary. (iii) Polar Transformation.

3 Feature Extraction

In this work SIFT feature extraction techniques have been used. The feature point description is found using the SIFT approach. Experimental results show that the proposed method is capable of discriminating between different iris patterns.SIFT [1] is a method of describing the features of an object such that the same object can be recognized with invariance to scale, rotation, and affine transformations. The method uses difference of Gaussian to locate points on an object that are stable in scale space and then describe these feature points by the relative gradient orientation of the feature point compared with surrounding points within some window size. This descriptor is made of 128 elements for each feature point using four bins in the x and y directions and eight bins for the orientation. The stability of feature points is important since comparison of two objects from different images is dependent on the comparison of the same feature points. Therefore, to ensure the most stable points, a 3-D quadratic function proposed by Brown and Lowe [2] is used to eliminate points that are too low contrast or along an edge, and therefore susceptible to instability from noise. In particular, this method chooses corner points based on the method proposed by Harris and Stephens [3]. In various applications of SIFT [4] [5] objects are identified by comparing the number of points that fall within a Euclidean distance threshold between two images.

3.1 Feature Point Selection

Features close to the pupil will remain close to the pupil and features on the left side of the iris will never be on the right side of the iris. Therefore, we can require that points only be compared if it makes sense to compare them. To accomplish this, we divide the annular iris area into two major regions: left, and right. Furthermore, the left and right regions are divided into 58×22 regions where the total height of the left and right regions is equal to the limbic diameter and the width is equal to the distance between the limbic and pupil boundaries. The top and bottom region is not considered as occlusion typically occurs in this area.

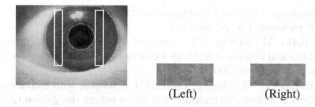

(Left)   (Right)

Fig. 3. Iris Feature Ponit Selection using SIFT

4 Matching

The Euclidean distance is one way of defining the closeness of match between two iris feature templates. It is calculated by measuring the norm between two vectors X and Y respectively of two images under consideration.

$$EM1 = \sqrt{(y1-x1)^2 + (y2-y1)^2 + ...}$$

$$ED = \min(FI, FD) \tag{1}$$

5 Results and Performance

In this paper, an efficient method for personal identification by means of human iris patterns is presented. We tested our project on 50 pictures, using a Mata lab® and obtained an average correct recognition rate 97% with an average computing time of 6.896s.From the experimental results, we are conceived that the proposed system.

Table 1. Runtime Results for Iris Recognition

Algorithm	Localization (Sec)	Feature Extraction (msec)	Comparison (msec)	Total Time (sec)
Daugman	8.7	682.5	54	9.436
Wildes	8.3	210	401	8.911
Proposed	1.42	5216	26	6.896

References

1. Lowe, D.: Object recognition from local scale-invariant features. In: Proceedings of the international conference on computer vision, Corfu, Greece, September 1999, pp. 1150–1157 (1999)
2. Brown, M., Lowe, D.G.: Invariant features from interest point groups. In: British machine vision conference, Cardiff, Wales, pp. 656–665 (2002)

3. Harris, C., Stephens, M.: A combined corner and edge detector. In: Fourth Alvey vision conference, Manchester, UK, pp. 147–151
4. Kelman, A., Sofka, M., Stewart, C.V.: Keypoint descriptors for matching across multiple image modalities and non-linear intensity variations. In: IEEE conference on computer vision and pattern recognition (2007)
5. Mortensen, E.N., Deng, H., Shapiro, L.: A SIFT descriptor with global context. In: IEEE computer society conference on computer and vision pattern recognition (2005)

A Framework for Priority-Based Inter Vehicle Communication for Highway Safety

A. Kumar[1], R.K. Chauhan[2], and Rajan Vohra[3]

[1] Assistant Professor, IT Dept., Lingaya's University, Faridabad
09.arzoo@gmail.com
[2] Chairman, Dept. Of Computer Science and Appl., Kurukshetra University
www.dcsakuk.com
[3] Professor, Dept. of Computer Science, DIT, Dehradun
rajanv12@gmail.com

Abstract. On demand set up, fault tolerance and unconstrained connectivity are a couple of advantages that why mobile computing continues to enjoy rapid growth. The original motive behind vehicular communication was safety on roads, because million of lives were lost and much more injuries have been incurred due to car crashes. Safety messages which are of highest priority need to be delivered to the destination node on time to prevent from accidents. To guide priority scheduling we use meta data. This meta data is in fact priority data which is updated dynamically. Its advantage involve providing more flexibility to the system design and empowering decision makers at the operational level.

Keywords: Vehicular Network, Message dissemination, decision controller.

1 Introduction

With the advent of wireless ad hoc network as packet radio networks in the 1970's, it became an interesting research subject in computer world. Now a days, one of the most attractive research topics in the area of Intelligent Traffic Control is Inter-Vehicle Communication. An ongoing European project, eCall[2] aims at providing automatic call service by 2009 using existing cellular infrastructure If the mobile nodes are vehicles then this type of network is called VANET(vehicular ad-hoc network). This paper is aimed to create a priority based decision support system for vehicular networks using controller and meta data information. In our proposed scheme, we utilize the directionality of data and vehicle for information propagation. The organization of the paper is as follows – first we take literature survey of some related work. Then a co-operative architecture for an intelligent decision support system is proposed. Finally we conclude with a summary and future research direction.

2 Literature Survey

The most related work is [3], in which the wireless ad hoc routing protocols are defined and then their performance is compared. But our focus is to study such routing

V.V Das et al. (Eds.): BAIP 2010, CCIS 70, pp. 531–534, 2010.
© Springer-Verlag Berlin Heidelberg 2010

protocols those support high mobility of nodes. One approach to reduce traffic is to divide the network into clusters. The description of cluster based routing is given in [6]. The research paper [4] defines the general technical issues for vehicle control applications from vehicle communication point of view.FleetNet-bringing car-to-car communication into real world[1]. Vehicle Safety Communication(VSC) Project[5] is a program initiated in 2004 to identify vehicle safety application enhanced or enabled by external communication, evaluate 5.9 GHz DSRC vehicle communication technology and influence proposed DSRC communication protocols to meet the needs of vehicle safety application. [7] presents the concept of local danger warning that is one of the most promising safety application in VANET. In [8] Little and Agarwal have proposed an information propagation scheme for VANET i.e. directional propagation protocol(DPP). The algorithm is distributed in nature and which does not require a global naming function and can perform irrespective of the traffic density.They have shown that cost of message exchange is a function of c,speed of vehicle, v, speed of message propagation and different traffic condition.

3   Existing Information Propagation Scheme for Vehicular Networks

Due to large number of vehicles on a highway in dense traffic condition, it is essential to implement a clustering scheme to manage network collisions. There are many techniques for cluster formation based on node ID and node mobility. We adopt a technique suited for the characteristic of our vehicular network. Vehicle travelling on the same directed pathway form an interconnected blocks of vehicles. It is common highway behavior of vehicles where vehicles tend to travel in block with gaps occurring between consecutive blocks. Vehicles that are within the range r and maintain connectivity for some time t said to be a part of cluster.

There is an exciting research exploring vehicle to vehicle communication such as directional propagation protocol DPP[8]. Each cluster containing a block of vehicles within the radio range of each other. Each cluster has a header and trailer, located at the front and rear end of cluster. Each head and trailer perform the task of communication with other cluster. We are not considering the selection criteria of electing the cluster head or trail. For our assumption we elect the node/vehicle as cluster head/trail that is at minimum distance d within the radio range..With multi-hoping architecture the message is sent to destination.

4   Proposed Scheme

In our proposed scheme, we add the meta data information to guide priority scheduling. For this we propose a model shown below.

To enable early reaction, we assume the use of multi-hop routing in clusters of connected vehicles to achieve a propagation rate that exceeds the speed of individual carrier vehicle.Warning messages from all the vehicles in same clusters are sent to header/trailer. All the messages are queued up in simple first in first out fashion.If the warning message is for the destination in same direction it is removed from the queue

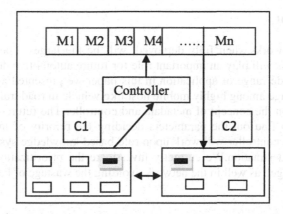

Fig. 1. Communication between two Clusters using metadata information

and sent to next cluster head. In this paper we add the logic of priority queue. When important emergency message gets priority and based on the priority of message, it is hopped next to cluster. The job of deciding the priority is done by controller. Here the controller assumed to work as an intelligent controller that maintains a meta data table which is updated dynamically as the relatively fast movement of vehicles. The corresponding flow chart represents the course of action.

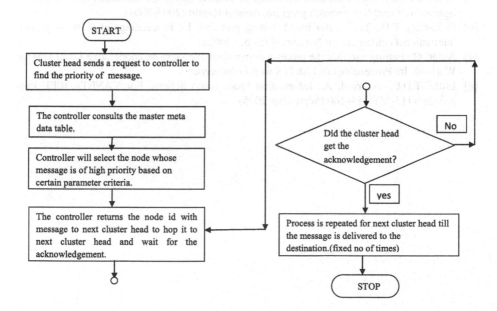

Fig. 2. Steps in proposed algorithm

5 Conclusion

Inter vehicle networks,when fully deployed, will be the largest open mobile ad-hoc network.VANETs will play an important role for future automotive development since they enable a wide range of application.In this paper we presented a approach to disseminate a message among highly mobile host like vehicle in road traffic.The proposed model is based on the concept of metadata and controller.The future work of this proposed scheme to find out the parameters deciding the priority of message.Based on those parameters controller will work upon rule based knowledge system to propagate the message to destination.We currently investigate the prioritization of message so that load is managed as well in the network avoiding the wastage of bandwidth.

References

[1] Festag, A., Fubler, H., Sarma, S.: FLEETNET-bringing car to car communication into the real world. In: Proceedings of 11th world congress on ITS, Japan (October 2004)
[2] Brussels: E-Call, European Project (February 2005)
[3] Broch, J., Maltz, D.A., Johnson, D.B., Jetcheva, J.: A Performance Comparison of Multi-Hop Wireless Ad Hoc Network Routing Protocols. In: Proceedings of ACM/IEEE, MOBICOM (October 1998)
[4] Aoki, M., Fujii, H.: Inter-Vehicle Communication: Technical Issues on Vehicle Control Application. IEEE Communication Magazine (October 1996)
[5] Vehicle Safety Communication Consortium, Vehicle Safety Communication Projcet, IVT light vehicle enabling research program, Annual Report (2003-2004)
[6] Hollerung, T.D.: The cluster based routing protocol. In: Proceedings of IEEE Singapore international conference on Network (October 2003)
[7] Adler, C.: Putting together the pieces-a comprehensive view on cooperative Local Danger Warning. In: Proceedings of 13th ITS world conference
[8] Little, T.D.C., Agarwal, A.: Information Propagation Scheme For VANETs. IEEE Proceedings (13-15), 155–160 (September 2005)

Data Compression on Embedded System

P.S. Revankar[1], Vijay B. Patil[2], and W.Z. Gandhare[1]

[1] Govt. College of Engg., Aurangabad. (MS), India
[2] Maharashtra Academy of Engg., Pune (MS), India
prevankar@gmail.com, patil_viju@rediffmail.com,
wz_gandhare@yahoo.com

Abstract. The development of efficient compression software to compress text is a challenging task. This paper presents how LZW Data Compression technique can be used to compress & decompress the text. The main goal of the system is to make use of LZW data compression technique to compress & decompress the text file on an Embedded Processor such as ARM. We present a way by which we can implement data compression algorithm on an embedded system. Given the set of text program to be compressed, the algorithms runs on Embedded processor and analyzes the code, gathers other relevant information and performs text compression or decompression . Implementation of LZW on embedded processor gives better result as compare to Huffman Compression.

Keywords: Data Compression, LZW compression, Embedded System.

1 Introduction

The spread of computing has led to an explosion in the volume of data to be stored on hard disks and sent over the Internet. This growth has led to a need for "data compression". The essential figure of merit for data compression is the "compression ratio"[2]. The proposed system uses dictionary based compression technique called as LZW.

1.1 Literature Survey

LZ-77 is an example of what is known as "substitution coding". There are other schemes in this class of coding algorithms. Lempel and Ziv came up with an improved scheme in 1978, appropriately named LZ-78, and it was refined by a Mr. Terry Welch in 1984, making it LZW [2,3,]. LZ-77 uses pointers to previous words or parts of words in a file to obtain compression. LZW takes that scheme one step further, actually constructing a "dictionary" of words or parts of words in a message, and then using pointers to the words in the dictionary.

The LZW algorithm stores strings in a "dictionary" with entries for 4,096 variable length strings. The first 255 entries are used to contain the values for individual bytes, so the actual first string index is 256. As the string is compressed, the dictionary is built up to contain every possible string combination that can be obtained from the message,

V.V Das et al. (Eds.): BAIP 2010, CCIS 70, pp. 535–537, 2010.

starting with two characters, then three characters, and so on. we scan through the message to build up dictionary entries.

The LZW coder simply uses dictionary as a tool to generate a compressed output. It does not output the dictionary to the compressed output file. The decoder constructs the dictionary as it reads and uncompressed the compressed data, building up dictionary entries from the uncompressed characters and dictionary entries it has already established.

2 Implementation

The LZW algorithm developed using C is implemented on ARM processor. We have used the arm-linux–gcc compiler for cross compiling the C source code into ARM executable. Output of Compilation with arm-linux-gcc is the executable file. Fig 1 shows the typical development setup of ARM (SBC9302) board .This file is then transferred to the program memory of the ARM processor. Finally the executable file is executed on ARM processor which takes source code as input and produces the compressed code of the source code provided as output. [1]. Processor compresses the source code and stores the result in data memory as a bit file. The parameters that were considered for compressed file are Compressed File Size (CFS), Compression Ratio(CR) and Average Code Length(ACL) Same process is repeated for decompressing the compressed file on ARM processor.

3 Experimental Results

Table 1 shows the results obtained after executing the LZW and Huffman compression algorithm on ARM processor for different file types as input. Obtained results of LZW and Huffman compression are compared with respect to the Compression Ratio (CR), Compressed File Size (CFS), Average code length (ACL) etc. Comparative results of LZW and Huffman are as shown in Fig 2. The compression ratio obtained in LZW compression is Higher than Huffman Compression. Highest compression ratio is obtained in a file where same group of words are repeated more frequently.

Table 1. Results of LZW Compression and Huffman Compression on ARM

Parameters	SFS	LZW Compression			Huffman Compression		
Files	(in Bytes)	CFS	CR	ACL	CFS	CR	ACL
Alice29.txt	152089	72321	53	3.804	87690	42.34	4.61
Comp.c	7843	3933	50	4.011	5039	35.76	5.14
Attendance.xls	18944	4568	76	1.929	6344	66.51	2.68
Grammar.lsp	3721	2115	44	4.541	2172	41.64	4.67
Nano.xml	15979	5957	63	2.982	10064	37.02	5.04

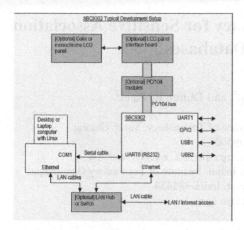

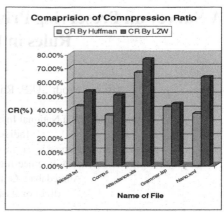

Fig. 1. Typical Development setup of ARM (SBC9302) Board

Fig. 2. Comparison of Compression Ratio

4 Conclusions

This work demonstrates a methodology for compress and decompresses data using enhanced LZW technique on embedded processor. Finally, the enhanced LZW technique is useful for text file format such as doc, PDF and txt. Based on the experimental results it is analyzed on a embedded processor to compare the memory size of the compressed file in light of memory consumed by the compression algorithm on the embedded processor.

References

1. Rein, S., Gühmann, C., Fitzek, F.: Compression of Short Text on Embedded Systems. Journal of Computers 1(6) (September 2006)
2. Blelloch, G.E.: Introduction to Data Compression, October 16 (2001)
3. Al-laham, M., El Emary, I.M.M.: Comparative Study between Various Algorithms of Data Compression Techniques. In: Proceedings of the World Congress on Engineering and Computer Science, WCECS 2007, San Francisco, USA, October 24-26 (2007)

A Survey on Preserving Privacy for Sensitive Association Rules in Databases

Chirag Modi[1], U.P. Rao[1], and Dhiren R. Patel[2]

[1] Sardar Vallabhbhai National Institute of Technology, Surat, Gujarat
India-395007
cnmodi.956@gmail.com, upr@coed.svnit.ac.in
[2] Dept. of Computer Science & Engineering, Indian Institute of Technology Gandinagar,
Ahmedabad, Gujarat, India-382424
dhiren@iitgn.ac.in

Abstract. Privacy preserving data mining (PPDM) is a novel research area to preserve privacy for sensitive knowledge from disclosure. Many of the researchers in this area have recently made effort to preserve privacy for sensitive knowledge in statistical database. In this paper, we present a detailed overview and classification of approaches which have been applied to knowledge hiding in context of association rule mining. We describe some evaluation metrics which are used to evaluate the performance of presented hiding algorithms.

Keywords: Data Mining, Frequent Itemset Hiding, Association Rule Hiding.

1 Introduction

Although successful, the data mining techniques pose a threat to individual's privacy. Therefore to solve privacy problem, PPDM has become a hot directive in data mining and database security field. Researchers have proposed several approaches for knowledge hiding, in context of association rule mining.

In the following example, we show the necessity of sensitive association rule hiding in real life application. Consider, as a tea reseller we are purchasing tea at low price from two companies, Tata Tea Ltd. and Lipton Tea Ltd., while granting them to access our customer database. Suppose, the Lipton Tea supplier mines association rules related to the Tata Tea and by analyzing the rules, runs a coupon scheme that offers some discount on items (items which are frequently purchased with Tata Tea) with purchase of Lipton Tea. So, the amount of sales on Tata Tea is down rapidly and Tata Tea supplier cannot offer tea at low price to us as before and Lipton monopolizes the tea market and is not offering tea at low price to us as before. As a result, we may start losing business to our competitors. So, releasing database with sensitive knowledge is bad for us. This scenario leads to the research of sensitive knowledge (or rule) hiding in database.

The rest of this paper is organized as follows:- In section 2, we discuss some related background, while a detailed overview and classification of existing approaches are

V.V Das et al. (Eds.): BAIP 2010, CCIS 70, pp. 538–544, 2010.
© Springer-Verlag Berlin Heidelberg 2010

discussed in section 3. In section 4, we describe important performance evaluation metrics and in section 5, we discuss and conclude our study by defining some future trends.

2 Theoretical Background and Preliminaries

Association rule can be defined as follows. Let I= {i_1,...,i_m} be a set of items. Database D={T_1,....,T_n} is a set of transactions, where $T_i \subseteq I$. A transaction T supports X, a set of items in I, if $X \subseteq I$. The association rule is denoted by $X \Rightarrow Y$, where $X \subset I$, $Y \subset I$ and $X \cap Y = \emptyset$. The rule with support s and confidence c is called, if $|X \cup Y|/|D| \geq s$ and $|X \cup Y|/|X| \geq c$ respectively. Because of interestingness, we consider thresholds for support and confidence respectively. A detailed overview of association rule mining algorithms and computationally efficient algorithms are presented in [18].

Association rule hiding should achieve at least one of the following goals: (i) All the sensitive association rules must be hidden in sanitized database. (ii) All the non sensitive rules can be mined from sanitized database. (iii) No any new rule that was not previously found in original database can be mined from sanitized database.

3 Classification of Privacy Preserving Association Rule Mining Algorithms

We classify some existing approaches for knowledge hiding in to five different classes.

3.1 Heuristic Based Approaches

These approaches replace 0's by 1's or vice versa in selected transactions for reducing significance of rules. So they can be used to address the complexity issue.

Data Distortion Techniques. M.Attallah et al. [1] were the first to propose heuristic algorithms which decrease significance of the rules. The algorithm selects the parent itemset with maximum support at each level of itemset graph. Then it sets selected parent itemset to be hidden. By iteratively following these steps, algorithm identifies large 1-itemset ancestor of initial itemset and by selecting supporting transactions for selected large 1-itemset and initial large itemset, algorithm removes large 1-itemset from the transactions. The authors also proved NP-hardness of optimal sanitization.

Verykios et al. [8] proposed five algorithms which reduce the support or confidence of sensitive rules by removing or inserting some items in selected transactions. These algorithms hide only one sensitive rule or sensitive item at a time and provide certain privacy. But they generate undesirable side effects in sanitized database.

Oliveira et al. [2] proposed approach which prevents the disclosure of sanitized rules from nonsensitive rules. The proposed algorithm concerns two types of attacks named forward inference attack and backward inference attack in sanitization process. It blocks some inference channels while ensuring better privacy.

Y-H Wu et al. [11] proposed a method to reduce the side effects, which formulates set of constraints related to the possible side effects and allows item modification based on more significant constraint. For rule hiding, a new scheme uses templates [11].

Based on templates, the hiding algorithm selects and applies them that are considered as least producing side effects in database.

K.Duraiswamy et al. [15] proposed an efficient clustering based approach that clusters the sensitive rules based on common item in R.H.S. of the sensitive rules and hides the R.H.S. items in each cluster by reducing support of it. This approach has high efficiency than others. But it hides the only rule which has single R.H.S. item.

Data Blocking Techniques. Y.Saygin et al. [4][12] were the first proposed blocking approach to increase or decrease the support of item by placing unknowns ("?") in place of 1's or 0's .So, It is difficult for an adversary to know the value behind "?".The safety margin is also used to show how much below the minimum threshold new significance of a rule should. This approach is effective and provides certain privacy.

Wang and Jafari [14] proposed more efficient approaches than other approaches as in [4][12]. They require less number of database scans and prune more number of rules, while hiding many rules at a time. But they produce undesirable side effects.

3.2 Border Based Approaches

Sun and Yu [7] were the first to propose border approach that uses the border of non-sensitive frequent item and computes the positive and negative borders in the itemset. Then it selects minimal affecting modifications. To reduce the support of a sensitive itemset from negative border, it calculates impact of the item deletion. Then it deletes minimal affecting item. This approach maintains database quality in terms of frequency of items. But, there is a small degradation in efficiency.

The authors in [10] proposed similar approaches as in [7] that use the revised positive and negative borders and try to remove all the sensitive itemsets belonging to negative border. They select positive border item with highest support and maximum distance from the border, which determines item through which the hiding of the itemset will incur. These approaches are more efficient than other approaches in [7].

3.3 Exact Approaches

Gkoulalas and Verykios [3] proposed method to find an optimal solution for hiding problem, that uses the itemset in the revised positive and negative borders to identify the itemsets for hiding while reducing its original size. Then it formulates a hiding problem to a constraint satisfaction problem (CSP). All the constraints become linear by constraint degree reduction process and solved by binary integer programming (BIP). If no optimal solution exists in the database, the relaxation (heuristic) approach is applied to gain good solution. This approach achieves good efficiency.

The authors in [9] proposed a similar approach as in [3] that extends original database by synthetically generated database and formulates it as a CSP which is solved by BIP. Then it exploits underutilized synthetic transactions to proportionally increase the support of nonsensitive itemsets. A partitioning approach is introduced, which provides better scalability and database quality than inline approach [3].

3.4 Reconstruction Based Approaches

Mielikainen [6] was the first to analyze the computational complexity of inverse frequent set mining and showed the problem is computationally difficult. The author showed that finding a dataset compatible with a given collection of frequent itemsets is NP- complete. For privacy preservation the results state that publishing frequent set might not cause threat to privacy because the inverse frequent set mining is difficult.

Y. Guo [13] proposed a FP tree based algorithm to reconstruct the original database by using non characteristic of database. It generates database using nonsensitive frequent itemsets. Compared with heuristic approaches, this approach is performed over the set of frequent itemsets which is much closer to the association rules than data. This algorithm provides good efficiency and a number of secure databases.

3.5 Cryptography Based Approaches

Vaidya and Clifton [5] proposed a secure approach for sharing association rules when data are vertically partitioned. Proposed approach uses the scalar product over the vertical bit representation of itemsets inclusion in transaction, in order to compute the frequency of the corresponding itemsets. The authors proposed a secure two party algorithm for discovering frequent itemset. This approach is quite effective in terms of communication cost. But it is very expensive for large datasets.

The authors in [16] addressed the secure mining of association rules over horizontal partitioned data. The proposed algorithm uses the secure set union to get the union of candidate association rules. Then summation and secure comparison is used to filter candidate items that are not supported globally. This approach mines association rules securely with reasonable communication cost and computation cost.

4 Comparative Performance Evaluation Metrics

Hiding Failure (HF). It quantifies the percentage of sensitive rules that are still not hidden in the sanitized database and it is derived by,

$$HF = \frac{|Rs\,(D')|}{|R_S(D)|} \qquad (1)$$

Where, |Rs(D')| and |Rs (D)| are number of sensitive rules appearing in the sanitized database and original database respectively. Higher value of HF affects the privacy.

Lost Rules cost. It quantifies the percentage of nonsensitive patterns which are accidentally hidden in sanitized database by hiding process, that is called misses cost(MC) in [17]. It measures utility of database and can be derived by,

$$MC = \frac{|R_{NS}(D)| - |R_{NS}\,(D')|}{|R_{NS}\,(D)|} \qquad (2)$$

Where, |R_{NS}(D)| and |R_{NS}(D')| are number of nonsensitive association rules found in the original database and sanitized database respectively.

Ghost Rules Cost. It measures the percentages of rules that are not previously found in the original database can be derived from sanitized database. These rules are called artifactual patterns (AP) in [17] and computed by,

$$AP = \frac{|R'| - |R \cap R'|}{|R'|} \qquad (3)$$

Where, |R| and |R'| are set of association rules can be generated from original database and sanitized database respectively. Ghost rules give wrong prediction to user.

Communication Cost. It measures the time taken to send information to each involving party in distributed environment.

Dissimilarity. It quantifies difference between original database and sanitized database. It can be calculated by,

$$DISS(D, D') = \frac{1}{\sum_{i=1}^{n} f_D(i)} \times \sum_{i=1}^{n} [f_D(i) - f_{D'}(i)] \qquad (4)$$

Where, $f_D(i)$ and $f_D'(i)$ means frequency of item i in the original database and sanitized database respectively.

Side-Effect Factor (SEF). It quantifies the percentage of nonsensitive rules are hidden as a side effect by sanitization process. It is defined by,

$$SEF = \frac{|R| - (|R'| + |R_S(D)|)}{|R| - |R_S|} \qquad (5)$$

Recovery Factor (RF). It expresses the possibility of an adversary recovering a restrictive rule based on non-restrictive rules. The idea behind it is that downward closure property of itemset. If adversary recover all subsets of an itemset, the recovery factor for such an itemset is possible, thus RF assign by value 1; otherwise RF=0.

Efficiency. It is measured in terms of CPU-time, space requirements and communication requirements for hiding process.

Scalability. It is measured based on the decrease in the performance of the algorithm or the increase of the storage requirements, when larger datasets are applied.

Data Quality. Some data quality parameters are as follows: (i) Accuracy measure the proximity of a sanitized value to the original one. (ii) Completeness evaluates the degree of missed data in the sanitized database. (iii) Consistency measures relationships that to hold among the different data items in a sanitized database.

Privacy Level. It measures the degree of uncertainty according to which, the protected information can still be predicted. The information entropy, the level of privacy etc. are some of the metrics used to quantify the privacy level gain by a hiding algorithm.

5   Conclusion and Future Scope

In this paper, we have surveyed existing approaches regarding knowledge hiding problem by their performance and limitations. Performance evaluation metrics are also discussed to evaluate performance of hiding algorithm.

A more efficient hiding solution can be found by using unknowns. A lot of time is required to solve CSPs which can be improved by further reducing inequalities in CSP. For reconstruction approach, the open problem is to restrict the number of transactions in the new database. An efficient solution can be found to reduce high communication cost for cryptography approaches. For databases in which presence and absence of item is not important, a better hiding solution can be found.

References

1. Atallah, M., Bertino, E., Elmagarmid, A.K., Ibrahim, M., Verykios, V.S.: Disclosure limitation of sensitive rules. In: Proc. of the 1999 IEEE Knowledge and Data Engineering Exchange Workshop (KDEX 1999), pp. 45–52 (1999)
2. Oliveira, S.R.M., Zaïane, O.R., Saygın, Y.: Secure Association Rule Sharing. In: Dai, H., Srikant, R., Zhang, C. (eds.) PAKDD 2004. LNCS (LNAI), vol. 3056, pp. 74–85. Springer, Heidelberg (2004)
3. Gkoulalas-Divanis, A., Verykios, V.S.: An Integer Programming Approach for Frequent Itemset Hiding. In: Proc. ACM Conf. Information and Knowledge Management (CIKM 2006), pp. 748–757 (2006)
4. Saygin, Y., Verykios, V.S., Clifton, C.: Using Unknowns to Prevent Discovery of Association Rules. ACM SIGMOD 30(4), 45–54 (2001)
5. Vaidya, J., Clifton, C.: Privacy preserving association rule mining in vertically partitioned data. In: Proc. Int'l. Conf. Knowledge Discovery and Data Mining, pp. 639–644 (2002)
6. Mielikainen, T.: On inverse frequent set mining. In: Proc. 3rd IEEE ICDM Workshop on Privacy Preserving Data Mining, pp. 18–23. IEEE Computer Society, Los Alamitos (2003)
7. Sun, X., Yu, P.S.: A Border-Based Approach for Hiding Sensitive Frequent Itemsets. In: Proc. Fifth IEEE Int'l. Conf. Data Mining (ICDM 2005), pp. 426–433 (2005)
8. Verykios, V.S., Elmagarmid, A.K., Bertino, E., Saygin, Y., Dasseni, E.: Association rule hiding. IEEE Transactions on Knowledge and Data Engineering 16(4), 434–447 (2004)
9. Gkoulalas-Divanis, A., Verykios, V.S.: Exact Knowledge Hiding through Database Extension. IEEE Transactions on Knowledge and Data Engineering 21(5), 699–713 (2009)
10. Moustakides, G.V., Verykios, V.S.: A Max-Min Approach for Hiding Frequent Itemsets. In: Proc. Sixth IEEE Int'l. Conf. Data Mining (ICDM 2006), pp. 502–506 (2006)
11. Wu, Y.H., Chiang, C.M., Chen, A.L.P.: Hiding Sensitive Association Rules with Limited Side Effects. IEEE Transactions on Knowledge and Data Engineering 19(1), 29–42 (2007)
12. Saygin, Y., Verykios, V.S., Elmagarmid, A.K.: Privacy preserving association rule mining. In: Proc. Int'l. Workshop on Research Issues in Data Engineering (RIDE 2002), pp. 151–163 (2002)
13. Guo, Y.: Reconstruction-Based Association Rule Hiding. In: Proc. of SIGMOD 2007 Ph.D. Workshop on Innovative Database Research (2007)
14. Wang, S.L., Jafari, A.: Using unknowns for hiding sensitive predictive association rules. In: Proc. IEEE Int'l. Conf. Information Reuse and Integration (IRI 2005), pp. 223–228 (2005)
15. Duraiswamy, K., Manjula, D.: Advanced approach in sensitive rule hiding. Modern Applied Science 3(2) (2009)

16. Kantarcioglu, M., Clifton, C.: Privacy preserving distributed mining of association rules on horizontally partitioned data. IEEE Transactions on Knowledge and Data Engineering 16(9), 1026–1037 (2004)
17. Aggarwal, C.C., Yu, P.S.: Privacy-Preserving Data Mining: Models and Algorithms, pp. 267–286. Springer, Heidelberg (2008)
18. Han, J., Kamber, M.: Data Mining: Concepts and Techniques, pp. 227–245. Morgan Kaufmann Publishers, San Francisco (2001)

Boon and Bane of Curvelet Transform

G. Geetha, V. Ragavi, K. Thamizhchelvy, K. Mariappan,
V. Lalitha, and S. Shanmuga Priya

Department of MCA, Sathyabama University, Rajiv Gandhi Salai, Chennai, India
{drggmca,ragaviprabhu,thamizhchelvy,mari.tvtg}@gmail.com
{sowmi.sund,shanmugapriya.s}@gmail.com

Abstract. Candes and Donoho introduced a new system of multiresolution analysis called the curvelet transform. Curvelets take the form of basis elements, which exhibit a very high directional sensitivity and are highly anisotropic. In this paper, we applied the curvelet transform, to generate Tamil OCR, to detect melanoma from microscopic images and to develop a stego system. Curvelet transform is a threat to the security of web applications where Image CAPTCHAs are used to dintinguish man from bots.

Keywords: Curvelet Transform, Image Recognition, Tamil OCR, Watermarking, CAPTCHA.

1 Introduction

Curvelet transform[1] has been developed to overcome the limitations of wavelet and Gabor filters. Curvelet transform intially implemented the concept of discrete ridgelet transform [2]. Since its creation in 1999 [3], ridgelet based curvelet transform has been successfully used as an effective tool in image denoising [4], image decomposition [5], texture classification [6], image deconvolution [7], astronomical imaging [8] and contrast enhancement [9], etc. But ridgelet based curvelet transform is not efficient as it uses complex ridgelet transform [10]. In 2005, Candès et al. proposed two new forms of curvelet transform based on different operations of Fourier samples [11], namely, unequally-spaced Fast Fourier Transform (USFFT) and wrapping based fast curvelet transform. Wrapping based curvelet transform is faster in computation time and more robust than ridgelet and USFFT based curvelet transform [10].

In Sections 2 to 4, the usefulness of curvelets in various application areas are illustrated. In Section 5, it is demonstrated how the curvelets can be a threat to the security of web applications.

2 Curvelet to aid Tamil Font Character Recognition

In this section we discuss how curvelets aid in the development of Tamil OCR. Our first step is to obtain the pattern to be recognized. Each pattern is an image containing black and white pixels. Patterns of the same character may not be identical to one another. To obtain a pattern, a character available in a paper is scanned using a camera.

V.V Das et al. (Eds.): BAIP 2010, CCIS 70, pp. 545–551, 2010.

The second step is to introduce noise. This noise introduction is to show that the system works even in noisy situation. In this work, the following types of noise are introduced in the pattern (a) Salt noise (b) Pepper noise. Noise removal is considered to be part of pre-processing a pattern. Preprocessing is done as in [12].

Third step is skeletonizing. Skeletonizing a pattern consists of deleting the block pixels along the edges of the strokes of the pattern until the pattern is thinned to a line drawing, which is called the patterns skeleton. We apply SPTA (Safe Pixel Thinning Algorithm)as in [13]. It is a skeletonization algorithm used to delete the selected black pixels in the pattern. The recognition of the character must be insensitive to its position, size and orientation. A break pixel is a black pixel whose deletion would cause a connected pattern to no longer remain so. An end pixel is a black pixel at the end of the stroke pixels are black pixel lying the edges of the strokes of pattern. SPTA executes passes over a given pattern and in each pass flags edge pixels. At the end of the each pass SPTA deletes the flagged pixels.

Next, we apply curvelets. Curvelets are known to provide a very good representation of edges in an image. By thinning or thickening an image morphologically, the position of the edges can be changed. Using the curvelet transform, the variation in position of edges are encoded in the transformed domain. In this work two thickened and thinned versions of the image are made. Along with the morphologically changed images, the original image is also used.

Finally we appeal to Naïve Bayes Classifier. It individually recognizes the pattern, rather than classifying the pattern separately. By assuming that the attributes in one pattern are independent of the attributes in another pattern. The Bayesian classifier performs the least misclassifications as compared to any other classifier. Thus curvelets is an important component part of this Tamil OCR system.

3 Curvelet to Identify Malignant Melanoma

Malignant melanoma is among the most frequent types of skin cancer and one of the most malignant tumors. Its incidence has increased faster than that of almost all other cancers and the annual incidence rates have increased at the rate of 3-7% in fair-skinned populations in recent decades [14]. Advanced cutaneous melanoma is still incurable, but melanoma diagnosed in early stages can be cured without complications. However, the differentiation of early melanoma from other pigmented skin lesions is not trivial even for experienced dermatologists. The issue has attracted many researchers who have developed systems and it is well discussed in [15]. Wavelet transform was demonstrated by Sachin et al., [16] to classify melanoma.

The multi resolution is an evolving process and the time-frequency analysis is the trade off between accurate localization of information in the spatial and the spectral domain. Curvelet Transform is a new multi-scale representation most suitable for objects with curves. The curvelet transform enables a multilevel decomposition of the image so that the magnitudes of the curvelet coefficients signify intensity variations on their level of detail. Hence, edges are detected when intensity variations are large on a selected scale. The curvelets provide a near-optimal representation of C^2-edges, considering the number of curvelet coefficients needed to represent the edge to a given accuracy[17]. This property makes curvelets useful for denoising of images with edges[18,19].

The efficient detection of edges and elongated features in images of intracellular and multicellular structures acquired using light or electron microscopy is a challenging and time consuming task in many laboratories. As curvelets are good at representing the edges, it outperforms the existing techniques used in identifying melanoma detection. This study helps to detect malignant melanoma at its early stage and thus save many lives.

The system developed using Curvelet Transform outperform Canny edge detector and an edge detector based on Gabor filters[20]. Discrete Curvelet Transform has absorbed the advantages of both the Gabor filters and canny edge detector while overcoming the disadvantages of both these methods.

For the automated detection of malignant melanoma we employ a variety of methods for image acquisition, feature definition and extraction, and lesion classification from features. It is clear from fig.1 that our scheme detects the vesicle membranes better than the other two methods. Our curvelet based scheme is less sensitive to the small circular artefacts.

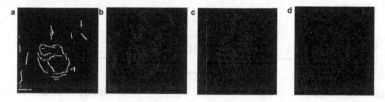

Fig. 1. Edge detection scheme comparison on the vesicle image. a) raw output from out curvelet-based scheme; b) Canny edge detector with thresholds 0.12 and 0.35; c) odd Gabor filter with $\sigma = 2$ and $\psi = 0.5$.; d) odd Gabor filter with $\sigma = 6$ and $\psi = 0.33$.

4 Unidentifiable Data Hiding in Images

Design of secure and survivable stego system is a challenging task. Here we appeal to the curvelet transform for developing an unidentifiable stego system.

Cox et al. [21] noted that in order for a watermark to be robust to attack, it must be placed in perceptually significant areas of the image. Xia, Boncelet, and Arce [22] proposed a watermarking scheme based on the Discrete Wavelet Transform (DWT). The watermark, modeled as Gaussian noise, was added to the middle and high frequency bands of the image. The decoding process involved taking the DWT of a potentially marked image. Sections of the watermark were extracted and correlated with sections of the original watermark. If the cross-correlation was above a threshold, then the watermark was detected. Otherwise, the image was decomposed into finer and finer bands until the entire, extracted watermark was correlated with the entire, original watermark. This technique proved to be more robust than the DCT method [21] when embedded zero-tree wavelet compression and halftoning were performed on the watermarked images.

a   b

c   d

Fig. 2. a) Noisy image, b) filtered images using the decimated wavelet transform, c) the un-decimated wavelet transform, d) curvelet transform

We apply the Curvelet Transform for watermarking the image. Using trous algorithm, the curvelet coefficients of low and high frequency bands of watermark is embedded to the most significant coeffients at low and high frequency bands of the curvelet transform of an image,respectively. A multiresolution nature of curvelet transform is exploited in the process of edge detection. The proposed watermarking method is robust to Discrete Cosine Transform(DCT) and Wavelet based lossy image compression techniques. Curvelet transform can be best suited for unidentifiable data hiding in images.

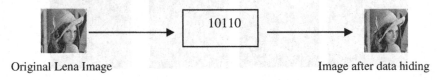

Original Lena Image   Image after data hiding

Fig. 3. Unidentifiable data in Lena image

5   Curvelets – Threat to the Security of Web Applications

Completely Automated Public Turing Tests to Tell Computers and Humans Apart (CAPTCHAs) are now an almost standard security mechanisms for defending against undesirable and malicious bot programs on the Internet. CAPTCHAs generate and grade tests that most humans can pass but current computer programs can't[23]. Such tests—often called CAPTCHA challenges—are based on hard, open artificial intelligence problems. Thus the basic requirement of a CAPTCHA is that computer programs must be slower than humans in responding correctly. To that purpose, the *semantic gap* [24] between human understanding and the current level of machine intelligence is exploited. Several types of CAPTCHAs already exist. The types of tasks they require include: image recognition, text recognition, and speech recognition. Most current CAPTCHAs are text-based. Commercial text-based CAPTCHAs have been broken using object-recognition techniques [25], with accuracies of up to 99% on EZ-Gimpy. Image-based CAPTCHAs such as Microsoft's Asirra, IMAGI-NATION [23,26,27] have been proposed as alternatives to the text media.

Curvelet transform has been developed as a robust mechanism which improves CBIR performance and a complete coverage of the spectral domain to capture more orientation information. In this section, we describe how curvelet transformations are used to identify the distorted images. Texture feature representation and its use in CBIR is an important research issue. Using discrete curvelet texture descriptor is a new and promising direction in image retrieval. In order to understand the effectiveness of the curvelet features for Content Based Image Retrieval, we had made a systematic analysis, application and evaluation of this feature in this section.

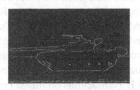

Fig. 4. Distorted Image

Fig. 5. Image after applying edge detection algorithm

Images described by curve segments, particularly line segments, can be obtained by applying curvelet transform to them, as shown in the above figure. They are usually called shape primitives or image silhouette primitives. After obtaining the curve segment description, we label the segments. The description of the image can be obtained from line segments derived by the application of Hough Transform. The segmentation of an image into distinct regions is often used as a means of obtaining structural description of images, e.g., based on proximity relations of region centroids and using labels related to the image properties of the regions such as perimeter, area, color, light intensity and texture.

After identifying the image if it is Microsoft's Asirra[28], it will click the respective images (cats/dogs) or if it is IMAGINATION[29] CAPTCHA Part II, it will identify the image and then it will select the respective option.

A key area of research that would greatly benefit from narrowing the semantic gap is content-based image retrieval (CBIR). Now that we have an attempt to build a system that can identify images that are semantically similar to query images and get the text respective to it, the limitations of the state-of-the-art in image content analysis, which we saw as an opportunity for system security is now been eroded.

6 Conclusion

Curvelet Transform can become a powerful tool in pattern recognition as demonstrated in this paper. We have shown how curvelet transform can be applied to character recognition, medical images, watermarking, pattern matching. There is a vast scope for further research in Geology, remote imaging, etc. Curvelet Transform, as proved by us can be a destructive tool and could emerge as a major threat for web applications where image based CAPTCHAs are used. Security experts can no more utilize the semantic gap for securing the applications. Thus Curvelet Transform can be a boon as well as a bane.

References

[1] Candes, E.J., Donoho, D.L.: Curvelets: A surprisingly effective nonadaptive representation for objects with edges (December 2006),
http://www.curvelet.org/papers/Curve99.pdf

[2] Candès, E.J., Donoho, D.L.: Ridgelets: a key to higher-dimensional intermittency? Philosophical Transactions of the Royal Society of London A 357, 2495–2509 (1999)

[3] Candès, E.J., Donoho, D.L.: Curvelets - a surprisingly effective nonadaptive representation for objects with edges. In: Cohen, A., Rabut, C., Schumaker, L.L. (eds.) Curve and Surface Fitting: Saint-Malo. Vanderbilt University Press, Nashville (1999)

[4] Starck, J.-L., Candès, E.J., Donoho, D.L.: The Curvelet Transform for Image Denoising. IEEE Transactions on Image Processing 11(6), 670–684 (2002)

[5] Starck, J.-L., Elad, M., Donoho, D.L.: Image Decomposition Via The Combination of Sparse Rrepresentations and a Variational Approach. IEEE Transactions on Image Processing, 1570–1582 (October 2005)

[6] Arivazhagan, S., Ganesan, L., Kumar, T.G.S.: Texture classification using Curvelet Statistical and Co-occurrence Features. In: The 18th International Conference on Pattern Recognition, ICPR 2006 (2006)

[7] Starck, J.-L., Nguyen, M.K., Murtagh, F.: Wavelets and Curvelets for Image Deconvolution: a Combined Approach. Signal Processing 83, 2279–2283 (2003)

[8] Starck, J.-L., Donoho, D.L., Candes, E.J.: Astronomical Image Representation by the Curvelet Transform. Astronomy & Astrophysics 398, 785–800 (1999)

[9] Starck, J., Murtagh, F., Candès, E.J., Donoho, D.L.: Gray and Color Image Contrast enhancement by the Curvelet Transform. IEEE Transactions on Image Processing 12(6), 706–717 (2003)

[10] Fadili, M.J., Starck, J.-L.: Curvelets and Ridgelets. Encyclopedia of Complexity and System Science (2007) (in press)

[11] Candès, E.J., Demanet, L., Donoho, D.L., Ying, L.: Fast Discrete Curvelet Transforms. Multiscale Moeling and Simulation 5, 861–899 (2005)

[12] Iliescu, S., Shinghal, R., Teo, R.Y.: Proposed heuristic procedures to preprocess character patterns using line adjacency graphs. Pattern Recognition 29(6), 951–75 (1996)

[13] Naccache, N.J., Shinghal, R.: SPTA: A proposed algorithm for thinning binary patterns. IEEE Transactions on System, Man and Cybernectics SMC-17(3), 409–418 (1984)

[14] Marks, R.: Epidemiology of melanoma. Clin. Exp. Dermatol. 25, 459–463 (2000)

[15] Maglogiannis, I., Kosmopoulos, D.I.: Computational vision systems for the detection of malignant melanoma. Oncology Reports 15, 1027–1032 (2006)

[16] Patvardhan, S.V., Dhawan, A.P., Relue, P.A.: Classification of melanoma using tree structured wavelet transforms. Computer methods and Programs in Biomedicine 72(3), 223–239 (2003)

[17] Candès, E.J., Donoho, D.L.: New tight frames of curvelets and optimal representations of objects with piecewise C-2 singularities. Commun. Pur. Appl. Math. 57, 219–266 (2004)

[18] Candès, E., Demanet, L., Donoho, D., Ying, L.X.: Fast discrete curvelet transforms. Multiscale Model Sim. 5, 861–899 (2006)

[19] Sivakumar, R.: Denoising of computer tomography images using curvelet transform. ARPN J. Eng. Appl. Sci. 2, 21–26 (2007)

[20] Gebäck, T., Koumoutsakos, P.: Edge detection in microscopy images using curvelets. BMC Bioinformatics 10, 75 (2009)

[21] Cox, I., Kilian, J., Leighton, F., Shamoon, T.: Secure Spread Spectrum Watermarking for Multimedia. IEEE Transactions on Image Processing 6(12), 1673–1687 (1997)

[22] Xia, X., Boncelet, C., Arce, G.: A Multiresolution Watermark for Digital Images. In: Proc. IEEE Int. Conf. on Image Processing, October 1997, vol. I, pp. 548–551 (1997)

[23] Von Ahn, L., Blum, M., Langford, J.: Telling Humans and Computers Apart Automatically. Comm. ACM 47(2), 56–60 (2004)

[24] Smeulders, A.W.M., et al.: Content-Based Image Retrieval at the End of the Early Years. IEEE Trans. Pattern Analysis and Machine Intelli. 22(12), 1349–1380 (2000)

[25] Mori, G., et al.: Recognizing Objects in Adversarial Clutter: Breaking a Visual CAPTCHA. In: Proc. IEEE Conf. Computer Vision and Pattern Recognition (2003)

[26] Chew, M., et al.: Image Recognition CAPTCHAs. In: Proc. 7th Info. Security Conf. (2004)

[27] Rui, Y., et al.: ARTiFACIAL: Automated Reverse Turing Test using FACIAL features. Multimedia Systems 9(6), 493–502 (2004)

[28] Elson, J., Douceur, J.R., Howell, J., Saul, J.: Asirra: A CAPTCHA that Exploits Interest-Aligned Manual Image Categorization. In: Proc. ACM Conference on Computer and Communications Security (2007)

[29] Datta, R., Li, J., Wang, J.Z.: IMAGINATION: A Robust Image-based CAPTCHA Generation System (2008)

Security in High Performance Computing

Urvashi Chugh and Amit Chugh

Department of CSE,
Institute of Technology and Management, Gurgaon
Urvashimutreja1984@gmail.com, amitchugh_9@rediffmail.com

Abstract. This paper proposes a solution for applying security to high performance computing systems (HPCS). Providing security in high performance computing is a challenging task. Internet, operating systems and distributed environments currently suffer from poor security support and cannot resist common attacks. The paper aims to apply various technologies at different levels of security on HPCS. HPCS[2] aims for receiving help to do complex and large computations in an environment where work is performed by many communicating computers on a single task which leads to an increased rank of security. The paper intends to achieve three major tasks. First, it divides the security in levels, second it covers how to define these levels on architectures and third it proposes the existing technologies of TCP/IP on the levels defined here.

Keywords: HPCS, Grid Security, Cluster Security.

1 Introduction

High performance computing is best achieved by parallelism. Parallelism (using parallel computers) is one of the best ways to overcome the speed bottleneck of single processors. Many computer systems supporting high performance computing have emerged like MPP, SMP, Distributed Systems, Cluster, and Grid. Their taxonomy is based on how their Processor, memory and interconnect are laid out. Cluster and Grid both are sincere source of High Performance computing.

Cluster is type of distributed processing system which consists of a collection of interconnected standalone computers working together as a single integrated computing resource. *Grid* as a system that coordinates distributed resource using standard, open general purpose protocol and interfaces to deliver non trivial quality of services.

Security is very important in every work platform. *Security* in Cluster and Grid deals with the issues of 1.*Security at Resource level* 2.*Security at Communication level* 3.*Security at User level*. Security [4] *disciplines* are 1.Authentication 2.Delegation 3.Single sign on 4.Credential life span and renewal 5.Authorization 6.Privacy 7.Confidentiality 8.Message Integrity 9.Policy Exchange 10.Secure Logging 11.Assurance 12.Manageability13. Firewall Traversal.

V.V Das et al. (Eds.): BAIP 2010, CCIS 70, pp. 552–556, 2010.

A. Security Facilities in the TCP/IP Protocol Stack[6]

IPsec [6] provide security to IP layer. It provides the capability to secure communication across a LAN and across the internet. IPsec encompasses three functional areas 1.Authentication 2.Confidentiality 3.Key Management. Authentication Header (AH) protocol, Encryption Security Payload (ESP), Internet security Association and key management protocol (ISAKMP) are the working protocols of IPsec. *Secure Socket layer* (SSL)[6] make use of TCP to provide a reliable end to end secure services. SSL is combination of four Protocols. i)SSL Record Protocol. ii)SSL Handshake Protocol. iii)SSL Change Cipher Specification Protocol. iv) SSL Alert Protocol.

Application layer security is achieved by all theses facilities. One of them is Kerberos. *Kerberos* is an Authentication service designed for use in a Distributed Environment. Kerberos makes use of a trusted third part Authentication service that enables client and server to establish authenticated communication. *Secure/ Multipurpose(S/MIME)* [6] internet mail extension is a security environment to the MIME internet.

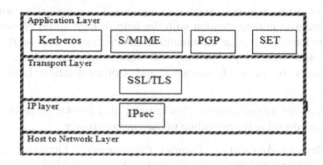

Fig. 1. Security Facilities in the TCP/IP Protocol Stack

E-Mail format standard, based on technology from Rivest Shannon Algorithm data security. *Pretty Good Policy(PGP)[6]* Provides Confidentiality and Authentication service that can be used for electronic mail and file storage application. PGP provide five services i) Authentication ii) Confidentiality iii) Compression iv) E-Mail Compatibility v) Segmentation.

Secure Electronic Transaction (SET)[6] it is an open Encryption and security specification designed to protect credit card transaction on the internet.

2   Security Applying in Cluster Architecture

Cluster Architecture [6] Fig.2 here by includes High Speed Network/Switch layer, PC workstation, communication software, and Network Interface Hardware layer SSI and Availability infrastructure, Sequential, Parallel Application Parallel Programming Environments.

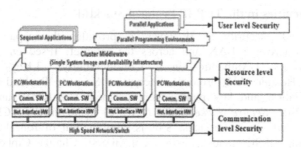

Fig. 2. Cluster Architecture

High Speed Network/Switch layer- This part in the Cluster Architecture is responsible for the communication in between the nodes. Every Node in the Cluster is attached to this i.e. Gigabit Ethernet and Myrinet. So need of Communication Level Security is arrived here.

PC workstation, communication software, Network Interface Hardware layer- This layer consist of many high performance computers. Communication software offers fast and reliable data communication with the help of high speed Network. Network Interface Hardware acts as a Communication Processor and is responsible for transmitting and receiving packets of data between cluster nodes via network/interfaces so need of Resource and Communication Level Security is required here.

SSI and Availability infrastructure- This layer is also known as cluster middleware layer which is responsible for providing unified system image.

*Sequential, Parallel Application Parallel Programming Environments-*This layer includes Applications and tools like Compiler, PVM and MPI. That is the reason that's why User Level Security is applying here.

3   Security Applying in Grid Architecture

Grid Architecture [1, 3, 7] fig. 3 is layered Architecture it includes four layers these are Fabric, Resource and Connectivity, Collective and finally User Application Layer.

Fabric Layer- The Fabric layer provides the Resources to which shared access is required .So need of Resource Level security is arrived here.

Resource and Connectivity Layer- Resource Layer include two types of protocols one is information and another one is Management for Resources. Connectivity layer defines core communication and authentication protocols. Communication protocols enable the exchange of data between fabric layer resources .So need for both Resource and Communication level security is arrived.

Collective Layer- Contains protocols and services not associated with anyone specific resource but instead capturing interaction across collection of resources. It provides directory, co-allocation, and scheduling, brokering, monitoring, data replication services. So, need of communication level security is arrived here.

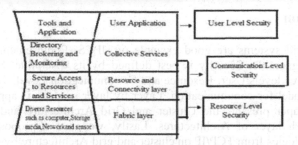

Fig. 3. Grid Architecture

User Application Layer- The final layer n our Grid Architecture comprises the user application that operate within a VO environment. So, here User level security is needed.

4 Security Achievement through Existing Technologies

There are many technologies existing that are following different security disciplines. Here we are applying technologies that were actually applied on TCP/IP model and then we will propose these technologies to security levels. Table 1 is defining this relationship between levels, disciplines, and technologies. like to say User application level need to follow Authentication, Authorization and Confidentiality etc. According to TCP/IP model Application Level Security can be achieved by Kerberos, S/MIME, PGP, SET technologies and these technologies can satisfy the disciplines required to follow at User/Application level. Communication Level Security need to follow Privacy in communication Message Integrity required policy.

Exchange is required to negotiation between two authorized parties. Firewall Traversal, Delegation, Single Sign On, Credential life span and renewal are also required at communication level. SSL/TLS work on Transport layer in TCP/IP model so some of disciplines required at communication level can be satisfied by this. Although we need some technologies extra then SSL/TLS yet it solve purpose up to some extent. Resource level security need to follow Secure logging, Assurance, Manageability disciplines. IPsec is working on IP layer so it can provide resource level security up to some extent.

Table 1. Technologies applied on different levels

LEVEL	DISCIPLINE	TECHNOLOGIES
USER/APPLICATION	Authentication Authorization Confidentiality	Kerberos S/MIME PGP SET
COMMUNICATION	Privacy Message Integrity Policy Exchange Firewall Traversal Delegation Single sign on Credential life span and renewal	SSL/TLS
RESOURCE	Secure Logging Assurance Manageability	IPsec

5 Conclusion

Cluster and Grid systems are good example of HPCS. Requirement of security in HPCS is not ignorable. Security is best defined by its discipline. Security can be divided into three levels User, Resource and Communication Level. TCP/IP model is well known model for communication. Layer by layer security is applied in TCP/IP model. This paper presents the Cluster and Grid Architecture and security level applied on each layer of Architectures. Lastly, we gave a proposal of applying existing technologies from TCP/IP on cluster and grid Architecture by security levels.

Every security technology is having constraints. Constraints of technology and architecture should be compatible like no. of users in communication like key management issues like intrusion detection and policy management.

References

1. Kacsuk, P. (ed.): Journal of Grid Computing Main. Springer, Netherlands; ISSN: 1570-7873 (print version) Journal no. 10723
2. Gerndt, M., Kranzlmüller, D. (eds.): HPCC 2006. LNCS, vol. 4208, p. 938. Springer, Heidelberg (2006),
   http://www.springerlink.com/content/8157133852440k02/
   ?p=7f9b43a84c124f1c92bb1cf057ddf7cf&pi=0
3. Fang, X., Yang, S., Guo, L., Zhang, L.: Research on Security Architecture and Protocols of Grid Computing System,
   http://www.springerlink.com/content/1g03cbplaq63m90x/
4. Lalande, J.-F., Rodriguez, D., Toinard, C.: Security Properties in an Open Peer-to-Peer Network. International Journal of Network Security & Its Applications, Academy & Industry Research Collaboration Center 1(3), 73–89 (2009)
5. Stallings, W.: Cryptography and Network security principles and practices; ISBN-81-203-3018-8
6. Buyya, R.: High performance Cluster Computing; ISBN-978-81-317-1693-9
7. Foster, I., Kesselman, C.: The Grid: Blueprint for a New Computing Infrastructure. Morgan Kaufmann, San Francisco (1999)

Trust Worthy Architecture for Mobile Ad Hoc Network Environment

V.R. Sarma Dhulipala[1], B. Vishnu Prabha[2], and RM. Chandrasekaran[3]

[1] Lecturer (Physics), Center for Convergence of Technologies/Anna University,
Tiruchirapalli, Tamil Nadu, India
[2] Student, Anna University Tiruchirapalli, Tamil Nadu, India
{dvrsarma, vishnuprabha.be}@gmail.com
[3] Registrar, Anna University Tiruchirapalli/Tamil Nadu, India
aurmc@hotmail.com

Abstract. A mobile ad hoc network is a kind of wireless communication network that does not rely on a fixed infrastructure and is lack of any centralized control. The wireless and distributed nature of Manet poses greater challenges of the system and networks for fruitful working are scalability, mobility, security, reliability and other attributes of trust worthy system. We propose an architecture for mobile ad hoc networks that provides holistic approach that considers challenges of the system and networks and focus on the collaborative mechanism providing architecture called Trust Worthy Architecture for Mobile Ad Hoc Networks. We characterize open distributed-system network-oriented architectures capable of fulfilling critical security, mobility, reliability, scalability, and performance requirements, while being readily adaptable to widely differing applications, different hardware and software providers, and changing technologies.

Keywords: MANET, Security, Mobility, Reliability and Quality of Service.

1 Introduction

Mobile Ad-Hoc Network (MANET) is a collection of wireless mobile nodes spread over in the mobile ad-hoc environment that communicate with each other without any centralized access points, infrastructure, or centralized administration. Mobile Ad-hoc Networks are more prone to physical threats because of the dynamically changing network topology [1]. The secure routing and key management mechanism are used to discover secure paths and subsequent communications [2].

Providing trust worthiness for a MANET is a major issue. In this paper we provide trust worthy architecture for mobile ad-hoc network and pseudo code implementation. It provides trusted services, as well as protection of confidential information, secure communication, secure routing protocol usage, secured mobility model, reliable communication and optimum quality of service metrics for the mobile ad hoc networks.

V.V Das et al. (Eds.): BAIP 2010, CCIS 70, pp. 557–560, 2010.

2 Trust Worthy Architecture

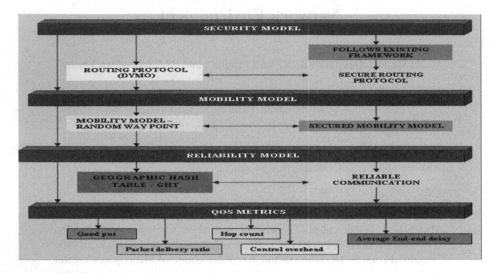

Fig. 1. Trust worthy Architecture

2.1 Security Model

Security is difficult to achieve in such networks as the networks are not conducive to centralized trusted authorities [3]. The security solutions that have been deployed for wired networks are not directly portable to ad hoc networks. The difficulty arises as a result of sporadic wireless medium, dynamic network topology and constraint battery resources. The security of the Trust Worthy architecture is achieved using key management mechanism between the sender and receiver [4]. Key exchange (symmetric and asymmetric) occurred only between the trusted parties. Trust worthy Architecture only allows authenticated node to the further processing.

Secure ad hoc routing protocols (SAR) are used for routing packets. In our architecture we are using DYMO for security purpose. In ad hoc networks, routing protocol should be robust against topology update and any kinds of attacks [3]. The attacks may include injecting erroneous routing information, replaying old routing information, and distorting routing information [5].

2.2 Mobility Model

The mobility model is designed to describe the movement pattern of mobile users, and how their location, velocity and acceleration change over time. The security in mobility model is urging because of intrusion and malicious attacks are easily happened during the node movement.

In our architecture we are using random way point mobility model [7] in which nodes move independently to a randomly chosen destination with a randomly selected velocity [7]. Prevention of intrusion, malicious attacks and flooding attacks are possible because the movement pattern is randomly selected from time to time.

2.3 Reliability Model

The number of packets received by different members of a group is highly variable [8]. Reliability model provides Reliable delivery of messages and Error free delivery of messages [4] [9].The trust worthiness of the MANET is achieved only through the reliable communication between the nodes in a mobile ad-hoc environment. The characteristic of Trust worthy Architecture such as security, mobility and scalability is validated only through the reliable communication.

2.4 QoS Metrics for MANET

The optimum quality of service of the MANET is achieved only when the node and the ad hoc environment is trust worthy. Various QoS metrics [10] considered for the analyses are Good put, delay, PDR, control overhead, jitter and hop count [10].

3 Trust Worthy Architecture Pseudo Code Implementation

```
1.  Mobile node enter in to the Mobile Ad-hoc Environment
2.  Node checking for authentication
3.  n=xy & f(n)=pq where p=x-1,q=1  x and y are two random variables is of
       the required bit length, e.g. 1024 bits.
4.  n = xy  &  f(n) = pq. Where p=x-1,q=y-1 n is known as the modulus
5.  Choose an integer e, 1 < e < φ(n), such that gcd(e, f(n)) = 1.
6.  Compute the secret value  d, 1 < d < f(n), such that ed ≡ 1 mod f(n).
7.  Asymmetric key is (n, e) and the symmetric key is (n, d). e is known as the
       asymmetric, d is known as the symmetric.
8.  Obtains the receiver node asymmetric key (n, e).
9.  Represents the original information as a positive integer m.
10. Computes the Encrypted informationt c = m^e mod n.
11. Sends the Encrypted informationt c to receiver node.
12. Uses sender node symmetric key (n, d) to compute m = c^d mod n.
13. Extracts the Original information from the integer representative m.
14. Trust worthiness of Secure ad hoc routing protocol is compared
15. Select DYMO Routing protocol for routing packets
16. Selection of the mobility model
17. Random WayPoint mobility model is choosen
18. Reliablity of Communication is validated
        a.    Reliable Communication under process
        b.    Else Node id enter in to the Geographic Hash Table
19. Go to the step 2. till network finishes the communication
20. Communication under process
```

4 Results and Conclusion

Our framework for Trust Worthy Architecture consists of a security module, Mobility module, Reliability module and provides optimum quality of service metrics. The pseudo code implementation of the Trust Worthy Architecture is verified with the help of C language. The initial check out is performed with the help of network simulator NS2. The results may better help the other researchers working in this area and construct better working environment with better parameterization.

5 Future Work

In future we plan to analyze the performance of the Trust Worthy Architecture and evaluate of the trust worthiness of the mobile nodes and the network. We are in the process of a constructive approach to analyze the performance issues of the mobile ad hoc network environment.

References

1. Balakrishnan, V., Varadharajan, V., Tupakula, U., Lucs, P.: Trust Integrated Cooperation Architecture for Mobile Ad-hoc Networks. In: 4th International Symposium on IEEE Wireless Communication Systems, ISWCS 2007, Macquarie Univ., Sydney, October 17-19, pp. 592–596 (2007)
2. Han, I.-S., Kim, J.-M., Hwang-Bin: Service Discovery and Delivery System Based on Trust in Mobile Ad-Hoc Network. In: International Conference on Information Science and Security, ICISS 2008, January 10-12, pp. 171–176 (2008)
3. Balakrishnan, V., Varadharajan, V., Tupakula, U., Lucs, P.: TEAM: Trust Enhanced Security Architecture for Mobile Ad-hoc Networks. In: 15th IEEE International Conference on Networks, ICON 2007, Macquarie Univ., Sydney, pp. 182–187 (2007)
4. Campo, C., Almenarez, F., Diaz, D., Garcia-Rubio, C., Lopez, A.M.: Secure Service Discovery based on Trust Management for ad-hoc Networks. Journal of Universal Computer Science, J. UCS 12, 340–356 (2006)
5. Ngai, E.C.H., Lyu, M.R.: Trust- and clustering-based authentication services in mobile ad hoc networks. In: IEEE 24th International Conference on Distributed Computing Systems Workshops, March 23-24, pp. 582–587 (2004)
6. Trivedi, A.K., Arora, R., Kapoor, R., Sanyal, S., Sanyal, S.: A Semi-distributed Reputation-based Intrusion Detection System for Mobile Adhoc Networks. India Journal of Information Assurance and Security, 265–274 (2006)
7. Camp, T., Boleng, J., Davies, V.: A survey of mobility models for ad hoc network research. In: Interscience conference on Wireless Communications and Mobile Computing, September 11, vol. 2(5), pp. 483–502 (2002)
8. Viejo, A., Sebé, F., Domingo-Ferrer, J.: Aggregation of Trustworthy Announcement Messages in Vehicular Ad Hoc Networks. In: IEEE Vehicular Technology Conference, VTC Spring 2009, Harbin, China, April 26-29, pp. 1–5 (2009) ISBN: 0-7695-3072-9
9. Chandra, R., Ramasubramanian, V., Birman, K.P.: Anonymous Gossip: Improving Multicast Reliability in Mobile Ad-Hoc Networks. In: 21st IEEE International Conference on Distributed Computing Systems, p. 275 (2001)
10. Sivaraman, R., Sarma Dhulipala, V.R., Sowbhagya, L., Vishnu Prabha, B.: Comparative Analysis of QoS Metrics in Mobile Ad Hoc Network Environment. Accepted on Academy publishers IJRTE 2009, pp. 69–71 (2009)

A Cross Layer Approach for Fault Management Framework in Wireless Sensor Networks

V.R. Sarma Dhulipala[1], K. Kavitha[2], and RM. Chandrasekaran[3]

[1] Lecturer (Physics), Center for Convergence of Technologies/Anna University,
Tiruchirapalli, Tamil Nadu, India
[2] Student, Anna University Tiruchirapalli, Tamil Nadu, India
{dvrsarma, kavithakumar87}@gmail.com
[3] Registrar, Anna University Tiruchirapalli, Tamil Nadu, India
aurmc@hotmail.com

Abstract. Wireless sensor network (WSN) is a collection of sensor nodes which are randomly deployed in distributed environment. Fault detection and management is major criteria in wireless sensor networks. Cross layer approach is used to implement Fault management plane in wireless sensor networks. Cross-layer approach (XLA) is developed, which replaces the traditional layered approach (TLA) that has been used in Wireless sensor networks. The design principle of XLA is both the data and the functional operations of traditional communication layers are melted in a single protocol. The objective of this paper is creating a cross layer approach (XLA) algorithm for fault management and it is verified using high level language.

Keywords: WSN, Fault Management, Fault tolerance, XLA, TLA.

1 Introduction

A Wireless Sensor Network (WSN) is a collection of small, lightweight sensor nodes deployed in large numbers to monitor the ambient conditions. WSN have a numerous advantages, but the fault detection and management is major criteria in wireless sensor networks. Cross layer approach is used to implement fault management framework in wireless sensor networks. XLA provides reliable and efficient communication [1]. XLA is developed, which replaces the TLA that has been used in Wireless sensor networks [2]. The principle of cross layering is the information and the functional operations of traditional communication layers are combined into a single protocol. The XLA is governed by the concept of initiative calculation. This concept provides freedom for each node to decide on participating in communication. XLA improves the efficiency of the communication than the traditional layered approach [2].

1.1 Planes in Protocol Stack

There are three management planes in wireless sensor networks. They are Power management plane, Mobility management plane and Task management plane [3].

V.V Das et al. (Eds.): BAIP 2010, CCIS 70, pp. 561–564, 2010.
© Springer-Verlag Berlin Heidelberg 2010

Power management plane manage a sensor node how to use its energy efficiently [4]. Mobility management plane detect the movement of sensor nodes in a particular region. Task management plane balances and schedules the tasks given to a specific node. These three management planes are necessary, so that each sensor node can work together in an energy efficient way [5]. Our contribution is implementing fault management plane using cross layer approach in existing protocol stack [6]. The objective of the proposed XLA is highly reliable communication with minimal energy consumption and fault tolerance [7].This results reliable and efficient communication in wireless sensor networks.

2   Proposed Protocol Stack

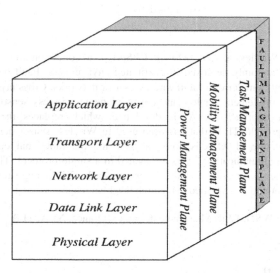

Fig. 1. Proposed protocol stack

3   Design Flow

Cross layer approach is based on the concept of initiative calculation. Wireless sensor networks have traditional layered approach and cross layered approach. Traditional layered approach has low power transmission. Cross layered approach is developed which replaces the traditional layered approach that has been used in wireless sensor networks. As already said cross layer approach is based on initiative calculation concept. This concept used for each node to decide on participating in communication. The problem in cross layer approach is difficult to implement [8]. Fault management plane is introduced in different layers using XLA [9] [10]. Our design principle is complete unified cross layering such that both the data and functional operation of traditional communication layers are melted in a single protocol. Energy consumption is major criteria in WSN [11]. The objective of the proposed cross layer approach is highly reliable communication with minimal energy consumption and fault tolerance. From XLA the system is achieving fault management to provide efficient communication. The figure shows the design flow model of XLA.

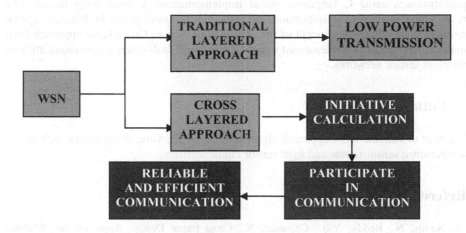

Fig. 2. Design flow

3.1 XLA Algorithm

Cross Layer Approach (XLA) algorithm provides implementation of Fault management plane in wireless sensor networks.

Step 1:   In the layered stack of WSN, identify is there any fault;
Step 2:   If it has any fault go to Step 4;
Step 3:   Go to Step 10, if there is no fault
Step 4:   Create Fault Management Plane using Cross layer approach;
Step 5:   Node initiate transmission by broadcasting an RTS packet using
          Initiative calculation concept in XLA;
Step 6:   Calculate Ni (TH);
Step 7:   Calculate $SNR_{(RTS)}$
Step 8:   If $N_i (Th) < = SNR_{(RTS)}$;
              Where $I_n = 1$;
                  Node decides to participate in communication;
              Else
Step 9:   Node cannot participate in communication;
Step10:   Based on decision, the system results Fault tolerant and efficient
          Communication;

Notations

XLA   → Cross layer approach, $N_i (Th)$ → Threshold Value for a node
RTS   → Request to send, I_n → Initiative of a node
$SNR_{(RTS)}$→ Signal to noise ratio of RTS Packet.

4 Result and Conclusion

We conducted the analysis of sensor nodes with XLA algorithm, and verify its performances using C language. Initial implementation is done using tinyos. The results clearly shows the importance of Fault management plane in Wireless sensor networks. Based on the concept of initiative calculation in Cross layer approach fault management plane is implemented to get efficient and fault tolerant communication in wireless sensor networks.

5 Future Work

We plan to validate XLA approach algorithm using hardware, using motes such as temperature sensor motes and light sensor characteristics.

References

1. Smith, N., Reddy, Y.B., Gajendar, N.: Cross-Layer Design Approach for Wireless Networks to Improve the Performance. IEEE Computer Society, Los Alamitos (2009)
2. Akyildiz, I.F., Vuran, M.C., Akan, O.B.: A Cross-Layer Protocol for Wireless Sensor Networks, pp. 1102–1107. IEEE Computer Society, Los Alamitos (2006)
3. Schott, W., Gluhak, A., Presser, M., Hunkeler, U., Tafazolli, R.: e-SENSE Protocol Stack Architecture for Wireless Sensor Networks, pp. 1–5. IEEE Computer Society, Los Alamitos (2007)
4. Vijay, S., Sharma, S.C.: A Wireless Sensor Network for Distributed Fault Management in Power Systems. In: Proceedings of the World Congress on Engineering, WCE 2008, vol. III, London, UK, July 2-4 (2008)
5. Akyildiz, I.F., Su, W., Sankarasubramaniam, Y., Cayirci, E.: Wireless sensor networks: a survey. Computer Networks 38, 393–422 (2002)
6. Salehy, I., Eltoweissyy, M., Agbariax, A., El-Sayedz, H.: A Fault Tolerance Management Framework for Wireless Sensor Networks. Journal of Communication 2(4) (June 2007)
7. Canli, T., Nait-Abdesselam, F., Khokhar, A.: A Cross-Layer Optimization Approach for Efficient Data Gathering in Wireless Sensor Networks. IEEE Computer Society, Los Alamitos (2008)
8. Mundarath, J.C., Ramanathan, P., Van Veen, B.D.: A cross layer scheme for adaptive antenna array based wireless ad hoc networks in multipath environments. Wireless Netw. 13, 597–615 (2007)
9. Yu, M., Mokhtar, H., Merabti, M.: A Survey on Fault Management in Wireless Sensor Networks (2007); ISBN: 1-9025-6016-7 © 2007 PGNet
10. Asim, M., Mokhtar, H., Merabti, M.: A Fault Management Architecture for Wireless Sensor Network. In: IWCMC apos; 2008, International, 779–785, August 6-8 (2008)
11. Sivaraman, R., Sarma Dhulipala, V.R., Aarthy, V., Kavitha, K.: Energy Comparison and Analysis for Cluster Based Environment in Wireless Sensor Networks. IJRTE, 89–91

Security Solutions to the Phishing: Transactions Based on Security Questions and Image

Aruna Kumari Devarakonda[1], Prasamsa Tummala[2], and Indra Praveen Sandrala[2]

[1] Asst.Professor
[2] IV/IV B.Tech, Department of Electronics and Computer Engineering,
Koneru Lakshmaiah University,
Vaddeswaram, Tadepalli(m.d), Guntur(Dist)-522502, India
enteraruna@yahoo.com, prasamsa5@gmail.com, indraadc@gmail.com

Abstract. One of the latest computer-related problems to arise is phishing, which is the criminally fraudulent process in which e-mails lure unsuspecting victims into giving up user names, passwords, Social Security numbers, and account information after linking to counterfeit bank, credit card, and e-commerce Web sites. Phishers are mainly targeting the customers of banks and online payment services. It is so pervasive that even corporate and government sites are actively informing the users on this issue. This paper presents a solution, which aims to protect users against email phishing attacks. Main key words which are used are a user ID and password, and the other is an authenticating question. An e-mail that a bank sends to user contains some image and preselected question which the phisher couldn't have, that the user chose when setting up the account. This proves to the user that the e-mail came from the bank or business, not a phisher, and that it is safe to use the provided link. The user is asked to provide his ID and the bank checks if the ID is valid or not. If the ID is valid, the user is asked to load the image which has been mailed and answer his preselected question along with a request for their logon password. After receiving the correct password, user is allowed to access the Web site.

Keywords: Phishing, Image authentication, Security system.

1 Introduction

Phishing is just one of the many ways that the Internet can be used to get people to unknowingly provide their personal financial information to fraudsters. A phishing attack is most often initiated with a special type of spam (unsolicited email) containing a link to a misleading domain name, which appears to be a legitimate site. The email tricks the recipient into visiting the spoofed web site-one that mimics a site where the person would normally feel comfortable entering a username and password or other personal information.

Phishing has also been explained as leveraging or exploiting the design of web pages in a social engineering attack that tricks the user into thinking that they are in a legitimate and secure web session with a trusted site. Actually, the phishing site is

V.V Das et al. (Eds.): BAIP 2010, CCIS 70, pp. 565–567, 2010.
© Springer-Verlag Berlin Heidelberg 2010

designed to install malicious software or acquire personal information, including credit card number, personal identification numbers (PINs), social security numbers, banking numbers and passwords. This information is then used by the phisher for identity theft, to steal money, or to commit other fraudulent schemes.

Recipients of the email are prompted to react immediately. They then click on a link provided in the email body, which actually directs them to the phishing Web page. The intent is to lure recipients into revealing sensitive information such as usernames, passwords, account IDs, ATM PINs, or credit card details. Like the phishing email, the phishing Web page almost always possesses the look and feel of the legitimate site that it copies, often containing the same company logos, graphics, writing style, fonts, layout, and other site elements. This spoofed Web page may also include a graphical user interface (GUI) intended to lure the user into entering their bank account information, credit card number, social security number, passwords, or other sensitive information. Either the phisher, or an anonymous remote user that is sent the information, can then use the stolen information.

2 Proposed System

Phishing attacks are increasing in frequency and sophistication. The Anti-Phishing Working Group (APWG; www.antiphishing.org) recently reported that the number of attacks is growing by 50 percent per month, with roughly 5 percent of recipients falling victim to them. Phishing Web pages generally use similar page layouts, styles (font families, sizes, and so on), key regions, and blocks to mimic genuine pages in an effort to convince Internet users to divulge personal information, such as bank account numbers and passwords.

If we hope to design web browsers, websites, and other tools to shield users from such attacks, we need to understand which attack strategies are successful, and what proportion of users they fool. However, the literature is sparse on this topic.

Several anti-phishing approaches are becoming popular. One key to many of these approaches is having Internet service providers (ISPs) close phishing Web sites. However, this can be time consuming and expensive. And it can be useless to even try closing sites in countries that lack or don't enforce anti-hacking laws. Meanwhile, companies whose Web sites are targeted by phishers must battle public perception that they can't protect their customers[1].

To confront those challenges, we came up with a solution. The words which are used to present this solution are a user ID and password, and the other is an authenticating question that the user pre-selects with a bank and an image sent by the bank which is random[2][3].

An e-mail that a bank sends to user contains preselected question which the phisher couldn't have, that the user chose when setting up the account and some randomly generated image which changes for every mail sent by the bank. This proves to the user that the e-mail came from the bank or business, not a phisher, and that it is safe to use the provided link as the pre-selected question is known only to the bank and the user[4]. After the user opens the link of the bank, the user is asked to provide his ID and the bank checks if the ID is valid or not. If the ID is valid, the user is asked to load the image which has been mailed (latest) and answer his preselected question along with a request for their logon password. After receiving the correct password, user is allowed to access the Web site[5][6].

This solution provides security to both the user and the bank. The email which has been sent by the bank and phisher can be distinguished by the user. This provides safety to the user in not opening the link if the mail is sent by phisher. On the bank side, only the user has the latest image sent by the bank and only he can upload the image. This provides the bank to give access only to the right user.

3 Conclusions

Phishing is a form of online identity theft that aims to steal sensitive information from users such as online banking passwords and credit card information. The last years have brought a dramatic increase in the number and sophistication of such attacks. Although phishing scams have received extensive press coverage, phishing attacks are still successful because of many inexperienced and unsophisticated Internet users. Attackers are employing a large number of technical spoofing tricks such as URL obfuscation and hidden elements to make a phishing web site look authentic to the victims.

The most effective solution to phishing is training users not to blindly follow links to web sites where they have to enter sensitive information such as passwords. However, expecting that all users will understand the phishing threat and surf accordingly is unrealistic. There will always be users that are tricked into visiting a phishing web site. Therefore, it is important for researchers and industry to provide solutions for the phishing threat.

References

[1] Microsoft. Anti-Phishing Technologies (2005), http://www.microsoft.com
[2] Microsoft. Browser Helper Objects: The Browser the Way You Want It (2005), http://msdn.microsoft.com
[3] Microsoft. Sender ID Framework Overview (2005), http://www.microsoft.com
[4] Anti-Phishing Working Group
[5] CRM Today. Financial Insights Evaluates Impact of Phishing on Retail Financial Institutions Worldwide, CRM Today, July 15 (2004)
[6] Cranor, L., Egelman, S., Hong, J., Zhang, Y.: Phinding phish: An evaluation of anti-phishing toolbars. Technical report, Carnegie Mellon University (November 2006)

CloneManager: A Tool for Detection of Type1 and Type2 Code Clones

E. Kodhai[1], S. Kanmani[2], A. Kamatchi[2], R. Radhika[2], and B. Vijaya Saranya[2]

[1] Department of IT, Sri Manakula Vinayagar Engineering College, Puducherry, India
[2] Department of IT, Pondicherry Engineering College, Puducherry, India

Abstract. Over the last decade, many clone detection tools have been proposed with good results. However, these tools are still unsatisfactory and either incomplete or inefficient. In particular, the recall and precision on the average remain unresolved. We introduce, *CloneManager*, a tool specifically proposed for the detection of functional Code Clones and to evaluate the precision and recall in C source code. It relies on the formulated metrics and those values are utilized during the detection process. Our tool is also compared with the two other existing techniques for the open source project Weltab.

Keywords: Clone Detection, Functional Clones, Software Metrics, String-matching.

1 Code Clones

Code cloning or the act of copying code fragments and making minor, non–functional alterations, is a well known problem for evolving software systems leading to duplicated code fragments or code clones. *Type1* is classified as an exact copy and *Type2* as only variable or function identifiers have been changed. The results of the code clone detection are given as clone pairs and clone clusters.

2 Proposed Method

The proposed tool is implemented in java and it detects functional code clones in C source codes using textual analysis and metrics. The tool initially parses through the given input source code and identifies the various methods present. Then a built-in hand-coded parser[4] parses the various methods following an island-driven approach[4]. Then the formulated metrics are applied to each method and their metrics values are entered in the database. These metrics values are used to extract all the possible clone pairs in given source code and are further put forth for the textual comparison. It detects both type1 and type2 clone fragments in given source code. Fig 1. Is the architectural diagram for our tool.

The input is given by the user as a form of source code, which is written in C language. First, it concatenates all the files of the same project into a single large file. The comments, whitespaces and the pre-processor statements are removed from the integrated file. Source code is re-structured to the standard format. Fig 2 illustrates a case in source code standardization and normalization.

V.V Das et al. (Eds.): BAIP 2010, CCIS 70, pp. 568–570, 2010.

Fig. 1. Architectural Diagram

Fig. 2. Before & after Standardization

Fig. 3. Before & after Template Conversion

The tool then converts the source code into a template form which is nothing but the transformation of the inputted source code in to a pre-defined defined set of statements or conversion into standard form. Refer figure 3. It identifies the actual clone methods in the standardized source code by adopting an island-driven parsing approach. The function definitions are extracted by means of a hand-coded parser and saved for further reference.

A set of 7 existing method level metrics are used for the detection of type-1 and type-2 clone methods. The tool computes these metrics values for each of the clone methods identified and finally the values are stored in a database. Then the tool short-list the clone methods having similar metric values from the database record and the selected candidates are only considered for textual analysis to confirm as clone pairs. They are as given in table 1.

Our tool detects type-1 and type-2 methods. Line by line comparison of the standardized and normalized source code is taken up for the identification of the type-1 clone methods while comparison of the template methods is taken up for the type-2 clone methods. Then, the tool clusters the "potential clone pairs" which is nothing but the identified cloned methods. Clustering is done separately for each type and then the clusters are uniquely numbered. Clustering is nothing but associating similar pairs into a single group called a cluster or a class. Each clone cluster may be defined as a unique set of methods that are similar within themselves.

Finally the obtained clone pairs and clone clusters for the given source code from the tool are stored in a database and they are also grouped according to their clusters. The output is nothing but the clone pairs and clone clusters obtained by the tool.

3   Experimental Results

We experimented our tool with Weltab[1] which is of approximately 11,000 lines. Having computed the results for type-1 and type-2 cloned methods we compared our results with two of the existing tools. The first is the Phoenix based clone detection tool[2], reported exact match function clones in these systems allowing differences of function names and data-types only. In case of weltab our tool identified eight exact match clone classes from 27 clone pairs while Tairas and Gray obtained only six exact match clone classes. Secondly, Our tool reported 8 exact-match and 18 near-miss clone clusters which are nothing but the type-1 and type-2 clone clusters found in Weltab which is same as the results of NICAD. Though NICAD has proved to effectively detect the functional clones, the initial phases that are performed employ an external parser TXL. While our tool uses a hand-coded parser, external parsers have not been deployed. Results are in table 2.

Table 1. Metric Values

S. No	Metrics	Values
1.	No. of lines of code	17
2.	No. of argum ents passed	5
3.	No. of local variables declared	6
4.	No. of function calls	1
5.	No. of conditional statem ents	1
6.	No. of looping statem ents	1
7.	No. of return statem ents	2

Table 2. Clone Pairs/clusters from weltab

Type	Phoenix-based			Nicad			Proposed method		
	FN	CP	CC	FN	CP	CC	FN	CP	CC
Type-1	123	21	4	123	27	8	12	27	8
Type-2		-	-		98	18	3	98	18

4 Conclusion

In this paper we have proposed a light-weight tool to detect functional clones with the computation of metrics combined with simple textual analysis technique. Our tool improved the precision and also reduced the total comparison cost by the usage of metrics with which the comparison of the various functions has been avoided. Since the string matching is performed over the short -listed candidates, a higher amount of recall could be obtained. The early experiments prove that this type of lightweight tools can do at the least as well as the existing systems in finding and classifying the function clones in C. In future we are planning to explore our tool to other languages while also continuing with type3 and type4 detection.

References

[1] Roy, C.K., Cordy, J.R.: NICAD: Acccurate Detection of Near-Miss Intentional Clones Using Flexible Pretty-Printing and Code Normalization in ICPC, pp. 172–181 (2008)

[2] Tairas, R., Gray, J.: Phoenix-based Clone Detection using suffix trees. In: ACM-SE, pp. 679–684 (2006)

[3] Ducasse, S., Nierstrasz, O., Rieger, M.: On the effectiveness of clone detection by string matching. Journal on Software Maintenance and Evolution 18(1), 37–58 (2006)

[4] Merlo, E.: Detection of Plagiarism in University Projects Using Metrics-based Spectral Similarity. In: The Dagstuhl Seminar: Duplication, Redundancy, and Similarity in Software (2007)

Document Image Segmentation Using Recursive Top-Down Approach and Region Type Identification

Dharamveer Sharma[1] and Bibanjot Kaur[2]

[1] Department of Computer Science, Punjabi University, Patiala, Punjab, India
dveer72@hotmail.com
[2] M.Tech(ICT), Department of Computer Science, Punjabi University, Patiala, Punjab, India
er.bibanjotkaur@gmail.com

Abstract. Document image analysis refers to algorithms and techniques that are applied to images of documents to obtain a computer-readable description from pixel data. This paper presents a Top-down approach for document image segmentation based on recursively finding rectangular blocks in the image. The proposed algorithm recursively finds the rectangular regions in the image document using vertical and horizontal profiles and each identified block is further analyzed to identify its type whether it is text, picture or table. The method used is not language specific. Documents of different languages have been tested and satisfactory results have been obtained. In this paper we have also briefly described the existing algorithms and the methods that are used for document segmentation.

Keywords: Document Image Segmentation, OCR, Document Region Type Identification.

1 Introduction

A document image consists of various regions such as text, image, table etc. Objective of the project work is to segment the document into above mentioned different regions and find out efficient algorithm for segmentation. Segmentation is the task of defining boundaries between paragraphs in the document image where the document image is composed of various regions such as text blocks, figures, tables etc. Thus, the document image can comprise of merely a single segment, or perhaps several different segments. The organization of this paper is: Section 2 covers literature survey. Section 3 includes the proposed scheme followed by some experimental results in Section 4. Concluding remarks are made in Section 5 and references are given in Section 6.

2 Literature Survey

A wide variety of algorithms for segmentation of document images have been proposed. An algorithm known as X-Y Cut Algorithm [1] which is based on

V.V Das et al. (Eds.): BAIP 2010, CCIS 70, pp. 571–576, 2010.

top-down approach divides a document image into sections based on valleys in their projection profiles. The algorithm repeatedly partitions the document by alternately projecting the regions of the current segmentation on the horizontal and vertical axes. The splitting is stopped when a particular criterion that decides the atomicity of a region is met. The Whitespace Analysis Algorithm [2] analyses the structure of the white background in document images. The objective is to find a set of maximal white rectangles (called covers) whose union completely covers the page background and none of them overlaps with any of the connected components on the page.

There is an another algorithm based on bottom-up approach, The Docstrum Algorithm [3] which is based on the k nearest neighbour clustering of connected components of the page. Docstrum is a plot of distance and angle tuples for all nearest neighbours on a page. Run-length Smearing Algorithm [4] is used for line extraction. It merges two black pixels which are less than a threshold apart, into a continuous stream of black pixels. Two distinct bit maps are generated by applying this method firstly row-by-row and then column-by-column. A logical AND operator is applied to combine the two results.

Payne et al. [5] basically described the application of a novel texture recognition strategy which deals with the assembling of nth order co-occurrence information within a processing window. The co-occurrence method is better in terms of processing time and ease of implementation. Kasturi et al. [6] in their paper discussed about the basic building blocks of document analysis system. Khedekar et al. [7] in their paper discussed about the techniques for page segmentation and layout analysis which are top-down, bottom-up and hybrid. In this paper they had used top-down, projection-profile based algorithm for separating text blocks from image blocks in a Devanagari document. Hu et al. [8] presented a two step method for layout comparison. They use different methods to compute the distance between image rows after segmentation into a grid of equal-sized cells.

Wang et al. [9] in their paper implemented a robust algorithm of document segmentation and classification based on the top-down strategy called Recursive X-Y Cut due to the fast processing speed and reliability of top-down approach. The algorithm which was implemented works well for the properly aligned and correctly scanned documents but it still requires improvements and enhancements, for example to cater for large skew angle. Lee and Ryu [10] proposed a parameter-free method for segmenting the document images into maximal homogeneous regions and identifying them as texts, images, tables, and ruling lines. A pyramidal quadtree structure is constructed for multiscale analysis and a periodicity measure is suggested to find a periodical attribute of text regions for page segmentation. To obtain robust page segmentation results, a confirmation procedure using texture analysis is applied to only ambiguous regions. Karim et al. [11] in the paper presented their approach of automatic page decomposition algorithm developed for the First International Newspaper Segmentation contest. The approach used by them decomposes the newspaper image into image regions, horizontal and vertical lines, text regions and title areas. The technique proposed by them for newspaper segmentation is based on splitting and merging zones. Mitchell and Yan [12] in their paper presented an algorithm which performs automated segmentation and classification of newspaper images. The algorithm implemented by them is based upon bottom-up approach which is used to segment the image, classify patterns and extract text lines. Shafait et al. [13] in their paper presented a quantitative comparison of six algorithms for page segmentation which includes X-Y cut, smearing, whitespace analysis, constrained text-line finding, Docstrum, and Voronoi-diagram based.

3   Proposed Method

The presented algorithm is recursive in nature with identifies the number of rectangular blocks present in a given rectangular image. The present algorithm is a two phase algorithm. In the first phase, the algorithm starts with considering the whole image as a rectangle and then inserting the image rectangle in a queue. Then a recursive function is called, which successively removes the blocks from the image and checks the presence of sub blocks in it using horizontal and vertical projection profiles.

Having found the rectangular blocks in the image the second step is to identify the type of each block. Broadly, the algorithm works as under.

Phase 1: Image Segmentation
Step 1: Get the enclosing rectangle R of the image and insert it in the queue.
Step 2: Repeat steps 3 to 8 till the queue is empty.
Step 3: Get the first rectangle R from the queue and call SegmentRect(R).
Step 4: In the SegmentRect(R) function create the Horizontal Project Profiles (HPPs) and find horizontal gaps, more than or equal to HorizontalGapThreshold (HGT), in the image. Each gap represents a dissecting point. Create rectangles R of the image.
Step 5: If number of rectangle found in the image rectangle R are more than one then create Vertical Project Profiles (VPPs) for each of the Rs and find vertical gaps, more than or equal to VerticalGapThreshold (VGT), in the Rs. Each vertical gap represents a further dissecting point. From such dissecting points create final rectangles FRs and insert each of the rectangles in queue.
Step 6: if number of rectangles found in the image rectangle R in step 4 are equal to one, then that means no horizontal gaps could be found in the image. In such case create VPPs of the image and find vertical gaps, more than or equal to VGT, in the image. Each vertical gap represents a dissecting point. Create rectangles R of the image.
Step 7: If number of rectangle found in the image rectangle R are more than one then create HPPs for each of the Rs and find horizontal gaps, more than or equal to HGT, in the Rs. Each horizontal gap represents a further dissecting point. From such dissecting points create final rectangles FRs and insert each of the rectangles in queue.
Step 8: If there is only one final rectangle FR in step 5, then insert FR in array of final blocks.

Phase 2: Block Type Identification

Step 1: For each final rectangle create HPPs and VPPs.

Step 2: From the HPPs, count the number of horizontal gaps which are less than HGT.

Step 3: Find average height of the block by diving total height of the image with number of horizontal gaps.

Step 4: If average height is less than one fourth of the width of the image and horizontal gaps are more than one then the block may be text or table.

Step 5: From the VPPs of the block, count the number of horizontal gaps which are less than VGT. If number of vertical gaps is more than 1 then the block is of type table else it is of type text.

Step 6: If any condition in step 4 is false then the block is of type picture.

Having identified the types of all the blocks, next different coloured rectangles are drawn around each block to represents the area of the block and its type. The colour codes used to represent different type of blocks are given in table 1.

Table 1. Colour codes used for representation of block types

Colour Code	Type of block
GREEN	Text
RED	Picture
BLUE	Table

4 Results

Results of document image segmentation are given following. As mentioned earlier, the algorithm developed is language independent, we have considered document images of different languages collected from internet, news papers and magazines. In all 240 images have been considered belonging to 7 different languages. Of these 227 were properly segmented resulting in accuracy of 94.58 percent. Partially segmented images were 7 and 6 images were not segmented at all. There are some failure cases which arise due to the absence of rectangular blocks in case of text as well as image. If image background is dark, if text is wrapped around a non-rectangular image, if image partially overlaps two or more columns and text is wrapped around it then no gaps are found in horizontal and vertical profiles making it difficult to segment the document in different blocks.

Table 2. Performance Evaluation

Cases	Accuracy	Percentage
Successful cases	227	94.58
Partially successful cases	7	2.92
Failed cases	6	2.50
Total Cases	240	100.00

Following are some of the results obtained after applying the segmentation algorithm developed.

(a) Sample Input Document Image   (b) Result of segmentation of Document Image

Fig. 1. Example of an English language document image segmentation

5 Conclusions

We have explored segmentation technique and implemented this technique on various document images including English, Hindi, Punjabi, Bangla, Malyalam etc. which in turn gave quite satisfactory results. Although there are certain failure cases in which document images have not been segmented due to the presence of text/image in some irregular layout fashion which are not recognized by rectangular blocks formed during segmentation.

References

1. Namboodiri, A.M., Jain, A.K.: Document Structure and Layout Analysis. Digital Document Processing, 29–48 (2007)
2. Breuel, T.M.: Two Geometric Algorithms for Layout Analysis. In: Proceedings of the Fifth International Workshop on Document Analysis Systems, pp. 188–199. Princeton, NY (2002)
3. O'Gorman: The Document Spectrum for Page Layout Analysis. IEEE Transactions on PAMI 15, 1162–1173 (1993)
4. Wong, K.Y., Casey, R.G., Wahl, F.M.: Document Analysis System. IBM Journal of Research and Development, 647–656 (November 1982)
5. Payne, J.S., Stonham, T.J., Patel, D.: Document Segmentation Using Texture Analysis. IEEE, 380–382 (1994)
6. Kasturi, R., O'Gorman, L., Govindaraju, V.: Document Image Analysis: A Primer vol. 27, Part 1, pp. 3–22 (February 2002)

7. Khedekar, S., Ramanaprasad, V., Setlur, S., Govindaraju, V.: Text-Image Separation in Devanagari Documents. In: Proc. of the 7th ICDAR, August 3-6, pp. 1265–1269 (2003)
8. Hu, J., Kashi, R., Wilfong, G.: Document Classification using Layout Analysis. In: Proc. of the 1st International Workshop on Document Analysis and Understanding For Document Database, Florence, Italy, pp. 556–560 (1999)
9. Wang, H., Li, S.Z., Ragupathi, S.: Document Segmentation and Classification with Top-Down Approach. In: Proc. of the 1st First International Conference on Knowledge-Based Intelligent Electronic System, May 21-23, pp. 243–247 (1997)
10. Lee, S.W., Ryu, D.S.: Parameter-Free Geometric Document Layout Analysis. IEEE Transactions on PAMI 23(11), 397–400 (2001)
11. Hadjar, K., Hitz, O., Ingold, R.: Newspaper Page Documentation using a Split and Merge Approach, pp. 1186–1189. IEEE, Los Alamitos (2001)
12. Mitchell, P.E., Yan, H.: Connected Pattern Segmentation and Title Grouping in Newspaper Images. In: Proc. of the 17th ICPR (ICPR 2004), August 23-26, pp. 397–400 (2004)
13. Shafait, F., Keysers, D., Breuel, T.M.: Performance Comparison of Six Algorithms for Page Segmentation. In: IUPR, pp. 368–379 (2006)

An Analysis to BER Performances of Differential OFDM Systems

Kaur Inderjeet

Department of CSE, Ajay Kumar Garg Engineering College, Ghaziabad, India
inderjeetk@gmail.com

Abstract. In an OFDM system, various modulation methods can be used in order to encode the binary information. If a differential phase modulation scheme is chosen, data can be encoded in the relative phase of consecutive symbols in each subchannel or in the relative phase of symbols in the adjacent subchannels. The two methods exhibit two essentially different behaviors in fading conditions. In this paper, we shall analyze the BER performances of both modulation types. The performance will be analyzed by considering a multipath fading channel, as in mobile communication systems.

Keywords: OFDM, differential, multipath fading, ISI.

1 Introduction

OFDM (Orthogonal Frequency Division Multiplexing) is one of the most promising modulation techniques that were proposed for being used in the 4th generation wireless systems. In a typical mobile radio channel the transmitted signal is subjected to multipath fading which generally exhibits time selectivity (also known as Doppler Effect) and frequency selectivity [1], [2]. The influence of the ISI (Inter-Symbol Interference) can be reduced by increasing the duration of the transmitted symbol. Using OFDM, the high-rate data sequence to be transmitted is split into a large number of lower speed symbol streams, each of them modulating a different carrier. The carrier spacing is selected such that all carriers used are orthogonal each other over a symbol interval. In addition, a cyclic prefix is inserted at the beginning of each OFDM symbol, in order to counteract the inherent time dispersive nature of the channel, preventing two or more symbols to interfere each other [3], thus inducing ISI. The lengthening of the symbol duration, introduced in order to combat the frequency selectivity is however limited by the time-variant nature of the channel that generates the Doppler Effect. Larger the symbol duration, higher the probability that the channel parameters vary during the transmission of an OFDM frame giving rise to frequency offsets of the carriers, thus destroying their orthogonality and generating inter-carrier interference (ICI). The transmitter and receiver for OFDM can be efficiently implemented using Fast Fourier Transform (FFT), a rapid mathematical algorithm of processing Discrete Fourier Transform (DFT). The data symbols that modulate multiple orthogonal carriers in OFDM are obtained using a classical digital modulation scheme. Various modulation methods could be employed such as BPSK, QPSK (also with their differential form) and QAM with several different signal

V.V Das et al. (Eds.): BAIP 2010, CCIS 70, pp. 577–581, 2010.
© Springer-Verlag Berlin Heidelberg 2010

constellations. If a differential phase modulation is chosen (the particular case of an OFDM-DBPSK system) there are two options to perform it. Thus, data can be encoded in the relative phase of consecutive symbols in each subchannel, obtaining an inter-frame differential modulation. On the other hand, data can be encoded in the relative phase of symbols in adjacent subchannels (consecutive samples of an OFDM symbol), achieving an in-frame differential modulation. The two methods exhibit two essential different behaviors in fading conditions. In this paper we realize a performance comparison of the two methods, focusing on the differences between them. The performance evaluation of both methods is analyzed by considering a multipath fading channel, as in mobile communications systems.

2   System Description and Fading Channel Model

In OFDM, the available bandwidth is partitioned into N subchannels. The desired high-rate symbol stream is achieved by simultaneously transmitting N slower rate sub streams using N orthogonal subcarriers. The binary data to be transmitted is differentially encoded using a DBPSK modulation scheme, obtaining a sequence of complex data symbols (fig. 1).

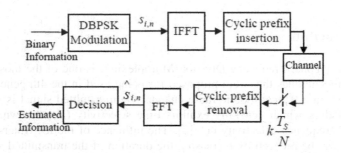

Fig. 1. OFDM Transceiver Model

There are two possibilities to perform differential modulation in the presented OFDM scheme. Data can be encoded in the relative phase of adjacent symbols in each subchannel or in the relative phase of samples transmitted in adjacent subchannels, that is consecutive samples of an OFDM symbol (Fig. 2).

Since the IFFT block accepts N parallel samples to its entry, the whole difference of the two methods can be thought as follows: if the phase modulation is separately achieved on each of the N parallel streams that constitute the entry to the IFFT block, then we are in the case of the first presented modulation type, namely an inter-frame modulation is performed (fig. 2a). If the modulation is made on the serial stream, prior to the parallel conversion required by IFFT, then an in-frame modulation is chosen, since N consecutive serial samples will simultaneously modulate N orthogonal carriers, forming an OFDM symbol (fig 2b). Both methods have an irreducible error rate because of the random change of the relative phase, caused by the fading channel. In the first method the distortion caused by the multipath fading is indicated by the

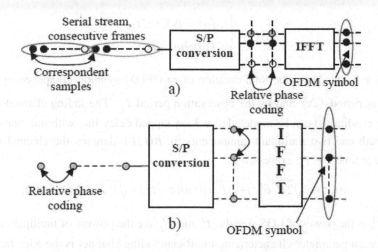

Fig. 2. (a) Inter-frame Modulation (b) In-frame Modulation

Doppler spectrum. In the second case, the channel multipath intensity profile and the length of the OFDM symbol indicate the phase change rate due to fading conditions. Therefore, the two methods exhibit essentially different behaviors although both encode the data differentially. After the differential encoding of the binary message using one of the two methods presented above, the sequence $S_{i,n}$ is obtained, $S_{i,n}$ denoting the nth symbol of the ith frame. The nth carrier is modulated by the samples $\{S_{i,n}, -\infty < i < \infty\}$ and the modulated carriers (orthogonal one-another) are added together to form the OFDM symbol to be transmitted. In order to combat the inter-symbol and inter-carrier interference introduced by the frequency selectivity and the time selectivity of the radio channel, each OFDM symbol is preceded by a cyclic prefix of L samples. The ith transmitted symbol (including the prefix) contains $N+L$ time domain samples, of which the mth sample is given by the equation below:

$$g_i(m) = \sqrt{\frac{E_S}{N+L}} \sum_{n=0}^{N-1} S_{i,n} e^{j2\pi\frac{nm}{N}}, m = -L...N-1 \quad (1)$$

Assuming the data symbols are statistically independent and having a unit average energy, the transmitted average energy per symbol equals E_S. The transmitted signals can be expressed in complex form as:

$$s(t) = \sum_{i=-\infty}^{\infty} p(t - iT_S) g_i(t). \quad (2)$$

where $g_i(t)$ represents the analogical waveform corresponding to the OFDM symbol, obtained after a DAC conversion of the sequence $\{g_i(m)\}, m = 0,1,....,N-1$. $p(t)$ is the pulse-shaping waveform of each symbol as:

$$p(t) = \begin{cases} 1, & for -\Delta \le t \le t_s \\ 0, & otherwise \end{cases}. \tag{3}$$

$T_S = \Delta + t_s$ stands for the total duration of an OFDM symbol, composed by the cyclic prefix period (Δ) and by the observation period t_s. The fading channel (assuming Rice conditions) can be modeled as a 3-ray tapped delay line with one line-of-sight (LOS) path and two multipath components. If $h(t, \tau)$ denotes the channel impulse response at time $t - \tau$, expressed as:

$$h(t, \tau) = \sqrt{2P_S}\, \delta(\tau) + \sqrt{P_1}\, a_1(t)\delta(\tau - \tau_1) + \sqrt{P_2}\, a_2(t)\delta(\tau - \tau_2). \tag{4}$$

where P_S is the power of LOS signals, P_1 and P_2 are the powers of multipath replicas. An important parameter characterizing the Rician fading channel is the Rice factor, defined as the ratio of the deterministic LOS component power P_S and the multipath components power $P_m = P_1 + P_2$, i.e. $K = P_S / P_m$. As a special case, the channel is AWGN when $K \to \infty$, while Rayleigh fading conditions are met for $K = 0$. The received signal can be written as [4]:

$$r(t) = \int_0^\infty s(t - \tau) h(t, \tau) d\tau + n(t). \tag{5}$$

where $n(t)$ is a complex Gaussian noise and $h(t, \tau)$ is the impulse response of the multipath fading channel at the time $t - \tau$. At the receiver, the output of each mth subchannel can be obtained as:

$$r_{m,i} = \frac{1}{t_S} \int_{iT_S}^{t_S + iT_S} \left\{ \int_0^\infty s(t - \tau)h(t, \tau)d\tau + n(t) \right\} \times e^{-j2\pi f_D(t - iT_S)} dt. \tag{6}$$

Finally, the differential detector decides what symbol was transmitted.

3 Results and Discussions

The BER performance of an OFDM system with both DBPSK in-frame and inter-frame modulation was analyzed. To simplify the cyclic prefix duration is considered to be equal to the serial symbol duration, i.e. $T = \Delta$. Two-ray Rayleigh fading conditions, with equal power of the two multipath components are considered for channel analysis. The BER computation was averaged over 20000 transmitted OFDM symbols. A comparison of the two methods is made, studying the influence of the block length N, of the channel multipath delay spread and of the Doppler shift introduced by the time-variant character of the channel on the BER performance in both in-frame and inter-frame DBPSK-OFDM system. The BER performances of the DBPSK-OFDM system in a Rayleigh fading channel, is a function of the normalized delay of the second multipath τ_2/T. It has been observed that the inter-frame modulation is significantly more sensitive to the Doppler shift than the in-frame modulation. Thus, at the two normalized Doppler shifts $(f_D * T_S)$ taken into account, the performance of the in-frame DBPSK system is almost identical, especially for an important multipath delay of the channel. It is shown that the maximum Doppler shift has a significant influence on the BER, especially when the delay of the second multipath is small. For large delays of the second multipath the main amount of errors is brought by the ISI introduced by the multipath components, which confirms the conclusion in [5], respectively in [4] for an in-frame DBPSK modulation.

4 Conclusions

In this paper we have discussed the BER performance of an OFDM-DBPSK system with two distinct phase modulation types. The principles of both in-frame and inter-frame modulation in an OFDM transmission scheme were briefly covered, accentuating on their differences. The essential different behavior in multipath fading conditions had also been emphasized. The inter-frame modulation system, while generally performing better has though shown to be more sensitive at the variation of the Doppler shift parameter. The in-frame modulation method allows significant performance improvement by increasing the data-block length. The multipath delay spread degrades the BER performance of both studied modulation types.

References

1. Marius, O.: BER Performances of a Differential OFDM Systems in Fading Channels. Transactions on Electronics and Communications, 389–393 (2004)
2. Lupea, E.: BER Performance of Frequency Selective Channels with Cyclic Prefix Based Equalizers, Buletinul Stiintific al Universitatii Politehnica Timisoara, Tom 47 (2002)
3. Sklar, B.: Rayleigh Fading Channels in Mobile Digital Communication Systems- Part I: Characterization. IEEE Communication Magazine (1997)
4. Sklar, B.: Rayleigh Fading Channels in Mobile Digital Communication Systems- Part II: Mitigation. IEEE Communication Magazine (1997)
5. Bingham, J.A.C.: Multicarrier Modulation for Data Transmission, An Idea Whose Time Has Come. IEEE Communication Magazine 31(5) (1990)

MPCS: An Account-Based Secure Mobile Payment Consortia System for Educational Institutions

S. Britto R Kumar[1] and S. Albert Rabara[2]

[1] Dept. of Computer Science, Bishop Heber College (Autonomous),
Trichirappalli – 620 017, Tamil Nadu, India
brittork@gmail.com
[2] Dept. of Computer Science, St. Joseph's College (Autonomous),
Trichirappalli – 620 017, Tamil Nadu, India
a_rabara@yahoo.com

Abstract. Mobile Payment services have become an essential for every human being at the personal level and professional level. To create global and open standard solutions for mobile payments, there are number of consortia that have taken the initiatives. However, none of the consortia is widely accepted due to lack of security and many companies participate in more than one consortium. The current status of the consortia is at infancy stage. A study reveals that there is no specific and global mobile payment consortium for educational institutions to collect the fees as well as for student community to pay the fees. To overcome, an innovative model has been proposed namely, Mobile Payment Consortia System which provides an end-to-end security among the mobile user, institution, MPCS server and the institution bank using Public Key Infrastructure (PKI). This paper mainly focuses on secure communication between the mobile user and the payment gateway namely, MPCS Server.

Keywords: Mobile Payment Consortia, Mobile payment, Security PKI.

1 Introduction

Mobile Commerce is an emerging discipline that involves mobile devices, applications, middleware and mobile networks. Mobile phones are well suited to carry out the business transactions to the customers anywhere and at any time. Mobile Payment is an essential service of everybody's daily life, specifically for mobile commerce applications such as Mobile banking, Mobile advertising, etc., and which has raised the attention of researchers in the last few years. Mobile Payments are a natural evolution of e-payment schemes that will facilitate mobile commerce.

A study reveals that different approaches came to the market for mobile payment system to address the existing needs of common man. However, there is no standard and global Mobile Payment Consortia System specifically for Educational Institutions to collect the fees as well as for student community to pay the fees. The proposed model namely, Mobile Payment Consortia System (MPCS) is well suited for the academic institutions to carry out the payments and financial services in a secured manner using mobile device anywhere and at anytime [1,2].

V.V Das et al. (Eds.): BAIP 2010, CCIS 70, pp. 582–585, 2010.
© Springer-Verlag Berlin Heidelberg 2010

The paper is organized as follows: Section 2 presents the review of security issues on existing Mobile payment consortia. Section-3 illustrates the secure communication between MPCS server and mobile payment user. The implementation of the proposed system is presented in Section 4. Section 5 is conclusion.

2 Literature Review

Security is the most important issue for any payment services. Jun Liu et al., proposed a new model based on SEMOPS by introducing the third parties to reduce the trust dependence on the payment processors. However, the performance will be degraded due to the involvement of third parties [3]. The existing mobile payment consortia such as MNO driven, Bank driven, Cross industry driven, Device manufacture driven, Technology driven and Identity driven are discussed in [4].

A.Vilmos et al., narrated the architecture and business model of Secure Mobile Payment Service (SEMOPS). The SEMOPS uses 1024 RSA technology to encrypt the sensitive user data and non-repudiation is achieved by using digital signature. To authenticate the users, SEMPOS uses PIN, password, OTP, and digital signature [5].

Mobey Forum [6] is a global, financial industry driven forum aiming to develop a secured mobile financial services. Mobey architecture uses PKI infrastructure for strong authentication and stores functions in Security Element (SE). Based on the existing mobile payment consortia systems, a novel model namely Mobile Payment Consortia System is proposed. The framework and the architectural design of MPCS are discussed in [1]. This paper mainly focuses on secure communication between the mobile user and the payment gateway namely, MPCS Server.

3 Secure Communication between MPCS and MP User

The proposed model includes student, institution, student bank, institution bank and Mobile Payment Consortia System (MPCS), which acts as a payment gateway between institution server and institution bank that operates under the institution private network. During the communication with the MPCS server, the client sends the PR to the institution server. Once the client is authenticated, the institution server sends the users profile. After receiving the user profile, MPCS server starts the PR authorization service by sending the interface to the mobile user. When the MPCS initiates the communication with the mobile user, it validates the IMEI number of the user device for device authentication. Then the user interface for PR authorization is enabled. The user interface consists fee options such as semester fee, exam fee, etc., and fee amount. The payment user can choose an option from a list. The option-id and fee amount are hashed using SHA-1 algorithm to produce unique message digest that ensures integrity of the data. The hashed option-id and the fee amount are then encrypted using the client's private key to create the digital signature for user authentication and non-repudiation.

While sending the hashed message to the server, the MPCS model encrypts option-id and fee amount using the secret key to support high security. Since the secret key is known only by the user and the institution, it authorizes the user to carry out the payment transactions and ensures data confidentiality. Both the digital signature and the encrypted message are concatenated and which is encrypted using a part of an IMEI number. This avoids data theft and eavesdropping. To protect from identity theft as well as to ensure data confidentiality, the IMEI number is encrypted using the institution's public key. Finally, the payment application creates digital envelop with encrypted concatenated message (M1) as well as with encrypted IMEI number (M2) and sends it to the MPCS server that ensures message confidentiality.

Once the digital envelop is received, the MPCS server decrypts the messages M1 using the part of an IMEI number and the message M2 using the institution's private key. The MPCS server also validates the remaining part of an IMEI number in order to identify the user and splits the encrypted message digest i.e. digital signature as well as encrypted option-id and fee amount. Then the server decrypts the encrypted message digest using the client's public key and encrypted option-id and amount using the secret key, which in turn retrieves both the message digest as well as option-id and amount. Finally, the MPCS server creates message digest for option-id and amount and compares the message digest sent by the client as well as newly generated message digest. If both are matched, the integrity of the message is ensured and if fee amount is matched with MPCS's database, successfully the user PR is authorized. The process flow of the client and server functionalities are shown in Fig. 1.

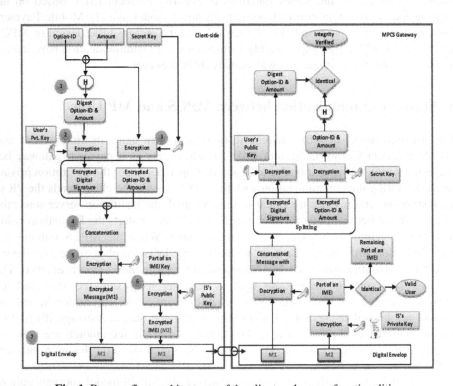

Fig. 1. Process flow architectures of the client and server functionalities

4   Implementation Using J2ME

The GUI for the MPCS has been developed using J2ME that include login and payment details. The implementation screenshots taken from the mobile phone using My Phone Explorer are presented in Fig. 2.

Fig. 2. Implementation screenshots are taken from the mobile phone

5   Conclusion

The mobile payments will remain the de facto standard for personal payments in the near future. Mobile Payment Consortia System is a novel model to carry out the financial transactions from the bank to the academic institutions for the payment of fees by students through mobile phone with end-to-end security using PKI infrastructure. This model can be extended to integrate all academic institutions so as to help the necessary payments by the students through mobile devices.

References

1. Britto, S., Kumar, R., Albert Rabara, S., Ronald Martin, J.: MPCS: A Secure Mobile Payment Consortia System (MPCS) for Higher Educational Institutions. In: 4th ACM International Conference on Computer Sciences and Convergence Information Technology, Seoul, South Korea, vol. 2, pp. 571–579. ACM, New York (2009)
2. Britto, S., Kumar, R., Arun Gnana Raj, A., Albert Rabara, S.: A Framework for Mobile Payment Consortia System (MPCS). In: International Conference on Computer Science and Software Engineering, Wuhan, China, vol. 2, pp. 43–47. IEEE, Los Alamitos (2008)
3. Liu, J., Liao, J., Zhu, X.: A System Model and Protocol for Mobile Payment. In: 3rd International Conference on e-Business Engineering, China, pp. 638–641. IEEE, Los Alamitos (2005)
4. Karnouskos, S., Vilmos, A.: The European Perspective on Mobile Payments. In: IEEE Symposium on Trends in Communications, Bratislava, Slovakia, IEEE, Los Alamitos (2004)
5. Vilmos, A., Karnouskos, S.: SEMOPS: Design of a New Payment Service. In: 14th International Workshop on Database and Expert Systems Applications, Prague, Czech Republic, pp. 865–869. IEEE, Los Alamitos (2003)
6. Kanniainen, L.: The Preferred Payment Architecture Executive Summary-Requirements for manufacturers and standardisation bodies. Technical Report, Mobey Forum (2001)

Team Automata Based Framework for Spatio-Temporal RBAC Model

N. Jaisankar, S. Veeramalai, and A. Kannan

Department of Computer Science and Engineering, Anna University-Chennai,
Chennai – 600 025, Tamil Nadu, India
jaisasi_win@yahoo.com, Veera2000uk@gmail.com,
kannan@annauniv.edu

Abstract. In this paper a framework called Team Automata (TA) has been introduced for capturing notions like co-ordination, collaboration and cooperation in distributed systems. It consists of component automata, combined in a coordinated way such that they can perform shared actions. Moreover, we consider a Spatio -Temporal Role Based Access Control Model (STRBAC) in the context of the team automata model, it describes the usage of the model and utility for capturing information security structures as well as critical coordination between these structures on the basis of Spatio -Temporal metaphor. In this work, Known access control strategies are given a formal description in terms of synchronization in TA.

Keywords: Team Automata, Spatio -Temporal Role Based Access Control (STRBAC), Timed Automata, Component automata, Input/output Automata.

1 Introduction

Team Automata [2] are inspired by-and form an extension of input/output automata IOA [1] like input/output automata. It forms a flexible framework for modeling communication between components of distributed systems. A logical architecture of a system can be modeled by describing it solely in terms of an automaton, the roles of actions and synchronization between these actions. Moreover, it is composed of component automata (CA), which are ordinary automata without final states and with a distinction of their actions into input, output and internal actions. In each state, it must be possible to execute every input action. A whole lot of TA which are distinguishable only by their synchronization can be composed over the set of CA. In particular, contrary to the case of IOA, in TA output actions may also be synchronized upon. The rigorous setup of these frameworks allows to formulate and verify general and specific logical properties of complex (distributed, reactive) systems in a mathematically precise way. Based on the idea of a synchronization of common actions the components of TA connected in order to collaborate. Within each component, a distinction has been made between internal actions which are not available for synchronization with other components and external actions are used to synchronize components which are subjected to synchronization restrictions. By assigning different roles to actions, many type of collaboration are made. Consequently, for each external action a separate decision is made as to how and when the components should synchronize on this action.

V.V Das et al. (Eds.): BAIP 2010, CCIS 70, pp. 586–591, 2010.

Our spatial temporal access control metaphor uses different spatial-temporal constraints for performing different actions in the groupware systems. The rest of the paper is organized as follows: section2 provides the literature survey. We present the preliminary definitions of TA in section 3 and subsequently we represent the behavior of each component of the model in terms of automata and combine them into TA model in section 4 and section5 provides a conclusion on this work and suggests some possible future enhancements.

2 Literature Survey

Team automata have originally been introduced by ter Beek et.al [3,4] in the context of computer supported co operative work. Ter Beek et. al [2] presents a survey of the use of team automata for the specification and analysis of some issues from the field of security. Kleijn [1] presented a survey of works that use team automata for the specification and analysis of phenomena from the field of computer supported cooperative work. Lynch et. al [5] have described team automata an extension of Input/Output automata (IOA) and are flexible framework for modeling communication between components of distributed systems. ter Beek et. al [6] demonstrate the potential of TA for capturing information security, protection structures and critical co ordinations between these structures. In [7], the authors have showed the potential of TA for modeling secure multicast and broadcast communication. Schneider [10] defines a Security Automata as a form of Buchi automata and applies them to a simple access control model. Mondal et. al. [11] discussed how TRBAC can be mapped to timed automata and various features of timed automata are effectively used to represent the characteristics of a role. Yu et al. [12] proposed a location based temporal authorization model it focuses on controlling access to the different locations. For example, access rules can have temporal constraints to specify when a user can enter or leave a location or how many times a user can enter a location. Moreover, Role-based access control model [13] is used for addressing the access control needs of commercial organizations. Covington et al. [14] introduced environment roles in a generalized RBAC model (GRBAC) to provide access control to private information and resources in ubiquitous computing applications.

3 Team Automata

In this section we present the definitions of CA and Team Automata, a TA is composed of component automata (CA), which are ordinary automata without final states and with a distinction of their sets of actions into input, output and internal actions. Their internal actions have observable by other CA and are used for communication between CA. Now both of these automata can be defined as follows.

Definition 1. A component automaton (CA) *is a construct* $C = (Q \ (\Sigma_{inp}^C, \Sigma_{out}^C, \Sigma_{int}^C), \delta, I)$ *with underlying automaton* $(\Sigma_{inp}^C \cup \Sigma_{out}^C \cup \Sigma_{int}^C), \delta, I)$ *and pair wise disjoint sets* Σ_{inp}^C, *of input,* Σ_{out}^C, *of output, and* Σ_{int}^C *of internal actions.* Σ^C *denotes the set* $\Sigma_{inp}^C \cup \Sigma_{out}^C \cup \Sigma_{int}^C$ *of actions of C and* Σ_{ext}^C *denotes its set* $\Sigma_{inp}^C \cup \Sigma_{out}^C$ *of external actions. We* discard C from these notations when no confusion can arise.

Definition 2. A team automaton (TA) *over* S *is a construct* $T = (\Sigma_{inp}^{\tau}, \Sigma_{out}^{\tau}, \Sigma_{int}^{\tau}), \delta, I)$, *with* $Q = \Pi_{i \in [n]} Q_i, \Sigma_{inp}^{\tau} = (U_{i \in [n]} \Sigma_{i,inp}) - \Sigma_{out}^{\tau}, \Sigma_{out}^{\tau} = U_{i \in [n]} \Sigma_{i,out}, \Sigma_{int}^{\tau} = U_{i \in [n]} \Sigma_{i,inp}, \delta \subseteq Q \times \Sigma^{\tau} \times Q$, *where* $\Sigma^{\tau} = \Sigma_{inp}^{\tau} \cup \Sigma_{out}^{\tau} \cup \Sigma_{int}^{\tau}$ *is such that* $\{(q, q')|(q, a, q') \in \delta\} \subseteq \Delta_a(S)$, *for all* $\alpha \in \Sigma^{\tau}$, *and* $\{(q, q')|(q, a, q') \in \delta\} = \Delta_a(S)$, *for all* $\alpha \in \Sigma_{int}^{\tau}$ *and* $I = \Pi_{i \in [n]} I_i$. Each choice of synchronizations thus defines a TA. It is important to observe that *every TA is again a CA.*

4   Construction of Team Automata for STRBAC

To model system as TA, first the components of STRBAC are user, role and permission are identified and the behavior of these components is represented is terms of automata. These automata has many nodes, known as control states, which are connected using directed edges labeled by spatio – temporal constraints and the actions that are indentified by the target. The different states of each STRBAC component are represented by one or more control states. In STRBAC model three states namely disabled, enabled and active state are considered. To represent the behaviors two additional control states which are labeled as "Disabled" and "Enabled" are created. Where this "Disabled" is considered as the initial state. Transitions from "Disabled" to "Enabled" and vice versa are annotated using some synchronization actions. In other words, a role is said to be enabled if it satisfies the spatio– temporal constraints needed to activate it. Moreover, the role enabling and disabling behavior are represented as in figure1. Now considering an active state of a role, an enabled role becomes active when user acquires the permissions associated with it. So, with the first user assignment, an enabled role goes to the active state. When all the users are unassigned from the role, then the role goes back to the enabled state. From enabled or active state, a role can go back to the disabled state.

While considering role hierarchy the users of a senior role can directly activate a junior role provided the junior role is already in enabled state. To capture this behavior in the automaton, a control location labeled as "Active" is added. Now the transition is carried out from enabled to active. This action is represented as activate_r_i (id) where r_i is the role under consideration and id is the user id to activate the role. Moreover, a self loop labeled with activation action is provided at the "Active" Location to reflect the fact that when role is in active state, it remains in the same state. These transitions are labeled by an action deactivate_ r_i(id). Spatio – temporal constraints are also applicable on the permission assignment relation with the constraint when a role active the permission associated with it are made available on satisfying given spatio – temporal constraints. The states are labeled as A_{po}, A_{p1}... A_{pm}, in Figure 1. From each such state, a permission access request is sent using synchronization action access_p_i, where $I = I_D$ ....m-1. Similarly from the locations E_{po} .... $F_{p(m-1}$, another synchronization action deny_p_i is used. A permission timed automata shown in figure 2 is developed using access_p_i locations inactive to active. Transition from inactive to active is labeled with the actions access_p_i and term with from and active to initiative is labeled with deny_p_i. So with the first access request, the permission role timed automata is in the Active State the term self loop transitions also added in the active location.

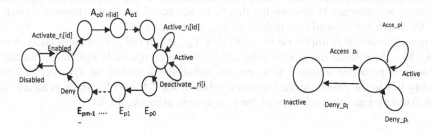

Fig. 1. Role Automata   **Fig. 2.** Permission Automata

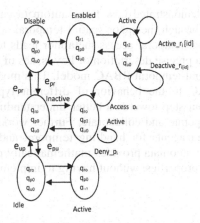

Fig. 3. Team Automata

It is observed that the basic structure of role assignment automaton is the same for all roles except for the action names. This is also true for permission assignment automata but representation of user behavior is not same. So, depending upon user behavioral characteristics, different types of user interaction are identified and represented in terms of automata [15]. The three different component automata called role assignment M_r, permission assignment M_p and user behavior M_u have been modeled to represent its behavior. The states of M_r, M_p and M_u are q_{ro}, q_{po}, q_{uo} and q_{r1}, q_{p1}, q_{u1} are initial states and active states respectively It clearly forms a composable system and we combine them into a team automata T_{urp}. Each of the team automata is a combination of a state from M_r, a state from M_p and a state from M_u.

Initially T_{rpu} is in state (q_{ro}, q_{po}, q_{uo}), a combination of initial states from the component automata. This means, one state is in action, while other two states are inactive assuming that one can have only one kind of action to do at a time, the other two should be idle at any moment in time. We let the automata synchronize on the external actions e_{rp}, e_{pr}, e_{pu} and e_{up}. Each such synchronized external action of T_{rpu} corresponds to current action while starting in another action. Synchronization of action e_{pr} models a move from role assignment to permission assignment this move is represented by (q_{ro}, q_{po}, q_{ro}), $e_{rp}(q_{ro}, q_{p1}, q_{ro})$ showing that is automata M_r we assign a user to a role, in automata M_p we assign permission. In each of the above component automata, one automata is idle while other is in active all internal actions are maintained the reachable state of thus is defined T_{rpu} as in figure 3.

At this moment, it is important to stress that T_{rpu} is not only team automaton over M_r, M_p, M_u. In general there is no unique TA over a composable system S, but this framework is provided within which one can constraint a variety of TA over S. The flexibility lies in the choice of the transition relation for TA over S, which is based on but not fixed by transition relations of the component automata in S.

5 Conclusion

In this paper we have demonstrated how team automata can be used for modeling spatio-temporal RBAC through metaphor spatial-temporal access. Our framework of team automata and spatial temporal access metaphor leads to a powerful abstraction which is well suited for a precise description of key issues of access control with state transition model for spatial-temporal RBAC model. This model maps the behavior of components of STRBAC to the behavior of different types of interaction. This framework is a significant step towards a better understanding of the ways in which people and systems cooperate and collaborate. Further works in this direction could be the use of specialized agents for handling temporal and spatial constraints and modeling AC using team automata provides mathematically precise analysis tools for providing crucial design properties, without having to implement one's design.

References

1. Kleijn, J.: Team Automata for CSCW – A Survey. In: Ehrig, H., Reisig, W., Rozenberg, G., Weber, H. (eds.) Petri Net Technology for Communication-Based Systems. LNCS, vol. 2472, pp. 295–320. Springer, Heidelberg (2003)
2. Ter Beek, M.H., Lenzini, G., Petrocchi, M.: Team automata for security -a survey. Electronic Notes in Theoretical Computer Science, vol. 128, pp. 105–119. Elsevier, Amsterdam (2005)
3. Ter Beek, M.H., Ellis, C.A., Kleijn, J., Rozenberg, G.: Synchronizations in team automata for groupware systems, Computer Supported Cooperative Work. The Journal of Collaborative Computing 12(1), 21–69 (2003)
4. Ellis, C.A.: Team Automata for Groupware Systems. In: Proc. GROUP 1997, pp. 415–424. ACM Press, New York (1997)
5. Lynch, N.A., Tuttle, M.R.: An Introduction to Input/Output Automata. CWI Quarterly 2(3), 219–246 (1989); Tech. Memo MIT/LCS/TM-373 (1988)
6. Ter Beek, M.H., Ellis, C.A., Kleijn, J., Rozenberg, G.: Team Automata for Spatial Access Control. In: Proc. ECSCW 2001, pp. 59–77. Kluwer, Dordrecht (2001)
7. Ter Beek, M.H., Lenzini, G., Petrocchi, M.: Team Automata for Security Analysis of Multicast/Broadcast Communication. Technical Report 2003-TR-13, Istituto di Scienza e Tecnologie dell'Informazione, Consiglio Nazionale delle Ricerche. Presented at WISP 2003 (2003)
8. Ter Beek, M.H., Lenzini, G., Petrocchi, M.: Team Automata for Security Analysis. Technical Report. TR-CTIT, pp. 04–13. Centre for Telematics and Information Technology, University

9. Focardi, R., Martinelli, F.: A Uniform Approach for the Definition of Security Properties. In: Wing, J.M., Woodcock, J.C.P., Davies, J. (eds.) FM 1999. LNCS, vol. 1708, pp. 794–813. Springer, Heidelberg (1999)
10. Schneider, F.B.: Enforceable Security Policies. ACM Transactions on Information and System Security 3(1), 30–50 (2000)
11. Mondal, S., Sural, S.: Security Analysis of RBAC with temporal and constraints-A Model Cheking Approach. Journal of Information Assurance Security 4, 319–328 (2009)
12. Yu, H., Lim, E.-P.: LTAM: A Location-Temporal Authorization Model. In: Jonker, W., Petković, M. (eds.) SDM 2004. LNCS, vol. 3178, pp. 172–186. Springer, Heidelberg (2004)
13. Ferraiolo, D.F., Sandhu, R., Gavrila, S., Kuhn, D.R., Chandramouli, R.: Proposed NIST Standard for Role-Based Access Control. ACM Transactions on Information and Systems Security 4(3) (August 2001)
14. Covington, M.J., Long, W., Srinivasan, S., Dey, A., Ashamed, M., Abode, G.: Securing Context-Aware Applications Using Environment Roles. In: Proceedings of the 6th ACM Symposium on Access Control Models and Technologies, Chantilly, VA, USA, May 2001, pp. 10–20 (2001)
15. Mondal, S., Sural, S., Atlari, V.: Towards Formal Security Analysis of GTRBAC using Timed Automata. In: SACMAT 2009, Italy, June 3-5, pp. 33–42 (2009)

Knowledge Discovery in Feedback System Using Pixel Oriented Technique

Malay Bhatt, Rituraj Jain, and C.K. Bhensdadia

Dept. of Comp. Eng., Dharmsinh Desai University, Nadiad, Gujarat – 387001
{malaybhatt202,jainrituraj}@yahoo.com, ckbhensdadia@ddu.ac.in

Abstract. To achieve excellence in education and produce quality students which can be absorbed by the organizations, feedback of students is collected to identify holes in the current teaching methodology and other services by institutions. A large amount of data is generated every semester and it is worthless to collect these data unless it is utilized for knowledge discovery. Visual data mining is most appropriate for representation when data size grows to Terabytes.

Proposed solution is divided into various stages: Data collection, Data preprocessing, Data representation and Data mining. An online feedback system is developed in-house for data collection. Preprocessing stage retrieves relevant fields of the data base for representation. Preprocessed data is visually represented using pixel oriented technique which generates an image of entire data. In data mining state, the knowledge patterns are discovered from generated image.

Keywords: Feedback, Pixel Oriented Technique, Visual Data Mining.

1 Introduction

Several organizations are working to provide quality education at various levels. Goal of an institute is to give quality education which is possible if they have plenty of resources. All these resources become wastage if they are not properly utilized. In any field, best critics are the users of the resource. The Students are the users and there feedback plays a significant role [2]. Visualization techniques can be used for explorative analysis, confirmative analysis or presentation of large amount of data. Visual data mining can also be used to show intermediate result of simulation [3]. Relationship between data, interaction technique and visual data mining technique is shown in Fig.1 (a) [1].

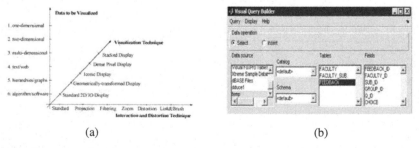

(a)   (b)

Fig. 1. (a) Relationship between data, interaction and visual data mining technique **(b)** Visual Query Builder showing Feedback table

V.V Das et al. (Eds.): BAIP 2010, CCIS 70, pp. 592–594, 2010.
© Springer-Verlag Berlin Heidelberg 2010

2 Proposed Solution

Each course contains various semesters which in turn covers various subjects and feedback of each subject by all students is covered through a set of questions. This process is a recursive process which leads to increase in data size over the years. Feedback data for students is collected through on-line feedback system and stored as a relational database in Oracle. 'Feedback' table is shown in Fig.1(b). Block diagram of proposed solution is shown in Fig.2(a).

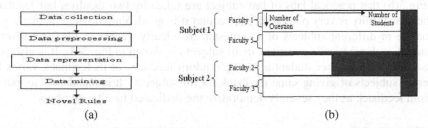

(a)   (b)

Fig. 2. (a) Block Diagram of Proposed Solution, (b) Subject wise feedback data representation

Suppose for example each semester is composed of n subjects. Each subject covers theory classes and labs. Let's assume that semester is handled by p faculties. It may be possible that p>=n. Each semester has strength of m students. Each subject will be evaluated using a set of parameters and these parameters can be ranked as bad(red), average(green), good(blue) and best(white) by setting 20 questions (15 questions) for theory (lab). So, Total size to represent individual semester's feedback is m*n*20 (m*n*15) pixels with the assumption that p=n otherwise feedback size will be higher.

Subject (theory or practical) wise feedback data representation for one semester is shown in Fig.2(b). Y-axis represents 3 dimensions (subjects, faculty and questions) nested into one another. X-axis represents Number of students giving feedback. Separation between various subjects is shown by thick dark horizontal black line. Similarly, faculty wise feedback data representation can be obtained by interchanging faculty and subject dimension in Fig. 2(b).

3 Experimental Results

Below is the list of questions which can be directly visualized with the integration of visual data mining technique into feedback system. Implementation of the visual data mining technique is done using MATLAB 7.5.0. Fig.3(a) represents subject wise theory feedback of one semester. Each subject's feedback is separated by dark black color horizontal line. Fig.3(a) contains feedback of 6 different subjects. Each subject can be taken by more than one faculty member. It is clear that first subject is taken by 2 faculty members in both divisions. If one faculty member is taking full subject in one division and half subject in another division then feedback for first faculty member will be given by students of both division and feedback of second faculty will be given by students of one division only which is clearly visible in third subject of Fig.3(a). It is clear from first subject's theory feedback that first faculty getting 'good' feedback while second faculty is getting 'average' feedback.

Table 1. Sample questions visualized by pixel oriented technique

1	Feedback for theory load for a particular subject conducted by multiple faculties.
2	Feedback of all students regarding specific Question for a given faculty
3	Overall performance of faculty in all semesters
4	Overall feedback of a particular semester in all subjects for all questions
5	Batch wise feedback for a given subject

Feedback of practical for all subjects is shown in Fig.3(b). It is observable from the Fig.3(b) that practical labs of last subject are taken by two faculties but feedback of the first faculty is very poor while for second it is good. Variations in faculty's performance in different subjects of a semester are clearly visible in Fig.3(c). Overall impact of each practical's questions in all subjects is shown in Fig. 3(d). It is also possible to identify whether student is giving random feedback or its feedback varies for different subjects or giving same feedback for all subjects. It is mandatory to extract random feedback as they severely demoralize the dedicated faculty members.

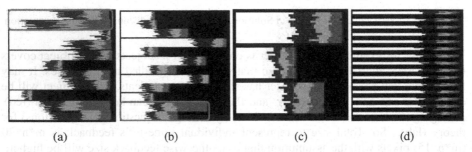

(a)   (b)   (c)   (d)

Fig. 3. **(a)** Subject wise Theory feedback of faculties, **(b)** Subject wise practical feedback of faculties, **(c)** Subject wise practical feedback of single faculty, **(d)** Question-wise Practical Feedback

4 Conclusion

Feedback system with visual data mining highlights holes in teaching methodology, resources etc. more clearly as compared to existing methods. It is difficult to gain knowledge in a single snapshot using existing approaches which are not coupled with visual data mining.

References

1. Keim, D.A.: Information Visualization and Visual Data Mining. IEEE Transactions on Visualization and Computer Graphics 7(1) (2002)
2. Bhatt, M.S., Jadav, P.M., Bhensdadia, C.K.: Integration of OLAP into Feedback System. In: Proceedings of International conference on Sensors, Security, Software and Intelligent Systems, Coimbatore (2009)
3. Auber, D., Novelli, N., Melancon, G.: Visually Mining the Datacube using a Pixel-Oriented Technique. In: Proceedings of the 11th international Conference information Visualization (2007)

Analysis and Simulation of a Low Leakage Conventional SRAM Memory Cell at Deep Sub-micron Level

N.K. Shukla, Shilpi Birla, and R.K. Singh

Institute of Technology & Management,
Sect.23, Gurgaon, India
neerajkshukla@itminida.edu, shilpi.birla@spsu.ac.in,
rksinghkec12@rediff.com

Abstract. The High leakage current in deep sub-micrometer region is becoming a significant contributor to power dissipation in CMOS circuits as threshold voltage, channel length, and the gate oxide thickness are reduced. As the standby current in memories is critical in low-power design. By lowering the supply voltage (VDD) to its standby limit, the data retention voltage (DRV), SRAM leakage power can be reduced substantially. The DRV increases with transistor mismatches. In this paper, we demonstrated the drowsy cache technique which shows a decrease in the leakage current dissipation in deep sub-micron designs of memory cells and embedded memories. The focus of this work is to simulate an effective scheme for SRAM leakage suppression in battery-powered mobile applications.

Keywords: Data Retention Voltage, Drowsy Cell, Deep Sub-Micron, SRAM, Drowsy Cache, 90nm Technology.

1 Introduction

Recent surveys shows, a roughly around 30% of the semiconductor business (worldwide) is due to semiconductor memory chips. In recent years as the need of leakage reduction in high-processors and microcontroller architectures, memory structures increases, there have been many research activities on low-voltage SRAM dynamic and standby techniques. Most of the researchers reported circuit techniques in this area focusing on the designs at the sleep mode, .g., an array of dynamically-controlled sleep transistors was used to provide a finely programmable standby V_{DD} [1].

2 SRAM Cell Architecture

An SRAM Cell incorporates the standard designs as decoders, memory core, multiplexer, pre-charge, sense amplifier, input and output tri-state buffer with control logic. The address decoding circuit is divided into two stages, pre-decoder and decoder. The output of the decoder drives the word lines of the SRAM. The SRAM Core is a 6T SRAM Cell. The column multiplexer is based on pass transistor logic. This connects the core to the sense amplifier and write buffer. The sense amp is connected to the read buffer. During a write operation, the data from the data bus is sent to the write buffer at the onset of the Write Enable signal. The write data is then transferred to the desired columns by the column multiplexer.

V.V Das et al. (Eds.): BAIP 2010, CCIS 70, pp. 595–597, 2010.
© Springer-Verlag Berlin Heidelberg 2010

3   Techniques for Leakage Reduction

The amount of leakage current is increased with advancement of technology generation. Reduction in dimension, increase of doping, reduction of V_T etc causes the increase of leakage current in every generation. So, leakage reduction technique is the
demand of modern age. Here we have discussed theoretically the two good techniques
for leakage reductions, the Data Retention Gated Ground and Drowsy Scheme. The
simulation model is presented for the drowsy cell technique.

3.1   Drowsy Cache Scheme

In it the Cache is put in low-power drowsy mode, when information preservation is
needed, to a high-power mode before access of its contents. Leakage current reduces
with voltage scaling. Reduced leakage and supply voltage gives large reduction in the
leakage power.

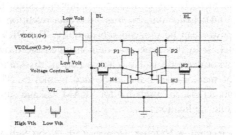

Fig. 1. Architecture of Drowsy Memory Cell

In the SRAM operation there is mainly two stages. One is when read or write operation is done. This can be assumed as active mode when actual data transaction
takes place. On the other hand when there is no data transaction only information preserve is done by the latching phenomena of memory. It is found that there is very low
supply voltage needed for preservation of data. Drowsy cache method puts memory in
a low power supply drowsy mode when only data preservation is needed. It uses multiple supply voltage sources. It supply high voltage when access of memory contents
is needed [7,9]. Leakage current is decreased as supply voltage decreases. Reduced
supply voltage and reduced leakage current together make a huge reduction in leakage
current [5]. Fig.4, shows the Drowsy Technique for leakage reduction. Thus, the
memory core is put in the low-power drowsy mode when the information prevention
is required and in the high-power mode before the access of the contents. The leakage
current reduces with the voltage scaling. This reduced leakage and supply voltage
results in a huge reduction of the leakage power [9].

4   Simulation

Simulation is done in the Cadence Platform at 90nm Technology.
    The design has been simulated in the Cadence Platform at 90nm Technology.
Without applying the leakage reduction technique to a 6T SRAM cell, the leakage

simulated as 1.8nA. The Drowsy Cache Scheme working correctly in 90 nm technology. An improvement in the leakage current is simulated before the application of pulse, a current of nearly, 108pA is flowing, whereas after the application of pulse a current of 84pA is present in the conventional 6T SRAM memory cell.

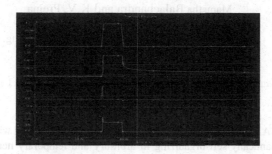

Fig. 2. Power Consumption Waveform for Drowsy Cache Scheme

References

[1] Zhang, K., et al.: SRAM design on 65-nm CMOS technology with dynamic sleep transistor for leakage reduction. IEEE Journal of Solid-State Circuits 40(4), 895–901 (2005)

[2] Kim, C.H., Kim, J., Chang, I., Roy, K.: PVT-Aware leakage reduction for on-die caches with improved read stability. IEEE Journal of Solid-State Circuits 41(1), 170–178 (2006)

[3] Khellah, M., Somasekhar, D., Ye, Y., Kim, N.S., Howard, J., Ruhl, G., Sunna, M., Tschanz, J., Borkar, N., Hamzaoglu, F., Pandya, G., Farhang, A., Zhang, K., De, V.: A 256-Kb Dual-VCC SRAM Building Block in 65-nm CMOS Process With Actively Clamped Sleep Transistor. IEEE Journal of Solid-State Circuits 42(1), 233–242 (2007)

[4] Agarwal, A., Li, H., Roy, K.: DRG-Cache:Adata retention gated ground cache for low power. In: Proc. Design Automation Conf., pp. 473–478 (2002)

[5] Taur, Y., Ning, T.H.: Fundamentals of Modern VLSI Devices, ch. 2, pp. 94–99. Cambridge Univ. Press, New York (1998)

[6] De, V., Ye, Y., Keshavarzi, A., Narendra, S., Kao, J., Somasekhar, D., Nair, R., Borkar, S.: Techniques for leakage power reduction. In: Chandrakasan, A., Bowhill, W., Fox, F. (eds.) Design of High-Performance Microprocessor Circuits, ch. 3, pp. 48–52. IEEE, Piscataway (2001)

[7] Roy, K., Mukhopadhyay, S., Mahmoodi-Meimand, H.: Leakage Current Mechanisms and Leakage Reduction Techniques in Deep-Submicrometer CMOS Circuits. Proceedings of the IEEE 91(2) (February 2003)

[8] De, V., Ye, Y., Keshavarzi, A., Narendra, S., Kao, J., Somasekhar, D., Nair, R., Borkar, S.: Techniques for leakage power reduction. In: Chandrakasan, A., Bowhill, W., Fox, F. (eds.) Design of High-Performance Microprocessor Circuits, ch. 3, pp. 48–52. IEEE, Piscataway (2001)

[9] Flautner, K., Kim, N.S., Martin, S., Blaauw, D., Mudge, T.: Drowsy caches: simple techniques for reducingleakage power. In: Proc. 29th Annual Int. Symp. Computer Architecture, pp. 148–157 (2002)

Enhancing the efficiency of On-demand Routing Protocol for Mobile Ad Hoc Networks

Mamatha Balachandra and K.V. Prema

[1] Department of Computer Science and Engineering,
Manipal Institute of Technology,
Manipal, India, 576104
mamthabc@yahoo.co.in, prema.kv@manipal.edu

Abstract. A Mobile Ad-hoc Network (MANET) is a system of wireless mobile nodes dynamically self-organizing in arbitrary and temporary network topologies. People and vehicles can thus be inter-networked in areas without a pre-existing communication infrastructure. The design of network protocols for MANETs is a complex issue. Dynamic Source Routing (DSR) and Ad-hoc On demand Distance Vector (AODV) protocol are two well-known on-demand routing protocols. A major disadvantage of these two protocols is, the problem associated with routing of packets through flooding, resulting in congestion. Path accumulation feature of DSR can be used in AODV and then an efficient path for the routing can be discovered using Minimum Route Spanning Tree Protocol.

Keywords: MANET, DSR, AODV, MRST, AODV-APM.

1 Introduction

A Mobile Ad-hoc Network (MANET) is a temporary wireless network composed of mobile nodes, in which an infrastructure is absent. There are no dedicated routers, servers, access points and cables. A central challenge in the design of ad-hoc networks is the development of dynamic routing protocols that can efficiently find routes between two communicating nodes. DSR and AODV[1][2] are the two well-known on-demand routing protocols for MANETs. A major disadvantage of these two protocols is, the problem associated with routing of packets through flooding, resulting in congestion and unnecessary traffic in the network. There exists minimal flow control in the network. The proposed protocol makes use of the minimum route spanning tree algorithm. Thus, DSR[3] and AODV[4] are combining into one hierarchical routing protocol. Using this technique an efficient path for the routing of packet is discovered and instead of flooding, the packet is sent through the Minimum route spanning tree path.

2 Path Accumulation

AODV can be modified to enable path accumulation[5] as in the case of DSR, during the route discovery cycle. Each node also updates its routing table with all the

V.V Das et al. (Eds.): BAIP 2010, CCIS 70, pp. 598–600, 2010.
© Springer-Verlag Berlin Heidelberg 2010

information contained in the control messages. Each RREQ and RREP contains a source route for the nodes along the path, so that each node can have a routing table entry to the rest of the nodes. The main benefit of obtaining the additional routing entries is to reduce the route discovery overhead by eliminating some of the RREQs that would be required to discover these nodes. Since RREQs are the major source of control overhead due to flooding the whole network, any reduction in RREQs is expected to improve the performance significantly. The tradeoff is that the RREQ and RREP packet header will become larger to accommodate the source route. Fig.1 (inspired by[6]) clarifies the difference between route discovery without path accumulation and route discovery with path accumulation.

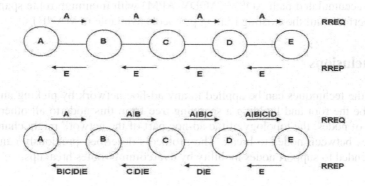

Fig. 1. Route Discovery Mechanism Without and With Path Accumulation

To configure alternative routes to the same destination, nodes are allowed to respond to the same route solicitation if it is received through different paths. Therefore, if a Route Request (RREQ) is received after a previous RREQ from the same origin has been responded, a node can decide to send a new Route Reply (RREP) message to the origin to build up a different path. In order to avoid long paths and to reduce interferences and power consumption in the nodes, this decision is assumed to be taken if the new detected path has a lower number hops (or optionally a lower cost) than the previously configured route.

3 Minimum Route Spanning Tree

The Minimum Route spanning tree (or MRST for short), always uses the tree route that is discovered by the MRST algorithm. In other words, MRST simply invokes the sendSpanningTree(s, d, message) method for each message. The advantage of this protocol is that once a tree is built, it does not waste any messages on path searching. Its only cost comes from the fact that messages are sent along sub-optimal routes. Notice that flood-based route discovery procedures propagate a route request through the network using broadcasts. In order to avoid the known Broadcast storm[7] effect, a broadcast jitter randomly delays the retransmission of the query and therefore the procedure is delayed. Since the tree-based route discovery procedure uses point-to-point communication, no such jitter mechanism is necessary, so no random artificial delay is required. Consequently, the overall delay is shorter and more predictable.

4 Result Analysis

1. In addition to the reduction in route discovery overhead, path accumulation improves the data path length in terms of number of hops, reducing the number of transmissions required in delivering a packet between source and a destination.
2. According to survey result, AODV-APM (AODV-Accumulated path metric) outperforms DSR-APM.
3. The accumulated path AODV (AODV-APM) with minimum route spanning tree outperforms all the existing routing protocols available in MANETs.

5 Conclusions

Clearly, the techniques can be applied to any ad-hoc network by picking an arbitrary node to be the root and building a spanning tree from this node to all others. Due to mobility of nodes, the topology of the ad-hoc part of the network might change, causing routes between nodes to break. The protocols described previously can be naturally extended to support nodes mobility by overcoming routes breakups.

References

1. Josh, B., et al.: A Performance Comparison of Multi-Hop Wireless Ad Hoc Network Routing Protocols. In: Proceedings of the Fourth Annual International Conference on Mobile Computing and Networking (MobiCom 1998). ACM, Dallas (1998)
2. Samir, R.D., et al.: Performance Comparison of Two On-demand Routing Protocols for Ad hoc Networks. IEEE Personal Communications Magazine special issue on Ad hoc Networking, 16–28 (February 2001)
3. Johnson, D.B., Maltz, D.A.: Dynamic source routing in ad hoc wireless networks. In: Imielinski, K. (ed.) Mobile Computing, vol. 353. Kluwer Academic Publishers, Dordrecht (1996)
4. Charles, P., Elizabeth, R.: Ad hoc on-demand distance vector routing. In: Proceedings of the 2nd IEEE Workshop on Mobile Computing Systems and Applications, February 1999, pp. 90–100 (1999)
5. Charles, E.P., et al.: Ad Hoc On Demand Distance Vector (AODV) Routing, IETF RFC 3561
6. Roy, F., et al.: Efficient route discovery in hybrid networks. Journal of Elsevier (2008)
7. Sze-Yao, N., et al.: The broadcast storm problem in a mobile ad hoc network. In: Proceedings of the 5th annual ACM/IEEE international conference on Mobile computing and networking, pp. 151–162 (1999)

Design Issues for Replacing Credit Card on Mobile Phone

Sukhwant Kaur, H.K. Kaura, and Mritunjay Ojha

Computer Department
Fr.C.Rodrigues Institute of Technology,
Vashi Navi, Mumbai-400703, Maharashtra
sukhwantsagar@gmail.com, hkkaura@gmail.com,
mritunjayojha@rediffmail.com

Abstract. Money Transaction has become common, frequent and a necessity in the current living and carrying cash always with a person is not a practical solution. The current trend of carrying the credit cards have become a crucial part of life and carrying of multiple cards is common nowadays. There is a risk involved when a credit card is stolen. Every one carries mobile phone. Our solution approach is to develop a system in which functions of the credit card is incorporated in mobile phone. The mobile phone is then used as a credit card and it replaces the function of swapping of the credit card each time we shop. Our system will have credit card application stored on mobile phone. This application will have all the information related to credit card operation, stored in encrypted form in the mobile phone. Further, this information is protected by a password. When a person desires to make any transaction through the mobile phone, the credit card data is passed from the mobile to the vendor machine through a Bluetooth communication interface. The vendor machine validates the credit card data with the corresponding bank in standard fashion and issue the receipt. Thus this eliminates the need for carrying credit card physically. This will require modification on mobile software for safe storage of credit card information and few hardware modifications (add-on) to the vendor terminal for communication using Bluetooth. This paper focuses on various design issues of this application where mobile phone will act as a credit card.

Keywords: Mobile Application, Credit card, Encryption, Bluetooth, Sim-Memory, NFC, PIN, IMEI, CVV, SMS.

1 Introduction

The current trend of carrying the credit card is increasingly becoming popular and is replacing cash transactions as it eliminates the inherent risk of carrying huge amount of cash for day-to-day transactions. But this existing credit card system has many problems. Credit card along with the PIN (Personal Identification Number) information are delivered to the customers by the banks through couriers and during this process, there is a high chances of misusing the cards if it goes into wrong hands and the customer will not be quickly able to realize the theft. The authentication used on all cards is a signature panel or photograph along with the signature panel in some credit cards but signatures are easy to forge and vendors do not bother to see the photograph on the credit card holder.

V.V Das et al. (Eds.): BAIP 2010, CCIS 70, pp. 601–604, 2010.

We are proposing a solution that will eliminate the need of using credit card physically. The credit card information such as type of card, name of cardholder, expiry date, credit card number, CVV (Card Verification Value) etc. which is there in magnetic stripe will be stored in encrypted form in the mobile phone memory. The mobile phone will then act as a credit card that will hold multiple types of credit cards of all the banks. The mobile-based system will facilitate any purchase made by the user. The transaction through mobile phone will be passed to the vendor machine through the Bluetooth communication interface of the mobile phone. The vendor machine or point-of-sale terminal will authenticate the credit card holder from the bank and get the receipt of the transaction in standard fashion.

2   Proposed Mobile Based Credit Card System

We are proposing a system that will eliminate the need of swapping the card at vendor terminal. The actual proposed system is as shown in figure 1.

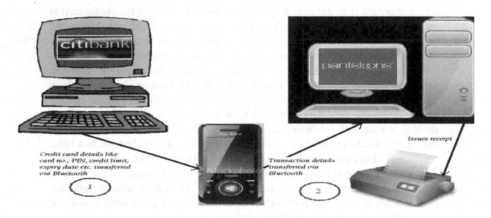

Fig. 1. Proposed system

The application is installed in the mobile phone. When the user runs this application, it will ask for the password. After validating the password, it will show multiple cards a particular user can choose. Then the user will select the proper credit card and enter the pin for that particular card along with the amount. All these information will then be sent to the vendor terminal using Bluetooth communication interface and then the receipt will be generated in standard fashion. This saves user for taking many credit cards in his wallet.

Advantages of our proposed system

   a)   Credit card information is stored in mobile phone in encrypted form. This information is further protected with a password ensuring double security.

   b)   Nobody can use the data even if mobile is stolen.

   c)   There is much more convenience to user as he/she need not carry multiple credit cards.

3 Design of the Application

Our application is organized in the form of modules as described below:

a) Bluetooth Connection Module: In this module, we have understood the working of Bluetooth functionality [6]. Credit card details like the credit card number, PIN, credit limit, expiry date etc. will be transferred to the user mobile by the bank through Bluetooth. The key features of Bluetooth technology are robustness, low complexity, low power and low cost. In this, Bluetooth functionality of desktop PC is enabled with the help of Bluetooth adapter. We have used USB Bluetooth adapter along with installation CD of Toshiba Corporation and Nokia 9500 communicator and LG KP500 mobile for transferring files from PC to mobile and vice versa. This module helps to understand the connection between two Bluetooth enabled devices.

b) Transfer Module: The transfer module is responsible for putting data in mobile phones from the bank application. The information related to the credit card cannot be stored as raw data as it is very confidential data. Therefore, it is being encrypted first and then stored. Further, this application is protected by two passwords. First password is required for using the application itself that is, only authorized user of the credit card can use the application. Second password is required to view the credit card details. Further, the credit card details are stored as read-only data so that no user can modify it. In addition, the credit card details are stored in phone memory because sim-memory of the phone is limited to 32kb or 64kb, which is not enough for such kind of application and external memory is not suitable for storing the data as it can be stolen.

We have simulated a bank application using Java Swing [7] and backend is developed using MS-Access. The bank will take details like name, mobile number, IMEI (International Mobile Equipment Identity) number, address, type of card, etc. from the user and store it in bank application database. The bank will then transfer the encrypted form of data (card number, PIN, credit limit, expiry date etc.) to the users mobile phone number through Bluetooth. The validations such as none of the text fields should be blank, mobile number should be of 11-digits, IMEI number should be a 16 digit unique number and credit card number should have only 16-digits etc are performed.

c) Transaction Module: The user will enter the master pin to view the application and to view the number of cards he/she is carrying. If the password is authenticated the application will display the list of credit cards available to the user. The user will then select the card and enter the PIN for that particular card. If the PIN is validated then it will display the amount user wants to pay to the vendor. If the amount is less than the credit limit then the transaction will be done and data will be sent to Point-of-Sale terminal through Bluetooth.

d) Point-of-Sale authentication: The receipt of transaction will be generated after authentication of the user, which will contain the name of the merchant and the amount paid through credit card. The same amount will then be deducted from the credit limit of the user's credit card.

4   Conclusion

The current trend of carrying the credit cards have become a crucial part of life. Everyone possesses multiple credit cards, which increases the risk of misuse when stolen. In this paper, we are proposing a system where mobile phone acts as a credit card. The credit card details are stored in phone memory of the mobile phone and will be in read only form. Further, the usage of application will be protected by password. The transactions are being carried in mobile phone and data is passed to point-of-sale terminal through Bluetooth. The simulation of Bank application and Bluetooth communication module is completed. Even if the mobile phone is lost, nobody can use the credit card information in it. All this will require modification on mobile software and few modifications (add-on) to the vendor terminal.

References

1. Al-Kwaja, A.H.: Proposal for an Open Minimal Standard-Processing, Financial Transactions using Mobile Phones, Gelszus Banker Trendcheck, CEBIT (2002)
2. Overview Advantages of J2ME,
   http://www.articlesbase.com/software-articles/
   overview-advantages-of-j2me-286725.html
3. Advantages of Wallet Phones Brooklyn NY,
   http://articles.directorym.com/Advantages_of_Wallet_Phones_
   Brooklyn_NY-r1132547-Brooklyn_NY.html
4. Keogh, J.: J2ME: The Complete Reference
5. Credit Card Fraud, http://en.wikipedia.org/wiki
6. Bluetooth, http://en.wikipedia.org/wiki/Bluetooth
7. Swing, http://en.wikipedia.org/wiki/Swing
8. Symbian Operating System, http://en.wikipedia.org/wiki/Symbian_OS
9. How Credit Cards Works,
   http://money.howstuffworks.com/personal-finance/
   debt-management/credit-card1.htm
10. Japanese Get First Mobile Wallet,
    http://news.bbc.co.uk/2/hi/technology/3551070.htm
11. http://stackoverflow.com/questions/609254/
    j2me-app-vs-browser-on-a-handset
12. Credit Card Transaction Lifecycle, http://technotes.towardsjob.com

Unknown Key Share Attack on STPKE' Protocol

R. Padmavathy[1] and Chakravarthy Bhagvati[2]

[1] Department of Computer Science and Engineering,
National Institute of Technology, Warangal, India
r_padma3@rediffmail.com
[2] University of Hyderabad, Hyderabad, India
chakcs@uohyd.ernet.in

Abstract. Three-party authenticated key exchange protocol is an important cryptographic technique in the secure communication areas, by which two clients, each shares a human-memorable password with a trusted server, can agree a secure session key. Recently, Lu and Cao proposed a simple three party password-based key exchange protocol (STPKE protocol). They claimed that their protocol is secure, efficient and practical. Unlike their claims, Kim & Choi proved that the STPKE protocol is vulnerable to Undetectable on-line password guessing attacks, and suggested an enhanced protocol (STPKE' protocol). In this paper, an Unknown key share attack on STPKE' protocol is demonstrated. The attack is implemented using a comprehensive set of experiments and reported. Additionally, the countermeasures to resist the above attack are discussed.

Keywords: STPKE' protocol, Unknown Key share attack, STPKE protocol.

1 Introduction

To communicate securely over an insecure public network, it is essential that secret session keys be securely exchanged. The shared session key may be subsequently used to achieve some cryptographic goals such as confidentiality or data integrity. Password-authenticated key exchange (PAKE) protocols [1,2] allow two or more specified parties to share a secret session key using only a human-memorable password. Password-based authenticated key exchange protocols, however, are vulnerable to password guessing attacks [3] since users usually choose easy-to-remember passwords. The goal of the attacker, is to obtain a legitimate communication party's password, can be achieved within a reasonable time. Thus, the password guessing attacks on password-based authenticated key exchange protocols should be considered realistic.

In general, the password guessing attacks can be divided into three classes [3].

Recently, Lu and Cao [4] proposed a simple three-party key exchange (STPKE) protocol based on the chosen-basis computational Diffie-Hellman (CCDH) assumption. They claimed that their protocol can resist various attacks and is superior to similar protocols with respect to efficiency. Kim and Choi [5] found that the STPKE protocol is vulnerable to undetectable on-line password guessing attacks by using formal description and proposed an alternative protocol (STPKE' protocol).

V.V Das et al. (Eds.): BAIP 2010, CCIS 70, pp. 605–608, 2010.

A	B	C	S

$x, a \in Z_p$

$X \leftarrow (g^x \oplus g^a) \cdot M^{pwA}$

$ID'_A \leftarrow ID_A \cdot g^a$ $ID'_A \| X$

$\xrightarrow{\hspace{3cm}}$ $y, b \in Z_p$

$Y \leftarrow (g^y \oplus g^b) \cdot N^{pwB}$

$ID'_B \leftarrow ID_B \cdot g^b$ $ID'_A \| X \| ID'_B \| Y$

$\xrightarrow{\hspace{4cm}}$

(**C** intercepts this message i.e it gets
ID'_A, ID'_B which will be used in later steps)

$w, c \in Z_p$

$W \leftarrow (g^w \oplus g^c) \cdot N^{pwc}$

$ID'_c \leftarrow ID_c \cdot g^c$ $ID'_A \| X \| ID'_c \| W$

$\xrightarrow{\hspace{4cm}}$

$g^a \leftarrow ID'_A / ID_A, g^c \leftarrow ID'_c / ID_c$
(As 'S' believes that 'A' &
'C' wants to establish a
session key it divides ID'_A,
ID'_C with ID_A & ID_c)

$g^x \oplus g^a \leftarrow X / M^{pwA}$,

$g^x \leftarrow (g^x \oplus g^a) \oplus g^a$

$g^{xz} \leftarrow (g^x)^z$

$g^w \oplus g^c \leftarrow W / N^{pwc}$,

$g^w \leftarrow (g^w \oplus g^c) \oplus g^c$

$g^{wz} \leftarrow (g^w)^z$

$X' \leftarrow g^{wz} \cdot H(ID'_A, ID'_B, ID_S, g^x)^{PWA}$

$W' \leftarrow g^{xz} \cdot H(ID'_B, ID'_A, ID_S, g^w)^{PWC}$

$X' \| W'$

$\xleftarrow{\hspace{4cm}}$

$g^{xz} \leftarrow W' / H(ID'_B, ID'_A, ID_S, g^w)^{PWC}$

$\alpha \leftarrow H(ID'_A, ID'_B, g^{xwz})$

$X' \| \alpha$ $g^{xwz} \leftarrow (g^{xz})^w$

$\xleftarrow{\hspace{4cm}}$

$g^{wz} \leftarrow X' / H(ID'_A, ID'_B, ID_S, g^x)^{PWA}$

verify α

$\beta \leftarrow H(ID'_A, ID'_B, g^{xwz})$

$SK_A \leftarrow H'(ID'_A, ID'_B, g^{xwz})$

β

$\xrightarrow{\hspace{6cm}}$

Verify β

$SK_B \leftarrow H'(ID'_A, ID'_B, g^{xwz})$

Fig. 1. Unknown key share attack on STPKE' protocol

In the current study, an Unknown key share attack is proved on the STPKE' protocol, A client 'C' not supposedly involved in a protocol run can end up sharing a session key with client 'A' but 'A' is thinking it is sharing with client 'B'. This is achieved through the field elements M and N used in the protocol. Neither they are random nor shared between the clients and the server, this motivated to design a Unknown Key Share attack. Moreover, the proposed protocol is analyzed on a set of experiments.

The paper is organized as follows: Section 2 describes the Unknown key share attack on STPKE' protocol. Section 3 reports the experimental results and the concluding remarks are made in section 4.

2   Unknown Key Share Attack on STPKE' Protocol

The Kim-Choi (STPKE') protocol falls to an unknown key share attack. A client 'C' not supposedly involved in a protocol run can end up sharing a session key with client 'A' but 'A' is thinking he is sharing with client 'B'.

Fig.1. illustrates Unknown key share attack on STPKE' protocol.

3   Experimental Results

The STPKE' protocol is implemented and the Unknown key share attack is successfully mounted. Table 1 shows the selected list of problems solved and the running time to mount the unknown key share attack.

Table 1. Running time to mount unknown key share attack on STPKE' protocol

Sl. no	Prime (p)	Running time to mount unknown key share attack (microsec)
1	200501759	1,00,929.3

4   Conclusion

In the present paper, an unknown key share attack on STPKE' protocol is demonstrated, this is developed due to two field elements in G i.e. M, N. The countermeasure is to make those two elements M, N (the two elements in G) shared between server, A and server, B respectively.

References

[1] Chen, T.H., Lee, W.B.: A new method for using hash functions to solve remote user authentication. Comput. Electr. Eng. 34(1), 53–62 (2008)

[2] Yeh, H.T., Sun, H.M.: Password authenticated key exchange protocols among diverse network domains. Comput. Electr. Eng. 31(3), 175–189 (2005)

[3] Ding, Y., Horster, P.: Undetectable on-line password guessing attacks. ACM Operat. Syst. Rev. 29(4), 77–86 (1995)

[4] Lu, R., Cao, Z.: Simple three-party key exchange protocol. Comput. Secur. 26(1), 94–97 (2007)

[5] Kim, C.: Enhanced Password-based simple three-party Key exchange protocol. Computers and Electrical Engineering 35(1), 107–114 (2008) (in press)

An Effective SOA Model for Developing Efficient Systems

Sasmita Pani[1] and Mahamaya Mohanty[2]

[1] Department Of Information Technology
NMIET, Bhubaneswar
susmitapani@gmail.com
[2] School Of Computer Engineering
KIIT University, Bhubaneswar
mahamayamohanty@yahoo.co.in

1 Introduction

Service Oriented Architecture is an architectural paradigm and discipline that may be used to build infrastructures enabling those with needs (consumers) and those with capabilities (providers) to interact via services across disparate domains of technology and ownership. Services act as the core facilitator of electronic data interchanges yet require additional mechanisms in order to function. Services comprise intrinsically unassociated, loosely coupled units of functionality that have no calls to each other embedded in them. Instead of services embedding calls to each other in their source code, they use defined protocols that describe how one or more services can "talk" to each other.. SOA may be used for business applications, or in government and the military.

2 Proposed Approach an Effectual SOA Model

The SOA for any system is proposed to have five layers and sub-layers within each layer which starts with the user's need and ends with modified layer as shown in Fig 1. The different layers are Application layer, Service Layer, System Specification Layer, System Evalution Layer and Modified layer.

The constituents of different layers are as follows:

The first layer is Application Layer consists of Requirement determination, Initial requirement specification, Feasibility Analysis and Final Specification.

The second Layer is Service Layer consists of Hardware study and Software study.

The third Layer is System Specification Layer which consists of System Design and Implementation of System Design.

The fourth Layer is System Evaluation Layer which is composed of Expected Output, Actual Output and the difference between two outputs.

The fifth and final Layer is Modified Layer.

V.V Das et al. (Eds.): BAIP 2010, CCIS 70, pp. 609–612, 2010.
© Springer-Verlag Berlin Heidelberg 2010

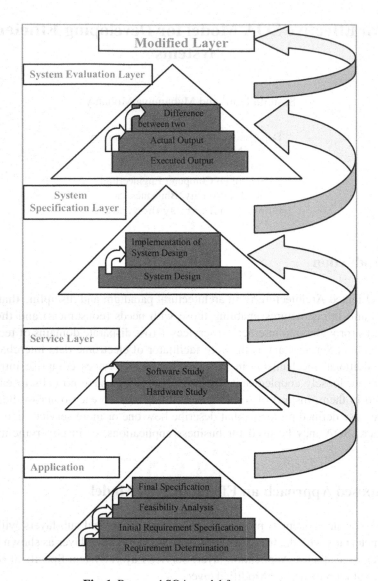

Fig. 1. Proposed SOA model for any system

3   Working Principles of the Proposed Approach

Step 1: At first the user's need is noted.

Step 2: The Application Layer is proposed to performs the following functions

The first sub-layer that is Requirement Determination determines what information is needed by an organization.

The second sub-layer that is Initial Requirement Specification determines the priority of the information that is what requirement is required at first.

The third sub-layer that is feasibility analysis assess if it is possible to meet the requirements specificed subject to all the constraints such as human resource, budget etc i.e. we prepare a report of available resource and the resources that are required which is known as feasibility report.

The fourth sub-layer that is final specification shows the overall functioning of the model how a user can do without knowing how the system is built.

Step 3: The Service Layer gives a clear understanding of hardware and software requirements for a system i.e. it determines the type of computer system and software tools needed to meet the final system specification.

Step 4: The System Specification Layer consists of the following sub-layers.

The first sub-layer is System Design where we design the programs, databases and test plans.

The second sub-layer is the Implementation of System Design where we show the working of the system in real-life examples like e-banking, e-learning, e-business etc.

Step 5: The System Evaluation Layer gives the difference between and the expected output and the expected output where the difference layer depicts whether the model is profitable/suitable or not which depends on the actual output.

If the actual output > expected output then the model can improve the system

If the actual output < expected output the model needs some change for the system an improved one.

Step 6: The final layer is the Modification Layer which depends on evaluation layer and according the modification is done.

Step 7: Stop

4   Conclusion

The proposed framework aims to support the development of new models in e-systems. The model that has been proposed here is simpler and clearer as each layer is broken down into different sub-layers. Each sub-layer of the architecture acts as its basic unit which directly implies what function is to be carried out in a particular instance of time. The future scope of Service Oriented Architecture lies on developing a testing tool to test each of the proposed layers for its reuse. It can also be implemented with the concept of Linked List which can be used in the System Evaluation Layer where different function such as insertion, deletion can be performed. One obvious and common challenge faced involves managing services metadata. SOA-based environments can include many services that exchange messages to perform tasks. Depending on the design, a single application may generate millions of messages where managing and providing information on how services interact is a complicated task. The second challenge involves the lack of testing in SOA space. There are no sophisticated tools that provide testability of all headless services (including message and database services along with web services) in a typical architecture. Lack of horizontal trust requires that both producers and consumers test services on a continuous basis. SOA's main goal is to deliver *Agility to Businesses*. Therefore it is important to invest in a testing framework (build or buy) that would provide you with the visibility required to find the culprit in your architecture in no time. Thirdly another challenge relates to provide appropriate levels of security. Security models built into an application may no longer suffice when the capabilities of the application are exposed as services that can be used by other applications. That is, application-managed security is not the right model for securing services.

References

[1] Zdun, U., Hentrich, C., van der Aalst, W.: A survey of patterns for service-oriented architectures. International Journal of Internet Protocol Technology 1(3), 132–143 (2006)

[2] Zimmermann, O., Krogdahl, P., Gee, C.: Elements of service-oriented analysis and design: an interdisciplinary modeling approach for SOA projects (2004)

[3] Gerede, C.E., Hull, R., Ibarra, O., Su, J.: Automated composition of e-services: Lookaheads. In: Proceedings of the International Conference on Service Oriented Computing (ICSOC 2004), NewYork, pp. 252–262 (2004)

[4] Greenfield, J., Short, K.: Software Factories: Assembling Applications with Patterns, Frameworks, Models and Tools. J. Wiley and Sons Ltd., Chichester (2004)

[5] Hentrich, C., Zdun, U.: Patterns for process-oriented integration in service-oriented architectures. In: Proceedings of 11th European Conference on Pattern Languages of Programs (EuroPlop 2006), Irsee, Germany (2006)

[6] Stahl, T., Voelter, M.: Model-Driven Software Development. J. Wiley and Sons Ltd., Chichester (2006)

[7] Di Mare, J.: Service-Oriented Architecture: A practical guide to measuring return on that investment, IBM Institute for Business Value (2006)

Refactoring Interprocedural Dynamic Slicing for Handling Pointers

Santosh Kumar Pani, Priya Arundhati, and Mahamaya Mohanty

School Of Computer Engineering
Kalinga Institute Of Industrial Technology
Bhubaneswar, India
spanifcs@kiit.ac.in
priya.arundhati@yahoo.com
mahamayamohanty@yahoo.co.in

Abstract. This paper presents a interprocedural dynamic slicing for handling pointers in programs. The use of pointers presents serious problems for software productivity tools for software understanding, restructuring, and testing. Pointers enable indirect memory accesses through pointer dereferences, as well as indirect procedure calls (e.g., through function pointers in C). Such indirect accesses and calls can be disambiguated with pointer analysis. In addition to a conservative analysis, we propose an optimistic algorithm that reflects common program's slicing. This paper uses the proposed pointer alias analyses to infer the types of variables in C programs and shows that most C variables are used in a manner consistent with their declared types. The proposed concepts for interprocedural dynamic slicing we have proposed here is more efficient then the existing concepts as it gives a detailed idea about the slices that can be obtained for one dimensional pointers, two dimensional pointer, pointer to arrays, dynamic memory allocation.

Keywords: Interprocedural Slicing, Active data Slice, Active Control Slice, Active Call Slice, Dynamic Slice, Pointer Analysis.

1 Introduction

Slicing reduces the program to a minimal form which still produces the same behavior. The reduced program, called a "slice", is an independent program guaranteed to faithfully represent the original program. The use of pointers presents serious problems for software productivity tools for software understanding, restructuring, and testing. Pointers enable indirect memory accesses through pointer dereferences, as well as indirect procedure calls. The chief difficulty in dealing with an indirect reference through a pointer or an array element reference is that the memory location referenced by such an expression cannot, in general, be determined at compiled time. Further, when such a reference occurs inside a loop, the memory location referenced may vary from one loop iteration to another. The difficulty is compounded if the language used is not strongly-typed and permits integer arithmetic over pointer variables.

V.V Das et al. (Eds.): BAIP 2010, CCIS 70, pp. 613–616, 2010.
© Springer-Verlag Berlin Heidelberg 2010

Such indirect accesses and calls can be disambiguated with pointer analysis. In this paper we evaluate the interprocedural slicing precision for one- dimensional pointer, two-dimensional pointers, pointers and array and dynamic memory allocation.

2 Basic and Proposed Concepts for Finding Slices

i) (Def(dvar)):
If dvar is a variable in a program P. A node u of CDG Gp is said to be a Def(dvar) node if u is definition statement that defines the variable dvar.
ii) (Use(dvar)):
If dvar is a variable in a program P. A node u of CDG Gp is said to be a Use(dvar) node if he statement u uses the value of the variable dvar.
iii) (Defvarset(u)):
Let u be a node in the CFG Gp of a program P. The set DefVarSet(u)={dvar:dvar is a data variable in the program P, and u is a Def(dvar) node}.
iv) (Usevarset(u)):
Let u be a node in the CFG Gp of program P. The set UseVarSet(u)={dvar:dvar is a data variable in the program P, and u is a Use(dvar) node}.
v) (ActiveControlSlice(s)):
Let s be a test node(predicate statement) in, the CDG Gp of a program P and UseVarSet(s)={var1,var2,......vark}.

Before execution of the program P, ActiveControlSlice(s) = Ø. After each execution of the node s in the actual run of the program, ActiveControlSlice(s)= {s}UActiveDataSlice(var1)..U.......ActiveDataSlice(vark).....U...... ActiveControlSlice(t), where t is most recently executed successor node of s in Gp. If s is a loop control node and the present execution of the node s corresponds to exit from loop, then ActiveControl-Slice(s)= Ø.
vi) (ActiveDataSlice(var))
We have distinguished here the variables into 3 categories i.e
(1) data variable denoted as dvar
(2) address variable(pointer) denoted as avar.
Address variable can be 1-Dimensional or multidimensional.
A 1-D pointer (address variable) stores the address of a single data item.
A 2-D pointer (address variable) stores the address of a 1-D pointer(address variable)
A n-D pointer (address variable) stores the address of a (n-1)-D pointer (address variable).
For a 2-D pointer we consider the 2-D pointer as address variable and 1-D pointer as the data variable.
For a n-D pointer we consider the n-D pointer as address variable and (n-1)-D pointer as the data variable.
We assume an address variable (avar) stores the address of a data variable (dvar).
Whenever an avar is assigned with the address of a data variable, the dynamic slices of dereference of address variable (*avar) is same as that of dvar. It need not be stored at a separate place.
Whenever an address variable is updated (If storing the address of an array variable) the *avar must be changed to the corresponding array member.(As the algorithm is

computing dynamic slices the value of array subscript must be known at execution time)

(3) Array variable with index i is denoted as arvar[i] .

(i) (ActiveDataSlice(dvar)):

Let dvar be a data variable in a program P.

Before execution of the program P, ActiveDataSlice(dvar)=$\emptyset$. Let u be a Def(dvar) node, and UseVarSet(u)={dvar1,dvar2,..dvark}. After each execution of the node u in the actual run of the program, ActiveDataSlice(dvar)= {s}UActiveDataSlice(dvar1)U ....UActiveDataSlice(dvark)UActiveControlSlice(t), where t is most recently executed successor node of s in Gp.

(ii) (ActiveDataSlice(avar)):

Let avar be an address variable in a program P.

Before execution of the program P, ActiveDataSlice(avar)= $\emptyset$ and Active-DataSlice(*avar)= $\emptyset$.

Let u be a Def(avar) node, u can be of the following forms

(a) avar = &dvar

(b) avar = &arvar[i]+n where n is an unsigned integer value and i is size of the array

(c) avar = avar1+n where n is an integer value

(d) avar = (type*)malloc(unsigned int)

for case(a)

ActiveDataSlice(avar)={u}U ActiveControlSlice(t)

ActiveDataSlice(*avar)={u}UActiveDataSlice(dvar)U ActiveControlSlice(t)

for case(b)

ActiveDataSlice(avar)={u}UActiveControlSlice(t)

ActiveDataSlice(*avar)={u}UActiveDataSlice(arvar[i+n])UActiveControlSlice(t)

for case(c)

ActiveDataSlice(avar)={u}UActiveDataSlice(avar1)U ActiveControlSlice(t)

ActiveDataSlice(*avar)={u}UActiveDataSlice(*(avar1+n))U ActiveControlSlice(t)

for case(d)

ActiveDataSlice(avar)={u}U ActiveControlSlice(t)

ActiveDataSlice(*avar)= $\emptyset$

vii) (DyanSlice(s,var)):

Let s be a node of the CDG Gp of a program P,and var be a variable in the set De-fVarSet(s) U UseVarSet(s). Before execution of the program P,DyanSlice(s,var)=$\emptyset$. After each execution of the node s in the actual run of the program, the dynamic slice DyanSlice(s,var) w.r.t the slicing criterion <s,var> corresponding to the execution of s is updated as DyanSlice(s,var)=ActiveDataSlice(var)U ActiveControlSlice(t),where t is the most recently executed successor node of s in Gp.

3 Conclusion

We have reported here a new concept of interprocedural slicing for pointers. While debugging, we normally have a concrete testcase that reveals the fault and we wish to analyze the program behavior for that particular testcase. Similarly we can go for pointer analysis with structures, unions, function pointer etc. Dynamic program slices help us for finding the inter statement dependencies for a given testcase. In this paper we have shown that we can find accurate dynamic slices in the presence pointers. The approach outlined provides a uniform framework for handling pointers as well as it can be extended to find slices even if some illegal pointers are also present. Future works can be done to identify client problems such as optimizations or program understanding tools.

References

[1] Burke, M., Carini, P., Choi, J.-D., Hind, M.: Flow-insensitive interprocedural alias analysis in the presence of pointers. In: Proceedings from the 7th Workshop on Languages and Compilers for Parallel Computing. Extended version published as Research Report RC 19546, IBM T. J. Watson Research Center, September 1994 (1995)

[2] Choi, J.-D., Burke, M., Carini, P.: Efficient flow-sensitive interprocedural computation of pointer-induced aliases and side effects. In: 20th Annual ACM SIGACT-SIGPLAN Symposium on the Principles of Programming Languages, January 1993, pp. 232–245 (1993)

[3] Emami, M., Ghiya, R., Hendren, L.J.: Context-sensitive interprocedural points-to analysis in the presence of function pointers. In: SIGPLAN 1994 Conference on Programming Language Design and Implementation, June 1994. SIGPLAN Notices, vol. 29(6), pp. 242–256 (1994)

[4] Choi, J.-D., Cytron, R., Ferrante, J.: Automatic construction of sparse data ow evaluation graphs. In: 18th Annual ACM Symposium on the Principles of Programming Languages, January 1991, pp. 55–66 (1991)

[5] Weiser, M.: Programmers use slices when debugging. Communications of the ACM 25(7), 446–452 (1982)

[6] Weiser, M.: Program slicing. IEEE Transactions on Software Engineering 10(4), 352–357 (1984)

[7] Mund, G.B., Mall, R.: RMall. An efficient interprocedural dynamic slicing method. The Journal of Systems and Software 79, 791–806 (2006)

[8] Horwitz, S., Reps, T., Binkley, D.: Interprocedural slicing using dependence graphs. ACM Transactions on Programming Languages and Systems 12(1), 26–61 (1990)

[9] Korel, B., Laski, J.: Dynamic slicing of computer programs. Journal of Systems and Software 13, 187–195 (1990)

Image Segmentaion and Steganography for Secured Information Transmission

Mamta Juneja and Parvinder Singh Sandhu

Department of Computer Sciences, Rayat and Bahra Institute of Engineering
and Bio-technology, Punjab, India
er_mamta@yahoo.com

Abstract. Image steganography is a covert communication method that uses an image as the cover to hide the truth from potential attackers that some secret message hidden in the image is being transported. In other words, steganography is a collection of cryptographic techniques that provide protection to the secret message by offering it the appearance of an image. In this paper, a specific image based steganography technique for communicating information more securely between two locations is proposed. The author incorporated the idea of secret key and password security features for authentication at both ends in order to achieve high level of security. As a further improvement of security level, the information has been permuted, encoded and then finally embedded on an image to form the stego image. Besides this segmented objects extraction and reassembly of the stego image through normalized cut method has been carried out at the sender side and receiver side respectively in order to prevent distortion of the Stego image during transmission.

Keywords: Steganography, Cover Image, Stego Image, Normalized Cut.

1 The Proposed Model

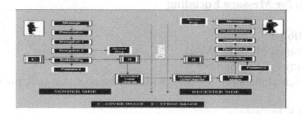

Fig. 1. Proposed secret key steganography model

Solution Methodology: The proposed system(Figure 1) consists of following two windows(Figure 2), one at the SENDER SIDE and the other at the RECEIVER SIDE. The user will be someone who is familiar with the process of information hiding and will have knowledge of steganography systems. Some cryptographic method will be included as an option prior to steganography for generation of the secret key. The user

V.V Das et al. (Eds.): BAIP 2010, CCIS 70, pp. 617–620, 2010.
© Springer-Verlag Berlin Heidelberg 2010

should be able to select a plaintext message from a file, an image to be used as the carrier (cover image) and then use the lsb steganographic method, which will hide the selected message in the selected carrier image and will form the stego image. The user at the receiver side should be able to extract the message from the stego image with the help of different reverse process in sequential manner to un hide the message from the stego image.

Fig. 2. GUI based steganography system

2 Algorithms

In this section, algorithms for different processes used both in the sender side and receiver side are discussed.

2.1 Algorithm for Message Permutation

   I. Input the message.
  II. Every 4th character of the message are append to the trailing part of the original message.
 III. Copied the newly generated message in reverse sequence to form the permuted message.
 IV. At the receiver side, the message is again re-permuted in reverse sequence to get back the original message.

2.2 Algorithm for Message Encoding

2.2.1 Encryption 1
   I. Input Permuted Message (Msg).
  II. Let K be any random number.
 III. Replace each alphabet in the Msg with an alphabet that is K positions down the order.
 IV. Increment K by one.
  V. If K is less than 26 then continue else stop.
 VI. Encoded message (Msg1) is generated.

2.2.2 Encryption 2
   I. Write Msg1 row– by–row in a rectangle of predefined size.
  II. Read Msg1 column-by-column based on some random sequence.
 III. The message thus obtained is the encrypted message (Msg2).

2.3 Extraction of Cuts of the Stego Image

Segmentation and cut extraction of the stego image is done through combining normalized cut and region growing method.

2.3.1 Algorithm for NCUT

   I. Define the weight function.
  II. Prepare the weighted graph G= (V, E) and compute weight matrix using the weight function.
 III. Compute (D-W)x=eDx for eigenvectors with smallest eigen values.
 IV. Use the eigenvector with second smallest value for bi-partitioning the graph.
  V. If the segmented subdivisions are re-partition-able then go to step 2.

2.3.2 Algorithm for Dividing the Regions and Cut Extraction

   I. Prepare the Ncut mask, where only the cuts are defined, from the segmented image.
  II. Mark each region in the mask with a unique number.
 III. Set each pixel in the mask to the region number where it belongs to.
 IV. For each region in the mask, if any pixel in the mask is within the region then keep the same pixel in the original image and set all other pixels in the image to zero.
  V. Repeat step 4 till all the regions are covered.

3 Analysis of the Results

In this work an attempt has been made to increase the level of security of the steganography model by incorporating the idea of secret key, password along with the use of permuted and encoded form of the original message. Further the object extraction of the Stego image, reassembly and feature matching has also been used to increase the level of security. The Levels of security incorporated in the proposed model:-

   1. Permutation of the secret message.
   2. Two level encryption method used in the permuted message.
   3. Embedding encrypted form of the message in image.
   4. Use of password and secret key.
   5. Segmentation, Reassembly of objects and feature matching of the Stego Image.

All the processes both in sender side and receiver side must be executed in proper sequence.

4 Concluding Remarks

The work dealt with the techniques for steganography as related to image science. The results of the test in order to check the security level is quite satisfactory. The security level may be increased combining the approach of text steganography and image steganography. As far as extending this research goes, segmented object extraction method may be substituted with multi-level thresholding and feature based merging to generate optimum objects. The wavelet based image compression over the stego image would be the best candidate to receive further attention.

References

[1] Simmons, G.J.: The Prisoners' Problem and the Subliminal Channel. In: Proceedings of CRYPTO 1983, pp. 51–67. Plenum Press, New York (1984)
[2] Stretching the Limits of Steganography. In: Anderson, R.J. (ed.) IH 1996. LNCS, vol. 1174, pp. 39–48. Springer, Heidelberg (1996)
[3] Kahn, D.: The Codebreakers - the comprehensive history of secret communication from ancient times to the Internet, Scribner, New York (1996)
[4] Shi, J., Malik, J.: Normalized Cuts and Image Segmentation. In: Int. Conf. Computer Vision and Pattern Recognition, San Juan, Puerto Rico (June 1997)
[5] Craver, S.: On Public-key Steganography in the Presence of an Active Warden. In: Aucsmith, D. (ed.) IH 1998. LNCS, vol. 1525, pp. 355–368. Springer, Heidelberg (1998)

Ant System Embedded with Local Search for Solving Facility Layout Problem

Surya Prakash Singh

Dept. of Operations Management and Decision Sciences,
Xavier Institute of Managment Bhubaneswar,
Bhubaneswar 751013, India
surya.singh@gmail.com

Abstract. The goal of this paper is to present an **ant** system embedded with local search named as ANTELS for quadratic assignment problem (QAP) which is a widely accepted mathematical formulation for facility layout problem (FLP). The performance of the proposed ANTELS is compared to other well known heuristics/ Meta-heuristics of FLP as well as other existing ant system. The computational results show that the proposed ANTELS provides promising result.

Keywords: QAP, Facility Layout Problem, Heuristic, Ant System.

1 Introduction

The FLP is a well researched problem. Koopmans and Beckman [1] first modelled FLP as the QAP. The QAP has been shown to be NP-hard (Sahni and Gonzalez [2]). Nowadays, the results achieved by applying the best existing exact algorithms (Branch and Bound) are modest: generally instances of the QAP of sizes larger than 30 cannot be solved optimally in a reasonable time. Thus, the interest lies in the application of heuristic and meta-heuristic methods to solve large QAP instances. In this direction one such approach that has given encouraging results is the ACO method (Maniezzo et al. [3], Gambardella et al. [4], Stutzle and Dorigo [5], Middendorf et al. [6], Dorigo and Blum [7], Solimanpur et al. [8]). Other approaches that can be used to solve FLP can be found from Loiola et al. [9], and Singh and Sharma [10].

This paper proposes an ANTELS based approach for solving the FLPs. The literature relevant to the application of classical Ant system in solving the FLP (modelled as the QAP) is reviewed in section 2. Mathematical formulation of QAP is given in section 3. A detailed description of proposed ANTELS is presented in section 4. Section 5 deals with the computational results and discussions. Lastly, the conclusion of the paper is given in section 6.

2 Past Work

Papers that deal with the past work related to ACO in connection with FLP are considered for brief discussion. Since the first application of ant system to the QAP

V. V Das et al. (Eds.): BAIP 2010, CCIS 70, pp. 621–628, 2010.
© Springer-Verlag Berlin Heidelberg 2010

(Maniezo et al. [3]), several improved ACO applications to this problem have been proposed. All ACO algorithms for QAP first construct solutions, then improve it by a local search, and finally update it. Ant System (AS) is the first ACO algorithm which has been applied and is widely referred as AS-QAP and was coined by dorido et al. [11]. Stutzle and Hoos [12] proposed another improvement over AS-QAP that is widely referred in literature as MMAS-QAP. Taillard and Gamberdella [13] proposed ACO for the QAP and called it Fast Ant System (FANT-QAP). HAS-QAP (Gambardella et al. [4]), although inspired by previous work on ant algorithms, differs rather strongly from the previously presented ACO algorithms. The major difference is that pheromone trails are not used to construct new solutions from scratch but to modify the current solutions. Maniezzo et al. [3] proposed an improved ACO algorithm and called it ANTS which introduces several modifications with respect to AS-QAP. Talbi et al. [14] implemented a parallel ant algorithm for QAP. Solimanpur et al. [8] developed ant colony approach for QAP. They compared the performance of the proposed ant algorithm with other well knwon facility layout algorithm and ant colony based approach for QAP. Demirel and Toksari [15] developed an ACO algorithm to solve QAP where they applied simulated annealing method for local search of solution. Hani et al. [16] applied a hybrid ant colony optimization approach coupled with a guided local search, applied to a facility layout problem which was modelled as a QAP, they compared the proposed approach with some of the best heuristics available in literature for this problem. Experimental results show that the proposed approach performs better for small instances, while its performance is still satisfactory for large instances. The conclusion, after this brief review, is that there have only been a few attempts made to modify ACO for improving the solution quality. In the present work, an attempt is made to deal such issue.

3 Mathematical Formulation

Consider the problem of locating 'n' facilities in 'n' locations. Each location can be assigned to only one facility, and each facility can be assigned to only one location. There is material flow between the different departments and cost (material handling) associated with the unit flow per unit distance. Thus, different layouts have different total material handling costs depending on the relative location of the facilities. F_{ik} is the flow between facilities 'i' and 'k', and D_{jl} is the distance between locations 'j' and 'l'. The FLP has been formulated as follows.

$$\sum_{\substack{i=1 \\ i \neq k}}^{n} \sum_{\substack{j=1 \\ j \neq l}}^{n} \sum_{k=1}^{n} \sum_{l=1}^{n} F_{ik} * D_{jl} * X_{ij} * X_{kl} . \tag{1}$$

$$\sum_{j=1}^{n} X_{ij} = 1 \quad \forall \ i = 1,...,n . \tag{2}$$

$$\sum_{i=1}^{n} X_{ij} = 1 \quad \forall \ j = 1,...,n \ . \tag{3}$$

$$X_{ij} \in \{0,1\}. \tag{4}$$

$X_{ij} = 1$ if facility 'i' is located/ assigned to location 'j' and $X_{ij} = 0$ if facility 'i' is not located/assigned to location 'j'. Where 'n' is the number of facilities in the layout. In equation (1) we seek to minimize the sum of flow multiplied by the distance for all pairs of facilities in a given layout. Equation (2) ensures that each location contains only one facility. Equation (3) ensures that each facility is assigned only one location. The QAP solution is represented as permutation 'π'.

4 Proposed ANTELS

A colony of ants cooperates to find best solutions, which are an emergent property of the ants' coperative interaction. The main traits of artificial ants are: (1) existence of ants as colonies of cooperating individuals, (2) indirect communication of ants by depositing pheromone, (3) using a sequence of local moves for finding the best possible solution, and (4) applying a stochastic decision policy by using local information. This section describes the proposed ANTELS. The development of ANTELS is based on following notations:

K	index for ants
m	number of ants
r,s	indices for random positions in permutation π
π^K	permutation of machines for current ant k
π^*	best permutation
q, α_1, α_2, Q	constants
τ_{ij}	pheromone matrix
τ_{ij}^0	initial pheromone matrix
P	probability value
I^{max}	maximum number of iterations
R	total number of iterations for pheromone updates
S	minimum number of iterations required for diversification
Z	objective value obtained
Z_{best}	best known objective value
$Z(\pi)$	Objective value for a given permutation
$Z(\pi^*)$	Improved objective value

4.1 Initialize Trials and Parameters

In first step of ANTELS, we set parametric values and generate the solution randomly and hence the initial pheromone matrix is initialized. An ant is associated with an integer permutation of $\pi = 1,2,...,n$. The pheromone matrix is initialized as equation (5).

The current solution of each ant is a transformed function of the pheromone matrix. We apply step 2 to further improve the initialized pheromone matrix.

$$\tau_{ij}^0 = \frac{1}{100} \times Z\left(\pi^*\right).$$ (5)

4.2 Local Search

Solution construction and an improvement are based on pheromone trail based modification. Pheromone trail based modification is applied by each ant to its own permutation πK. It starts with πK and produces $\tilde{\pi}K$. The pheromone trail based modification works on following two steps.

Step 1: Indices selection
In the first step, randomly select two different indices say 'r' and 's', $1 \le r, s \le n$ and r $\neq$ s. 'r' is chosen randomly between 1 and n i.e. $r \in [1, n]$. Then another index 's' is chosen with a probability 'q' proportional to the values contained in the pheromone trial as per equation (6).

$$q = \frac{\tau^K_{r\pi_s} + \tau^K_{s\pi_r}}{\sum_{j \neq r} (\tau^K_{r\pi_j} + \tau^K_{j\pi_r})}.$$ (6)

Step 2: Swapping
In second step, swapping of two randomly selected pheromone trial at step first is performed. The swapping is done in the following ways. Generate a random number 'R1' and a random integer 'Rn', $R1 \in [0, 1]$ and $Rn \in [1, n]$. Let the probability $q = 0.9$ and the Rn is considered as r^{th} position. If R1 < q, then apply Rule 1, Else rule 2.

Rule 1: Here, we select a random position of 's' such that $s \in [1, n]$ and $r \neq s$. If the corresponding $\left(\tau^K_{r\pi_s} + \tau^K_{s\pi_r}\right)$ value is maximum, then swap r^{th} and s^{th} position.

Rule 2: Generate a random number 'R2' such that $R2 \in [0,1]$. Find the value of $\dfrac{\tau^K_{r\pi_s} + \tau^K_{s\pi_r}}{\sum_{j \neq r}(\tau_{r\pi_j} + \tau_{j\pi_r})}$, where K is the current ant. Initialize a probability value $P = 0$.

Update P by P + $\dfrac{\tau^K_{r\pi_s} + \tau^K_{s\pi_r}}{\sum_{j \neq r}(\tau_{r\pi_j} + \tau_{j\pi_r})}$ for each generation of R2. If R2<P, then swap rth

position and sth position, Else not. In this study, $\dfrac{n}{3}$ numbers of swapping exchanges are applied. Local search is based on 2-way exchange process. It is designed to examine $\dfrac{n(n-1)}{2}$ number of swapping. For problem size n = 4, number of pairs of facilities will be swapped resulting in 10 different permutations. For an example, if a permutation of $\begin{bmatrix} 3 & 2 & 4 & 1 \end{bmatrix}$ is a considered, then six swap has to perform to examine the neighborhood of size 10. In the above permutation, facility 5 is located at position 1 and facility 3 is located at position 2 and so on. The possible swaps are (3,2), (3,4), (3,1), (2,4), (2,1), and (4,1). If any improvement is obtained in a local search, then the improved solution is stored as the best solution.

4.3 Intensification

Intensification is to explore the neighborhood of good solutions more completely. For $I^{max} = n/3$ number of times the intensification mechanism is active, if improvement is produced. The intensification is active while at least one ant succeeds in improving its solution during iteration.

4.4 Updating Pheromone Matrix

Pheromone trail matrix is updated in order to simulate the evaporation process. First the pheromone matrix values are reduced with the equation (7), where $0 < \alpha_1 < 1$. Secondly, the pheromone matrix values are reinforced with the best solution found. The pheromone matrix values are reinforced with the equation (8). In all computational experiments the values of parameter α_1 and α_2 was set as 0.1.

$$\tau_{ij} = (1-\alpha_1)\tau_{ij}. \tag{7}$$

$$\tau_{i\pi_i^*} = \tau_{i\pi_i^*} + \alpha_2/Z(\pi^*). \tag{8}$$

4.5 Diversification

When the best solution obtained is unable to improve during $S = n/2$ number of iterations, the diversification task is executed. It will force the ANTELS to start from new set of solutions with new random permutations. The working methodology of ANTELS is based on the hybridization of ant colonies with greedy local search. In this work an attempt is made to hybridize an ant system with a population pool of good permutations of twice the problem size i.e. n and to explore the 2-way exchange mechanism of greedy local search along with the initial population pool size i.e. m.

5 Computational Results and Discussions

Tables 1 show the results of randomly selected instances taken from QAPLIB with four different values of 'm'. Tables shows an improvement when the population size was set as $m = 2n$. In this section we also compared the performance of ANTELS with other existing approaches viz. tabu search from Taillard [17], reactive tabu search (RTS) from Battiti and Tecchiolli [18], simulated annealing from Connolly [19], the HAS-QAP cited from Gambardella et al. [8], and hybrid ant system from Talbi et al. [14] in a same computational time. Results are shown in table 2.

Table 1. Solution quality of ANTELS for randomly selected instances from QAIPLIB

S.No.	Instance	n	BKS	M			
				n		$2n$	
				OFV	%Dev.	OFV	%Dev.
1	Bur26a	26	5426670	5426670	0	5426670	0
2	Bur26b	26	3817852	3817852	0	3817852	0
3	Bur26c	26	5426795	5426795	0	5426795	0
4	Bur26d	26	3821225	3821225	0	3821225	0
5	Bur26e	26	5386879	5386879	0	5386879	0
6	Bur26f	26	3782044	3782044	0	3782044	0
7	Bur26g	26	10117172	10117172	0	10117172	0
8	Bur26h	26	7098658	7098658	0	7098658	0
9	Chr25a	25	3796	3866	1.84	3796	0
10	Kra30a	30	88900	90090	1.34	88900	0
11	Kra30b	30	91420	91490	0.08	91490	0
12	Nug20	20	2570	2570	0	2570	0
13	Nug30	30	6124	6136	0.20	6128	0.07
14	Sko42	42	15812	15812	0	15812	0
15	Sko49	49	23386	23418	0.14	23398	0.038
16	Sko56	56	34458	34478	0.06	34458	0
17	Sko64	64	48498	48556	0.12	48498	0
18	Sko72	72	66256	66346	0.14	66278	0.03
19	Sko81	81	90998	91154	0.17	91048	0.048
20	Sko90	90	115534	115612	0.07	115562	0.02
21	Tai40a	40	3139370	3199422	1.91	3199332	0.442
22	Tai40b	40	637250948	637250948	0	637250948	0
23	Tai50a	50	4938796	5064316	2.54	5008926	1.42
24	Tai50b	50	458821517	459739160	0.20	458821517	0
25	Tai60a	60	7205962	7378436	2.39	7377002	2.37
26	Tai60b	60	608215054	608215054	0	608352112	0.02
27	Tai80a	80	13527910	13851227	2.39	13687539	1.18
28	Tai80b	80	818415043	818415043	0	818415043	0

Table 2. Comparison of ANTELS with other known ANT based approaches. Figure shows % deviation from the best known solution (BKS).

S.No.	Instance	BKS	TT	RTS	SA	HAS-QAP	ANTabu	ANTELS
1	Bur26a	5426670	0.0004	---	0.141	0	0	0
2	Bur26b	3817852	0.0032	---	0.182	0	0.017	0
3	Bur26c	5426795	0.0004	---	0.074	0	0	0
4	Bur26d	3821225	0.0015	---	0.005	0	0	0
5	Bur26e	5386879	0	---	0.123	0	0	0
6	Bur26f	3782044	0.0007	---	0.157	0	0	0
7	Bur26g	10117172	0.0003	---	0.168	0	0	0
8	Bur26h	7098658	0.0027	---	0.126	0	0	0
9	Chr25a	3796	6.9652	9.889	12.49	3.082	0.895	0
10	Kra30a	88900	0.47	2.008	1.465	0.629	0.267	0
11	Kra30b	91420	0.059	0.712	0.194	0.071	0	0.08

Table. 2. (*continued*)

S.No.	Instance	BKS	TT	RTS	SA	HAS-QAP	ANTabu	ANTELS
12	Nug20	2570	0	0.91	0.07	0	0	0
13	Nug30	6124	0.032	0.872	0.121	0.098	0	0.07
14	Sko42	15812	0.039	1.116	0.114	0.076	0	0
15	Sko49	23386	0.062	0.978	0.133	0.141	0.038	0.038
16	Sko56	34458	0.08	1.08	0.11	0.1	0.002	0.002
17	Sko64	48498	0.064	0.861	0.095	0.129	0.001	0
18	Sko72	66256	0.148	0.948	0.178	0.227	0.074	0.03
19	Sko81	90998	0.098	0.88	0.206	0.144	0.048	0.048
20	Sko90	115534	0.169	0.748	0.227	0.231	0.105	0.02
21	Tai40a	3139370	1.01	0.623	1.307	1.989	0.442	0.442
22	Tai40b	637250948	0.208	---	4.56	0	0.464	0
23	Tai50a	4938796	1.145	0.834	1.539	2.8	0.781	1.42
24	Tai50b	458821517	0.2943	---	0.81	0.191	0.253	0
25	Tai60a	7205962	1.27	0.831	1.395	3.07	0.919	1.08
26	Tai60b	608215054	0.3904	---	2.137	1.048	0.275	0.02
27	Tai80a	13527910	0.854	0.467	0.995	2.689	0.663	1.18
28	Tai80b	818415043	1.435	---	1.438	0.667	0.718	0

6 Conclusions

A new approach of ant system embedded with 2-way local search approach named ANTELS is proposed. ANTELS is tested on a large set of benchmark instances taken from QAPLIB. Paper also compares ANTELS with previous ant systems for the QAP (HAS-QAP and ANTabu). Results show an increase in performance compared to other metaheuristics. It can be concluded that the proposed ANTELS might lead to improved methodology for other combinatorial optimization problem as well.

References

1. Koopmans, T.C., Beckmann, M.: Assignment Problems and the location of Economic Activities. Econometric 25, 53–76 (1957)
2. Sahni, S., Gonzalez, T.: P-complete approximation problem. Journal of Associated Computing Machinery 23(3), 555–565 (1976)
3. Maniezzo, V., Dorigo, M., Colorini, A.: The Ant System Applied to the Quadratic Assignment Problem. Technical Report IRIDIA/94-28, Universite Libre de Bruxelles, Belgium (1998)
4. Gambardella, L.M., Tailard, E.D., Dorigo, M.: Ant Colonies for the Quadratic Assignment Problem. Technical Report IDSIA-4-97, IDSIA, Lugano, Switzerland (1997)
5. Stutzle, T., Dorigo, M.: ACO algorithm for the quadratic assignment problem. In: Corne, D., Dorigo, M., Glover, F. (eds.) New ideas in Optimization. McGraw-Hill, New York (1999)
6. Middendorf, M., Reischle, F., Schmeck, H.: Multi colony ant algorithm. Journal of Heuristics 8(3), 305–320 (2002)

7. Dorigo, M., Blum, C.: Ant colony optimization theory: a survey. Theoretical Computational Science 344, 243–278 (2005)
8. Solimanpur, M., Vrat, P., Shankar, R.: Ant colony optimization algorithm to the inter-cell layout problem in cellular manufacturing. European Journal of Operational Research 157, 592–606 (2005)
9. Loiola, E.M., Abreu, N.M.M., Boarenture-Netto, P.O., Hahn, P., Querido, T.: An analytical survey for the Quadratic assignment problem. European Journal of Operational Research (2007) (in press)
10. Singh, S.P., Sharma, R.R.K.: A review on different approaches to facility layout problems. International Journal of Advanced Manufacturing System 30, 425–433 (2006)
11. Dorido, M., Maniezzo, V., Colorni, A.: The Ant System: Optimization by a Colony of Cooperating Agents. IEEE Transaction on Systems, Man, and Cybernetics–Part B 26(1), 29–41 (1996)
12. Stutzle, T., Hoos, H.: MAX_MIN ant system. Future Generation Computer Systems 16(8), 889–914 (1997)
13. Taillard, E.D., Gambardella, L.: Adaptive memories for the qudratic assigment problem. Technical Report, IDSIA, Lugano, Switzerland, pp. 87–97 (1997)
14. Talbi, E.G., Roux, O., Fonlupt, C., Robillard, D.: Parallel Ant Colonies for the quadratic assignment problem. Future Generation Computer System 17, 441–449 (2001)
15. Demirel, N.C., Toksari, M.D.: Optimization of the quadratic assignment problem using an ant colony algorithm. Applied Mathematics and Computation 183(1), 427–43 (2006)
16. Hani, Y., Amodeo, L., Yalaoui, F., Chen, H.: Ant colony optimization for solving an industrial layout problem. European Journal of Operational Research 183(2), 633–642 (2007)
17. Taillard, E.D.: Robust Tabu Search for the Quadratic Assignment Problem. Parallel Computing 17, 443–455 (1991)
18. Battiti, R., Tecchiolli, G.: The reactive tabu search. ORSA Journal of Computing 6, 126–140 (1994)
19. Connolly, D.T.: An improved annealing scheme for the QAP. European Journal of Operational Research 46, 93–100 (1990)

Strategic Initiatives and Automated Decision Support with ERP System Environment

Asim Gopal Barman[1], Ranjan Bhattacharya[1], and Sudip Kumar Deb[2]

[1] Department of Production Engineering, Jadavpur University,
Kolkata – 700 032, West Bengal, India
asimgopal.research@gmail.com, agbarman_ju@yahoo.co.in
[2] Department of Mechanical Engineering, Assam Engineering College,
Guawahati – 781 013, Assam, India

Abstract. Enterprise Resource Planning (ERP) systems are presently offering some attractive features to incorporate some sorts of decision support capabilities. Still ERP system itself cannot make decisions but it keeps the data and records of organizational transactions in a very systematic and logical manner. The operational level managers and middle level managers for regular organizational transactions and analysis and reporting mainly use ERP systems. We argue that automated decision supports and strategic initiatives can be made with the present ERP system environment. This paper proposes a conceptual model of Automated Decision Support System with ERP (ADSSERP) system environment. The model can encompass some major decision making problems and strategic initiatives having mid term and long term decisional scopes based on a present ERP system for an enterprise without affecting the architecture of existing ERP system.

Keywords: ERP, Database, Automated Decision Support, Strategic Initiatives.

1 Introduction

Purpose of generic ERP system is to keep organization-wide transactional data and records & make available whenever necessary. ERP system consists of business function modules that amalgamate all standard business processes and information throughout the organization. ERP systems allow information to flow across the organization and provide improved control and management of the organization's resources. But management and implementation of ERP systems have tended to concentrate on their transactional and record keeping aspects, rather than on their decision-support capabilities. Speed is the most important competitive elements in many modern business environments. With this in mind, many organizations are adopting Enterprise Resource Planning (ERP) Systems. Business Intelligence (BI), Artificial Intelligence (AI) etc. are finding place in ERP systems just of late to help make better decisions. Operational level & middle level managers are the key users of present ERP systems of an ERP-controlled organization. "Sense-and-respond" strategy directs to offer more even for top-level managers with ERP systems. Various vendors (e.g. – SAP, Oracle, Microsoft etc.) of ERP systems are trying to introduce some new

V. V Das et al. (Eds.): BAIP 2010, CCIS 70, pp. 629–635, 2010.
© Springer-Verlag Berlin Heidelberg 2010

features of intelligence with their new versions. Emerging demand for additional decision making capabilities with ERP system environment is very much palpable in recent literature also. Most of the very large organizations all over the world have already adopted ERP, and increasingly small- and medium-sized enterprises (SMEs) too are finding it cost effective and a competitive necessity to follow suit [1]. They typically support the different departments and functions in the organization by using a single database that collects and stores data in real time [2]. An ERP system does not operate using functions as in old systems, but it adopts processes, which are activities that involve several modules [3]. They do not, however, help answer the fundamental questions of what should be made, where, when, and for whom [4]. ERP adopters currently perceive a moderate level of decision-support characteristics [5]. The need for further innovation on planning and management system have been recognized [6]. The demand for more effective decision making tools has seen the move away from Decision Support Systems to more complex solutions [7]. One strategic enterprise resource management (SERM) has also been conceptualized [8].

In this scenario we still argue that (1) automated decision support (ADS) is possible and is an emerging need with ERP system environment, (2) scopes of further improvements lie mainly in tactical and strategic level, (3) strategic initiatives and decision making process must be faster with ERP system environment, (4) some tactical or strategic decisions are not required everyday to make, but decision supports must be ready to make any decision at any time, (5) Artificial Intelligence (AI), Business Intelligence (BI), Operations Research (OR) algorithms and optimizing heuristics must find more space to accrue real benefits out of these with ERP system environment and (6) existing ERP systems should accommodate the proposed model of ADSSERP without any major modifications.

2   Lineage of ERP System Evolution and Fitting the Proposed Model

Material Requirement Planning (MRP) systems were developed in the 1970s which involved mainly planning the product or parts requirements according to Bill of Materials (BOM) and the Master Production Schedule (MPS). In the 1980's the concept of

Table 1. Evolving ERP systems and their main components and features

Time Frame	Evolving Systems	Main components & Features
1960s	MRP	BOM +MPS + Inventory Records
1970s	Closed Loop MRP	MRP + Capacity Planning + Feedback
1980s	MRP-II	Closed Loop MRP + Shop Floor Management + Distribution Management Activities (Sales)
1990s	ERP	MRP-II + Financial Management + Quality Management + Maintenance Management + HRM
2000s	Extended ERP	ERP + SCM + CRM + e-business functionalities + Reporting & Analytical tools
2010s	ADSSERP (proposed)	Extended ERP + ADS + Strategic Management Features

Manufacturing Resources Planning (MRP-II) evolved. Table 1 shows the various components and features of evolving ERP systems.

3 The Proposed Model – Automated Decision Support System with Enterprise Resources Planning (ADSSERP) System

The basic components of any ERP system are the ERP application platforms (e.g. – Microsoft Dynamics, SAP AG, Oracle Applications etc.) and a dedicated database (e.g. – SQL Server, DB2, Oracle etc.) at the core. Sometimes Workflow Management System (WfMS) is also integrated with ERP system as per requirement [9].

3.1 The Model

The access to the database equipped with the decision making component must serve the aim of Automated Decision Making without connecting the ERP application platform into action. We describe the proposed model in simple form in Fig. 2.

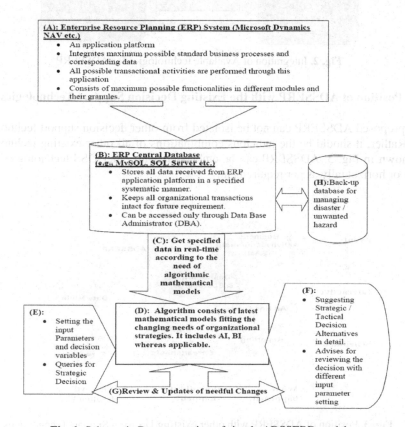

Fig. 1. Schematic Representation of simple ADSSERP model

3.2 Available Technologies

We consider, for ready reference, Sturts Framework [10] of JAVA based technologies for implementing the D, E, F and G parts of our ADSSERP (in Fig. 1). Model (D), View (F) and Controller (E) (MVC 2 implementation) model of struts framework can be best suited for the final implementation of ADSSERP model. WfMS can be of use for final execution of the total system [9] as shown in Fig. 2.

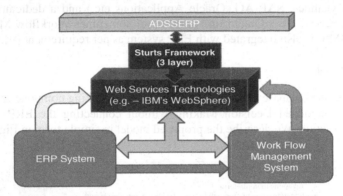

Fig. 2. Integration of Available technologies for ADSSERP

3.3 Position of ADSSERP with the Existing Decision Support Technologies

The proposed ADSSERP can not be isolated from other decision support technologies [7]. Rather, it should be the judicious combinations of all other existing technologies as shown in Fig. 3. ADSSERP can be embedded with other DSS technologies vertically or horizontally as per requirement.

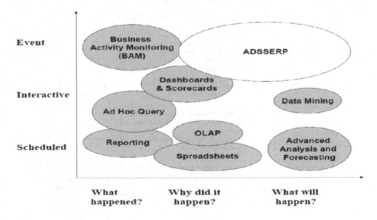

Fig. 3. Position of ADSSERP with other existing Decision Support Technologies

4 Possible Decisions with the ADSSERP

4.1 Strategic Planning and Decisions

The overall modifications in business strategy includes defining (i) the market and market areas in which the enterprise competes. ADSS suggests avoiding the managers' performance measurement only on return on investment (ROI). (ii) the level of investment.(iii) the means of allocating resources to and integrating of separate business units. (iv) the locating and relocating manufacturing facilities and distribution centers. (v) capacity growth planning (vi) the Operations Strategy.

4.2 Management of Technology

Many companies are currently under pressure to be more responsive to shifts in demand and to pressures for faster new product introductions and modifications [12]. The management of technology encompasses the management of research, product and process development, and manufacturing engineering [11]. Which product line or services are to deploy where and when is a great concern for a technology dependant enterprise. Demand pattern for a particular line of product or services can be one of the main inputs in making these sorts of decisions.

4.3 Decisions due to Economic Unrest

Changes in economic policies of government and fluctuations in market badly affect all organizations. Changes in taxation structures, various monetary policies, commercial agreements, political decisions, ups and downs in stock exchanges, time value of money and many more aspects related to economic issues must be factored into the decision making processes in an ADSSERP. Balanced Score Card (BSC) can be considered to be one of the most effective tools for ADSSERP in this respect [13].

5 Benefits of ADSSERP

The expected benefits of ADSSERP are: (i) It delivers strategic decision in real-time. Strategic planning process gets boost for making quick decision and may be a great help for top and middle level managers to some extent of organization. (ii) It can be made a robust decision making system with fixing the ever-changing needs of the organization and responding to external environment in real time. (iii) It is believed to put the vision and strategy into action. It insists middle level managers and operational level managers of organization to contribute inputs for making decisions at the top level. (iv) Management of technology concept and related planning and decisions are expected to be a great boost for marketing department. (V) The ADS engine has been connected with the ERP database in the proposed model without disturbing the existing configuration of ERP system. This approach can be exercised without any assistance from vendor of the ERP system. Only the database administrator (DBA) and business intelligence (BI) expert are able to make ADSSERP. (vi) It can easily be improved by exploiting AI, BI, and OR applications [14] to stay ahead of peers.

6 Concluding Remarks

The main challenge for a successful ADSSERP is to acquire data from database by matching the requirement of the decision making engine (D) as shown in Figure 1. A strong knowledge of central database structure is a very essential prerequisite for properly capturing the data. It is acknowledged that the decisions made by DSS might not be applicable directly. The decision alternatives need to be reviewed before implementing those. However decision making process can be pushed forward some steps ahead to make it a final. The future scopes of research lie in this respect with a great demand worldwide. A robust ADSS under ERP system environment through the application of AI and BI is great challenge in future. No doubt, ADSSERP is very comprehensive for organizational decision making but a true comprehensive package with ERP system environment is future demand.

References

1. Klaus, H., Rosemann, M., Gable, G.G.: What is ERP? Information Systems Frontiers 2(2), 141–162 (2000)
2. Davenport, T.H.: Mission Critical: Realizing the Promise of Enterprise systems. Harvard Business School Press, Boston (2000)
3. Quiescenti, M., Bruccoleri, M., La Commare, U., Noto La Diega, S., Perrone, G.: Business process-oriented design of Enterprise Resource Planning (ERP) systems for small and medium enterprises. International Journal of Production Research 44(18-19), 3797–3811 (2006)
4. Simchi-Levi, D., Kaminsky, P., Simchi-Levi, E., Shankar, R.: Designing and Managing the Supply Chain: Concepts, Strategies, and Case Studies, 3rd edn., pp. 435–436. Tata McGraw-Hill Publishing Company Limited, New York (2008)
5. Holsapple, C.W., Sena, M.P.: The Decision –Support Characteristics of ERP Systems. International Journal of Human-Computer Interaction 16(1), 101–123 (2003)
6. Bullinger, H.-J., Schweizer, W.: Intelligent production – competition strategies for producing enterprises. International Journal of Production Research 44(18-19), 3575–3584 (2006)
7. Hawking, P., Foster, S., Stein, A.: Investing Business intelligence (BI) Solution Adoption in Australian Companies: An ERP Perspective. In: 17th Australian Conference on Information Systems (ACIS). Adelaide, Proceedings (Association for Information Systems), December 6-8 (2006)
8. Oztemel, E., Polat, T.K.: Ageneral framework for SERM (strategic enterprise resource management). Production Planning & Control 18(1), 64–71 (2007)
9. Cardoso, J., Bostrom, R.P., Sheth, A.: Workflow management Systems and ERP systems: Differences, Commonalities, and Applications. Information Technology and Management 5, 319–338 (2004)
10. IBM developerWorks: Resources for Java developers,
    http://www.ibm.com/developerworks/ibm/library/j-struts
    (accessed on 12/12/2009)
11. Gattiker, T.F.: Enterprise resource planning (ERP) systems and the manufacturing – marketing interface: an information-processing theory view. International Journal of Production Research 45(13), 2895–2917 (2007)

12. Erickson, T.J., Magee, J.F., Roussel, P.A., Saad, k.N.: Managing Technology as a Business Strategy. Engineering Management Review, 34–38 (Spring 1991)
13. Kaplan, R.S., Norton, D.P.: Using the Balanced Scorecard as Strategic management System. Harvard Business Review (January-February 1996)
14. Gayilis, S.P., Tatsiopoulos, I.P.: Design of an IT-driven decision support system for vehicle routing and scheduling. European Journal of Operational Research 152, 382–398 (2004)

A Case Study of Strategic Design Management

Fumihiko Isada

Business School, Nagoya University of Commerce and Business, 1-20-1,
Nishiki, Naka, Nagoya, 460-0003, Japan
isada@nucba.ac.jp

Abstract. Many manufacturers want to improve their product design. However, most manufacturers cannot readily produce a good design, even though they recognize the importance of design. The case of IKEA was considered as an example of how the design bureau in a company should be managed to bring about a good design. It can be summarized as a) concept (a policy is advocated, and a concept is produced), b) Environment (an environment that brings about concept innovation is supplied), c) Risk-Taking (decisions are made that involve risk).

Keywords: design management, strategic decision making, case study.

1 Introduction

Many manufactures want to improve their product design. However, most companies cannot readily produce a good design, even though they recognize the importance of design. IKEA, the target company of this research, is a Swedish company that departs from this trend, successfully producing products with high-quality design characteristics. This paper focuses on how the design section of the company should be managed so as to produce a good design given prevailing conditions.

IKEA started as a business in Sweden in 1943, and to date has opened 267 stores in 24 countries around the world, mainly on the strength of its furniture sales. The main factor that has been accepted by many consumers is good design and pricing of the products (Jungbluth (2006)). From the consumer's viewpoint, IKEA supplies fashionable goods and furniture, at a good price (North Europe style editorial department). In this paper, I discuss why IKEA succeeds in terms of design and price.

2 Analysis Framework and Review of Previous Works

In this paper, three important points are stressed: Concept, Environment, and Risk taking. In other words, the management comes up with the concept for a good design, so the environment is given, and it is necessary to take a risk to complete the task.

2.1 Concepts

The concept is important as the first step in producing designs and is a basis for evaluating, judging, and gauging the design. According to Kametani (2007), the design

V. V Das et al. (Eds.): BAIP 2010, CCIS 70, pp. 636–640, 2010.

is merely a series of expressions starting with the concept. Toda (2007) divides the stages of a design into concept, design plan, and brushing up. All designs are built from a concept, which becomes a basis of the design plan.

The management side creates a concept as a policy for the section in charge of design, and the direction of the design must be clear. Furthermore, according to Yoshida (2007), the steps in the development process of the design is sorted as form, interaction, new experience, and the philosophy (culture) of the company.

The form of the design process tends to be affected by company philosophy (culture), so that a design (or brand) is a reflection of the company. The characteristics of the company can often be seen in its design concepts. Kametani (2007) stated that the purpose of designs in business is to successfully convey a message to the customer. For example, Sony is seen as an advanced electronics company, and Mazda reflects its status as a sporty car company in its product design.

2.2 Environment

Thus, what should be done in design management is to provide an environment conducive to good design. The environment controls whether a good design can be substantially realized. One important aspect of environment concerns the building of an innovative working environment.

With ongoing threats of commoditization, good design is one of the ways to ensure survival (Vogel. M. C, Cagan. J, & Boatwright. P (2005)). Growth through innovation is the only way to win in a global marketplace where suppliers are chosen only in terms of low cost, since it can change the value proposition toward the selection of the best or the most strategic product (Kelly, et al. (2005)).

Abernathy and Clark (1985) classified innovations into four categories, which are regular, revolutionary, architectural, and niche creation. Innovations in the field of furniture are generally classified into regular innovation. However, IKEA has sometimes developed a new market, which is classified into niche creation. In other words, it may be said that a designer can create concept innovation in this field.

Kelly et al. (2005) describe important reasons for having a process for innovation. Innovation is not merely something that can produce an attractive new product or services. Rather, it describes the creative process itself: the stimulation provided the collaboration through which designs are realized, and the wonderful energy it brings to the progress of an organization. Kelly et al. (2005) explain that a design section will play a role by providing uniformity in concept innovation, in his book, The Faces of Innovation. Effectiveness comes about through a mix of people, all experts in various fields, including the person in charge of the design. Sugawara (2007) stated that it is better to develop a design with several people than with one.

However, the team is not merely the sum of its combined parts. An innovative environment is built by giving the person in charge discretion, and a reasonable evaluation method is proposed here. Discretion involves authority, including management of people and budget. The budget need not be large, but should be sufficient to cover overhead and allow designers to carry out their creative activity. Research is necessary for creativity. It is necessary to constantly pursue new materials and colors, mechanism designs, fashion trends, and ergonomics. Without these inputs, the output of the design process will dry up.

An environment that fosters collaboration and allows advice to be given freely is important. Ed Catmull (2008) states that the decision making and communication structure should be distinguished. Reasonable personnel evaluation from the management side is indispensable for producing such a climate. Production does not come merely from desk work, since innovation cannot be driven by hard evaluations. In design management, it is important to provide an environment in which concept innovation can easily occur. We need an evaluation method that allows the exercising of discretion. In this way, designers will actively work towards concept innovation, and collaboration will be fostered.

2.3 Risk Taking

Ed Catmull (2008), a cofounder of Pixar Animation Studios, stated: Anyone is apt to avoid a risk. Managers will thus be encouraged to copy their peers, which are why imitation is so rampant in the movie industry, and so many similar movies are released each year. This is also why so few truly superior works exist.

When a design is a new product line to attract the market's attention, rather than a minor update of an existing line, risk-taking is done during decision-making for the design. It may be said that decision-making is the primary element in design management in a company. There may be times when decision making is not possible for the risk taking. As development, sales, and support departments spring up, the originality of the design may be lost. Upper management may want to avoid risk to maintain sales numbers, forcing the designer to make changes in the design to hedge the risk. Then how should the risk in the design be reduced?

In some companies, such as Apple, risk-taking for a design is performed by the top-down. However, bets can be hedged in other ways, such as by limiting the production quantity of the product. According to the BearingPoint (2006), risk reduction is to limit the amount of surfaced loss and/or to decrease the frequency of occurrence of the loss phenomenon. Thus, risk can be reduced by the control activity and the portfolio effect. One of the solutions to reduce the scale of loss without changing the design is to reducing the production quantity of products. According to Arnault. B (Wetlaufer, S. (2001), some brands of LVMH decide the production quantity beforehand. In other words, additional quantities are not produced even if a product succeeds, and this strict regimentation reduces the risk of new product design for the brand. Another method could be to begin with a small lot, and then increase it if the design is highly evaluated.

3 Case Study

3.1 Strategic Design of IKEA

The success of IKEA is based on both design and price. The furniture field in which IKEA is involved is one in which it is easy to bring about a design-oriented product. Also, IKEA realizes low prices from the planning stage, the production stage, and every each stage of distribution.

3.1.1 Design That Is Premised on Low Prices

To result in low price, it is important that the product is designed with low price from the first. At IKEA, the price is designed before the product is designed. The selling price and the cost price are decided first, and then a design that can realize these prices is chosen later. This flow allows IKEA to arrive at the best result without having to perform cost-price and design-related trade-offs, playing a great role in realizing the strategy of IKEA.

3.1.2 Decreasing Physical Distribution Costs through the Flat Pack and Customer-Driven in-Store Purchasing

A signature characteristic of the distribution of IKEA products is the flat pack. It was around 1956 that IKEA first introduced the flat pack. It can be assumed that the flat pack played an important role in IKEA's pricing strategy from an early stage in the company's history. There are two major merits to the flat pack.

First, flat pack allows the physical distribution costs from the manufacturer to the store to be kept low. Beyond promoting efficiency of inventory control in the warehouse, the self-service concept is enabled in the store and transportation of the product becomes easy. Each of the two points above plays an important factor in supporting the low price of the IKEA product.

Furthermore, one of the key corporate identities of IKEA is the concept of taking the flat pack all the way to the customer with a self-service shopping method, which, incidentally, provided a distinctive shopping experience that helped IKEA to penetrate the market. The IKEA development process assumes a flat pack throughout the product design stage, including a package technician whose primary function is to enable a flat pack. When the design is such that a flat pack is impossible, then the product is not manufactured. It may be said that the one of the symbols signaling the thorough price focus of IKEA is the flat pack.

3.2 The Design Management of IKEA

3.2.1 Concept

In IKEA, two points form the concept, Being Sweden furniture, and Cost first. Product development for IKEA is performed in Scandinavia. IKEA recognizes that it is connected to its location and adopts a public identity in other countries that associates itself with product development in Sweden. In IKEA, the process that begins with setting of the cost is a clear concept throughout the design and development stage. When a designer designs to these two points, it is clear as an evaluation criterion. Furthermore, it is a point that strengthens IKEA's brand in the minds of consumers. A meaningful design is only created for a company after such a concept exists. Therefore, it is important that the management side creates and publicizes a definite concept.

3.2.2 Environment

A product developer, a product editor, and a designer are all involved in product development at IKEA. Furthermore, the cooperation with the business side to realize low price is addressed positively, and it may be said that the environment fosters the creation of innovative products. In the development of products for IKEA, the most innovative environment exists in the process where the prototype is produced in a production plant. Price is controlled thorough collaboration all the way until the product is produced, and continued improvement of functionality and design characteristics also takes place. This process is described in the IKEA way to design superior furniture, and the fact that IKEA attaches much importance to this process can be seen.

3.2.3 Risk-Taking

It may be said that the risk of the design is reduced by the broad product portfolio of IKEA. Because a product is merely one of 9,500 products, risk-taking in the design is enabled. It may be said that the encouragement of risk-taking in the design is enabled by the construction of a good product portfolio.

4 Conclusion

The case of IKEA was considered as an example of how the design bureau in a company should be managed to bring about a good design. It can be summarized as follows:

a) Concept (a policy is advocated, and a concept is produced)
b) Environment (an environment that brings about concept innovation is supplied)
c) Risk-Taking (decisions are made that involve risk)

I believe that the design management technique based on the success of IKEA can be utilized to other companies. The discovery of problems may be made easier by returning to these three points when managing the design process.

References

1. Catmull, E.: How Pixer Fosteres Collective Creativity. Harvard Business Review, 65–72 (September 2008)
2. Jungbluth, R.: Die 11 Geheimnisse des IKEA-Erfolgs. Campus Verlag GnbH, Frankfurt (2006)
3. Kametani, T.: Design strategy to lead innovation. Think! (22), 33–37 (Summer 2007)
4. Kelly, T., Littman, J.: The Ten Faces of Innovation. Broadway Business (2005)
5. Sugawara, A.: Design intellectual power in five keyword. Think! (22), 24–30 (Summer 2007)
6. Vogel, M.C., Cagan, J., Boatwright, P.: The Design of Things to Come: How Ordinary People Create Extraordinary Products. Wharton School Publishing (2005)
7. Wetlaufer, S.: The Perfect Paradox of Star Brands: An Interview with Bwenard Arnault of LVMH. Harverd Business Review 79(9), 117–123 (2001)
8. Yoshida, M.: Samsung electronic design strategy. Hitotsubashi Business Review, AUT 55(2), 36–46 (2007)

The Effects of Mannequins on Consumers' Perception and Shopping Attitude

N. Anitha and C. Selvaraj

Department Of Management Studies,
Velammal College of management and computer studies, Ambattur Red hills road,
Chennai – 600066, Tamilnadu
anithamba@rediffmail.com, selvaraj1971@gmail.com

Abstract. This research focuses on the effects of mannequins on consumer's perception and shopping attitude in the context of retail clothing sales. Mannequins impact customers by giving them a look to aspire to. Mannequins are great for showing just how certain garments can be worn. A research was conducted based upon the mannequin displays in the retail stores. According to the results, consumers seem to have a more positive perception of color display, design, appearance. Consumers perceiving the displays positively and feels that it is creating a new sense and life style by providing complete visualization.

Keywords: Mannequins, Perception, Shopping attitude, Life style, Clothing retail, visualization.

1 Introduction

In recent years the contemporary retailing revolution has made tremendous changes in the shoppers buying pattern. Today's consumers are very choosy while making purchase and swifts from an un organized retailing formats to organized retailing formats due to the influence of various factors in addition to the retailers innovative strategies adopted from western markets. The cross cultural strategies are attracting the consumers too in terms of shelves arrangement, in store music and internal and external ambience, convenient mode of payment and self service facilities .communication instruments have an effects on consumers shopping attitude in a competitive market place. In particularly garment sector visibility plays a vital role in consumers purchase decision. In the modern scenario mannequins add more value to the product visibility.

Mannequin displays give a wide variety of information about a store as well as product. Mannequins will make the features of the product more visible. Even if they would have never looked twice at the clothes on the rack, seeing them on the mannequin almost forces them to consider it. It offers an overall image by displaying the fashion and seasonal goods and a store can show that it is contemporary.

By showing the eye catching displays that have a little to do with its merchandise offering, a store can attract pedestrians' attraction. Therefore consumers may often obtain information about a product category and a retail clothing store through the

V. V Das et al. (Eds.): BAIP 2010, CCIS 70, pp. 641–647, 2010.

mannequin displays. Although mannequin displays have a very important effect on consumers, there has not been significant empirical evidence regarding the effect of displays on consumers shopping attitudes.

The mannequins are powerful strategically used tool by the retailers to win in merchandising. It is not the retailers' intelligence but it is the direction of retailers intelligence that determine the pace of retailing progress and retailers intelligence can be directed if only they know how to display its features.

Displays have great power; one right direction and display at the right time can change the psychological perception of the consumers and thus change the direction of their life style. This study examines the effects of mannequins in consumer's perception and shopping attitude.

2 Literature Review

A number of previous studies have supported the idea that the store image attributes play an important role in affecting consumers shopping attitude and patronage behaviors. In these studies a link has been found between the consumers' perception of mannequins and shopping attitudes such as intention to buy the product.

A large body of literature suggests that consumers likelihood of using a particular informational input to make a decision depends on its accessibility and perception, certain types of information culled from mannequin displays and to make a store entry decision. More specifically, mannequin displays can act as a more direct point of purchase promotional device by stimulating the purchase probability of the displayed mannequins.

Our brains are geared to make snap decisions and create first impressions. This gives us the ability to quickly judge levels of danger, distinguish likes and dislikes, as well as be subjective about something's significance or insignificance to us. Using this information in a retail setting is very beneficial. The window display is a prime example of where this psychological structure can be put to good use. When a customer approaches a retail store, the first thing they notice is the window display. The window displays should give the customer a lot of information. They should also have a lot of subtle cues to buy as well. (Mary Wagner January 2005). Merchandise display, according to Zentes et al. (2007: 209), is a term frequently used in the context of in-store marketing. It refers to the way products are presented in a retail outlet. While this expression has been used with a focus on merchandise display (e.g. the choice of fixtures to be used and the method of product presentation), it relates to overall store design, store layout and other facets of the store environment.

McIntosh (2007) illustrates that merchandising is more than simply the arrangement of products on the shelf. It is an integral component of the business image. It should be considered when designing the retail mix. Opinions suggest that merchandising and display are frivolous extra expenses for the small business owner who is just starting up. The implication is that expenses such as marketing, rent, inventory, utilities and staffing are serious expenses, while merchandising and display are frills. Merchandising and display are an important part of the retail environment, and should have a reasonable budget allocated even for a retailer operating on a shoestring. In today's competitive retail environment, a retailer cannot afford to consider merchandising as a frill. Everyone is competing for the customers' rand. There are more choices out there for consumers than ever before. By rotating merchandise and changing displays, the customers feel that there is always something new for them to see or experience. Including merchandising in the retailing plan and budget makes sense. It can make the difference between selling a product and having it sit on the shelf.

Appealing displays by retailers can lead shoppers to sacrifice the time and effort required to go further to more distant stores. This technique suggests that consumers shop at the stores where they can maximize their satisfaction (i.e. efficiency), considering both retail attributes and shopping costs. Pleasant shopping atmosphere positively affects the shopping time and the money that customers spend in a store as well as the emotion of shopping (Kim and Jin, 2001: 236).

Kerfoot *et al.* (2003: 143) maintain that initial findings, suggest that liking of display does not totally determine purchase, but does make it four times more likely. Visual stimulation and communication have also been considered important aspects of retailing by practitioners. Merchandise display is, therefore, concerned with both how the product and/or brand is visually communicated to the customer. The themes that linked most strongly to purchase intention are: merchandise colours, presentation style, awareness of fixtures, path finding, sensory qualities of materials and lighting. The importance of attaining appropriate merchandise display has meant that within the retail environment, numerous methods have been used to display merchandise and communicate product and retailer brand. This diversity in merchandise display methods has also stemmed from the vast array of goods and services that are sold by retailers.

Favourable merchandise display entices consumers to browse through the store and results in purchasing. This pattern is supported in previous research studies with results showing that merchandise display results in increasing purchasing patterns. The themes that linked most strongly to purchase intention are: merchandise colours, presentation style, awareness of fixtures, path finding, sensory qualities of materials and lighting (Kerfoot *et al.*, 2003: 143).

3 Research Methodology

3.1 Research Objectives

- To determine the influence of mannequins over the consumers' purchase decision making.
- To identify the likeliness of the consumers on mannequin displays.
- To identify the motivation created by the mannequins on consumers.

3.2 Methodology

A Questionnaire was developed to measure the consumers' perception on mannequins and attitude.   These were measured by using the rating scale and validated. Convenient sampling method was used for data collection and 150 samples were identified for data collection in different locations of Chennai City.

4 Findings from the Study

- The research findings show that 35 percent of respondents are post-graduate, 27 percent are graduates and 38 percent are qualified in other way. It shows that 62 percent of respondents are highly literate and qualified people.
- Majority of the respondents are in the age group of 35 years and above. It shows that definitely they must have very good purchasing power and can able to take a decision rationally.
- 54 percent of respondents are having monthly income of Rs.10000-15000. 43 percent of respondents are having more than Rs.20000 as their monthly income.
- Consumers are having different types of purchase habit on garments. 65 percent of respondents are having the habit of purchase during any festival or season. It shows that respondents are having some reason to purchase the garments.   Only 16 percent of respondents are purchasing garments frequently.
- Majority (59 percent) of the respondents prefer general type of merchandise retail outlets for purchase of garments.   38 percent of respondents prefer branded retail outlet and 32 percent prefer exclusive retail outlets for purchase of garments.
- Variety is the major element influencing the consumer preference towards selecting a retail outlet. Display is least factor attracting the consumer to select a retail outlet. May be Indian consumers are giving much importance to value for concept, because the price is second major element in selection of retail outlet.
- Majority of the respondents have accepted that the mannequins are influencing their purchase decision in garment selection.
- 57 percent of respondents have said that mannequins are inducing them to have a glance over a product and 38 percent have said it is forcing them to purchase.
- Majority of the respondents are observed that sarees and pant & shirts mostly displaed throught the mannequins. Next to sarees and shirts, the consumers observed that inner wears, hair dresses and Tie.
- 54 percent of respondents accepted that mannequin provides complete visualisation of the product. Around 8 percent disareed with that. 23 percent of respondents are strongly agreed that mannequin provides complete visualisation of the garments.
- Majority of respondents felt that the through mannequins could able to understand the new style and fashion. It shows that mannequins plays vital role to exhibit new trend in the narket.
- The mannequin display can able to provide to the consumers an insight whether the product is suitable them or not. Majority of respondents agreed that mannequin display would provide a visualisation whether the product is suitable for them or not.
- Consumers perceives that mannequins are inducing a new sense and lifestlye on them. It shows that people can able to undrstand and perceive a new sense and lifestyle through mannequins.

- More than 50 percent of respondents are accepted   that they are preferring retailoutlet based on its display. It shows that now a days visual merchandising plays an improtant role to attract the customers.
- Mannequin display provides a complete information over colour, design and appearnce of the product. It would reduce the time taken by the consumer to over view and even for trail of that product.
- Majority of the respondents are perceived that mannequins display are saving time by visualisation or otherwise people will go for trail.
- Respondents perceived that mannequins are restricting the consumer choice or alternatives. Because they may restrict their choice or fashion only with what is displayed on the mannequins.
- Most of the respondents do not have opinion over the mannequin display of inner wears. Around 20 percent of respondents agreed that inner wear displays are irritatting them. May be country like india consumer have of traditional oriented attitude and behaviour.
- More than 30 percent of respondents agreed that manneqin display are better than trail of the garments. It would reduce considerable time and protect the consumer privacy.

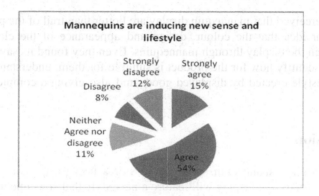

Fig. 1. Inducement of Mannequins on new sense and lifestyle

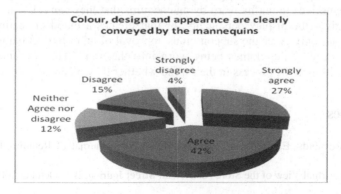

Fig. 2. Colour, design and appearance conveyed by the mannequins

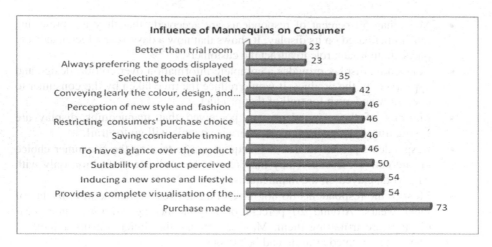

Fig. 3. Influence of Mannequins on consumers

5 Discussion

Consumers perceived that mannequin display are better than trail of the product. They have the clear idea that the colour, design and appearance of the cloth is clearly convey through the display through mannequins. Even they found its saves their time, could able to identify how for the product is suitable for them, understanding the new sense and lifestyle created by displayed goods and also giving a complete picture of the products.

6 Conclusion

People like to see a mannequin showcase in stores because it gives them fashion ideas. A lot of times, the display will feature a new style that someone hasn't thought of. Displaying clothes on a mannequin won't automatically make sales for you. You have to be creative enough to give your mannequin displays feeling. People can envision themselves in outfits worn by mannequins that they can relate to. Develop a scene that gives the display personality, or that creates a mood or feeling. Using a mannequin not only gives the subconscious approval of other human beings, but also forces the image of the clothes being worn into the mind. The consumer instantly starts going through the process in their mind whether they planned to or not.

References

Arnold, J., Reynolds, E.: Hedonic Shopping Motivations. Journal of Retailing 11(2), 77–79 (2003)

Byron, E.: A Virtual View of the Store Aisle. Wall Street Journal, B.1 (October 2007)

Darley, W.K., Lim, J.S.: Effects of store image and attitude toward secondhand stores on shopping frequency and distance traveled. International Journal of Retail & Distribution Management 27(8), 311–31 (1999)

Kent, T.: Creative space: design and the retail environment. International Journal of Retail & Distribution Management 35(9), 734–745 (2007)

Koo, D.M.: Inter-relationships among store images, store satisfaction, and store loyalty among Korea discount retail patrons. Asia Pacific Journal of Marketing and Logistics 15(4), 42–71 (2003)

Newman, A.J., Foxall, G.R.: In-store customer behaviour in the fashion sector: Some emerging methodological and theoretical directions. International Journal of Retail & Distribution Management 31(11/12), 591–601 (2003)

Paulins, A.V., Geistfeld, L.V.: The effect of consumer perceptions of store attributes on apparel store preference. Journal of Fashion Marketing and Management 7(4), 371–385 (2003)

Knowledge Transfer: Do Instructor Characteristics Matter?

Jaya Chitranshi and Shailja Agarwal

Jaipuria Institute of Management, Vineet Khand, Gomti Nagar, Lucknow, India
jaya@jiml.ac.in
shailja@jiml.ac.in

Abstract. Research studies the transfer of knowledge with a very technical perspective while studies also establish various dimensions that make a teacher liked by students or that render a teacher effective (for e.g. Barnett, 2003; Bettinger and Long, 2005) but whether or not do such dimensions affect the knowledge receptivity of students is highly debatable. This study is an attempt to address this contentious issue. The study has revealed that there are many instructor characteristics that may lead to an instructor's overall effectiveness, students' liking for the instructor and their positive evaluation of the instructor but they may not necessarily impact the knowledge receptivity of students.

Keywords: Knowledge transfer, knowledge receptivity, instructor characteristics, classroom.

1 Introduction

The process of acquiring of knowledge is possible primarily through education. Over the years, there has been a great deal of scholarly interest in the transfer of knowledge in higher education system (Akintunde, 2007; Kourik and Maher, 2008) The focus has been on academicians who often participate in the knowledge transfer process, as in a classroom setting, the teacher is the source of knowledge and in control of teaching material and learning pace.

Research studies the transfer of knowledge with a very technical perspective. An immense focus has been on on-line transfer of knowledge (Roberts J., 2000; Tsai, 2001), rhetoric knowledge (Julie, 2004), explicit and tacit knowledge (Polanyi, 1998; Tsoukas, 1996) and so on. On the other hand, studies establish various dimensions that make a teacher liked by students or that render a teacher effective (for e.g. Barnett, 2003; Bettinger and Long, 2005) but whether or not do such dimensions affect the knowledge receptivity of students is highly debatable. This study is an attempt to address this contentious issue.

2 Literature Review

2.1 Various Perspectives on Knowledge

Knowledge, by positivists is viewed as an objective existence that is man-made, static, modal, and permanent and whose value does not vary with time. It can be easily

V. V Das et al. (Eds.): BAIP 2010, CCIS 70, pp. 648–655, 2010.

conveyed, infinitely used, and accumulated. Based on this perspective, knowledge has become an experience or information that can be shared. As to the meaning of "knowledge transfer", the focus is placed on the acquisition (capture/recording) of internal knowledge, sharing (shared use), transmission (delivery), and application (Grant, 1996; Hansen., 1999; Sabherwal & Becerra-Fernandez, 2003). A professor's ability to facilitate the knowledge of transfer is not limited to what he or she communicates verbally (Carr, Davies and Lavin, 2009, 2009). Research points out that elements like attire, attitude etc contribute significantly in influencing the students (Carr *et al*, 2009; Morris, Gorham, Cohen, Stanley and Huffman, 1996). Are these factors significant enough to impact upon the receptivity of knowledge of a student? Research does not yet provide a clear answer to this. Studies indicate that educators must not only pay attention to the content of their courses but must also consider how the image that they convey influences those around them (Scott, O'Neal and Cheatham, 1994). However, little work has been done to understand if this image affects knowledge receptivity in any way amongst the taught.

There is little argument that the single most important factor in the transfer of knowledge is knowledge itself. Understandably, both hard and soft skills of the teacher and the taught are involved in the successful transfer of both- tacit and explicit knowledge. While research is replete with studies on factors that may influence a student (Faranda and Clarke, 2004; Myers, 2004; Barnett, 2003), there appears to be a wide gap in trying to assess if characteristics of that instructor, who is here the channel of knowledge transfer, play any role in receptivity of knowledge intended to be transferred. That the instructor characteristics have been assessed as influencing students liking for the instructor (Tootoonchi, Lyons, Hagen, 2002) and evaluation of the course (Centra, 2004; Marsh and Roche, 1997), is a well established fact but there is little evidence to ascertain whether these characteristics have any positive or negative impact on the process of knowledge transfer.

2.2 Factors Leading to Students Liking of an Instructor

A vast literature argues that teaching is a multi-dimensional process (Boex, 2000) comprising a number of separable dimensions or instructor attributes (Centra, 2004; Arreola 1995; Marsh and Roche, 1997). There is a broad consensus within the education literature which recognizes that an instructor's overall effectiveness depends on a combination of these instructor attributes, such as clarity of the instructor's lectures, the course's organization, the degree to which the instructor motivates the students and the instructor's success in building an interpersonal rapport with the students. A number of studies define and measure such instructional dimensions (Centra, 2004; Arreola 1995; Marsh and Roche, 1997; Schmelkin, Spencer and Gellman, 1997).

3   Research Questions

The following research questions are raised:

1. Do instructor characteristics have some role in receptivity of knowledge?

2. If yes, which categories of instructor characteristics influence receptivity of knowledge?

4 Method

4.1 Participants and Procedure

Based on the various factors discussed in the review of the literature, a survey questionnaire was prepared with the objective of finding which instructor-based factors, if any, influenced the knowledge receptivity of post graduate students of management colleges of India. Six hundred eighty seven adult students enrolled in a Post Graduate Diploma in Business Administration program of eight management institutes of India participated in the study. Out of these, four hundred forty filled questionnaires were rendered usable. Students in the chosen classes were asked, through several instructor and instruction-related questions, for their opinion on how the professor's characteristics, behavior, style and attitude impacted their receptivity of the knowledge the professor tried to transfer. All the respondents were Indians and full-time business management students in the final year of their course. The average age of the respondents was 22 years with 27 years as the highest and 21 years as the lowest age. 55% of the respondents were males. 84.4% students had 0-1 year of experience while 11.4% had 1.1- 2 years of experience prior to joining the programme.

The survey instrument was based on a five-point Likert scale, with 1 as 'strongly disagree' and 5 as 'strongly agree' and consisted of 34 statements. Apart from this, there were demographic questions on gender, academic background. Age, nationality and work experience.

5 Results and Discussion

The study was undertaken to determine the variables which may influence the knowledge receptivity of students and thus affect the process of knowledge transfer. Based on the analysis of data, it can be concluded that instructor characteristics do have a significant impact on the knowledge receptivity of students. This was verified by 88 % of respondents saying that instructor characteristics did effect their knowledge receptivity.

The frequencies in percentage were calculated to determine which instructor characteristic significantly influenced the learning experience of the students. Out of all the instructor characteristics, the receptivity of knowledge is greatly influenced by the following characteristics outlined in the sample taken for the study:

93.1 % students agreed to the role of good communication skills of the instructor in the receptivity of knowledge. Witcher, Onwuvgbuzie, Collins, Filer & Wiedmaier (2003)and Tootoonchi, Lyons & Hagen (2002) suggested 'communication' as an important characteristic for effective college teaching and learning by students. Ramasamy, Goh & Yeung (2006) also advocated that 'communication' is one of the most important channels of knowledge transfer. 84.1 % students agreed to the polite behavior of the instructor as influencing receptivity of knowledge. Hamacheck (1985) found that the best teachers possessed a warm and polite attitude. 97.9% students favored good command over subject as a characteristic of the instructor influencing the receptivity of knowledge. Witcher, Onwuvgbuzie, Collins, Filer & Wiedmaier (2003) suggested that 'knowledgeable about the subject matter' is an important characteristic for effective college teaching. Personal guidance and counseling provided by the instructor, as a characteristic for the receptivity of knowledge, was chosen by 86.4% students. Seriousness and positive attitude of the instructor towards the course, as a characteristic affecting receptivity of knowledge, was selected by 88.6% students. Administrative authority and clout of the instructor, as a characteristic affecting receptivity of knowledge, was chosen by 84.1 % respondents. Provision of a lot of scope for class-room participation, as a characteristic affecting receptivity of knowledge, was selected by 88.6% students. Nemanich, Banks & Vera (2009) found that social richness of the class-room learning environment enhances course receptivity. Tootoonchi, Lyons & Hagen (2002) suggested 'class-room discussion' as an important characteristic for effective college teaching and learning by students. Use of effective tests and exercises, as a characteristic affecting receptivity of knowledge, was agreed to by 84.1% students. Good class control, as a characteristic affecting receptivity of knowledge, was chosen by 88.1% students. Fluent classroom delivery, as a characteristic affecting receptivity of knowledge, was selected by 81.8% students. Tootoonchi, Lyons & Hagen (2002) suggested that 'class-room discussion' is an important characteristic for effective college teaching. Provision for easy access to the course material, as a characteristic for receptivity of knowledge, was agreed to by 88.8% students.

To further study the categories in which instructor characteristics important in knowledge receptivity would fall, Factor Analysis was used on the data-set for 440 respondents for 32 specific instructor characteristics traced out in literature survey.

The Kaiser- Meyer- Olkin Measure of Sampling Adequacy value (.39) indicates that the data-set is adequate.

Bartlett's Test of Sphericity indicates existence of significant sphericity and cohesiveness and thus finds the data-set fit for factorization.

The total variance accounted for by each of the six components explains nearly 58% of the variability in the original 32 variables. So we can reduce the original data set by using these six components (Eigen values greater than 1).

The rotated factor matrix, the study shows six factors (which represent the six characteristics of Receptivity of Knowledge) derived from 32 variables (which represent various Instructor Characteristics in determining Receptivity of Knowledge).

Factor 1 can be labeled as   **Competence and Quality of Teaching**
Factor 2 can be labeled as   **Instructor's Attitude**
Factor 3 can be labeled as   **General Personality**
Factor 4 can be labeled as   **Personal Liking**
Factor 5 can be labeled as   **Class-room Behaviour**
Factor 6 can be labeled as   **Authority and Clout**

The results indicate that the instructor characteristics, which influence the receptivity of knowledge, can be classified into the six broad factors given above.

Regression Factor Scores show that independent variables, "Competence and Quality of Teaching" (.43) and "Instructor's attitude" (.39), are found to be significantly correlated with the dependent variable, "Receptivity of Knowledge".

Discussion

The present study was an attempt to focus on the concept of 'knowledge transfer' among management students. For effective 'knowledge transfer' characteristics of the instructor have an important role to play. Since all the instructor characteristics could not be taken up for this piece of research, a few based on the basis of literature-review done, were taken up for in-depth analysis to outline and evaluate their role in influencing the 'receptivity of knowledge' among management students. The study, therefore, focused on the various 'instructor characteristics' which influence 'receptivity of knowledge'.

'Receptivity of Knowledge' is found being influenced by a number of instructor characteristics.

Seriousness and attitude towards the course, class room interaction, use of effective tests and exercises, fluent class-room delivery are some of the instructor characteristics which are related with the instructor's teaching style. Encouraging and motivating attitude, personal guidance and counseling provided and friendliness with the students are the characteristics which are related with the behavioural aspects of the instructor. Good communication skills of the instructor and good class control are skills of the instructor.

With the help of Principal Component Analysis, all the 32 instructor characteristics are grouped into six components. Considering the item falling into a particular cohort, component-labelling is done.The six components are labeled as Competence and Quality Teaching, Attitude, Impression, Personal Liking, Class-room Behaviour and Authority and Clout.

Factor1, 'Competence' incorporates the instructor-chracteristics related with command over subject, seniors' feedback, age and high maturity level while 'Quality ofTeaching' incorporates strict marking in exams, personal guidance and counselling provided, lot of use of visual aids, use of effective tests and exercises, class-room delivery, objective and fair assessment and fluent class-room delivery.

Factor 2, 'Instructor's Attitude' includes items about instructor's seriousness towards the course, encouragement and motivation provided, personal rapport, politeness, marking leniently in exams and the instructor's young age.

Factor 3, 'General Personality', incorporates items about industrial exposure of the instructor, the formal way of dressing and well-dressing, high academic qualifications of the instructor, pre-existing impressions and smart bearing of the instructor.

Factor 4, 'Personal Liking', incorporates items on physical appearance, instructor's complexionand gender.

Factor 5, 'Class-room Behaviour', incorporates items about good communication skills, providing easy access to course material, promoting class-room interaction and good class control.

Factor 6, 'Authority and Clout', incorporates items on the influence and authority the instructor possesses.

The correlations between 'instructor–characteristics' and 'receptivity of knowledge' show a significant correlation existing between 'Competence and Quality Teaching' and 'Receptivity of Knowledge' (.43) and the ' Instructor's Attitude' and

'Receptivity of Knowledge' (.39). Competence, quality of teaching and instructor's attitude are observed to be having a significant impact on receptivity of knowledge.

6 Conclusion

The study has revealed that there are many instructor characteristics that may lead to an instructor's overall effectiveness, students' liking for the instructor and their positive evaluation of the instructor but they may not necessarily impact the knowledge receptivity of students. In fact, certain characteristics like formal attire, instructor being a female, physical appearance of the instructor, smart bearing of the instructor etc have emerged to be having a very insignificant impact on the knowledge receptivity of students which otherwise have a high significance on the students' overall impressions of the instructor.

Based on the analysis and subsequent discussion, it can now be concluded that:

1. 'Instructor characteristics' do influence 'Receptivity of Knowledge'.
2. The 'Instructor Characteristics' lie in the following categories or factors:

- Knowledge and Quality of Teaching
- Instructor's Attitude
- Impression
- Personal Liking
- Class-room Behavior
- Authority and Clout

References

Akintunde, O.A.: Education and Knowledge Transfer: A Priority for the Future. International Food & Agribusiness Management Review 10(4), 129–136 (2007)

Arreola, R.: Developing a comprehensive faculty evaluation system. Anker Publishing Company, Inc., Bolton (1995)

Barnett, J.E.: Do Instructor-Provided On-Line Notes Facilitate Student Learning. Paper presented at the Annual Meeting of the American Educational Research Association, Chicago, IL (2003)

Bettinger, E.P., Long, B.T.: Do Faculty Serve as Role Models? The Impact of Instructor Gender on Female Students. In: AEA Papers and proceedings, pp. 152–157 (2005)

Boex, L.F.J.: Journal of Economic Education (2000)

Carr, D., Davies, T., Lavin, A.: The effect of business faculty attire on student perceptions of the quality of instruction and program quality (2009),
http://findarticles.com/p/articles/mi_m0FCR/is_1_43/
ai_n31438318/

Centra, J.A.: Will Teachers Receive Higher Student Evaluations by Giving Higher Grades and Less Course Work? Research in Higher Education 44(5), 495–518 (2004)

Faranda, W.T., Clarke III, I.: Student Observations of Outstanding Teaching: Implications for Marketing Educators. Journal of Marketing Education 26(3), 271–281 (2004)

Grant, R.M.: Toward a Knowledge-Based Theory of the Firm. Strategic Management Journal 17, 109–122 (1996)

Hamachek, D.E.: Humanistic-Cognitive Applications to Teaching and Learning: Theoretical-Philosophical Bases. In: Annual Convention of the American Psychological Association, 93rd, Los Angeles, CA (1985)

Hansen, M.T.: The Search-Transfer Problem: The Role of Weak Ties in Sharing Knowledge across Organization Subunits. Administrative Science Quarterly 44 (1999)

Julie, D.F.: Knowledge transfer across disciplines: Tracking rhetorical strategies from a technical communication classroom to an engineering classroom. IEEE Transactions on Professional Communication 47(4), 301–315 (2004)

Kourik, J.L., Maher, P.E.: Does Practice Reflect Theory? An Exploratory Study of a Successful Knowledge Management System. World Academy of Science, Engineering and Technology 45, 5–12 (2008)

Marsh, H.W., Roche, L.A.: Making students' evaluations of teaching effectiveness effective: The critical issues of validity, bias, and utility. American Psychologist 52(1), 1187–1197 (2008)

Morris, T.L., Gorham, J., Cohen, S.H., Huffman, D.: Fashion in the classroom: Effects of attire on student perceptions of instructors in college classes. Communication Education 45(2), 135–148 (2008)

Myers, S.A.: The Relationship between Perceived Instructor Credibility and College Student In-Class and Out-of-Class Communication. Communication Reports 17 (2004)

Nemanich, L., Banks, M., Vera, D.: Enhancing Knowledge Transfer in Classroom Versus Online Settings: The Interplay Among Instructor, Student, Content, and Context. Decision Sciences Journal of Innovative Education 7(1), 123–148 (2009)

Polanyi, M.: The tacit dimension. In: Prusak, L. (ed.) Knowledge in Organization. Butterworth Heineman, Boston (1998)

Roberts, J.: From Know-how to Show-how? Questioning the Role of Information and Communication Technologies in Knowledge Transfer. Technology Analysis and Strategic Management 12(4), 429–443 (2000)

Sabherwal, R., Becerra-Fernandez: An Empirical Study of the Effect of Knowledge Management Processes at Individual, Group, and Organizational Levels. Decision Sciences 34(2), 225–260 (2003)

Sadker, M.: Gender Equity in the Classroom: The Unfinished Agenda. College Board Review 170, 14–21 (1994)

Schmelkin, L.P., Spencer, K.J., Gellman, E.S.: Faculty Perspectives on Course and Teacher Evaluations. Research in Higher Education 38(5), 575–592 (1997)

Scott, J.L., O'Neal, J.W., Carole, C.: Nonverbal communication and image building: Their importance to the business professor. Journal of Management Education 18(1), 105–110 (1994)

Tootoonchi, A., Lyons, P., Hagen, A.: MBA students' perceptions of effective teaching methodologies and instructor characteristics. International Journal of Commerce and Management 12(1), 79–93 (2002)

Tsai, W.: Knowledge Transfer in Intra-organizational Networks: Effects of Network Position and Absorptive Capacity on Business Unit Innovation and Performance. The Academy of Management Journal 44(5), 996–1004 (2001)

Tsoukas, H.: The firm as a distributed knowledge system; a constructionist approach. Strategic Management Journal 17, 11–25 (1996)

Witcher, A.E., Onwuegbuzie, A.J., Collins, K.M.T., Filer, J., Wiedmaier, C.: Students' perceptions of characteristics of effective college teachers. Paper presented at the annual meeting of the Mid-South Educational Research Association, Biloxi, MS (2003)

Wood, D.R.: Professional Learning Communities: Teachers, Knowledge, and Knowing. Theory into Practice 46(4), 281–290 (2007)

Strong and Weak Formulations of Single Stage Uncapacitated Warehouse Location Problem

Priyanka Verma and R.R.K. Sharma

Department of Industrial and Management Engineering,
Indian Institute of Technology, Kanpur, 208016, India
{pmodi,rrks}@iitk.ac.in

Abstract. Some researchers have not used the 'strong' formulations for single and multistage warehouse location problems despite it being well known earlier. In this paper we give 'strong' and 'weak' formulations of the single stage uncapacitated warehouse location problem (SSUWLP) by borrowing from the literature on capacitated version of the problem. The constraints borrowed are 'weak' constraints, demand side 'strong' constraints and the supply side 'strong' constraints. We give four different formulations of the SSUWLP and also empirical results for the relative strengths of their linear programming (LP) relaxations.

Keywords: Single Stage Uncapacitated Warehouse Location Problem, Strong and weak formulations, Linear Programming Relaxations.

1 Introduction and Literature Review

Single stage uncapacitated warehouse location problem (SSUWLP) arise when the distances between plants and markets are large and it becomes necessary to route the suppliers through warehouses. The set of potential warehouses are known, with each having an associated fixed cost with it. The problem is to choose a sufficient number of warehouses such that the sum total of fixed location cost and transportation costs is minimized. In addition to the assumption of unlimited capacity of warehouses, we assume a single commodity for distribution.

In this work location of facility at single stage is considered. This is attempted by [1] and [2] and very interestingly they have given completely different formulations. Reference [3] also attempted a variant of this problem and has used quantity flow variables as x_{ijk} indicating flow from plant 'i' to warehouse 'j' to market 'k'; as against [2]. In this work we have used the formulation style of [4] to formulate SSUWLP. It is also shown by [1],[2] and [3] that they have used 'weak' formulation of the problem instead of strong formulation despite of it being well known earlier [5],[6]. Reference [7] gave weak and variety of strong formulations based on different 'strong' and 'capacity' constraints for the single stage capacitated warehouse location problem (SSCWLP); and empirically verified its efficacy. We provide the 'strong' formulations and then determine their superiority over the 'weak' formulations of SSUWLP.

V. V Das et al. (Eds.): BAIP 2010, CCIS 70, pp. 656–659, 2010.
© Springer-Verlag Berlin Heidelberg 2010

2 Mathematical Formulation of SSUWLP

We use the index 'i' ($i = 1,...,$ I), 'j' ($j = 1,...,$ J) and 'k' ($k = 1,...,$ K) to represent respectively the sets of plants, warehouses and markets. To meet the absolute demand D_k at the kth market, i^{th} plant supplies S_i amount of commodity. We represent supply from i^{th} plant and demand at the kth market as a fraction of the total market demand, respectively as $s_i (= S_i / \sum_k D_k)$ and $d_k (= D_k / \sum_k D_k)$. Fixed cost of locating an uncapacitated warehouse at site 'j' is represented by f_j. The transportation cost of supplying $\sum_k D_k$ quantity of goods from plant 'i' to warehouse 'j' and from warehouse 'j' to market 'k' is represented respectively as csw_{ij} and cwm_{jk}. The decisions variables similarly are given by XSW_{ij} and XWM_{jk}, which represent respectively the quantity of goods from plant 'i' to warehouse 'j' and from warehouse 'j' to market 'k'. These two variables are also used in the model as a fraction of the total market demand, respectively as $xsw_{ij} (= XSW_{ij} / \sum_k D_k)$ and $xwm_{jk} (= XWM_{jk} / \sum_k D_k)$. In addition, we use a location binary variable y_j, which is 1 if warehouse is located at point 'j', 0 otherwise. Based on the parameters and decision variables defined here, we present the mathematical formulation of SSUWLP below.

$$Min \sum_{ij} csw_{ij} xsw_{ij} + \sum_{jk} cwm_{jk} xwm_{jk} + \sum_j f_j y_j \qquad (1)$$

Subject to:

$$\sum_j xsw_{ij} \leq s_i \qquad \forall i \qquad (2)$$

$$\sum_j xwm_{jk} \geq d_k \qquad \forall k \qquad (3)$$

$$y_j \geq \sum_k xwm_{jk} \qquad \forall j \qquad (4)$$

$$y_j d_k \geq xwm_{jk} \qquad \forall j,k \qquad (5)$$

$$y_j s_i \geq xsw_{ij} \qquad \forall i,j \qquad (6)$$

$$xsw_{ij} \geq 0 \ \forall i,j \qquad xwm_{jk} \geq 0 \ \forall j,k \qquad (7)$$

$$y_j \in \{0,1\} \qquad \forall j \qquad (8)$$

$$\sum_i xsw_{ij} = \sum_k xwm_{jk} \qquad \forall j \qquad (9)$$

3 Strong and Weak Formulations and Their Relaxations

Here we propose four formulation SSUWLP_R1 – SSUWLP_R4, comprising of constraints given above.

SSUWLP_R1: (1), subject to (2)-(4), (7), (8), (9); weak formulation of SSUWLP [7].
SSUWLP_R2: (1), subject to (2), (3), (5), (7), (8), (9); 'demand side' strong formulation [7].
SSUWLP_R3: (1), subject to (2), (3), (6), (7), (8), (9); 'supply side' strong formulation [7].
SSUWLP_R4: (1), subject to (2), (3), (5), (6), (7), (8), (9); strong formulation involving demand and supply based constraints, (5) and (6).

In above four formulations if (8) is relaxed to relax the integrality of y_j ($0 \le y_j \le 1$,) we get respective linear programming (LP) relaxations, referred to as LP_SSUWLP_R1 – LP_ SSUWLP_R4.

4 Experimental Setup

Random problems of sizes: 10x10x10, 15x15x15, 20x20x20, 25x25x25 and 30x30x30 (plants x warehouses x markets) are created for SSUWLP. The four formulations and their LP relaxations are solved using LINGO on a 512 MB RAM, 2.4 GHz PC. Four categories of problems are considered, $\sum_i s_i = m$ (m = 1, 1.5, 2, 6) depicts the scenario when level of 'over supply from the plant' is in abundance of 'm' times the demand. For each category of problem size we created 50 problems (total 1000 problems). Fixed cost is varied as U (1, 1000) and all transportation costs are varied as U (1, 100).

5 Results and Discussion

t-test is carried for comparisons of the bounds obtained by LP relaxations; and comparison of the bound obtained by the best LP relaxation and optimal (SSUWLP_R1 to SSUWLP_R4). For each SSUWLP_Rm-SSUWLP_Rn (m, n = 1, 2, 3, 4), 't' calculated is for difference between objectives of (LP_SSUWLP_Rm/LP_SSUWLP_Rn) and 1.

All 't' values in table-1 and 2 are compared with the standard t values at different significant levels as given above. From the results, it is clear that LP_SSUWLP_R4 is giving the best bound while LP_SSUWLP_R1 is giving the weakest bound. Also LP_SSUWLP_R2 provides better bounds than LP_SSUWLP_R3.

Table 1. t test for bounds given by LP_SSUWLP_R3–LP_SSUWLP_R1 and LP_SSUWLP_R2–LP_SSUWLP_R3

Problem Size	Problem Category to compare LP_SSUWLP_R3–LP_SSUWLP_R1				Problem Category to compare LP_SSUWLP_R2–LP_SSUWLP_R3			
	A	B	C	D	A	B	C	D
10x10x10	5.48^{+++}	6.4^{+++}	5.8^{+++}	4.3^{+++}	-0.98	2.12$^+$	3.66^{+++}	4.42^{+++}
15x15x15	9.34^{+++}	8.07^{+++}	7.84^{+++}	6.46^{+++}	0.11	3.14^{+++}	4.96^{+++}	6.24^{+++}
20x20x20	9.78^{+++}	10.3^{+++}	9.1^{+++}	8.22^{+++}	-0.41	5.52^{+++}	5.63^{+++}	6.06^{+++}
25x25x25	11.22^{+++}	10.54^{+++}	10.15^{+++}	7.98^{+++}	-0.21	5.11^{+++}	7.24^{+++}	6.96^{+++}
30x30x30	13.78^{+++}	16.46^{+++}	13.95^{+++}	11.39^{+++}	-0.76	5.8^{+++}	8.9^{+++}	10.3^{+++}

Table 2. t test for bounds given by LP_SSUWLP_R4–LP_SSUWLP_R2 and SSUWLP_Rm–LP_SSUWLP_R4

Problem Size	Problem Category to compare LP_SSUWLP_R4–LP_SSUWLP_R2				Problem Category to compare SSUWLP_Rm–LP_SSUWLP_R4			
	A	B	C	D	A	B	C	D
10x10x10	4.3^{+++}	3.86^{+++}	2.64^{++}	1.12	-0.71	1.41	3.13^{+++}	1
15x15x15	5.85^{+++}	5.63^{+++}	3.76^{+++}	1.85^{+}	2.04^{+}	1.05	1.01	1
20x20x20	6.16^{+++}	6.14^{+++}	4.02^{+++}	2.57^{++}	2.03^{+}	1.93^{+}	1.43	1.25
25x25x25	6.82^{+++}	6.05^{+++}	4.3^{+++}	1.77^{+}	2.81^{+++}	1.24	1.32	1
30x30x30	7.05^{+++}	7.95^{+++}	6.04^{+++}	3.36^{+++}	0.12	1	1.41	1.41

+ : α = 0.05 (1 tail, t-critical : 1.68); ++ : α = 0.01 (1 tail, t-critical : 2.40); +++ : α = 0.005 (1 tail, t-critical : 2.68)

6 Conclusions

In this work four new formulations of SSUWLP and their LP relaxations are developed. Random problems of different sizes and categories are created with varying supply limits; and these are tested empirically to establish the relationship between the bounds of different formulations. t-test has been conducted in order to compare. It is found that for different problem instances of SSUWLP, 'strong' formulations produce significantly better bounds compared to the bounds of 'weak' formulation. The empirical results show that the formulation with both supply and demand side strong constraints is the best compared to the rest three formulations and provide bounds closest to the optimal.

References

1. Geoffrion, A., Graves, G.: Multicommodity distribution system design by Benders decomposition. Management Science 20(5), 822–844 (1974)
2. Sharma, R.R.K.: Modeling fertilizer distribution system. Europ. J. of Operational Research 51, 24–34 (1991)
3. Kouvelis, P., Rosenblatt, M., Munson, C.: A mathematical programming model for global plant location problems: Analysis and insights. IIE Transactions 36, 127–144 (2004)
4. Sharma, R.R.K., Sharma, K.D.: A new dual based procedure for the transportation problem. Europ. J. of Operational Research 122(3), 611–624 (2000)
5. Nemhauser, G., Wolsey, L.: Integer and Combinatorial optimization. Wiley and Sons, New York (1988)
6. Rardin, R., Choe, U.: Tighter relaxations of fixed charge network flow problems. Technical Report J-79-18, Georgia Institute of Technology, Atlanta, Georgia (1979)
7. Sharma, R.R.K., Berry, V.: Developing new formulations and relaxations of single stage capacitated warehouse location problem (SSCWLP): Empirical investigation for assessing relative strengths and computational effort. Europ. J. of Operational Research 177(2), 803–812 (2007)

CRM in Pharmaceutical Sector: Meeting the Challenges of Changing Healthcare Environment

Ritu Sinha and Chandrashekhar Kaushik

Marketing Faculty
IES Management College & Research Centre,
VMD Lotlikar Vidya Sankul
Bandra (West), Mumbai-400050, India
Tel.: 91-022-61378349, 91-022-61378356
taffeta2006@yahoo.com, chandrashekhar.kaushik@gmail.com

Abstract. CRM has redefined the relationship between customers and the companies that serve them. It is premised on a simple logic of creating, maintaining and retaining customers for profitable long term association and maximizing the value through customer relationships. Even the pharma sector has also shown its confidence towards this upcoming expensive and technology intensive system. This article describes the concepts and mechanism of CRM for the pharma sector, illustrates its need for pharma sector and throws light on the benefits and pitfalls of CRM for pharma sector.

Keywords: CRM, Pharmaceutical industry, Customer, Relationship marketing.

1 Introduction

The pharmaceutical industry has witnessing growth even during recession times. Today Pharmaceutical industry is also undergoing major transformation phase. This sector is under immense pressure by factors like intensifying competition, poor pipeline productivity, regulatory barriers, falling margins, governments putting price caps, cost controls and running out on patents of medicines. These factors are also denting their industry earnings and forcing them to search for options to maximize value. Besides, they are also looking for strategies to remain competitive by continuously developing new drugs and extending the indications of marketed drugs in the view of imminent patent expiration. They are streamlining product development processes, implementing the right lifecycle management strategy to survive in competitive environment. The development process of a single drug requires the investment of hundreds of millions of dollars ranging from ten to fifteen years. Their research requires exchange of project data and disease knowledge between scientists in the various stages of a drug project. There is enormous need for the analysis of experimental data from discovery to developmental phase and even extending to the post-marketing phase. This sector is also characterized by existence of multiple touch points across a diverse customer base (patient, providers and payers) and shows its affinity for the data where new data is dispensed into the organization

V. V Das et al. (Eds.): BAIP 2010, CCIS 70, pp. 660–664, 2010.
© Springer-Verlag Berlin Heidelberg 2010

every month. These firms are in need of some automation for the speedy analysis of data which helps them in extrapolating the evolving trends across the enterprise and offer a competitive advantage for these firms.

2 Characteristics of Pharma Industry

The pharma industry is distinguished by its over-dependency on research and development (R&D) and technological development. Technology works at two levels: upstream and downstream. Upstream deals with drug discovery and its delivery whereas downstream caters to the manufacturing and marketing. It has traditionally been considered as a high margin business and do not focuses too profoundly on maximizing every margin point. But with the changing market environment, it has now started looking at optimizing its existing assets and infrastructure. It mostly relies on the development and sales and marketing of high-volume products i.e. `blockbusters drugs' to physicians, hospitals, and wholesalers. Now, this strategy is no longer effective owing to the expiry of patents and the dearth of new blockbuster molecules coming to market. With increasingly well-informed patients and internet-based initiatives of `e-healthcare', pharma companies can no longer afford to be product specific and have realized the importance of effective in selling drugs. Earlier, their strategy for selling more drugs was to employ more sales reps and equip them with the right technology. But with the intensifying competition and changing market dynamics, they are required to be more effective in selling drugs. They have to evolve beyond traditional sales and marketing strategies and search for the latest technology solutions that will help them to execute a highly effective sales and marketing strategy.

3 Objective of CRM

CRM, in present era, can be viewed as a technological link between the company and customer that strives to integrate the employees, the process and the technology to improve an organization relationship with its customers. It is nothing but all about knowing the customers better so as to meet their latent needs in a more effective way. It can be considered as database marketing where promotional aspects of marketing are linked to database efforts. It involves collecting client data, putting it together, analyzing it and utilizing the results to respond to the needs of current and potential customers. The basic objective of CRM is to remain in touch with customers after the sales is made so as to build closer relationship with existing customers and converting them into loyal customers. This helps in expanding co-operative and collaborative relationship between firms and its customers. The data collection through CRM initiative can also aid in understanding the competitor's strategy.

4 Role of CRM in Pharma Sector

The customer oriented approach of CRM is usually typically supported and automated by an IT application known as the CRM system in pharma. These are mainly used as tools for sales reporting system and for the segmentation of target groups. These systems capture the customer preferences and transaction data and make it uniformly available to marketing, sales, and customer service operations. This enables the firms to focus on each customer in a customized way, winning the loyalty and satisfaction of the customers. In addition to that, it can be used for coordinating a discussion with the healthcare environment, working on the brand image and reputation of the company among doctors, healthcare personnel and other stakeholders. It helps in enhancing productivity with the wider access to data and functionality and fosters a streamlined user experience. At the same time it also helps in streamlining business processes by making use of enhanced design tools given to the end users, developers, and IT professionals. It helps in extending improved reporting tools built for end users.   Intelligent management of data empowers in preserving the integrity and accuracy of the database. It also meets the challenges of global business by offering support for multiple languages, currencies, and time zones. Centralized management tools and self-healing capabilities help IT staff work more efficiently so they can concentrate on strategic initiatives, thereby improving management efficiency. This system enables pharmaceutical companies to improve the efficiency of customer related activities, allowing them to multiply their revenues without adding much on resource spending. It facilitates the coordination between sales, marketing, and regulatory and customer service departments, extending the one face to the customer. This helps the organization in branding themselves in the top of mind of doctors and other key stakeholders.

With increasing number of representatives covering per doctor, the effectiveness of pharmaceutical promotion to individual prescribers is losing ground. The endless availability of information by virtue of internet offers an alternative viewpoint in decision making for therapy and drug selection. CRM system offers information that states the preferences, concerns, interests and needs of stakeholders and can help in generating relevant stakeholder information based on their requirement. This can further help in carrying out segmentations augmented with methods of profiling for specific campaigns, and can examine the trends that could be relevant for one's business. This profiling looks for the behavioral segmentation of prescribers which will also direct the process, substance and communication style of representative's calls. This in turn helps in generating more effectiveness of calls. This will give rise to focused account management than just a promotion effort by representatives only. It aims at building support and information to prescribers and users of the drugs thereby enhancing compliance, satisfied experience with the treatment. So, when we talk of Pharmaceutical CRM, there are four parameters, sales force automation, customer care automation, marketing automation and analytical CRM. A Sale force automation helps in shortening the sales cycle, increase sales, improves account management and gathers customer data. Customer care automation helps in improving customer service and decreases the cost of customer service. Marketing automation enhances efficiency, personalize Campaign, use customer data to increase success rates and decrease cost. The Analytical CRM leads to one to one marketing, up selling and cross Selling, improved Customer service and link the overall performance.

5 Customer Orientation In Pharma Industry

One of the most distinguishing traits of pharma sector is the profile of the end customer. The customer is approached not directly but by utilizing the *Doctor channel* owing to its regulatory constraints. While manufacturers in other sectors deal with the end customer directly, pharma companies are entangled in a web of relationships with physicians (who prescribe but do not buy medicines), pharmacies and hospitals (who buy but do not prescribe) and patients (who buy but do not decide on products). As firms don't sell directly to the consumer, they have to service the prescribing professionals and retailers to do the job of maintaining customer relationship. Firms in turn maintain their relationship with the doctors and the stockiest/retailers. Service quality has become a priority for today organizations and they have realized the fact cost of dissatisfying a customer is many more times greater than the cost involved in assuring that every customer contact is satisfying. Apart from this, customer has become very demanding and patients are much more informed about drugs than they were before. They demand more value at lower prices and ask for more freedom of choice regarding healthcare providers. They have found their faith more on internet rather than accepting a physician's traditional role as a decision-maker. The access to doctors is getting restricted in evolving pharma market place. The number of visits of the pharma sales representative has been diminished due to increased number products, sales representative and number of players, dwindling numbers of prescriptions.

6 Pitfall of CRM

CRM on the whole is highly dependent on technology. But, the ability to deploy and control this program is not easy mission. In addition, technology also creates data proliferation and new risks. The reasons for the CRM failures range from user incompetence, bad technology and overblown expectations to failure on companies' behalf to make the necessary cultural and policy changes that allowed the technology to work. These systems were complex, expensive and failed to deliver on all their promises. In many big pharmaceutical companies CRM turned out to be one of most expensive and un-successful implementation projects. The reason responsible for this is the high complexity and unclear processes among the pharmaceutical IT, sales directors and sales and marketing staff. These CRM programs should be driven from the top down. For example, if a senior management wants a reporting on sales, the pipeline, forecast, etc then the sales team should be taken in the loop to make available quality information into the system. The long deployment time also adds to the cost involved in implementing the CRM projects. Before buying a CRM, the organization is required to identify with their own requisite for a particular business and its future requirements. It should be flexible enough and can be modified when the organization needs to adapt to future changes. Different modules launched at various intervals helps in gradual adoption. Also, the company should focus on the customer rather than on technology and strategy. The first alphabet in CRM stands for customer, so the customer should be the first when thinking about any CRM strategy.

7 Conclusion

Intensifying competition, deregulation, cost pressures, and electronic distribution channels are compelling pharma companies to adopt customer oriented strategies. The ultimate objective of CRM is to drive sales and improve the bottom line. New segmentation methods, account management and differentiation between accounts will make the difference in effectiveness and efficiency of CRM systems. But, with declining productivity and ROI, mounting pressures to improve profit margins and market share are driving pharmaceutical companies to rethink and redesign their business model and their CRM strategies. In the near future, the key to an effective CRM implementation includes discovery of the most successful CRM strategies, maximizing its ROI, improving the customer retention, supporting market development and reducing operating costs. Too often, businesses limit the scope of CRM implementation and level of integration within an enterprise and fail to recognize that CRM is as much about changing employee skills and business processes as it is about technology. By investing intelligently in CRM, companies can bring genuine improvement across business functions and reap the rewards of higher ROI.

References

Global pressures force Pharma Industry to re-think role, priorities of IT, says Datamonitor,
    http://industry.tekrati.com/research/8980/
Wahlberg, O., Strandberg, C., Sundberg, H., Sandberg, K.W.: Trends, Topics And Under researched Areas in Crm Research - A Literature Review. International Journal of Public Information Systems, 3 (2009)
The importance of CRM,
    http://www.ngpharma.eu.com/article/The-importance-of-CRM
Atul Parvatiyar, A., Sheth, J.: Customer Relationship Management:Emerging Practice, Process, and Discipline. Journal of Economic and Social Research 3(2) (2002); 2001, 2002 Preliminary Issue (1-34)
Agrawal, M.L.: Customer Relationship Management & Corporate Renaissance. Journal of Service Research 3(2) (October 2003-March 2004)

HR Roadmap: Becoming a Strategic Business Partner

Shweta Maheshwari

HR Faculty
IES Management College & Research Centre
VMD Lotlikar Vidya Sankul
Bandra (West), Mumbai-400050, India
Tel.: 91-022-61378356
zoomshweta@hotmail.com

Abstract. HR for long has been viewed as being purely a process driven function. In today's competitive environment where everyone is being asked about contribution in terms of value addition, HR is no exception. HR's true strategic opportunity lies in its ability to evolve from focusing primarily on tactical administrative transactions to becoming an outcome driven function, where it is seen as a function that adds value. Adding value calls for integrating the people strategies with business strategies in a way that advances bottom line. The paper analyses how HR functions in organizations that are Best Employers in India have demonstrated the role of strategic business partner.

1 Introduction

In 2007, organizations were on a roll with double digit growth rates, high employee payouts and optimism all around. This wave of optimism was suddenly pushed back by last year's global meltdown. The same organizations having massive growth and investment plans in 2007, started resorting to initially conservative and then extreme measures to survive in the changing environment. While some organizations were struggling to keep pace with the changing environment, others were juggling for their mere viability and survival. Best workplaces stood against this tough time by focusing on to their most important asset, their people and the HR functions of these organizations facilitated this by aligning its people with the changed business needs. Dave Gartenberg, HR director at Microsoft UK, said: "In turbulent times more than any other, there is not only the opportunity, but the need for HR to provide leadership to the business. The ability to attract and retain workers when times are tough really requires leaders to be at their best."

2 Some Key Statistics

The Best Employers in Asia Study 2009 done by Hewitt indicates that the performance assessment process in best organizations is actually helping to improve performance. Hewitt studies also confirm that Best Employers consistently deliver higher

V.V Das et al. (Eds.): BAIP 2010, CCIS 70, pp. 665–669, 2010.

revenue growth and stronger growth in profitability. A 2007 global study jointly conducted by consulting firm Deloitte Touche Tohmatsu and The Economist Intelligence Unit showed business leaders do not see HR as a key to people strategies. Only 23 percent of corporate leaders see their HR departments as currently playing a crucial role in coming up with a corporate strategy that would have significant impact on operating results. They do, however, recognize people as a key intangible portion of a company's market value. But only 52 percent of HR leaders believe they are major contributors in shaping a company's culture. These statistics suggest that while the HR function does play a significant role in improving performance, many business leaders fail to recognize this.

3 Objectives of the Study

a) Examination of the role of HR as a strategic business partner as demonstrated by Best Employers in India
b) Understanding how HR can become a strategic business partner

4 Research Methodology

This is an empirical study. The Research Methodology comprises the following:

- Detailed analysis of data obtained from Best Employers Survey Report published by leading research firms.
- Surveys conducted by research organization on how HR practices can affect the financials of an organization and enable them to achieve greater business results were studied.

5 Limitations and Further Research

- This study is based only on the data obtained from Best Employers Survey Report published by leading research firms. There is no mention of any specific organization.
- To analyze the subject in detail the study needs to be extended to a detail mass of organizations having progressive HR practices.

6 Literature Review

The inclusion of HR into the strategic role is a two-party game between the business and the HR leaders. The more aligned are their objectives, interests and capabilities, the tighter will be the bond. (SHRI Research Center). Dave Ulrich (1997), a true visionary has been writing and demonstrating about the need for HR to become a strategic business partner. He says "Today's HR professionals are often labeled business partner. Too often however, the term business partner is narrowly defined as an HR professional working with general managers to implement strategy, that is, working as a strategic partner." He pointed out that this original conception has changed and to-day, a more dynamic, encompassing equation replaces the concept of business part-ner. Business partner = Strategic partner (aligning HR systems with business strategy) + Administrative expert (efficient design and delivery of HR systems) + Employee champion (ensure employees contribution to business remain high) + Change Agent (help business through transformations and adapt to changing business conditions). "HR professionals often find themselves in dilemma. While their organizations are asking them to become leaders and partners in running business, they are frequently asked to implement initiatives and programs with which they have no formal authority One solution is to find an appropriate balance between supporting and challenging organization's leadership. The HR professional must find a way to become a true partner with CEO" (Michael Seitchik, 2002).

7 Best Employers Study

HCL Technologies shifted its focus to employees by bringing in "Employees First" policy in 2005. HCL's entire HR policy was revisited to bring in a qualitative shift towards employees. Exposure was increased and skills were updated to enhance knowledge. Employees were empowered to have views about the company and given opportunities to express them.

Cisco, Best Employers HR function went through a major overhaul in 2005 to help the company move from a statutory board to a private company. HR function which was doing purely administrative functions geared it to take up the role of a strategic business partner by aligning its people processes to the changing business needs.

The Human Resources department at Eureka Forbes believes in a performance driven culture. They continuously monitor attrition rate and feel it helps them align the employee base with regular performers which in turn helps the business and, in turn, the people who run it.

8 Analysis, Findings and Key Learning

Analysis of actions taken by HR functions of Best organizations which clearly differ-entiate them from the rest show that HR can play the role of a strategic business part-ner by adopting 5 steps model as discussed below:

1. Building credibility by understanding business
The first important task for any HR professional is to understand business dynamics to gain credibility. Most of the HR professionals are not involved in strategic decision making because of their lack of business knowledge. Every HR professional must spend considerable time in understanding strengths, weaknesses, threats and opportu-nities of the organization and the environment within which it operates. Understand-ing business goals, strategies, customer base and most importantly expectations of key stakeholders will take HR professionals into a strategic platform.

2. Organize for performance and perform for organization

For any successful HR function its first important to organize itself to deliver robust HR solutions. This can be done in a similar fashion as RMSI, the winner of Best Employer Award by Great Place to Work Institute has done:

- Aligning organizational structure in a way that there are right number of resources in right roles, levels and costs both internally and externally
- Streamlining HR processes as per key business needs
- Leveraging technology optimally make HR delivery strong, giving room for HR to concentrate on business imperatives while reducing administrative burden
- Building HR competencies and skills that are aligned to business

3. Build an employee value proposition

Employee value proposition in simple terms means the rewards and benefits an employee receives in return of performance at the workplace. It is important to link performance with pay and reward innovation. This also calls for building trust with the employees by listening and responding to them and communicating with them continuously. HR professionals should engage their employees and thereby enhance their commitment and boost their morale. Employee value proposition is a key driver for of talent attraction, engagement and retention.

4. Provide leadership

HR professionals must become leaders by focusing on clear business priorities and pulling its employees in the right direction. They must keep the future in perspective and reshape behavior for organizational change. They must embrace change and balance by developing HR processes and programs to help organization transform itself on one hand and supporting new behavior of employees to keep up with the competition on other hand.

5. Measure HR

While HR spends a lot of time in appraisal cycle and measuring performances of its employees, most often HR function is just measured keeping in mind how happy the employees are. In order to become a strategic partner it is important for the HR function to become accountable to all the key stakeholders (customers, shareholders and managers) and not just the employees.

9 Conclusion

As described by Terence Brake, Partnering' implies higher levels of commitment to shared goals and objectives than do terms 'team member', 'colleague', or 'associate'. Commitment is not enough for partnership to work. Partners must be able to move beyond words and intentions to actions and these actions must produce results. Partners must continually demonstrate that they add value to the relationship; otherwise the partnership will not survive. Every HR activity must be challenged with such questions as "What value does this add? How does this increase our viability? What is the link between this activity and our business strategies?" Meeting these challenges is vital if HR is to be seen more than just an expense item on the balance sheet.

References

Ulrich, D.: Human Resource Champions (1996)
Ulrich, D., Brockbank, W.: The HR Business Partner model, HBR
Losey, M., Ulrich: Future of Human Resource Management
Joynt, P., Morton, B.: The Global HR Manager
NHRD Network: HRD Newsletter 24(11,12), 25(2, 4, 5)
HRM Review, vol. IX(II, III, V, XI). ICFAI University Press
Seitchik, M.: Dilemmas in the HR Partnership, HBR
Jamrog, J.J.: Building a strategic HR Function-Continuing the evolution, HBR
Saha, J.: From HR to strategic business partner, SHRI Research Centre
Lawler III, E.E., Mohram, S.: HR as a strategic business partner-What does it take it to make it happen, HBR
Best Employers Study 2007, 2009 Global HR Study, Best Employers in Asia Study 2009, Cost reduction and engagement survey 2009, Hewitt Associates: HR of the future
Great Place to work Study of Best Employers in India (2009)
NHRD Network, Mumbai: Presentation made by RMSI and Fed Ex

Recent Trends in Indian Technical and Management Education W.R.T. Maharashtra

J.S. Kadam[1], J.J. Nirmal[2], and M.Y. Khire[1]

[1] Pad. Dr. Vithalrao Vikhe Patil Foundations College of Engineering, Ahmednagar
js_kadam@rediffmail.com, mykhire@gmail.com
[2] P.D.V.V.P.F. Institute of business Management and Rural Development, Ahmednagar (M.S.)
jayashree_nirmal@rediffmail.com

Abstract. The Indian Technical &management education sector is undergoing drastic changes in the past. The focus is shifted from public sector to private sector up in technical education. The Govt. has come with a number of regulations and targeted the private sector investment in education. The Govt. is all set to introduce a law for regulation of foreign university entry in the country. The Govt. is also starting to focus on primary and secondary education sectors by providing same plans and policies for these sectors. This paper mainly focus on development in education sector in post independence period and recent trend in technical education; an Indian perspective.

1 Introduction

Better management can yield better results. Now a days the value of the manager and especially the professional Engineers & managers has increased manifold and for that matter the value of technical and management education has increased specifically.

Technical and management education is one of the more significant components of the development spectrum with great potential for adding value to products &overall service to the national economy and improving quality of life of the people.

Technical & management Education has got a lot of importance for national development of a country. Technical education plays a vital role in H R development of the country by creating a skilled manpower, enhancing industrial productivity & imparting the quality of life technical education covers courses &program's courses in engineering technology management architecture Pharmacy applied arts & crafts [1,2].

2 Role of Government in Education Sector

Allocation of responsibility for various subjects to different tier of government is ultimately laid down in the Constitution. From 1950, when the Constitution came into force, till 1976, Education was essentially a State subject, with role of Central Government being limited to Technical & Management are making the most of their resources. one college is taking smart approach to acquiring equipment for hands-on-learning in fox valley Technical college & management institute in Appleton[4]. In Maharashtra

V.V Das et al. (Eds.): BAIP 2010, CCIS 70, pp. 670–673, 2010.

state Government passed resolution regarding starting a privet unaided Technical & Management, Pharmacy „Architecture institution in 1983. There was a drastic change in rural educational management and now Indian government started a new policy about technical institute under one roof known as "Integrated Campus".

2.1 National Policies on Education

There have so far been mainly two comprehensive statements of the National Policy on Education, viz. those of 1968 and 1986. The former contained decisions of the Central Government on the recommendations of the National Commission on Education, 1964-66. The latter was a result of the renewed priority assigned to Education by the government of the Late Shri Rajiv Gandhi, who was Prime Minister during 1984-89. The 1986 policy was reviewed by a Committee constituted in 1990 under the chairmanship of Acharya Ramamurti. On the basis of the recommendations of this Committee, certain provisions of the 1986 policy were modified in 1992. Thus, in all, the following three comprehensive national policy statements exist on Education:[5,6].

3 Size of the Indian Education System

In keeping with its billion-plus population and high proportion of the youth, India has a large formal Education System. Its target group (children and young persons in the 6-24 years age group) numbered around 410 million in 2005, or about 38% of the country's population. Following are some indicators of the size of India's Education System:[3,4].

Table 1. Statistical Data

Target Population (6-26 years age group) (Estimate during 2009)	425 million (All Over India)
Number of Technical &management Educational Institutions in Maharashtra	Tech 350 , Management 240
Total Enrolments In maharashtra Technical &management schools	71000 K In Technical & 19000 K In management during 2009
Universities Maharashtra (as on 14/12/2009)	9Universities + 7 Deemed Universities +2 Institutions of National Importance +11 autonomus

3.1 Growth and Important Achievements

The Indian higher technical education system has been continuously witnessing impressive growth post liberalization. Student enrollments in the country have grown to over 12 Million, from just 0.1 Million in 1947. This revolution has come around with the emergence of a whole new class of education providers, including private institutes, distance education providers, self-financing courses in public institutions and foreign education providers.

Over the decades, the Department has also established or substantially funded a number of premier institutions, which have come to acquire a reputation for excellence. Some of these are:

- 13 Indian Institutes of Technology (IITs)
- 7 Indian Institutes of Management (IIMs)
- Indian Institute of Science (IISc), Bangalore
- 23 Central Universities
- Indian School of Mines, Dhanbad
- 4 Indian Institutes of Information Technology (IIITs)
- 20 National Institutes of Technology (NITs)

The above list does not include premier institutions in the field of Medical, Agricultural and Legal Education, which are looked after by other Ministries of the Government of India.

4   Factors Influencing Quality of Technical Education

The factors that influence economic development of any country depend on the stage of development of that particular country. At the initial stages of development, the factors that are important are the effective use of basic inputs such as land, labour and capital. As the countries advances, the factors that influence the economic development are higher reliance on international trade and attracting FDI. As countries reach high income status, they need to generate high levels of innovation and commercialization of new technologies (Porter, Sachs and Macarthur, 2001). Thus, it is important to create a positive perception in the minds of the students as well as other stakeholders of the institution. This paper attempts to identify the factors that differentiate those institutions which are perceived as of high quality from those which are perceived as those of low quality. This paper is part of a wider study covering the quality aspects of a number of technical institutions in the state of Maharastra.[3,6]

5   Autonomy

Government of Maharashtra has adopted a proactive policy for growth of Technical and Management institutions. It has asked opinions and views of experts in education field to promote premier govt. aided and private institutes to the status of 'Autonomous Institute '. World bank was also involved through Govt. of India under the scheme "Technical Education Quality Improvement Programme" nicknamed as 'TEQIP'. A Large amount of funds were made available to premier institute under the condition of accepting the 'Autonomous 'states in due course of time subsequently.

6 Conclusion

Indian Technical &management Educational Institutions in maharashtra education sector is growing rapidly with gradual development in & around the world, Globalization & technological innovations brings about drastic changes in educational field use of IT revolutions, Distance learning , Multimedia learning etc are some of the examples. Government is also playing a vital role for improving the quality of education by providing necessary legislations & policies time to time.

References

1. Indian Growth and Development Review, vol. I, II
2. Raju, K.D.: Indian Education Sector Growth and Challenges
3. http://www.aicte.ernet.in/ApprovedInstitute.htm
4. http://www.indiaeducation.com
5. http://www.newsoutlookindia.com

Author Index